DATA ANALYSIS AND DATA MINING USING MICROSOFT® BUSINESS INTELLIGENCE TOOLS:

Excel™ 2010, Access™ 2010, and Report Builder 3.0 with SQL Server™

by

Robert S. Bussom, Ph.D.

ISBN: 978-0-9857428-3-6

www.zerobits.info

Table of Contents

Chapter 1 - Introduction

Welcome, analysts, power users, and others interested in Microsoft's Business Intelligence tools. From my perspective Microsoft has assembled the best, most accessible integrated set of BI tools for the desktop. This chapter contains short sections about the book's purpose and scope, its intended audience including expectations about readers' skills and knowledge, its organization and content, and the software utilized in it.

Purpose and Scope

I did not start writing about Business Intelligence (BI) to publish a book. Rather, my intention was to use writing as a way to better understand the topic for my consulting work and to satisfy my curiosity, but as I learned more about it, the writing evolved into this book. In learning about BI I found that I had to do considerable rooting around in "the literature" and that there was a lack of sources about using BI at an intermediate level. There are many introductory Excel and Access books and advanced books and other sources about SQL Server, data warehousing, and the like but not much in the middle for the advanced computer user who prefers to work in Excel and Access and can't or doesn't want to work primarily in SQL Server's BI applications: Analysis Services, Integration Services, and Reporting Services. In addition, some topics were difficult to track down, e.g., information about the Data Mining Extensions for SQL Server language. So, this book is a compilation of what I've found during this leaning process.

The book focuses on applying Microsoft's user-level data analysis (Excel 2010), data management (Access 2010), and reporting (Report Builder 3.0) tools in a BI context. While SQL Server's database engine, Analysis Services, and Reporting Services provide data and services in the background for the tools, there is little in the book about how to use them directly. Indeed, in this book we are on the outside of SQL Server looking in instead of inside looking out, an approach we would take if we were writing about SQL Server. In addition, the coverage of Excel and Access focuses on data acquisition, transformation, and analysis and with less emphasis on reporting and visualization such as charts and graphs. However, given that reporting is an important element of data analysis I have included coverage of Report Builder 3.0. Because the primary focus of the book in on data analysis and also to keep it to manageable

length coverage of Microsoft's SharePoint server and the Excel PowerPivot add-in is not included.
A few more words about the exclusion of PowerPivot may be in order. PowerPivot is great! It efficiently handles very large datasets, allows combining data from multiple sources, includes the Data Analysis Expression (DAX) language to create custom calculations, and much more. However, when you become experienced with using the tools covered in this book, especially designing queries and working with Analysis Services, then you can easily learn to use PowerPivot. In addition, adequately covering PowerPivot is considerably beyond the scope of this book. Indeed, there are books available about PowerPivot only. So, because of space considerations, avoidance of scope creep, the overlap among the tools covered here and PowerPivot, and the availability of other sources I decided to pass on the opportunity to not do it justice here.

Intended Audience

This book is intended for people who are knowledgeable about and comfortable with desktop applications, especially Microsoft Excel, on Windows-based computers, who perform and/or use data analysis, and who are curious about or need to use BI tools, particularly data mining. It may be of lesser use for information technology professionals with considerable experience in BI.

While writing the book I assumed that readers would have a moderate level of expertise in Microsoft Excel 2010 and Access 2010 meaning that you should be comfortable creating workbooks and worksheets, navigating in them, using formulas with absolute and relative cell references, formatting cells and ranges, and creating charts in Excel and creating and using Access databases with multiple tables, select queries, forms, and reports. However, just in case you are a little rusty or need some help with the basics I've included appendixes to get you "Up to Speed" with queries, Excel, and Access.,

While no statistical background is required for understanding the material in the book, statistics does play a prominent role in data analysis and is utilized as appropriate from time to time with minimal reliance on mathematical notation.

Contents

I took a guided tour approach to the topics in the book, and I've tried to provide explanations as appropriate to help you understand what's going on so that you can generalize beyond examples and screen shots, of which there are many. The contents of the book are briefly described below:

Chapter 2 (Business Intelligence Overview) defines BI, describes generic BI outputs and processes, and introduces data warehousing and Online Analytical Processing.

Chapter 3 (Microsoft SQL Server Business Intelligence Tools) describes the components in SQL Server 2008: the database server, the SQL Server Management Studio, the Business Intelligence Development Studio, Integration Services, the AdventureWorks sample database, Analysis Services including a brief description of Microsoft's data mining algorithms, and Reporting Services as background for connecting to or using SQL Server services during data analysis and mining in Excel.

Chapter 4 (Report Manager and Report Builder), describes how to use Report Manager, the browser-based user interface for Reporting Services, and Report Builder 3.0 to create and edit reports.

Chapter 5 (Data Analysis with Excel 2010: Part I) describes how to use Excel 2010 for data acquisition, inspection and cleaning, and transformation in preparation for data analysis.

Chapter 6 (Data Analysis with Excel 2010: Part II), a follow-on to Chapter 5, describes how to perform data analysis with Excel 2010 using Excel tables, pivot tables and pivot charts, Online Analytical Processing Cubes, statistical inference, and regression and correlation analysis.

Chapter 7 (Data Analysis with Access 2010) describes acquisition of data from external sources, using advanced query features, employing pivot tables and charts in Access, database management, and Access Data Projects as front-ends to SQL Server databases.

Chapter 8 (Time Series Forecasting with Excel 2010) describes time series forecasting fundamentals; how to do smoothing, time series linear regression, decomposition, time series linear regression, and autoregression in Excel 2010; and the Microsoft Time Series algorithm.

Chapter 9 (Data Mining with Excel 2010 Table Analysis Tools), describes how to use the Table Analysis Tools included in the Microsoft SQL Server 2008 Data Mining Add-ins for Microsoft Office 2007 and 2010. The Table

Analysis tool are a subset of Excel's data mining tools and are used for quick and easy data mining. The tools include Analyze Key Influencers, Detect Categories, Scenario Analysis, the Prediction Calculator, and Shopping Basket Analysis.

Chapter 10 (Data Mining with Excel 2010 Data Mining Tools), describes how to exploit Analysis Services' data mining capabilities with Excel 2010. Topics include an expanded description of Microsoft's data mining algorithms, using the data modeling tools, accuracy and validation, model usage and management, and prediction queries.

Appendixes: The six appendixes contain complementary, supplementary, and ancillary material. I tried to list all of the acronyms and abbreviations that I used in one place, Appendix A, so you don't have to hunt for them in the index. I included a few definitions as well. Appendix B, Some Notes about Data Analysis Concepts, is perhaps a remnant from my academic career but I included it because the topics in it have served me well in my excursions into data analysis. Expertise with queries is fundamental for working with databases, and queries are used frequently in the book so I included a query "how to" in Appendix C. Appendixes D and E are refreshers for Excel and Access, respectively. And finally, Appendix F provides an introduction to the Data Mining Advanced Query Editor and Data Mining Extensions language.

Software Utilized

Of course you'll need Microsoft Excel 2010, and I recommend Access 2010 as well. You can get along without Access but it sure makes working with some data easier. Excel and Access are included in Microsoft Office 2010 Professional but you can buy them separately. However, at retail the two separate applications cost about the same as the package. Microsoft Visio 2010, another Office application, has a few useful BI features, reverse engineering of existing databases to create database models and data mining diagrams, but my experience with it is that those benefits are not worth the cost if that's all that you're going to use it for. Please be aware that the SQL Server Data Mining Add-ins necessary to have access to the Table Analysis and Data Mining Tools (see below) at this time are not compatible with 64-bit Excel except when accessing SQL Server 2012. For prior versions of SQL Server you must have 32-bit Excel/Office 2010 installed.

Connection to SQL Server is absolutely necessary to utilize the Report Server for Report Builder 3.0, its table analysis and data mining capabilities for Excel, and AdventureWorks and other database samples. I used the 2008 R2 version for the examples in this book. (I will describe my experience using SQL Server 2012 on my Web site, www.zerobits.info, as time permits.) You may get by with SQL Server 2005 but you will miss some useful data analysis and mining features. Of course, if your organization uses SQL Server as its database management system, then you may be all set. However, it's likely that your access to it will be blocked or at best limited. Talk to your IT folks about your access options to SQL Server and what permissions they are willing to grant. An option is to install the SQL Server Developer Edition (inexpensive at about $50) on a local machine at least for learning and training. It has all of the capabilities of the Enterprise edition but is licensed for only one developer. Whatever you do, do not mess with production databases. Always work with copies or read only data warehouses.

Report Builder is a report authoring application that creates reports to be published on the Report Server. Report Builder 1.0 installed with SQL Server 2008 has been superseded by Report Builder 3.0 which is installed separately. Just search the Internet for Report Builder 3.0.

The Microsoft SQL Server 2008 Data Mining Add-ins for Microsoft Office 2007 and 2010 contains three components: Table Analysis Tools for Excel, the Data Mining Client for Excel, and Data Mining Templates for Visio. The first two are absolutely necessary. Search the Internet for the SQL Server 2008 Feature Pack or the Data Mining Add-ins for Office. Also in the Feature Pack are the Microsoft SQL Server 2008 Native Client (OLE DB provider and SQL ODBC driver) for use in creating data connections and the SQL Server 2008 Analysis Services 10.0 OLE DB Provider.

OLAP PivotTable Extensions is an Excel 2010 add-in that provides supplemental functionality to Excel when working with Analysis Services cubes. It is available for download from CodePlex, Microsoft's open source project hosting web site, at http://www.codeplex.com.

Most of the examples in the book utilize data from the AdventureWorks 2008 R2 sample databases which are also availa0ble from CodePlex. AdventureWorks sample reports for Reporting Services referred to in the book as are available there as well.

Chapter 1

The Northwind and PUBS legacy SQL Server databases mentioned in the book were available at the time of this writing from:

> http://www.microsoft.com/DOWNLOADS/details.aspx?familyid=06616212-0356-46A0-8DA2-EEBC53A68034&displaylang=en

Tips

We'll finish with a few software tips. We use Microsoft Query frequently in the book so if it was not installed with Office, you can do so by rerunning Office setup and selecting Microsoft Query from the Database Tools options.

The optional Developer tab for the Excel's Ribbon is particularly useful for recording macros and opening Visual Basic for Applications. To display it select Options then Customize Ribbon from the File tab and then select Developer from the Main Tabs list.

The Office Trust Center is a component in Microsoft's computer security repertoire. This is a great security feature but it can drive you nuts with unnecessary security alerts. You can designate directories (folders) as trusted locations to bypass Trust Center screening by adding locations in the Trusted Locations panel accessed with the Trust Center Settings button on the Trust Center tab of Excel Options. Trusted locations for Access 2010 are set the same way.

Check www.zerobits.info, for updates, for other information about BI and this book, to participate in a Business Intelligence Forum, and to report errors on the Contact Us page. I will correct errors as soon as possible and post errata. In addition, since some images in the book are quite large and will be difficult to view on a small screen, they are available at:

> http://www.zerobits.info/businessintelligencebook/bibookimages/

In the book each of the larger images has a link to this Webpage below the image title.

Chapter 2 - Business Intelligence Overview

About ten years ago I took an online graduate-level course in Decision Support Systems which emphasized decision support systems, executive information systems, expert systems, and artificial intelligence. During the course there was no mention of the term business intelligence that I can remember, and there is only a cursory reference to it in the text that we were using. At that time my IT bookshelf contained titles about databases, data warehousing, online analytical processing, and data mining but not business intelligence.

Flash-forward, the curriculum of that program in which I was enrolled now includes a freestanding business intelligence systems course, and I now have a number of BI titled books on my shelf. A search for "business intelligence" books on Amazon.com results in a number of pages of BI titles. BI has come of age encompassing a number of related topics from years past. So, what is BI? There are a plethora of definitions available. Here's my rendition pilfered in part from others.

BI: A Definition

To me Business intelligence (BI) is a set of concepts, methods, and computer related technologies used to transform an organization's data into information to enhance operational and strategic decision making. BI applications include data warehousing, online analytical processing, data and statistical analysis, forecasting, data mining, and reporting.

This definition emphasizes the transformation of data into information as discussed in Appendix B. It specifically recognizes that BI is used for operational as well as strategic decision making whereas the early approaches of OLAP and data mining seemed to focus on executive-level information needs. It also incorporates computer technologies without which BI would not be possible. It avoids reference to decision support systems as that term has expanded in generality and ambiguity, and it focuses on the organization's data which the organization routinely captures and stores, intentionally understating acquisition and analysis of data related to factors external to the organization such as would be implied by terms like "military intelligence" and "competitive intelligence."

Furthermore, it broadens the scope of BI beyond larger business and enterprises to be useful for organizations in general of all types and sizes. In the context of this book the term "business data" refers to the business of the organization whether it be commerce, government, education, not-for-profit, or whatever.

A Generic Business Intelligence Model

The intention of BI is to take a business's raw data, possibly from a variety of disparate sources, convert it into relevant, usable data and information, and transmit and present it to appropriate users. Most of the data sources in Figure 2-1 below should be familiar to you but just in case we'll review online transaction processing and relational databases later in this chapter. The BI processes may be as simple as an Excel worksheet on the desktop for a single user or as complex as the full use of the Microsoft SQL Server 2008 BI package at the enterprise level.

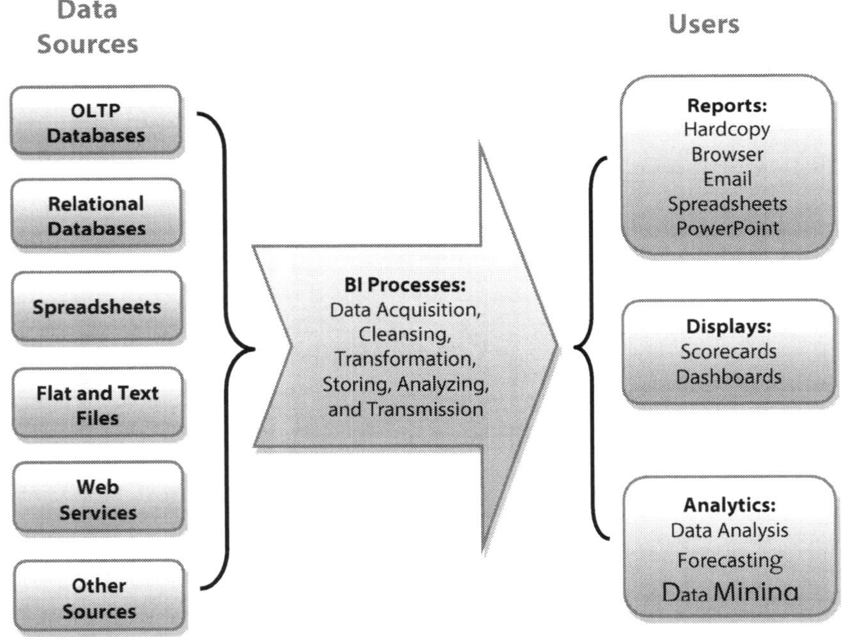

Figure 2-1 Generic Business Intelligence Model

Reports

Users may receive reports from the BI processes in a variety of forms including hardcopy (ugh!), on the organization's intranet or directly from SQL Server's Reporting Services with a browser, or pushed via email. BI reports follow a conventional report format by presenting data in an organized way perhaps including some data visualization such as charts or graphs. BI reports are similar to traditional hardcopy reports and may be static like the one in Figure 2-2 or more dynamic interactive reports with filter and drill-down capabilities and graphics as shown by the one in Figure 2-3 from the Microsoft AdventureWorks Sample Reports application.

FoodMart Store Sales

	Quarter (Store Sales)				
Store	Q1	Q2	Q3	Q4	Total
1	15,063	12,302	12,756	16,276	56,397
2	1,061	1,118	1,151	1,449	4,780
3	13,482	14,064	13,158	17,277	57,982
4	15,378	13,542	12,107	13,839	54,865
5	1,357	1,247	1,035	1,264	4,903
6	12,470	10,558	14,357	14,980	52,365
Total	58,811	52,831	54,565	65,085	231,291

Figure 2-2 Simple Static Report

The report in Figure 2-2 was created quickly using the Report Builder capability of Microsoft's Reporting Services from a cleaned up, upgraded version of the old FoodMart database included as an example, I believe, in SQL Server 2000. We'll get to using that later.

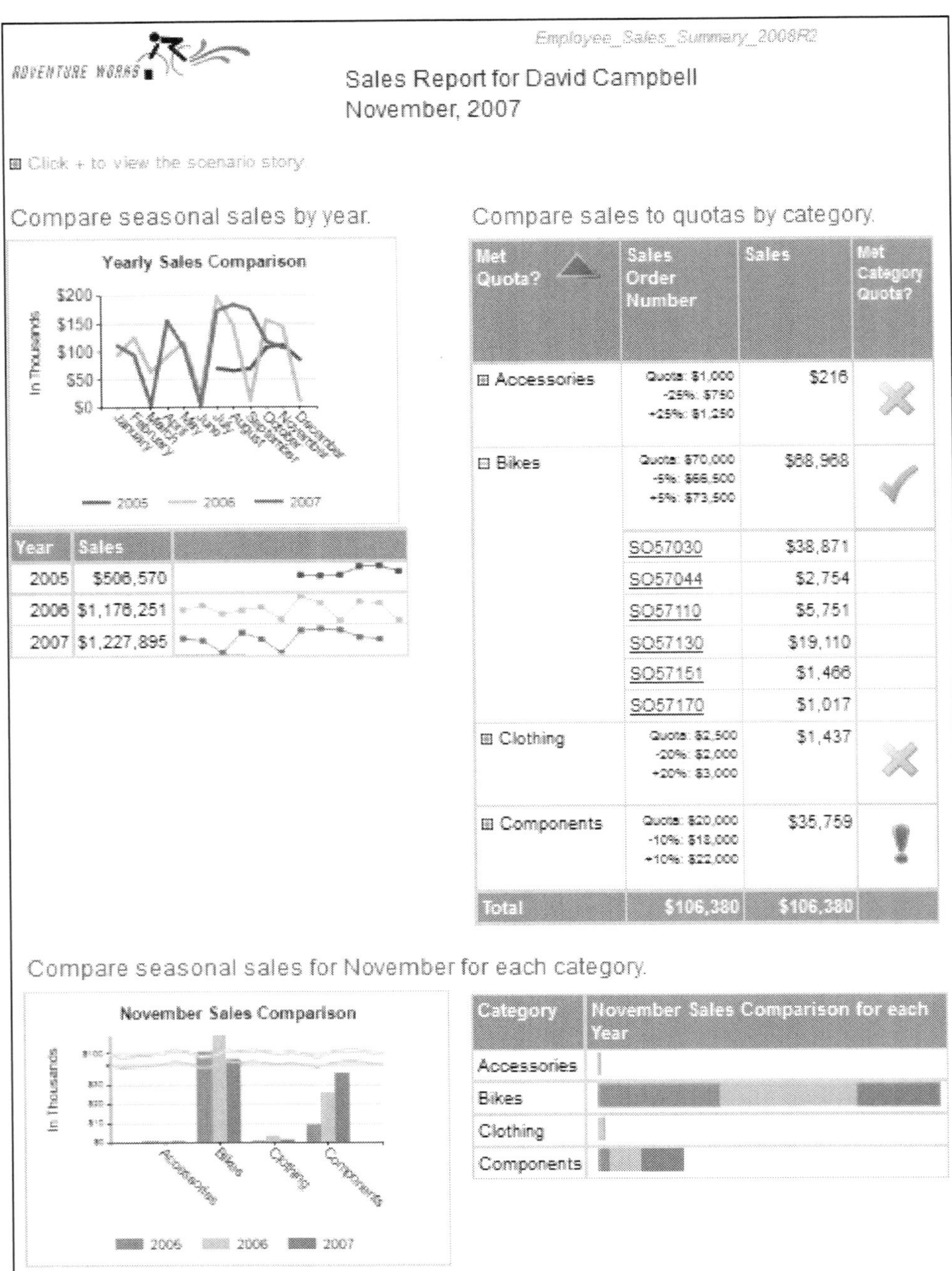

Figure 2-3 Dynamic (Drill-Down) Report

Notice the plus (+) and minus (-) buttons in the AdventureWorks sample report in Figure 2-3 which allows users to expand a section of the report to a lower level of detail. For example, the + button has been clicked to expand the Bikes product category to list product sub categories. This interactive process is called drilling-down. Hyperlinks to other reports as well as charts and graphs can be added to reports.

Displays

Data and information displays, primarily dashboards and scorecards, are different from reports. They are created to present a visual representation of the current status of processes and projects in the case of dashboards or of performance against some benchmark in the case of scorecards. Dashboards and scorecards are usually associated with executive-level managers but there is no reason that they cannot be used effectively by the rest of us. The differences between dashboards and scorecards are essentially unimportant, and in practice dashboards and scorecards usually are intermixed in a display.

Figure 2-4 shows a representative dashboard from MicroStrategy, an independent BI software provider. Notice how this image presents current performance, i.e., the dashboard is descriptive. In comparison the scorecard from Dashboards By Example shown in Figure 2-5 shows actual performances compared with target performance, i.e., the scorecard is evaluative.

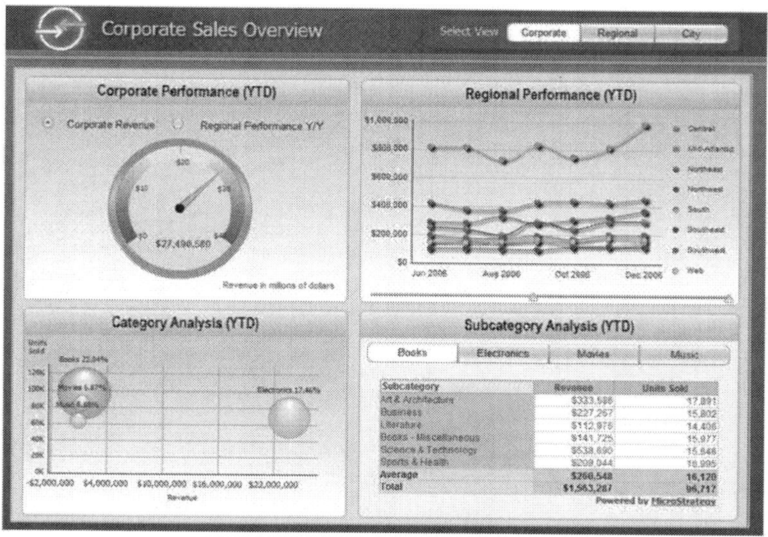

Figure 2-4 Example Dashboard from MicroStrategy

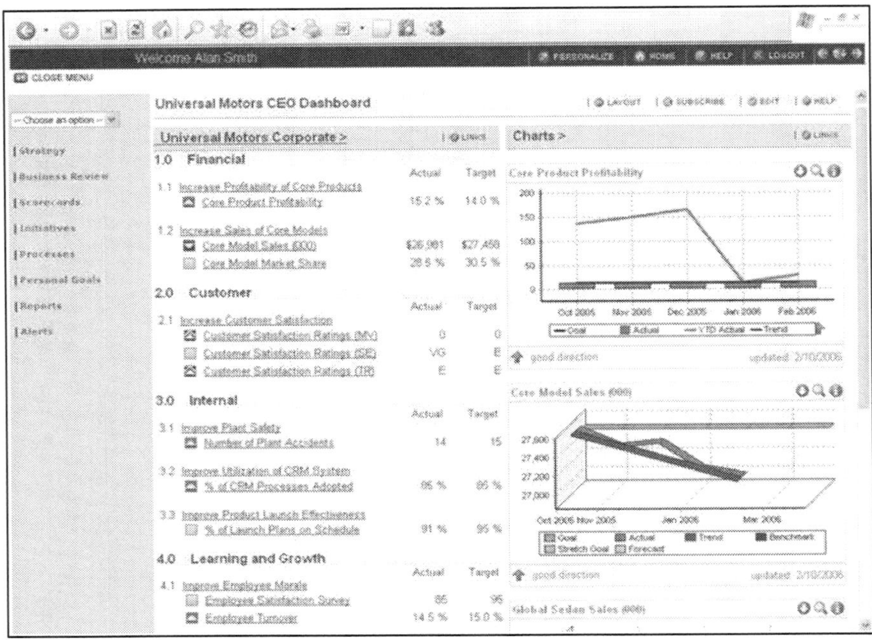

Figure 2-5 Example Scorecard from Dashboards By Example

Regardless of whether the display is called a dashboard or scorecard it presents a considerable amount information in a single visual representation, as in the hackneyed expression, a picture is worth a thousand words. Display designers must take care to represent data fairly in displays. Managers may make decisions based on these displays, and performance unintentionally misrepresented may lead to unintended consequences.

Analytics

In BI analytics we're talking about tools, methods, and models that help us extract information from the business's data. It helps us identify patterns and anomalies; It stimulates us to pose questions about business processes and strategies and to answer them; And it serves as the foundation for models that assist in decision making. Analytics are the primary focus of this book. We will also cover reporting as a way to transmit and publish our results but that is only secondary to producing information for answering important business questions. Reports can also serve as source of data for analysis.

In our generic BI model analytics includes data analysis, forecasting, and data mining. Each will be addressed in more detail in a later chapters. Data analysis can be an umbrella term covering all types of methods and models including quantitative data analysis, qualitative data analysis, exploratory data analysis, statistical analysis, forecasting, data mining, and so on. In this book we use data analysis to mean those methods, procedures, and models other than forecasting and data mining techniques that are relevant for understanding and using business data. With data analysis we will primarily focus on data exploration, data cleansing, cross tabulations and pivot tables, descriptive statistics, simple statistical analysis (an oxymoron?), and correlation and regression.

Forecasting is a standalone topic in its own right. There are two types of forecasting. Qualitative forecasting involves subjective predictions about the future and the business's environment. Fortunately, qualitative forecasting is not, at least yet, in the realm of BI. Quantitative forecasting utilizes historical numerical to identify patterns in data and then project those patterns into the future.

A number of other terms are jumbled in with data mining including exploratory data analysis, predictive analytics, and knowledge discovery. To avoid confusion about what data mining is for this book we'll use a variation on an operational definition, i.e., a definition that says what something does and what operations it performs. For our purposes then data mining is the set of methods that Microsoft uses in its data mining tools in Microsoft SQL Server 2008 and Excel 2010. This set includes association, clustering, and neural network algorithms among others. Data mining as the term is used in the Microsoft BI applications uses these sophisticated techniques to analyze large data sets in specific ways.

Business Intelligence Processes

Figure 2-1 lists data acquisition, cleansing, transformation, storing, analysis, and transmission as the major BI processes that get data from sources to users. We'll now explore the BI processes a bit here and more so in the next chapter. Figure 2-6 presents a simplified generic diagram of BI architecture.

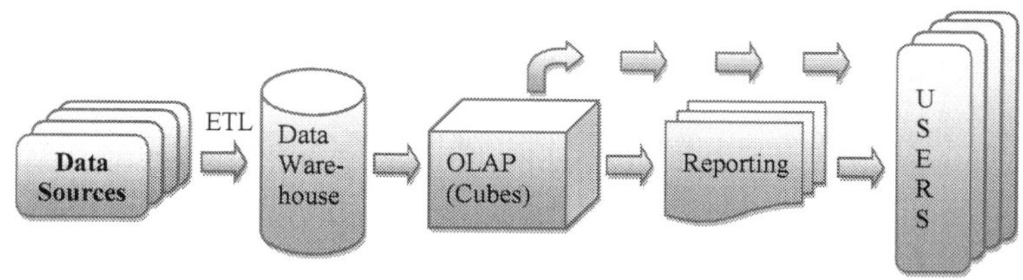

Figure 2-6 Simplified Generic BI Architecture

Original data are loaded into a data warehouse. Online analytical processing (OLAP) transforms the data in the warehouse into a multidimensional database (cube). In the main path of the architecture the reporting service utilizes the multidimensional data to produce reports for users. In the upper path users may access the multidimensional database directly for analysis, presentation, and data mining. Note that it is advisable to add a staging server between data sources and the data warehouse to contain copies of the data sources which the data warehouse extraction process would use instead of directly accessing the original data. This configuration eliminates the risk of damage to the data sources by the extraction process. The staging server is not shown in the diagram because it in inconsequential to our discussion, not because it is unimportant in data warehousing.

Data Warehousing

A data warehouse is a repository for the organization's historical data separate from and in addition to its raw data sources. A data warehouse is periodically updated from its raw data sources and usually has read only access by users. Data warehouses retain historical data which is important for analysis purposes whereas online transaction processing (OLTP) systems may limit historic data to one to a few years.

Some authors make a distinction between a data warehouse and a data mart saying that the warehouse is a larger entity, perhaps containing data for the enterprise, whereas a data mart is a smaller version, limited in scope to the data for a department, location, or organizational function. For our purposes this distinction is unimportant because we are interested in accessing the data that we need regardless of what the repository is called. Thus, for in this book for convenience we'll use data warehouse as the generic term for these types of repositories.

Online Transaction Processing

As discussed briefly above, the business's data may originate in a variety of sources and in a variety of forms. Most of the data will come from online transaction processing systems usually in the form of relational databases. OLTP systems acquire, store, manage, backup, and secure business transaction data like sales, orders, invoices, production, and inventory. The detail in the OLTP database is at event level, i.e., it contains the raw data about transactions, and it usually has a time dimension. For example, an order for a bicycle and accessories in the Microsoft SQL Server AdventureWorks sample database is a transaction listing the items sold, perhaps the prices paid, and the time and date of occurrence.

Generally, OLTP systems should not be directly used for other purposes such as data analysis for at least three reasons. First, OLTP databases are designed for efficiency in handling raw transaction data. They are relational databases that adhere to strict rules for creating, modifying, and managing transaction records. They are built for speed, data integrity, and security, not for usability, data exploration and analysis, or reporting. Although OLTP system usually produce routine reports, they are ill suited for the type of data access required for BI.

Second, OLTP systems are crucial for the continuing operation of the organization. You do not want to mess with them unnecessarily. Bullet proof security on them is imperative, and access to them should be strictly limited. And, rightly so. Consequently, only the database administrator may have direct access to transaction data with others accessing these systems via application programs or stored queries and reports. This means that if a user needs data different from that available, then someone in IT must create the query or report which causes delays, extra work, and perhaps stress and conflict.

Third, OLTP systems usually deal with high volumes of records and may be extremely busy during operating hours. In addition to transaction processing, these systems have other tasks to perform as well such as backup and replication. To avoid degrading system performance intrusions to execute ancillary tasks such as responding to user queries should be minimized.

Why Data Warehousing

OK, so one reason for using a data warehouse is because we can't or shouldn't access OLTP systems directly. Another is that raw data usually reside in disparate sources. For example, organizational functions may have different information systems. Marketing may use a sophisticated CRM; Production may use a homegrown job scheduling and tracking system; And Accounting may be plodding along on a legacy COBOL system. Or, a company using SQL Server merges with another using Oracle. Or, operational data is on a OLTP system but the annual budget is on a spreadsheet. For BI purposes the data from the various sources needs to be integrated to provide users with a single source for, if you will, one-stop data shopping. That's provided by the data warehouse.

Reason three for using a data warehouse is to clean up dirty data. The raw data in your organization may be clean and pure but, believe it or not, this may not be the case elsewhere. There may be inaccuracies, duplications, and empty records just to name a few possibilities. In the process of acquiring data from sources for the warehouse data are cleansed, transformed, and stored into a uniform structure. This process is called ETL for **E**xtracting data from the sources, congruously **T**ransforming it, and **L**oading it into the warehouse. In Figure 2-6 the ETL process is indicated above the arrow between data sources and the data warehouse.

Relational vs. Dimensional Database Architectures

This is one of those things that you should know about but can't do anything about unless you are the data warehouse designer or have the whole BI enchilada on your desktop computer. The conventional design for databases is the relational model. The fundamental structure in this model is a two dimensional table called a relation. A row in the table is an individual, unique record called a tuple, and a column is a field or attribute.

A section of the Orders Details table from the old Microsoft sample database, Northwind Traders, in Table 2-1 shows rows representing a sale of individual products with fields (columns) of OrderID, Product, Unit Price, Quantity, and Discount.

Order ID	Product	Unit Price	Quantity	Discount
10248	Queso Cabrales	$14.00	12	0%
10248	Singaporean Hokkien Fried Mee	$9.80	10	0%
10248	Mozzarella di Giovanni	$34.80	5	0%
10249	Tofu	$18.60	9	0%
10249	Manjimup Dried Apples	$42.40	40	0%
10250	Jack's New England Clam Chowder	$7.70	10	0%
10250	Manjimup Dried Apples	$42.40	35	15%
10250	Louisiana Fiery Hot Pepper Sauce	$16.80	15	15%
10251	Gustaf's Knäckebröd	$16.80	6	5%

Table 2-1 Orders Detail Table

A relational database usually contains numerous tables which are linked by relationships among fields in the tables. Figure 2-7 shows the relationships among the tables in the Northwind database. The Order Details table described above is linked to the Products table and the Orders table. In turn the Products table is linked to the [product] Categories and Supplier tables. The Order Details table is a special type of table called an associative entity used to connect two tables both of which have many to many relationships.

The tables in a relational database are normalized, i.e., they adhere to a set of requirements that insure that the database is efficiently organized by eschewing data redundancy (at least theoretically) and requiring that each table has a single subject or theme. Normalization usually results in databases with many tables.

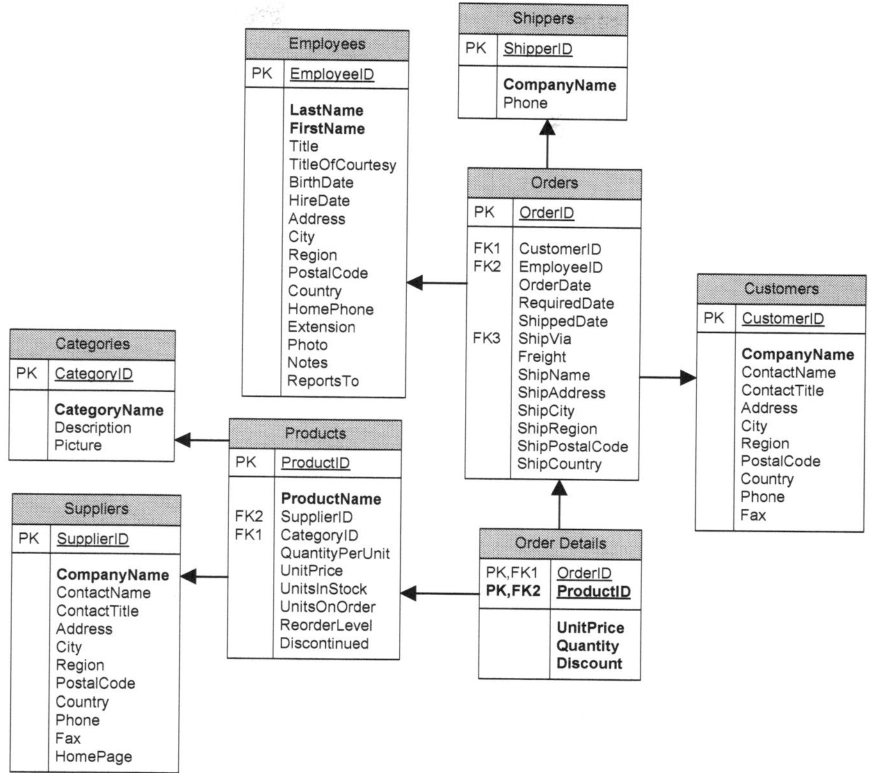

Figure 2-7 Northwind Relational Database Diagram

(For better viewing of this image, go to http://www.zerobits.info/bibook/bibookimages/)

Tables are linked by special fields called keys. A primary key (PK) is a field with a unique identifier, usually a number generated automatically when a row is added to the table. A foreign key (FK) in a table is a primary key from another table that is used to link a record in that table with a record in the other table. For example, the Employees table has EmployeeID as the primary key which is used in the Orders table as a foreign key to identify the employee that took an order. Some tables use composite primary keys which are made up of two or more fields to create a unique identifier. The OrdersDetail table has a composite key of OrderID and ProductID which are also foreign keys. Confused yet? What we need to remember about keys is that regardless of how they are constructed they identify a unique row in a table and allow us to link rows between tables.

The links facilitate selecting specific data from the database even though the data may reside in different tables. This is accomplished by constructing queries. Table 2-2 provides an example of a query in the Northwind database to list sales by product category. This query requires data from four tables: Orders, Orders Details, Products, and Categories.

Sales by Category

Category Name	Product Name	Product Sales
Meat/Poultry	Alice Mutton	$14,123.85
Condiments	Aniseed Syrup	$1,544.00
Seafood	Boston Crab Meat	$9,796.33
Dairy Products	Camembert Pierrot	$22,413.48
Seafood	Carnarvon Tigers	$14,525.00
Beverages	Chai	$5,070.60
Beverages	Chang	$5,817.80
Beverages	Chartreuse verte	$2,295.90
Condiments	Chef Anton's Cajun Seasoning	$5,214.88

Table 2-2 Sales by Category Query

Relational databases use structured query language (SQL—pronounced sequel) to create queries. SQL is also used to create and manage databases as well. The Microsoft Access SQL for the sales by catalog query above is shown in Table 2-3. Although SQL is standardized, applications may use variations. For example, SQL used in Microsoft SQL Server, Transact-SQL, is not quite the same as that used in Microsoft Access. Fortunately, most of us don't have to write SQL because the applications that we use do it for us.

```
SELECT Categories.CategoryName, Products.ProductName,
Sum([Order Details Extended].ExtendedPrice) AS ProductSales
FROM Categories INNER JOIN (Products INNER JOIN
(Orders INNER JOIN [Order Details Extended] ON
Orders.OrderID = [Order Details Extended].OrderID) ON
Products.ProductID = [Order Details Extended].ProductID) ON
Categories.CategoryID = Products.CategoryID
WHERE (((Orders.OrderDate) Between #1/1/1997# And
#12/31/1997#))
GROUP BY Categories.CategoryID, Categories.CategoryName,
Products.ProductName
ORDER BY Categories.CategoryName;
```

Table 2-3 SQL for the Sales by Category Query

Segregating data into individual shallow tables in a relational database facilitates transaction processing but bogs down producing data for use in analysis and reporting. An alternative database architecture, the dimensional model, is specifically designed for complex data access. In a dimensional database data are consolidated into fact tables and dimension tables. Fact tables contain the numerical measures that will be of interest such as sales in units or dollars, cost data, or production counts. Dimension tables contain attributes of objects related to the facts such as products, employees, and customers. There is also usually a time dimension as well.

Figure 2-8 shows a simplified dimensional model diagram for the Northwest Traders database discussed above. In the diagram the dimension tables are located around the fact table. This is called a star schema because an abstraction of such a diagram resembles a star. (A schema defines the structure of a database. We'll use the term interchangeably with architecture.) The snowflake schema is another dimensional structure where one or more dimensions will have a sub-dimension(s). For example, we would have a snowflake schema if ProductCategory in the DimProduct table was split off as another table and linked back to the DimProduct table. We care about these different architectures if we are building data warehouses but if we're not, we use what they give us.

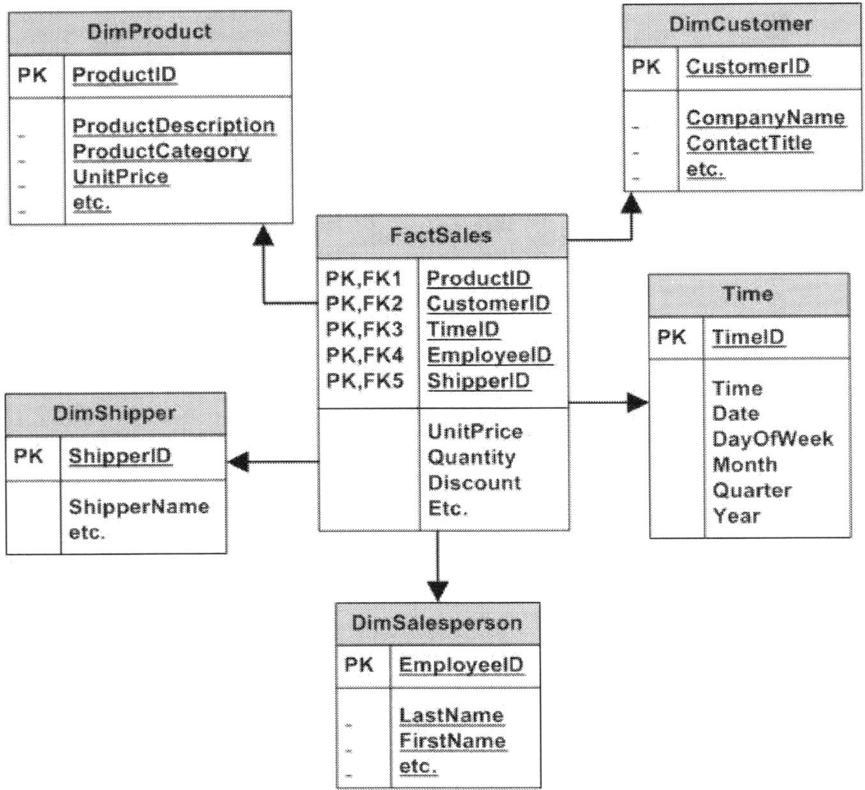

Figure 2-8 Northwind Dimensional Database Diagram

(For better viewing of this image, go to http://www.zerobits.info/bibook/bibookimages/)

The current wisdom seems to be that the dimensional architecture is preferable for data warehouses. However, OLAP can handle either relational or dimensional architectures, at least in Microsoft's BI toolset. By the way it's interesting to note that the sample AdventureWorks OLTP database has 68 tables and its dimensional data warehouse version, called AdventureWorksDWR2 (DW for data warehouse), has only 28 tables.

Online Analytical Processing

We said earlier that Online analytical processing (OLAP) transforms the data in the warehouse into a multidimensional database. This multidimensional database can be envisioned as a multidimensional dimensional cube—in fact it's called that—with dimensions on the axes and measures as cell values.

Figure 2-9 below shows a three dimensional cube representation of the Northwind example with Product, Customer, and Time as dimensions and sales as the cell values.

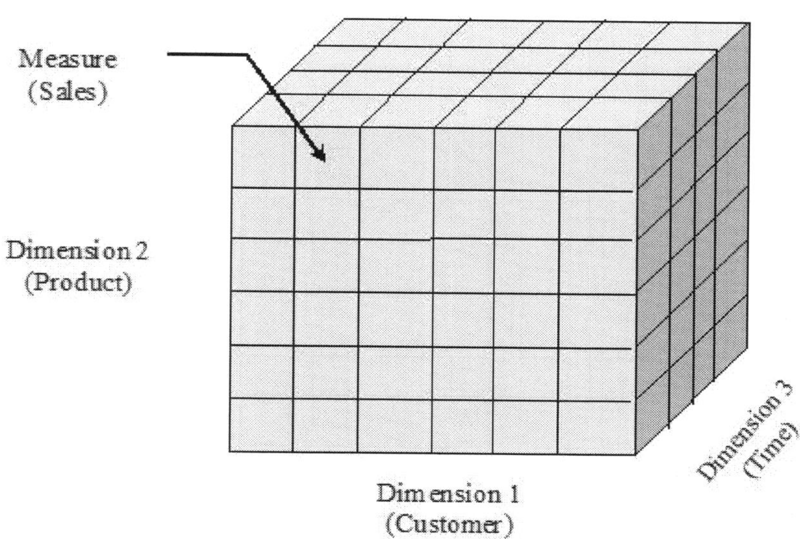

Figure 2-9 OLAP Cube

You can think of a multidimensional database as a stack of tables like the one in Figure 2-10. Here, Products and Customers are the row and column headings with sales in dollars in the intersecting cells. Each table contains sales for one day on the time dimension. In the example total sales for Product 5 to Customer 3 on April 5 were $274.61.

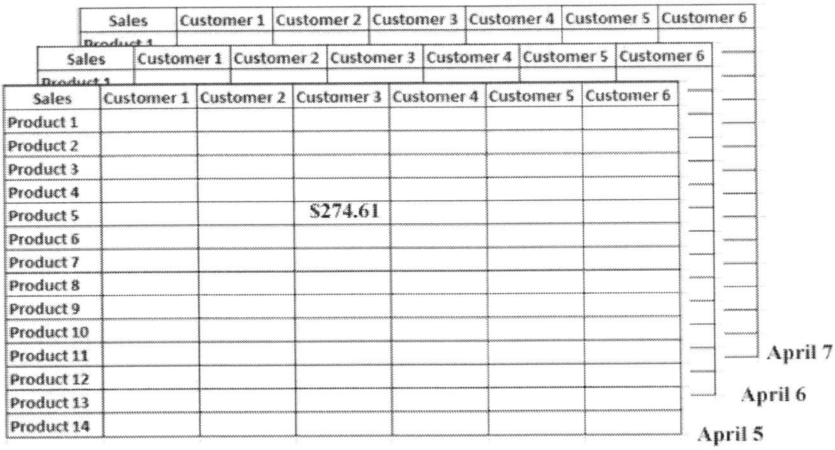

Sales	Customer 1	Customer 2	Customer 3	Customer 4	Customer 5	Customer 6
Product 1						
Product 2						
Product 3						
Product 4						
Product 5			$274.61			
Product 6						
Product 7						
Product 8						
Product 9						
Product 10						
Product 11						
Product 12						
Product 13						
Product 14						

April 7

April 6

April 5

Figure 2-10 OLAP Cube as Stacked Tables

OLAP performs queries very quickly because some of the data for queries is preprocessed at the time the data are loaded into the multidimensional database. In addition OLAP may aggregate fact values at higher levels of consolidation in advance. For example, in the Northwind OLAP example, OLAP may aggregate sales by week, month, quarter, and year. Thus, when a user requests, say, total sales for each product for the month of April, OLAP already has the values available and does not have to compute them from atomic-level data.

Atomic-level data is that at the lowest level of detail, and the level of detail is often referred to as the granularity or grain of the dimension or measure. The lowest level of detail in the Northwind database is an order with an order date and the products contained in it. If only the product category was included in Northwind, then the granularity would be coarser than if the product (a lower level of detail) is included as shown in Figure 2-7.

OLAP also gains efficiency by storing some or all of its data in the cube. There are three OLAP storage configurations: Relational OLAP (ROLAP) stores the database structure in cube but leaves the fact data in the warehouse; Multidimensional OLAP (MOLAP) stores everything in the cube; And Hybrid OLAP, a combination of ROLAP and MOLAP, stores the structure and aggregates in the cube but not the fact data. MOLAP is generally recommended, especially for retrieval speed. However, there are circumstances where ROLAP or HOLAP may be preferred. Again, we are fortunate that the BI system designers have to deal with this, not us.

OLAP may also supply calculated measures and key performance indicators. Calculated measures are values derived from and are available in addition to the fact data. For example, a Northwind cube may contain a gross margin measure that is calculated by OLAP from price and cost facts. We'll see later that users may create calculated measures themselves in Microsoft Excel.

Key performance indicators (KPIs) are OLAP facts compared with an objective and usually showing the trend of the measure. For example, a convenience store operator may have gross margin in cents per gallon of fuel as a KPI. A display of the KPI may show its current value, its trend direction from the previous value, and a goal value. KPIs are used in scorecards and dashboards. In fact, the scorecard in Figure 2-5 utilizes KPIs.

Users can extract a great variety of information from an OLAP cube, in various levels of detail, and from many perspectives. Of course, there is jargon to describe various views of and operations on the data. Users can drill-down/up, roll up, slice and dice, pivot, drill-through the cube, and more. To drill-down means to expand a dimension to a lower level of detail, and drill up means just the opposite—to summarize to a higher level of detail. For our purposes roll up is similar to drill up. An example of drilling down is expansion of the accessories product category as noted in Figure 2-3.

A slice is a sub layer of a dimension so slicing and dicing is looking at subsections of a cube. It is equivalent to filtering. Pivoting (or rotating) changes the axes of the displayed data. We'll learn more about pivoting when we use Excel pivot tables. Drill-through allows viewing related reports or views with one-click, similar in behavior to a hyperlink.

What's Next

I hope that this has been a useful overview of BI concepts and processes. Most of the topics above are in themselves quite deep and complex. For example, there are books available just about the ETL process. Fortunately again, that level of detailed knowledge is not necessary for using BI tools. The material that we've covered here will serve as a foundation for learning about those tools in subsequent chapters, and should also help you to communicate. more effectively with your IT colleagues.

In the next chapter we will look at Microsoft's rendition of BI, and how SQL Server 2008 approaches BI.

Chapter 3 - Microsoft SQL Server 2008 Business Intelligence Tools

In this chapter we'll survey SQL Server 2008 and its BI related services. In Chapter 1 I mentioned that I wrote this book assuming that users would have limited permissions to access SQL Server, i.e., they would be unable to utilize directly SQL Server's tools to build, modify, or manage BI services. So, why take time here to go over technology that you cannot use? Because, like broccoli, it's good for you? That may be part of it but the primary reason is because you will be using software applications, specifically Excel and Access 2010 and Report Builder 3.0, that utilize SQL Servers databases and services.

In addition, I believe that informed users are more efficient and effective users. By knowing what data and information the services can provide and how they are packaged users are better prepared to understand the data available to them and to access those data in forms that meet their needs. Furthermore, a general understanding about these BI services and the vocabulary associated with them will also help you to communicate more effectively with the IT folks.

Figure 3-1 provides a revision of Figure 2-6 incorporating SQL Server's BI services. Integration Services performs the extract, transform, and load processes (ETL) to build the data warehouse in a SQL Server database from data from various sources. Analysis Services creates the cubes including calculated measures and KPIs. A second function of Analysis Services is to build data mining models. Reporting Services produces reports that are accessed by users via the Report Server. Of course, users may also extract data from the cubes themselves for further analysis. As noted in Chapter 1 users may access data and reports via many different routes including browsers, Excel 2010, Access 2010, and SharePoint Server.

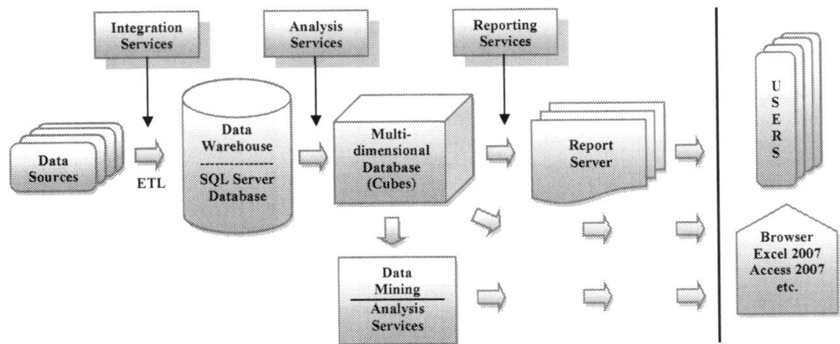

Figure 3-1 Simplified Microsoft BI Architecture

SQL Server is the mainstay of Microsoft BI. BI applications in Microsoft SQL Server go back to at least to SQL Server 7 (1998). While these applications were improved and expanded in SQL Server 2000, SQL Server 2005 included a significant overhaul of its BI technology. The debut of SQL Server Management Studio made it much easier to manage SQL Server databases; The Business Intelligence Development Studio integrated into Visual Studio 2005 provided an easy to use integrated development environment to develop and manage BI services; The Unified Dimensional Model was introduced to provide users with a single source for disparate raw data; And much more. Although SQL Server 2008 has some enhancements, the BI technology in it is very similar to that in the 2005 version. The major components of SQL Server from a BI perspective are the Database Server, the Business Intelligence Development Studio, Integrations Services, Analysis Services, and Reporting Services.

SQL Server Database Server

SQL Server is first and foremost a database management system (DBMS). In Chapter 2 we described a database in a roundabout way in our sketch of data warehousing—one of the uses for a DBMS. A database is an organized collection of records. DBMSs create and manage database structures and the data within them. They use tables with fields and records to hold the data, and they create relationships among the tables to use queries to extract the data for applications and users. The SQL Server Database Server does that work for SQL Server. As mentioned earlier SQL Server's version of structured query language is Transact-SQL or T-SQL for short.

There are many DBMSs available for every computer platform. SQL Server is Microsoft's premier DBMS for the Windows platform. In terms of market share for enterprise-level DBMSs SQL Server is third behind number two DB2 from IBM and number one Oracle.

SQL Server Management Studio

SQL Server Management Studio is used to develop and manage SQL Server databases. Figure 3-2 shows a partial screen shot of the SSMS integrated development environment (IDE) on my computer. An IDE is computer application with a graphical user interface (GUI) to support software development and testing.

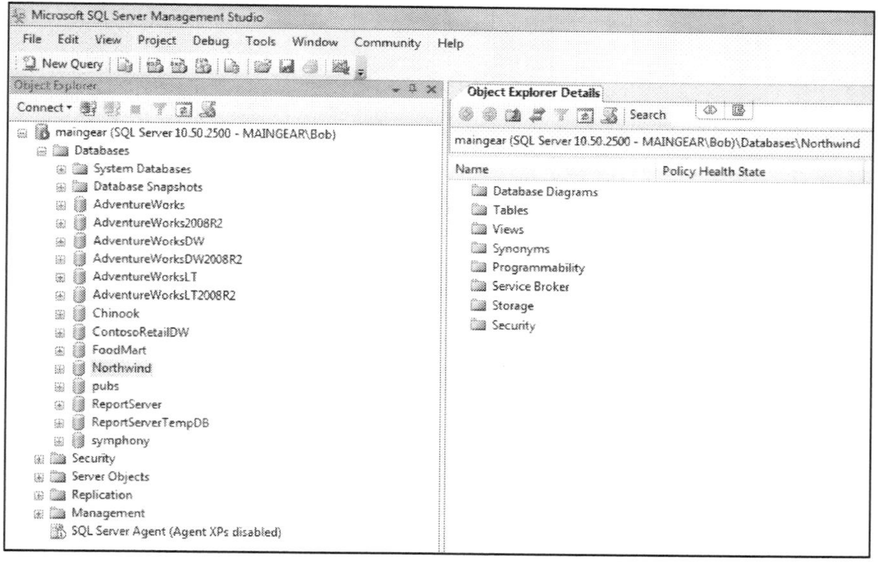

Figure 3-2 SQL Server 2008 Management Studio

The instance of SQL Server 2008 R2 (SQL Server version 10.50) that we're connected to in Figure 3-2 is named MAINGEAR. I've expanded the Databases folder in the Object Explorer on the left by clicking the + box to list all of the databases managed by this instance. AdventureWorks is the sample database for SQL Server 2008. FoodMart, Northwind, and Pubs databases are previous SQL Server sample databases. Chinook is a sample database alternative to Northwind, and Contoso is a BI demo dataset from Microsoft for the retail industry. Note again that Microsoft now provides sample databases from CodePlex, its open source project hosting Web site. Also note FYI that SQL Server databases have a file extension of "mdf."

The Object Explorer Details tab on the right side of Figure 3-2 lists the objects in the Northwind database. The same list would be shown in the Object Explorer itself if we had clicked the + box beside Northwind. The database diagram shown in Figure 3-3 is the first object listed in the Details tab. (Note that I created the diagram in Visio which is easier to work with than the SQL Server diagramming tool.) The database diagram presented here is a more complete than shown in Figure 2-7. The Employees table is now linked with an EmployeeTerritories table which in turn is linked to Territories and then Regions, and the Customers table now as an associative entity connected to it to link it to a CustomerDemographics table.

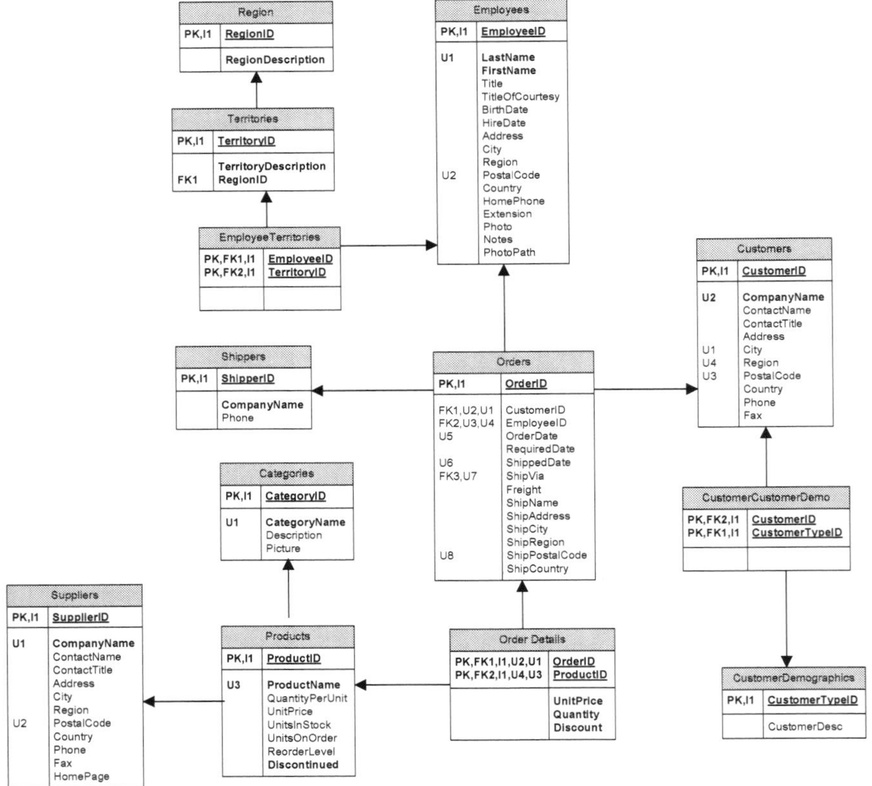

Figure 3-3 SQL Server 2008 Northwind Diagram
(For better viewing of this image, go to
http://www.zerobits.info/bibook/bibookimages/)

Figure 3-4 shows the expansion of the Northwind folder and its subordinate Tables folder. The tables listed are the same ones shown in Figure 3-3 above.

The Object Explorer Details tab displays rows of data from the Orders Details table.

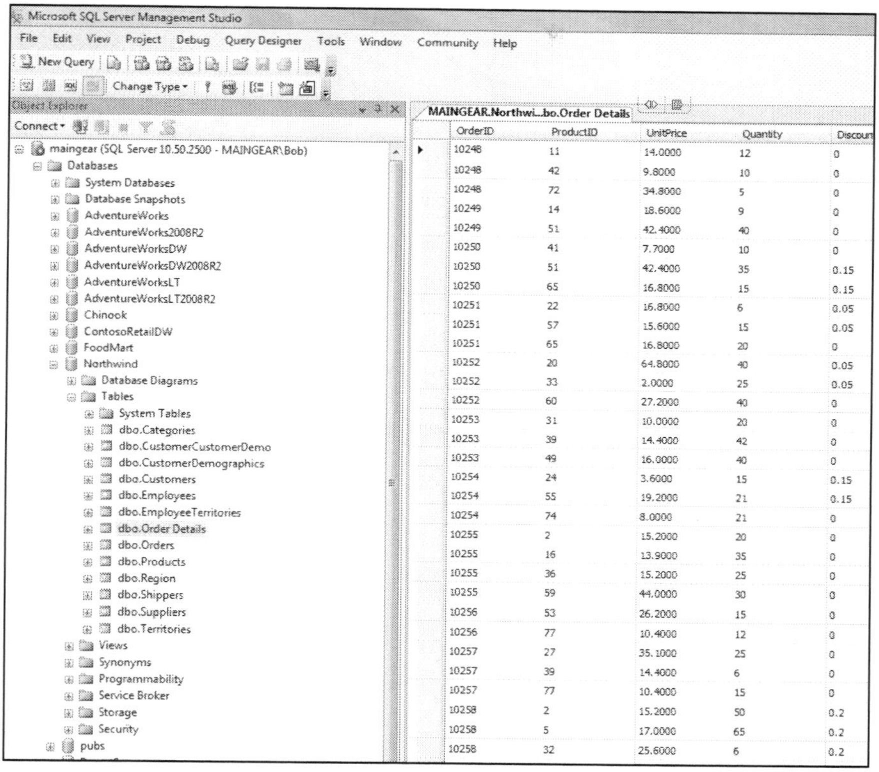

Figure 3-4 SQL Server 2008 Management Studio—Orders Detail

(For better viewing of this image, go to http://www.zerobits.info/bibook/bibookimages/)

In Figure 3-5 the expanded listing of the Views folder which is just below the Tables folder in the Object Explorer shows all of the views that have been created for the Northwind database. Views are stored queries. Some of the records in the Sales by Category view (previously shown in Table 2-2) appear in the Object Explorer Details tab on the right side of the screen shot.

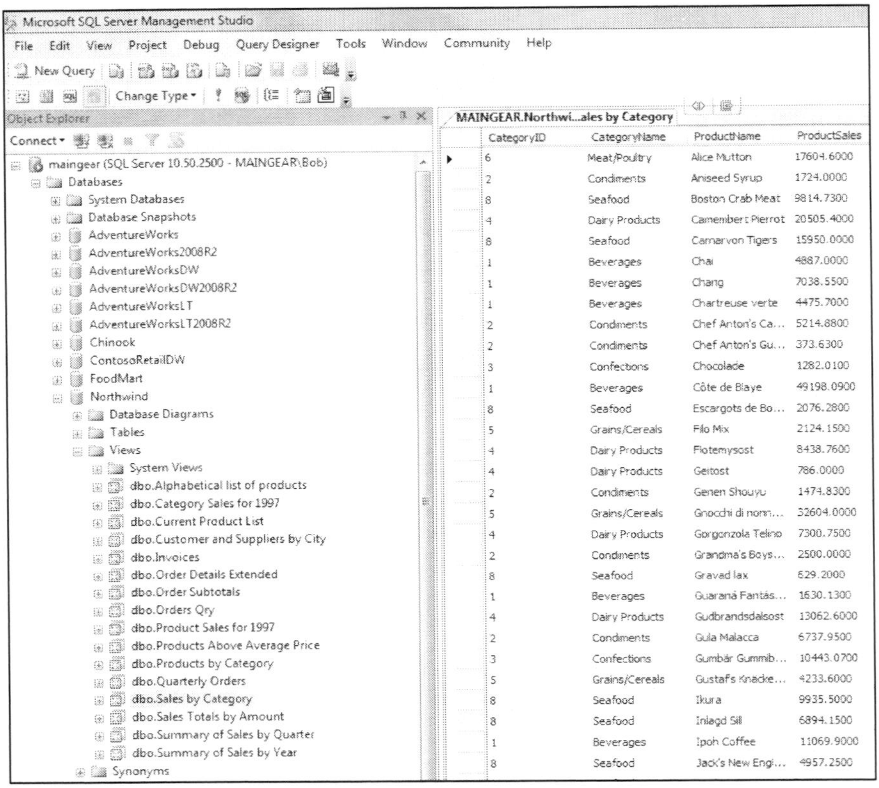

Figure 3-5 SQL Server 2008 Management Studio—Views

(For better viewing of this image, go to http://www.zerobits.info/bibook/bibookimages/)

Stored procedures, contained in the Programmability folder shown in Figure 3-6, are scripts (programs) written in T-SQL that can be executed to perform a variety of tasks. Of interest to us are stored procedures that return data like views only stored procedures can perform more complex operations on the data and values can be passed to them via parameters. The script of the CustOrderHist stored procedure in the Details Tab on the right is essentially a customer order history view with a parameter @CustomerID to specify the customer whose history should be presented.

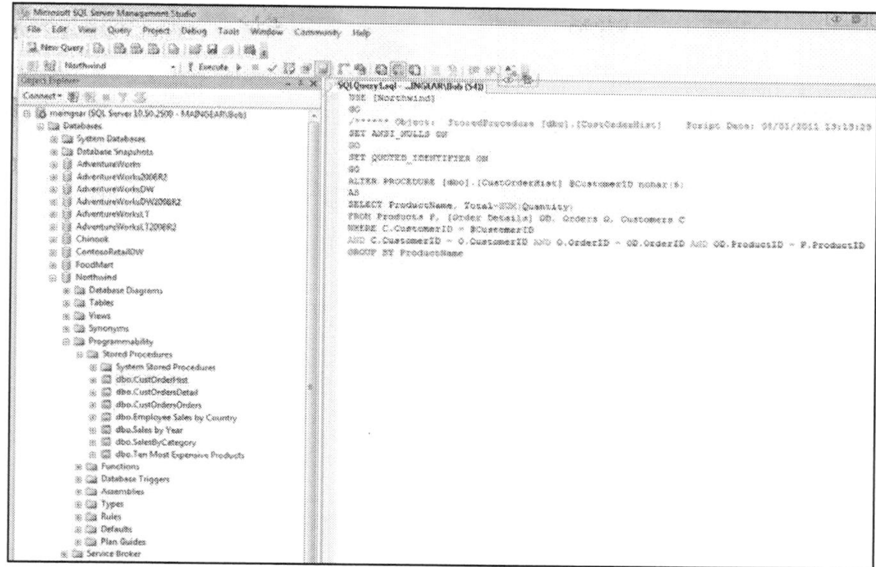

Figure 3-6 SQL Server 2008 Management Studio—Stored Procedures

The other folders listed within a database folder (see Figure 3-4) are not particularly applicable to us analysts and power users so we'll not discuss them here.

Figure 3-7 shows that SSMS can connect to the Analysis Server, Report Server, and Integration Services as well as the SQL Server Database Server. Although these services can be managed in SSMS, the primary development environment for using them is the Business Intelligence Development Studio described below.

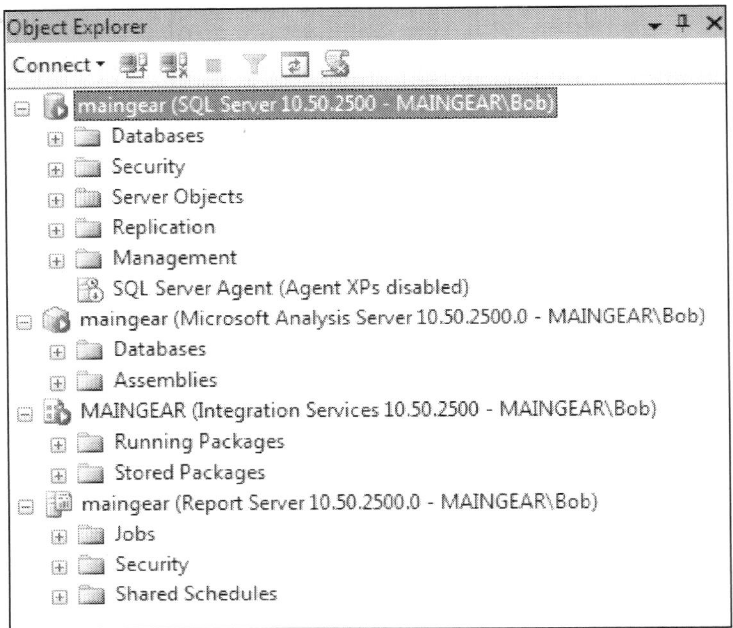

Figure 3-7 SQL Server 2008 Management Studio—Connections

Business Intelligence Development Studio

The Business Intelligence Development Studio (BIDS) is the IDE for developing Integration Services (ETL), Analysis Services (cubes and data mining), and Reporting Services applications. BIDS runs within Visual studio—you can consider it as a Visual Studio add-in. Figure 3-8 shows a partial screen shot of the BIDS (Visual Studio) Start Page. I have clicked on Create Project to open the New Project Dialog Box which lists the Visual Studio templates available for Business Intelligence Projects: Analysis Services Project, Integrations Services Connections Project Wizard, Report Server Project Wizard, Report Server Project, Import Analysis Services Database, Integration Services Project, and Report Model Project. Selecting a template with "Project" at the end of the name will create a new project of that type. Each of the three types of projects—Integrations Services, Analysis Services, and Reporting Services—have different functionality and IDE characteristics. We'll briefly look at each of these below.

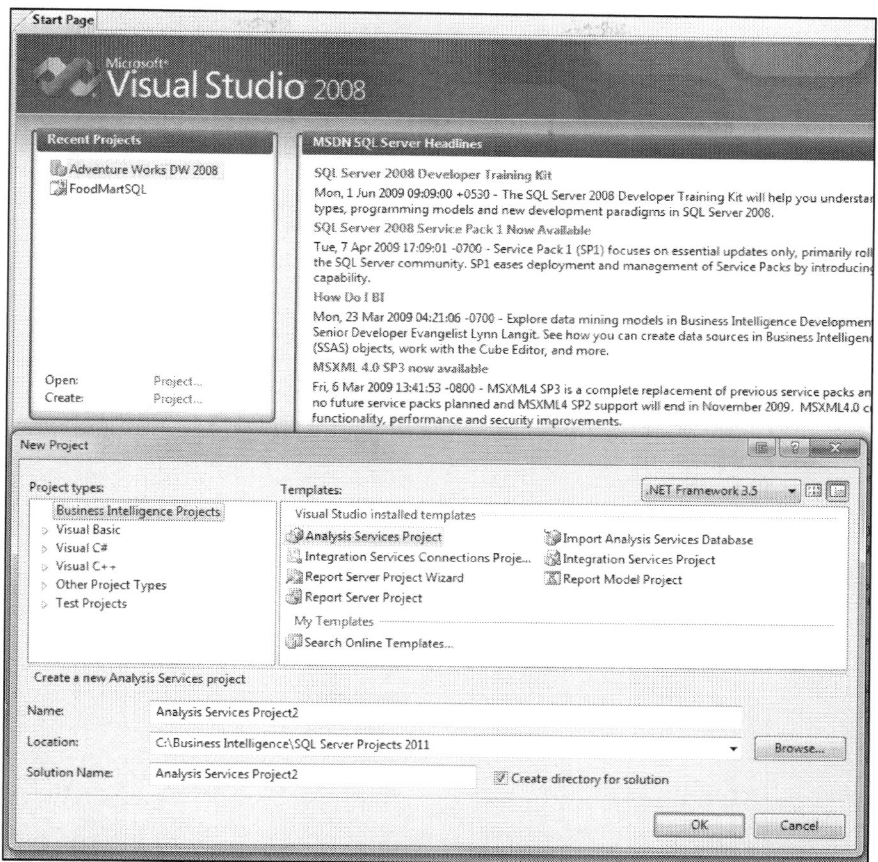

Figure 3-8 Business Intelligence Development Studio Start Page

(For better viewing of this image, go to http://www.zerobits.info/bibook/bibookimages/)

BIDS creates, edits, manages, and deploys BI projects and solutions. Think of a solution as a software application, say for example, an Application Services program to build a cube. There are one or more projects within a solution, although most solutions only have one project, at least in my case. Figure 3-9 shows a screen shot of BIDS. The left panel is the toolbox with objects that can be added to projects by dragging and dropping. The center panel is the designer window where developers create applications graphically or with code. The right panel in this case has two windows: the Solutions Explorer and Properties. The Solution Explorer contains all of the items in the solution. The Properties window lists the properties of the object selected.

SQL Server 2008 Integration Services (SSIS)

Integration Services is used to perform SQL Server's Extract, Transform, and Load (ETL) tasks. SSIS does its work with packages which are sets of instructions that tell SSIS what to do, somewhat like computer programs do. In Figure 3-9 the Solution Explorer in the right panel lists Load Product Dimension as the only package in the project so far.

Packages have control flow and data flow elements. Control flow does what its name implies—it manages a sequence of steps in a procedure. There is one control flow in a package. ETL designers can select a variety of control flow elements from the toolbox in the left panel. In this case I clicked on the Data Flow Task object, dragged it to the designer window, and then gave it a name, Load Products. I created two more Data Flow Tasks, Load Categories and Load Suppliers, and connected them with arrows to specify the task sequence to load the product dimension in a Northwind data warehouse—one somewhat similar to that shown in Figure 2-8.

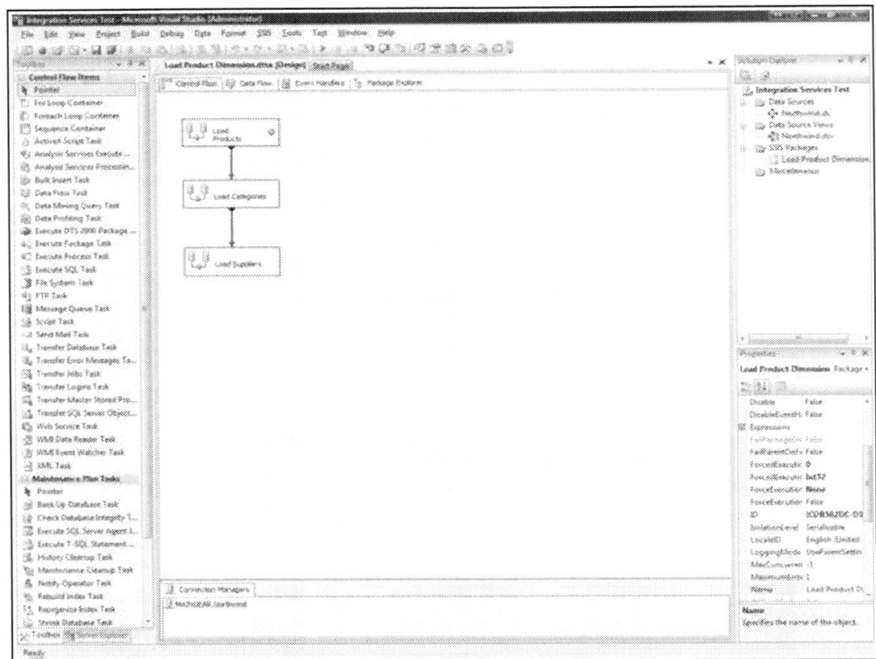

Figure 3-9 BIDS Integration Services Control Flow Example

If I double click on one of the data flow tasks, say the Load Products task, the designer window switches to the Data Flow tab and the toolbox changes to data flow objects: data flow sources, transformations, and destinations. Figure 3-10 shows the Data flow designer for the Load Products Data Flow Task.

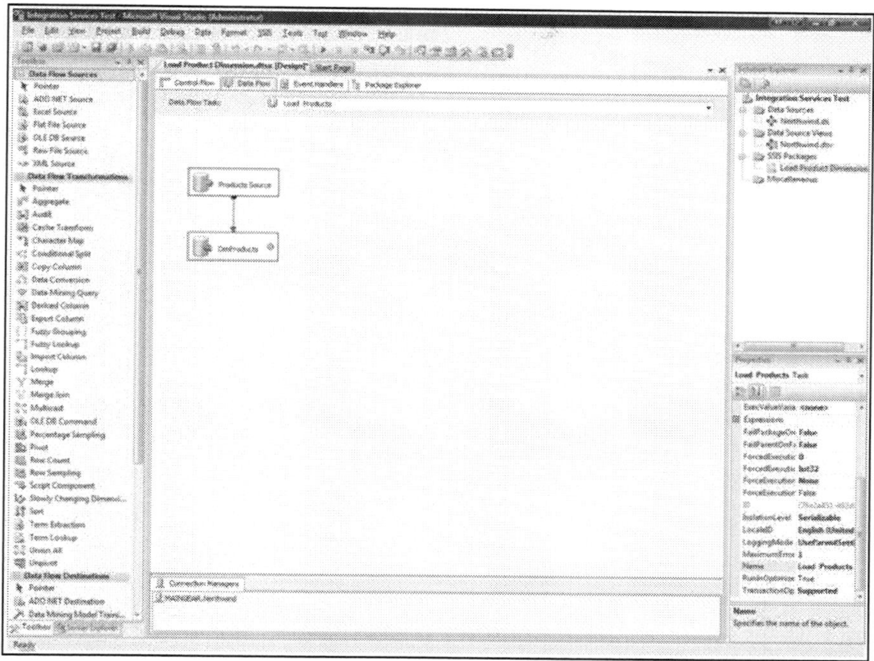

Figure 3-10 BIDS Integration Services Data Flow Example

This data flow only has two components which I dragged and dropped from the toolbox. The Products Source component defines a data source for the data flow. In this case the source would be the Northwind database. DimProducts defines the destination—the product dimension in the Northwind dimensional data warehouse. There was no transformation operation necessary for this simple data flow. To configure a data flow object, say Products Source, I would double click on it and use wizards, code, and/or scripts to complete the process.

Packages can be scheduled to run periodically or run in response to some event. For example, a data warehouse update package may be scheduled to run after the close of business each day, probably after the backup of the OLTP databases. Or a package could be triggered to run when a new record is inserted into a particular table in a data source.

We're now finished with the preliminaries and can move on the parts of SQL Server that will be more useful for data analysis. But before we do that let's look at the AdventureWorks samples.

AdventureWorks

AdventureWorks is a collection of SQL Server samples and examples provided by Microsoft. Sample databases are no longer installed automatically with SQL Server 2008—they must be downloaded from CodePlex and installed separately. The AdventureWorks samples that we will use are AdventureWorks2008DWR2, the dimensional data warehouse, and AdventureWorks Sample Reports.

Adventure Works sells bicycles that it manufactures and related products such as clothing, components, and accessories that it purchases to consumers online and to stores for resale. It is an international company with sales in North America, Europe, and Australia with its corporate headquarters in the Washington state with regional sales teams located in their primary markets. The Adventure Works OLTP database (AdventureWorks2008) containing data related to customers, human resources, production, purchasing, and sales is the data source for AdventureWorks DW (data warehouse).

AdventureWorks Data Warehouse

AdventureWorks DW as mentioned in Chapter 2 has 28 tables compared with its OLTP source with 68. This large difference in size is due to the compression of information in the dimensional model. Even the 28 table version is quite complex as shown by the illegible structural diagram of it shown in Figure 3-11.

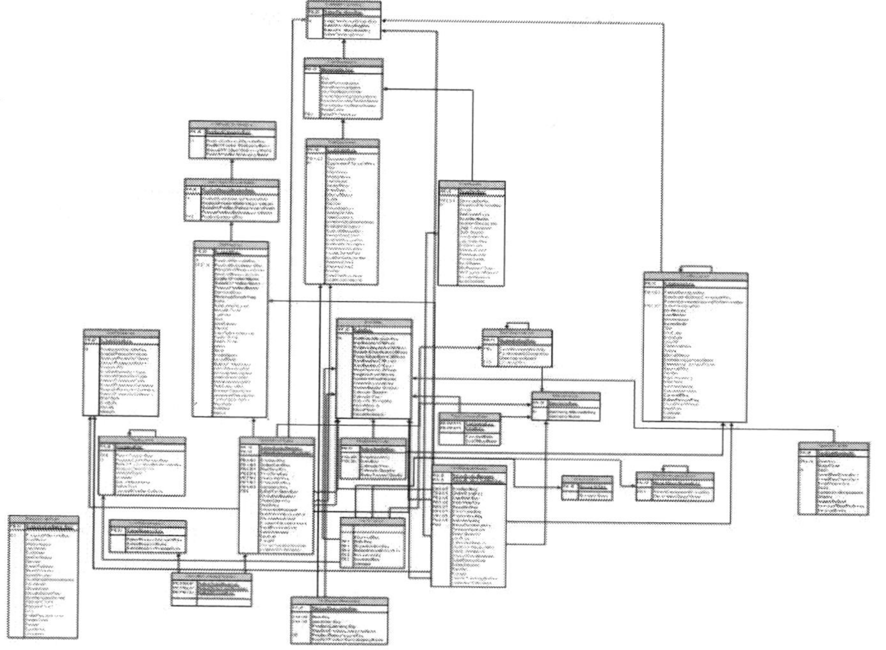

Figure 3-11 AdventureWorks DW Diagram

(For better viewing of this image, go to http://www.zerobits.info/bibook/bibookimages/)

Figure 3-12a shows the tables in AdventureWorks DW in a partial screen shot of the Object Explorer panel in the SQL Server management Studio. The AdventureWorks DW focuses on sales data although there is a bit of accounting data in the Finance fact table and Account dimension table and currency data in the CurrencyRate fact table and in the Currency dimension table. For our examples in this book we'll primarily use Internet sales data from the InternetSales fact table and dimensional data from the Customer, ProductCategory, and SalesTerritory tables. Figure 3-12b lists the dimensions and measures in the AdventureWorks cube contained in AdventureWorks DW. Data in the warehouse cover four years, 2005 through 2008.

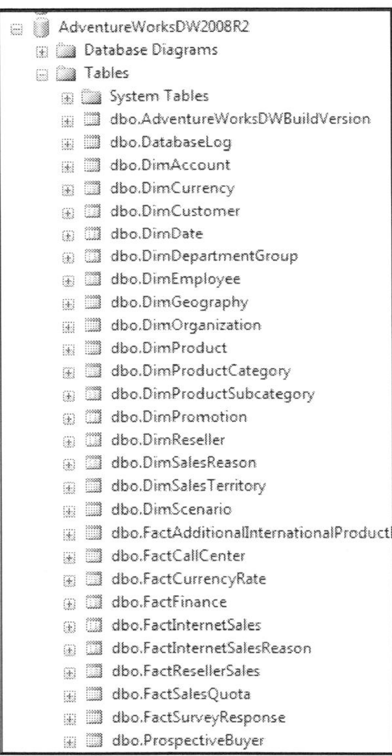

Figure 3-12a AdventureWorks DW Tables

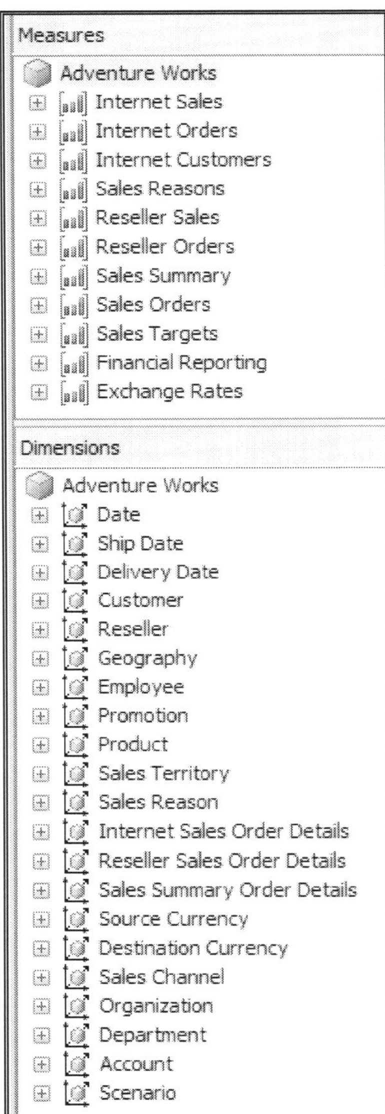

Figure 3-12b AdventureWorks Cube

Figure 3-12 AdventureWorks DW Structure

(For better viewing of this image, go to http://www.zerobits.info/bibook/bibookimages/)

SQL Server 2008 Analysis Services

Analysis Services is used to create and deploy cubes and data mining structures and models. A screen shot of the sample Analysis Services project for AdventureWorks DW in BIDS is shown in Figure 3-13. The Solution Explorer in the right upper panel shows the components in the solution. In creating an Analysis Services project you first define a data source(s) which is usually accomplished with the help of the Data Source Wizard. For example, the AdventureWorks.ds data source is connected to the AdventureWorks DW dimensional database.

Data Source Views are what Analysis Services uses as its data sources for processing. Think of them as queries. Data Source Views allow Analysis Services to be disconnected from the data source, and permits data from multiple sources to be used in a view. The views are created with the help of the Data Source View Wizard. The BIDS Designer pane in the middle of the screen shot displays the tables in the AdventureWorks.dsv (data source view) and the schema diagram of it. The Properties window in the lower right corner has little information so we'll ignore it here.

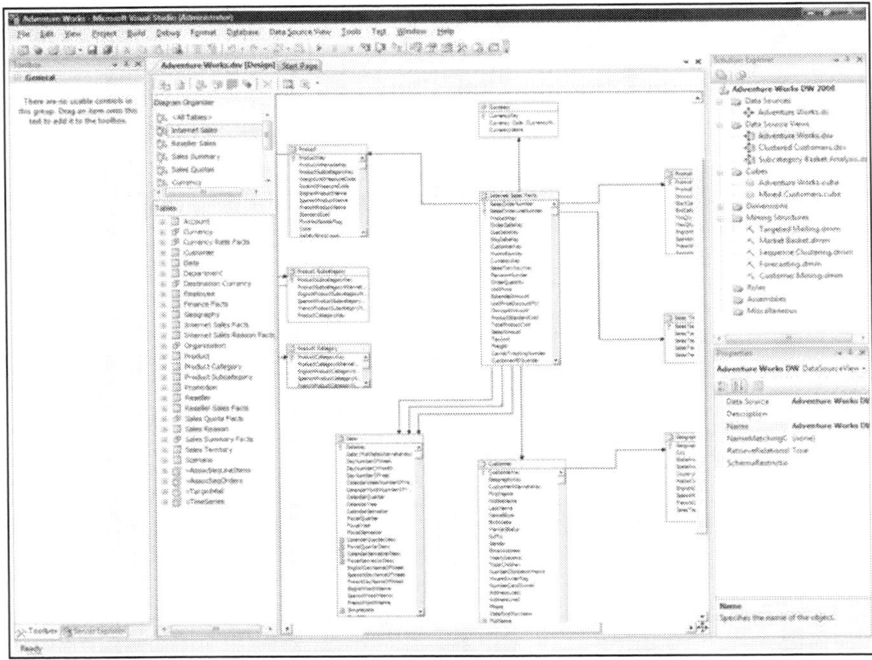

Figure 3-13 BIDS Analysis Services - Data Sources and Views

(For better viewing of this image, go to http://www.zerobits.info/bibook/bibookimages/)

Analysis Services uses the Microsoft Unified Dimensional Model (UDM), introduced in SQL Server 2005, to extract data from sources. UDM is called an abstraction layer but think of the it as a data broker that extracts the appropriate data from disparate sources and presents it to the user as an organized collection. For the UDM, and thus Analysis Services, the data do not have to be in data warehouses. In fact, with UDM we can go back and tap into the original raw data sources. However, as mentioned in Chapter 2 this is bad practice, and we should access data from a non-production, intermediate source like a data warehouse. In Analysis Services, data provided by UDM are used to create cubes and data mining models.

Analysis Services - Cubes

Recall that cubes are multidimensional structures with measures (facts) and dimensions. Cubes are created in Analysis Services with the help of the Cube Wizard. The AdventureWorks DW Analysis Services sample project contains two cubes as you can see in the Solution Explorer window. Clicking on the

AdventureWorks cube there changes the Designer window to the Adventure Works Cube Design shown in Figure 3-14.

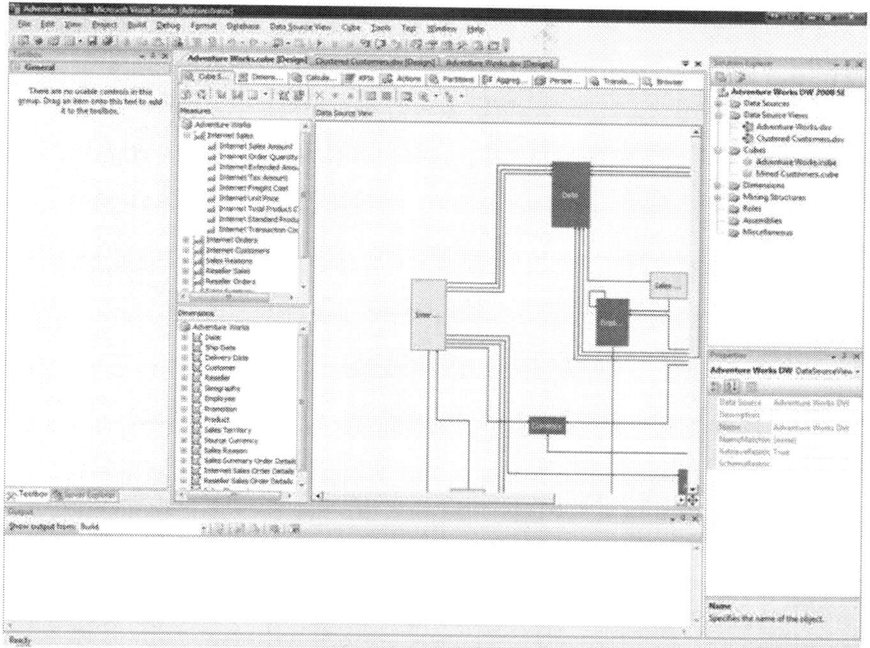

Figure 3-14 BIDS Analysis Services - Cubes

They're difficult to see but there are now a number of tabs across the top of the Designer window. The first, which is selected, is the Cube Structure partially shown in the view panel. On the left side of the Designer the top panel lists the measures available in the cube. I've expanded the Internet Sales measure category to show the specific measures. Similarly, the left lower panel lists the available dimensions.

A time/date dimension is almost always included in a cube to support temporal analysis of data. In fact, Date is the first dimension in the Dimensions list. The time dimension in a cube is particularly hierarchical. For Example, the Adventure Works DW Date dimension includes the following designed-in date attributes:

Date	Calendar week number	English day name of week
Day number of the week	Calendar month number	Spanish day name of week
Day Number of the year	Calendar quarter	French day name of week
Fiscal quarter	Calendar year	English month name
Fiscal semester	Calendar semester	Spanish month name
Fiscal year		French month name

If you want to compare sales by year by quarter by month, you can do so. If you want to look at sales by day of the week for a sales staffing needs analysis, you can do so. And so on. Some cubes may have time attributes down to the second or fraction of a second depending on the application.

Calculated Members

Calculations, i.e., calculated members mentioned in Chapter 1, is the third tab at the top of the Designer window shown in Figure 3-15. We'll pass the second tab, Dimensions, because it doesn't contain much. Calculated members use data from the original measures and create new ones using Multidimensional Expressions (MDX). MDX is a SQL type language for working with multidimensional databases.

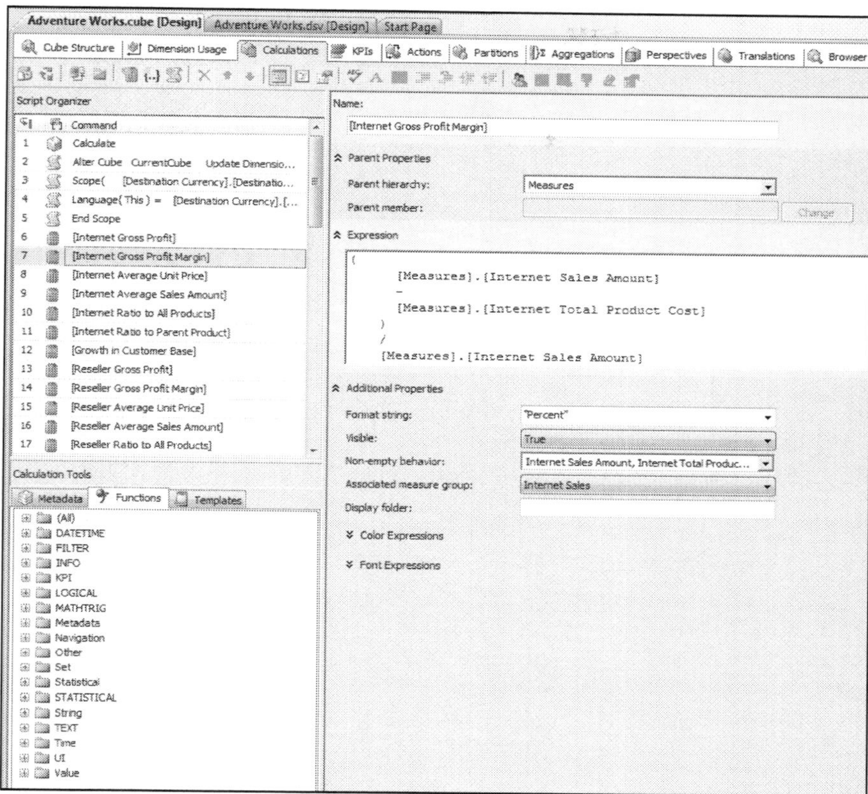

Figure 3-15 BIDS Analysis Services - Cube Calculations

(For better viewing of this image, go to http://www.zerobits.info/bibook/bibookimages/)

The Script Organizer on the top left of the Designer for the Calculations tab lists the calculated measures for the project. There are a bunch of them. Below that panel is a list of Calculation tools with the Functions tab selected. Functions can be dragged and dropped into expressions to perform various calculations. For example, the AVE statistical calculation function would be used to compute the arithmetic mean. The MetaData tab lists the measures and dimensions available in the cube, and the Templates tab lists a number of model measures such as net profit margin and moving average that can be tailored by the user. These can be dragged and dropped into an expression as well. The larger Designer panel to the right shows the calculation for the Internet Gross Profit Margin calculated measure in the Expressions code textbox. Remember, Internet Gross Profit Margin is not an original measure.

The expression to compute Internet Gross Profit Margin, shown is the Expression textbox, is a simple MDX formula:

> ([Measures].[Internet Sales Amount] - [Measures].[Internet Total Product Cost])/[Measures].[Internet Sales Amount]
>
> Or in English, sales less cost divided by sales

Other calculated measure expressions can become quite complicated with the addition of program control statements like IF - Then - Else and Case statements or the calculation tools mentioned above. Formatting options are selected in the Additional Properties area below the Expressions code textbox. Fortunately, we will use MDX only sparingly if at all.

Key Performance Indicators

In Chapter 2 we defined KPIs as OLAP facts compared with an objective and usually showing the trend of the measure. More specifically, a KPI is composed of a measure, its value, a goal its degree of accomplishment, and a trend indicator. KPIs can be used in reports, dashboards and scorecards, Excel, or other places where you can access Analysis Services or create your own. For example, a convenience store operator may have a KPI for the gross margin on gasoline in cents per gallon, i.e., the difference between the selling price and cost, with an objective of at least $.15. The KPI in a report would present the current value of the margin, say $.12, its relationship with the goal -$.03 below, and its trend, say upward if the pervious margin was $.11.

The Designer Window in Figure 3-16 lists the KPIs that have already been created in this cube: Growth in Customer Base, Net Income, etc. Calculation tools, the panel below it, is the same as described above except that the Metadata tab is selected in which the available measures (including calculated measures) and dimensions are listed.

Value, goal, status and trend expressions are constructed in the main Designer pane. In Figure 3-16 I selected the Product Gross Profit Margin KPI. The Value Expression is the calculated measure Gross Profit Margin dragged from the Calculation Tools panel.

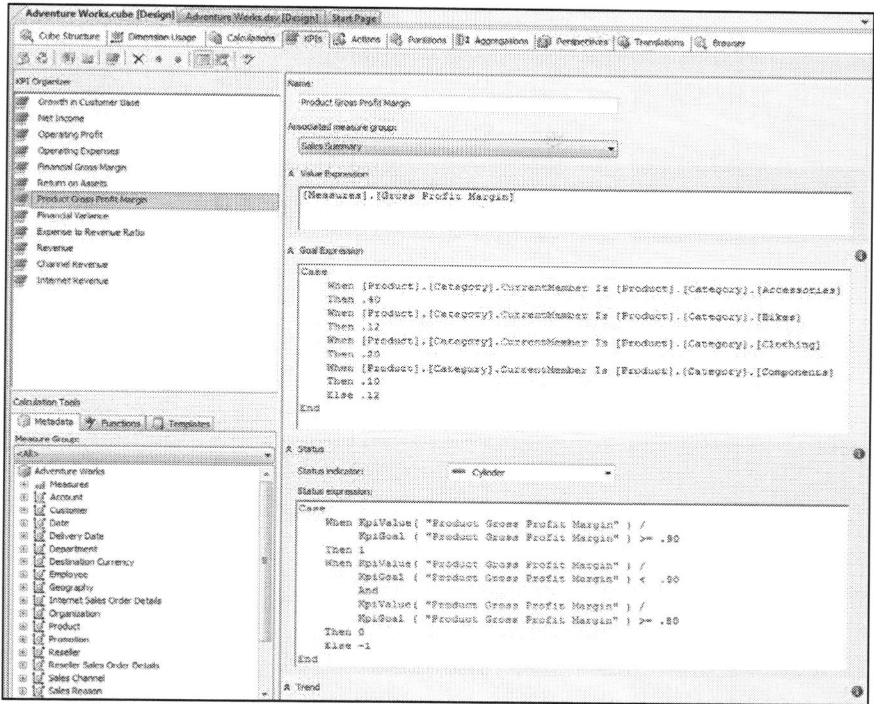

Figure 3-16 BIDS Analysis Services - Cube Key Performance Indicators

The Goal Expression defines the goal for the KPI using MDX. In this case it says:

> If the product category is Accessories, then the goal is .40 (40%)
> If the product category is Bikes, then the goal is .12 (12%)
> If the product category is Clothing, then the goal is .20 (20%)
> If the product category is Components, then the goal is .10 (10%)
> If the product category is anything else, then the goal is .12 (12%%)

Using MDX the Status Expression creates a status value between 1 and -1, i.e., -1 <= Status Value <= 1, to indicate the degree of goal achievement as follows:

Status Value	Meaning
1	Very Good or High
.5	Good
0	Acceptable or Medium
-.5	Not So Good
-1	Bad or Low

The Status Expression for the example says:

> If the KPI Value divided by the KPI Goal is greater than or equal to .90, then the Status Value is 1
>
> If the KPI Value divided by the KPI Goal is less than .90 and greater than or equal to .80, then the Status Value is 0
>
> If the KPI Value divided by the KPI Goal is anything else, then the Status Value is -1

The developer of this KPI choose not to use the intermediate status values of .5 and -.5.

So, suppose the gross profit margin for Accessories this period is .35 (35%), then the KPI Value divided by the KPI Goal would equal to .875 (.35 divided by .40 = .875), and, thus, the Status Value would be 0 or Acceptable.

The Status Value is represent visually by a Status indicator that is selected in the Status Indicator drop-down list which has Shapes selected for the Gross Profit Margin KPI. Other Status Indicator images are Cylinder, Traffic Light, Road Signs, Gauge, Reverse Gauge, Thermometer, Faces, and Variance Arrow.

Figure 13-17 shows a partial screen shot of an Excel 2010 pivot table that displays the data for the AdventureWorks Gross Profit Margin KPI for each product category. Here the green circle represents a Status Value of 1 (very good); a yellow triangle represents a value of 0 (acceptable); and a red diamond represents a value of -1 (Bad). In 2006 Accessories only achieved 76.5% of the goal of 40% (30.6% divided by 40% = 76.5%) resulting in a Status Value of -1 with a red diamond indicator.

A	B	C	D	E	F
	Column Labels				
Row Labels	Accessories	Bikes	Clothing	Components	Grand Total
CY 2005					
Product Gross Profit Margin	40.4%	14.8%	-5.6%	8.8%	14.5%
Product Gross Profit Margin Goal	40.0%	12.0%	20.0%	10.0%	12.0%
Product Gross Profit Margin Status					
CY 2006					
Product Gross Profit Margin	30.6%	9.1%	21.0%	11.8%	9.7%
Product Gross Profit Margin Goal	40.0%	12.0%	20.0%	10.0%	12.0%
Product Gross Profit Margin Status					
CY 2007					
Product Gross Profit Margin	48.1%	8.7%	15.3%	7.6%	9.3%
Product Gross Profit Margin Goal	40.0%	12.0%	20.0%	10.0%	12.0%
Product Gross Profit Margin Status					
CY 2008					
Product Gross Profit Margin	55.2%	15.4%	19.4%	6.6%	15.6%
Product Gross Profit Margin Goal	40.0%	12.0%	20.0%	10.0%	12.0%
Product Gross Profit Margin Status					
CY 2010					
Product Gross Profit Margin					
Product Gross Profit Margin Goal	40.0%	12.0%	20.0%	10.0%	12.0%
Product Gross Profit Margin Status					
Total Product Gross Profit Margin	**49.9%**	**11.1%**	**17.4%**	**8.8%**	**11.4%**
Total Product Gross Profit Margin Goal	**40.0%**	**12.0%**	**20.0%**	**10.0%**	**12.0%**
Total Product Gross Profit Margin Status					

Figure 3-17 Key Performance Indicator Visualization Example

In the very bottom of Figure 3-16 the top of the Trend section for the KPI is just visible. Scrolling down we would see a Trend expression textbox similar to the Status expression textbox discussed above. Trend shows the direction of change in the KPI from the previous value. Like the Status Expression the Trend Expression supports values between -1 and +1 in 0.5 increments.

Trend Value	Meaning
1	Upward Trend
.5	Mildly Upward Trend
0	Flat Trend
-.5	Mildly Downward Trend
-1	Downward Trend

For the Gross Profit Margin KPI the MDX code that you don't see in Figure 3-16 says:

If the change in Gross Profit Margin from the previous period is greater than .02, then the Trend Value is 1

If the change in Gross Profit Margin from the previous period is less than or equal to .02, then the Trend Value is 0

If the change in Gross Profit Margin from the previous period anything else, then the Trend Value is -1

Status arrows or faces can be selected as the trend indicator.

Figure 3-18, a partial screen shot of the KPI tab in the Designer window in its browser view, shows a listing of sample values and indicators for the 12 KPIs in the AdventureWorks cube. Note that the availability of these indicators is dependent on the client tool used to access the cube, e.g. Excel.

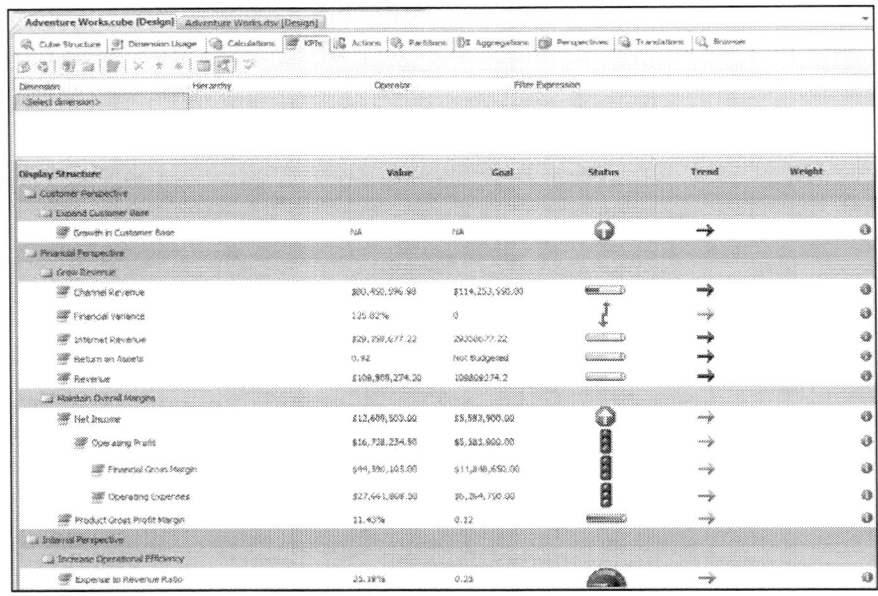

Figure 3-18 BIDS Analysis Services - Cube Key Performance Indicators

Data Mining with Analysis Services

In Chapter 1 we defined data mining operationally as the set of methods that Microsoft uses in its data mining tools in Microsoft SQL Server 2008 and Excel 2010. Data mining is a technical field, and an extensive presentation of it is beyond the scope of this book. Please search SQL Server Books Online for "data mining" to read Microsoft's definition and introduction to it. We will learn how to use data mining in later chapters.

Data mining applications use algorithms, solution methods with a finite number of steps, to build data mining models. Table 3-1 below briefly describes each of the nine data mining algorithms available in Analysis Services.

Algorithm	Description	Example Use
Association	Searches for items that appear together and creates rules about these associations.	Market basket analysis
Clustering	Assigns cases (individual items) into clusters with similar characteristics.	Market segmentation
Decision Trees	Develops predictive decision tree models for an output (dependent) variable using values from input (independent) variables. Uses a classification algorithm for discrete attributes and linear regression for continuous attributes. (See more about decision trees below)	Buyer behavior
Linear Regression	Uses least squares to determine the model that represents the best linear fit between a continuous dependent and continuous independent variables.	Forecasting sales as a function of leading indicators
Logistic Regression	Models the relationship between a discrete dependent outcome and discrete and/or continuous independent variables.	Buyer behavior

Algorithm	Description	Example Use
Naïve Bayes	A classification algorithm based on Bayesian statistics but with an assumption of independence among characteristics.	Buyer behavior
Neural Network	Based on models of biological neurons these algorithms create networks that learn by trial and error	Bankruptcy prediction
Sequence Clustering	A hybrid algorithm that uses clustering and Markov chains to model sequence data.	Identify patterns in Web site viewing
Time Series	Uses two algorithms specifically designed to model time series data	Project sales patterns over time into the future

Table 3-1 Microsoft Data Mining algorithms

(For better viewing of this image, go to http://www.zerobits.info/bibook/bibookimages/)

Some of the algorithms can be used for the same purpose as indicated by the multiple use of the buyer behavior example.

Microsoft categorizes the algorithms into five types: classification, regression, segmentation, association, and sequence analysis. Each will be briefly described below.

Classification

Classification algorithms use attributes in a dataset to predict one or more discrete variables. The decision tree algorithm is an example of a classification algorithm. A decision tree is a model depicting a series of independent decisions. The graphical representation is usually a horizontal tree structure with nodes for decision points and branches leading to other decision points or to the end of the tree. Microsoft decision trees represent sequential relationships among characteristics. (Note that this rendition of decision trees is somewhat different than that used in management science to model decision making under risk, if you are familiar with that.) An example of a hypothetical Analysis Services decision tree for discrete characteristics of bicycle buyer behavior is shown in Figure 3-19.

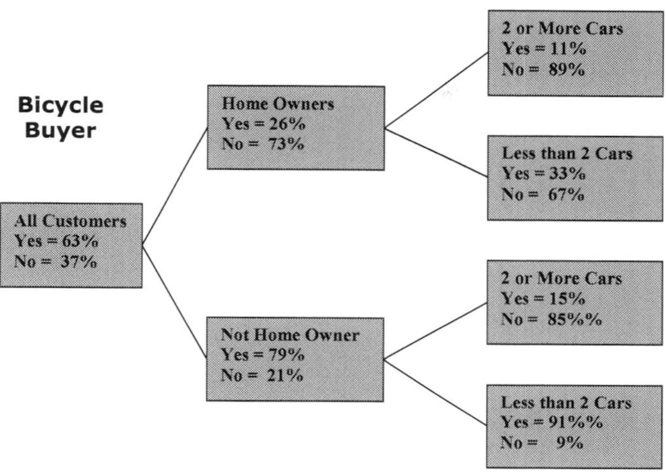

Figure 3-19 A Decision Tree Algorithm Example

In this example the decision tree algorithm predicts bicycle purchase behavior (a discrete yes or no variable) based on customer demographics: home ownership and number of cars owned. The marketing department could use this information in developing a promotion strategy.

Regression

Regression is a method for constructing mathematical relationships between a continuous dependent variable and one or more continuous independent variables. It's called regression because of the context in which it was originally used. Linear regression, probably the most used form, computes the parameters for a linear equation that best fits the data. For example, Figure 3-20 shows a chart of General Electric's annual net earnings and corresponding year-end Dow Jones Industrial average (DJIA) values for 1996 through 2009. These points are plotted with the diamond shaped markers. DJIA values are on the horizontal axis, and GE's net earnings in millions of dollars are on the vertical axis. You can see that there is a general upward trend to GE's Earnings as the DJIA increases. Indeed, the trend line shows this relationship quite well.

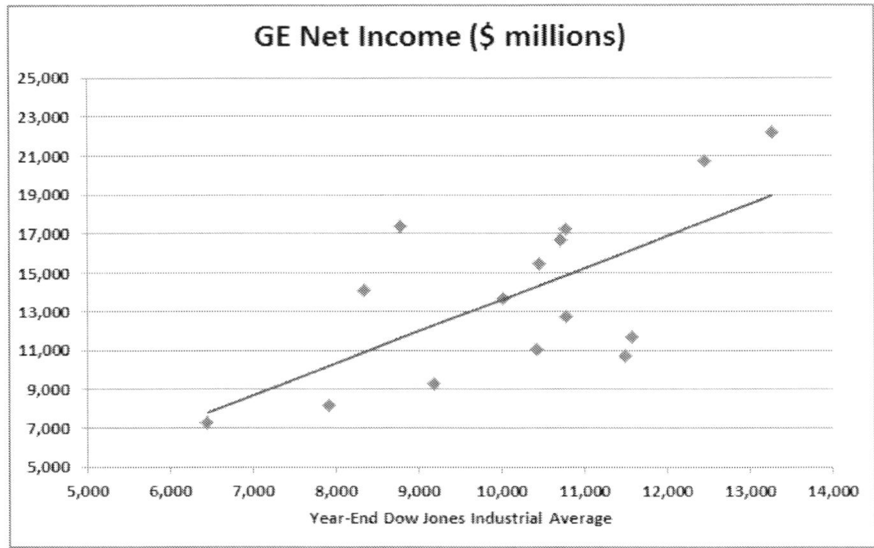

Figure 3-20 Linear Regression Example

Linear regression analysis in Excel 2010 produced the equation for the line of best fit. In the example the equation turns out to be:

GE Net Earnings = -3960.27+ 1.7886(DJIA)

So, knowing that the DJIA for 2010 was 11,577 we can "predict" GE's earnings for 2010 as $16,746. However, GE's actual earnings for 2010 was $11,644 so the model erred by 44 percent. Well, that's forecasting and the nature of the stock market. I remember a quote from somewhere at said that the only thing to be sure of in forecasting is that the forecast will be wrong. We'll talk more about linear regression in a subsequent chapter.

Segmentation (Clustering)

Segmentation algorithms arrange cases into groups of similar cases based on their attribute values. It essentially sorts objects into collections of like items as you might do when sorting a shoebox full of financial receipts and records. Only instead of sorting items into logical categories like household expenses, credit card statements, charitable contributions, etc., segmentation algorithms group items in natural clusters—ones that derive from the attributes of the items themselves.

Figure 3-21 shows a cluster diagram from an Analysis Services clustering algorithm applied to AdventureWorks DW sample customer data. The algorithm found that ten clusters best categorize the customers in the sample. Notice that at this point the clusters have the generic names of Cluster 1, 2, etc. It is up to the analyst to assign meaningful names to the clusters.

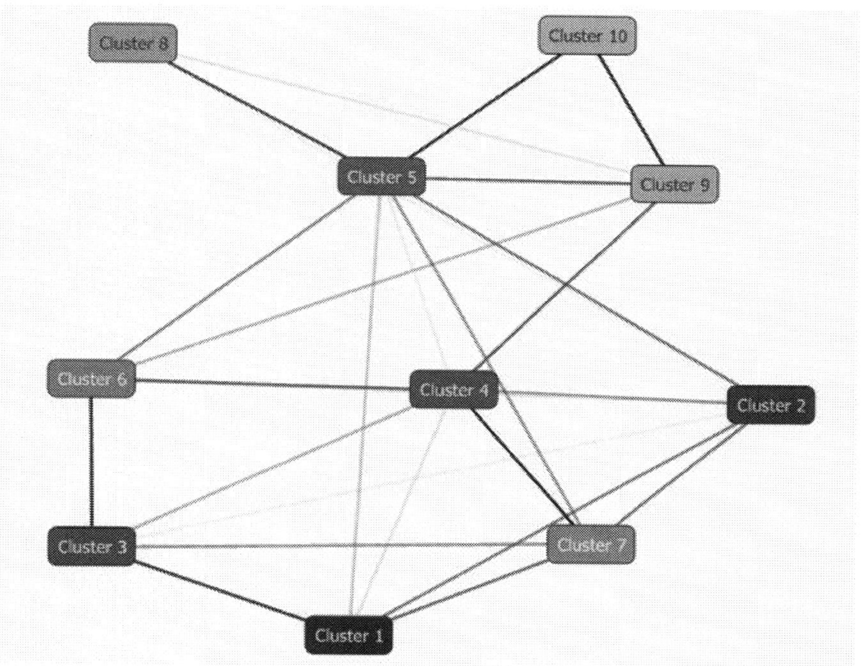

Figure 3-21 AdventureWorks Example Cluster Analysis Diagram

Suppose that the customers in one cluster are at least 50 years old, earned college degrees, own homes, and hold managerial positions. We'll might call them Baby Boomer Managers. Another cluster would have different characteristics, say younger than 30, single, with high school degrees, living in apartments. Relating these clusters to some behavior, say the propensity to buy a bicycle, AdventureWorks could develop a marketing strategy that would target customers in clusters with a higher propensity to purchase bikes.

Association

Association models are useful for market basket analysis and recommendation engines. Market basket analysis identifies items that have a higher probability of being purchased together, e.g., hot dogs and hot dog buns. Recommendation engines use a customer's previous buying behavior to recommend items to them to purchase or use market basket models to recommend other product for the customer to purchase after they have selected an item to buy. This type of analysis is also call Affinity Analysis.

Figure 3-22 shows an association dependency network diagram for products purchased from a hypothetical convenience store. (Note that this example is pure fiction.) For this store customers tend to buy a lottery ticket when they buy a newspaper and/or coffee but do not necessarily buy a newspaper or coffee with a lottery ticket. So, in a sense buying a newspaper predicts buying a lottery ticket but buying a lottery ticket does not necessarily predict buying a newspaper. Some items have two-way connection indicating that these items usually occur in the same market basket.

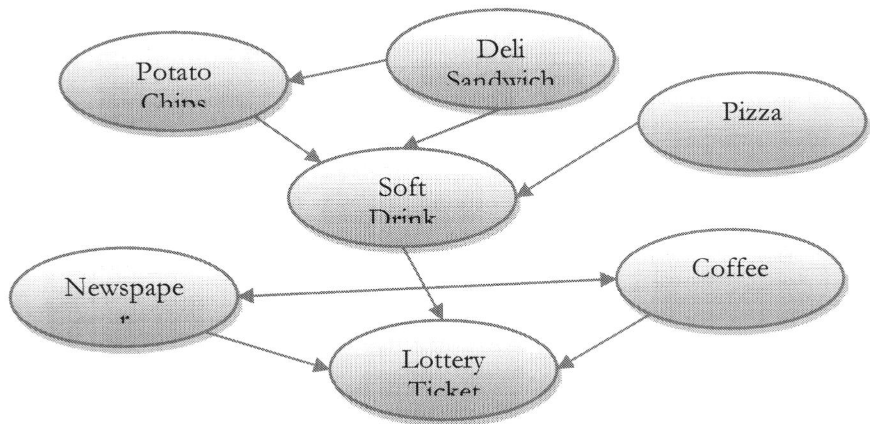

Figure 3-22 Example Association Dependency Diagram

Sequence Analysis

Sequence analysis is used to model sequential paths of events by representing the paths as Markov chains if you know what they are. If not, don't be concerned about it here. The usual example of sequence analysis is modeling Internet Web site navigation patterns, i.e., a network model showing the sequence of Web pages visited and the probabilities of moving from one page to another. Figure 3-23 depicts a trivial example of such a sequence model.

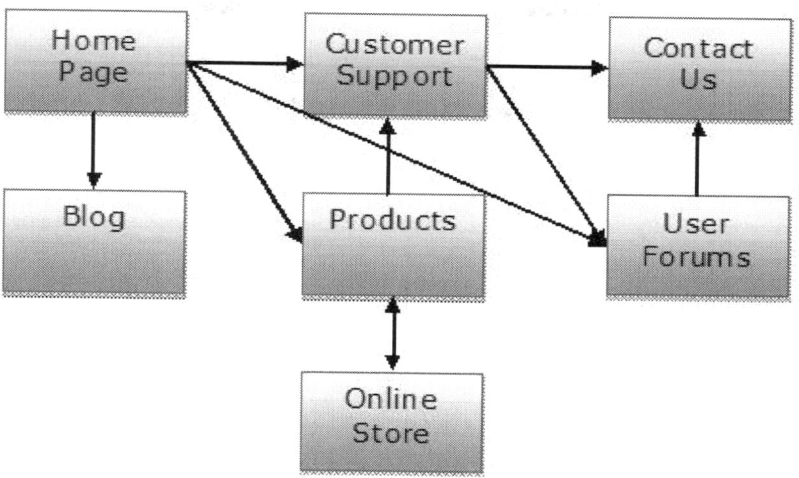

Figure 3-22 Example Web Site Navigation Paths

If data are available about visitor characteristics, say from their initial registration with the site, then clustering can be added to the analysis to track how different groups of visitors navigate the site. This could be helpful for Web site design, development of promotion strategies, etc. Analysis Services Sequence Clustering algorithm uses such a hybrid approach.

The AdventureWorks DW Analysis Services sample project contains five data mining examples as you may be able see in the Solution Explorer pane in Figure 3-13 in the list of Mining Structures. The Targeted Mailing structure uses four different algorithms—clustering, decision trees, naive Bayes, and neural networks—to independently identify customer types who are more likely to buy a bicycle. The four models can then be evaluated to select the most appropriate.

The Market Basket structure creates an association model to identify products that are purchased together for an AdventureWorks recommendation engine. The Forecasting structure forecasts AdventureWorks sales for each of their three geographical regions. And the Customer Mining structure builds the segmentation model for AdventureWorks Internet customers described above.

The Analysis Services Data Mining Wizard makes it fairly easy to build data mining models. You specify the data source—a database, warehouse, or existing cube—select the data mining technique to use, select source data characteristics, and then let the algorithm go to work. We'll look at data mining in more detail using Excel 2010 in later chapters. Now onto Reporting Services.

SQL Server 2008 Reporting Services

Reporting Services is a full-featured application for report creation and management to design, modify, store, and publish reports. You can schedule report processing, distribute reports according to a schedule, and build ad hoc reports. Reporting Services is accessed via BIDS. You can see in Figure 3-8 that a Report Server Project is one of the available selections for a new project. Just like an Integration Services or Analysis Services project a Report Server project begins with the specification of a data source with the Data Source Wizard, e.g., the AdventureWorks DW dimensional database. The report is constructed by using the Report Wizard which includes a graphical query designer to specify the fields that will be used and by dragging and dropping objects onto a report design canvas.

Reporting Services uses the Report Definition Language (RDL) to define reports, i.e., reports are saved to .rdl files in XML. A report definition contains data retrieval and layout information for a report. RDL is composed of XML elements that match an XML grammar created for Reporting Services.

There are two types of basic reports available in the Reporting Services: tabular and matrix. Tabular reports display lists of data in columns whereas matrix reports are like cross tabulations, i.e., fields (dimension attributes) appear is both rows and columns with values (measures) in the cell intersections. We saw an example of a matrix report in Figure 2-3.

Figure 3-24 is a screen shot of report layout in BIDS Reporting Services design view. The data source, the AdventureWorks Cube, is listed in the Solution Explorer in the right upper panel as well as the two reports that have been constructed in the project so far: the primary report, Sales by Product, and a subreport, Gross Profit Margin by Product. The Toolbox in the left lower panel shows the objects that can be dragged and dropped onto the design surface. There are seven objects on the design surface: a textbox for the report title, Sales by Product; an image of the AdventureWorks logo that I copied from the AdventureWorks report samples; a matrix directly below the report title that presents data for Internet sales by product category and subcategory; a subreport container (the grey rectangle); a graph; a gauge, and a textbox for the gauge. The objects in the report are configured and formatted with menus and by setting various properties.

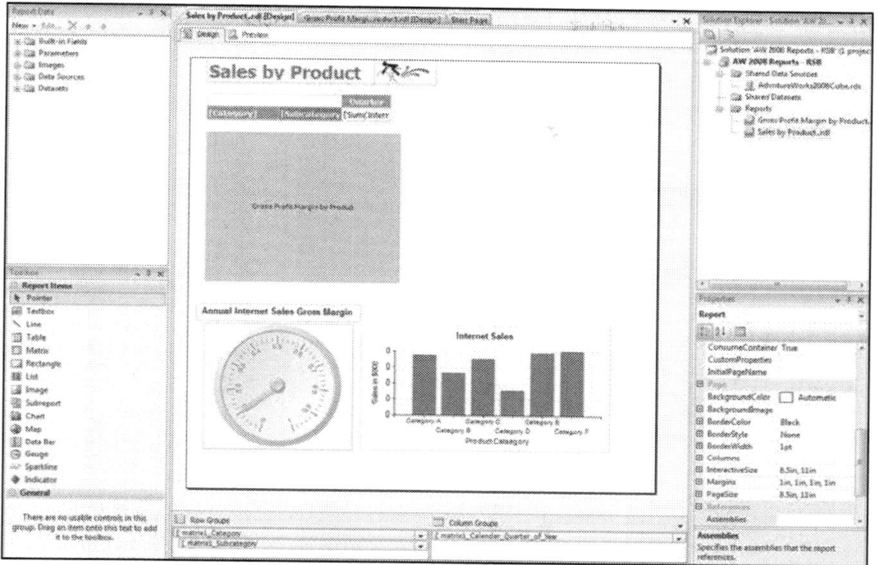

Figure 3-24 Reporting Services Design View

Figure 3-25 shows this report in preview view, i.e., how the report will actually appear. Now you can see the matrix-type tables for sales and gross profit margin that were shown as layouts in design view. A few comments about the report are in order. First, I constructed the report only to demonstrate the use of some of the tools available not to present a professional looking, useable report. I just dropped objects onto the design surface and did a little formatting and tinkering.

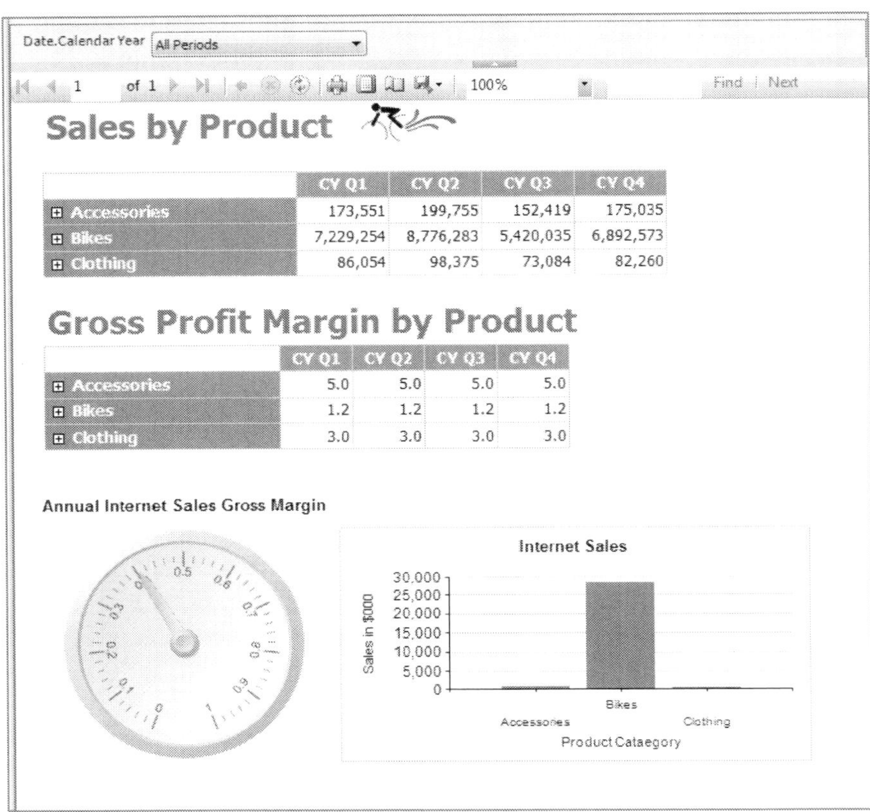

	CY Q1	CY Q2	CY Q3	CY Q4
⊞ Accessories	173,551	199,755	152,419	175,035
⊞ Bikes	7,229,254	8,776,283	5,420,035	6,892,573
⊞ Clothing	86,054	98,375	73,084	82,260

	CY Q1	CY Q2	CY Q3	CY Q4
⊞ Accessories	5.0	5.0	5.0	5.0
⊞ Bikes	1.2	1.2	1.2	1.2
⊞ Clothing	3.0	3.0	3.0	3.0

Figure 3-25 Reporting Services Preview View

(For better viewing of this image, go to http://www.zerobits.info/bibook/bibookimages/)

Second, the primary report has a filter for selecting the year(s) to present in the report which is accomplished by including a parameter in the query that underlies the report. Figure 3-26a shows the Report Data tab that you can barely see in the upper left panel of Figure 3-24. In addition to listing the data used in the report, SalesDataset and GaugeDataset, the Report Data panel shows the parameters in the report. In this case the only parameter specified is the DateCalendarYear field. If we click on the filter selection area in the upper left corner beside the parameter name, Date.Calendar Year, in the Design panel in Figure 3-25, the listbox shown in Figure 3-26b would drop-down where we can select the year(s) to display. There "All Periods" is selected which displays the data for all periods combined. To select other years deselect "All Periods" and click the years to select.

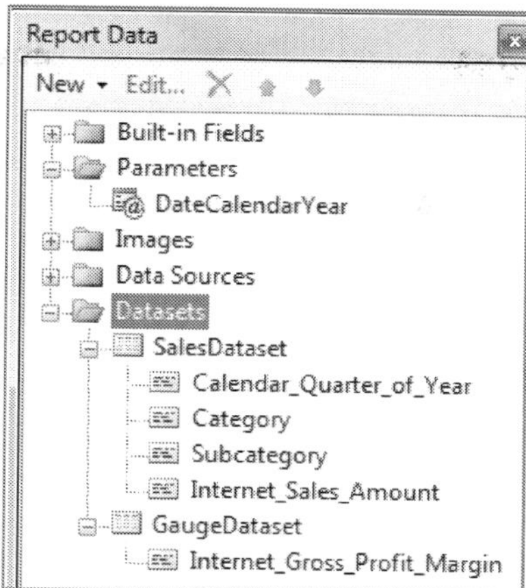

Figure 3-26a - Report Data

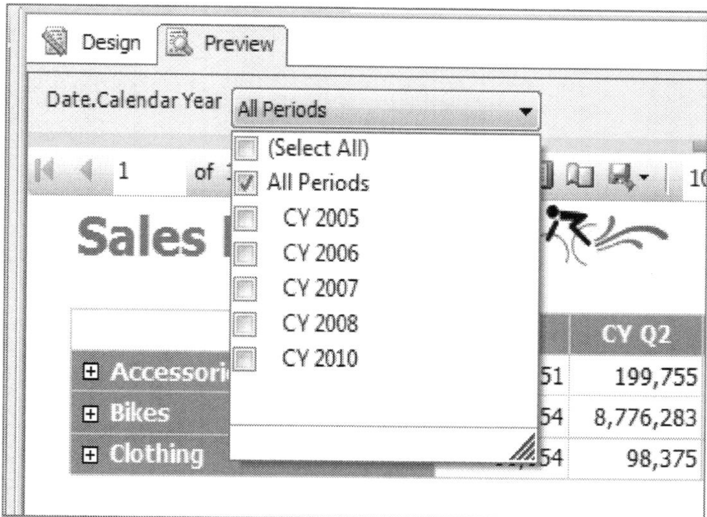

Figure 3-26b - Filter Selection List

Figure 3-26 Report Filter Example

Third, the subreport, Gross Profit Margin by Product is linked to the calendar year parameter in the primary report so when a year is selected for the primary report, the secondary report changes as well. Fourth, the two matrix-type tables are set up with drill-down capabilities as shown Figure 3-27 with the Accessories subcategory expanded in the Sales by Product table and the Bikes category expanded in the Gross Profit Margin by Product subreport table.

Fifth, it's possible to add drill-through capabilities to reports. In Chapter 2 we said that drill-through is similar to a hyperlink. It uses textboxes or images as buttons to navigate to other reports, bookmarks, or URLs. Our discussion in the next chapter about the Report Builder includes an example of drill-through.

Last, with the use of graphs, gauges, and tables reports can simulate dashboard and scorecard presentations. In fact, if the data source for the report is an Analysis Services cube, then KPIs can be added to reports just like in dashboards and scorecards.

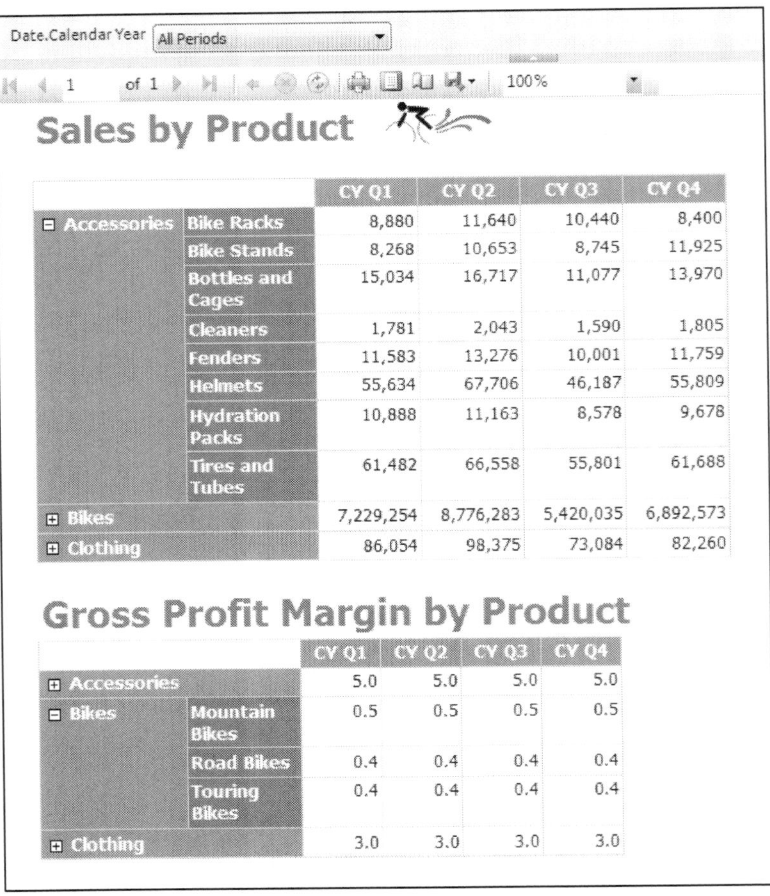

Sales by Product

		CY Q1	CY Q2	CY Q3	CY Q4
⊟ Accessories	Bike Racks	8,880	11,640	10,440	8,400
	Bike Stands	8,268	10,653	8,745	11,925
	Bottles and Cages	15,034	16,717	11,077	13,970
	Cleaners	1,781	2,043	1,590	1,805
	Fenders	11,583	13,276	10,001	11,759
	Helmets	55,634	67,706	46,187	55,809
	Hydration Packs	10,888	11,163	8,578	9,678
	Tires and Tubes	61,482	66,558	55,801	61,688
⊞ Bikes		7,229,254	8,776,283	5,420,035	6,892,573
⊞ Clothing		86,054	98,375	73,084	82,260

Gross Profit Margin by Product

		CY Q1	CY Q2	CY Q3	CY Q4
⊞ Accessories		5.0	5.0	5.0	5.0
⊟ Bikes	Mountain Bikes	0.5	0.5	0.5	0.5
	Road Bikes	0.4	0.4	0.4	0.4
	Touring Bikes	0.4	0.4	0.4	0.4
⊞ Clothing		3.0	3.0	3.0	3.0

Figure 3-27 Drill-Down Example

(For better viewing of this image, go to http://www.zerobits.info/bibook/bibookimages/)

What's Next

I hope that you are as impressed as I am with the BI capabilities built into SQL Server 2008. And there's more in the Microsoft BI toolkit: the Report Server to publish reports, the Report Builder for users to author reports, Excel and Access 2010 to manipulate and analyze data, Visio 2007 to present BI results, and SharePoint server to deliver BI information.

In the next chapter we peruse the Report Server and learn how to use Report Builder 3.0. In subsequent chapters we look using at Excel and Access for data analysis and Excel for forecasting and data mining. As mentioned earlier, SharePoint is beyond the scope of this book but there are many sources available about if you are interested.

Chapter 4 - Report Manager and Report Builder 3.0

Reports created in Reporting Services such as the one in Figure 3-23 are made available to users through the SQL Server Report Server. Figure 4-1 shows my conceptualization of the Report Server architecture. The Report Server has access to about any data sources available just like Integration Services and Analysis Services, and it manages a Report Server database. There are two sources for reports: those created by a developer using Reporting Services in SQL Server and those created by users using the Report Builder. Users use a browser to interact with the Report Manager and use Report Builder, a Windows application, to create reports. In SQL Server 2005 the Report Server ran under Internet Information Services (IIS), the Windows Web server. Now, Reporting Services 2008 handles HTTP requests itself so that IIS is no longer required for it. The Report Server includes Report Builder 1.0, a Microsoft Office-like application to design reports. Report Builder has been updated to Report Builder 3.0 available by download from Microsoft. We will first explore the Report Manager GUI and then learn how to use Report Builder 3.0.

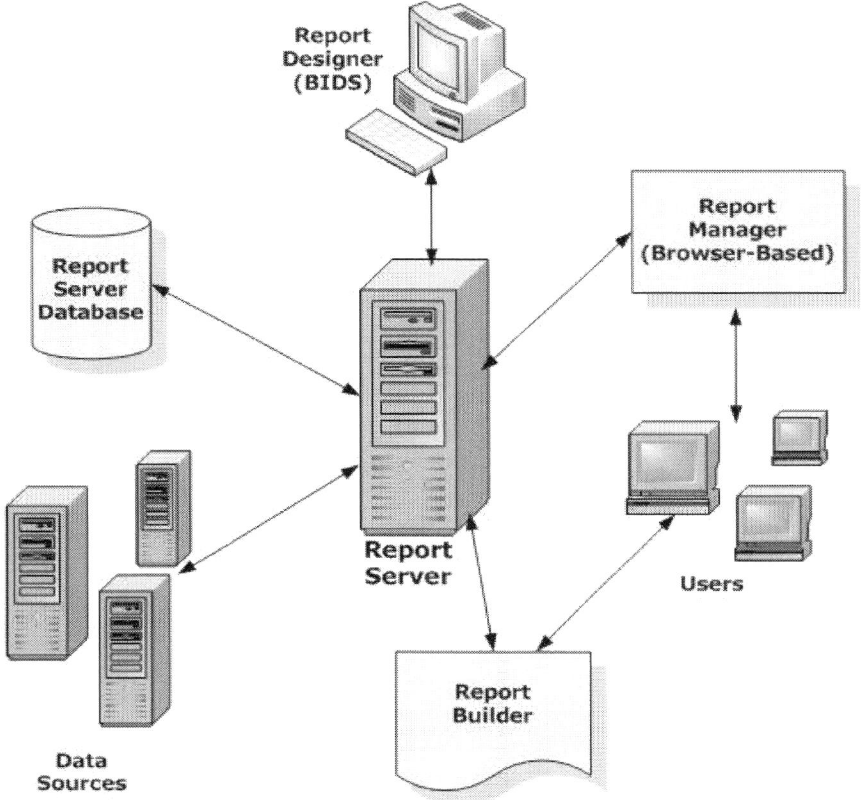

Figure 4-1 Report Server Architecture

(For better viewing of this image, go to http://www.zerobits.info/bibook/bibookimages/)

Report Manager

As we learned in Chapter 3 a developer using SQL Server Reporting Services creates and manages reports using the Report Designer in BIDS depicted at the top of Figure 4-1. There, the developer can also deploy (publish) the report to the Report Server for users to access. Deployment is an automated process initiated by the developer by selecting deploy from a project's menu. If the deployment is successful, the report will then show up in the list of available reports on the Report Server.

The Report Manager, the Report Server's user interface, is accessed in a browser at a URL something like http://<servername>/Reports. Of course,

Internet Explorer as a Microsoft product renders the Report Manager's pages accurately. However, using other browsers may be problematic. In Firefox try the IE Tab add-on.

Figure 4-2a shows a partial screen shot of the Report Manager home page using the URL http://MAINGEAR/Reports for my setup. MAINGEAR is the name of the server on my local machine and Reports refers to the Report Manager. You are probably not hosting SQL Server on your local machine unless you are working with the Developer edition so ask the IT folks for the URL for your Report Server. Note that the availability of the various capabilities in the Report Manager depends on the permissions granted to the user. For example, some users may only view reports whereas others may create and publish reports.

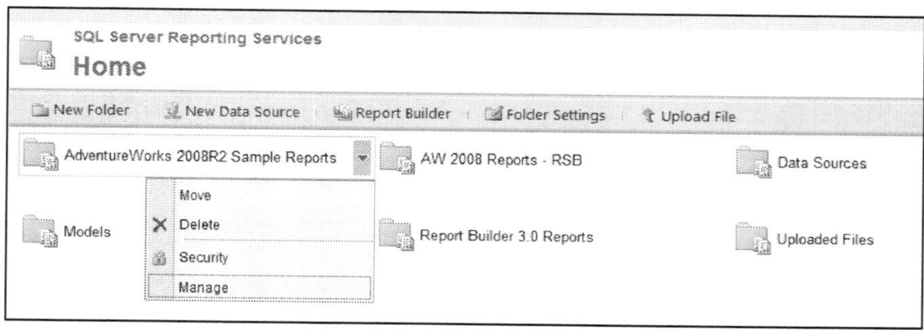

Figure 4-2 Report Manager in Internet Explorer

Objects available from the Report Manager are organized in a usual folder structure. You may perform operations on a folder by clicking the down arrow on the right which displays the box as shown in the figure for the AdventureWorks 2008R2 Sample Reports folder. In this example there are six folders. The first, the AdventureWorks Sample Reports folder, contains nine reports deployed from the Reporting Services AdventureWorks sample project downloaded from Microsoft. Figure 4-3 shows the contents of that folder, and Figure 4-4 shows part of the second report in the list, Employee Sales Summary 2008R2, which we saw a version of in Figure 2-3.

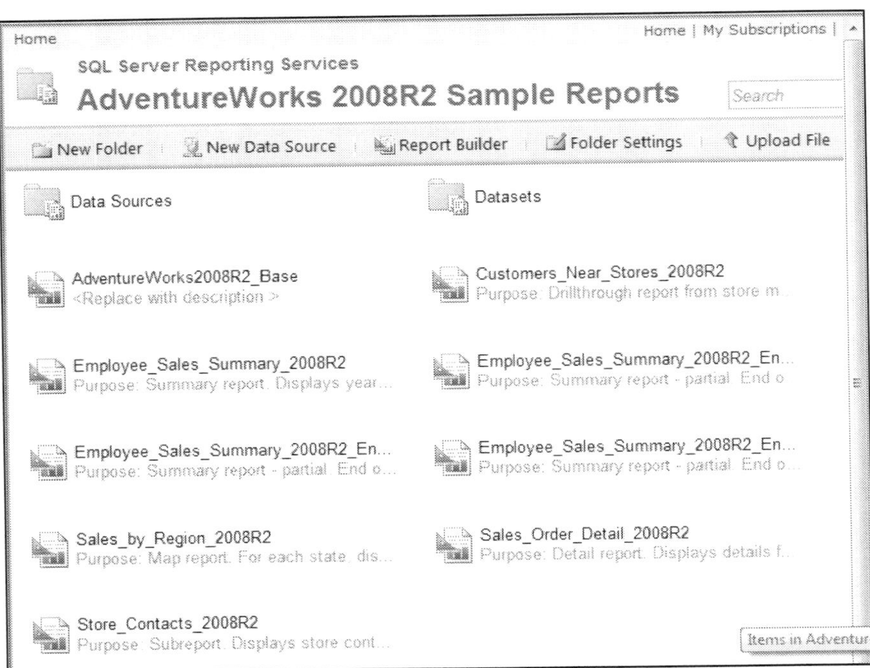

Figure 4-3 AdventureWorks Sample Reports Folder

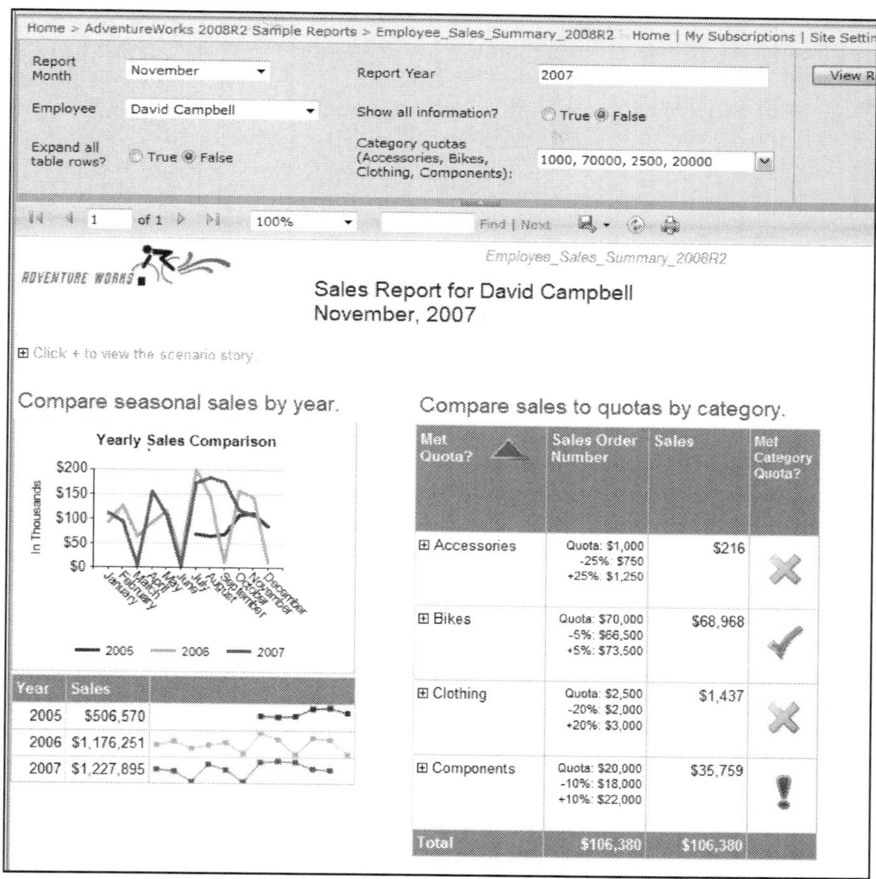

Figure 4-4 AdventureWorks Sample Report

(For better viewing of this image, go to http://www.zerobits.info/bibook/bibookimages/)

The AW 2008 Reports - RSB and the Report Builder 3.0 folders listed in Figure 4-2 contain reports that I created, deploying reports from Reporting Services for the former folder and using Report Builder 3.0 for the latter. Data Sources, Models, and Uploaded Files are special folders that we'll get to shortly.

New Folder

Creating a new folder is about the same as creating one on a Windows computer. Figure 4-5 shows a screen shot of the New Folder window. To create a new folder just specify a name, an optional description, and click OK.

Folders can be nested as usual. To create a folder within a folder just navigate to the parent folder and click New Folder.

Figure 4-5 New Folder Window in Report Manager

Data Sources

The Data Sources folder contain (surprise!) data sources. These data sources are used by the Report Builder to build reports with a shared data source. More on that in a bit. Three data sources are available in my Data Sources folder in Figure 4-6: The AdventureWorks OLTP database, the DW database, and the Analysis Services Cube. To create a new data source click on the New Data Source menu item to access the Data Sources properties page shown in Figure 4-7 which shows the data source properties for the AdventureWorks2008Cube: its name; the data source type, an analysis Services cube in this case, and the connection string. The connection string will usually be of the form:

data source=<SQL Server instance>;initial catalog=<source name>

In this example the server on my local machine is named MAINGEAR and the source is the cube from "Adventure Works DW 2008R2." Figure 4-8 displays the list of data source types available. Since the data source is a cube, the Microsoft SQL Server Analysis Services type is selected. The type of authentication credentials required to assess the data source is specified in the Connect using area. This example uses Windows integrated security.

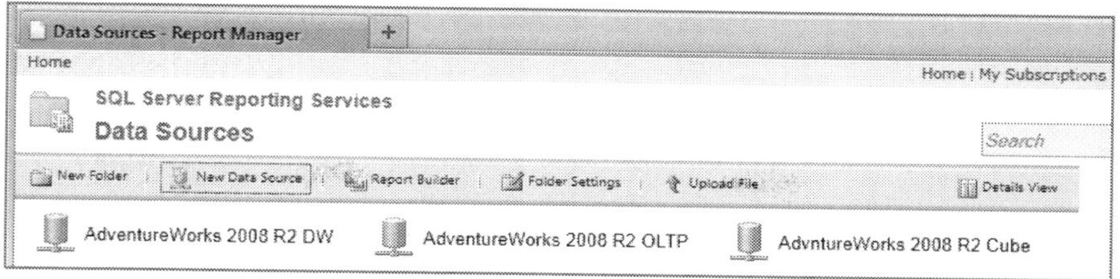

Figure 4-6 Data Sources Folder

AdvntureWorks 2008 R2 Cube - Repo...
Home > Data Sources
SQL Server Reporting Services
AdvntureWorks 2008 R2 Cube
Delete | Move | Generate Model
Properties
Subscriptions
Dependent Items
Security
Name: AdvntureWorks 2008 R2 Cube
Description:
Hide in tile view
Enable this data source
Data source type: Microsoft SQL Server Analysis Services
Connection string: Data Source=MAINGEAR;Initial Catalog="Adventure Works DW 2008R2"
Connect using:
Credentials supplied by the user running the report
Display the following text to prompt user for a user name and password:
Type or enter a user name and password to access the data so
Use as Windows credentials when connecting to the data source
Credentials stored securely in the report server
User name:
Password:
Use as Windows credentials when connecting to the data source
Impersonate the authenticated user after a connection has been made to the data source
Windows integrated security
Credentials are not required
Test Connection
Apply

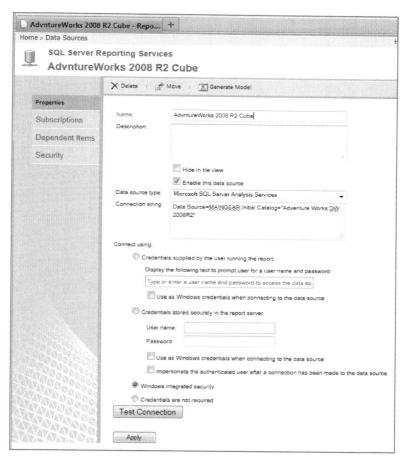

Figure 4-7 Data Sources Window

(For better viewing of this image, go to http://www.zerobits.info/bibook/bibookimages/)

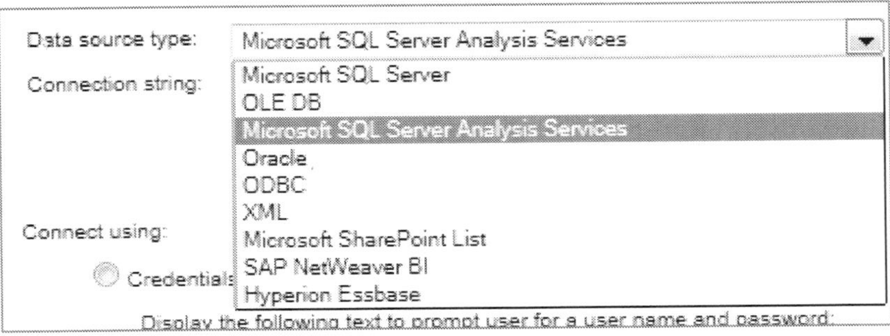

Figure 4-8 Data Source Types

Models

The Models folder in Figure 4-2 contains the list of data models available on the Report Server. In our case there is only one model listed, Adventureworks2008DW (not shown in a figure). Data models are representations of an underlying database that include relationships and queries. A data model created by a developer or database administrator can be used by Report Manager users as data sources for reports. This avoids the need for users to create a data source as discussed above.

Upload File

The Upload File menu action, of course, uploads a file to the Report Server and makes it available in the Report Manager. The usual file uploaded is a RDL file, i.e., a file containing a report definition prepared in Reporting Services, Report Builder, or some other application using the Report Definition Language (RDL). We mentioned RDL briefly in Chapter 3. However, other file types can be uploaded as well such as report model files (Semantic Model Definition Language—.smdl), images, or just about anything else. All files uploaded except RDL and SMDL file are stored as resources for the user or developer. For example I uploaded two files into a new folder called Uploaded Files: a jpeg image of the AdventureWorks logo and a Microsoft Word 2010 document. A partial screen shot of the Uploaded Files folder is shown in Figure 2-9a, and a view of the jpg file by clicking on its name is shown in Figure 2-9b.

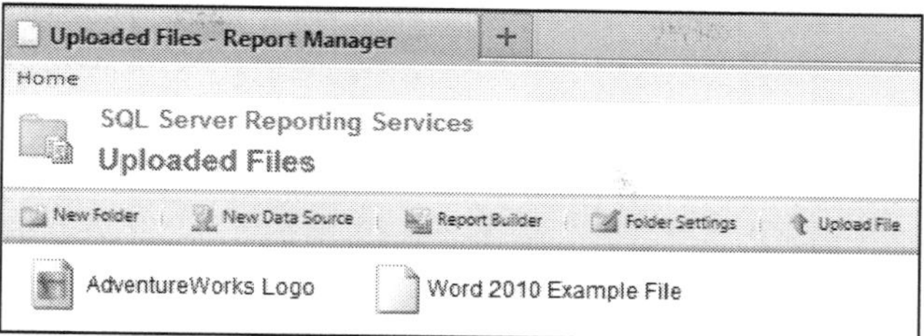

Figure 4-9a - Uploaded File List

Figure 4-9b - Uploaded File View

Figure 4-9 Uploaded Files Example

Folder Settings

Within a folder clicking on Folder Settings in the action bar will display the folder properties window as shown for the AdventureWorks 2008R2 Sample Reports folder in Figure 4-10 where you may change the folder name and description as well as delete or move the folder.

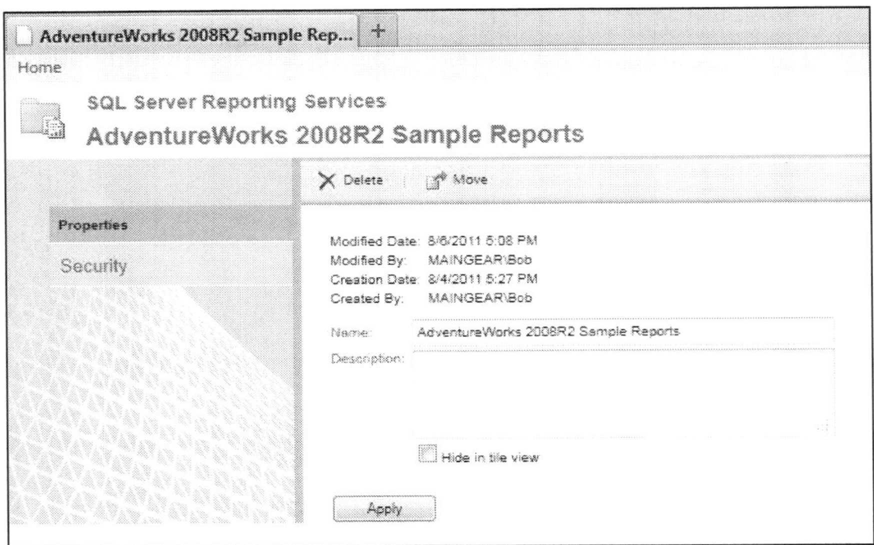

Figure 4-10 Folder Properties

Show Details

The Details View action on the far right of the menu area in Figure 4-2 is used to display object properties and to edit the properties or delete or move the objects. Figure 4-11 shows the detailed view of the Home page by clicking on the Details View button. Each row in the list represents an object on the page or folder. You may perform operation on a folder by using the drop down listbox as noted above.

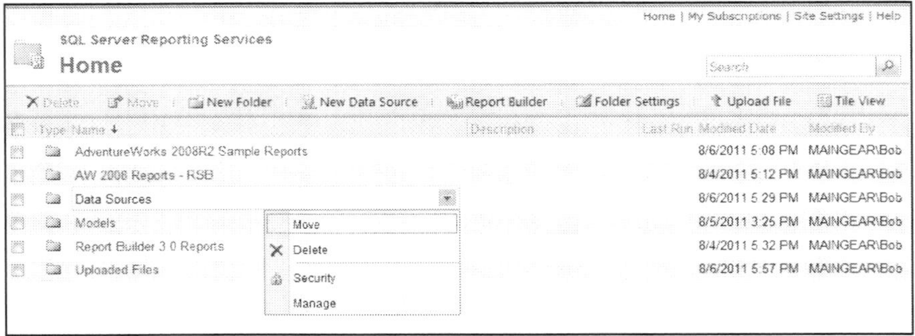

Figure 4-11 Details View

Clicking on the folder icon in the Type column in Figure 4-11 just lists the contents in the folder—the same as in Figure 4-3. Clicking on the check box in row enables the Delete and Move actions in the menu area. Clicking on Delete does just that. Clicking on Move opens the Move window in Figure 4-12. At the top of the window the object to move is identified, in this case the AdventureWorks 2008R2 Sample Reports folder. Below that the textbox indicates the location the object will be moved to, and the directory tree on the right allows the user to select the new location as I did here with the Data Sources folder. Note that the folders in the directory tree can be expanded as usual.

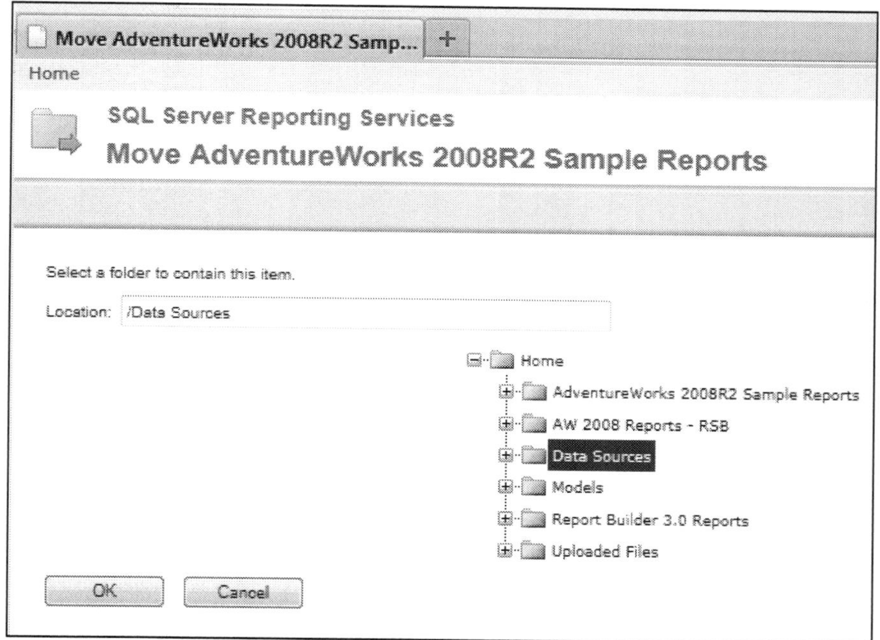

Figure 4-12 Show Details Move Window

Export and Print

You may export reports in a variety of formats. Figure 4-13 shows a partial screen shot of the Sales Report (Figure 4-4) where I clicked the small disk icon to display the export options. If you want to export the report to Microsoft Word, then just select Word in the list and then click Export. A dialog box will open asking if you want to open or save the file. Proceed from there as usual. The application that supports the format, e.g., Microsoft Word, must be available. Note that reports with interactive features like drill-down probably won't work in exported reports. Use the printer icon to print the report in a similar manner.

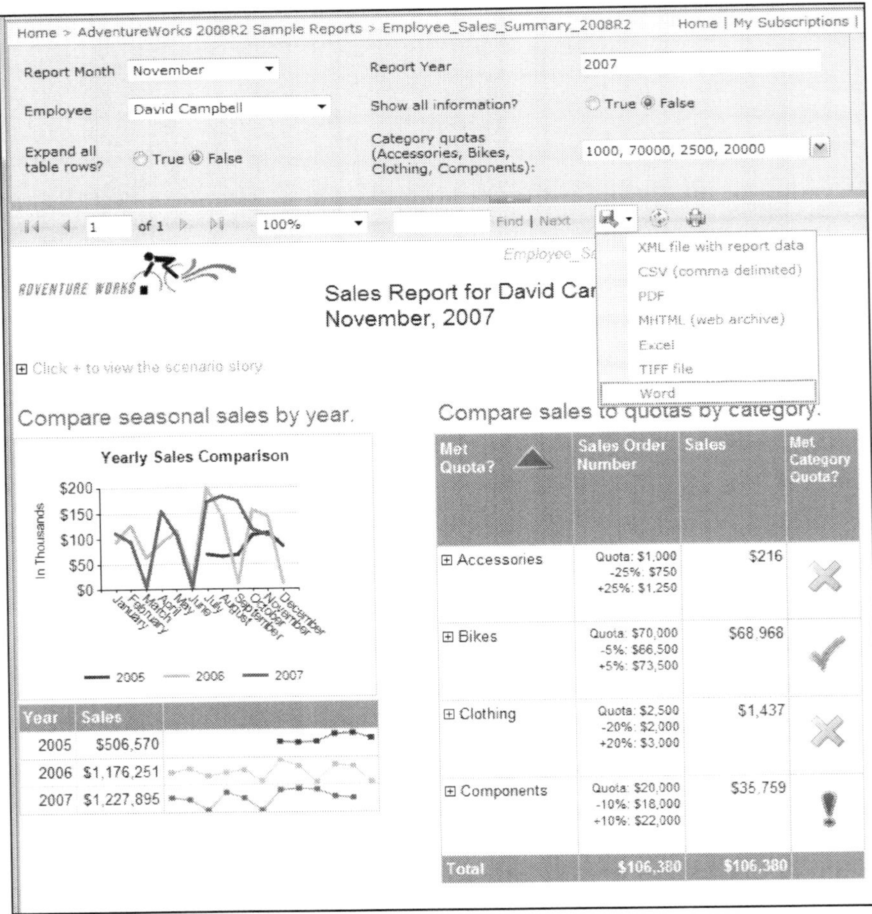

Figure 4-13 Report View Export Options

(For better viewing of this image, go to http://www.zerobits.info/bibook/bibookimages/)

Subscriptions

Instead of viewing reports with the Report Manager users may receive reports via email or a Windows file share. A subscription is created by selecting the Subscribe option in the drop down menu for a particular report as in Figure 4-14. This will open the Subscription page shown in Figure 4-15.

(Tip: you may receive an error message something like "subscription cannot be created because the credentials used to run the report are not stored . . . ." This may be because the data source for the report must be using stored credentials.

To remedy this go to the data source for the specific report. In Properties select Credentials stored securely in the report server. Enter a user name and password, check Use as Windows credentials when connecting to the data source, test the connection, and Apply.)

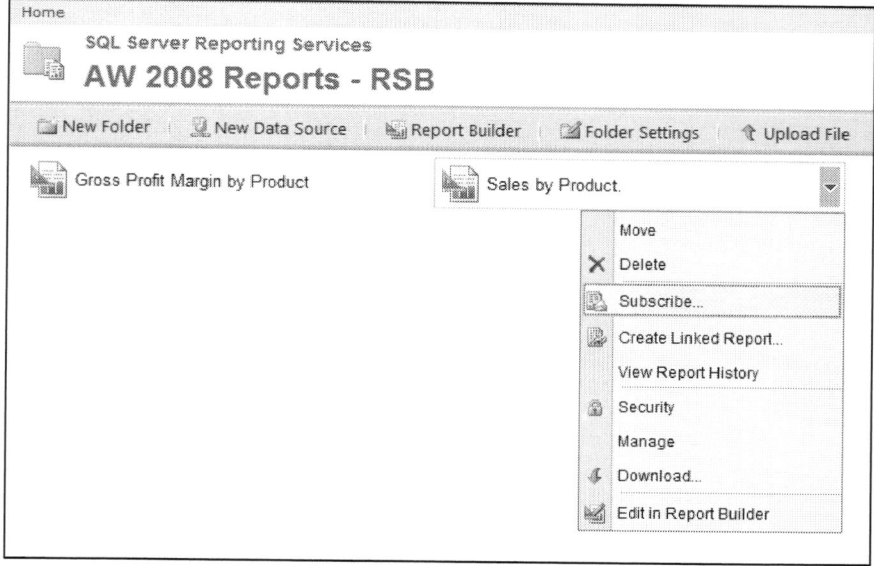

Figure 4-14 Report in the View Tab

Configuring the Subscription page is straightforward. Select the Delivered by mode, either email or Windows file share (if a file share is available). Fill in the recipient(s) information, select a delivery schedule by clicking on the Select Schedule button, and configure parameter values if parameters are available in the report. Clicking the Select Schedule button brings up the Schedule Details page shown in Figure 4-16 which is self-explanatory. The only parameter in this report is calendar year which is now set to All Periods, i.e., the data presented in the report will be the sum of all years. You could select one or more years for the report by using the listbox.

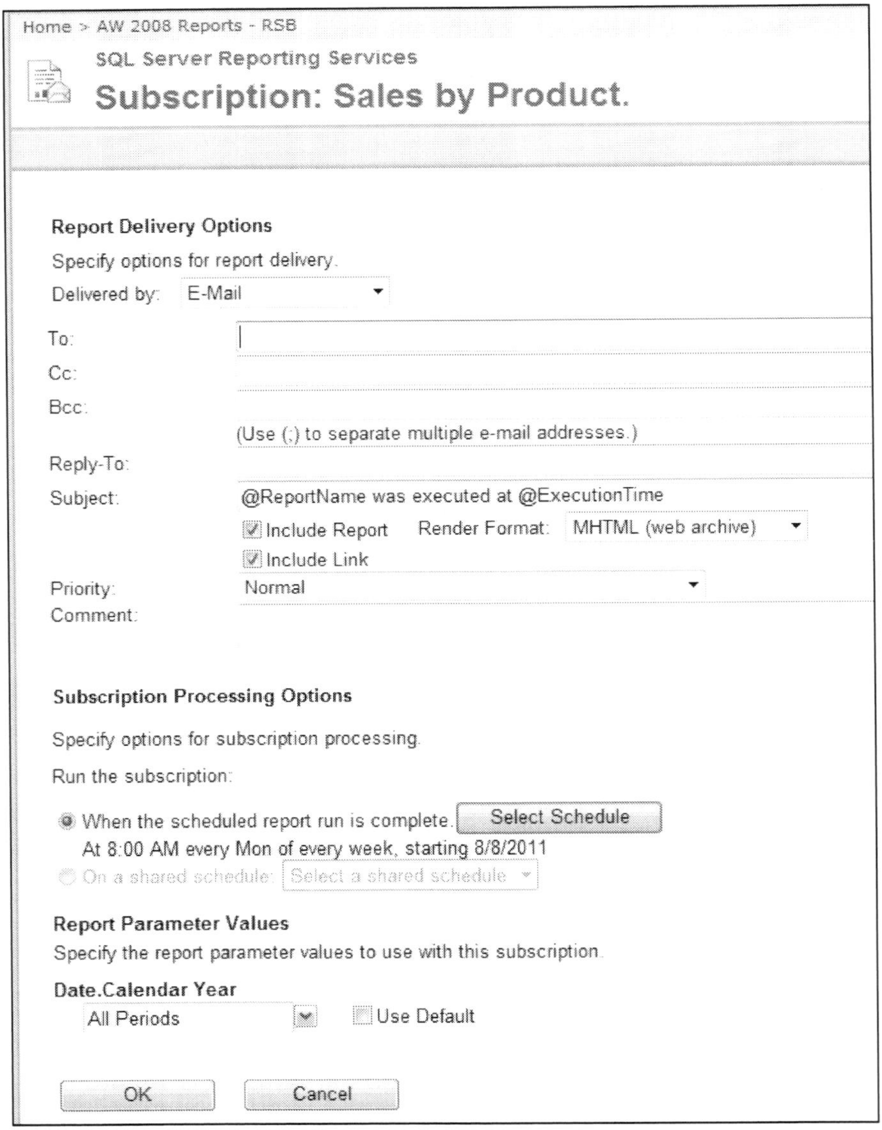

Home > AW 2008 Reports - RSB

SQL Server Reporting Services

Subscription: Sales by Product.

Report Delivery Options

Specify options for report delivery.

Delivered by: E-Mail

To:

Cc:

Bcc:

(Use (;) to separate multiple e-mail addresses.)

Reply-To:

Subject: @ReportName was executed at @ExecutionTime

Include Report Render Format: MHTML (web archive)

Include Link

Priority: Normal

Comment:

Subscription Processing Options

Specify options for subscription processing.

Run the subscription:

When the scheduled report run is complete. Select Schedule

At 8:00 AM every Mon of every week, starting 8/8/2011

On a shared schedule: Select a shared schedule

Report Parameter Values

Specify the report parameter values to use with this subscription.

Date.Calendar Year

All Periods Use Default

OK Cancel

Figure 4-15 Subscription Window

(For better viewing of this image, go to http://www.zerobits.info/bibook/bibookimages/)

Clicking OK to back out of the forms will return you to the report's subscription page as shown in Figure 4-16 which lists the new subscription. (By the way I successfully emailed this report to myself via my ISP.) You can also create a data-driven subscription as indicated by the New Data-driven Subscription action on the menu area in Figure 4-17 which is accessed by selecting Manage form the report options menu and then the Subscriptions tab. Data-driven subscriptions distribute reports to a recipient pool specified in a subscriber database. While configuration of data -driven subscriptions is beyond the scope of this book, information and tutorials are available about this in SQL Server 2008 Books Online and on the Web.

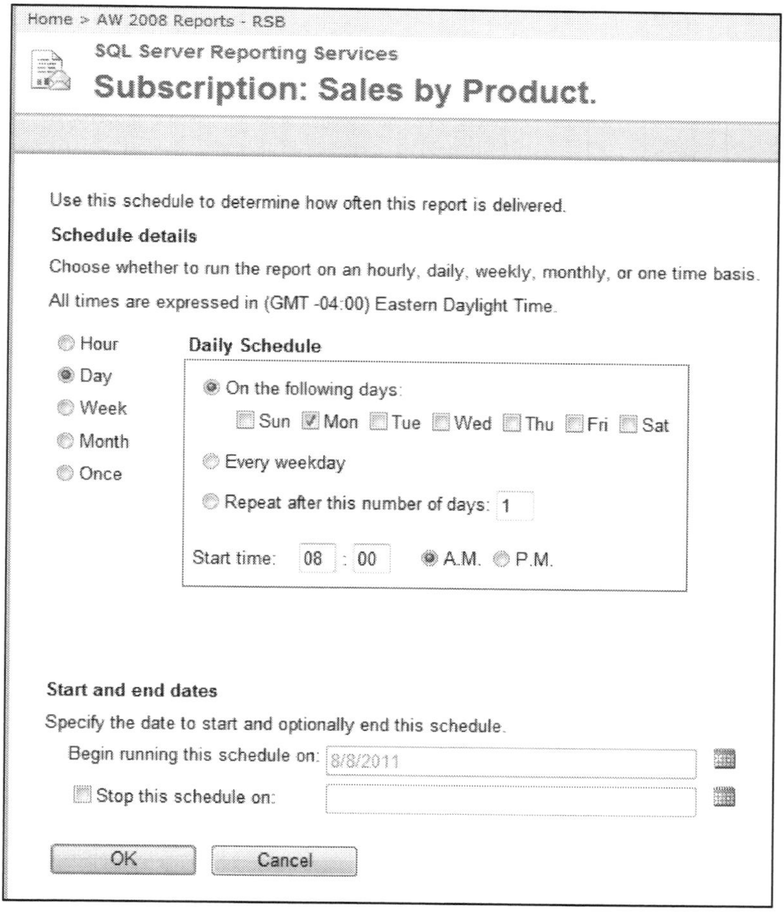

Figure 4-16 Subscription Delivery Schedule Details

(For better viewing of this image, go to http://www.zerobits.info/bibook/bibookimages/)

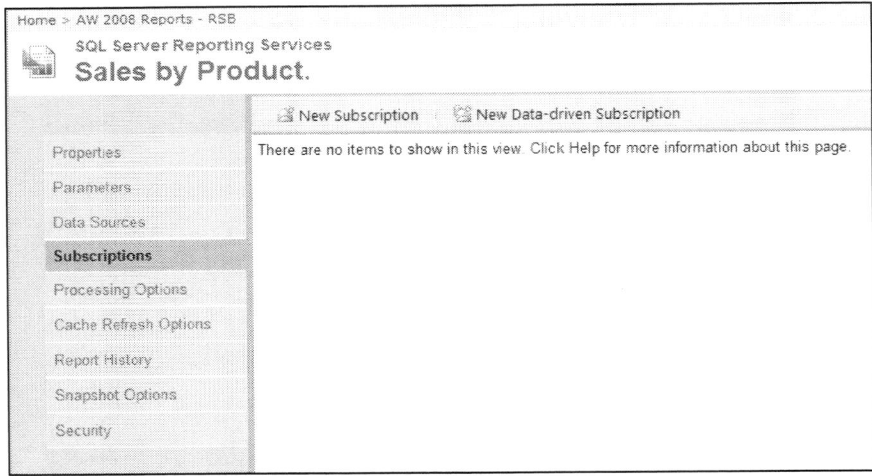

Figure 4-17 A Report's Subscription Page

The My Subscriptions navigation button in the Report Manager's toolbar in the upper right corner will display the My Subscriptions page shown in Figure 4-18. Here, all of your subscriptions will be listed, and from this page you can edit or delete them.

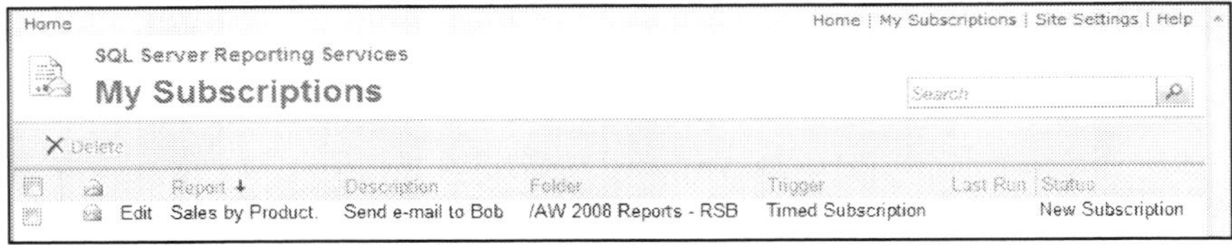

Figure 4-18 My Subscriptions Page

That's it for the tour of the Report Manager. Now on the Report Builder.

Report Builder 3.0

Report Builder is a report authoring application that creates reports to be published on the Report Server. As indicated at the beginning of this chapter Report Builder 1.0 which was installed with SQL Server 2008 has been superseded by Report Builder 3.0 (RB3). RB3 may be installed separately from a msi file downloaded from Microsoft. It requires the Microsoft .Net Framework version 3.5 to be installed on your computer.

RB3 offers a number of enhancements over version 1.0 including a Microsoft Office-optimized report authoring environment, a new Tablix data region that combines the table, matrix, and list formats from 1.0 version, and use of any data sources such as the SQL Server Database Engine, Analysis Services, Oracle, Microsoft Access, etc. instead of being limited to data sources and models in the Report Server. It now includes maps, Sparklines, databars, and a Report Part Gallery.

The following is only an introduction to RB3 and Reporting Services. There are a number of features that are slighted and some not even mentioned. Please see other sources such as RB3 Help, SQL Server Books Online, or books about Reporting Services for more complete coverage.

In RB3 you can use wizards to create tables, matrices, and map type reports or build reports from scratch. Most of report creation is done by dragging and dropping tools on a workspace, and you can add textboxes, images, gauges, subreports, and conditional formatting. You can modify data with filters, sort it, add drill-through reports, and add formulas and expressions. The reports can be saved to the report server or to your computer.

You start RB3 just like any other application by clicking on it in the Start menu, by double clicking on the exe file or a shortcut, or clicking on the Report Builder button in the Report Manager taskbar. Although it interacts with the Report Server, it is independent of it. Its appearance at start is shown in Figure 4-19. The Report Data panel is on the left, Properties on the right, the design surface (canvas) in the left center, the report part gallery in the right center. and groupings on the bottom. A Getting Started page is displayed on top where you may choose frequently used options. You may disable the Getting Started page by checking the box on the bottom.

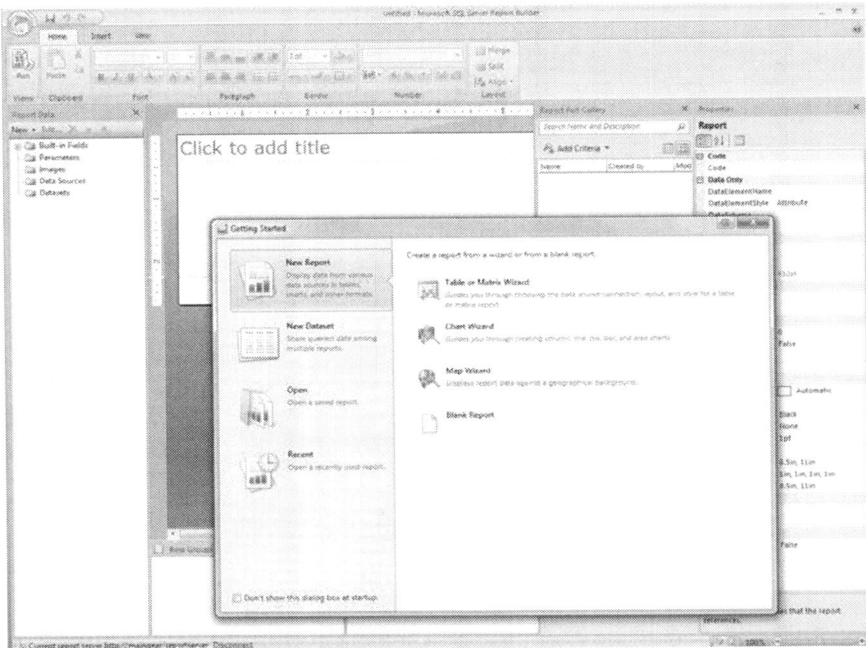

Figure 4-19 Report Builder 3.0 GUI

RB3 has the Office 2010-type ribbon user interface at the top with three tabs: Home, Insert, and View. Partial screen shots of those ribbons and the Report Builder button are shown in Figure 4-20. In the figure the Home ribbon essentially offers formatting options and the Run button on it to run and view a report. The Insert menu lists objects that can be used in a report with the Table, Matrix, Chart, and Map objects having drop-down menus which offer two options: using a wizard or inserting the object directly, e.g., for the table object the option would be Table Wizard or Insert Table. There is not a separate toolbox panel as in some other applications like BIDS. The View menu allows the selection of what appears on the interface surface: the data, properties, and groupings panels and the ruler. RB3 has a more simplified and streamlined GUI than the Report Designer in BIDS that we looked at in Chapter 3. The final image shows a drop-down menu similar to the File menu in Office 2010 applications. This is displayed by clicking on what I call the Report Builder button in the upper left corner of the window. There you can create new reports, open previous reports, save the current report, and display option menus.

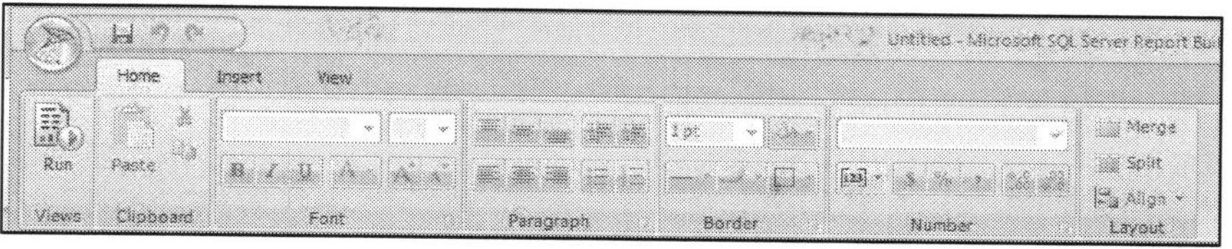

Home Tab

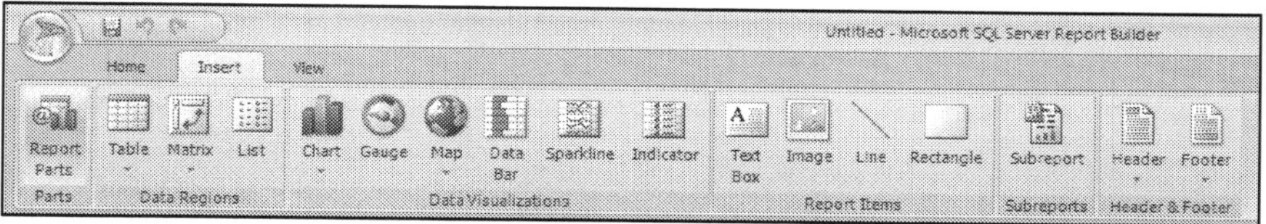

Insert Tab

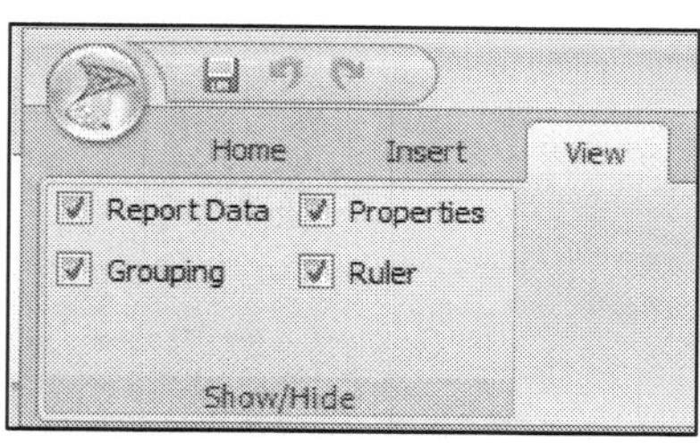

View Tab

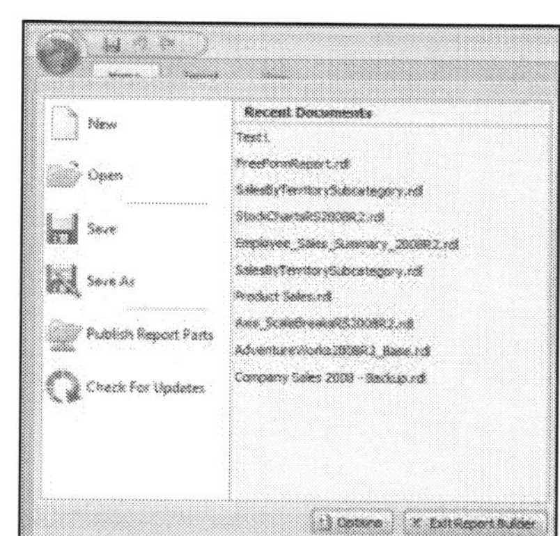

Report Builder Button Menu

Figure 4-20 Report Builder 3.0 Ribbons and Report Button Menu

(For better viewing of this image, go to http://www.zerobits.info/bibook/bibookimages/)

Now for three report fundamentals: data sources, query designers, and data regions.

Data Sources

Each report requires a data source. Data sources can be either shared or embedded. Shared data sources are stored on the Report Server and can be used in any reports given appropriate permissions. We discussed creating data sources in the Report Manager earlier in this chapter. Embedded data sources are local to the specific report. The connection information in an embedded report is contained only in that report and cannot be used for other reports. If an embedded data source is required in another report, the connection must be specified anew there as well. If a shared data source contains the data you need for a report, then use it. If a shared data source is not available, you have three options: use an embedded data source, go to the Report Manager and create a new shared data source, or ask the IT folks to create a shared data source using Reporting Services.

Data Sources with the Wizard

Regardless of whether you will use a shared or embedded data source or whether you will create your report with the wizard or manually, you will work with a data source or dataset properties dialog boxes like the one in Figure 4-21 for the Table wizard. If the data source that you need is not on the list, click on "Create a dataset" and then Next to display the Choose a connection to a data source window as in Figure 4-22. If the data source you want is not on the list, click the Browse button to view the shared data sources as in Figure 4-23. This file list is a view of the directory structure in the Report Manager shown previously in Figure 4-2. Click on any row in the list to view the contents of that folder. In this particular list only two folders contain shared data sources: Data Sources and Models. If you click on a folder that does not contain a data source, the resultant window will be blank.

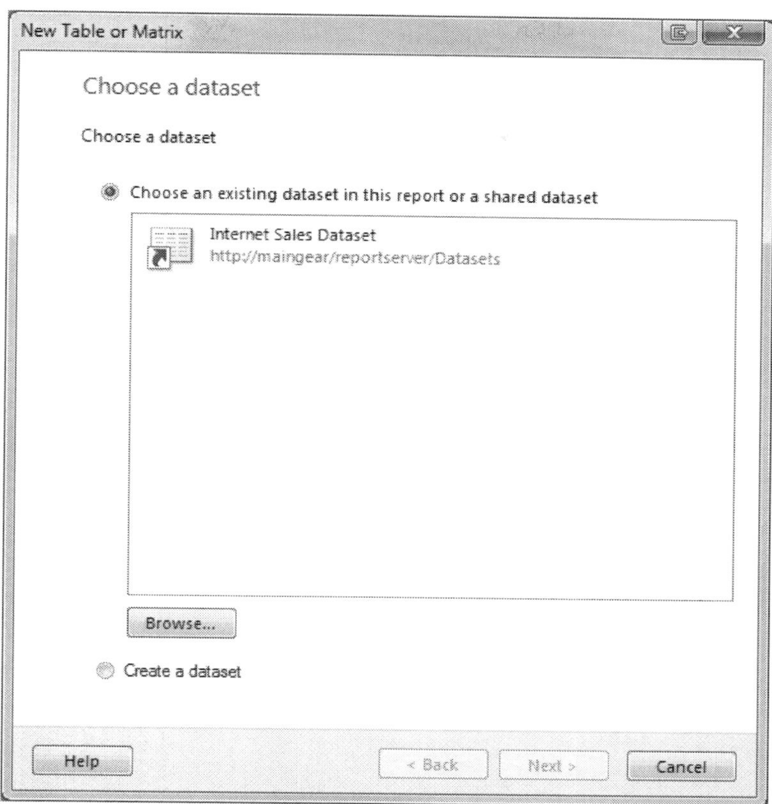

Figure 4-21 Initial Dataset Dialog Box for the Wizard

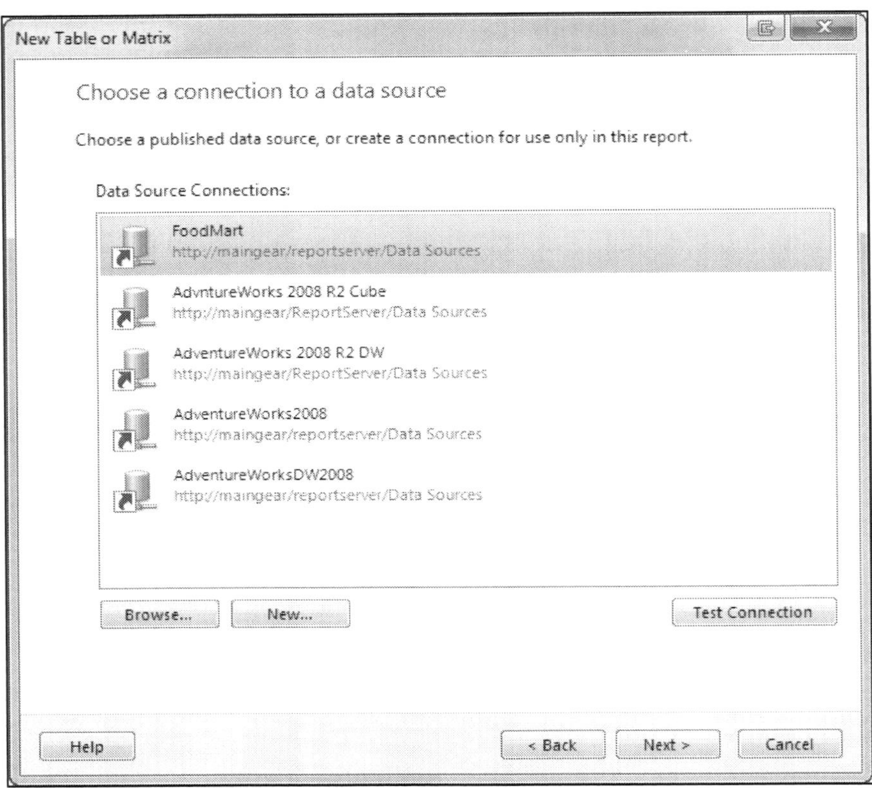

Figure 4-22 Connection Data Source

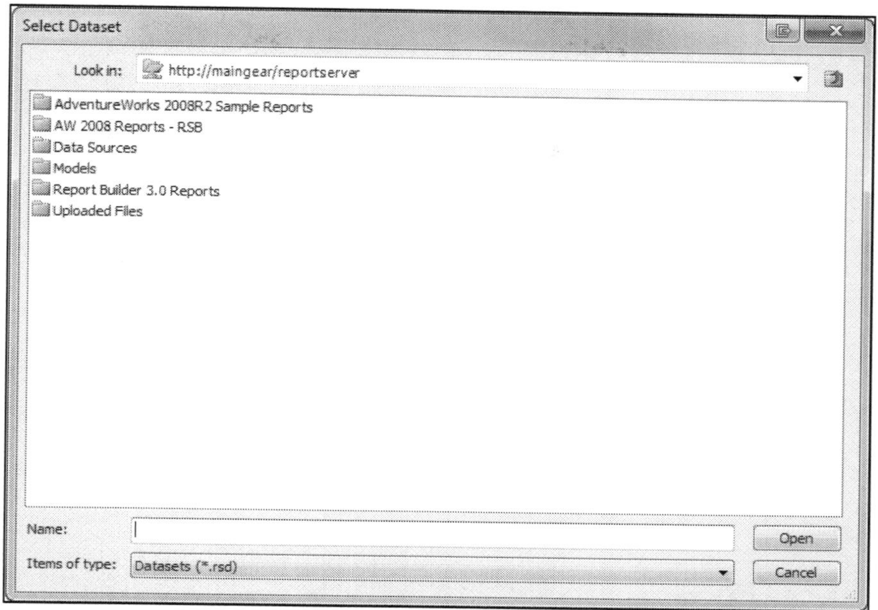

Figure 4-23 Browse for a Shared Data Source

If the data source that you need is not available as a shared data source and you cannot or choose not to create one or have one created for you, then you will have to use an embedded data source. In this case, click the "Create a dataset" button and the Next button in Figure 4-21 to bring up the Data Source Properties dialog box in Figure 4-23.

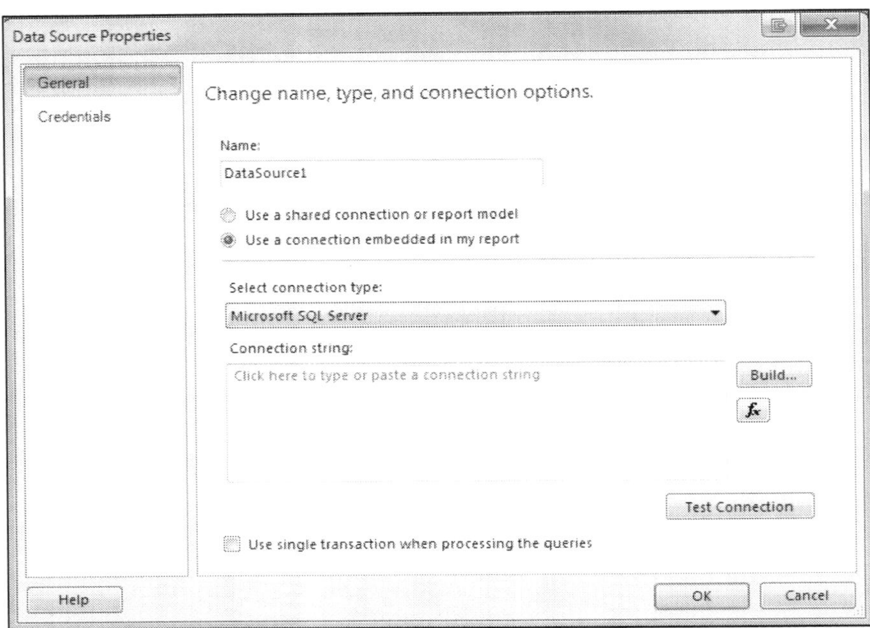

Figure 4-23 New Data Source Properties

To define a new embedded data source you give it a name (here DataSource1 is the default), select the connection type, and build the connection string. Figure 4-24 shows the listbox for the connection type. I used the SQL Server connection type to create data sources from databases on my instance of SQL Server 2008 and the Analysis Services connection type to create a data source for the AdventureWorks Cube. There many other connection types available as you can see in the figure. If one is not specifically identified on the list, then you can probably find what you need in the OLE DB connection type or define a connection via an ODBC connection string. For example, you could connect to an Access 2010 database by using the OLE DB connection type with the Microsoft Office 12.0 Access Database Engine OLE DB Provider. A database connection to the Northwind Access database is shown in Figure 4-25.

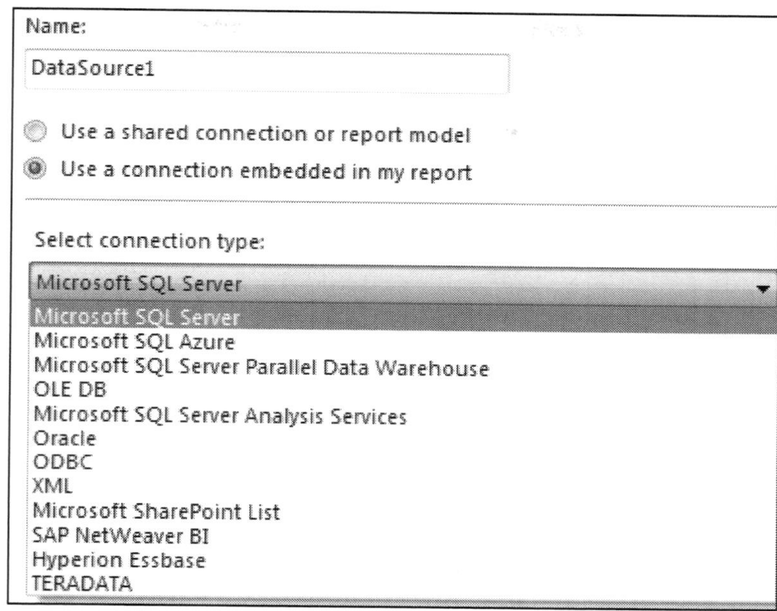

Figure 4-24 Data Source Connection Types

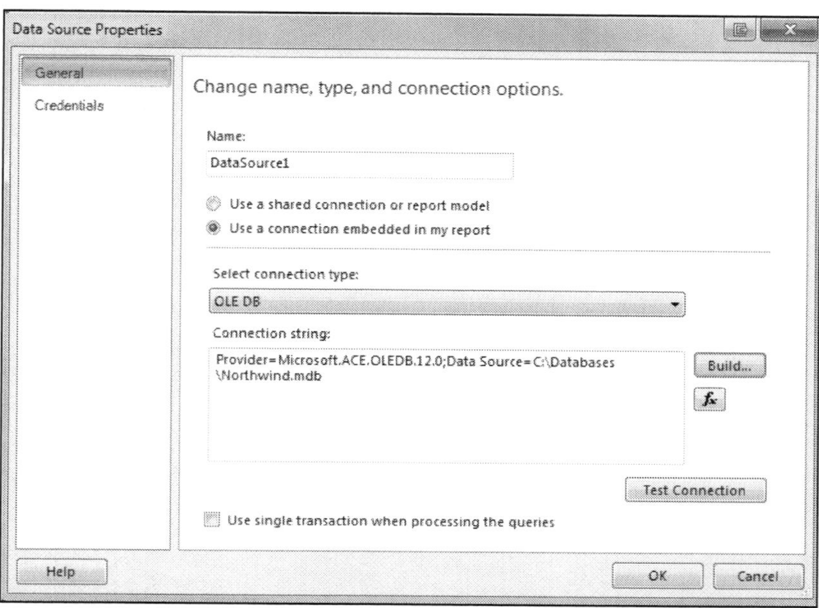

Figure 4-25 Access 2010 Data Source Connection

Since you will likely use SQL Server databases as data sources. let's look at how to build a connection to them. If you selected Microsoft SQL Server as the connection type as in Figure 4-24 and then clicked the Build button, a Connection Properties dialog box would be displayed as in Figure 4-26. You have the option of changing the data source type by clicking the Change button, and you select the server instance by entering its name in the Server Name textbox or selecting a server that is shown on a list when you click on the down arrowhead. In Figure 4-27 I entered my server's name, MAINGEAR. At this point you may test the connection by clicking the Text Connection button at the bottom. If the test succeeds, then you may select the database for the connection from the drop-down list. In Figure 4-27 I selected the old FoodMart database. Clicking the OK button at the bottom will take you back to the Data Source Properties dialog box (Figure 4-23) with the appropriate connection showing in the Connection String textbox, and clicking OK will take back to the to the next wizard page.

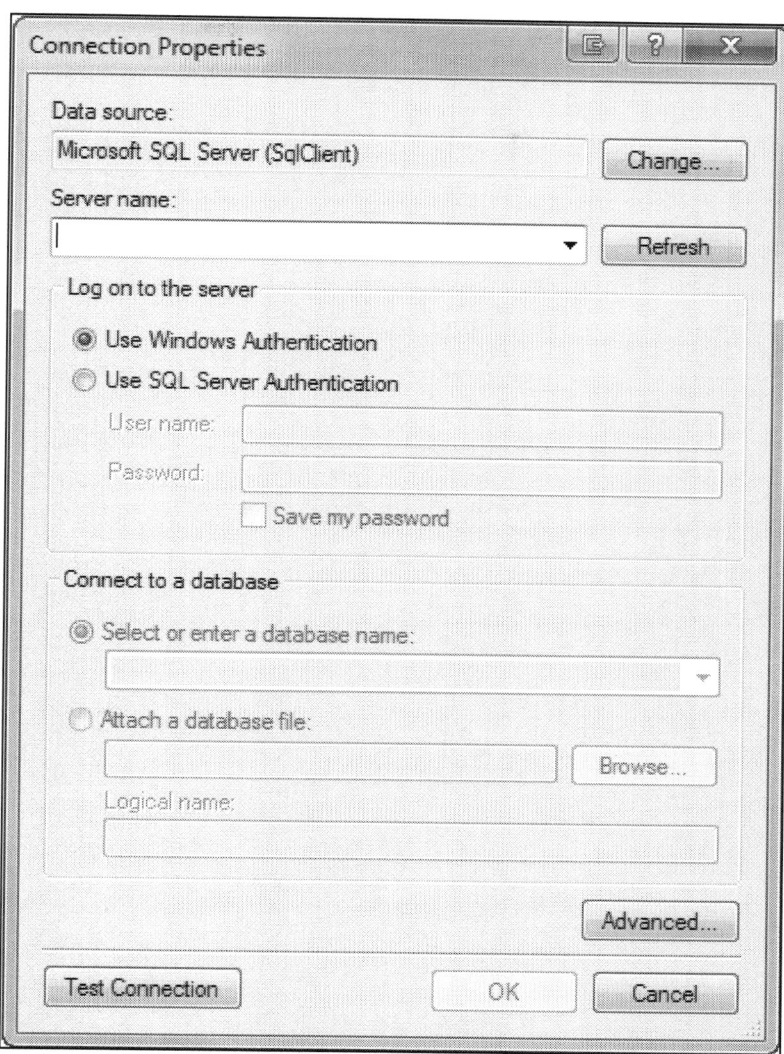

Figure 4-26 New Connection Dialog Box

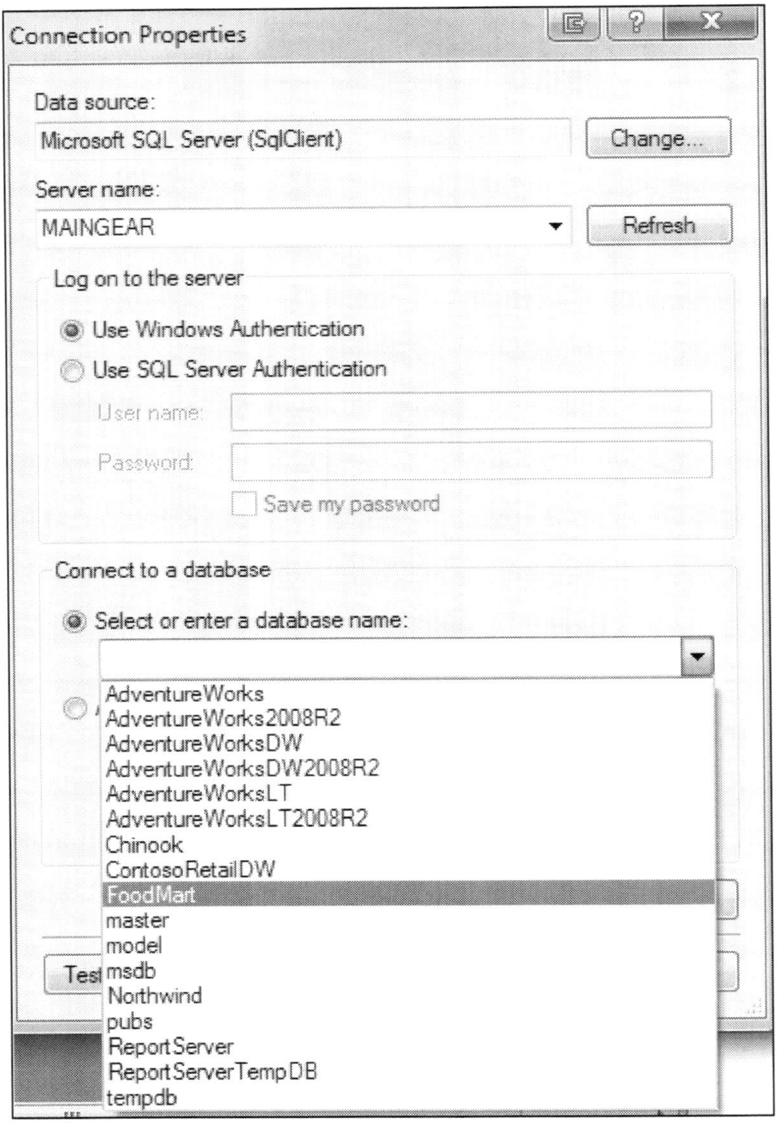

Figure 4-27 Connection to a SQL Server Database

Manual Data Source Connections

Starting with the initial RB3 window in Figure 4-19 we can create a new data source manually by clicking on New in the Report Data panel on the left which presents the drop-down listbox in Figure 4-28. Clicking on Data Source there brings up a Data Source Properties dialog box as in Figure 4-23. You may also right click on the Data Sources Folder to display that box. Selecting the shared connection option keeps you in this view where you may either select a shared connection used previously from the list or browse for other available shared connections by clicking on the Browse button which will bring up the Select Data source window shown in Figure 4-21. Selecting the embedded connection option will bring up a window similar to the one in Figure 4-22. Proceed to create the connection and return to the RB3 main window where a new data source has been added in the Report Data panel as in Figure 4-29. Double clicking on the new data source, DataSource1, will take you back to the dialog box in Figure 4-23.

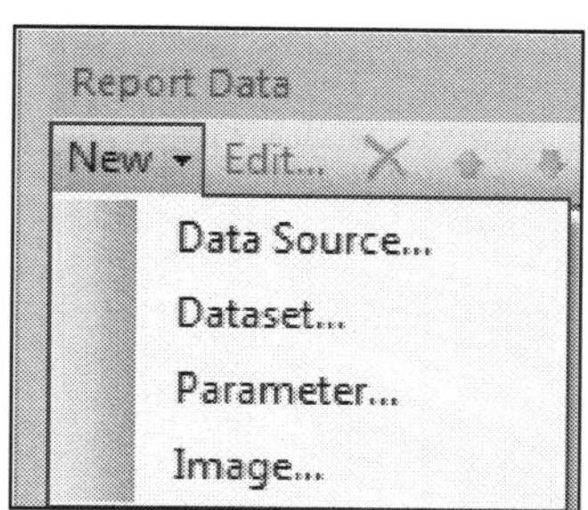

Figure 4-28 Report Data New List

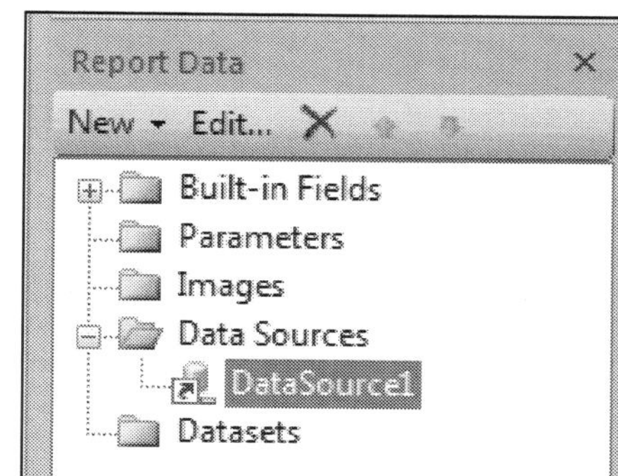

Figure 4-29 Data Source Added

The next step in manually creating a data source is to construct a dataset to be used in the report from the data source. When using the query designer with the wizard as discussed below, a dataset will be automatically be created. We'll cover constructing a dataset for a manually created data source later in the description of query designers.

Query Designers

Each report uses a query to specify the data, the columns and rows, that will be used in it. The query designer is an easy to use, drag and drop GUI that creates the query statement in the appropriate query language, e.g., SQL for relational databases, MDX for cubes, etc., unless only a text-based designer is supported. The presentation of the designer user interface varies depending on the type of data source: an Analysis Services cube, a relational database, a report model, and a few others. We will explore the Designer for an Analysis Services database.

The Query Designer shown in Figure 30 uses the AdventureWorks Cube as a shared data source. You may change the Analysis Services data source by clicking on the Cube Selection button, the one with the dots, to the right of the current cube name (AdventureWorks). Note that you are limited to changing to an available data source of the same type, in this case another cube. There are four main areas on the Designer surface: Metadata contains the list of data available – for our example measures, KPIs, and dimensions since we're using a cube; Calculated Members local to the report (there are none yet in this initial setup); the Design and Query View panel on the lower right; and the Filter panel above it.

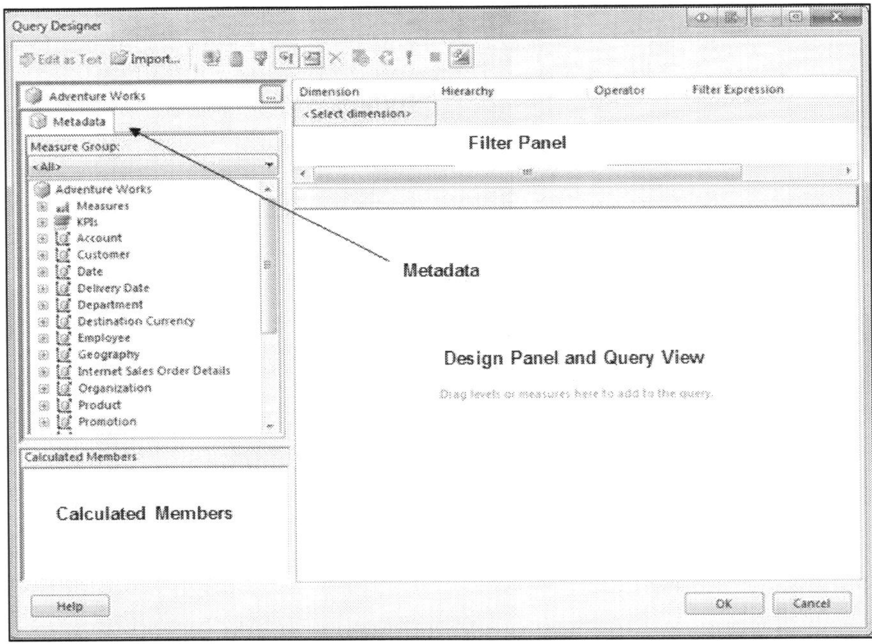

Figure 4-30 Report Builder Query Designer

Fields and values are added to a query by selecting an object in the Metadata panel, and then dragging and dropping it into the Design panel. Items selected and dropped will insert all items included beneath it into the query, e.g., if I dropped the Measures item into the designer, all of the measures in the cube would be inserted into the query. As an example of building a query, I expanded Measures to get to the list of measures in Figure 4-31a, and then the Internet Sales folder for the list of individual Internet sales measures in Figure 4-31b. I then dragged and dropped the Internet Gross Profit Margin and

Internet Sales Amount fields onto the design surface. I also dropped the Category and Subcategory attributes from the Products dimension and the Calendar Quarter from the Date dimension as shown in Figure 4-32. Last, I dropped Calendar year from the Date dimension into the Filter panel. This essentially completes the query.

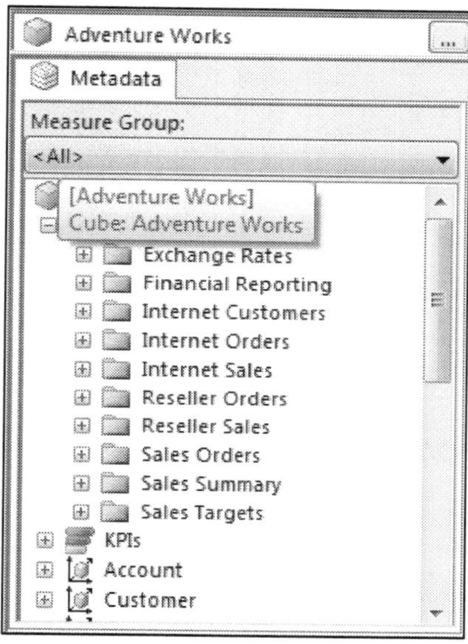

Table 4-31a Measures Expanded

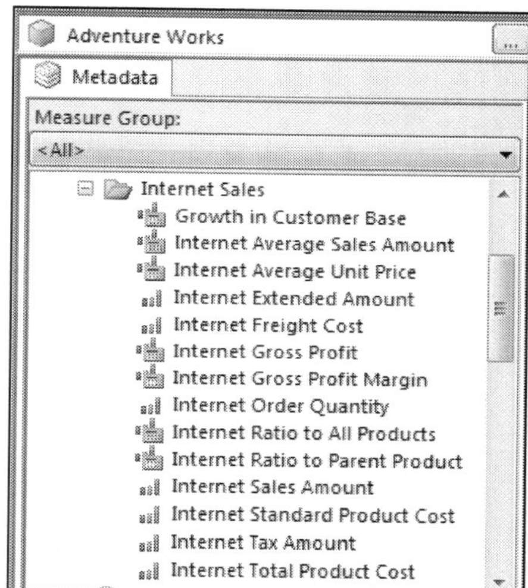

Table 4-31b Internet Sales Expanded

Figure 4-31 Query Fields Selection

By including the Calendar Year in the Filter panel the report based on the query will have its records limited(filtered) to the value(s) specified by the filter. If you click on the Date.Calendar Year box in the Hierarchy column, a drop-down list box allows you to change the filter attribute as shown in Figure 4-33a. Similarly, clicking on the box below the Operator heading brings up the operator-type listbox as in Figure-33b. The time period to display in this particular report is selected in the drop-down listbox accessed under the Filter Expression column heading as in Figure 4-33c.

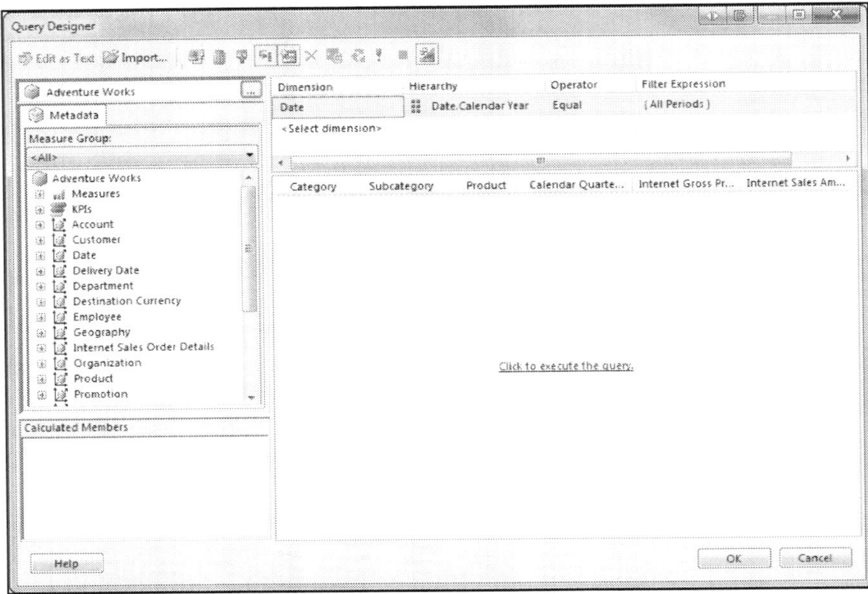

Figure 4-32 The Completed Query

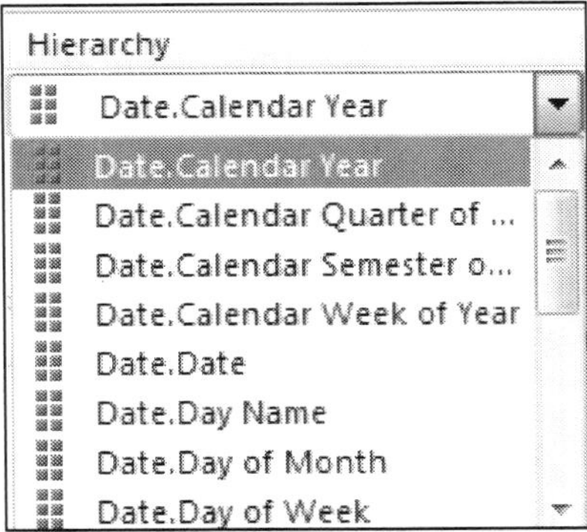

Figure 4-33a Hierarchy List

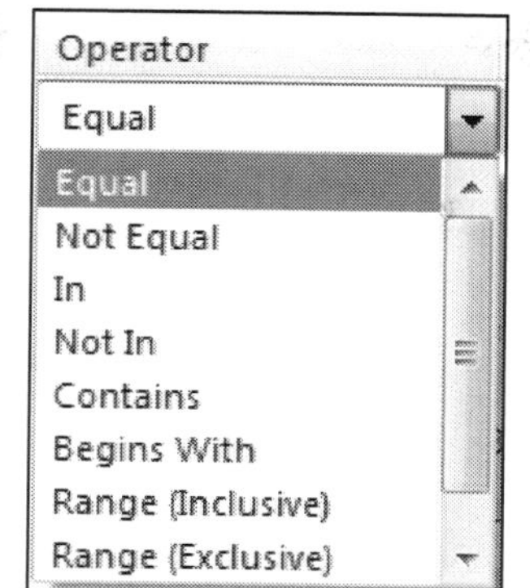

Figure 4-33b Operator List

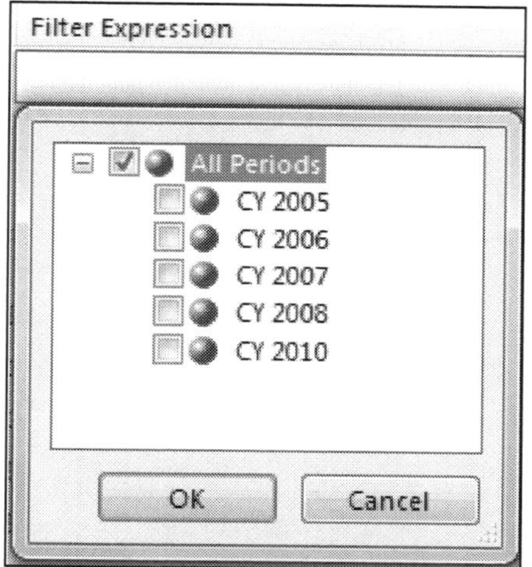

Figure 4-33c Filter Expression List

Figure 4-33 Filter Configuration Lists

If you prefer to have the filter act as a parameter in the report, i.e., an attribute whose value the user can specify when the report is viewed as shown in Figure 4-34 (All Periods are selected there), then click on the Parameter checkbox which is shown by moving the horizontal scroll bar at the bottom of the Filter panel all the way to the right as in Figure 4-34. With the parameter enabled the Filter Expression becomes the default presentation in the reports initial rendering. By including the Calendar Year in the Filter panel as a parameter the report based on the query will have the capability to display the data by the calendar year(s) selected by the user.

Dimension	Hierarchy	Operator	Filter Expression	Param...
Date	Date.Calendar Year	Equal	{ All Periods }	☑
<Select dimension>				

Category	Subcategory	Product	Calendar Quarter ...	Internet Gross Profit	Internet Sales Amo...
Accessories	Bike Racks	Hitch Rack - 4-Bike	CY Q1	5558.88	8880
Accessories	Bike Racks	Hitch Rack - 4-Bike	CY Q2	7286.64	11640
Accessories	Bike Racks	Hitch Rack - 4-Bike	CY Q3	6535.44	10440
Accessories	Bike Racks	Hitch Rack - 4-Bike	CY Q4	5258.4	8400
Accessories	Bike Stands	All-Purpose Bike S...	CY Q1	5175.768	8268
Accessories	Bike Stands	All-Purpose Bike S...	CY Q2	6668.778	10653

Figure 4-34 Filter Parameter Checkbox

To remove a field from the design surface just click on its name (the column heading) and drag it away from the panel. To execute the query, if it has not run already, click on the red exclamation point (!) button or the "Click to execute the query" message in the design panel. The results are displayed in Query View at the bottom of Figure 4-34. It's important to run the query at this point in case that there are execution errors.

The buttons at the top of the query designer appear above Table 4-1 which describes their function. Search for "Analysis Services MDX Query Designer User Interface" in RB3 Help for more information. Clicking on the last icon button in the list, the Design-Query mode toggle shows the query code in what was the Filter panel, in this case in MDX query language, as in Figure 4-35. Clicking again will return to design mode.

1 2 3 4 5 6 7 8 9 10

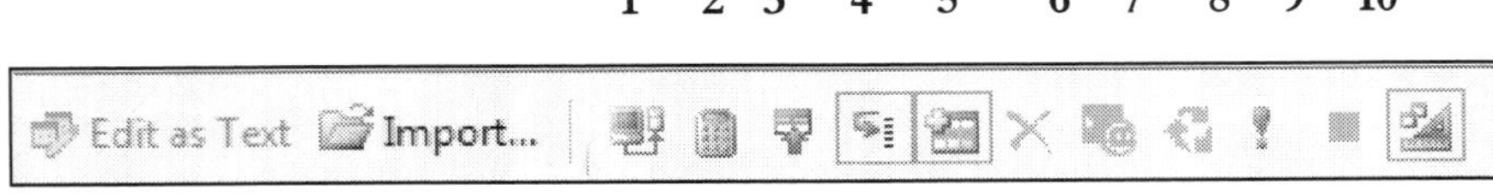

Button	Description
1	Refresh metadata.
2	Add calculated member.
3	Show empty cells.
4	Auto execute.
5	Show aggregations.
6	Query parameters.
7	Prepare query.
8	Execute query.
9	Cancel Query.
10	Design mode.

Table 4-1 Query Designer Buttons

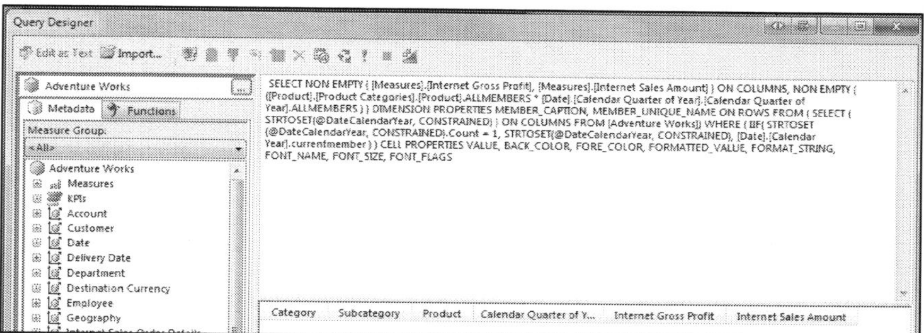

Figure 4-35 Query Mode

Calculated Members

Calculated members are dimensions or measures that do not exist in the data source but are calculated from those that are. You use a calculated member in the same manner as those that already exist in the cube.

You create a new calculated member by either clicking on the Calculated Member Builder icon button in the toolbar or right clicking on the Calculated Members panel. Either way you get to the Calculated Member Builder shown in Figure 4-36. First, give the new calculated member a name and select the Parent Hierarchy, the place in the Metadata list where the new calculated member will appear. I'll keep calculated members in Measures. Note that Parent Member is disabled if the Parent Hierarchy is Measures. Next, create the MDX expression by dragging and dropping Metadata and/or functions into the Expression textbox or by writing MDX code directly (Ugh!).

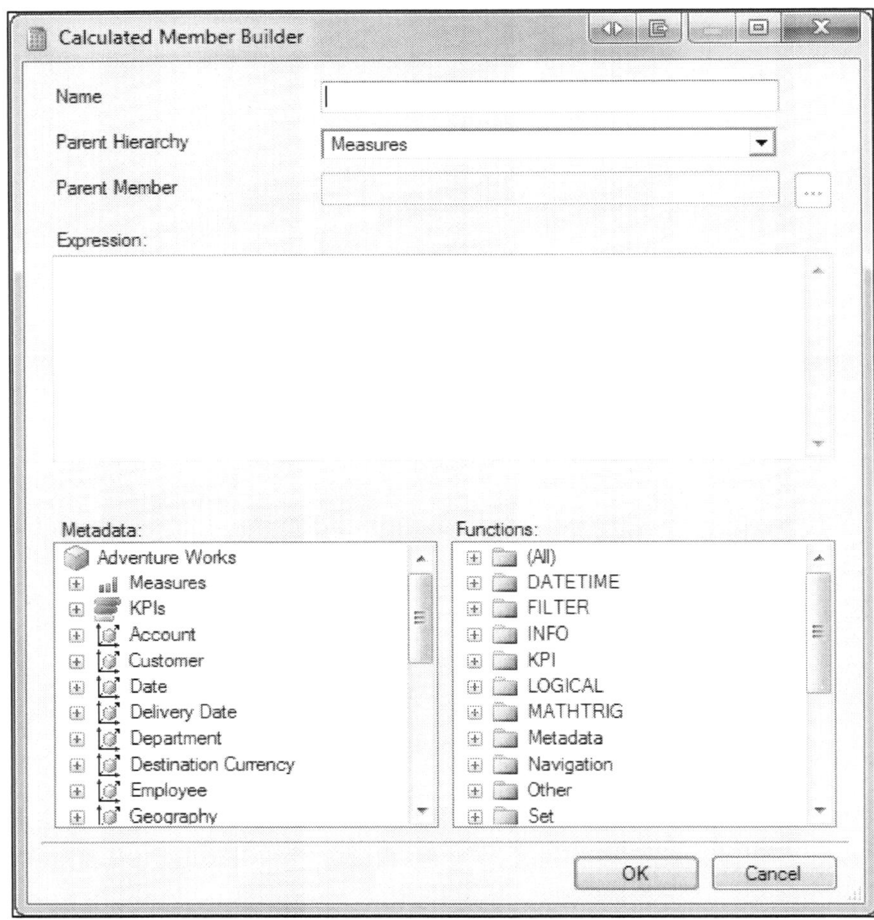

Figure 4-36 Calculated Member Builder

In Figure 4-37 I created a very simple calculated measure to compute the sales tax rate by dragging and dropping the Internet Tax Amount and the Internet Sales Amount from the Metadata panel in the Measures folder into the Expression textbox. I added the divide operator (/) and multiplied the result by 100 to compute a percentage. Click OK to return to the Query designer where the new calculated member will appear in the Calculated Members panel ready to use. Neat! Note that the calculated members created with BIDS in Analysis Services are still available and are listed in the Metadata. In fact we used one, Internet Gross Profit Margin, in building the example query above.

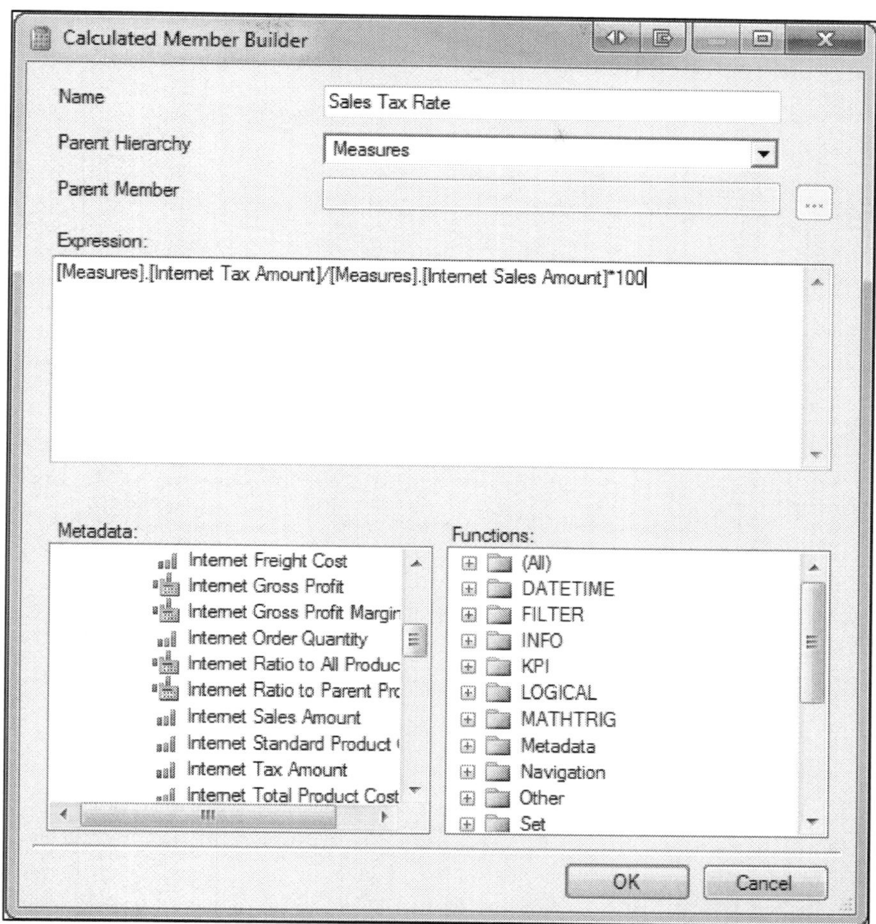

Figure 4-37 Calculated Member Builder Completed

Clicking OK will get you back to the query designer. Clicking OK in the query designer window will complete the query design and take you either further on in the report wizard or back to the RB3 main window depending upon where you started the query design process. When you return to the query designer main window you will find a new entry in the Report Data panel on the left of the RB3 main window in the background as shown in Figure 4-38. In this figure the entry "AdventureWorksCube" is the data source name, and the data fields to be used are listed under the dataset , InternetSales.

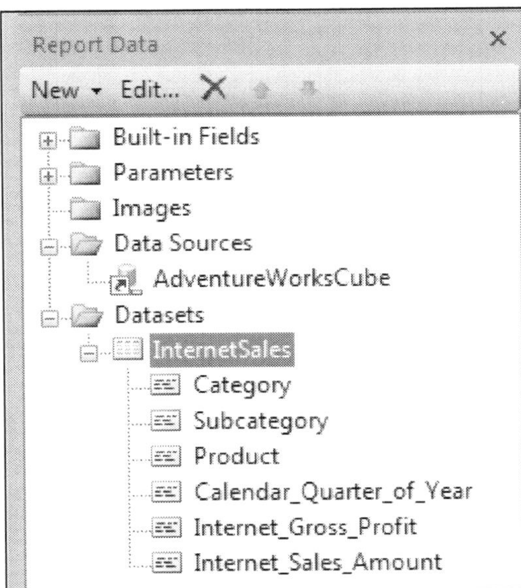

Figure 4-38 A New Query in the Report Data Panel

Manual Dataset Construction

Earlier we described how to create a data source manually as shown in Figure 4-28. Continuing with that here, a dataset is required to use data from the data source in a report. A dataset lists the fields and attributes that will be available to the report and is specified in a query as exemplified by the list under DataSet1 in Figure 4-38 above. You may create more than one dataset for a data source. To create a new dataset either click on New or right click on the data source in the Report Data panel and select Add Dataset. Either method will bring up the Dataset Properties dialog box shown in Figure 4-39. You may rename the dataset from its default name and select or create a new data source if the one showing is not correct. Clicking on the Query Designer button will take you to the query designer as in Figure 4-30. Clicking the Import button will take you to a file explorer where you can select items that already have datasets defined, e.g., report files (files with a rdl file extension), reports in the Report Manager, etc. Figure 4-40 shows the Dataset Properties window after I imported a dataset from another report.

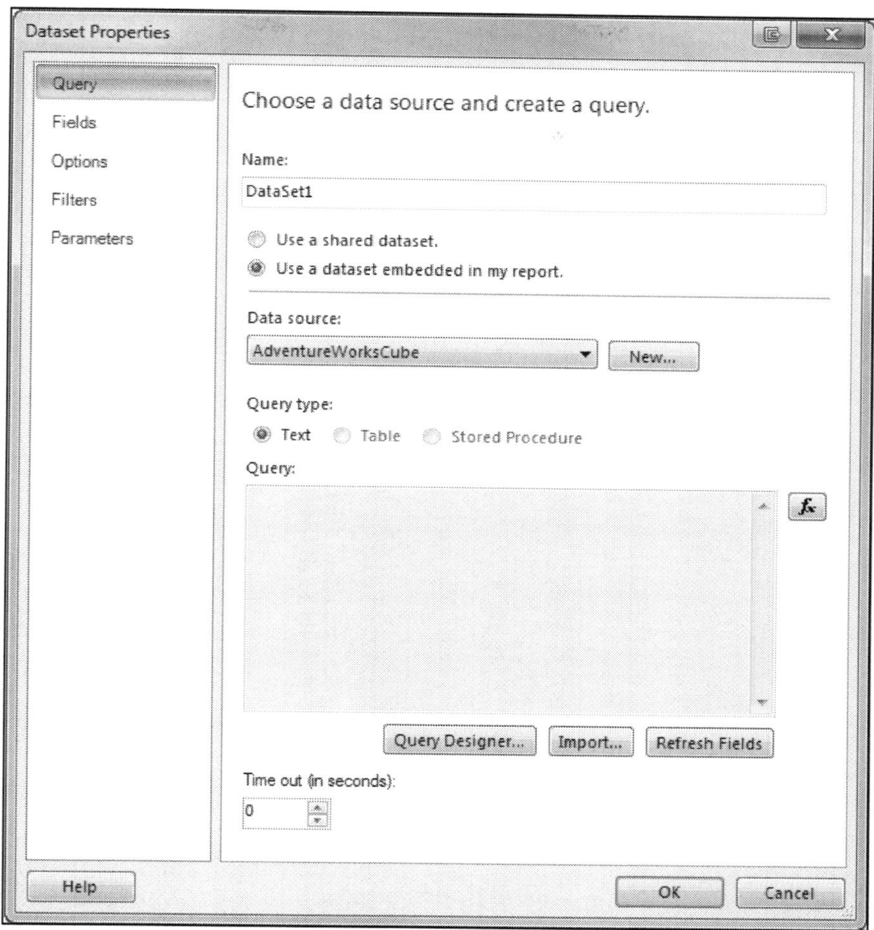

Figure 4-39 Dataset Properties Dialog Box

(For better viewing of this image, go to http://www.zerobits.info/bibook/bibookimages/)

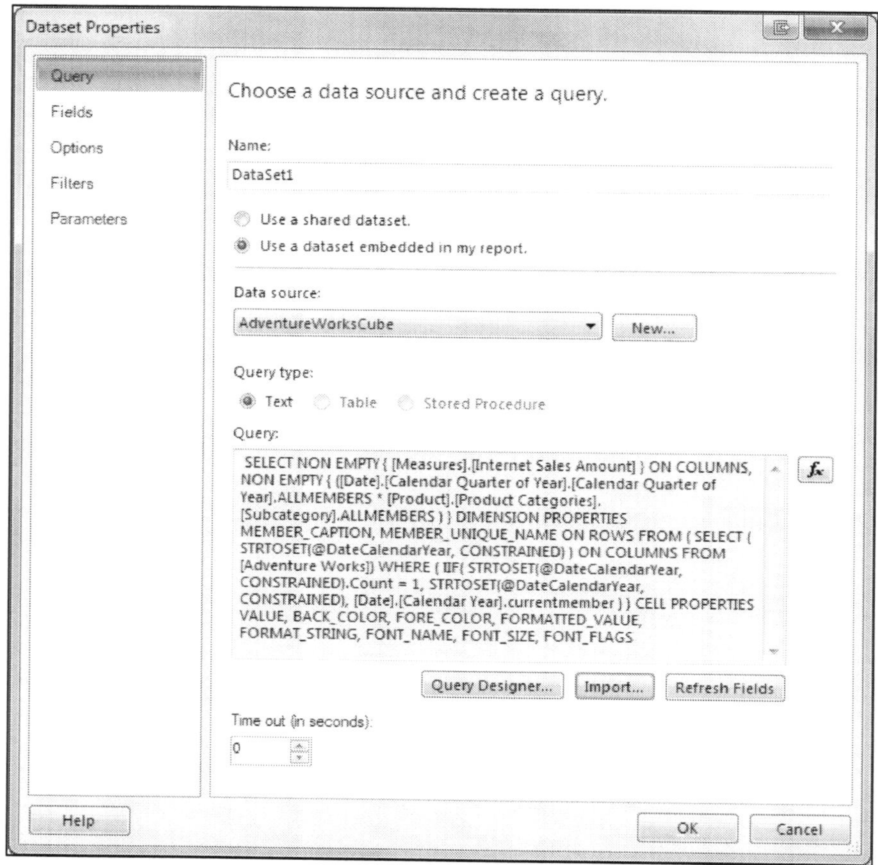

Figure 4-40 Imported Query

(For better viewing of this image, go to http://www.zerobits.info/bibook/bibookimages/)

After the query is specified you may configure the dataset by using one or more of the items in the list in the panel on left side: Parameters lists the existing parameters and allows deleting existing ones and adding new ones; Fields allows you to add or delete fields from the query; Options allows you to change collation, case sensitivity, and other options; And Filters allows you to add and delete filters. Since these actions are fairly straight forward, we'll not examine them in detail here. Clicking OK in the Query view returns you to the RB3 main page with the new dataset listed in the Report Data panel as shown in Figure 4-41.

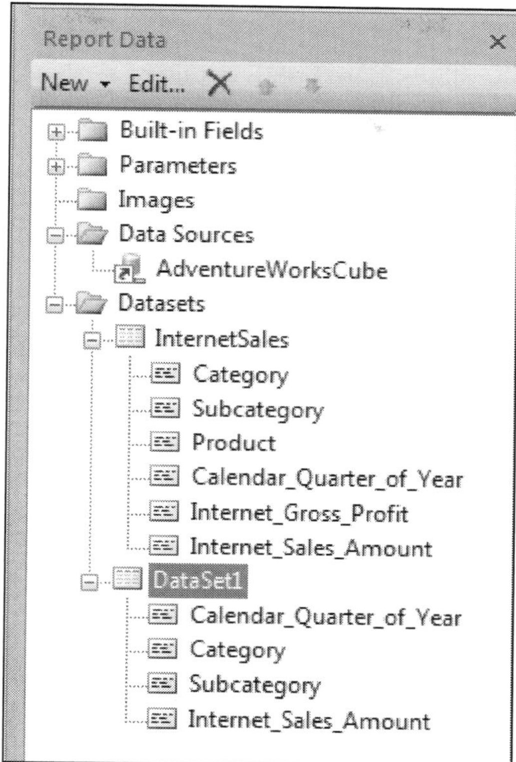

Figure 4-41 Completed New Dataset

Shared Datasets

You may store dataset configurations for reuse instead of having to recreate a dataset for each new report that uses it. To do that in RB3 select New Dataset from the Getting Started page or from the New Report or Dataset window which will display a data source list as in Figure 4-22 from which you specify the data source for the data set. After doing that, you will proceed to the Report Builder Query Designer (Figure 4-30) and proceed to build the query. Back in the Report Builder main page you would then save the dataset as a .rdl file to a folder in the Report Server or elsewhere. I save mine in a folder called Data Sets.

Data Regions

Data regions are used to display data in a report. There are three types of data regions in RB3: tables, matrixes, and lists. We will see how to use these data regions a bit later in this chapter. There can be more than one data region in a report, and data regions can be nested within other data regions.

Tables, matrixes, and lists are variations of the tablix data region which presents data in tabular form with rows and columns. The default cell in a tablix is a textbox but you can insert other report objects such as an image.

A Tablix without groupings presents data in the detail as defined by the underlying query. However, data may be aggregated in a Tablix by using groups for, say, drilling-down. Figure 4-42 shows the grouping panes at the bottom of the designer window. Groups are organized as a hierarchy in a tree-like structure. For example, row groups for products may have product category at the top of the hierarchy (the parent), product subcategory below and subordinate to the product category (its child), and then the product itself at the bottom of the hierarchy as the child of the product subcategory. Similarly, column groups could have calendar year as the parent with calendar quarter as its child. We'll see later how groups can be used to create interactive reports with drill-down capabilities. There's considerably more to learn about the tablix data region than we can present here. Please see Report Builder 3.0 Help for advanced topics.

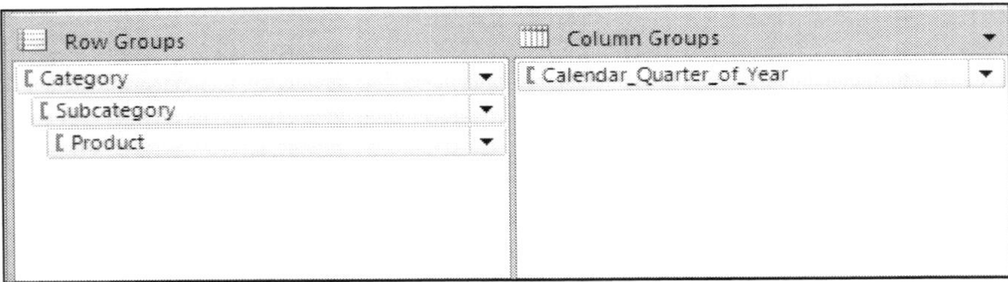

Figure 4-42 Tablix Groping Example

So far in this description of RB3 we have learned how to create data sources, data sets, and data regions but we have yet to build a report. There are two ways to do that: with a wizard or manually. We will examine both.

Using the Report Builder Wizard

The obvious way to start building a report is to click on one of the two option presented on the design surface of a new report as in Figure 4-19: Table or Matrix or Chart. The other way is to click on Table, Matrix, or Chart on the Insert Ribbon and select the wizard drop-down option. Either way will bring up the data source connection dialog box as in Figure 4-21 which leads to the Query Designer that we learned about above. When the query design is complete, click OK to move on to the next window to arrange the fields in the Tablix. Using the query that we created above the Arrange Fields window initially appears as in Figure 4-43 with the fields that we included in the query listed in the Available Fields panel. We can drag and drop these fields into positions for a table (just columns of data if you remember) or rows and columns for a matrix style report. The Values panel will contain the measures that will be the table's or matrix's cell values.

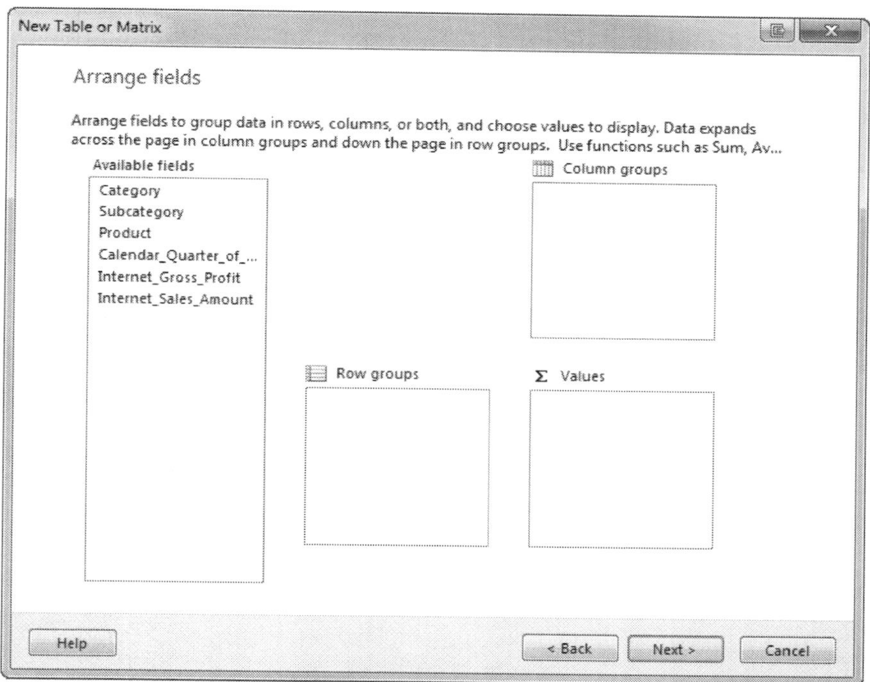

Figure 4-43 Initial Tablix Arrange Fields Window

In Figure 4-44 I dragged Calendar_Quarter_of_Year into the Column groups for the column heading, Category and Subcategory into Row groups for row headings, and Internet_Sales_Amount into Σ Values (Sum of Values) for cell values. I left the Internet_Gross_Margin calculated measure alone for now. Note that the row and column groups will appear in the report designer groupings panel per our discussion of Figure 4-42.

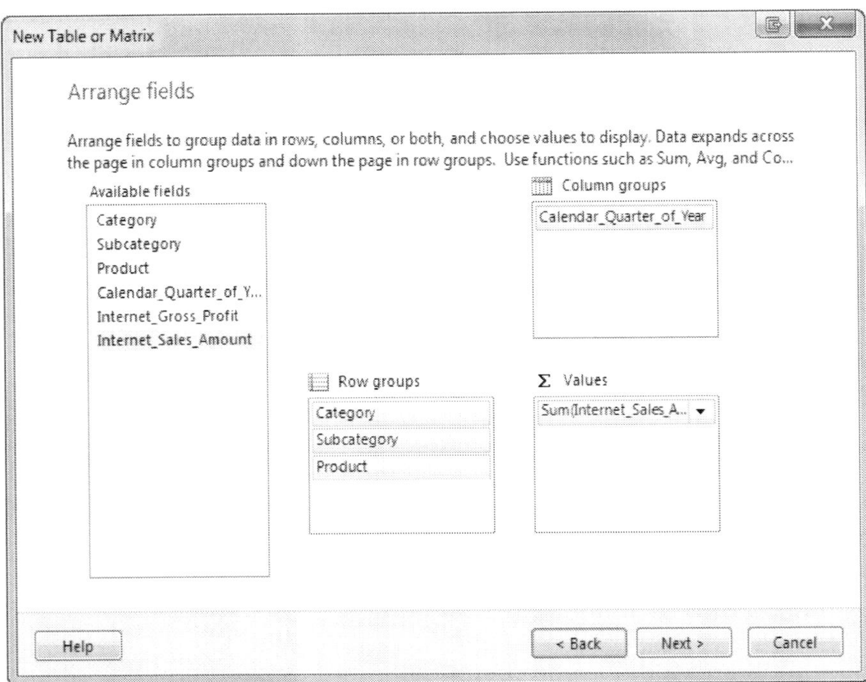

Figure 4-44 Completed Tablix Arrange Fields Window

You select the layout style in the next window shown in Figure 4-45. If you want subtotals and grand totals in the report, leave that box checked. Note that the Expand/collapse groups box it checked. This allows drill-down in the report. You can also set this toggle later by tinkering with the properties of groups in the Groupings panel.

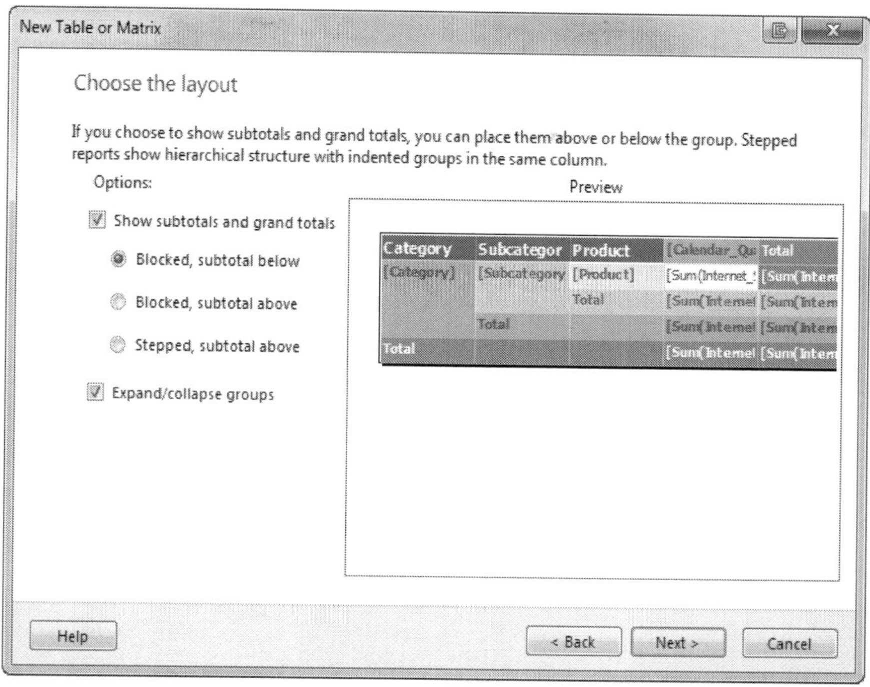

Figure 4-45 Layout Window

The next window in Figure 4-46 allows you to choose a report style. Just click on a style name to view a preview. Here the Ocean style is previewed.

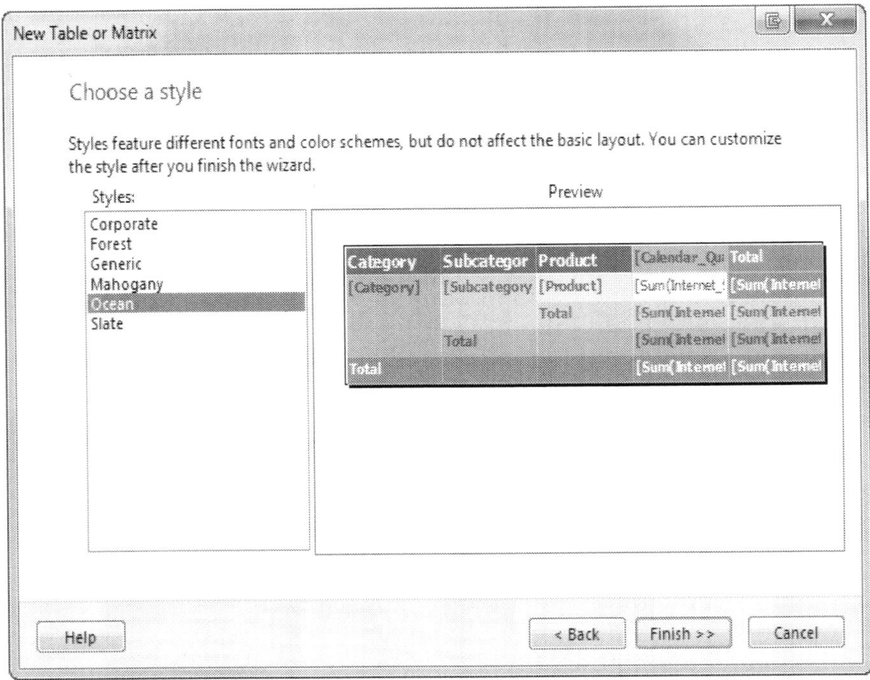

Figure 4-46 Style Window

When you click on Finish, you will return to the RB3 main page as in Figure 4-47 which now shows the report in design view on the design surface. You may now preview it by clicking on Run in the upper left corner of the window. If you did that, you would see the mess in Figure 4-48. (Note that the Report Server must be accessible to preview a report.) It's obvious that the report needs a lot more work to make it presentable.

The Run tab in Figure 4-48, the only tab on the Ribbon in preview view, contains actions and menus related to the report such as zooming, printing, and exporting. The Parameters button in the Options menu hides or unhides the parameters bar below the Ribbon if parameters are included in the report design. Note that with parameters visible, clicking on the button in the Parameters bar displays the drop-down listbox to select, in this case, the years to include in the report as we saw back in Figure 3-25. To return to design view just click on Design in the upper left corner.

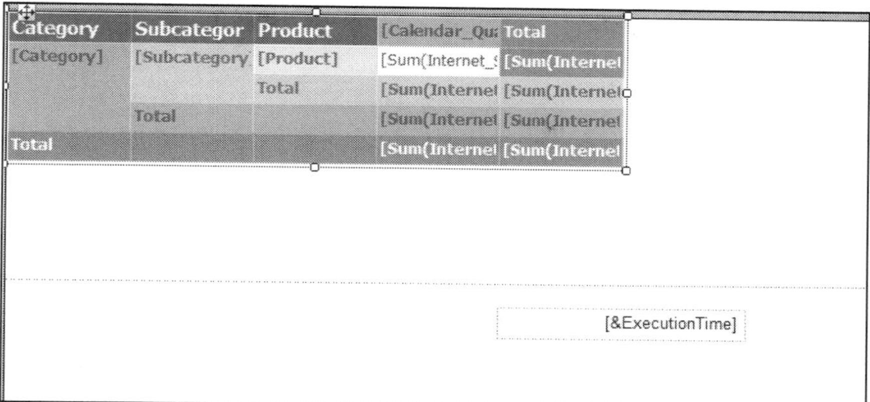

Figure 4-47 Initial Report in Design View

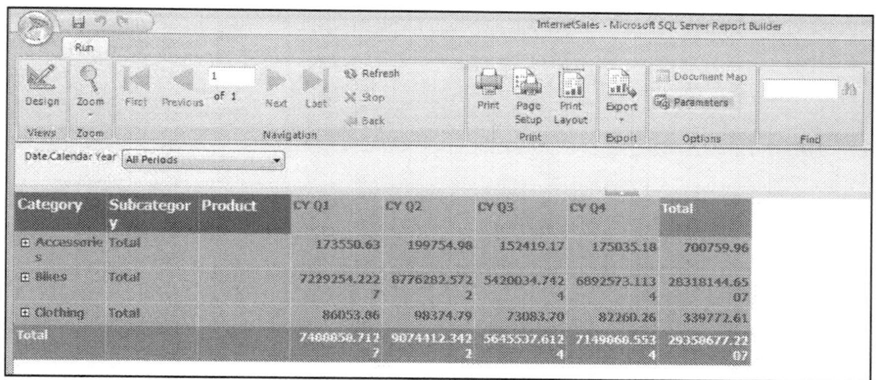

Figure 4-48 Initial Report Preview

A report can be saved as regular file in the usual way. I saved this report as "InternetSales.rdl" in a directory on my local hard drive. However, if you want the report to be available on the Report Manager, say so other users can view it, you can save it to the Report Server as well. To do that select Save As to bring up the Save As Dialog box and click Recent Sites and Servers which, in this case, lists the folders on my report server as in Figure 4-49. I saved the report in the Report Builder 3 Reports folder by clicking on that folder and then on Save. You can see in Figure 4-50 that the report was published to the Report Manager. We'll expand on saving reports at the end of the chapter.

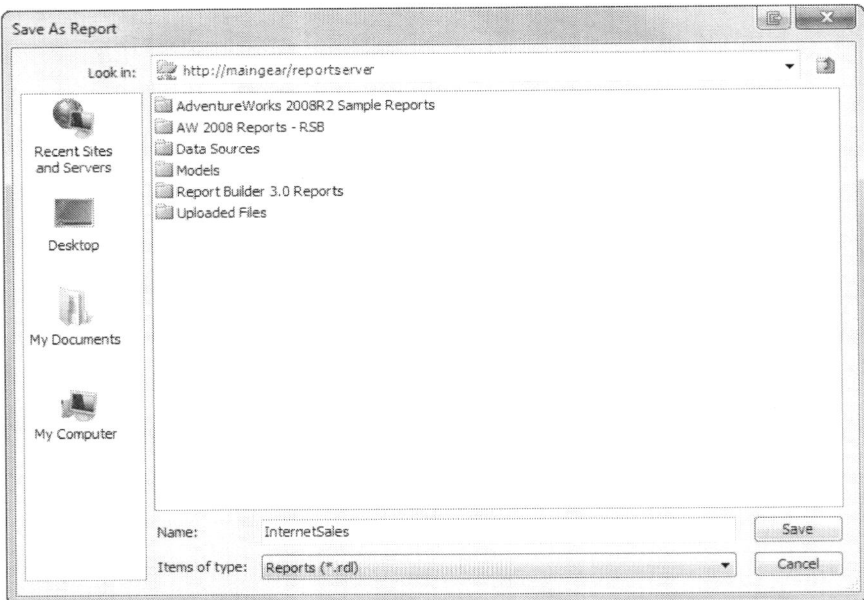

Figure 4-49 Save a Report to the Report Server

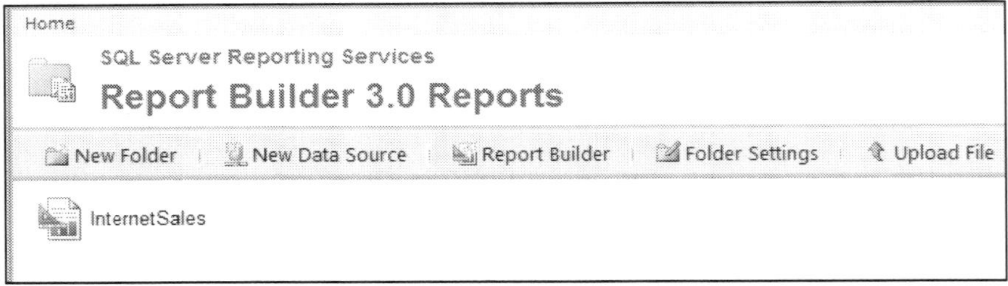

Figure 4-50 Report Available in Report Manager

Designing a Report Manually

When you open RB3 or click on New from the Office 2010-type button in the upper left corner you will be presented with the report designer as shown in Figure 4-19. Let's start out with a clean design surface as in Figure 4-51 by deleting all the items that RB3 creates when you begin. You do this by clicking on an object to select it (when selected a frame will appear around it) and then delete it. You may remove the footer by clicking on Footer on the Insert tab and selecting Remove Footer. Ok, now we have an empty surface. To resize the canvas just drag a border to the desired shape. By the way, we're using the report rdl file in which we created a data source and dataset back in Figure 4-41.

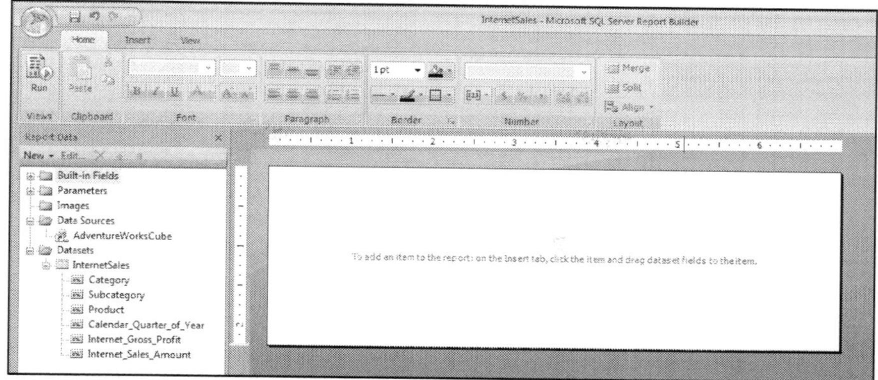

Figure 4-51 Clean Design Surface

For the example let's insert a matrix-type table into the report by clicking on Matrix on the Insert tab and selecting Insert Matrix. Then, move the mouse pointer to the design surface and draw a rectangle for the matrix. If there was no dataset defined, RB3 would bring up the Dataset Properties dialog box as in Figure 4-38. However, since a dataset exists already, it will create an empty matrix-type framework on the design surface as shown in Figure 4-52a. To change the design of the matrix click anywhere within it and boarders will appear on its perimeter. Then right clicking on an element within will display an options window. In the case of Figure 5-52 b I clicked on a column heading to display column options. I would then select Insert Columns and Inside Group Right to insert another column. Columns can be resized by dragging on their boarders.

Figure 4-52a Empty Initial Matrix

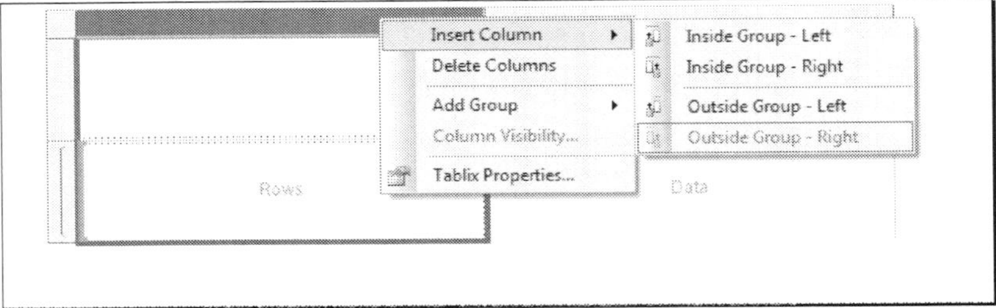

Figure 4-52b Initial Matrix with Options Menu

Figure 4-52 Matrix Framework on the Design Surface

Going back to Figure 4-52a now all that remains to complete definition of the report is to drag and drop objects from the Report Data pane onto the framework as shown in figure 4-53.

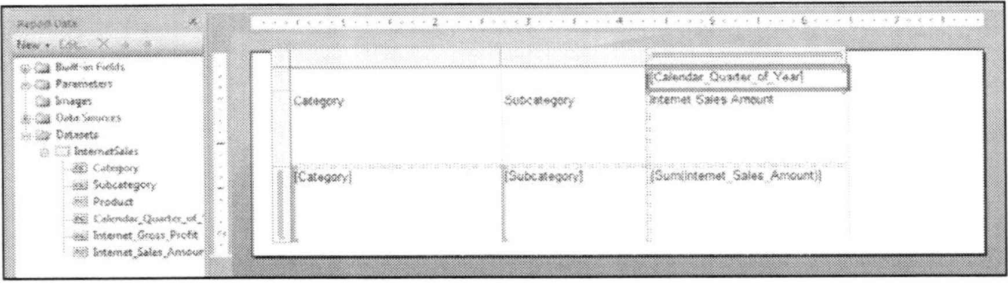

Figure 4-53 Objects Added to the Matrix Framework

This is essentially the same report that we built with the wizard above with calendar year as the row heading, product category and subcategory as column headings, and sales amount as the cell values. The dimensions were automatically added to the groupings panel at the bottom (not shown). Instead of dragging and dropping row and column to the cells in the framework, we could have dragged and dropped them into the grouping panel to achieve the same result. Figure 4-54 shows the preview of the report and how really basic the design is at this point. Notice that it does have the calendar year parameter that we specified in the query design.

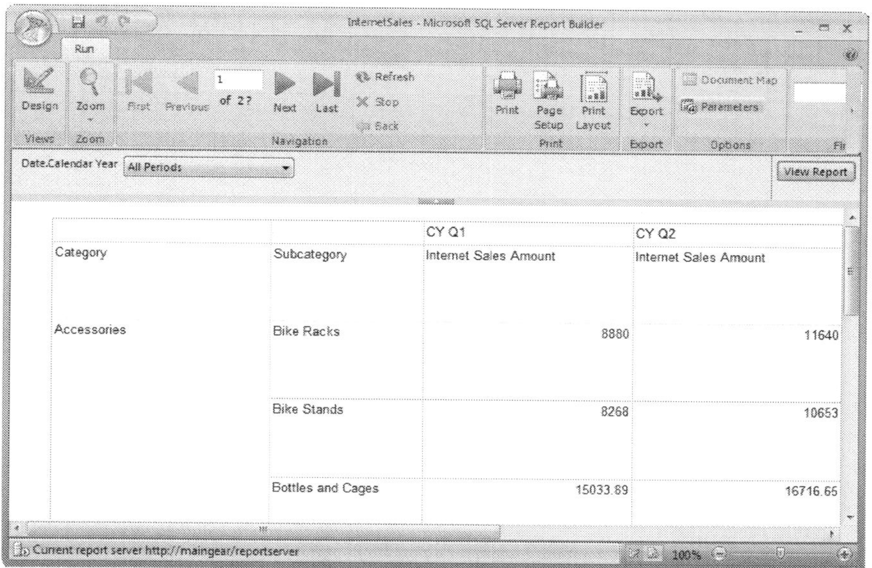

Figure 4-54 New Report Preview

The Properties panel on the right side of Figure 4-53 lists the properties for the object selected on the design surface. In that Figure the Internet_Sales_Amount cell is selected as indicated by that name appearing at the top of the panel. There are many properties, and you can change most of them by clicking on the property and either selecting or entering a value. However, I recommend that you do not change properties in the Properties panel unless you know what you are doing. There are other, safer ways to configure a report as we shall see in the next section. But, there are times when using the Properties panel is the only option. Now on to the making a report more presentable.

Tuning the Report

Both reports we have created so far, the ones in Figures 4-48 and 4-54, are not presentation quality to say the least. This is expected as all reports require tinkering to get into presentable form. Their initial construction is only a place to start the design process, and when the basic structure is there we can proceed to enhance and polish the layout. In the description below I'll try to cover the major design options including adding other objects to the report such as subreports, charts, and images; formatting the report; and adding drill-down and drill-through capabilities. There are other options that we will not examine but knowledge about the basic ones should allow you to proceed on your own with the others.

Basic Report Structure and Properties

The basic report structure is shown in the partial screen shot of an empty report (except for the three textboxes used to identify the sections) on RB3's design surface (canvas) in Figure 4-55. The Page Header will be displayed on the top of all pages, and the page footer at the bottom of all pages. Headers and footers can contain a variety of objects such as textboxes, images, shapes, and so on. The Body can contain any type of report object such as tables, charts, images, textboxes, etc. Note that the Body textbox has a frame around it which means that object is currently selected, and the four arrow icon there represents a point to click and drag to reposition the object on the surface. You can change the shape of the object by dragging the double arrows that appear when the mouse pointer is positioned over the small squares on the perimeter. Headers and footers can be inserted and removed via the Header & Footer menu on the Insert tab. Header, footer, and body areas can be resized using the double arrow to drag the boundary line.

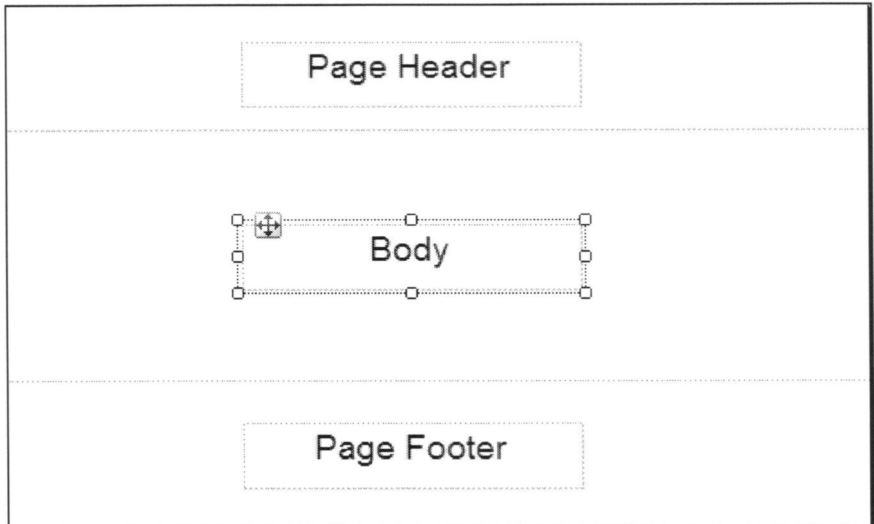

Figure 4-55 New Basic Report Design Surface

The size of the design surface canvas can be resized by moving the mouse over the perimeter boundary of the canvas until a double arrow appears, then clicking and holding the double arrow while dragging it to change the shape. Right clicking on the designer panel outside of the canvas displays the Report Properties dialog box as in Figure 4-56 where you can set various properties in the Page Setup view.

In Report Properties Code view presents an area to insert custom Visual Basic code into the report. (It appears to me that this is Visual Basic .Net and not Visual Basic for Applications code.) A few examples of custom code are listed below:

```
Public Const MyName = "Bob Bussom"
Public Dim NumberOfCopies as Integer =1
Public RecipientEmail as String = "someone@somewhere.com"

Public Function ChangeWord(ByVal s As String) As String
Dim strBuilder As New System.Text.StringBuilder(s)
If s.Contains("Bike") Then
strBuilder.Replace("Bike", "Bicycle")
Return strBuilder.ToString()
Else : Return s
End If
End Function
```

The first line defines a constant; the second an integer variable, and the third a string variable. The frivolous function copied from Report Builder 3.0 Help replaces the word Bike with Bicycle if the string passed to it contains the word Bike. Constants, variables and other custom code may be used in expressions which will be addressed later in this chapter.

The Reference view provides for setting references to assemblies and classes, specifically dll files if you know what they are. (References is an advanced topic so we'll pass by it here.) The Variables view allows adding other custom variables to a report.

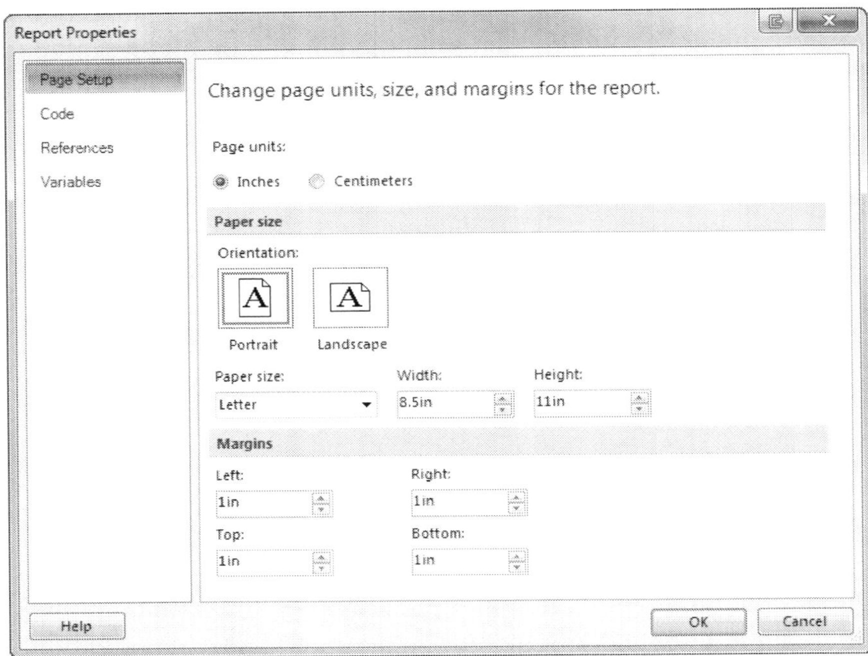

Figure 4-56 Report Properties Dialog Box

Back on the canvas right clicking on the header area and selecting Header Properties brings up the Page Header Properties dialog box as in Figure 4-57 where you can configure the header page, change the background fill color or insert a background image in the Fill view, and add a boarder in Border view. The same properties are available in the Page Footer Properties and Body Properties dialog boxes.

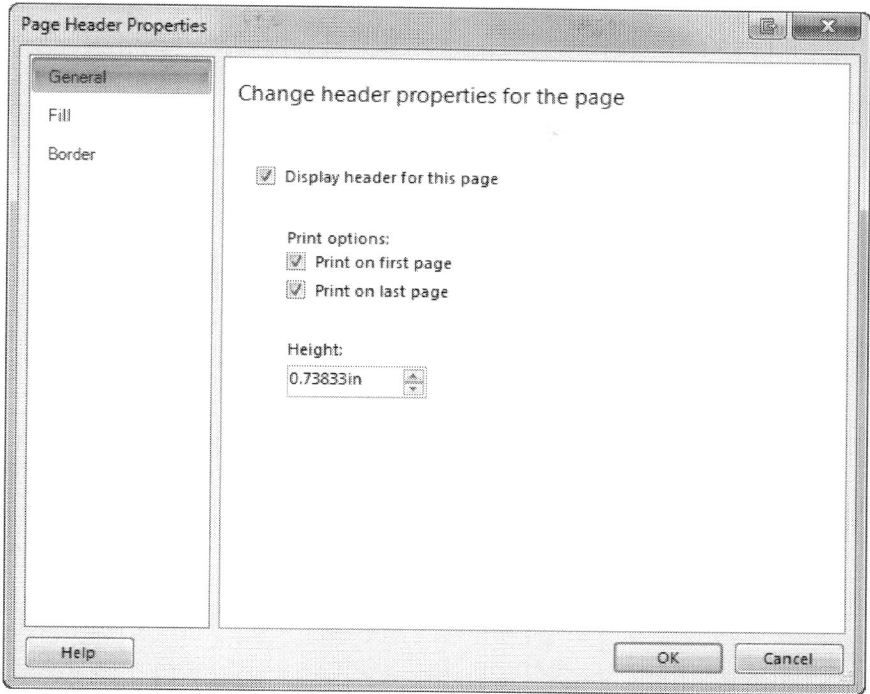

Figure 4-57 Page Header Dialog Box

Formatting a Tablix

Let's return to the report presented in Figure 4-47 and in preview view in Figure 4-48 where the formatting of the table needs some adjustments: (1) the numbers in cells and in the totals row and column should be in an acceptable format; (2) the headings in the top row should be centered; (3) the Category and Subcategory columns should be widened to avoid text wrapping; and (4) the fonts may need changing. But before we get to that notice that when the tablix was created with the wizard a title textbox and a footer with an execution datatime value were automatically added. We could remove them but we'll leave them for now.

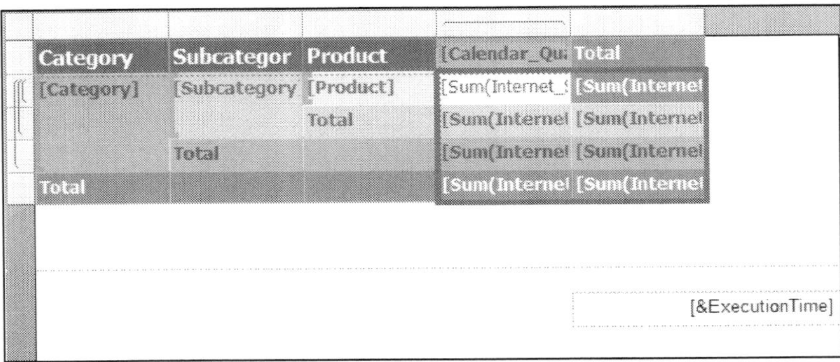

Figure 4-58 Matrix Formatting Example

1. To reformat the numbers, select all of the cells that display numbers as shown in Figure 4-58 (the dark border shows the selected area). You then have two optional approaches: use the Number menu on the Home Ribbon directly or the Text Box Properties dialog box. We'll look at both options.

   Number Menu: I want to format the numbers in a format with commas as the thousands separators but with no decimal places. So I selected number from the drop-down listbox in the Number menu that is currently set to default and then selected Number, clicked the comma box to activate separators, and then removed all decimal places by repeat clicking on the .00→0 box.

   Text Box Properties: Click on the tiny arrow at the bottom of the Number menu there to bring up the Text Box Properties Dialog Box as shown in Figure 4-59. There you can change the name of the box, value, and sizing options; format a number or date; change alignment; change the font; insert borders and fill; change when the report is visible; enable sorting, and specify an action (we will get into actions a bit later). So, I selected Number and checked Use 1000 separator to change the number format this way.

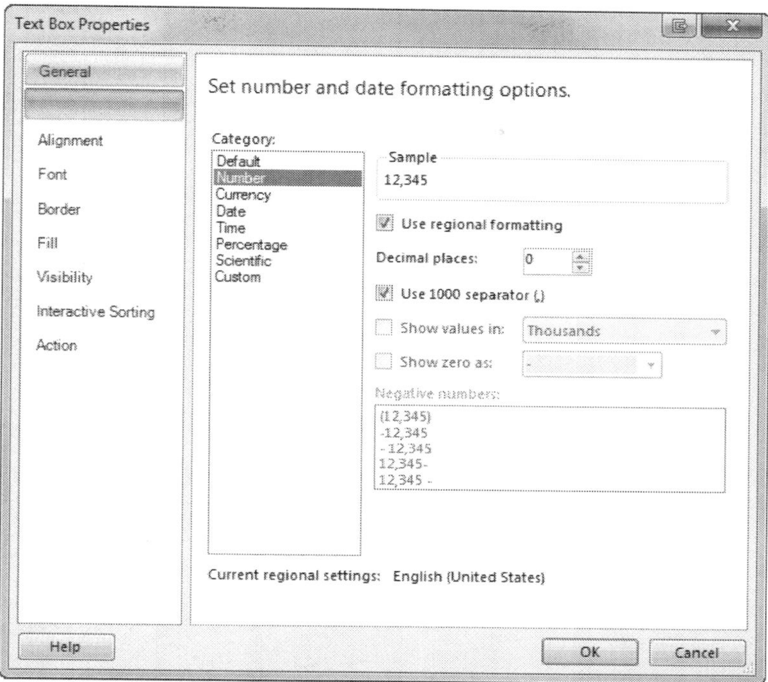

Figure 4-59 Textbox Properties Dialog Box

2. Centered Headings: Select the entire report heading row, and then click the center alignment icon just above the Paragraph title on the Home tab.

3. Column Width: As you can see in Figure 4-48 the Category and Subcategory columns need to be widened to avoid work wrap. So, I just dragged the right boundary in the gray area at the top of each of the column to widen them.

4. Font: Select the entire table, and then select the font characteristics from the Font menu on the Home Ribbon that you prefer. I selected the Verdana font and left all else as is for now.

I also took the liberty of adding a title to the report in the "Click to add title" textbox that was inserted by the wizard by just typing the it in the box. Regardless of the approach the report now looks like that in Figure 4-60. Much better, but it still need some work.

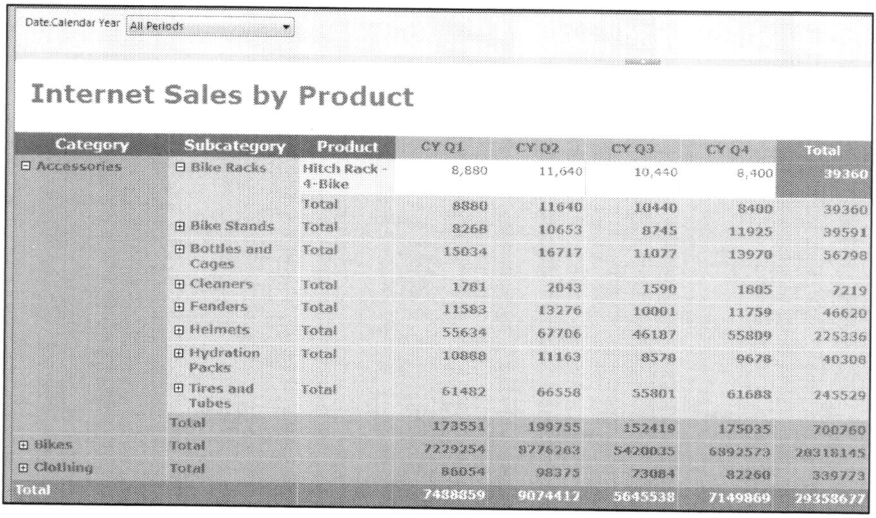

Date.Calendar Year: All Periods

Internet Sales by Product

Category	Subcategory	Product	CY Q1	CY Q2	CY Q3	CY Q4	Total
⊟ Accessories	⊟ Bike Racks	Hitch Rack - 4-Bike	8,880	11,640	10,440	8,400	39360
		Total	8880	11640	10440	8400	39360
	⊞ Bike Stands	Total	8268	10653	8745	11925	39591
	⊞ Bottles and Cages	Total	15034	16717	11077	13970	56798
	⊞ Cleaners	Total	1781	2043	1590	1805	7219
	⊞ Fenders	Total	11583	13276	10001	11759	46620
	⊞ Helmets	Total	55634	67706	46187	55809	225336
	⊞ Hydration Packs	Total	10888	11163	8578	9678	40308
	⊞ Tires and Tubes	Total	61482	66558	55801	61688	245529
	Total		173551	199755	152419	175035	700760
⊞ Bikes	Total		7229254	8776263	5420035	6892573	28318145
⊞ Clothing	Total		86054	98375	73084	82260	339773
Total			7488859	9074417	5645538	7149869	29358677

Figure 4-60 Reformatted Report

Adding a Chart

The Insert tab Ribbon in Figure 4-20 shows all of the items that can be added to a report. We have already seen how to add a table or matrix in a report so we won't repeat that here. To add a chart just click on Chart and select either Chart Wizard or Insert Chart from the drop-down list. If you go the Chart Wizard route, you will be lead through a series of windows starting with one to choose the dataset for the chart. If you choose to create a new dataset, you will proceed to a data source connections dialog box similar to the one in Figure 4-21. You would proceed on from there as usual. If you select an existing dataset, e.g., InternetSales in our example, then the Chart Type dialog box will appear as in Figure 4-61 where you select the chart type. You then move on to arrange the chart fields as in Figure 4-62. Note that the Categories list is displayed on the horizontal axis, the Values list on the vertical axis, and the series list creates series. (A series is a separate variable to plot. For example. in a line chart with multiple lines each line on the chart is a separate series.). Next you would select the chart style and then finish it. I selected a column chart.

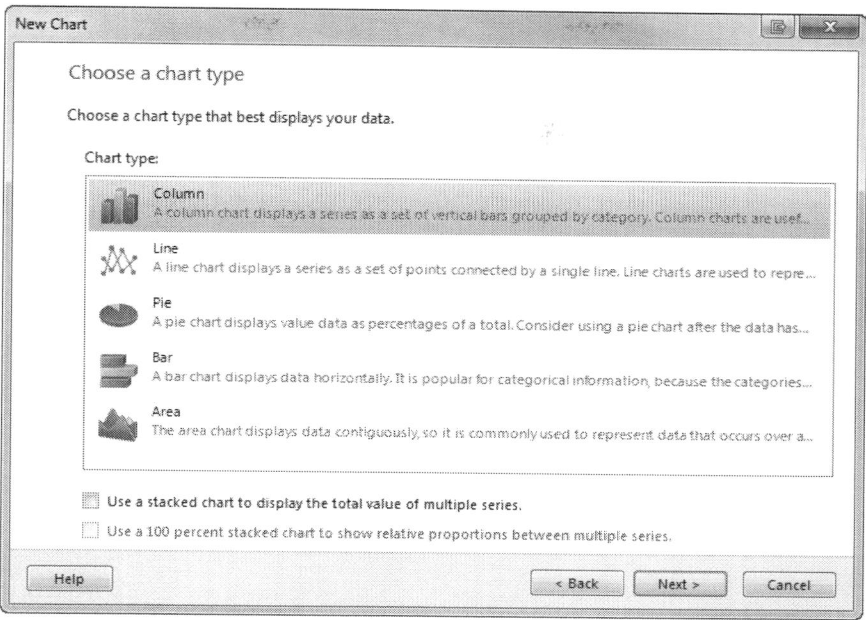

Figure 4-61 Chart Wizard - Chart Type

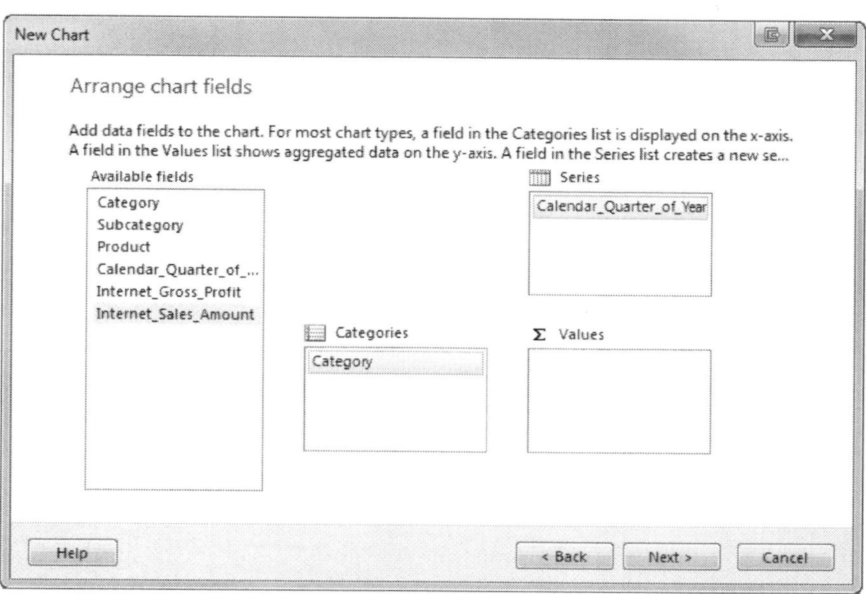

Figure 4-62 Chart Wizard - Chart Fields

When you return to the RB3 main page the new chart may be superimposed on some of the existing objects on the canvass. If so, just select the chart and move it to an appropriate place as I did in Figure 4-63. The image of the chart on the canvas in design view is only a stylized representation of it—the chart must be previewed to actually see it.

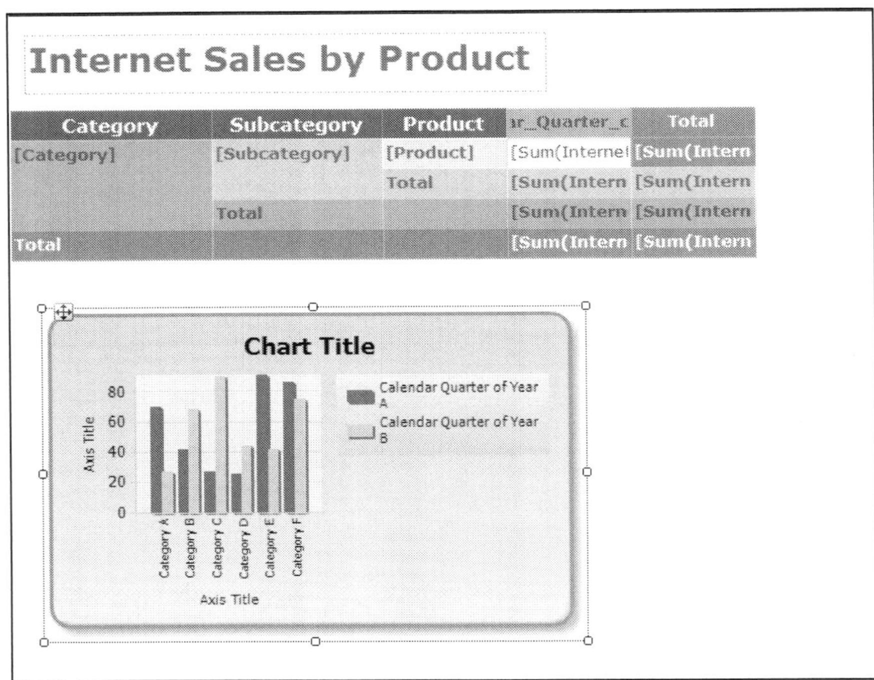

Figure 4-63 Example Chart on the Canvas

Figure 4-64 shows the report preview with the new chart. Notice that the bikes columns are far higher than those of accessories and clothing as you would expect by looking at the data in the table; the quarters of the year show up as series; the chart and axes need titles; and the vertical axis values need formatting. To change the title of an axis either double click it and enter the new title or go to the Axis Title Dialog Box by right clicking on the axis title. I used the former approach here. To reformat an axis either click on the axis and use the formatting controls on the Home tab or right click the axis to bring up the Axis Properties dialog box. I used the former approach to change the font on the horizontal axis categories to Verdana bold and the latter approach to reformat the vertical axis values.

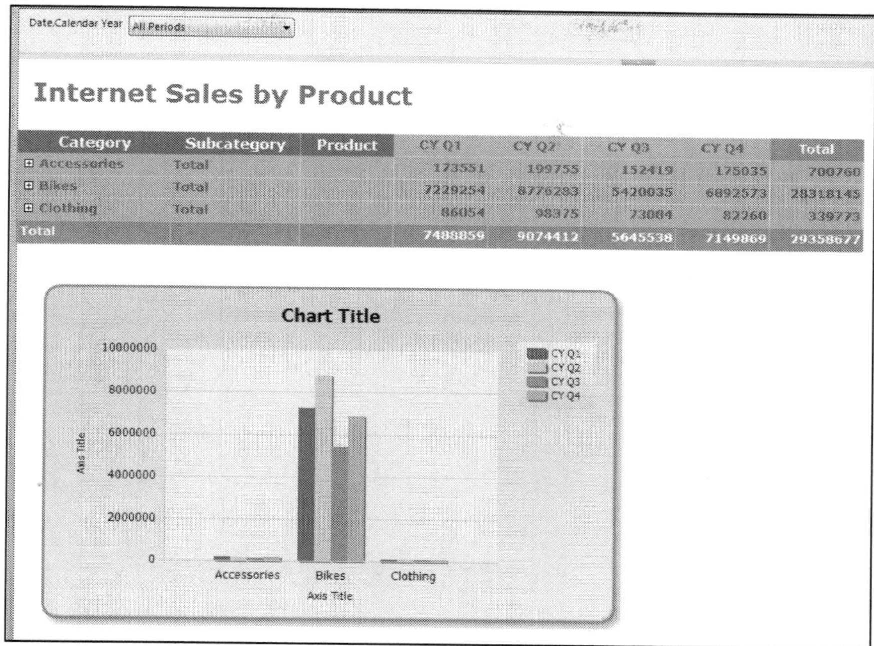

Category	Subcategory	Product	CY Q1	CY Q2	CY Q3	CY Q4	Total
⊞ Accessories	Total		173551	199755	152419	175035	700760
⊞ Bikes	Total		7229254	8776283	5420035	6892573	28318145
⊞ Clothing	Total		86054	98375	73084	82260	339773
Total			7488859	9074412	5645538	7149869	29358677

Figure 4-64 Example Chart in Preview

The Axis Properties dialog box for the vertical axis (called the Value axis by RB3) is shown in Figure 4-65. Properties can be changed there for axis options, labels, the font, number, tick marks, and the axis line. I used the Number view (see Figure 4-59) to set the number format to render sales in $000. I also inserted a chart title and changed to a bold font for the legend. The result is shown in preview view in Figure 4-66.

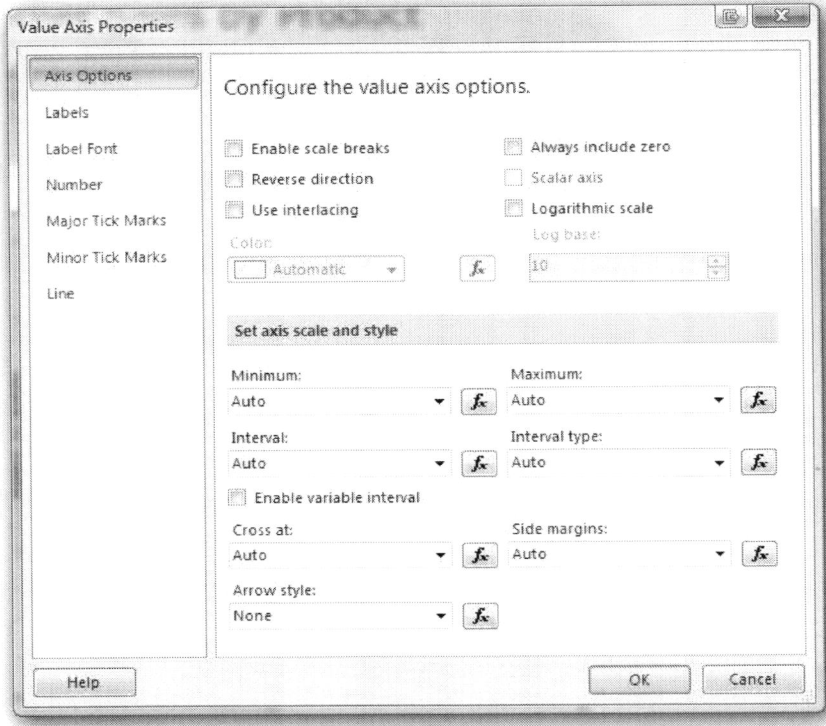

Figure 4-65 Axis Properties Dialog Box

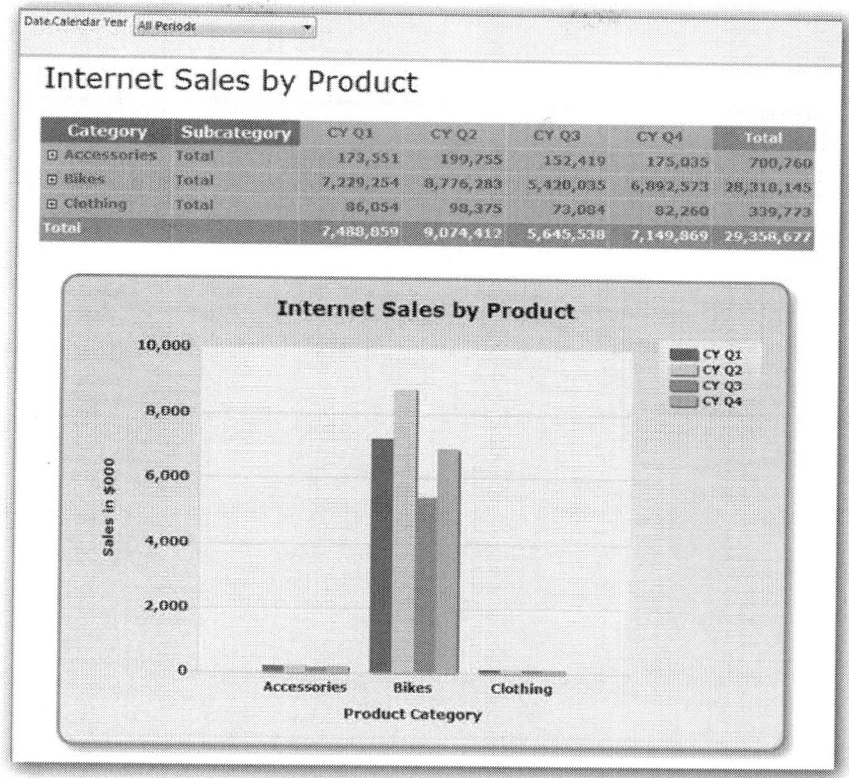

Category	Subcategory	CY Q1	CY Q2	CY Q3	CY Q4	Total
⊞ Accessories	Total	173,551	199,755	152,419	175,035	700,760
⊞ Bikes	Total	7,229,254	8,776,283	5,420,035	6,892,573	28,318,145
⊞ Clothing	Total	86,054	98,375	73,084	82,260	339,773
Total		7,488,859	9,074,412	5,645,538	7,149,869	29,358,677

Figure 4-66 Reformatted Chart

(For better viewing of this image, go to http://www.zerobits.info/bibook/bibookimages/)

The principle to learn here is that you can view and change the properties of any object in the chart by either clicking on it and using the Home tab controls or by right clicking on it to bring up a menu or dialog box. Indeed, these are basically the same approaches used in Microsoft Office 2010 applications, particularly Excel 2010. For example, if you right click anywhere on the chart background, the menu in Figure 4-67 pops up. In that menu you can change the chart type, change various properties, and so on.

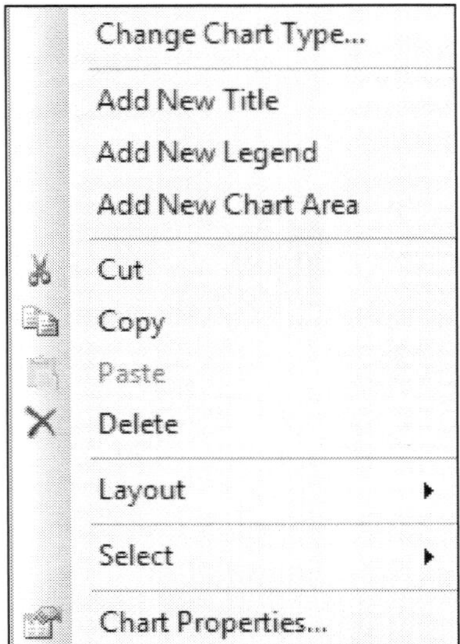

Figure 4-67 Chart Properties Menu

Adding a Gauge

Let's return to the report in Figure 4-47 and add a gauge. On the Insert tab you can either click on the Gauge icon and then draw a gauge on the canvas or double click on the Gauge icon. In either case the Select Gauge Type dialog box appears where, of course, you select the style of gauge that you want. There are twelve radial gauge templates all with some kind of dial and nine linear templates with thermometer or ruler images available. You use gauges to display data values.

Report Builder 3.0 identifies the gauge parts in the image below, and goes on to say that gauge forms cannot be interchanged as in Office 2010 application. Rather, the current gauge must be replaced with a new gauge. A gauge have at least one scale, and other scales can be added.

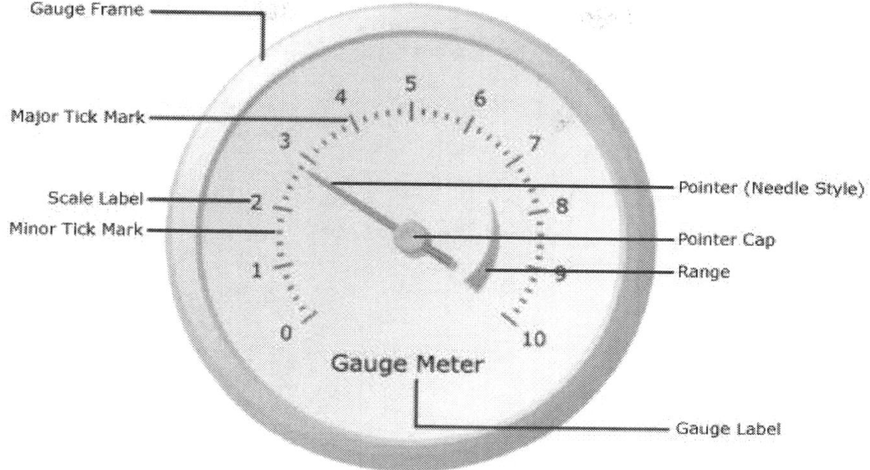

Gauges seem to be more difficult to work with than tables and charts, at least for me. Possibly this is because gauges only display one value on a scale. So, for example using a gauge to represent Internet Sales in our ongoing example in itself would be meaningless unless we added some maximum value so that the gauge would show the position of sales relative to that value. Additionally, a gauge displays aggregate sums or counts of a field, and, even if a group is included, the gauge only displays the value for the last member of the group. See Report Builder 3.0 Help or SQL Server 2008 Books Online for more info about this.

As an example I picked a simple radial gauge and selected Internet Gross Profit Margin as the metric to use because it has an absolute maximum value of 1.0 (100%). To add a data field to a gauge either drag the field from the Report Data pane to the drop zone that appears on the gauge image; display the drop zone by double clicking on the gauge image and then click on the tiny rectangular icon to show the list of available data fields; or right click on the gauge pointer and select pointer properties. I just dropped the Internet Gross Profit Margin field from the Report Data pane into the data drop zone. Figure 4-68 shows the drop zone with the gross margin field added to it in the lowest row in the drop-down table. Note that the field is initially set to the Sum of Internet Gross Profit Margin. I changed it to Avg (for Average) by clicking on the Internet Gross Profit row in the menu, clicking on Aggregate, and selecting Avg from the list. The figure also shows the menu list that appears when you right click the scale on the gauge.

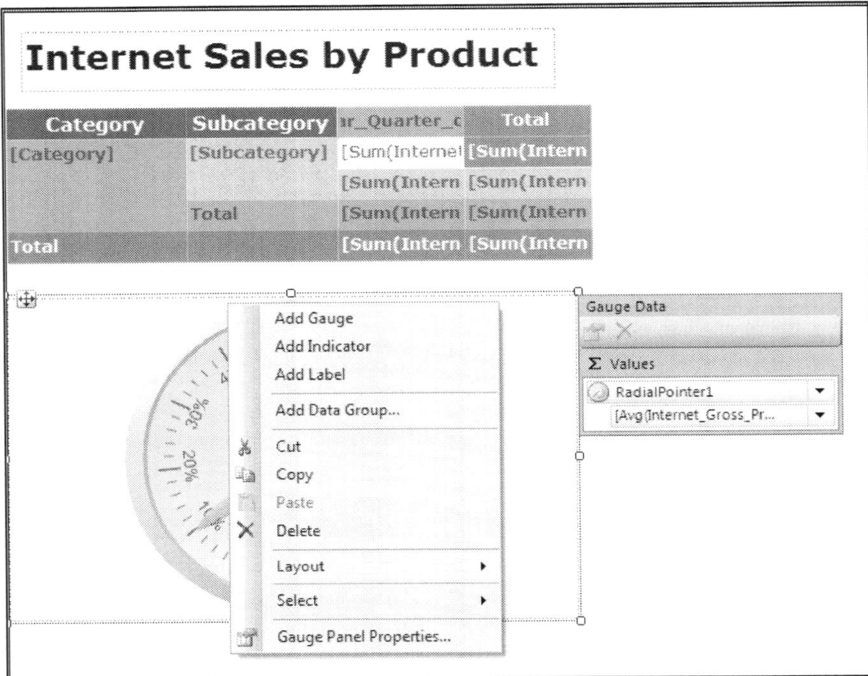

Figure 4-68 Gauge Example

To format the gauge scale click on scale properties to display the Scale Properties dialog box as in Figure 4-69 where I have changed the Maximum value from 100, its default value, to 1 so that the gauge will properly display the gross margin percentage. I also changed the scale values to percentage in the dialog box Number view and added a textbox. The resulting preview of the gauge is shown in Figure 4-70 indicating that the AdventureWorks Internet sales gross margin over all years is about 44 percent. If you change the parameter value in the upper right corner of the report to say 2008, the gauge pointer will move to the value for that year, and, of course, the matrix will be updated as well.

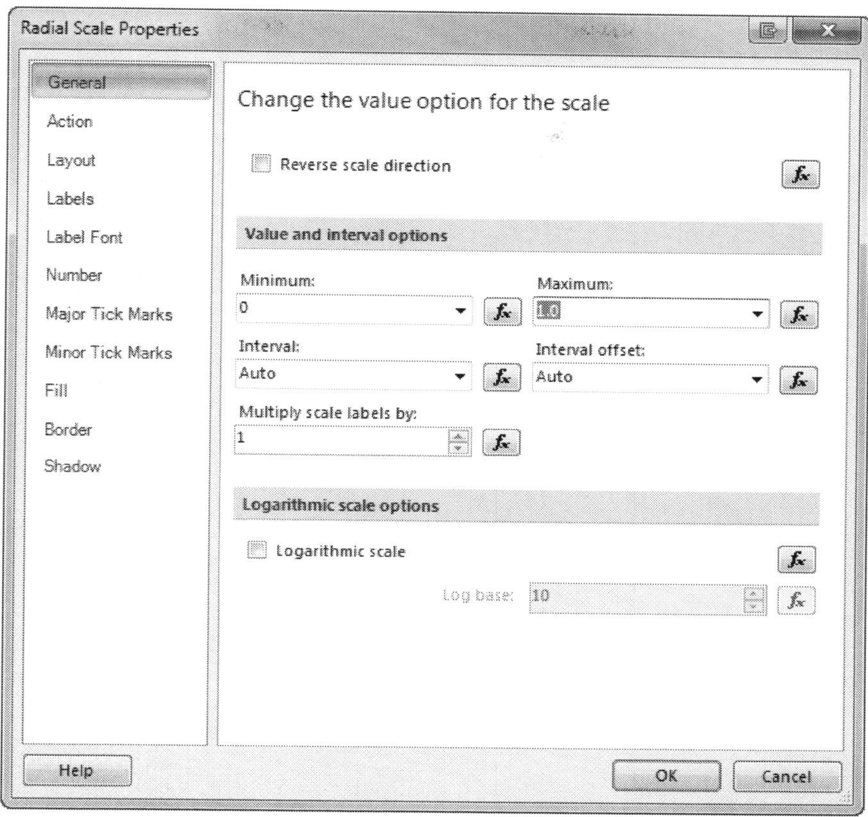

Figure 4-69 Scale Properties Dialog Box

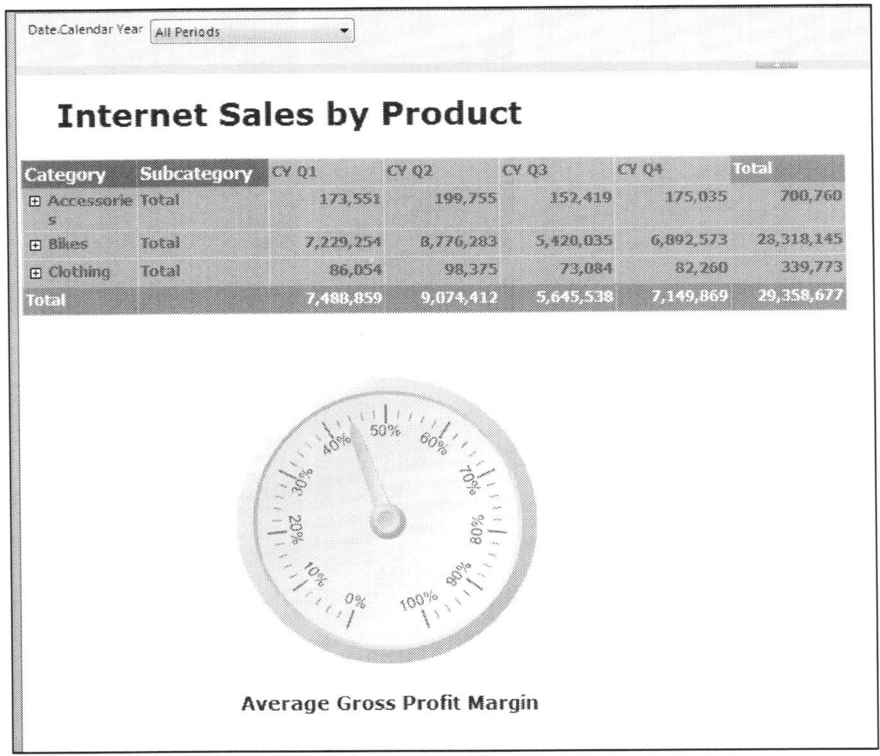

Date.Calendar Year
All Periods
Internet Sales by Product
Category
Subcategory
CY Q1
CY Q2
CY Q3
CY Q4
Total
Accessories
Total
173,551
199,755
152,419
175,035
700,760
Bikes
Total
7,229,254
8,776,283
5,420,035
6,892,573
28,318,145
Clothing
Total
86,054
98,375
73,084
82,260
339,773
Total
7,488,859
9,074,412
5,645,538
7,149,869
29,358,677
0%
10%
20%
30%
40%
50%
60%
70%
80%
90%
100%
Average Gross Profit Margin

Figure 4-70 Completed Gauge Example Preview

Adding a List

A list is a type of free-form Tablix data region into which you can drop data fields, textboxes, etc. Figure 4-71 shows three stages of adding a list to our report. Here I have removed the matrix table and other items in the report that we inserted previously. A list is added to a report by clicking on List in the Insert tab and then drawing a rectangle on the design canvas. When you do that, a rectangle appears with a frame (container) around it with sizing handles. Clicking on the rectangle displays the list space shown by the top box in Figure 4-71. I also right clicked on the bar at the top to bring up the menu that is visible. In the list space shown in the middle of the figure I dropped four data fields: Calendar Quarter, Category, Subcategory, and Internet Sales Amount. If we preview the report at this point we will get page after page of quarter-category-subcategory-sales raw data. The bottom list space has the list formatted including adding page breaks to display each set of values on a separate page. A preview of the report with the list is shown in Figure 4-72.

Note that only the bottom list in figure 4-71 is present in the actual report rdl file—I deleted the other two prior to running the report.

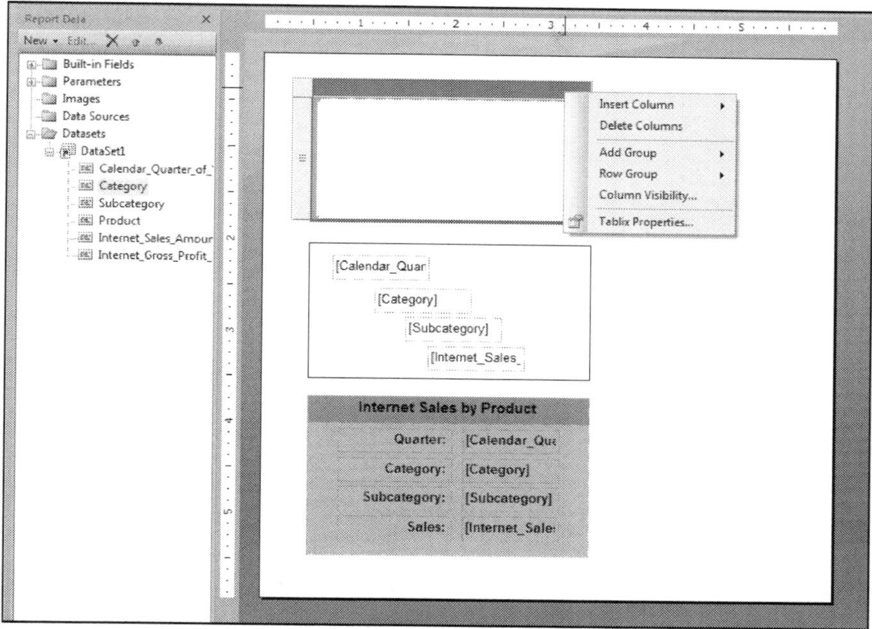

Figure 4-71 Adding a List to a Report

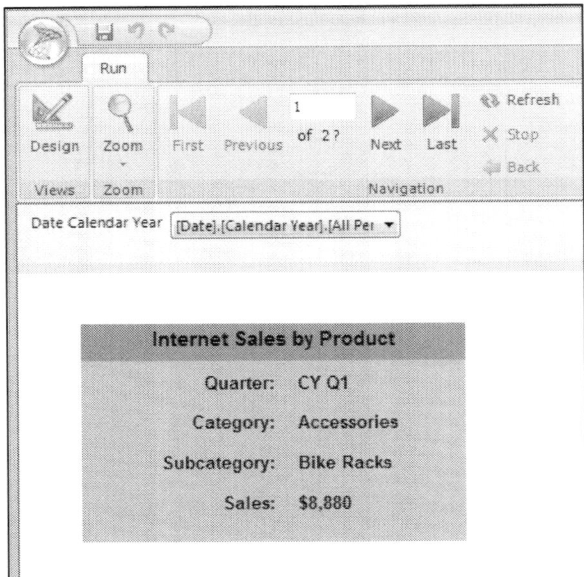

Figure 4-72 List in Preview

This list acts somewhat like a form in Visual Basic or Access with which you can scroll through individual records by clicking on the navigation buttons, the large arrow icons on the Ribbon. For example, clicking on Next will move to the next record: CY Q1, Accessories, Bike Stands. There are 633 pages (records) in the report for the combinations of quarter, categories, and subcategories.

Admittedly, this is a trivial example but it does demonstrate the potential for the List-type Tablix in a report. The List has additional functionality allowing it to serve as a container for other objects and grouped data. For example, you could incorporate a table and chart view in a listbox. Please see RB3 Help for more details.

Adding a Textbox, Image, Line, and Rectangle

The Insert tab in RB3 has four more sets of objects in addition to Data Regions: Data Visualizations, Report Items, Subreports, and Header & Footer. In Report Items double clicking on Text box, Line, or Rectangle adds that item to the report canvas. Double clicking on Image brings up the Image Properties dialog box shown in Figure 4-73 where you can name the image, create a tool tip, and select the file for the image from the General page. Images can be embedded in the report so that the report does not have to import them from an external source at the time the report is rendered. Or, you may use an external source by specifying a URL to it. You may also configure the image size, visibility, action, and border from the Image Properties dialog box. In this example I embedded the AdventureWorks Logo jpg into the report. Note that you use a similar process to add a background image to the body of a report or a tablix, textbox, or rectangle in it.

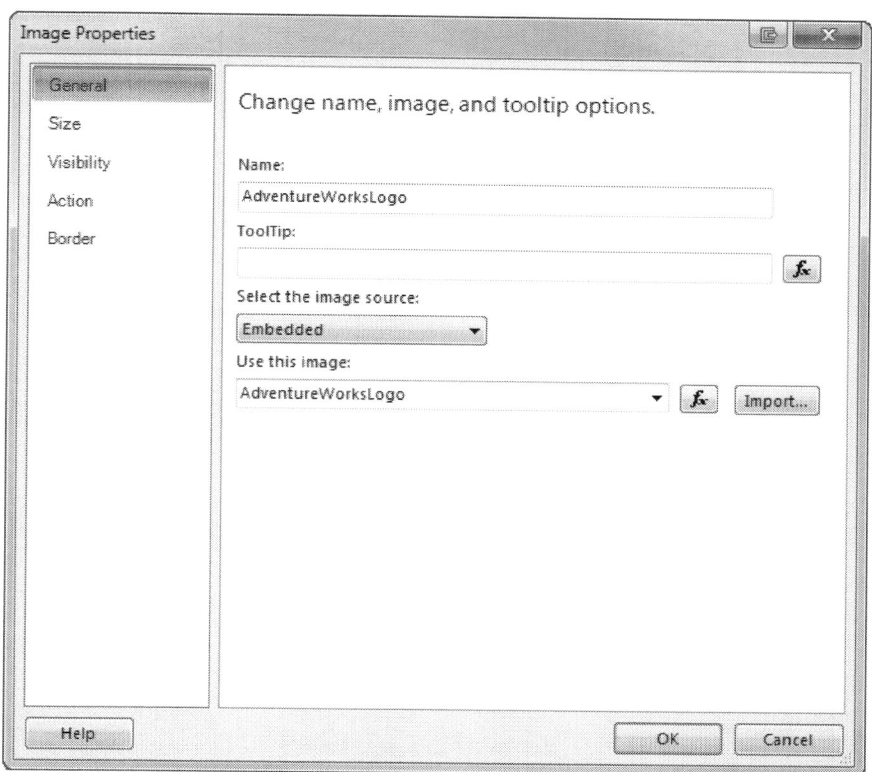

Figure 4-73 Image Properties Dialog Box

In Figure 4-74 I added a textbox, line, image and rectangle to the design surface and have selected all of them as indicated by the frames with sizing handles around them. The objects are formatted by right clicking on them, using the Properties panel on the right side of RB3, or using the formatting option on the Home tab . In the latter case, the formatting options on the Ribbon will enable only those options applicable to the type of object that you have selected. For example, when an image is selected only the Border formatting option is enabled.

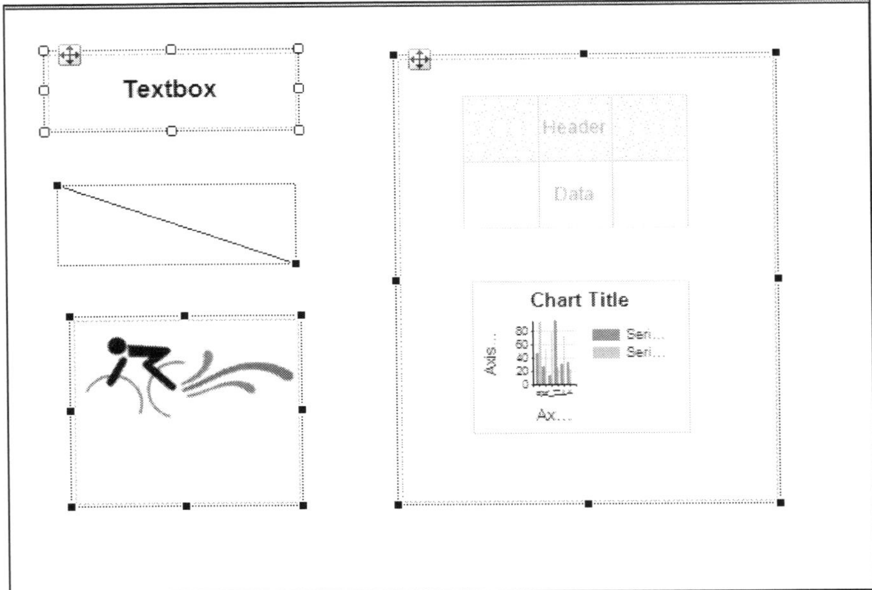

Figure 4-74 Image Properties Dialog Box

The rectangle, the object on the right side of Figure 4-74 acts as a container for other objects so that when the rectangle is moved the objects in it move with it. Here, I placed a table in the rectangle with a chart below it.

Adding Subreports and Page Headers and Footers

A subreport is just a separate report displayed inside the parent report. Both the report and its subreports are stored on the Report Server usually in the same folder. We saw an example of a subreport in Figure 3-23 and 3-24. You may pass parameters from the report to the subreport, and you may place a subreport in a Tablix data region.

We learned how to add headers and footers to a report in our discussion of Figure 4-55. Note that headers and footers here refer to page headers and footers and not to report headers and footers. When you display a report, headers and footers will be displayed on each page of the report. Report headers and footers are placed at the top and bottom of the report and appear only once at the top of the first page and the bottom of the last page of the report respectively.

Page headers and footers usually display something about the properties of the report or the page, e.g., page number, total pages, date, etc. For example, the report in Figures 4-47 and 4-48 includes a textbox holding a report execution datatime stamp.

Adding KPIs

There are three ways to incorporate KPIs into a report: by using background colors to represent different states of the KPI, by displaying the KPI on a gauge, and by using images to represent the KPI state. We use each approach in the example. For the new report in Figure 4-75 I created a new dataset containing the Category dimension and the Gross Profit Margin KPI fields using the AdventureWorks2008Cube as the data source and created a calculated value for the percentage of goal accomplishment. I added a textbox at the top of the report, a table below it, and a gauge at the bottom. The table has product categories as rows and KPI values, goals, and status as columns, i.e., I dragged those fields from the Report Data list and dropped them onto the tablix. The status value would normally not be visible but I included it here so that you could see it to compare the value to the visualization of it. For this example I ignored the KPI trend value but you treat it in the same way as we do the status value. The report in preview view after some tinkering is shown in Figure 4-76.

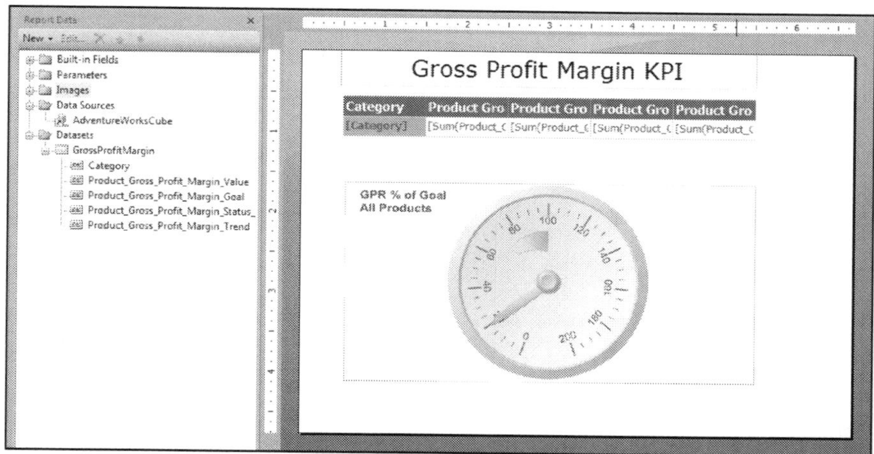

Figure 4-75 KPI Example in Design View

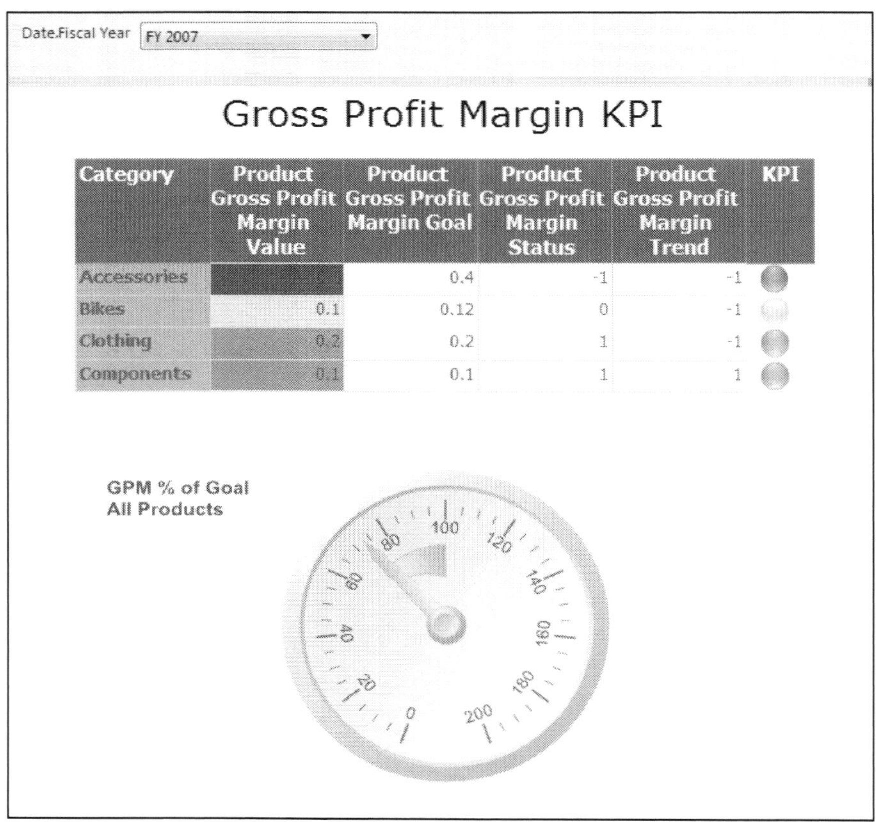

Figure 4-76 KPI Example in Preview View

Background Color Method: Recall from our discussion in Chapter 3 that KPI status takes on values between -1 and +1 in 0.5 increments. Also recall that the Gross Profit Margin status value is determined as follows:

GPM KPI/GPM Goal	Status Value
>= .90	1
>= .80 and < .90	0
< .80	-1

Using an expression (which we'll discuss below) I set the background fill color to green, yellow, and red for the status values of 1, 0, and -1 respectively as is shown in the figure. Neat!

Gauge Method: The gauge also uses an expression to determine its pointer value as a percentage:

= GPM KPI/GPM Goal*100

I set the gauge scale maximum to 200 (percent) because the KPI can exceed its goal, set the scale font to bold ,and added a label in the upper right corner.

Image Method: RB3 seems not use the status and trend images defined in the Analysis Services cube as described in Chapter 3 (see Figure 3-17).To use images to represent KPI values I added the column on the right side of the table titled KPI and then added an expression in Image Properties where it says "Use this image" (Figure 4-73) with reference to images of colored balls to represent the different status values. Prior to that I added three images to the report as shown in Figure 4-77. To add an image to Report Data right click on Images which will bring up a file 0pen dialog box and proceed from there as usual.

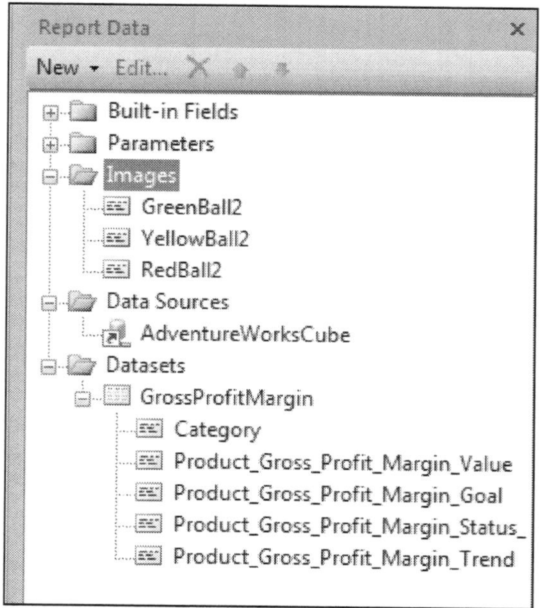

Figure 4-77 Background Images

Using Expressions and Built-in Fields

Expressions provide great flexibility in the design of a report. As you saw above we used expressions to set colors and images for KPI values. We can also use them to perform calculations, filter values, format data and objects, and so on.

To create or modify an expression click on the *fx* button (there are two in Figure 4-73) to bring up the Expression dialog box. The Expression dialog box for the gauge in Figure 4-76 is shown in Figure 4-78. All expressions begin with an equals symbol. You may write the expression manually but it's far easier to use category items to build it. For example, the fields available in the GrossProfitMargin dataset are listed in the Values listbox in Figure 4-78. I double clicked on the GPM Value field to insert it into the expression, added the divide operator, double clicked on the GPM Goal field, and added the multiplication operator and the number 100 to complete the expression.

The Category panel lists items that are commonly used in expressions. Constants, Parameters, and Variables list the ones available in the report. In our case there are no constants or variables but there would be if we had created them as discussed earlier. DateCalendarYear would be listed as the only parameter. Built-in Fields, the same ones as in the Report Data panel for this report shown on the left side of Figure 4-75, are listed in Figure 4-79a. This list contains global and user variables for the report which are usually used in headers and footers. For example, the report in Figure 4-19 uses the ExecutionTime built-in field to display the datetime that the report is run. Similarly, you may use the PageNumber and TotalPages fields to print "Page X of Y Pages" in a footer (see the bottom example in Table 4-2).

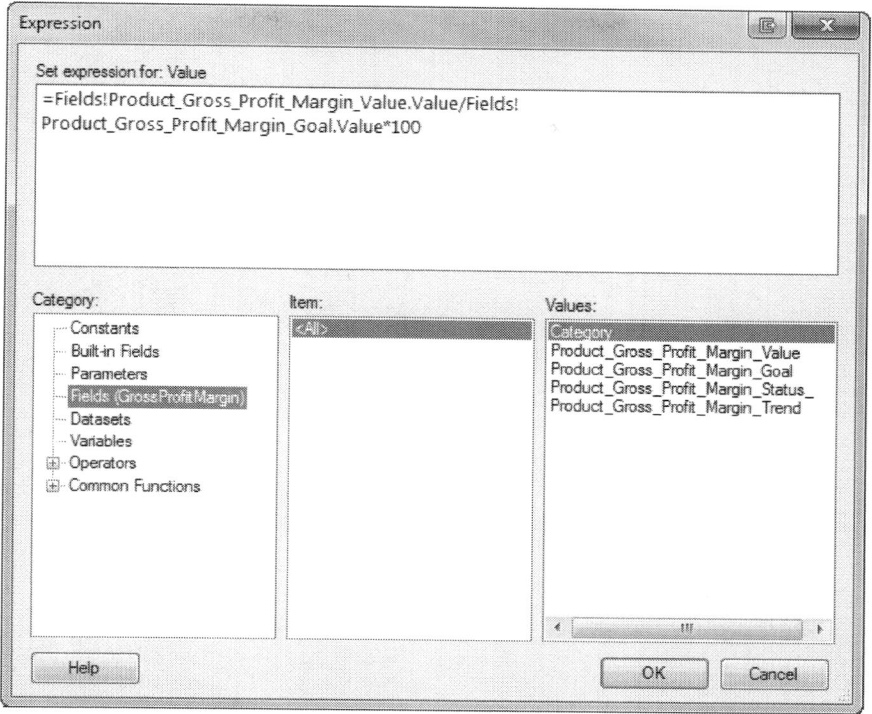

Figure 4-78 Expression Dialog Box

The Fields and Datasets categories list the ones available in the report. (The fields are shown in the figure above.) Operators lists the usual computer programming arithmetic, comparison, concatenation, and logical operators, in this case from Visual Basic. Common functions provide a number of categories of Visual Basic functions available as in Figure 4-79b where some of the date and time functions are displayed in the Item pane. Again, all you have to do to add one of the items to the expression is to double click on it.

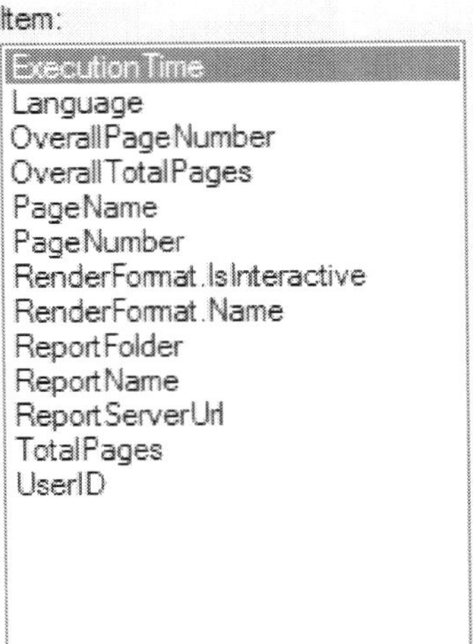

Figure 4-79a Build-in Fields

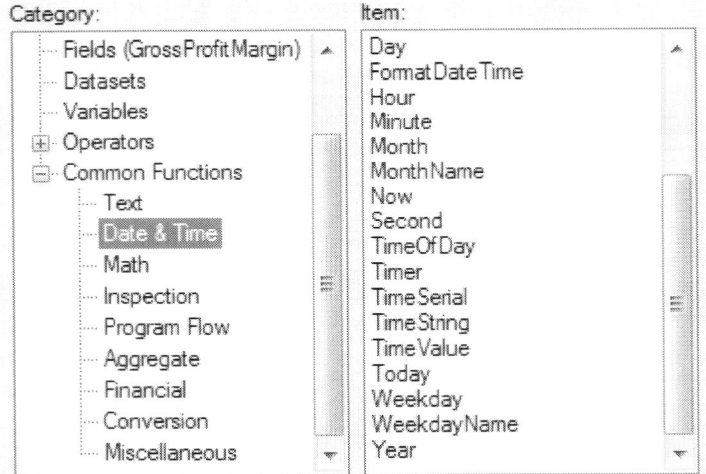

Figure 4-79b Common Functions

Figure 4-79 Expression Category Examples

If you are interested in the expression for the background color of the Product Gross Profit margin Value column in Figure 4-76, it uses the IIF function:

```
=IIF(Fields!Product_Gross_Profit_Margin_Status_.Value>=1,
"Lime",
IIF(Fields!Product_Gross_Profit_Margin_Status_.Value=0,"Yellow",
"Red"))
```

Note that for this expression the Constants category presents a color picker in the Values pane so all I had to do to set the color for a status value was to click the color. The expression for the background image for the KPI column also uses a similar IIF function:

```
=IIF(Fields!Product_Gross_Profit_Margin_Status_.Value>=1,
"GreenBall2",

IIF(Fields!Product_Gross_Profit_Margin_Status_.Value=0,"YellowBa
ll2", "RedBall2"))
```

To use custom code like the ChangeWord function example presented earlier use an expression something like: = Code.ChangeWord(<reference to word to change>). Please see Report Builder 3.0 Help for more examples of expressions.

Adding Databars, Sparklines, and Indicators

Databars and sparklines are small charts and indicators are small gauges without elements such as pointers. There are five types of sparklines: column charts, line charts, area charts, pie charts, and range charts. Databars are horizontal or vertical bars showing some sort of value(s). Indicators are used to display a single value such as the status of a KPI. There are four indicator image types: directional that show trend direction, symbols such as checkmarks and flags, shapes like the balls we used in Figure 4-76, and ratings such as stars, bars, and pie charts.

You add one of these objects to a report by clicking on it on the RB3 Insert ribbon and then clicking in the cell destination. For example, in a new report using the InternetSales dataset that we used previously I inserted four tables as shown in Figure 4-80. All use internet sales as the row field. The first, second, and fourth table use calendar year as the column field, and the third uses calendar quarter. I added a second column to each table to display the data visualization. You must manually enter the heading on that column.

After inserting the object you specify its data in a manner similar to what we used with gauges in Figure 4-68 by dragging a data item from the Report Data pane into the data drop-down box as shown in Figure 4-81a. This menu is displayed by clicking on the cell containing the object. The objects can be modified by using drop-down menus as displayed in Figure 4-81b by right clicking on the cell containing the object. Figure 4-82 shows the resultant report. Note that I used different sparklines for the second and third tables: a line chart for the second and a bar chart for the third.

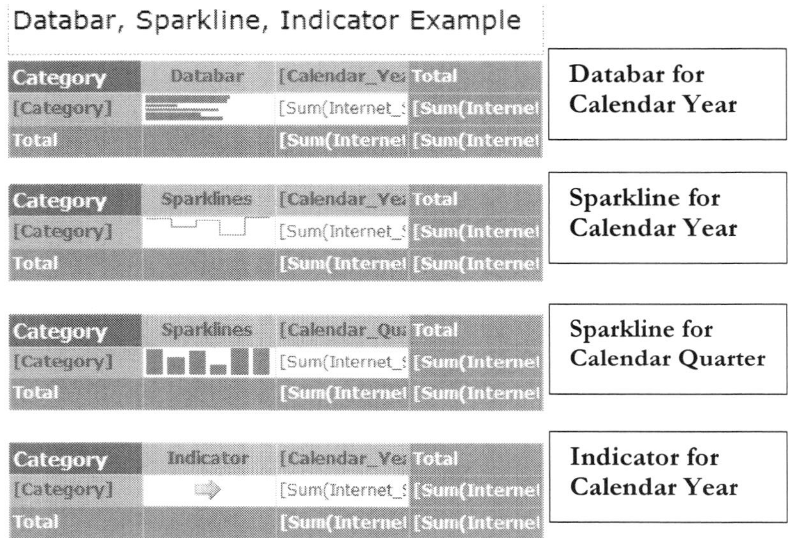

Figure 4-80 Databar, Sparkline, and Indicator Design Example

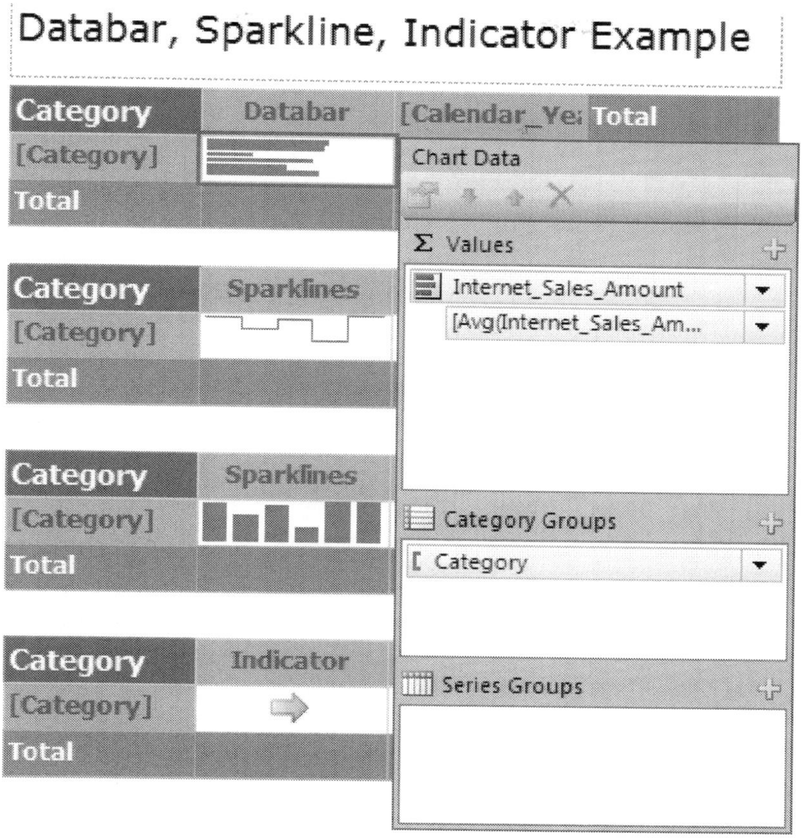

Figure 4-81a Chart Data Options

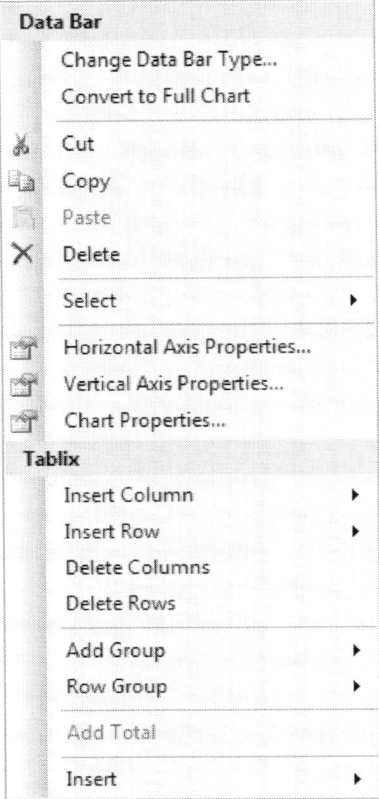

Figure 4-81b Databar Menu

Figure 4-81 Databar, Sparkline, and Indicator Design Example

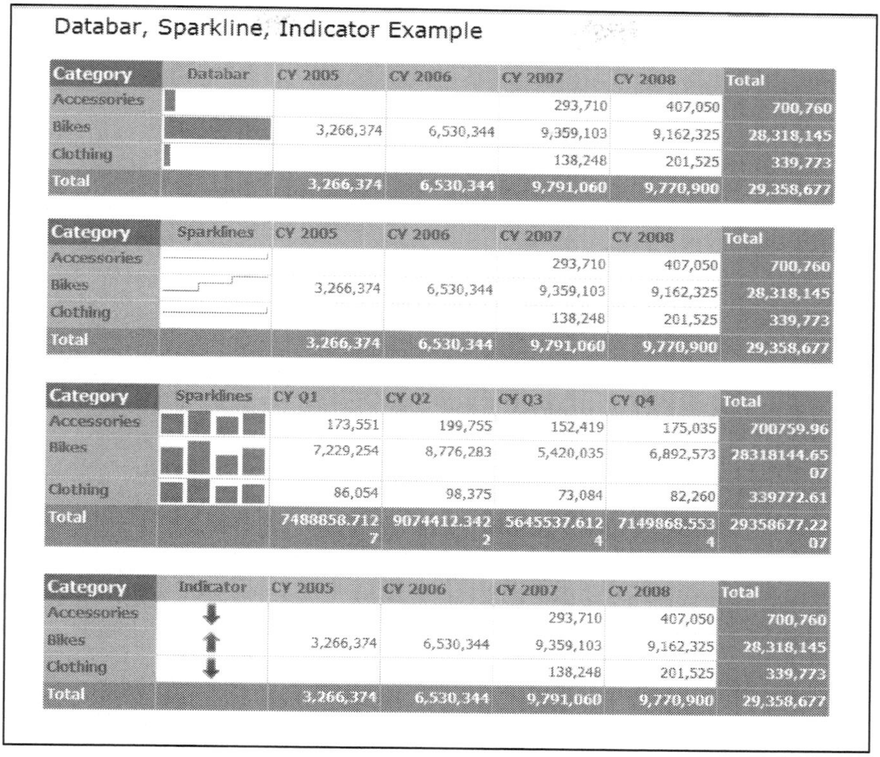

Databar, Sparkline, Indicator Example

Category	Databar	CY 2005	CY 2006	CY 2007	CY 2008	Total
Accessories				293,710	407,050	700,760
Bikes		3,266,374	6,530,344	9,359,103	9,162,325	28,318,145
Clothing				138,248	201,525	339,773
Total		3,266,374	6,530,344	9,791,060	9,770,900	29,358,677

Category	Sparklines	CY 2005	CY 2006	CY 2007	CY 2008	Total
Accessories				293,710	407,050	700,760
Bikes		3,266,374	6,530,344	9,359,103	9,162,325	28,318,145
Clothing				138,248	201,525	339,773
Total		3,266,374	6,530,344	9,791,060	9,770,900	29,358,677

Category	Sparklines	CY Q1	CY Q2	CY Q3	CY Q4	Total
Accessories		173,551	199,755	152,419	175,035	700759.96
Bikes		7,229,254	8,776,283	5,420,035	6,892,573	28318144.6507
Clothing		86,054	98,375	73,084	82,260	339772.61
Total		7488858.7127	9074412.3422	5645537.6124	7149868.5534	29358677.2207

Category	Indicator	CY 2005	CY 2006	CY 2007	CY 2008	Total
Accessories	⬇			293,710	407,050	700,760
Bikes	⬆	3,266,374	6,530,344	9,359,103	9,162,325	28,318,145
Clothing	⬇			138,248	201,525	339,773
Total		3,266,374	6,530,344	9,791,060	9,770,900	29,358,677

Figure 4-82 Databar, Sparkline, and Indicator Report

Instead of importing images for KPI visualization as we did in Figure 4-76 we could use indicators as shown in Figure 4-83. In design view I dropped an indicator object into the KPI value cell, selected the three color shapes type, and specified the value in the Value and States window of the Indicator Properties menu shown in Figure 4-84. In this case the value is [Sum(Product_Gross_Profit_Margin_Status_)] showing the trend of the Gross Profit Margin.

Using sparklines and indicators in Excel will be addressed in a later chapter.

Gross Profit Margin KPI

Category	Product Gross Profit Margin Value	Product Gross Profit Margin Goal	Product Gross Profit Margin Status	Product Gross Profit Margin Trend	KPI
Accessories	[illegible]	0.4	-1	-1	
Bikes	0.1	0.12	0	-1	
Clothing	0.2	0.2	1	-1	
Components	0.1	0.1	1	1	

Figure 4-83 KPI with Indicators

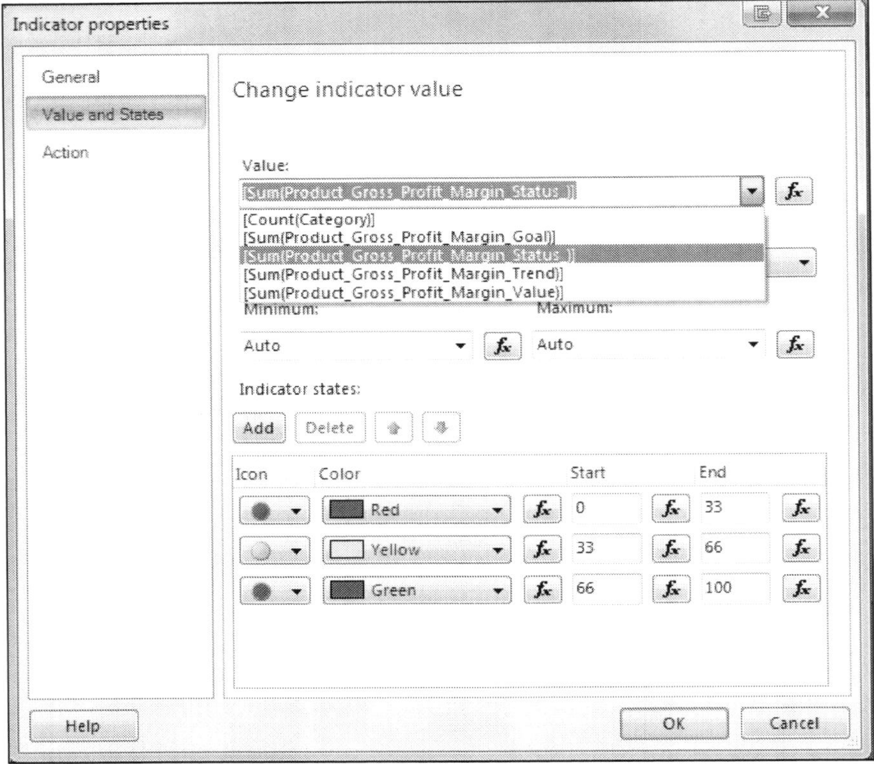

Figure 4-84 Indicator KPI Value

Adding Maps

RB3 can overlay data visualizations on geographical maps. These maps require both analytical data (values) and spatial data (locations). There are four sources for spatial data: the Map Gallery installed with RB3 that uses U.S. Census Bureau data; Environmental Systems Research Institute (ESRI) Shapefiles with geographic information in a vector data format; spatial data stored in a SQL Server database (see SQL Server Books Online); and custom locations created by the user (see RB3 Help). We do not have space for complete coverage of RB3 maps so I will only describe a simple example here, a map of the United States showing the value of AdventureWorks internet sales by state.

It's relatively easy to design maps using the Map Wizard. In design view click new in the Report Builder button menu and then select the Map Wizard. This will bring you to the New Map page in Figure 4-85a where there are three types of spatial data to choose from. We will use the Map Gallery that has maps for the United States. Within the Map Gallery I selected US by State Insert to select the type of map to use.

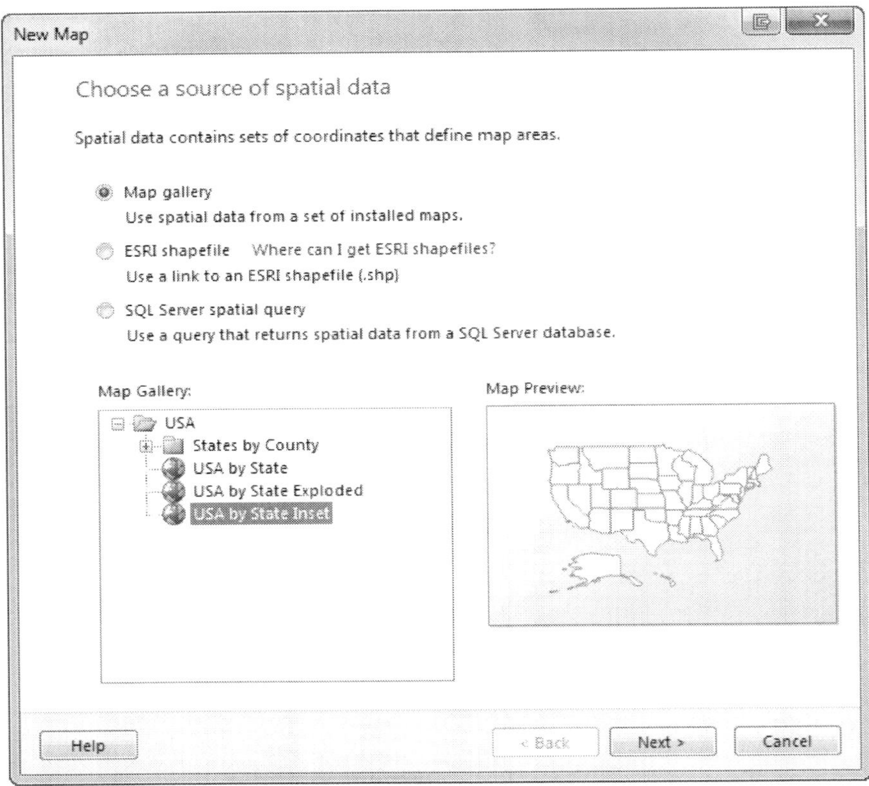

Figure 4-85a Map – Spatial Data

Clicking Next will take you to a page (Figure 4-85b) to select view options where you may use the directional arrows to change the shape of the map. I did not use the Bing Map Layer that lets you add roads and /or aerial views to the map. The next page shown in Figure 4-85c provides three map types: Basic, Color, and Bubble. I choose the Color Analytical Map.

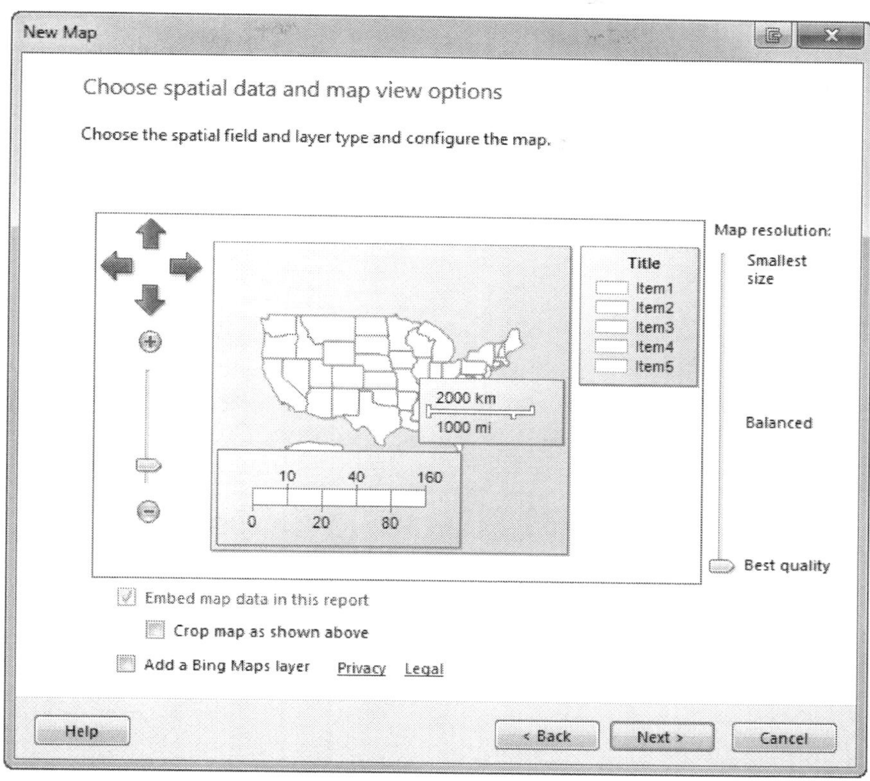

Figure 4-85b Map – View Options

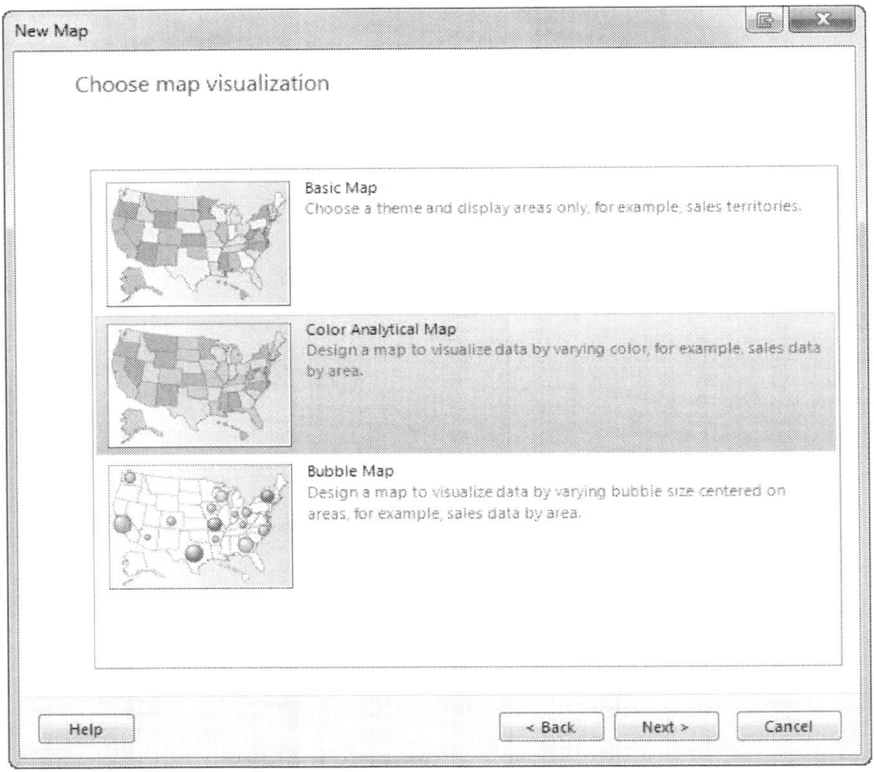

Figure 4-85c Map – Visualization Type

You specify the analytical dataset, the data to be overplayed on the map, in the next window (Figure 4-85d). Here you choose between an existing dataset or one that you will add. I choose add a dataset so I could construct the query for the map data. Clicking Next takes you to a data source page (Figure 4-85e) that you are familiar with. I selected the AdventureWorks Cube. Next in the Query Designer (Figure 4-85f) I dragged Internet Sales Amount from the Measures group and State-Province from the Customer Geography Fact list onto the design surface and Country and Calendar Year into the filter area. I selected United States for the Filter Expression for Country to only use US sales data and marked the Calendar Year filter as a parameter so that the user could select what data to display on the map. Note that you could also add a calendar quarter parameter to be able select quarters as well as years.

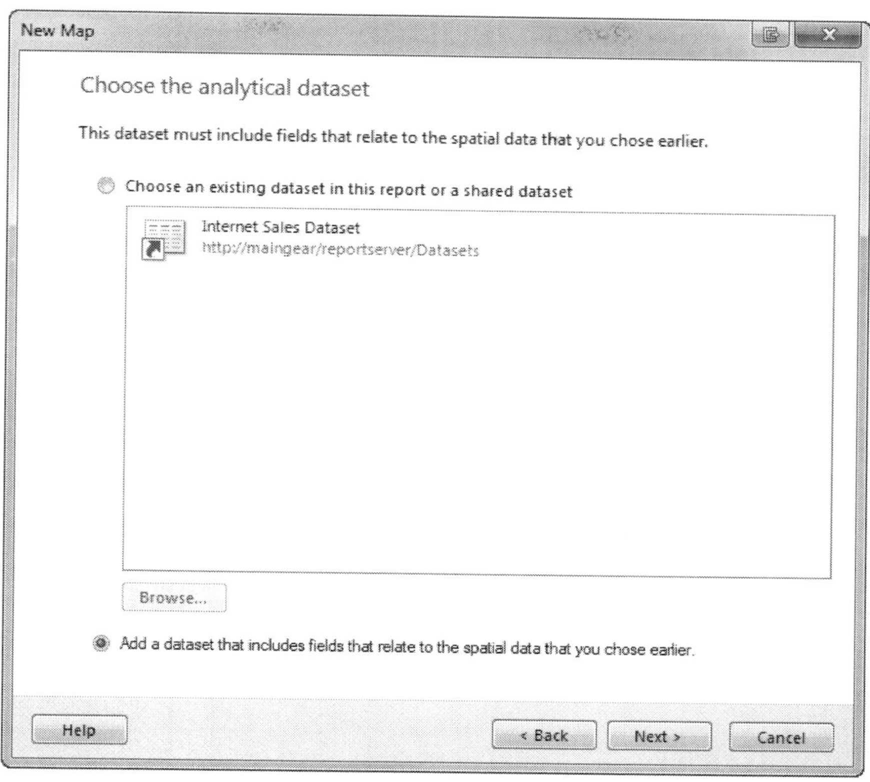

Figure 4-85d Map – Analytical Dataset

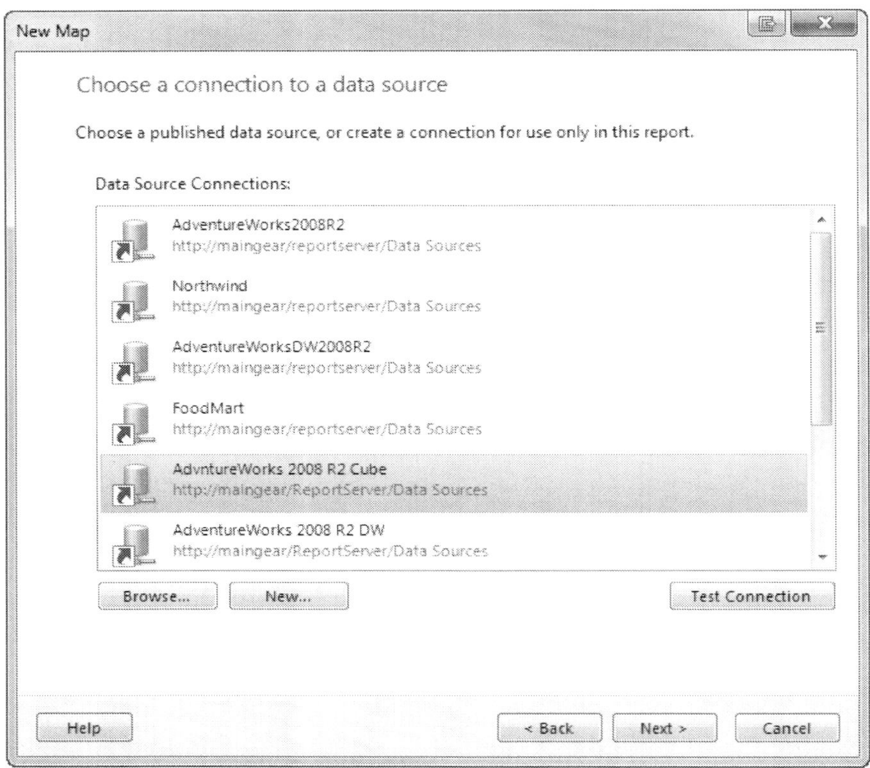

Figure 4-85e Map – Data Source

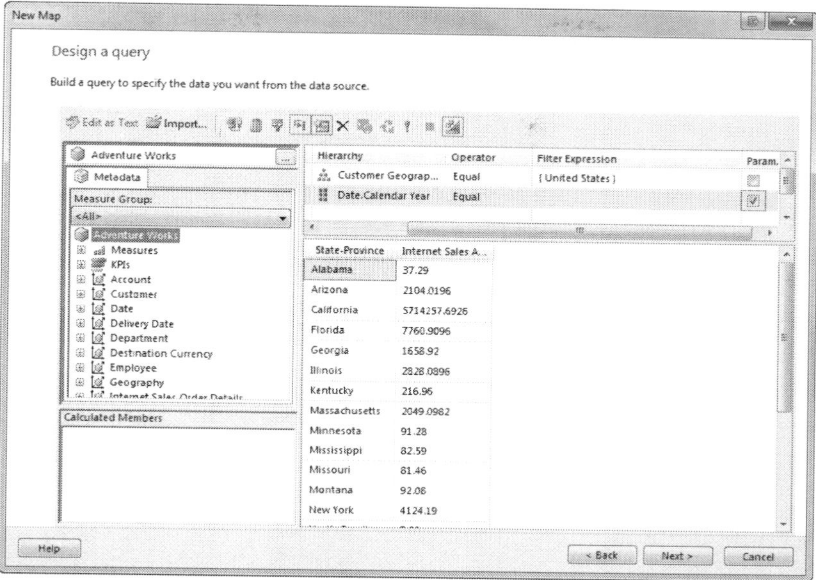

Figure 4-85f Map – Query Design

In the next window (Figure 4-85g) you match spatial and analytical data fields. In this case the spatial data are in the STATENAME field and the analytical data are in the State_Province field.

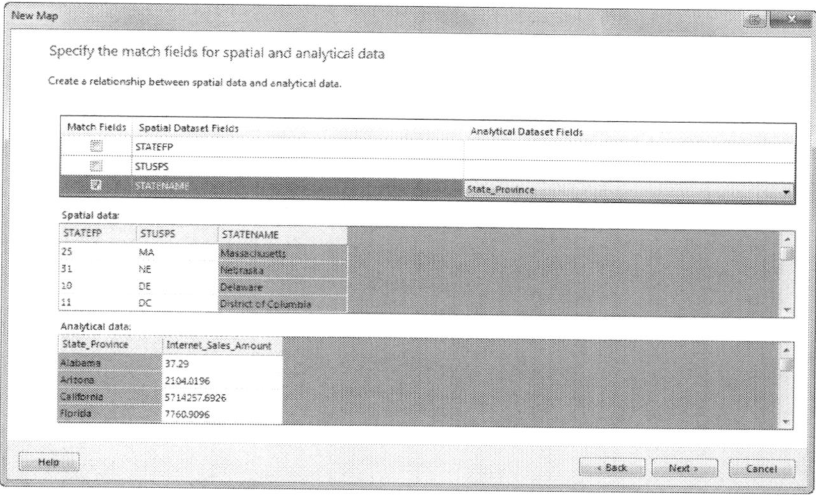

Figure 4-85g Map – Field Match

Next you choose the theme, data field to use, and the color rule for the map in Figure 4-85h. I left the theme at the default (Ocean); selected [Sum(Internet_Sales_Amount)] for the data to display, i.e., data will be summed for each state; and the Light-Dark color rule where states with lower internet sales will be show lighter and those with higher sales will be darker. You can see in the drop-down list that there are a number of color combinations.

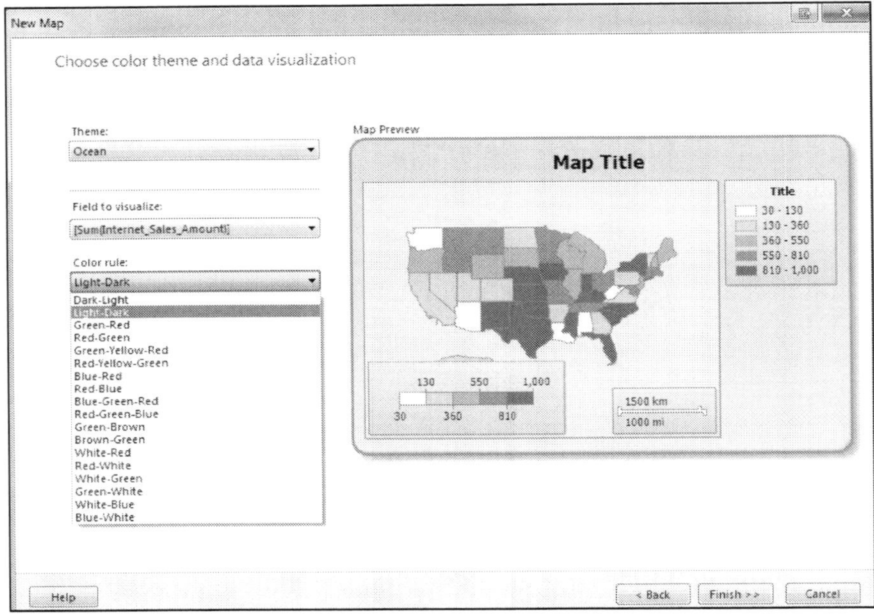

Figure 4-85h Map – Theme and Data Field

Figure 4-85i shows the completed map in design view, and Figure 4-85j the run view. In the run view it's obvious the AdventureWorks' sales are predominately on the West Coast something that AW's marketing department may want to investigate. Note that by changing map parameter values (not shown), i.e., changing years and/or quarters, the sales pattern change over time. Interesting.

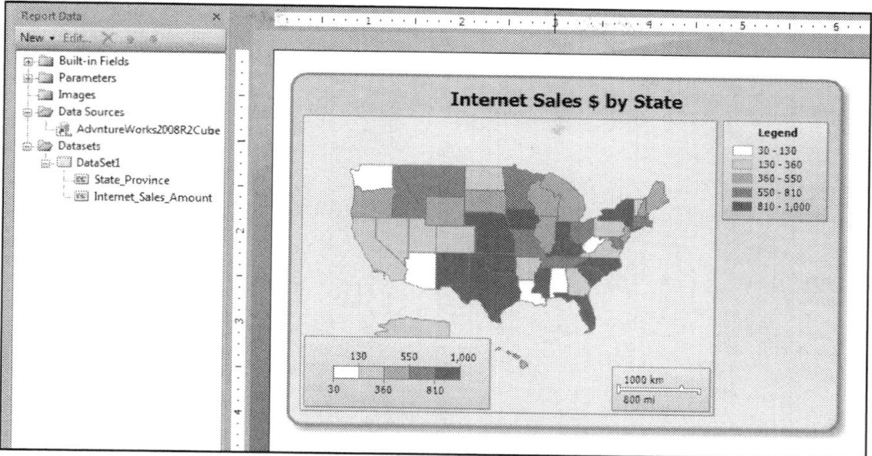

Figure 4-85i Map – Design View

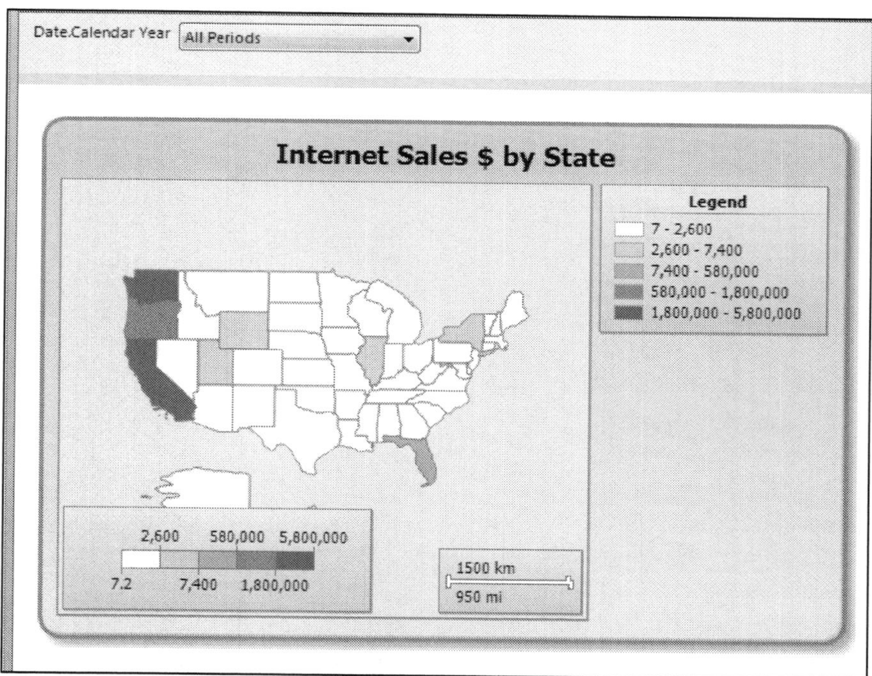

Figure 4-85j Map – Run View

Using Actions

Some report objects have Action as a property category along with General, Number, Font, Visibility, etc. Actions are essentially hyperlinks, i.e., clicking on an object with a defined action will navigate to the action's target: another report on the Report Sever, a bookmark, or hyperlink. You may create actions for textboxes, including those in a tablix, images, and maps. Figure 4-86 shows the action view for a Textbox Properties dialog box in which I specified the Gross Profit Margin KPI report we worked on above as the action target. That report already has a calendar year parameter so I did not add one here.

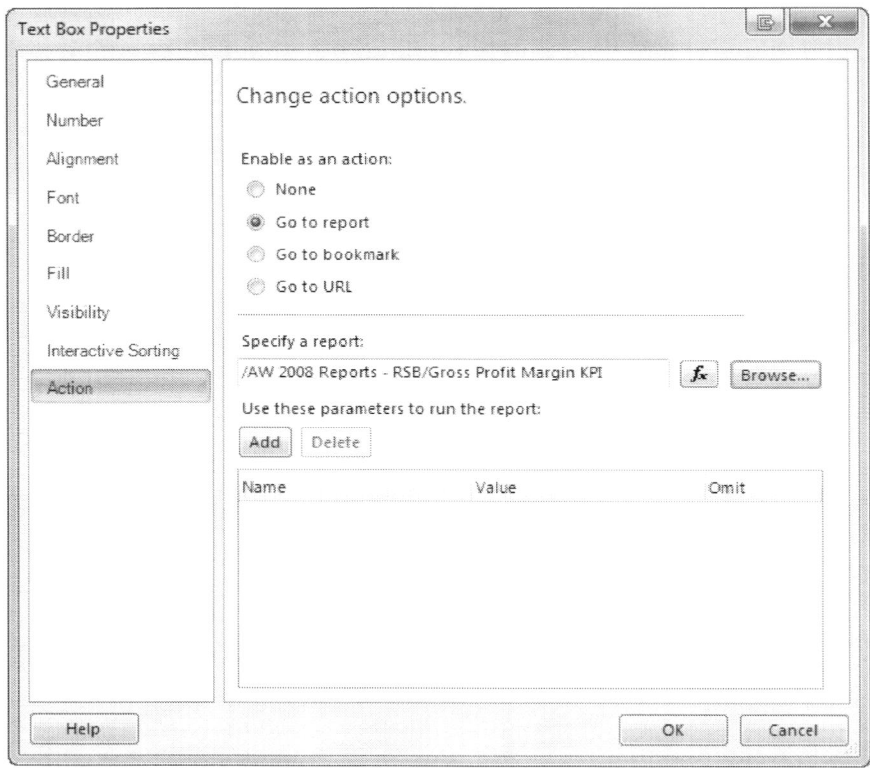

Figure 4-86 Action Properties

As an example the report in Figure 4-87 shows the report from Figure 4-60 with a textbox and image added to it, both of which have actions specified in them. The textbox "Go to KPI Report" uses the action defined in Figure 4-86 to navigate to the GPM KPI report. Note that a report specified in an action must be already published to the Report Server. The action for the Microsoft image is set to a hyperlink to the Microsoft home page. So, when the report in

Figure 4-81 is run, clicking on the KPI Report textbox will take you to that report and clicking on the Microsoft image will bring up the Microsoft home page in your default browser.

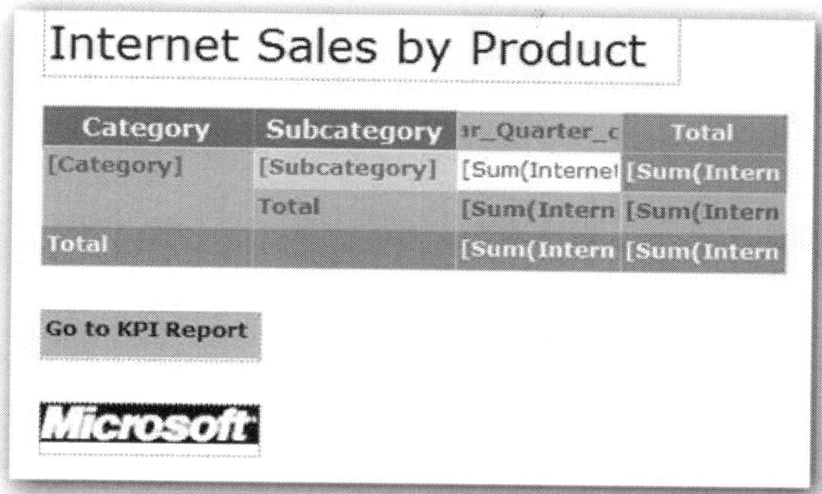

Figure 4-87 Action Example

You add an Action to an object by right clicking on the object to display the Properties dialog box, selecting Action and the Action type, and then specifying the target in the textbox provided.

Drill-through, Drill-down, Subreports, and Nested Data Regions

A drill-through report displays another report when the user clicks on a specific textbox in the parent report. For example, in the Internet Sales by Product report in Figure 4-87 I could right click on the [Subcategory] cell to bring up the Properties window and then proceed to define an Action to go to another report. Then, when the report runs and the user clicks on that cell, the other report will be displayed. A subreport is similar to a drill-through report except that the other report is displayed within the parent report.

The Internet Sales by Product report in Figure 4-60 has the drill-down capability whereby a dimension can be expanded to show the underlying detail as Accessories are expanded in the Figure to display product subcategories.

Similarly, nested data regions display other data regions, say a sub-table, or a data visualization, say an indicator, within another data region. The Gross

Profit Margin KPI report in Figure 4-76 is an example where the KPI is nested within the GPM table. Please see RB3 Help for more information about these topics.

Publishing Reports to the Report Server

As mentioned earlier reports are saved with an rdl file extension either to a storage device such as your local hard drive or to the Report Server or to both. If you save reports in both places, be aware that a changed report saved to one location does not automatically update the other version, i.e., the new version must be saved in both locations.

To publish a report to the report server that has not been saved there before either save it from RB3 to the Report Server or upload the file from the storage location by using the Report Manager. We addressed uploading earlier in this chapter. To save the file from RB3 to the Report Server click on Save As from the list displayed when clicking the RB3 button in the upper left corner to bring up the Save As Report dialog box shown in Figure 4-88. Select Recent Sites and Servers on the left and double click on the server URL in the right panel to list the folders available on the Server. Select a folder and then save the file. To save the report to a new folder either use Report Manager to create it prior to saving the report from RB3 or save it to an existing Server folder temporarily and then use the Report manager to create the new folder and move the report to it. Of course, you may change the file name of the report to how you want it to appear on the Server by entering the new name in the Name box or renaming it within the Report Manager.

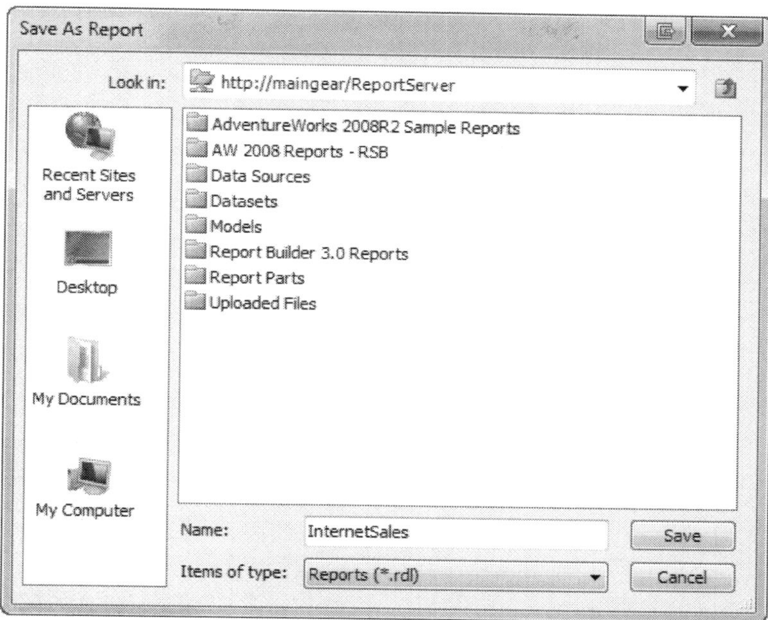

Figure 4-88 Save a Report to the Report Server

I published most of the reports that we used as examples in this chapter to my report server's AW 2008 Reports - RSB folder shown in Figure 4-89. Note that I changed the names of the reports to something more descriptive. After publishing the report to the Report Server, I would probably rename the locally stored version as well and include a version number in the name for backup purposes.

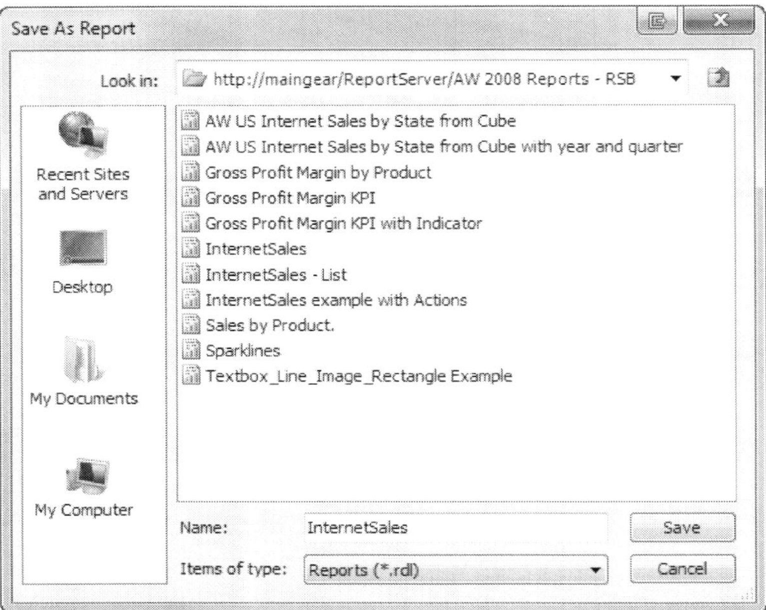

Figure 4-89 Reports on the Report Server

The Report Part Gallery

Report parts are report objects such as tables, charts, and images saved on the report server that can be used in other reports. You save report parts in RB3 by clicking on the RB button in the upper left corner to display the drop-down menu as in Figure 4-88. Clicking the Publish Report Parts button will bring up the window in Figure 4-89 where you select the setting to use for the parts. To publish all objects as is with default settings select the top option. To modify the properties select the bottom option that will take you to the Select report parts to publish window as in Figure 4-90 where you can select which reports and datasets to publish.

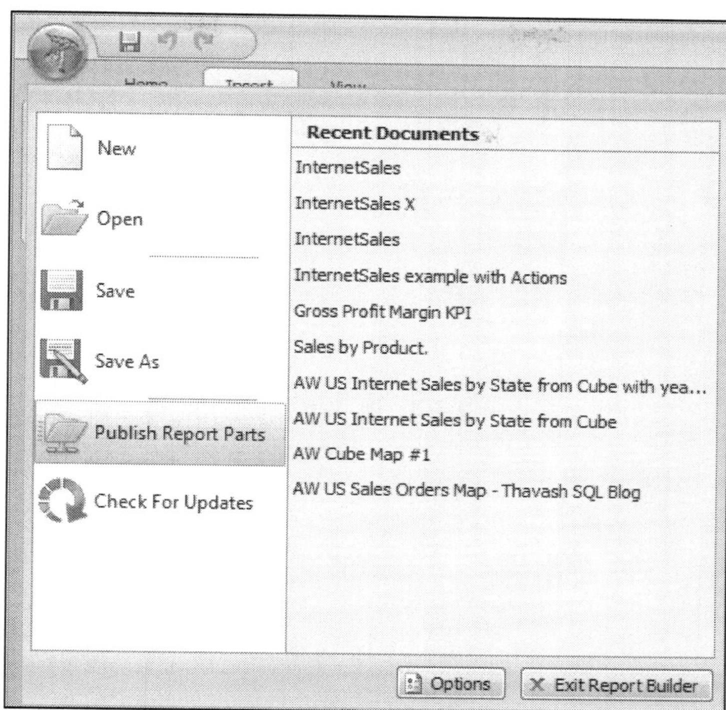

Figure 4-88 Action Example

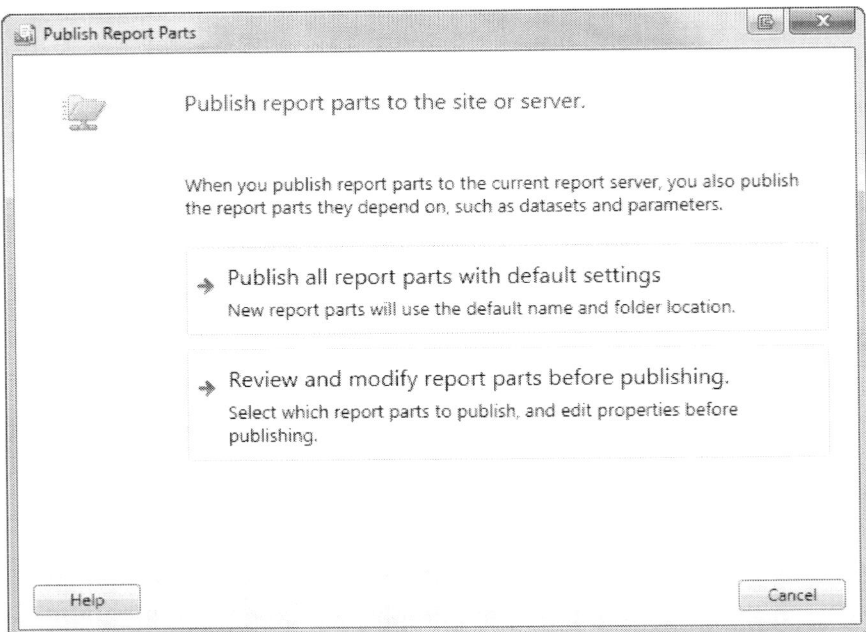

Figure 4-89 Report Parts Publish Options

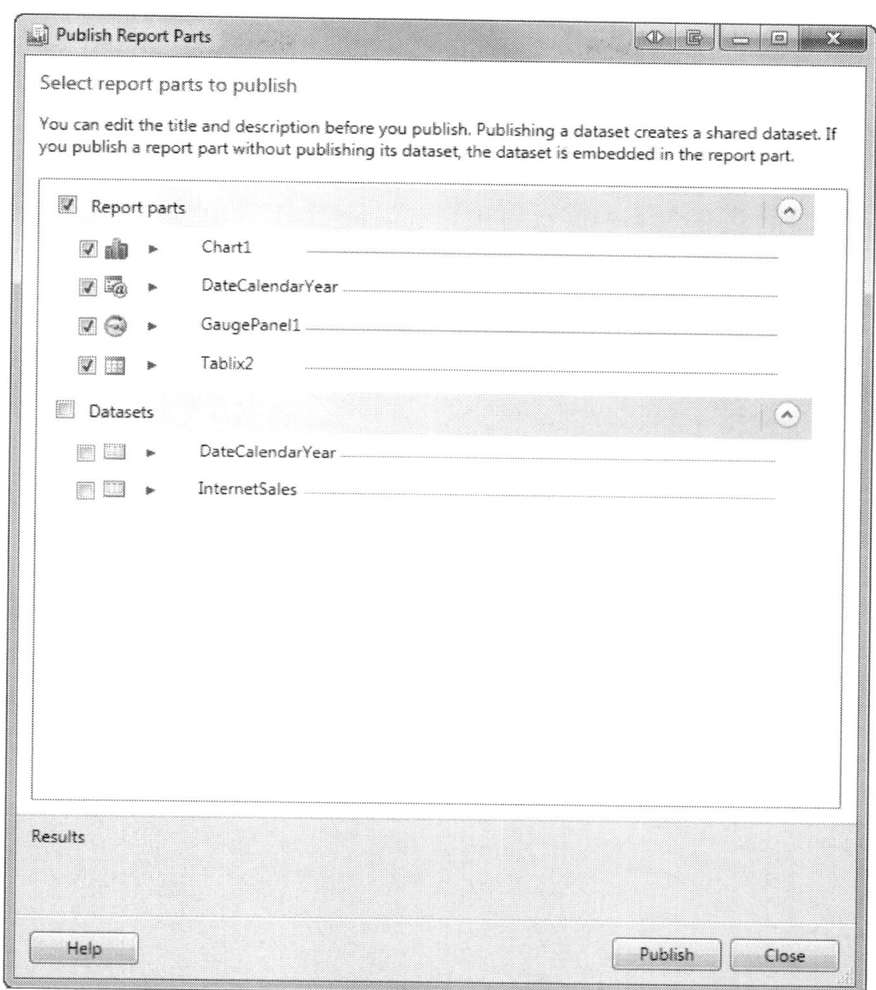

Figure 4-90 Review and Modify Report Parts Window

(For better viewing of this image, go to http://www.zerobits.info/bibook/bibookimages/)

The report parts will be published (saved) on the report server to the folder specified in the Report Builder Options window accessed from the RB3 button in the top left corner. I left the folder set to the default (Report Parts) where I saved objects from some of the reports we used earlier. Figure 4-91 shows the objects in the Maingear/Report Server/Report Parts folder which are also displayed in the Report Part Gallery on the right edge of the RB3 window as in Figure 4-92. In that Gallery you can specify search criteria such as created, modified, and type and set the server folder to search. Note that you must click on the magnifying glass button in the upper right corner to display a list of objects. To use an object in a report you may either drag and drop it the from the Gallery onto the design surface or double click it. Using RB3's report parts capability can significantly reduce report design time.

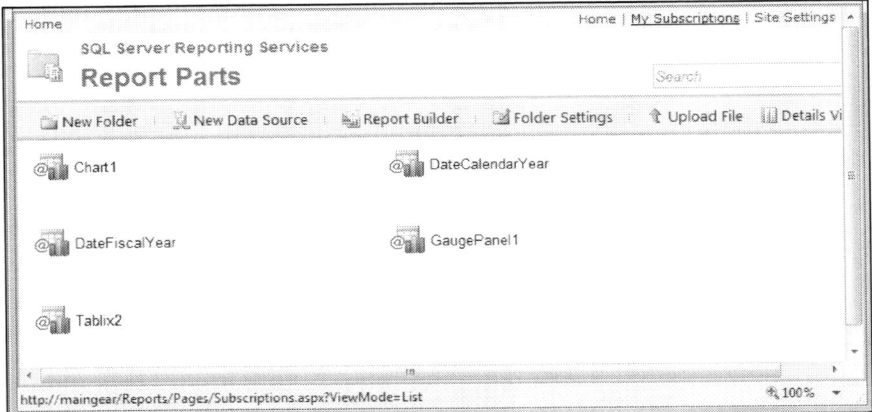

Figure 4-91 Report Parts Folder

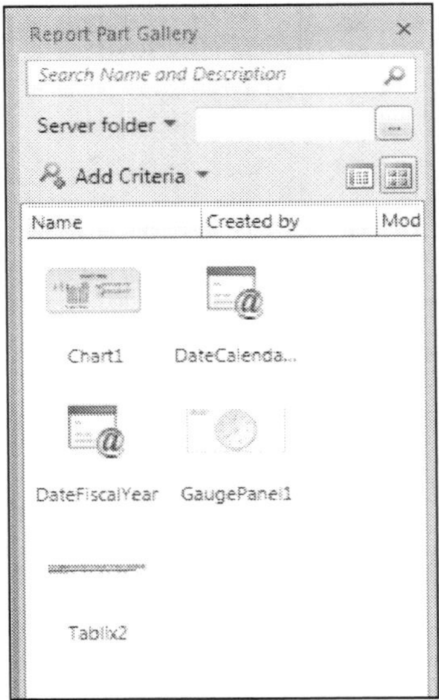

Figure 4-92 Report Part Gallery

What's Next

We have most definitively not covered all of the features of the Report Manager and especially of Report Builder 3.0, and for RB3 we have slighted many of the topics that we have addressed. However, as noted in Chapter 1 we cannot possibly cover any of the Microsoft BI tools in their complete depth so please see Books Online, RB3 Help, or other sources for coverage of more advanced topics.

In the next chapter we begin our investigation of data analysis using Excel.

Chapter 5 - Data Analysis with Excel 2010: Part I Data Acquisition, Data Inspection, and Data Transformation

A spreadsheet is a near ideal mechanism for analyzing data. In it data can be organized, manipulated, and transformed; analyzed with sophisticated mathematical and statistical processes; and presented in professional formats. This is accomplished with relative ease as compared with manual methods prior to the computer age and so too with computer-assisted analysis prior to VisiCalc, the first spreadsheet program. Microsoft Excel 2010 is the premier spreadsheet application for personal computers.

Before we get started with Excel data analysis in earnest I'd like to address a few preliminaries.

Preliminaries

In this and subsequent chapters we assume a moderate level of Excel expertise. This means that you should be comfortable creating workbooks and worksheets, navigating in them, using formulas with absolute and relative cell references, formatting cells and ranges, and creating charts. It does not mean that you must be familiar with using external data sources, pivot tables, or statistical methods. Those who are a little rusty can review some Excel basics presented in Appendix D. We also assume that you are familiar with the Office 2010 user interface especially the Ribbon. Also note that the intended scope of this presentation is limited to Microsoft Office Excel 2010 (hereafter referred to as Excel) although much of the material may apply to previous versions, especially Excel 2007. In addition, most, if not all of, Excel's capabilities can be related to data analysis in one way or another so it is impossible to cover all of them or even some of them in depth in two chapters. I have included those topics which seem to me to be most useful leaving others for more advanced study.

Set Up

Although we mentioned software set up in the Chapter 1 we'll cover it in a bit more detail here for Excel. First, if you haven't, set up your trusted locations because if you don't, the security alerts will drive you nuts. To do that, use the Office button in the upper left corner to access Excel Options. Select Trust Center, Trust Center Setting, and then Trusted Locations. Use the Add new location button to add secure locations that you will use for your Excel work. I limit my trusted locations to my local machine behind a good firewall.

Next, download and install the Microsoft SQL Server 2008 Data Mining Add-ins for Microsoft Office 2007 and 2010 and activate other appropriate add-ins. The Data Mining Add-ins include the Table Analysis Tools, the Data Mining Client for Excel, and the Data Mining Templates for Visio. Search the Internet for "Microsoft SQL Server 2008 Data Mining Add-ins" to find the download site. There are separate versions of the Data Mining Add-ins for SQL Server 2008 and SQL Server 2005. When using the Data Mining Add-ins in Excel 2010 you may get a dialog box when starting Excel that says that "Excel experienced a serious problem with the 'sqlserver.dmxladdiin' add-in. . . . . Do you want to disable this add-in?" Please click NO to keep the add-in enabled. If for some reason it becomes disabled, then go to Options on the File tab, then Add-ins. At the bottom of the window select Disabled items in the Manage textbox, select the Data Mining add-in from the list, and click Enable.

A number of add-ins are included with Excel but may not be activated at the time of installation. You will at least want to make sure that the Analysis Tool Pack (ATP) is enabled. Some Web sites say that the functions in the ATP are already included in Excel 2010 so it unnecessary to load it. Other sites provide instructions about how to activate it. To be on the save side check to confirm that it is enabled. To do that or to activate other add-ins use the Office button to get to Excel Options and select Add-ins. Toward the bottom of the Excel Options window open the Add-ins window, select Excel Add-ins in the Manage textbox, and click the Go button to bring up the Add-Ins dialog box as in Figure 5-1. Click the check boxes for the add-ins you want to enable and then OK.

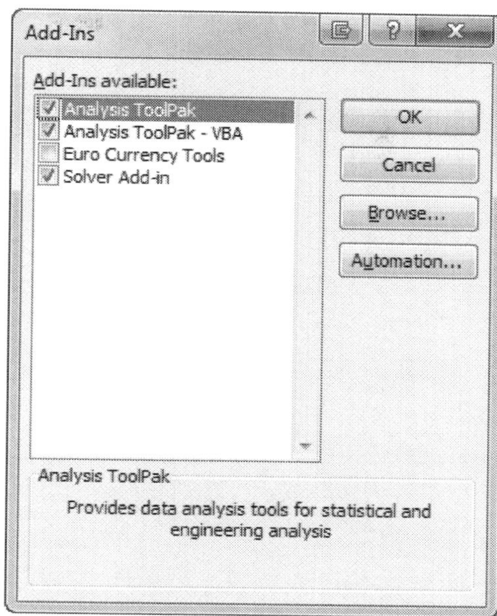

Figure 5-1 Add-Ins Dialog Box

Excel as a Database Management System

Excel has many strengths—database management is not one of them. However, Excel does contain many database-type functions such as filtering and sorting data and entering data via forms, and many of us start by using Excel as primary storage for data either out of naiveté, convenience, or lack of knowledge about database applications. I can say from more than one personal experience that doing this it is bad practice if the amount of data is even of moderate size. I recommend that you manage and store data in a database management application, especially if you expect to accumulate over a screen full of data, maybe 30-40 rows at most. I prefer Access 2010 for managing personal and small workgroup data and SQL Server for larger databases but there are many other options, including SQL Server Express which is free.

Excel Data Structures

Un-tabularized, Excel Table, and Pivot Table are the three forms for data in Excel. Un-tabularized, my term for data that is not in one of the other two forms, may be organized in a number of different ways. Data from a raw data source may be represented in Excel in un-tabularized form. Un-tabular does not necessarily mean unorganized—it just means that the data have not yet been defined as a table or pivot table.

A range of cells can be designated as an Excel Table. Doing so requires that the data are organized similar to a database table with rows as records and columns as fields. The first row in the range must contain the names of the fields. Data in an Excel Table can be easily sorted and filtered, calculated fields added, column values totaled, styles specified, and much more. In addition, an Excel Table enables the Table Tools tabs on the Ribbon which offer additional and valuable analysis and formatting options (Note that the Data Mining Add-ins mentioned above must be installed to have access to the Table Analyze Tools.). Structuring data as an Excel Table has much to offer. Most data imported from external sources will automatically become Excel Tables but an Excel table can also be defined manually by using the Table command in the Tables command group on the Insert tab. Excel tables can be formatted in a variety of ways using the Ribbon's Table Tools Design tab options.

As you know pivot tables are like interactive cross tabulations with rows and columns representing dimensions or attribute values such as time periods, locations, and product categories and the intersecting cells contain aggregate numerical values such as sums, counts, and averages . Row and column dimensions (attributes) can be and usually are nested, i.e., a dimension may have a sub-dimension that may have a sub-sub-dimension, etc. Dimensions may be expanded for drill-down, collapsed for drill-up, or filtered to present a subset of the data. Pivot Tables are similar in structure to OLAP cubes described in Chapter 2. In fact, an Analysis Services cube is usually represented in Excel by a pivot table.

Data Connection Refresh

If data from an external source is dynamic, i.e., that it changes over time, then you may want to periodically refresh it. You may refresh data in a specific table or pivot table manually by right clicking any cell in the table and selecting Refresh; clicking the down arrow head on the Refresh All option in the Connections command group of the Data tab; or clicking the Refresh option in the Table Tools Design tab. You can refresh all data connections in the workbook by clicking Refresh All in the Connections command group of the Data Tab or by clicking the down arrowhead on the Refresh option in the External Table Data command group of the Table Tools Design tab and selecting Refresh all. Whew! It sounds much more complicated than it is.

Data connections may also be refreshed automatically by configuring the Refresh Control in the Connection Properties dialog box shown a little later in Figure 5-3. There are three refresh possibilities there: Checking Enable background refresh means that you may continue to use the workbook while the data are being refreshed. You may specify a refresh interval ranging from 1 to 32,767 minutes, and also elect to refresh the data when the workbook is opened. These options are not mutually exclusive, i.e., you may select any or all of them.

Inserting Data into Excel

The last step after creating or selecting a data connection is to transfer data into Excel by identifying the location in Excel for it to be placed via the Import Data dialog box as shown in Figure 5-2.

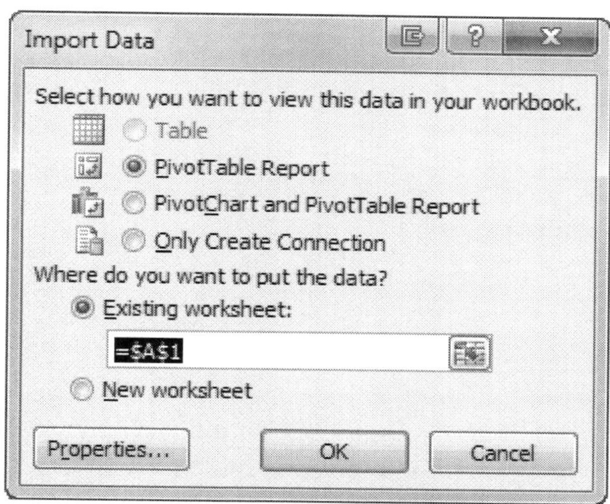

Figure 5-2 Import Data Dialog Box

The Import Data Dialog box for most connection types will offer options to insert the data as a table, pivot table, or pivot chart/pivot table combination. You must designate where to put the data in an existing or new worksheet for all connections. For an existing worksheet you may specify the cell location by selecting the cell reference in the Existing Worksheet textbox (the selection will have a black background) and then clicking on a cell in the worksheet. Clicking OK will import the data into Excel.

Before leaving the Import Data Dialog box you may bring up the Connection Properties dialog box (Figure 5-3) by clicking the Properties button where you can change the connection name and description and specify the refresh type in the Usage tab. The Definition tab in Figure 5-4 allows you to select another connection file to use, view the connection string (perhaps useful for establishing a connection using code), and export the connection file among other actions. The connection shown in Figure 5-4 is a view of data that I created in the AdventureWorksDW database. After importing data you can display the Connection Properties dialog box by selecting the Properties option in the Connection command group in the Data tab and then clicking the icon beside the connection name.

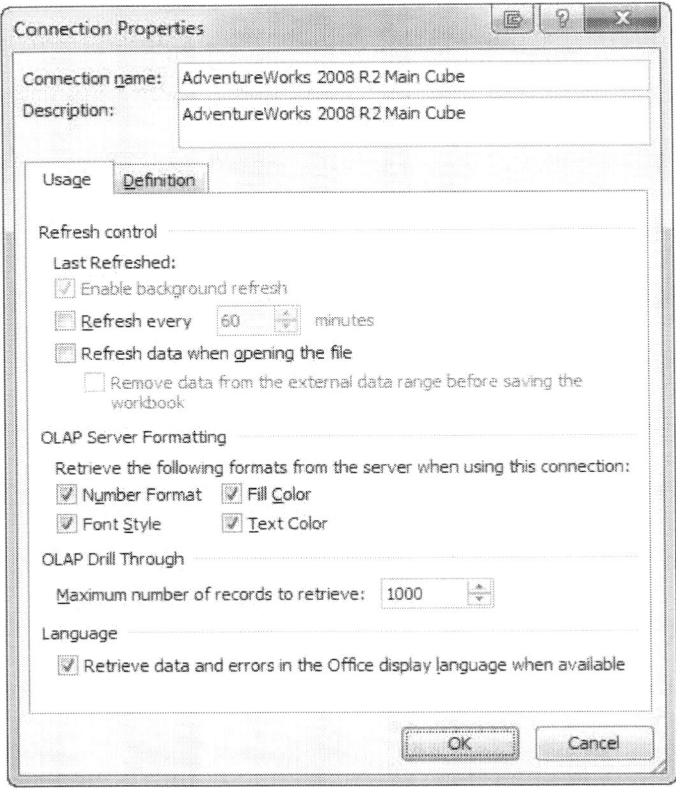

Figure 5-3 Connection Properties - Usage Tab

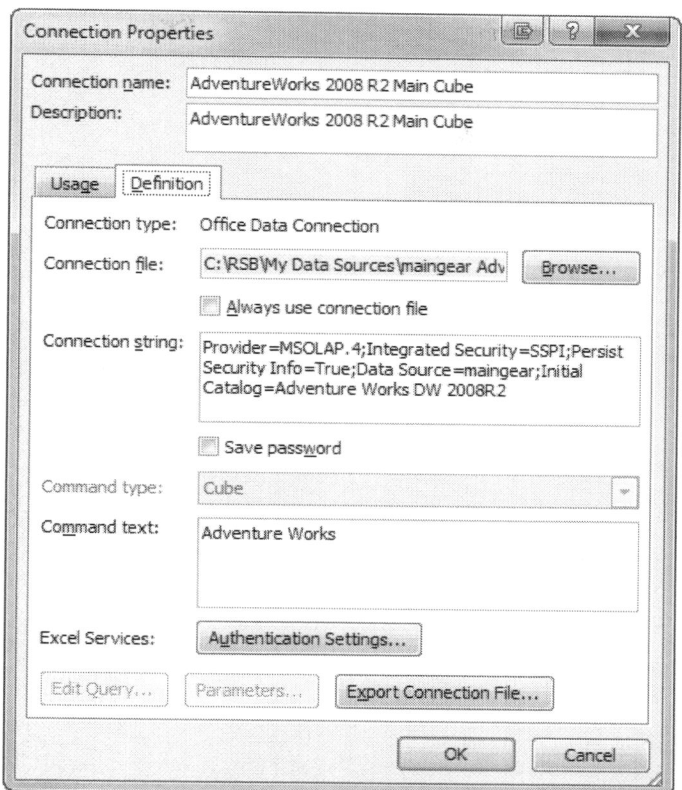

Figure 5-4 Connection Properties - Definition Tab

Table Analysis Tools

The Data Mining Add-ins for Microsoft Office 2007 and 2010 adds the Table Analyze tab to Excel's Table Tools menu. The Analyze tab in Figure 5-5 contains three command groups: Table Analysis Tools, Connection, and Help. Although we will use the majority of the tools in Chapter 9, Data Mining with Excel 2010 Table Analysis Tools, the Fill From Example and Highlight Exceptions tools will be helpful in data inspection, cleaning, and repair. Note that SQL Server 2008 Analysis Services must be running and accessible to use the Table Analysis Tools. When using the Table Analysis Tools for the first time you may need to establish a connection to your Analysis Services SQL Server instance through the Connections command.

Figure 5-5 Table Tool Analyze Ribbon

The Table Tools Design Ribbon in Figure 5-6 is part of Excel 2010 and is available whether the Data Mining Add-ins are installed or not. The Table Tools are only enabled when working inside an Excel table. Selecting a cell outside the table disables the tools and hides the Ribbon tabs. Table Tools are not enabled for pivot tables—separate Pivot Tables Tools Ribbons are available for them.

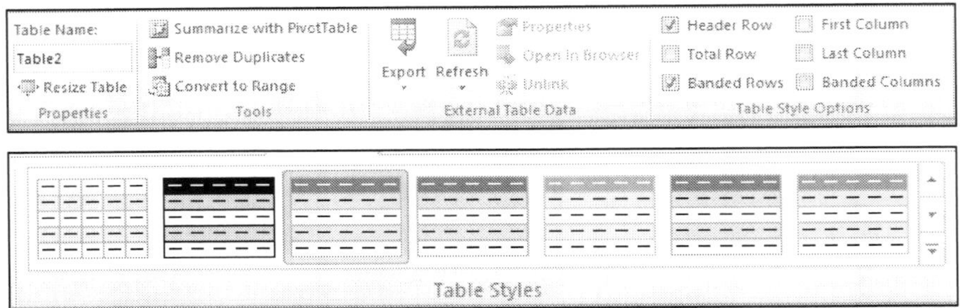

Figure 5-6 Table Tool Design Ribbon

Chapter Organization

The topics in this and the following chapter are organized somewhat in the order of the data analysis steps introduced in Appendix B, using only those steps that are applicable here and combining those with similar functions. We will discuss data acquisition; inspection and cleaning; and transformation in this chapter and data analysis with Excel tables, pivot tables and pivot charts, OLAP cubes, statistical inference, and correlation and regression in the next.

Data Acquisition

No doubt most, if not all, of the data you will use in Excel for data analysis purposes will come from external sources such as enterprise-level DBMSs, OLAP cubes, personal and workgroup DBMSs, the Web, text files, and XML files. We will look at examples of acquiring data from each of these types of data sources. However, we will not be going into detail here about queries and connections which are integral to acquiring data from external sources because those topics are addressed in Appendix C. In addition, we will focus on acquiring data from new data sources that do not have an established existing connection (see Appendix C for a bit more about existing connections) and emphasize ones that we did not cover in that appendix.

From SQL Server 2008 Databases

Assuming that you have access to a SQL Server instance and that you have been granted appropriate permissions, establish a new connection to a SQL Server table or view by following the example in Appendix C (Connections section—Figures C-6 to C-9) using the From Other Sources and From SQL Server options in Excel's Data tab. Proceed to create a connection to SQL Server, select a database and table/view for the source, save the data connection file, and then finish by specifying the location to put the data in with the Import Data dialog box shown in Figure 5-2. Using the From SQL Server option to establish a connection limits you to one table or view. The data from a SQL Server database may be inserted into Excel as a table, pivot table, or pivot chart/table combination. If you need data from multiple tables/views, use the From Microsoft Query option also described in the Appendix C.

In SQL Server more complex queries can be executed by using stored procedures which are scripts written in Transact-SQL in the SQL Server Management Studio. As far as I can determine, stored procedures cannot be accessed directly from Excel's Get External Data options. However, they can be run with VBA code. As an alternative you can create a Microsoft Access-like parameter query using Microsoft Query as discussed below and in Appendix C.

ODBC and OLE DB providers are available for other enterprise-level DBMSs such as Oracle, IBM's DB2, and Sybase so you can also connect to them from Excel using Microsoft Query.

From SQL Server 2008 Analysis Services Cubes

The procedure to connect to an Analysis Services data source is similar to connecting to a SQL Server database. Selecting the From Analysis Services command in the From Other Sources option in the Data tab will display the Connect to Database server dialog box. Enter the server name, select the type of authentication, and proceed to the Select Database and Table dialog box. Select the database and the cube or perspective that you want to use and then move on to the Save Data Connection File and Finish Dialog box to complete the process. Note that for Analysis Services cubes the Table view option is not available in the Import Data dialog box (Figure 5-2).

From Access 2010 Databases

Clicking on the From Access option in the Get External Data command group will bring up a Select Data Source dialog box (file finder) to select a MDB or ACCDB file. (Microsoft Access versions prior to 2007 use the MDB file extension whereas Access 2007 introduced the ACCDB improved file format. Access 2010 is backwards compatible with the MDB format.) Opening an Access file with the dialog box will display a Select table dialog box where you may select a table or query to bring into Excel. Then, click Open.

As with SQL Server, if you want data from multiple tables/queries, then you must use Microsoft Query in the From Other Sources option in the Get External Data command group. Microsoft Query will display the Choose Data Source dialog box shown in Figure 5-7. Select MS Access Database and click OK to display the File Finder as in Figure 5-8. There I navigated to my databases directory and selected the Northwind database that was upgraded to the 2007 format. Clicking OK will take you to the "column" selector as in Figure 5-9 where the fields for the query are selected. I selected OrderDate from the Orders table; Quantity, UnitPrice, and Discount from the OrderDetails table; CompanyName form the Customer table; and CategoryName from the Categories Table. Clicking Next may display a dialog box about joining the tables manualy. Please see Appendix C about how to do that. In this case you must add the Products table to the query to complete the relationships between the OrderDetails table and the Category table as shown in the completed query in Figure 5-10.

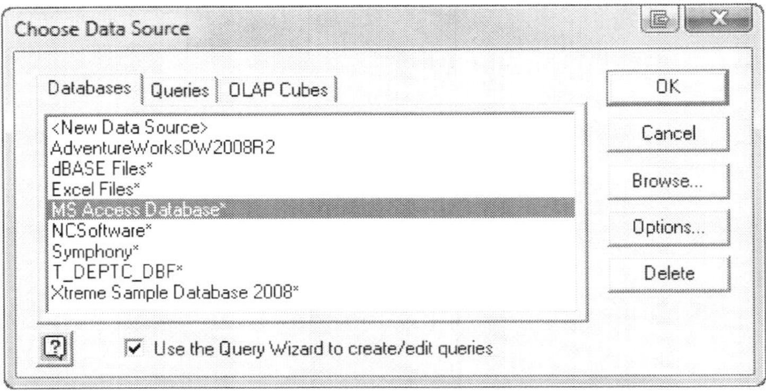

Figure 5-7 Microsoft Query Choose Data Source Dialog Box

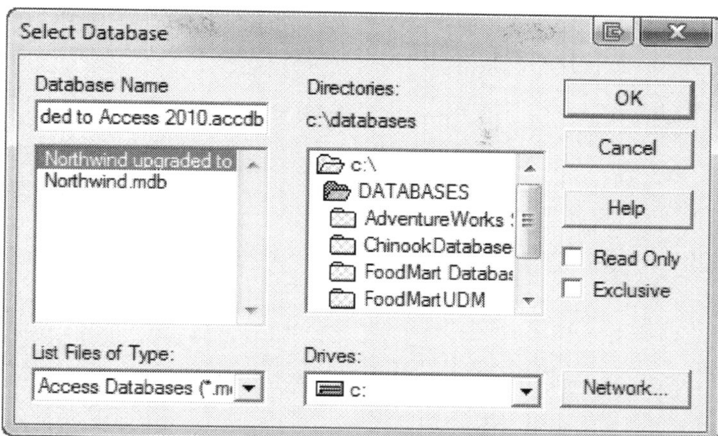

Figure 5-8 Microsoft Query File Finder

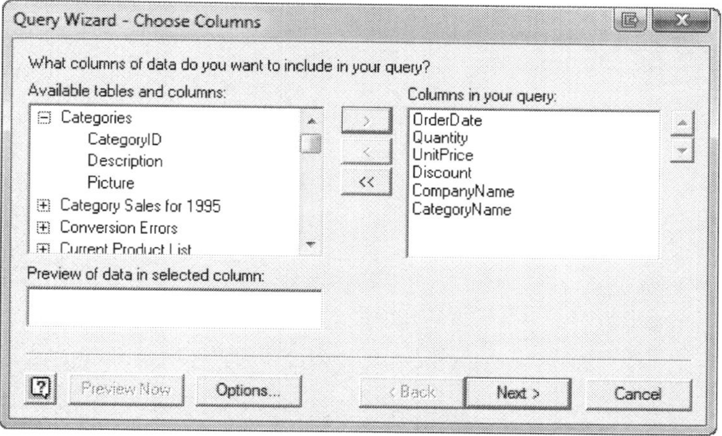

Figure 5-9 Microsoft Query Field Selector

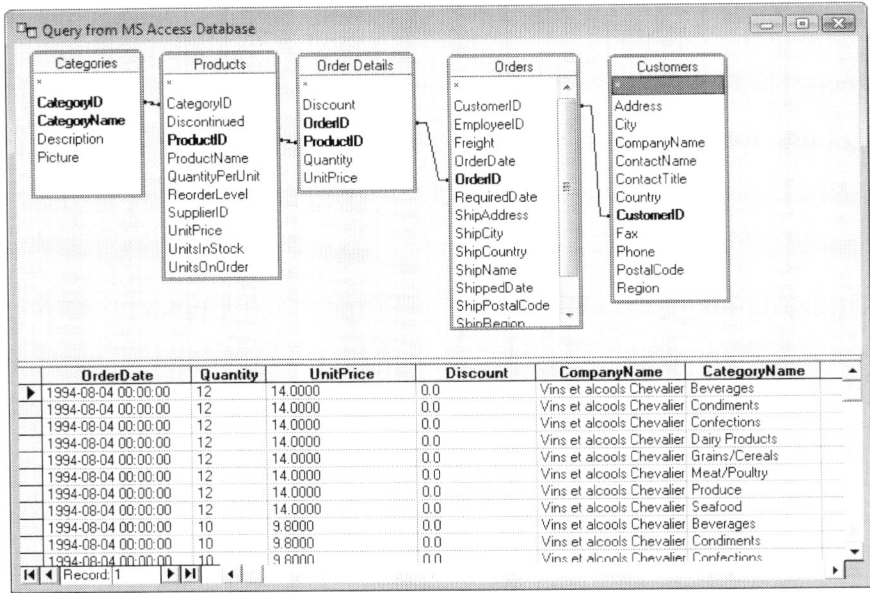

Figure 5-10 Completed Query

(For better viewing of this image, go to http://www.zerobits.info/bibook/bibookimages/)

From Text Files

Use the From Text option in the Data tab to bring up the Import Text File locator (file finder), select the file to import, and click the Open button. This will display a series of three Text Import Wizard dialog boxes (not shown) where you will specify the file type (delimited or fixed width), the delimiter character or the column widths, and the column data format. Clicking the finish button on the third dialog box will take you to the Import Data dialog box (Figure 5-2).

To import data from a Microsoft Word document just save it as a text file and then use the From Text external data option in Excel.

From XML Files

Both XML files on disk and XML data on the Internet can be imported into Excel by using the From XML Data Import command in the From Other Sources Option in the Data tab. Clicking the From XML Data Import command will display a Select Data Source dialog box (file finder) that you use to open a XML file. As usual, the From XML Data Import command will take you to the Import Data dialog box (Figure 5-2). XML files available on a Web page may be imported by inserting the URL into the File Name textbox of the Save Data source dialog box.

From Parameter Queries

In Appendix C we describe parameter queries as select queries that allow passing a parameter(s) to the query to specify a subset of the data to return, something like a dynamic filter. When a parameter query is executed, an Enter Parameter Value input box is displayed to prompt the user for the parameter value as shown in Figure 5-11 (a duplicate of Figure C-26).

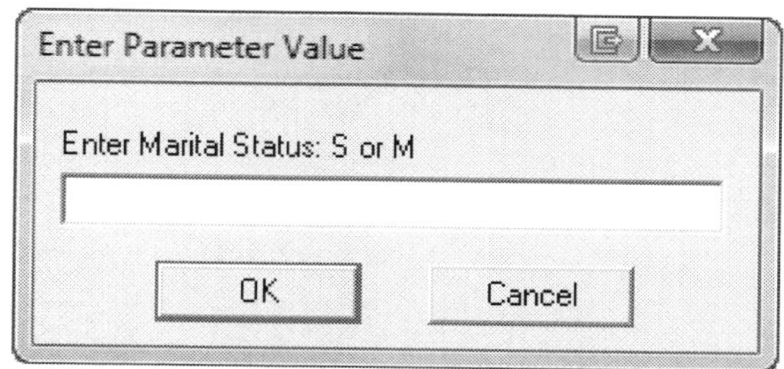

Figure 5-11 Input Box for Parameter Query Example

There are other ways to enter the parameter values than the prompts which can be bothersome. One way is to use a constant value for the parameter, and the other is to embed the parameter value in an Excel cell. All three approaches are managed by a Parameters dialog box. Before you can access that dialog box the underlying query must be run at least once in Excel to create an Excel Table there. Then, select any cell(s) inside the table and click Properties in the Table Tools Design tab External Table Data command group to display the External Data Properties dialog box as in Figure 5-12. Then, click the Connection Properties button directly to the right of the Name textbox to show the Connections Properties dialog box which has two tabs as shown in Figure 5-13. And finally, click the Parameters button on the Definition tab to bring up the Parameters dialog box in Figure 5-14 where the three options are listed.

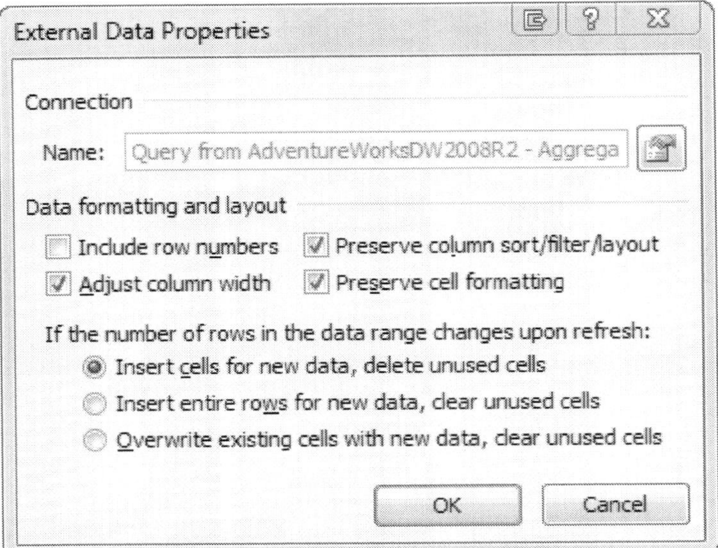

Figure 5-12 External Data Properties Dialog Box

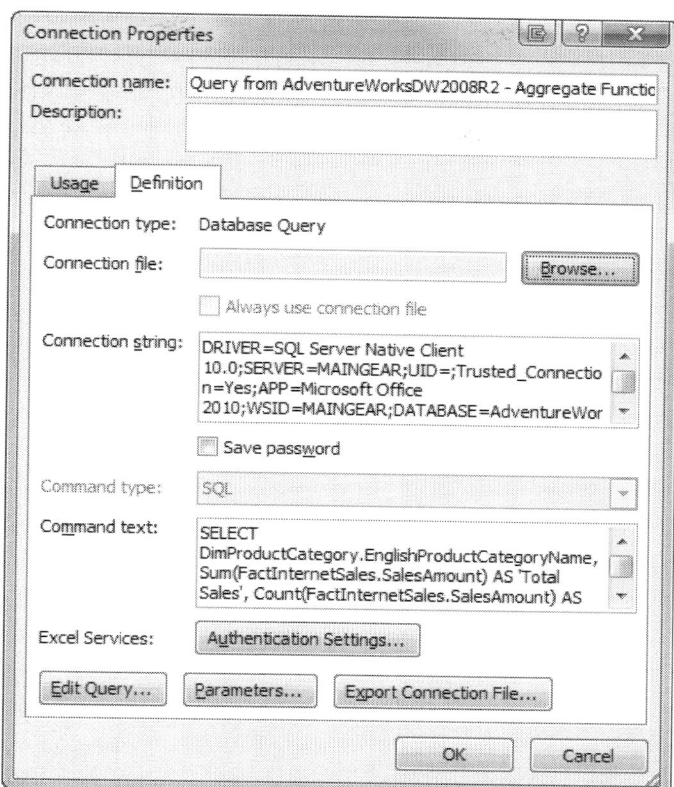

Figure 5-13 Connection Properties Dialog Box

The Parameters dialog box in Figure 5-14 is for a Microsoft Query on the AdventureWorks2008DW database which contains the Internet Sales Amount, Product, and Date fields. In addition, the query has two parameters: start date and end date. When values for these parameter are entered, the data returned will be limited to the records between these dates inclusively. In MS Query the expression in the Value parameter in the Criteria field for the date is "Between [Start Date] And [EndDate]." (Please refer to Appendix C for more information.)

Figure 5-15 shows a partial screen shot of the records from this query in an Excel table. Entering a string in the textbox for the first option for obtaining a parameter value in Figure 5-14 will result in that string appearing in the Enter Parameter Value input box, e.g., Enter Marital Status: S or M for the prompt in Figure 5-11. This prompt will override the one initially defined when the query was created. Selecting the Use the following value option and entering a valid value results in the query using that value without a prompt at each refresh. For example, if I selected Use the following value for the Start Date parameter and entered the value 9/1/2005, then the query would always use that as the start date until I changed the date or elected to use another parameter option.

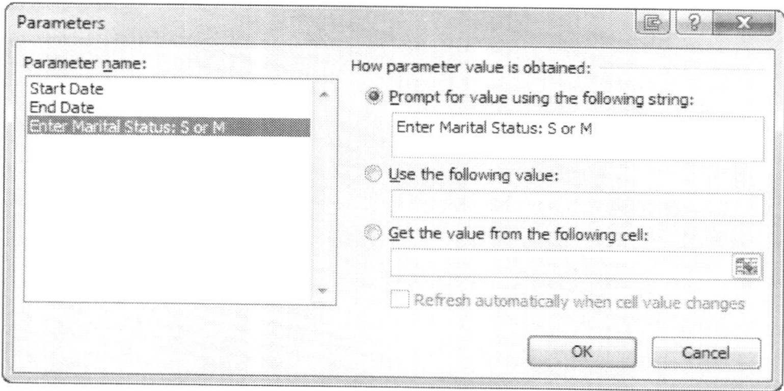

Figure 5-14 Parameters Dialog Box

Using the Get the value from the following cell option does just that—the query will use the value in the specified cell reference for the parameter value without prompting. To specify a cell for the parameter value select the Get the value option and then click in a cell in the Excel worksheet outside of the query table. A location something like ='Parameter Query'!,<cell reference> will be inserted into the textbox. For example, for the worksheet in Figure 5-15 I selected cell B1 for the start date and cell B2 for the end date. In addition, I labeled these values in the adjacent cells A1 and A2 so that I wouldn't forget what the values were. So, to change a parameter value I just enter a new value in the cell and, then refresh the table.

If an invalid data type is entered into a parameter value cell, Excel will display an error message. However, if the data type is valid, Excel will run the query even if the data value is out of range. For example, the earliest date in for Internet Sales in the AdventureWorksDW2008 database is 7/1/2005. If I entered a date for the Start Date parameter before that, the query would run producing the same results as in Figure 5-15. Entering 6/1/2001 as End Date parameter value would result in no records returned. One way to minimize parameter value errors is to use Excel data validation as described later in this Chapter.

	A	B	C
1	Start Date	8/1/2006	
2	End Date	8/10/2006	
3			
4	Sales Amount	Product Category	Date
5	2,443	Bikes	8/1/2006
6	1,000	Bikes	8/1/2006
7	1,000	Bikes	8/1/2006
8	2,443	Bikes	8/1/2006
9	783	Bikes	8/1/2006
10	2,443	Bikes	8/1/2006
11	2,049	Bikes	8/1/2006

Figure 5-15 Microsoft Query Example with Parameters

From the Internet

To import data from a table(s) on a Web page use the From Web option in the Data tab to display the New Web Query dialog box shown in Figure 5-16 which includes a bare-bones browser. Enter the URL for a Web page and click Go and the page will be displayed. Note that browser does not have a window maximize button in the upper right corner so to enlarge the window just drag the window boundaries. Importable tables on the page will be indicated by an arrow inside a small yellow box. When the box is clicked to select a table(s), the arrow will switch to a check mark. You may select more than one table on a page. If you do not save the table at this time as an IQY (Internet Query file), the connection will be embedded in and available only in the current workbook. If you want to access this table data in other workbooks, then save the connection as an IQY file via the Save Query button directly to the left of "Options. . ." on the toolbar. Then, click the Import button to bring up the Import Data dialog box as in Figure 5-2. Note that if you are connected to the Report Manager (see Chapter 4), then the initial URL and Web page displayed may be the Report Manager home page. And, yes you may import data from tables on the Report Server via the Report Manager. The connection in Figure 5-16 is to the MSN Money Central US Sector and Key Indexes Web page.

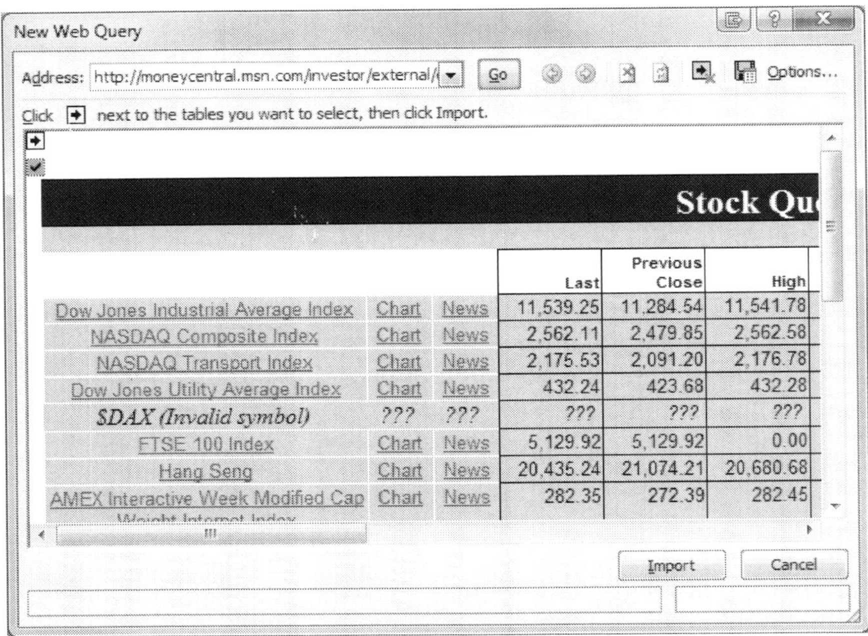

Figure 5-16 New Web Query Dialog Box

Web queries can also be parameterized when there is a parameter value(s) embedded in a URL. To create or modify parameterized Web queries you must work with IQY (Internet query files) files like the one for the Web query in Figure 5-16 presented in Table 5-1a. Note that the connection must have been saved as an IQY file before you can edit it. The first two lines in the file identify the query as a Web type version 1. From what I can determine both of these lines must be either present or absent in an IQF file. The next line is the URL followed by some attributes. All we need to do to turn this into a parameter query is to replace "usindex" in the URL with a parameter prompt expression such as ["Enter index name"]. Thus, the URL becomes http://moneycentral.msn.com/investor/market/["Enter index name"].aspx shown in Table 5-1b. To do this use Notepad to open the IQY file, make the modification, and then save it.

When the query is run, an Enter Parameter Value input box will pop up where the name of the financial index to import is entered, e.g., usindex for U.S. stock indexes like the Dow-Jones Industrials and the S&P 500, commodities for commodity prices, world markets for international stock indexes, etc. Executing this query returns a lot of unnecessary text along with the index data but it does demonstrate how to create a parameterized Web query.

```
WEB
1
http://moneycentral.msn.com/investor/external/excel/quotes.asp?
symbol=$INDU,$COMP,$TRAN,$UTIL,$DAX,$FTSE,$HSI,$IIX.X,$COMPX,$NI225,
$CAC,$SOX.X,$IUX,$OEX,$INX,$STI,$AOI,$CA:OSPTX

Selection=EntirePage
Formatting=All
PreFormattedTextToColumns=True
ConsecutiveDelimitersAsOne=True
SingleBlockTextImport=False
```

Table 5-1a Web Query IQY File

```
WEB
1
http://moneycentral.msn.com/investor/market/["Enter index name"].aspx
Selection=EntirePage
Formatting=All
PreFormattedTextToColumns=True
ConsecutiveDelimitersAsOne=True
SingleBlockTextImport=False
```

Table 5-1b Web Query with Parameter

Table 5-1 MSN Money Central IQY File

Data Acquisition Wrap-Up

The last point to make about data acquisition is that Visual Basic for Applications (VBA) can be used as a last resort for acquiring external data or for customizing its workbook location or its format. Please see other sources for information about VBA code.

Data Inspection and Cleaning

Inspection is the process of examining data to assess data quality by identifying errors and aberration; cleaning is the process of correcting those errors. To do this we need to understand the structure of the data, the nature of the data source(s), and the context in which the data are used. In this chapter we focus on tabularized data (Excel tables) from external data sources. Examples of data flaws that we should be on the lookout for when inspecting data are listed on the next page:

- Duplications, e.g., duplicate records or fields
- Misspellings
- Inconsistencies
- Unexpected values
- Null values
- Data type and format irregularities
- Invalid values
- Spurious values
- Multiple values for the same object type such as the title Doctor and Dr.
- Consistency among fields, e.g. area codes and geographic regions
- Outliers and exceptions
- Suspicious distributions of values
- Downright incorrect values (difficult to find)

The primary requisite in data inspection and cleaning is knowing your data. There are many flaws beyond the obvious such as misspellings, nulls, and perhaps duplications to detect that require intimate knowledge about the data. So, when dealing with new data take time to familiarize yourself in advance with the data source(s) by examining available metadata, schema, table designs, ETL processes, and other documentation. Next, eyeball the data to look for things that don't seem right and produce some quick plots to enhance your understanding of it. Then, proceed with Excel to identify and correct errors. Excel's tools that are particularly useful for inspection and cleaning are described below.

The example data that we will use is a sample of reseller sales data from the AdventureWorks2008DW database using the Order Date (FullDateAlternateKey), Order Quantity, Sales Amount, Product Category, Product Subcategory, Sales Territory, and Country fields. I created a sample of 35 records by using the Sample Data tool (see Chapter 10) on the Data Mining tab on an Excel table with all 60,855 records in it. A partial screen shot of the sample data is shown in Figure 5-21. I also added an additional record (row) with erroneous data, e.g., 9/1/1901 for the Order Date. This faulty record, highlighted in orange, is row 37 in the figure.

	A	B	C	D	E
1	Order Date	Order Quantity	Tota lProduct Cost	Product Name	Product Category
20	2/1/2007	1	$486.71	Road-650 Red, 62	Bikes
21	3/1/2007	1	$10.31	Cable Lock	Accessories
22	3/1/2007	3	$41.63	Sport-100 Helmet, Blue	Accessories
23	4/1/2007	6	$174.48	Long-Sleeve Logo Jersey, M	Clothing
24	5/1/2007	4	$62.68	Full-Finger Gloves, M	Clothing
25	7/1/2007	7	$10,373.57	Touring-1000 Blue, 50	Bikes
26	8/1/2007	1	$17.98	LL Mountain Pedal	Components
27	8/1/2007	4	$2,852.32	Road-550-W Yellow, 40	Bikes
28	12/1/2007	1	$77.92	LL Crankset	Components
29	1/1/2008	2	$2,165.02	Road-350-W Yellow, 44	Bikes
30	1/1/2008	2	$1,510.30	Touring-2000 Blue, 60	Bikes
31	2/1/2008	5	$207.86	Short-Sleeve Classic Jersey, L	Clothing
32	5/1/2008	2	$922.89	Touring-3000 Yellow, 44	Bikes
33	5/1/2008	3	$2.57	Patch Kit/8 Patches	Accessories
34	5/1/2008	1	$360.94	ML Road Frame-W - Yellow, 44	Components
35	6/1/2008	1	$1,481.94	Touring-1000 Blue, 50	Bikes
36	6/1/2008	1	$601.74	HL Touring Frame - Blue, 50	Components
37	9/1/1901	56	-$987.00		Bicycles
38					

Figure 5-21 Sample Data Set

Tagging suspect rows, say by changing the cell fill color as I did in Figure 5-21, is useful as you proceed through the various inspection tools. When inspection is completed, you can sort or filter the table by however you tagged the suspect rows so that you may work with them as a group. I tagged row 36 by clicking on its row index (37) and used the fill color button in the Font command group on Home tab.

Spelling Checker (Review tab)

The spell checker is located on the left side of the Review tab. To use it select a range of cells or one or more columns to check and then click Spelling. Note that if you click a field (column) name in the top row of a table, the spell checker will iterate through the entire table unless you terminate it.

Sorting

Sorting by a field(s) is an easy way to identify erroneous values, especially blanks and nulls. You can sort the data by using the down arrowheads on the column name or the Sort dialog box. For the former click an arrowhead and select the sort option that is appropriate. If the down arrowheads are not visible, click the Filter button in the Sort & Filter command group on the Data tab. If the column has a date format, then the options are oldest to newest or newest to oldest. For numbers the options are smallest to largest or largest to smallest. And, for strings A to Z or Z to A. To sort by multiple fields use a backwards sequence. For example, to sort the sample data by Order Date and

Order Quantity with Order Quantity sorted within Order Data first sort by Order Quantity and then by Order Date.

To display the Sort dialog box (Figure 5-22) click on Sort in the Sort & Filter command group on the Data tab. There you can add any number of levels (fields) to the sort and specify the sort order for each level. When you add a level use the drop-down listbox to select from the available fields. The sort depicted in the figure is the same one as described in the paragraph above. You may also select what to sort on (values, cell color, font color, or cell icon). The Options button allows you to choose to sort with case sensitive on or off.

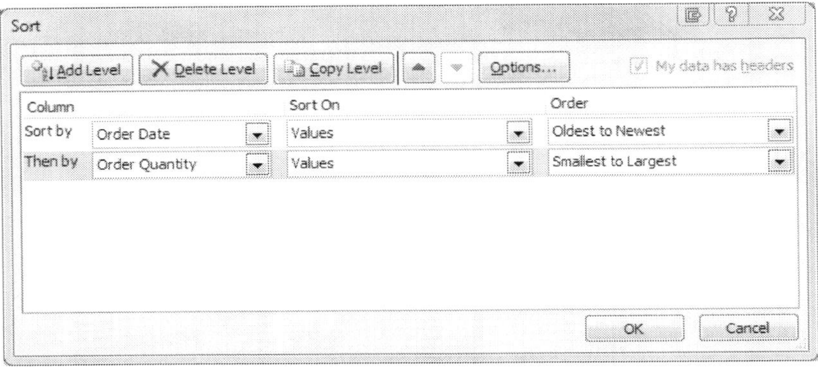

Figure 5-22 Sort Dialog Box

So, what good does it do? Erroneous values will usually rise to the top or fall to the bottom of the sort order so you can easily find them for repair or deletion. For example, when I sorted the sample data above the erroneous record sorted to the top because it had the earliest order date.

Filtering

Filtering helps to validate data, i.e., to check if the data in a field has the correct data type and within the acceptable range of values. There are two ways to filter data in a table. One is to use the down arrowhead on the column name to bring up the sort/filter menu as in Figure 5-23 for the Order Quantity field. The first thing to notice there is that all of the values in the column are shown in a list so you can filter values by selecting (keeping) or deselecting (hiding) them. Erroneous values will show up there as well. At the bottom of this list is the value "Blanks" which is great to use to identify blank entries. More advanced filters may be created by hovering the mouse pointer over the Number Filters bar to display the filter criteria menu on the right in Figure 5-23. Clicking one of the criteria options brings up the Custom AutoFilter dialog box in Figure 5-24 where you specify values in the textbox on the right side. In the example I am filtering Total Product Cost for values less than or equal to zero. When I clicked OK, the data were filtered showing only the one erroneous record with a Sales Amount of -$987.00. With this option the records will be filtered in place, i.e., only the records that satisfy the filter criteria will be displayed in the original location of the table. To turn off the filter and restore all of the hidden records click the Filter button (icon) in the Sort & Filter command group on the Data tab.

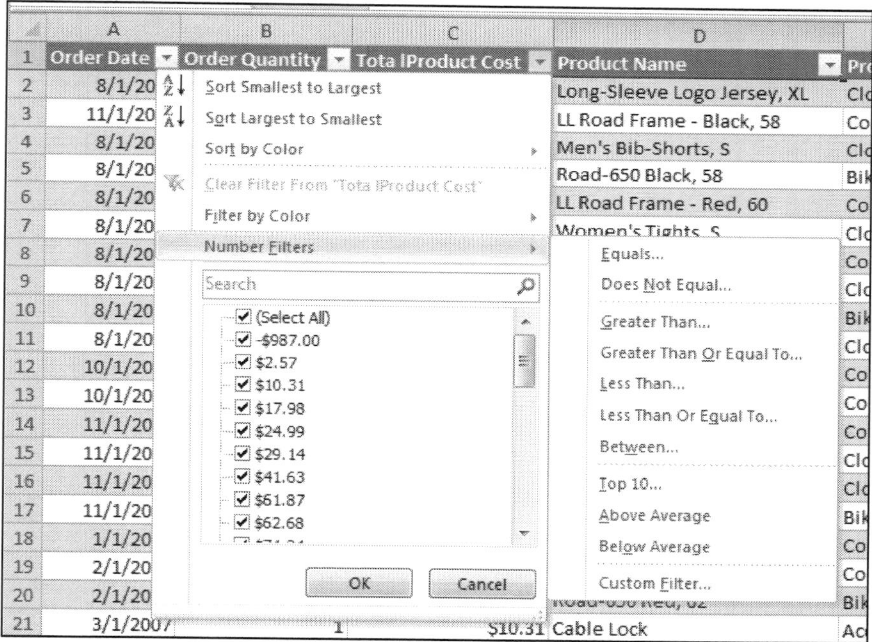

Figure 5-23 Sort/Filter Menu

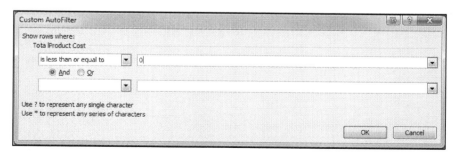

Figure 5-24 Custom AutoFilter Dialog Box

The other way to filter data is to click on Advanced in the Sort & Filter command group on the Data tab to display the Advanced Filter dialog box (Figure 5-25a). The radio buttons at the top set the location to which the filtered data will be returned: in-place as described in the first option above or to another location either on the current worksheet or a different worksheet. Note that in this case the term “list” is equivalent to table because we are working within an Excel table. However, we can also filter an un-tabularized range of data (a list) so the term “list” in the dialog box can refer to either format.

For the table that we are working in the List range should correspond to the table range. If not, adjust the List range accordingly. The Advanced Filter uses cells in a worksheet outside of the table range to specify the filter criteria somewhat like the values for parameter queries discussed earlier in this chapter. In the example, I set the criteria to Sales Amount greater than or equal to $1,000 and Product Category equals Bikes as shown in Figure 5-25b. To specify the criteria I copied the field names to be filtered to a location outside of the table range and specified the criteria below it. In this case the upper left cell in the criteria range is A39 as shown in the Criteria range textbox in Figure 5-25a. Note that Excel references the cells by the notation <‘worksheet name’>!<cell range>, e.g., Sample Data’!$G$7:$H$9 for cells G7 to H8 in the worksheet named Sample Data. (Note: ! is called the bang operator.) The filter criteria cells can be in the worksheet in which the table is located or a different worksheet.

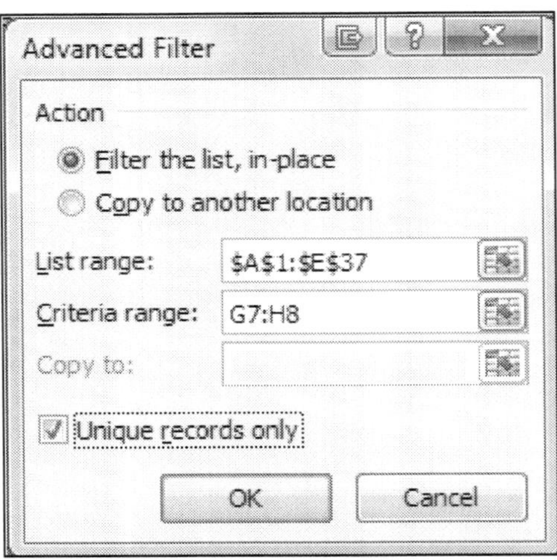

Figure 5-25a Advanced Filter Dialog Box

	G	H
7	Product Cost	Product Category
8	>=1000	Bikes

Figure 5-25b Advanced Filter Criteria

Figure 5-25 Advanced Filter Dialog Box and Criteria

The Copy to another location in Figure 5-25a will enable the Copy to textbox in which you select the upper left cell for the filtered record set. For example, if I clicked in the enabled textbox and then clicked on cell A42 of the worksheet in which the table is located, the Copy to cell reference would be changed to Sample Data'!$A$42. Clicking OK will insert the filtered records starting at that cell. Excel gets upset and displays the error message (Figure 5-26) if you try to copy the filtered data to another worksheet. A workaround is to start the filter in the worksheet in which you want the filtered records located. So, navigate to the different worksheet prior to initiating the Advanced Filter dialog box, select Copy to another location, click on the List range textbox, and then navigate to the worksheet containing the data table. There select the entire table, click the Criteria range textbox, and copy the range into it. Return to the new worksheet, enter the Copy to location, and finish by clicking OK. If checked, the Unique records only checkbox in Figure 5-25a returns only one row of a set of duplicate records.

Figure 5-26 Advanced Filter Error Message

Remove Duplicates Tool

Remove Duplicates in the Data Tools command group on the Data tab automatically finds and deletes records that contain duplicate values. It may also be accessed with the Remove Duplicates option in the Tools command group of the Table Tools - Design tab. The Remove Duplicates dialog box for our example Excel table is shown in Figure 5-27 where all of the fields in the table are listed and selected by default. Use the Unselect All button to do just that. Note the check on the My data has headers box. This essentially means that the data are in Excel table format. However, if you are working with un-tabularized data, unchecking the box results in the columns having their default names A, B, C, ... If I clicked Ok in Figure 5-27 as is, the records displayed would remain the same because there are no exact duplicates in this set. That is, the tool searches for duplicates with matches for the fields that are selected and so far all fields are selected. However, if I had selected the Order Data and Product Category fields only, then the returned set of records would contain only one record for a unique Order Date - Product Category combination. For example, since Row 21 and 22 in Figure 5-21 have duplicate values in the Order Data and Product Category fields, the result of applying this filter would remove one of those records from the set. To return to the full set of records after running this filter us the Undo action on the Quick Access Toolbar.

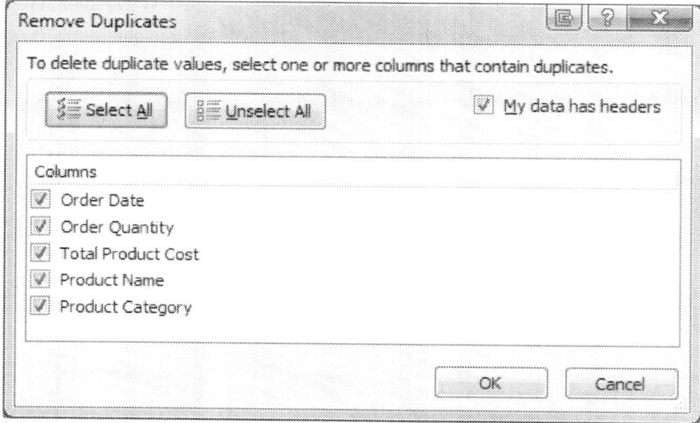

Figure 5-27 Advanced Remove Duplicates Dialog Box

Another way to find duplicate records is to use conditional formatting. Please see the section in the next chapter about that.

Highlight Exceptions Tool

The Highlight Exceptions tool is available on the Table Tools - Analyze tab. As you can see in the description provided in the Highlight Exceptions dialog box in Figure 5-28 this tool detects non-conforming rows and generates a report in a separate worksheet. Exclude unique identifier fields from the column selections so as to reduce having spurious exceptions displayed. I selected the fields shown in the figure for illustrative purposes only. When you click Run, another dialog box in Figure 5-29 will pop up showing the completion of a series of tasks. Since the processing is being done in SQL Server Analysis Services, it may take some time to complete, especially if there are many records in the data table.

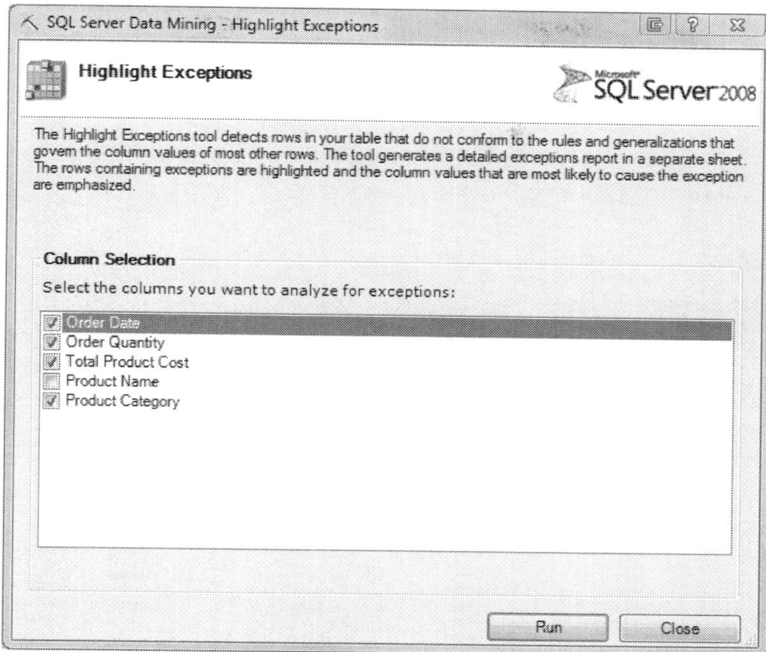

Figure 5-28 Highlight Exceptions Dialog Box

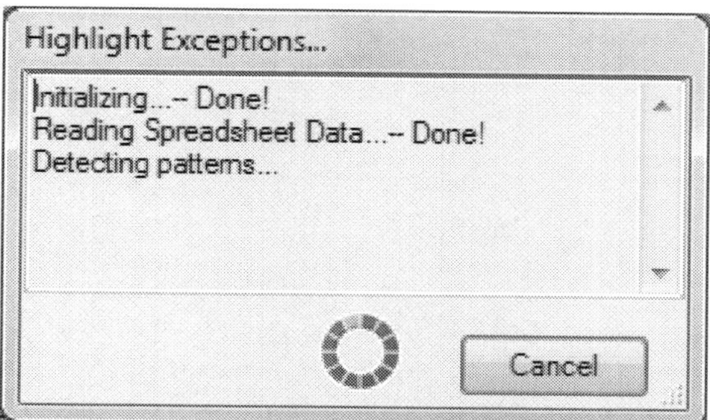

Figure 5-29 Highlight Exceptions Tasks

When processing is complete, a new worksheet containing the exception report named Selected Data Outliers will be created in the workbook as in Figure 5-30. The exception report has two columns: one showing the fields selected for processing and the other the number of outliers found in each field. Note that the colored bars in the outlier cells are like bars in a bar chart for the outlier frequencies. The Exceptions tool has an Exception Threshold parameter that can range between 0 and 100 with 0 selecting all rows in the table as exceptions and 100 selecting none. The default value is 75.

	A	B	C	D	E
1	Highlight Exceptions Report for Selected Data				
2	The outlier cells are highlighted in the original table.				
3					
4	Exception threshold (more or fewer exceptions)	75			
5					
6	Column	Outliers			
7	Order Date	0			
8	Order Quantity	1			
9	Total Product Cost	2			
10	Product Category	0			
11	Total	3			
12					

Figure 5-30 Highlight Exceptions Report

The Exceptions tool also highlights the records in the Excel table that it identified as possible exceptions as shown in Figure 5-31. The highlighting is linked to the Exception threshold so that changing the number of outliers will be dynamically reflected in the number of highlighted records. For a data table with many records you can sort a column by color to group all highlighted records for easier inspection. Remember that since the Exceptions tool uses Analysis Services for processing, SQL Server must be running and available to access it.

	A	B	C	D	E
1	Order Date	Order Quantity	Total Product Cost	Product Name	Product Category
2	8/1/2005	4	$126.90	Long-Sleeve Logo Jersey, XL	Clothing
3	11/1/2005	4	$704.80	LL Road Frame - Black, 58	Components
4	8/1/2006	4	$148.48	Men's Bib-Shorts, S	Clothing
5	8/1/2006	3	$1,460.12	Road-650 Black, 58	Bikes
6	8/1/2006	2	$374.31	LL Road Frame - Red, 60	Components
7	8/1/2006	2	$61.87	Women's Tights, S	Clothing
8	8/1/2006	2	$374.31	LL Road Frame - Red, 60	Components
9	8/1/2006	3	$29.14	Half-Finger Gloves, S	Clothing
10	8/1/2006	3	$1,460.12	Road-650 Red, 44	Bikes
11	8/1/2006	8	$247.47	Women's Tights, S	Clothing

Figure 5-31 Highlighted Exceptions in the Data Table

Data Analysis Option - Descriptive Statistics

If you have a good understanding about the data in a table, descriptive statistics may help you to decide if there are problems with it. Descriptive Statistics is one of the options available in the Analysis Tools as shown in the Data Analysis Dialog box (Figure 5-32) accessed from the Analysis command group on the Data tab. Clicking OK will bring up the Descriptive Statistics dialog box in Figure 5-33. There you specify the data range (I selected the Order Quantity column in the example data table); indicate how the data are grouped and if labels are in the first row; designate the output location; and select the statistics to present. The result is presented in a table as in Figure 5-34.

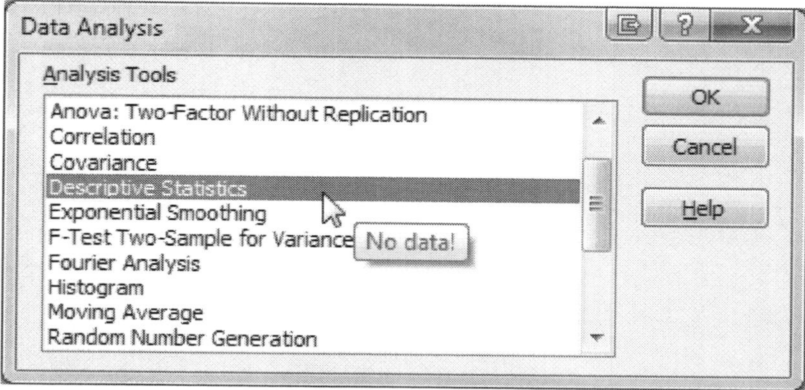

Figure 5-32 Data Analysis Tools

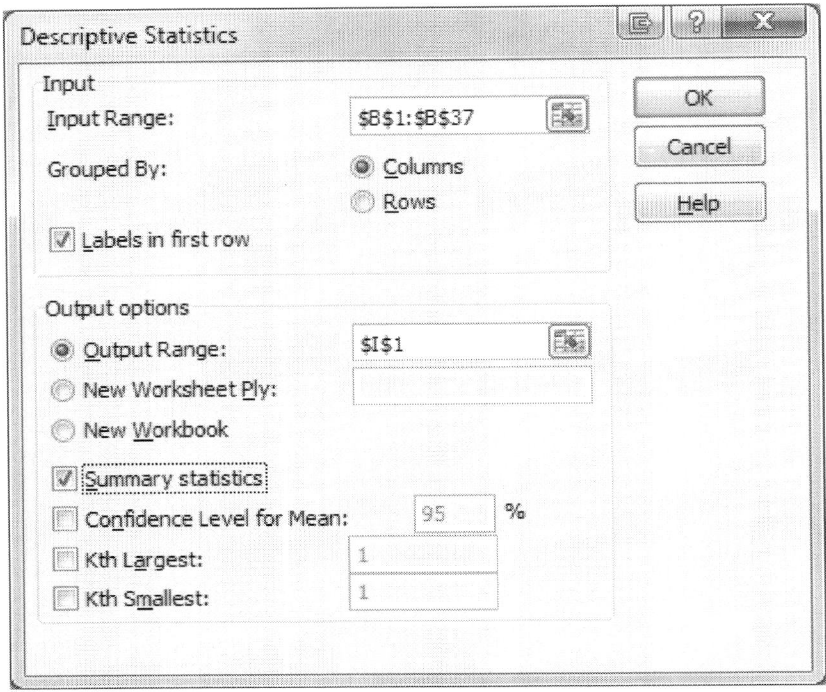

Figure 5-33 Descriptive Statistics Dialog Box

Order Quantity	
Mean	4.361111
Standard Error	1.510888
Median	3
Mode	1
Standard Deviation	9.065327
Sample Variance	82.18016
Kurtosis	32.44699
Skewness	5.575448
Range	55
Minimum	1
Maximum	56
Sum	157
Count	36

Figure 5-34 Sample Data Tool

I know what kurtosis and skewness are but I can never remember what the values mean so I ignore them. You can produce descriptive statistics for multiple columns but they must be contiguous, and they are only calculated for numerical data.

This is probably a good place to note that you can display descriptive statistics in a total row at the bottom of a table by checking Total Row in the Table Style Options command group on the Table Tools - Design tab. You may select one statistic from the list displayed for each column (field) by clicking the down arrowhead in a Total row cell as shown in Figure 5-35. The Total row in the figure calculates the sum of the values in the example's Order Quantity column.

33	5/1/2008	3	$2.57
34	5/1/2008	1	$360.94
35	6/1/2008	1	$1,481.94
36	6/1/2008	1	$601.74
37	9/1/1901	56	-$987.00
38	Total	157	
39		None	
40		Average	
		Count	
41		Count Numbers	
		Max	
42		Min	
43		Sum	
		StdDev	
44		Var	
45		More Functions...	

Figure 5-35 Total Row Value List

Two other descriptive statistics tools are available in the Analysis ToolPak: Histograms and Rank and Percentile. The Histogram tool creates a frequency distribution table based on value intervals that you specify (called Bins). An example histogram table for a sample of AdventureWorks2008 reseller data is shown in Figure 5-36a. The Rank and Percentile tool arranges numerical values in descending order and adds a cumulative percent column to the output table as in Figure 5-36b for a sample of ten rows of reseller data. You can easily create column charts for these tables by using Excel's charting tools.

Bin	Frequency
1000	28
2000	4
3000	2
4000	0
5000	0
6000	0
7000	0
8000	0
More	1

Figure 5-36a Histogram Output

C	D	E	F
Point	Column1	Rank	Percent
1	$10,373.57	1	100.00%
2	$2,165.02	2	88.80%
3	$1,481.94	3	77.70%
4	$704.80	4	66.60%
5	$486.71	5	55.50%
6	$360.94	6	44.40%
7	$207.86	7	33.30%
8	$77.92	8	22.20%
9	$41.63	9	11.10%
10	$10.31	10	0.00%

Figure 5-36b Rank and Percentile Output

Figure 5-36 Total Row Value List

Data Validation Tool

The Data Validation dialog box (Figure 5-37) is accessed by the Data Validation option in the Data Tools command group on the Data tab. To use it, first select the cell values in a table column that you want to validate (as an example I selected the Order Quantity column) and then bring up the dialog box. The default validation criteria, "Any value," does no validation. Selecting another criteria from the list will enable textboxes relevant to the particular criteria as shown in Figure 5-38a. When I choose Whole Number for the criteria (Figure 5-30a), the Data textbox in Figure 5-38b was displayed. After I choose the less than or equal to criteria, the Maximum textbox was enabled. Note again that these value boxes are peculiar to the specific criteria selected, e.g., the between criteria has a minimum and maximum textbox. The Input Message and Error Alert tabs in Figure 5-37 are useful for data entry but of no value during inspection so we'll leave them alone.

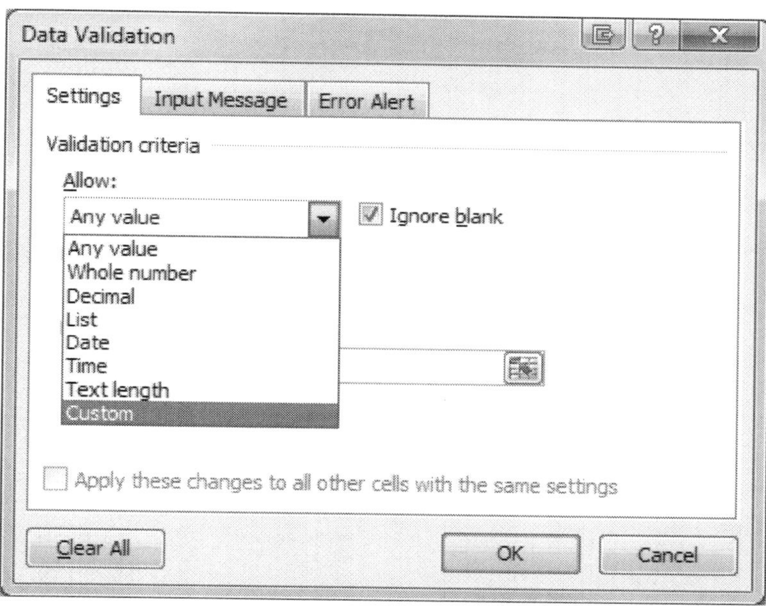

Figure 5-37 Data Validation Dialog Box

Figure 5-38a

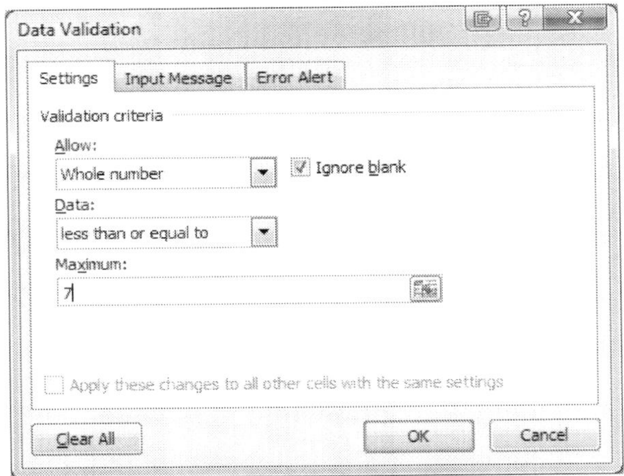

Figure 5-38b

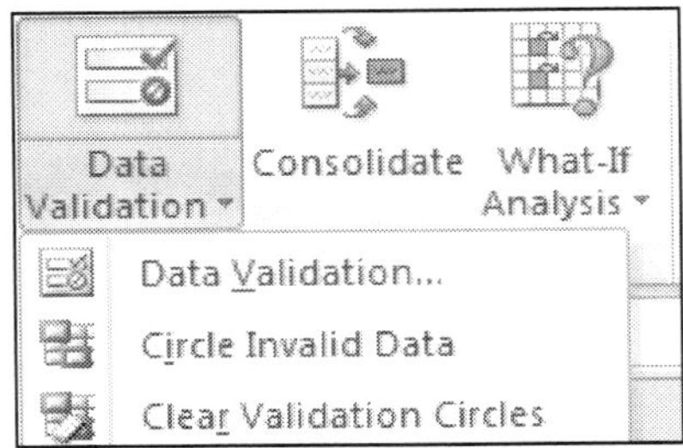

Figure 5-38c

Figure 5-38 Data Validation Options

When you are finished specifying the validation rule and click OK, nothing will appear to happen. But, if you return to the Data Validation option in the Data tab and click the Circle Invalid Data as in Figure 5-38c, then the invalid data will be circled as shown in the partial screen shot of the Excel table in Figure 5-39. Neat!

17	8/1/2006	2
18	5/1/2008	1
19	10/1/2006	3
20	8/1/2006	8
21	11/1/2006	8
22	2/1/2008	5

Figure 5-39 Data Validation Circled Invalid Data

Explore Data Tool

The Explore Data option in the Data Preparation command group on the Data Mining tab takes you through a series of three dialog boxes (Figures 5-39 a, b and c) to produce a histogram showing the frequency of occurrence of ranges of values in a particular field (column). You use the first dialog box to specify the data source (a table or range), and the second to select a field. The resulting histogram is displayed in the third as is shown for the Product Cost field. The Buckets combination box in Figure 5-40c controls the number of intervals that the data will be divided into for the histogram. A bucket is an interval of data. In this case it used eight buckets and displayed eight bars.

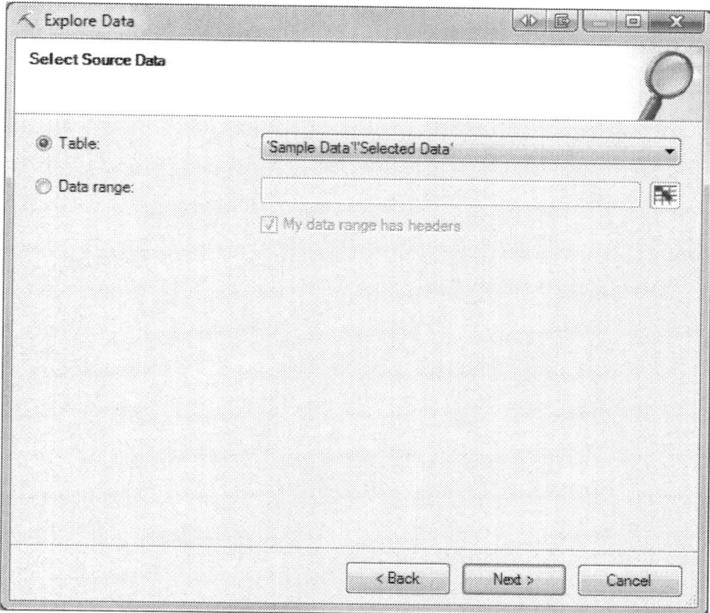

Figure 5-40a Explore Data Dialog Box - Window 1

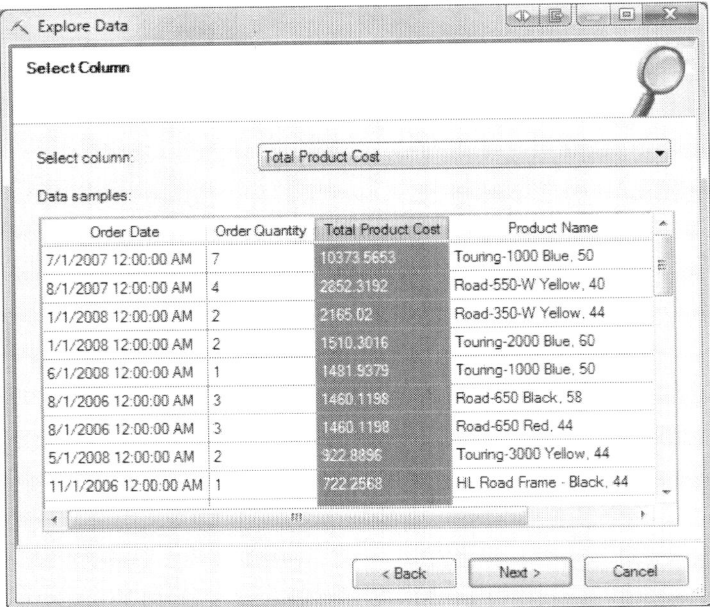

Figure 5-40b Explore Data Dialog Box - Window 2

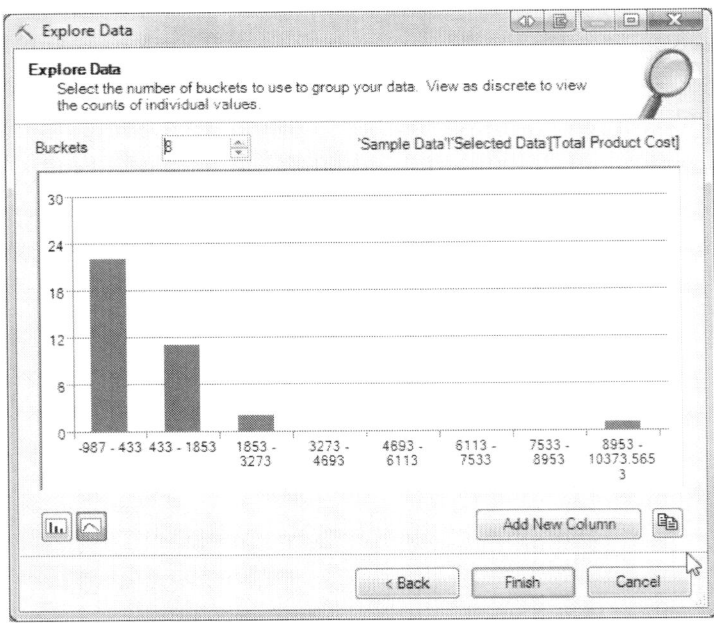

Figure 5-40c Explore Data Dialog Box - Window 3

Clean Data tool - Outliers

The Clean Data option is also available on the Data Mining tab. The Outliers Wizard identifies outliers in a field or data range. It uses the same dialog boxes as shown in Figure 5-40a and b to identify the data source and field to process and then displays the Specify Thresholds dialog boxes as in Figure 5-41a and b. The charts in that figures plot field values on the horizontal axis and frequency of occurrence on the vertical axis. In the line graph rendition selected by clicking the line graph icon in the lower left corner you use the Minimum textbox to specify low values to truncate and Maximum textbox high values. You may enter values in the textboxes or use the sliders to set them. The hatched area on the charts indicates those values that will be processed as outliers. In the example for the Order Quantity field I choose to tag those values over 10 as outliers. The Resolution textbox seems to control how many "intervals" are shown on the horizontal axis.

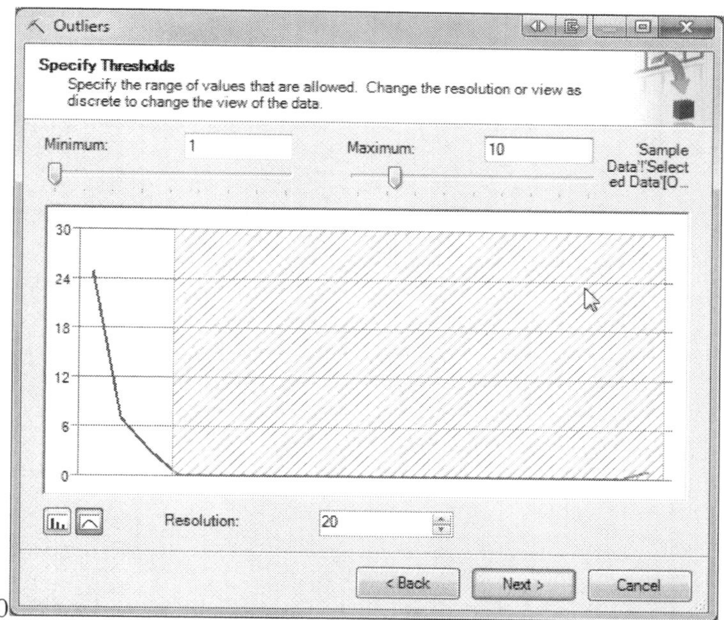

Figure 5-41a Outliers Wizard - Line Graph

The bar chart rendition (Figure 5-41b), displayed by clicking on the bar chart icon in the lower left corner, arranges values or categories in descending order on frequency, i.e., the highest frequency value is displayed on the left with the next highest on its right, and so on. The Minimum textbox sets the cut off frequency for the low end. In the example the Order Quantity the Minimum value of 2 defines all order quantities less than 2 as outliers. Order quantities of 5, 6, 7, and 56 only occurred once.

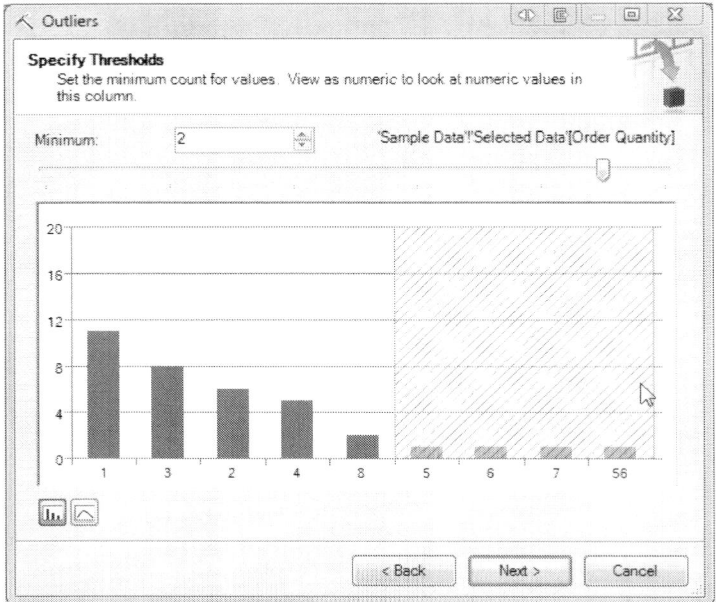

Figure 5-41b Outliers Wizard - Bar Chart

The final dialog box of the Outlier Wizard defines how the outliers will be handled. Figure 5-34a lists the options for the line graph rendition and Figure 5-42b for the bar chart rendition. The options are self-explanatory.

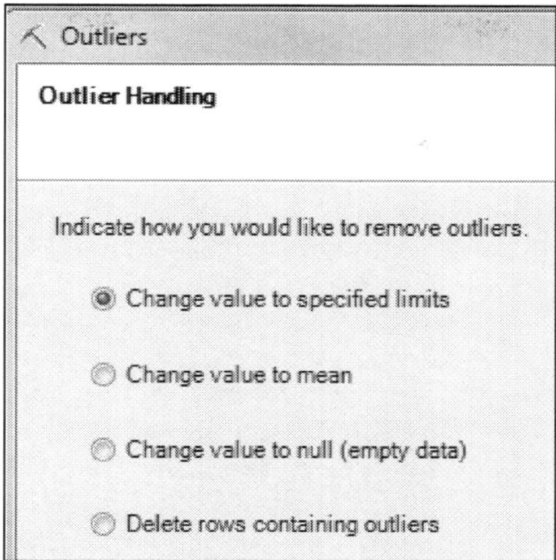

Figure 5-42a Line Graph

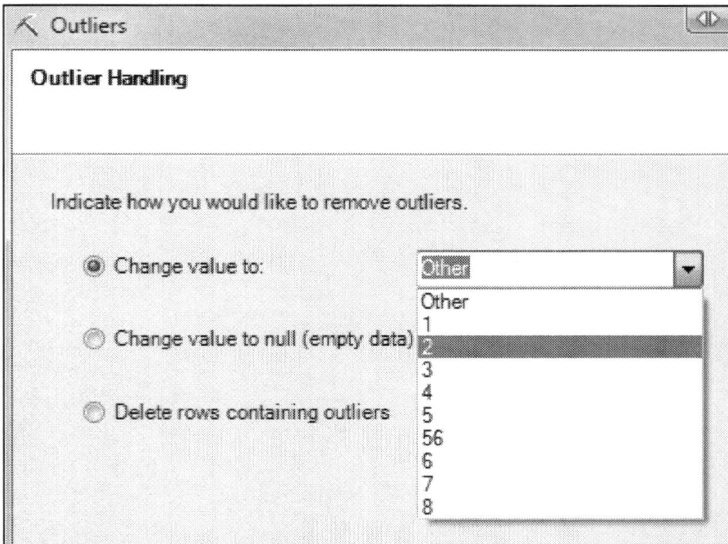

Figure 5-42b Bar Chart

Figure 5-42 Outliers Wizard - Outlier handling

An interesting example of using the Outliers tool is shown in Figure 5-43 for the Product Category field. Here the category error "Bicycles" is easily detected.

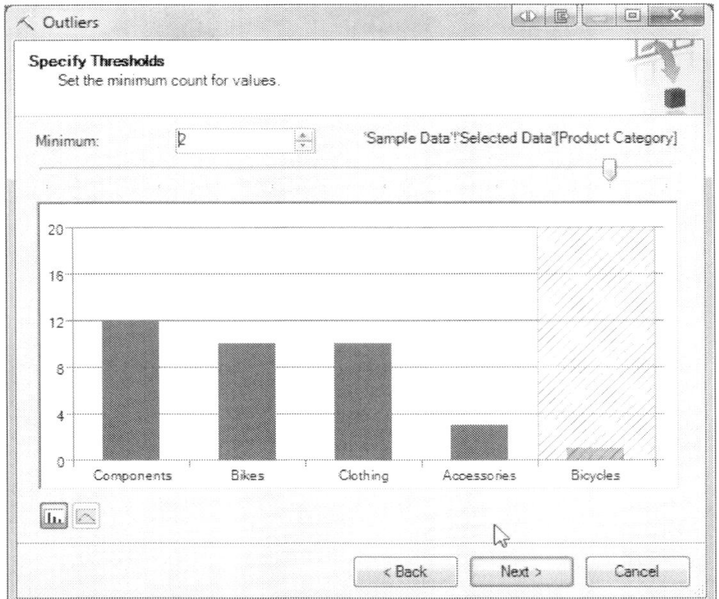

Figure 5-43 Outliers Wizard - Product Category Example

Removing Spaces and Non-Printing Characters from Text

Many of Excel's formulas are useful for cleaning data. Examples are the Clean, Trim, and Substitute functions that assist in removing pesky spaces and non-printing characters that crop up in string data. Clean removes the first 32 nonprinting characters from text; Trim removes the space character; And Substitute replaces specific text in a string.

Data Transformation

Data transformation takes data in one form and converts it into another form. Excel is really good at this and offers a multitude of functions for that purpose. We will only look at a few of those here along with some Excel tools that are particularly useful for data transformation. Please see other Excel books for more extensive coverage of additional functions.

Fill From Example Tool

The Fill From Example tool helps to fill in values for a partially populated field (column) or a new field that you have added to a table. In an example for 50 Internet Sales records I added a US Bikes field (column J) to the table (Figure 5-44) that will have values of US Bikes and Not US Bikes. For the moment ignore column K (USBikes_Extended). I rearranged the rows so that the ones that I wanted to tag as examples would be at the top so the whole worksheet would not have to be shown in the figure, and I entered the US Bikes column values for six of the records out of the 50 total. My intention is to have records with United States in the Country field and Bikes in the Product Category field tagged as US Bikes. All other records should be identified as Not US Bikes. This is a fairly useless example but it does demonstrate the process.

The Fill From Example tool will discern the pattern in the placement of the US Bikes - Not US Bikes tags that I inserted and then will apply that pattern to the 44 unclassified records. The Tool is initiated by clicking the Fill From Example button on the Table Tools - Analyze tab to display the dialog box in Figure 5-44 where you select the column containing the examples (US Bikes). At this point there are two alternative approaches: let the Tool select the columns to use for pattern recognition or specify those columns yourself. For the former just click the Run button; for latter click the "Choose columns to be used for analysis" phrase to open the Advanced Columns Selection dialog box (Figure 5-46), designate columns that should be used to identify a pattern, and return to the previous dialog box. Regardless of the approach, the Tool will insert a new column in the table, US_Bikes_Extended in this case, containing the values for the field that the pattern determined. This is column E in the example (Figure 5-44). You may use the tool iteratively so I if there are incorrectly tagged records, you can retag them and run the Tool again. Note that the more tags you supply the fewer errors the Tool should make.

	A	B	C	D	E
1	Sale Amount	Product Category	Country	US Bikes	US Bikes_Extended
2	3,578.27	Bikes	Australia		Not US Bikes
3	3,578.27	Bikes	United States	US Bikes	US Bikes
4	2,181.56	Bikes	Australia	Not US Bikes	Not US Bikes
5	2,071.42	Bikes	Germany		Not US Bikes
6	539.99	Bikes	United States	US Bikes	US Bikes
7	4.99	Accessories	United States	Not US Bikes	Not US Bikes
8	49.99	Clothing	United Kingdom	Not US Bikes	Not US Bikes
9	8.99	Accessories	France		Not US Bikes
10	69.99	Clothing	Australia		Not US Bikes
11	2,443.35	Bikes	Australia	Not US Bikes	Not US Bikes
12	539.99	Bikes	Germany		Not US Bikes
13	4.99	Accessories	United Kingdom		Not US Bikes
14	4.99	Accessories	United States	Not US Bikes	Not US Bikes
15	21.98	Accessories	United States		Not US Bikes

Figure 5-44 Fill From Example Data Table

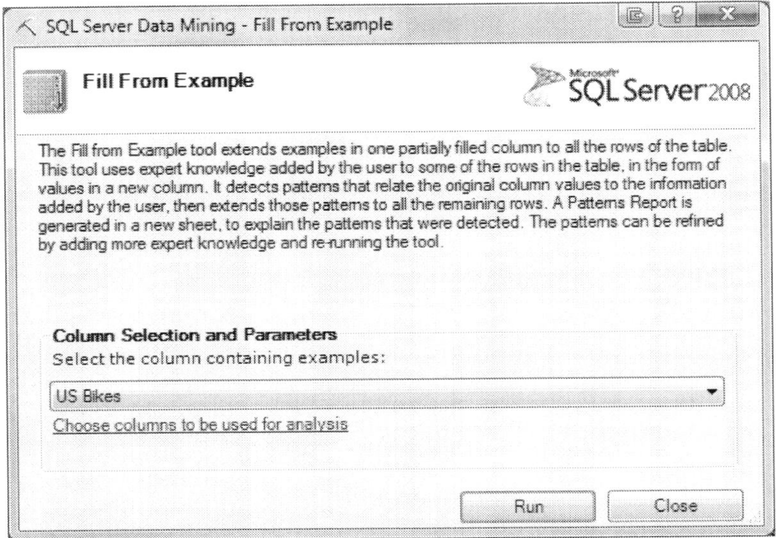

Figure 5-45 Fill From Example Dialog Box

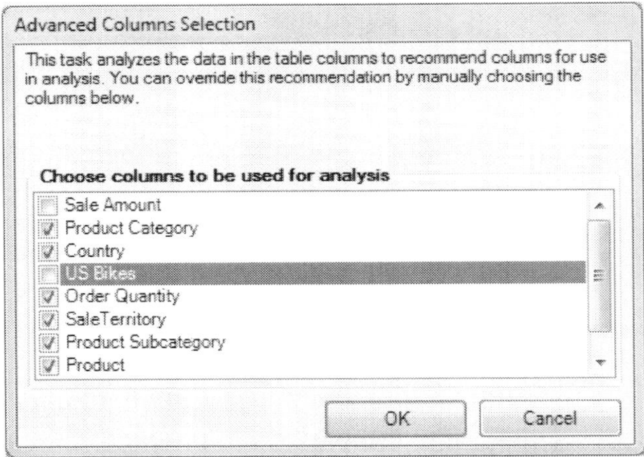

Figure 5-46 Fill From Example Column Selection

During processing the Tool also creates a Pattern Report in a separate worksheet (Figure 5-47) which shows how values in other fields relate to the field of interest and indicates the rules it used to assign new values. Figure 5-47 shows the report for when I let the Tool select the columns to process. The top four rows relate to categorizing Not US Bikes and the bottom eight rows US Bikes. For example, the Tool found that the Tires and Tubes products are probably not US Bikes (correct). Not all of the results make sense to me but maybe they do to the Tool.

	A	B	C	D
1	Pattern Report for 'US Bikes'			
2				
3	Key Influencers and their impact over the values of 'US Bikes'			
4	Filter by 'Column' or 'Favors' to see how various columns influence 'US Bikes'			
5	Column	Value	Favors	Relative Impact
6	Country	Australia	Not US Bikes	
7	Product Subcategory	Tires and Tubes	Not US Bikes	
8	Country	United Kingdom	Not US Bikes	
9	SaleTerritory	Australia	Not US Bikes	
10	Country	United States	US Bikes	
11	Sale Amount	2,168.120 - 3,578.270	US Bikes	
12	Product Category	Bikes	US Bikes	
13	SaleTerritory	Northwest	US Bikes	
14	SaleTerritory	Southwest	US Bikes	
15	Date	4/15/2006 12:00:00 AM - 12/8/2006 1:24:12 PM	US Bikes	
16	Product Subcategory	Road Bikes	US Bikes	
17	Sale Amount	1,257.592 - 2,168.120	US Bikes	

Figure 5-47 Fill From Example Pattern Report

Clean Data tool - Re-label

Another way to reclassify records is to use the Clean Data tool - Re-label in the Data Preparation command group of the Data Mining tab. Re-label is the second option in this tool—the other is the Outliers option discussed earlier. After selecting the source data with the Explore Data dialog box (Figure 5-40a), use the Select Column dialog box (Figure 5-48) to identify the field to use for input into the re-labeler, and then bring up the Re-label Data dialog box as in Figure 5-49. Specify a new label for each of the original labels by using the drop-down list box or by clicking twice on the new label box to enter a new name. Then, move on the next dialog box to select the destination (Figure 5-50) Click next and voila, in this case a new column (column G) with the new labels is inserted into the table (Figure 5-51).

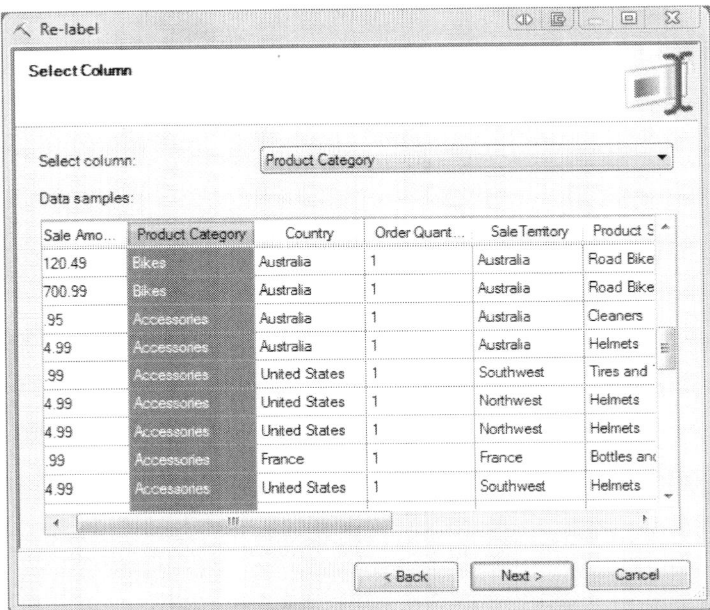

Figure 5-48 Re-label - Select Column

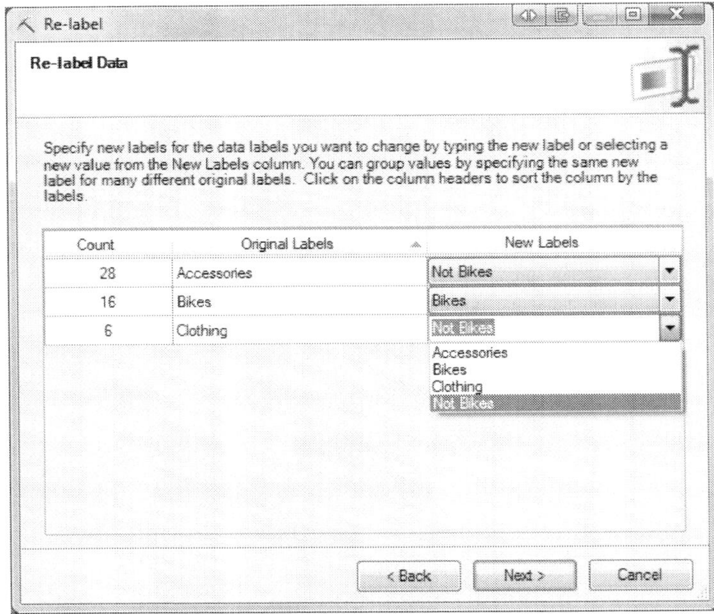

Figure 5-49 Re-label Data Dialog Box

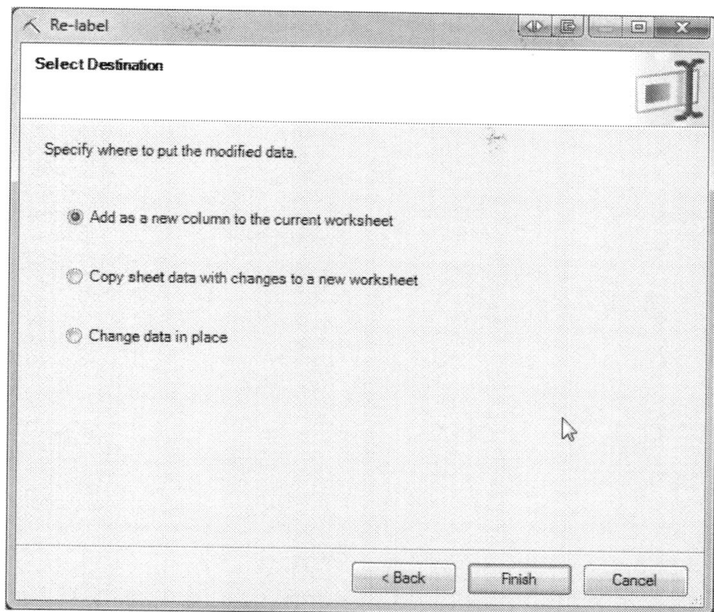

Figure 5-50 Re-label - Select Destination

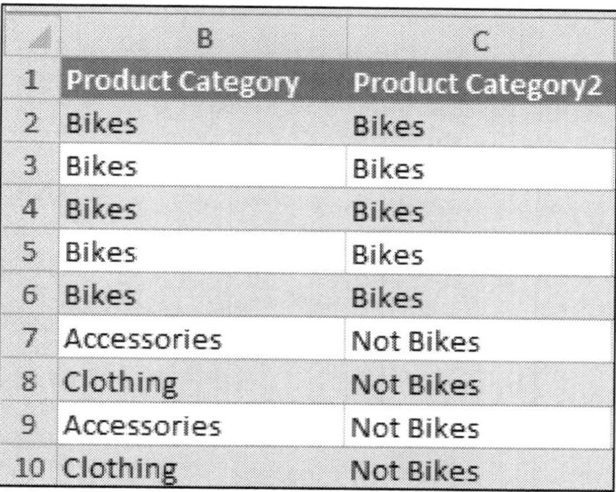

	B	C
1	Product Category	Product Category2
2	Bikes	Bikes
3	Bikes	Bikes
4	Bikes	Bikes
5	Bikes	Bikes
6	Bikes	Bikes
7	Accessories	Not Bikes
8	Clothing	Not Bikes
9	Accessories	Not Bikes
10	Clothing	Not Bikes

Figure 5-51 Re-label - Results

Calculated Fields

Many times new fields calculated from values of existing fields are useful in data analysis. For example, suppose an imported database has order quantity and price per unit fields but no total sale field. We can create a new total sale field in an Excel table by just multiplying quantity by price. It is only necessary to insert the formula into one cell of a new field and it is automatically copied to the other cells in the column. In our example we need a revenue per unit sold field so I inserted the expression for the computation into one cell in the empty column contiguous to the table and Excel created the following formula:

=[@[Total Sales]]/[@Quantity]

	A	B	C	D	E
1	Total Sales	Quantity	Category	Country	Revenue per Unit
2	138,690.63	7,004	Accessories	Australia	$19.80
3	8,852,050.00	4,472	Bikes	Australia	$1,979.44
4	70,259.95	1,869	Clothing	Australia	$37.59
5	103,377.85	5,365	Accessories	Canada	$19.27
6	1,821,302.39	924	Bikes	Canada	$1,971.11
7	53,164.62	1,331	Clothing	Canada	$39.94
8	63,406.78	3,344	Accessories	France	$18.96
9	2,553,575.71	1,444	Bikes	France	$1,768.40
10	27,035.22	770	Clothing	France	$35.11
11	62,232.59	3,273	Accessories	Germany	$19.01
12	2,808,514.35	1,600	Bikes	Germany	$1,755.32
13	23,565.40	752	Clothing	Germany	$31.34
14	76,630.04	4,057	Accessories	United Kingdom	$18.89
15	3,282,842.66	1,858	Bikes	United Kingdom	$1,766.87
16	32,239.51	991	Clothing	United Kingdom	$32.53
17	256,422.07	13,049	Accessories	United States	$19.65
18	8,999,859.53	4,907	Bikes	United States	$1,834.09
19	133,507.91	3,388	Clothing	United States	$39.41

Figure 5-52 Calculated Field

Discretizing Data

Discretizing is the process of converting continuous data into discrete categories, e.g., converting family annual income into ranges such as $0 to $20,000, $20,001 to $40,000, and so on. Some of the data mining tools automatically discretize data where the data are divided into buckets, categories representing ranges of values. There are at least three other ways to discretize data in Excel: using the Explore Data tool, the IF function, and Visual Basic for Applications (not addressed).

The procedure for using the Explore Data tool is the same here as described earlier (Figures 5-39 a, b, and c) except that you use the Add New column button to insert the buckets (categories) into the table. Figure 5-53 shows the Explore Data dialog box for the new calculated field, RevenuePerUnit, described above. The new populated RevenuePerUnit column is inserted into the table in Figure 5-54 column F.

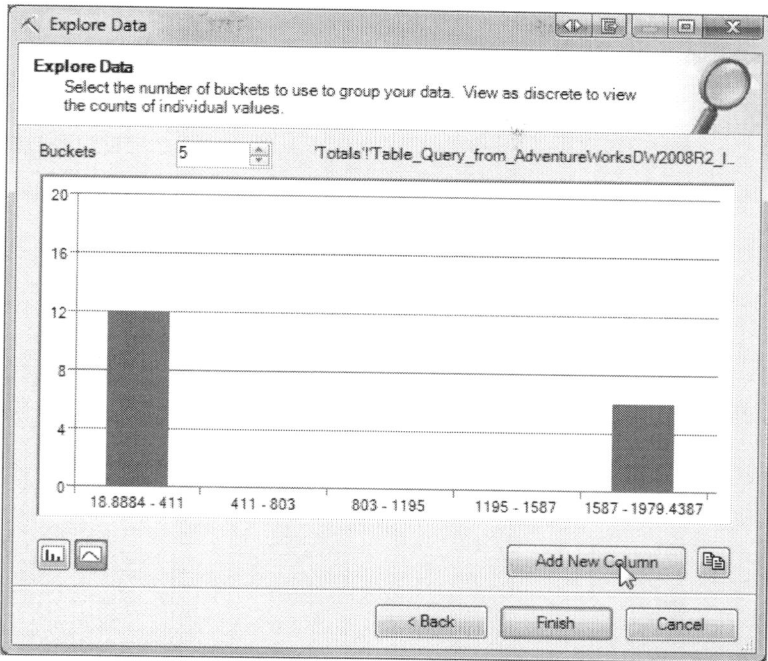

Figure 5-53 Discretizing Data Using the Explore Data Tool

D	E	F
Country	Revenue per Unit	Revenue per Unit2
Australia	$19.80	18.8884 - 411
Australia	$1,979.44	1587 - 1979.4387
Australia	$37.59	18.8884 - 411
Canada	$19.27	18.8884 - 411
Canada	$1,971.11	1587 - 1979.4387
Canada	$39.94	18.8884 - 411
France	$18.96	18.8884 - 411
France	$1,768.40	1587 - 1979.4387
France	$35.11	18.8884 - 411

Figure 5-54 Discretized Data

Another way to discretize data is to use the IF function which has the form:

IF(<logical test>, <value if true>, <value if false>)

IF functions can be nested, i.e., an IF function can take the place of a "value if" expression above. For example, I created the following IF expression to discretize the RevenuePerUnit field into three categories of low, medium and high Total Sales. The formula is shown below and the result in Figure 5-55. Note that the reference Sample_Data[[#This Row],[RevenuePerUnit]] was created by Excel because I was working in an Excel table.

```
=IF([@[Total Sales]]<1000000,"Low",
 IF([@[Total Sales]]<5000000, "Medium", "High"))
```

	A	B
1	Total Sales	Revenue Category
2	138,690.63	Low
3	8,852,050.00	High
4	70,259.95	Low
5	103,377.85	Low
6	1,821,302.39	Medium
7	53,164.62	Low
8	63,406.78	Low

Figure 5-55 Discretized Data Using the IF Function

Microsoft Access users please note that the Access' IIF Function which provides the same functionality as the Excel IF function does not work in Excel. I learned about that the hard way.

Date Values

We frequently use time periods, e.g., year, quarter, or month, as attributes or independent variables in data analysis so I thought that we should spend a little time on converting date values with some of the more useful date functions. I expect that you are familiar with using datetime values and with the various datatime formats. And, you probably know that Excel keeps track of dates using the reference point of January 0, 1900 so that January 1, 1900 has the date of 1. This way of keeping track of dates allows us to perform arithmetic operations on them. For example, if I subtract the date 1/1/2008 (39448) from 12/31/2008 39813) the result is 365. Note that the result cell must be formatted as General to display the number of days between the values. If necessary, you can switch over to the 1904 date system used on the Mac by selecting that in Excel Options – Advanced. When calculating this workbook section from the Office Button. Table 5-2 lists the data function that I if find most useful. Most of them provide a means to discretize date data.

Function or Value	Purpose	Example Cell A1 contains 8/14/2009 Cell A2 contains 5/23/2007 Formula	Result
DATE(year, month, day)	Converts a date in a date format to a serial number.	=DATE(2009,8,14)	40039
DATEDIF(Date 1, Date2, Interval)	Calculates the difference between two dates where interval = y for years, m for months, and d for days.	=DATEDIF(A2,A1,"m")	26
DATEVALUE(string)	Converts a date in string format to a serial number date format.	=DATEVALUE("September, 9, 2009")	40065
NOW()	Current datetime.	=NOW()	Current
YEAR(Date)	Extracts the year from a date.	=YEAR(A1)	2009
MONTH(Date)	Extracts the month from a date.	=MONTH(A1)	8
Quarter	Uses the ROUNDUP and MONTH functions: ROUNDUP(MONTH(date)/3, 0)*	=ROUNDUP(MONTH(A1)/3,0)	3
WEEKDAY(date)	Identifies the day of the week (1 - 7)	=WEEKDAY(A1)	6
Age in years	Calculates years from date of birth until a particular date or NOW: =DATEDIF(birth date,reference date,"y")	=DATEDIF(A2,NOW(),"y") where NOW = 3/6/2007	1
Season	Use the IF function	=IF(AND(MONTH(A2)>=6,MONTH(A2)<=11), "Hurricane Season", "Not Hurricane Season")	Hurricane Season

*Thanks to Pearson Software Consulting (2009) for this tip.

Table 5-2 Useful Date Functions

Note that many of these functions require a parameter expressed as a serial date value, the number of days since January 0, 1900. This is automatically taken care of if the parameter is entered as a cell reference. However, to enter a date in a date format, say 11/5/2009, directly into one of the functions it must first be converted to the serial date value using the DATE function. Example: DAY(DATE(2009, 8,9)) returns 9.

I frequently use year, quarter, and month fields in data analysis. A dimensional database like AdventureWorks2008DW may already have those fields but other data sources may not. In the latter case I will create new columns in the Excel table or pivot table for these values.

Parsing Text Values

At times it's necessary to extract a part of the text in a string. For example, if a name field contains full names—first name, middle initial, and last name—and you wanted to sort the records on last name, then you could strip out the last name into a new field and use that field for sorting. The most useful functions for parsing text are listed in Table 5-3.

Function	Purpose
LEN	Returns the number of characters in a string.
MID	Returns the characters from the middle of a string, given a starting position and length.
FIND	Returns the starting position of one string within another (case sensitive).
SEARCH	Returns the number of the character at which a specific character or string is first found (not case sensitive)
LEFT	Returns the specified number of characters from the start of a string.
RIGHT	Returns the specified number of characters from the end of a string.

Table 5-3 Useful Functions for Parsing Text

Covering all of these text functions will get into too much detail so we'll limit the presentation to the full name example. Suppose we know for sure that the full name field will always have a first name followed by a space, a middle initial followed by a period and a space, and a last name without following spaces. We could use the following function to extract the last name.

=RIGHT(A1,(LEN(A1)-FIND(". ",A1)-1))

The formula says subtract the position of the ". " characters from the length of the string, subtract one, and then return that number of characters from the right end of the string. Suppose cell A1 contains the name Larsen E. Whipsnade. Thus, LEN will return 19, FIND 9, and RIGHT(19-9-1) "Whipsnade." Of course, this is a concocted example, and in actuality name fields are not likely to have this standard form. For example, the formula does not work correctly with the name "W. C. Fields." To do that I would use a short custom function in Visual Basic for Applications that parses a full name into a last name as in Figure 5-56.

B15 | fx =LastName(A15)

	A	B	C
14	Full Name	Last Name	
15	Kayla Alexander	Alexander	
16	Julio E. Vazquez	Vazquez	
17	Connor G. Kumar	Kumar	
18	Lauren R. Washington	Washington	
19	Jeremy Bryant	Bryant	
20	Jesse D Howard	Howard	
21	Faith D. Bailey	Bailey	
22	B. C. Cox	Cox	
23	Bianca F. Wu	Wu	
24	Cameron L. Gonzales	Gonzales	

Figure 5-56 Custom Visual Basic Function Results

For those interested the Visual Basic code follows. In it the beginning location of the last name is identified by the location of the first space character from the right end of the string as computed in the Bloc statement. Then, the last name is assigned to the function name, LastName, using the Mid function which extracts the last name characters from the string. Thus, the function parses the last name correctly regardless of the format for the first name and middle initial or middle name. To use it just enter LastName with an equal sign in the function textbox as shown in the top right corner of Figure 5-56.

```
Public Function LastName(Name As String) As String
    Dim Length As Integer, Bloc As Integer
```

```
    Length = Len(Name)
    Bloc = InStrRev(Name, " ")
    LastName = Mid(Name, Bloc, Length - Bloc + 1)
End Function
```

What's Next

We could go on and on about other types of transformation but it's time to move on. What we've looked at here should give you a sense how to transform data. I hope that you will explore other possibilities on your own. Now on to real data analysis.

Chapter 6 - Data Analysis with Excel 2010: Part II Excel Tables, Pivot Tables and Pivot Charts, OLAP Cubes, Statistical Inference, and Correlation and Regression

Data Analysis With Excel Tables

We introduced Excel tables at the beginning of the previous chapter and thereafter described a number of tools that can be used for inspection, cleaning, and transformation. Most of those tools are also useful for data analysis. So, in this segment we won't cover those again but we'll add a few more tools to your Excel repertoire. We will also use data in Excel tables in sections in this and other chapters.

Hiding and Rearranging Columns

It's useful to see data in side-by-side columns. Columns can be arranged side-by-side by either hiding columns not of interest or arranging the columns of interest to be contiguous. For the former approach select the columns to be hidden by ctrl-clicking on the column designator (A, B, C, . .), then either use the Hide & Unhide menu in the Format option in the Cells command group on the Home tab or right click within the selection and click Hide. To unhide columns select the columns within which the columns are hidden and use one of the operations as above. Note that if column A is hidden, you may have to select the entire worksheet and then unhide it.

The other way to arrange columns side-by-side is to rearrange columns. To do that select one or more field in a table that are contiguous, move the mouse pointer to a border of the selection for it to become a move pointer (four perpendicular arrows), hold the ctrl key, and drag the selection to the new location.

As an example, I wanted to see if there is a relationship between the country of sale and the revenue from the sale in the AdventureWorksDW data that we have been using so I arranged the Country, Product Category, and RevenueCategory fields side-by-side, in this case by hiding a field between them. I then sorted the records by Product Category as shown in Figure 6-1. The results may suggest that US costumers buy higher priced bikes. To explore this relationship we could use a variety of other tools including using statistical inference to test the validity of the hypothesis or applying some of the data mining tools. We cannot conclude anything about the accessories and clothing categories because of the inadequacy of our revenue categorization scheme. Regardless, this example shows how hiding or rearranging columns can help in data analysis.

B	D	E
Revenue Category	Category	Country
Low	Accessories	Australia
Low	Accessories	Canada
Low	Accessories	France
Low	Accessories	Germany
Low	Accessories	United Kingdom
Low	Accessories	United States
High	Bikes	Australia
Medium	Bikes	Canada
Medium	Bikes	France
Medium	Bikes	Germany
Medium	Bikes	United Kingdom
High	Bikes	United States
Low	Clothing	Australia
Low	Clothing	Canada
Low	Clothing	France
Low	Clothing	Germany
Low	Clothing	United Kingdom
Low	Clothing	United States

Figure 6-1 Hide/Rearrange Columns Example

Data Sampling

The example data we've been using contains over 60,000 records—way too many to comprehend visually. Sometimes it's worthwhile to take a small sample for preliminary exploration purposes. In addition, a number of tools to be covered later in this and other chapters use different sets of data for training and testing usually with a proportion of the complete data set used for training and the remainder used for testing. The Sample Data tool in the Data Preparation command group of the Data Mining tab provides a means to divide a data set into two parts, say a small one for preliminary analysis or one for training and one for testing.

Clicking on the Sample Data tool button displays the Select Source Data dialog box that we've used before where we can select data from a table or data range in Excel or from an external data source. In our example we will use a table containing all of the 60,000 plus records from the AdventureWorks2008DW internet sales data set. The sampling method is selected the next dialog box as in Figure 6-2a and b. As explained in the descriptions random sampling selects a subset of the data at random and oversampling insures that the resultant sample contains a specified ratio of records for category values, e.g., males and females. We will use random sampling in our example.

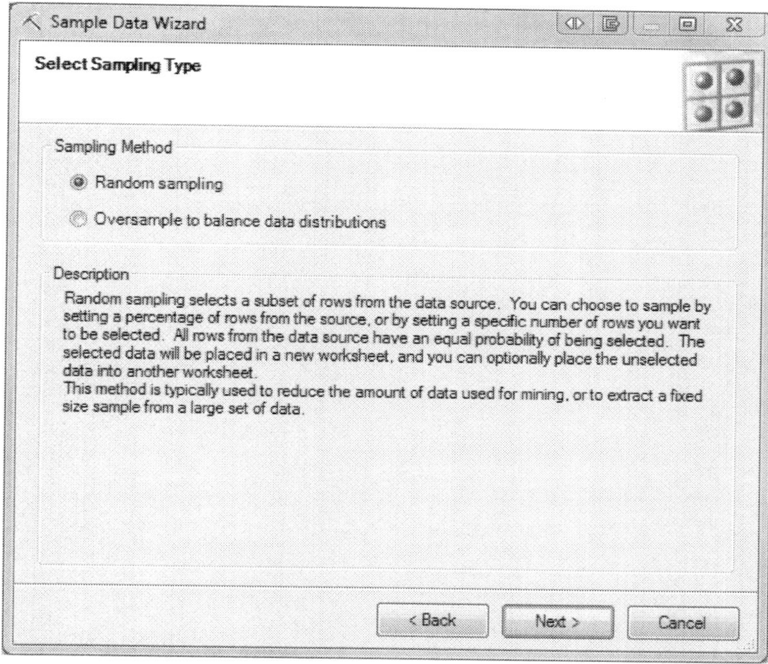

Figure 6-2a Select Random Sampling

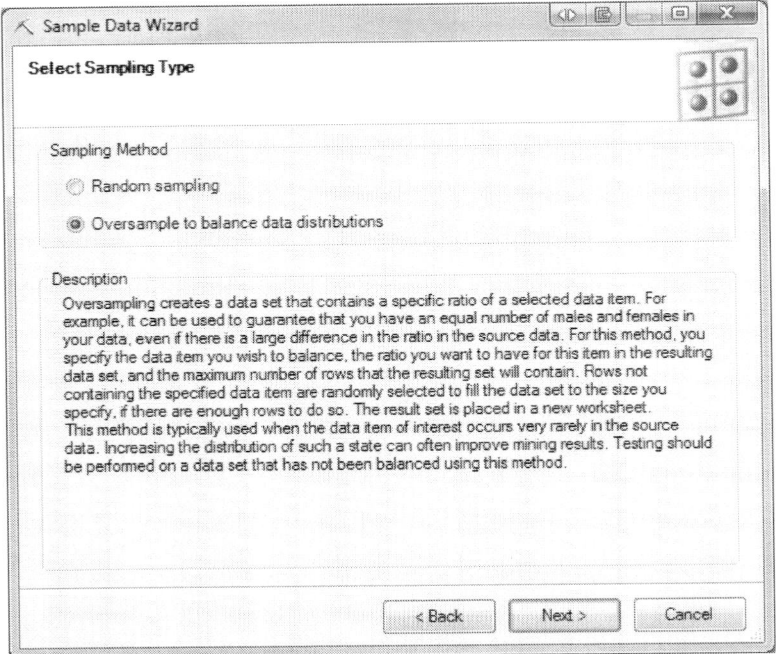

Figure 6-2b Select Sampling Type

In the Random Sampling dialog box (Figure 6-3) you can specify either a percentage of the data records or a specific row count for the sample. For this example I specified ten percent for the sample size as compared with the default of 70 percent. In an earlier example of reseller sales data I specified 35 rows for the sample. The next and final dialog box (Figure 6-4) allows you to name the worksheets for the sample data and for the unselected data if you choose that option. Clicking the Finish button will insert the data in to the workbook.

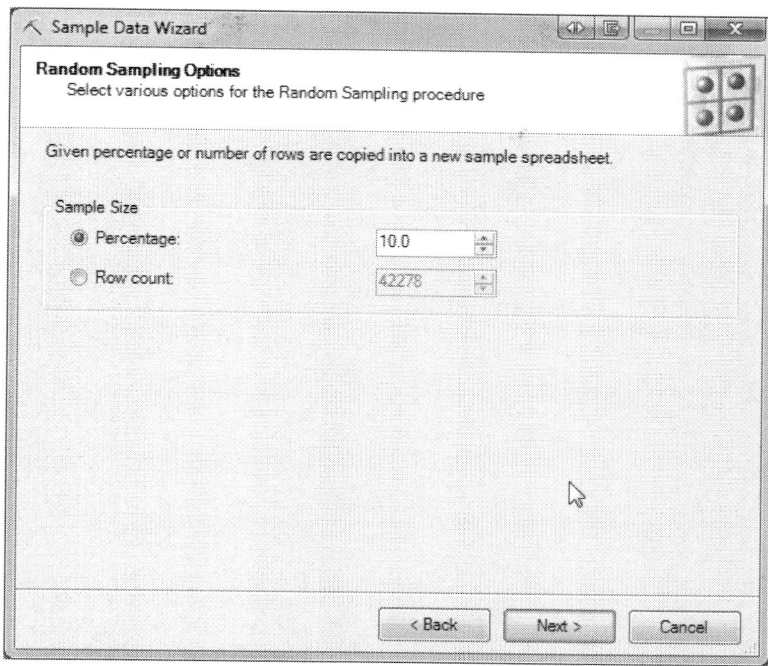

Figure 6-3 Random Sampling Options

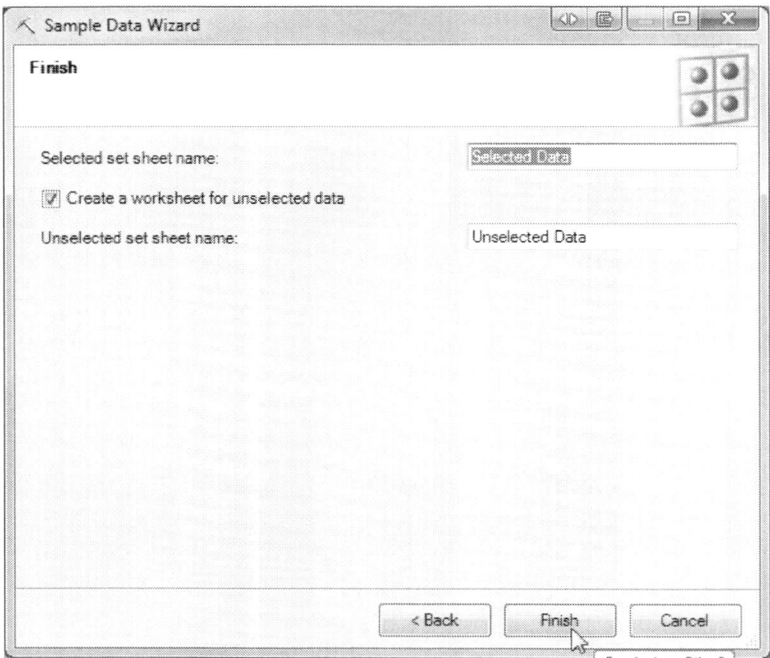

Figure 6-4 Sample Data Finish Dialog Box

Conditional Formatting

Conditional formatting changes the format of cells based on conditions that you specify, e.g., a red background color for values less than or equal to zero and a green background color for values greater than zero. Conditional formatting helps to focus your attention on records that are of particular interest. There are five types of conditional formats as shown by the menu in Figure 6-5a which is displayed when you click the down arrowhead on Conditional Formatting in the Styles command group on the Home tab. The options for the Highlight Cell Rules, Top/Bottom Rules, Data Bars, Color Scales, and Icon Sets are shown in Figure 6-5b through f respectively.

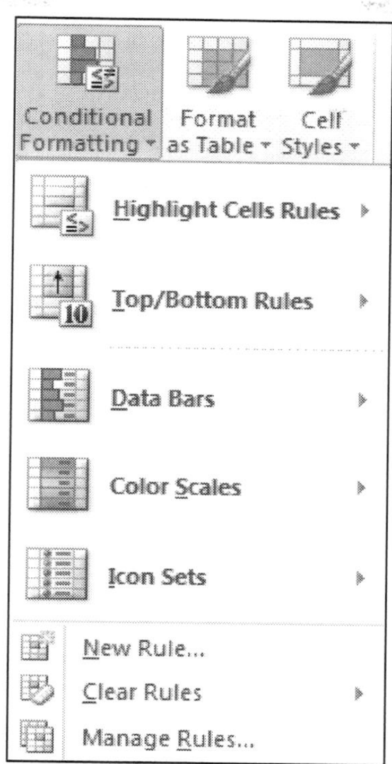

Figure 6-5a Menu

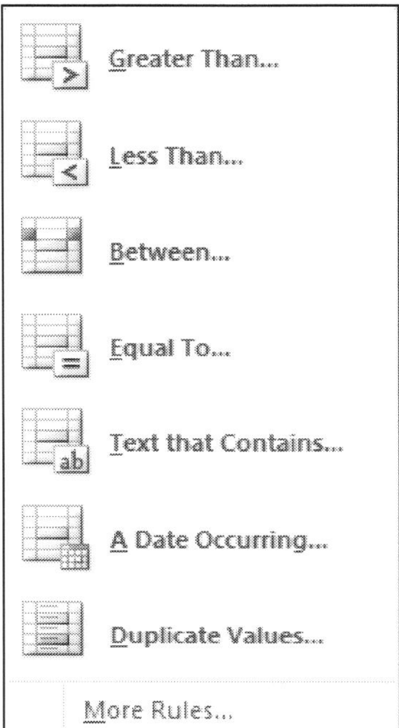

Figure 6-5b Highlight Cells

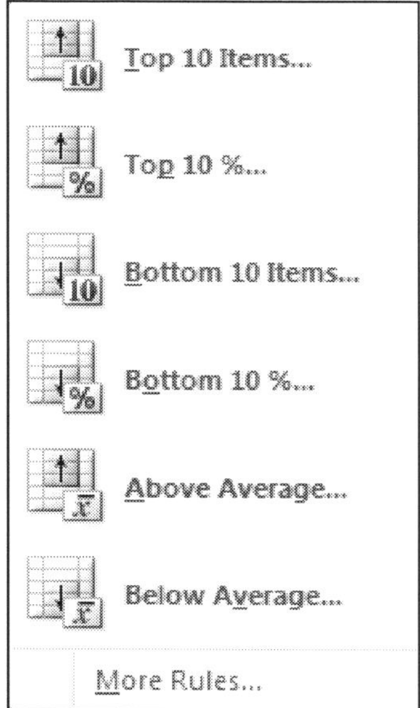

Figure 6-5c Top/Bottom

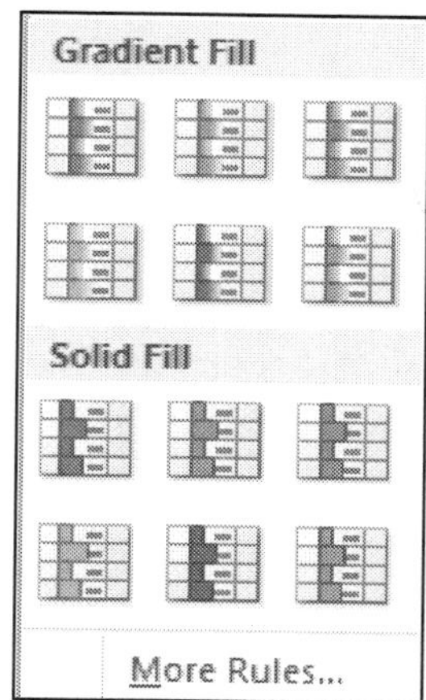

Figure 6-5d Data Bars

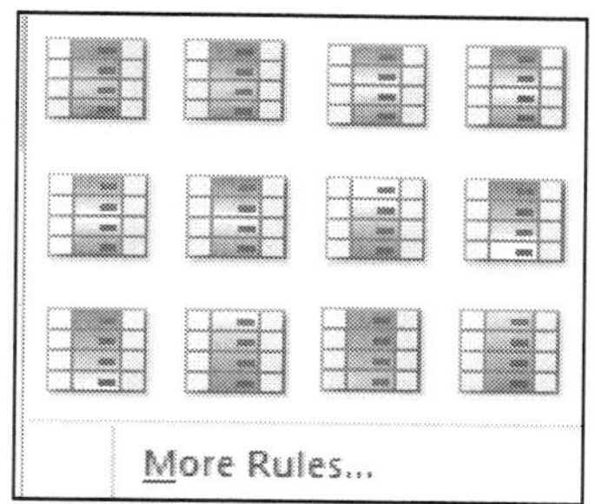

Figure 6-5e Color Scales

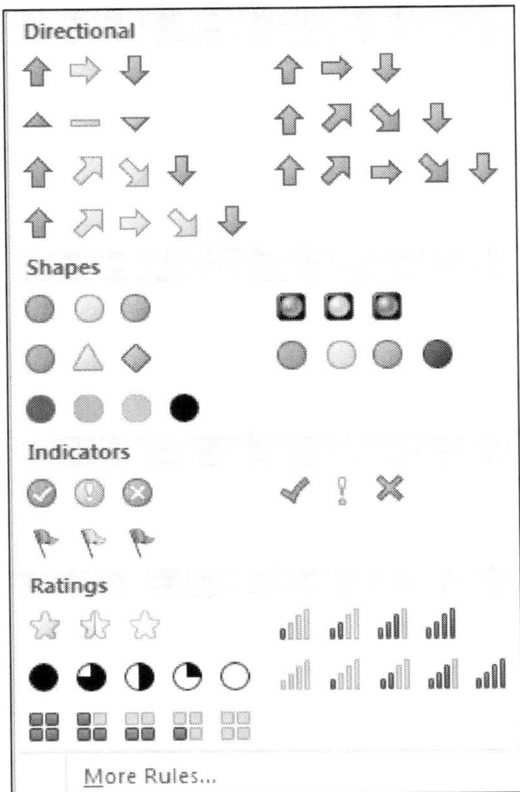

Figure 6-5f Icon Sets

Figure 6-5 Conditional Formatting Options

(For better viewing of this image, go to http://www.zerobits.info/bibook/bibookimages/)

Most of the options are self-explanatory. For example, the Greater Than option in Highlight Cells Rules highlights those cell in the range selected, in our case an Excel table field, that are greater than the specified value. The More Rules button, available at the bottom of each option menu, displays a New Formatting dialog box as in Figure 6-7 in this case for Highlight Cells Rules where you have access to the full range of conditional formats. In that dialog box the Edit the Rule Description area on the bottom half of the box will change according to the type of rule selected.

Figure 6-6 Conditional Formatting Options

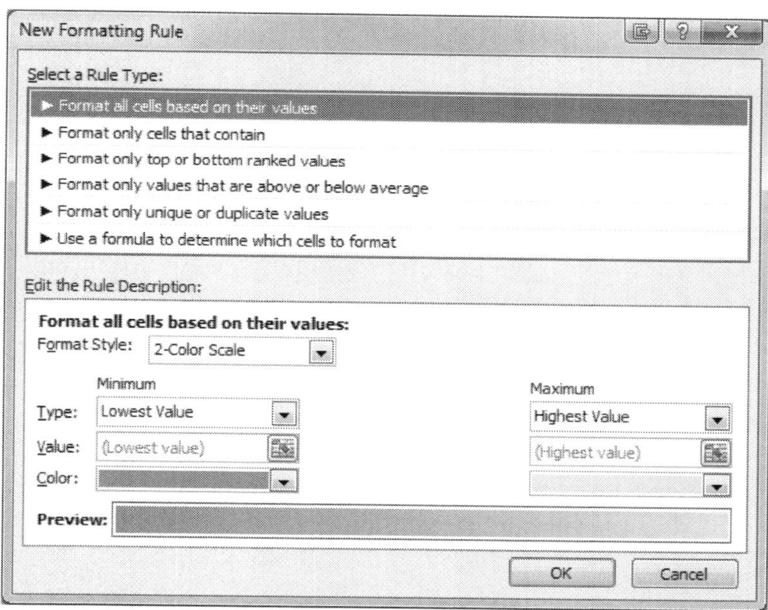

Figure 6-7 New Formatting Rule Dialog Box

Selecting the Clear Rules option on the Conditional Formatting menu (Figure 6-5a) offers four choices: clearing the rules from selected cells, the entire worksheet, a table, or a pivot table. Selecting the Manage Rules option on the Conditional Formatting menu (Figure 6-5a) brings up the Conditional Formatting Rules Manager as in Figure 6-8 where you can create a new rule or edit or delete an existing one. Note that the Duplicate Values option on Highlight Cells menu (Figure 6-5b) is another way to identify duplicates; that conditionally formatted cells can be filtered and sorted by that formatting; and that multiple conditional formatting rules can be applied to the same cells. Figure 6-9 shows a few example of conditional formatting.

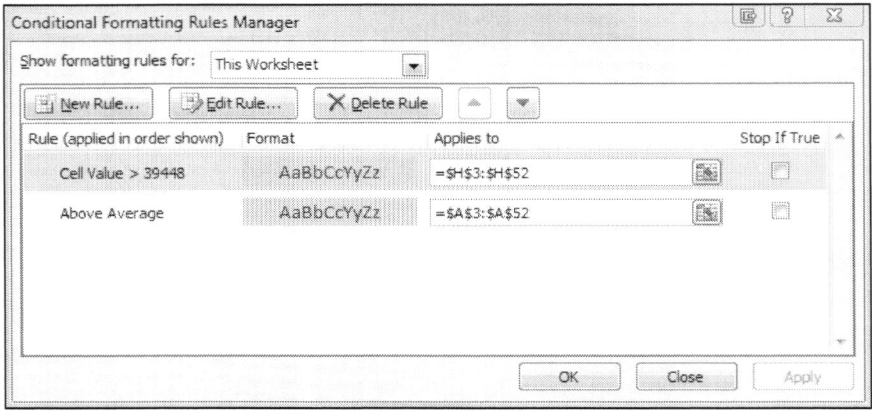

Figure 6-8 Conditional Formatting Rules Manager

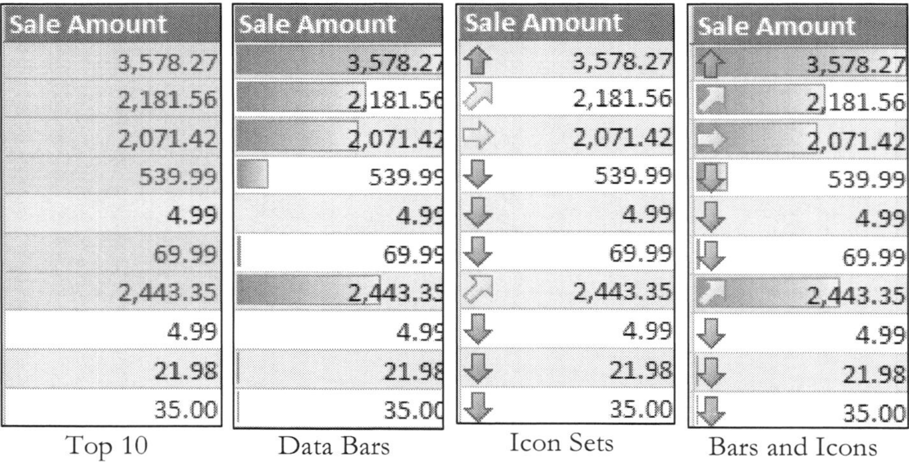

Sale Amount	Sale Amount	Sale Amount	Sale Amount
3,578.27	3,578.27	3,578.27	3,578.27
2,181.56	2,181.56	2,181.56	2,181.56
2,071.42	2,071.42	2,071.42	2,071.42
539.99	539.99	539.99	539.99
4.99	4.99	4.99	4.99
69.99	69.99	69.99	69.99
2,443.35	2,443.35	2,443.35	2,443.35
4.99	4.99	4.99	4.99
21.98	21.98	21.98	21.98
35.00	35.00	35.00	35.00
Top 10	Data Bars	Icon Sets	Bars and Icons

Figure 6-9 Conditional Formatting Examples

Data Analysis With Pivot Tables and Pivot Charts

At the beginning of Chapter 5 we said that pivot tables are like interactive cross tabulations where rows and columns represent dimensions or attribute values; that the intersecting cells contain aggregate numerical values; that row and column dimensions can be and usually are nested; and that dimensions may be expanded for drill-down, collapsed for drill-up, or filtered to present a subset of the data.

A pivot table (Figure 6-10a) has two main components: the pivot table on the left and the Pivot Table Field List on the right which is only visible when a cell or range is selected in the pivot table. Selecting a cell outside of the pivot table range will hide the Pivot Table Field List and the PivotTable Tools tabs. There are four regions in a pivot table: row dimensions (Row Labels), column dimensions (Column Labels), the cell value area (Σ Values), and filters (Report Filter). In the example, the row dimensions are year and quarter; the column dimension is product category; the cell values are aggregate sales; and the filter is country. So, you can see that sales for Bikes in all countries combined for the third quarter of 2005 totaled $1,453,523.

The items in these regions are managed by adding, deleting, or moving fields from the PivotTable Field list on the left in Figure 6-10b into the drop zones in the lower part of the panel shown on the right side of the figure. Fields can be added to a region three ways. The easiest is to drag a field from the available fields list in the top panel into one of the drop zones. Another way is to right click on a field in the available fields list to display a menu that lists the four drop zones. The third way is to click the check box beside a field in the available fields list and let Excel insert it in one of the drop zones. I avoid the latter method because Excel doesn't always put the field in the correct zone.

For users of previous versions of Excel an option is provided to permit dragging and dropping fields directly onto the pivot table. To enable this feature select a cell or range in the pivot table, open the PivotTable Options dialog box by clicking Options in the PivotTable command group of the PivotTable Tools Options tab, select the display tab, and then check the Classic PivotTable layout check box on the Display tab. An easier way is to right click on a cell in the pivot table, select pivot table option, and proceed from there.

	A	B	C	D	E
1	Customer Geography	All Customers			
2					
3	Internet Sales Amount	Column Labels			
4	Row Labels	Accessories	Bikes	Clothing	Grand Total
5	CY 2005		3,266,374		3,266,374
6	CY Q3		1,453,523		1,453,523
7	CY Q4		1,812,851		1,812,851
8	CY 2006		6,530,344		6,530,344
9	CY Q1		1,791,698		1,791,698
10	CY Q2		2,014,012		2,014,012
11	CY Q3		1,396,834		1,396,834
12	CY Q4		1,327,799		1,327,799
13	CY 2007	293,710	9,359,103	138,248	9,791,060
14	CY Q1		1,413,530		1,413,530
15	CY Q2		1,623,971		1,623,971
16	CY Q3	118,675	2,569,678	55,988	2,744,340
17	CY Q4	175,035	3,751,923	82,260	4,009,218
18	CY 2008	407,050	9,162,325	201,525	9,770,900
19	CY Q1	173,551	4,024,025	86,054	4,283,630
20	CY Q2	199,755	5,138,299	98,375	5,436,429
21	CY Q3	33,745		17,096	50,841
22	Grand Total	700,760	28,318,145	339,773	29,358,677

Figure 6-10a Pivot Table Example

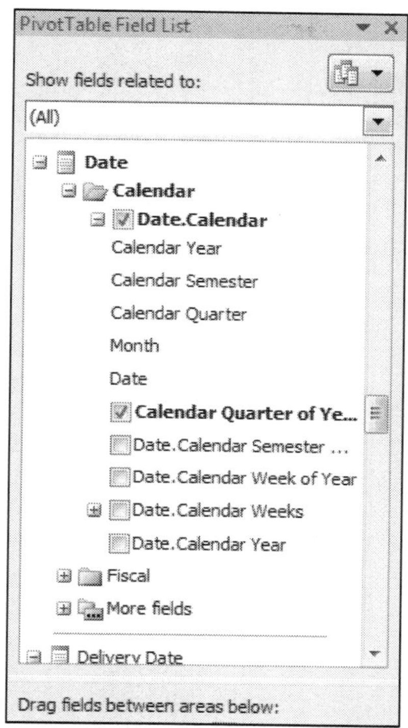

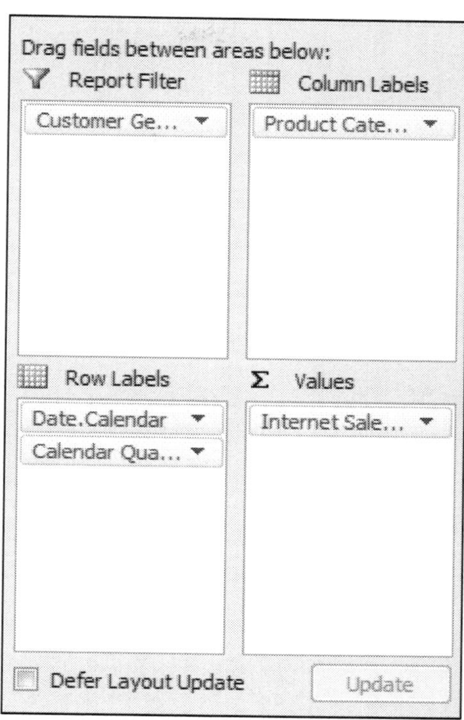

Figure 6-10b Pivot Table Field List

The example data are from a SQL Server 2008 view (query) that I created in the AdventureWorks2008DW database for Internet sales and customer demographic data. The view includes three calculated fields: year and quarter calculated from the order date field and age from the customer birth date field.

Pivot Table Data Sources

Data for pivot tables can come from either an Excel table or directly from an external data source. To convert an Excel table into a pivot table use the Summarize with Pivot Table option in the Tools command group on the Table Tools Design tab. Data from some external sources may be imported directly as pivot tables by making that selection in the Import Data dialog box as in Figure 6-11 (previously shown as Figure 5-2). In the dialog box if you imported the data as a table, then to use it in a pivot table you would convert it as described above. Using the PivotTable Report option skips the Excel table step and creates a pivot table in the worksheet. The PivotChart and PivotTable Report option will create a pivot chart along with the pivot table. We will look at pivot charts later in this chapter.

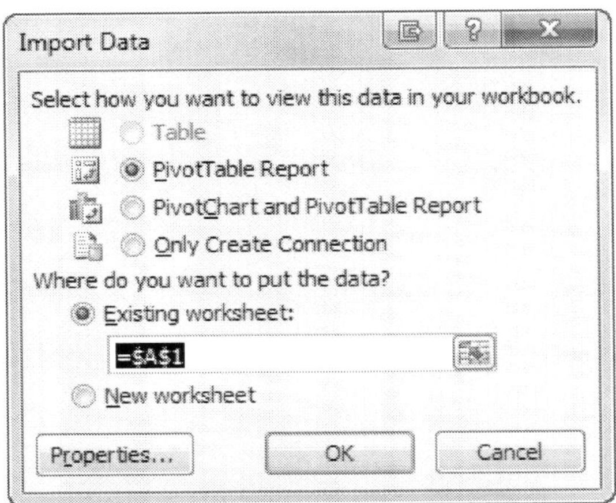

Figure 6-11 Importing External Data as a Pivot Table

Pivot tables are disconnected from their data sources just like Excel tables. Thus, pivot tables (like Excel tables) must be refreshed to update the data from the source. While Excel table data is stored directly in the table itself, pivot table data is stored in memory in a pivot cache. The pivot table cache data may be saved with the Excel workbook or not. Saving the cache will result in a larger xls file size but with the workbook possibly opening faster. Use the Pivot Table Options dialog box to enable/disable this option. It is enabled by default.

If you have multiple pivot tables using the same data source, there are two options: creating a new connection for each pivot table with each having its own cache or using one pivot cache for all pivot tables. The benefit of the latter approach is a reduction in main memory usage. A possible disadvantage is that any modifications in the pivot table data will be reflected in all of the tables. For example, if a calculated field is added in one table, it will show up in all other versions as well. To use the same pivot cache for a new pivot table just copy and paste the existing pivot table to a new location. The new pivot table will use the existing cache as its data source.

Blank values in pivot table cells seem to cause problems. To avoid this problem set the For empty cells show option to zero (0) in the Layout & Format tab of the Pivot Table Options dialog box.

Sorting and Filtering

You may select sort and filter options for row and column dimensions by clicking on the down arrowhead beside the Row Labels or Column Labels box to bring up the menu shown in Figure 6-12 or by right clicking on a dimension and selection sort or filter from the menu. Sorting can also be accessed by selecting the Sort option on the Data or Pivot Table Tools Options tabs tab.

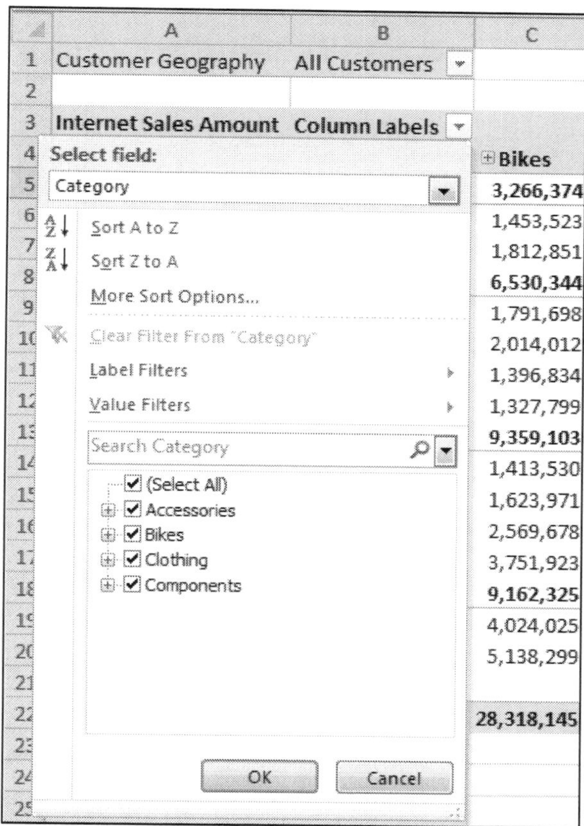

Figure 6-12 Pivot Row and Column Sort and Filter Menu

Aggregate Calculations

The values displayed in the intersections of rows and columns may be changed if allowed by opting for a different aggregate calculation which include sum, count, average, max, and min. To change the aggregate calculation type right click on a value cell and using the Field Settings dialog box (see below). The default setting is usually sum.

Pivot Table Tools Design Tab

Again, when a cell or range in a pivot table is selected, the Pivot Table Tools Design and Options tabs are visible. The right side of the Design tab presents a PivotTableStyles command group similar to the one in the Table Tools Design tab. The left side of the Design tab (Figure 6-13) presents some layout options. The ***Subtotals option*** displays a menu to specify whether subtotals will be shown in rows at the top or bottom of each group in a dimension or not shown at all. For example, in Figure 6-10a subtotals are displayed at the top of the dimension group. Similarly, grand totals for rows and/or columns can be turned on or off by the ***Grand Totals option***.

The ***Report Layout option*** has three alternatives on its menu: compact form, outline form, and tabular form. The compact form is shown in Figure 6-10 and the outline form in Figure 6-14.

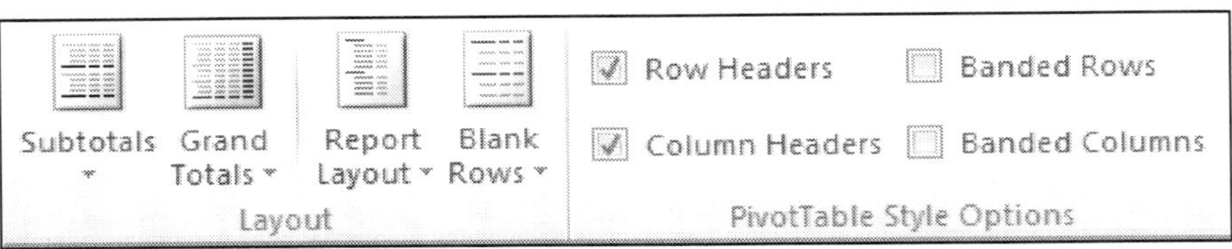

Figure 6-13 PivotTable Tool Design Tab - Left Side

	A	B	C	D	E	F
1	Customer Geography	All Customers				
2						
3	Internet Sales Amount		Category			
4	Calendar Year	Calendar Quarter of Year	Accessories	Bikes	Clothing	Grand Total
5	CY 2005			3,266,374		3,266,374
6		CY Q3		1,453,523		1,453,523
7		CY Q4		1,812,851		1,812,851
8	CY 2006			6,530,344		6,530,344
9		CY Q1		1,791,698		1,791,698
10		CY Q2		2,014,012		2,014,012
11		CY Q3		1,396,834		1,396,834
12		CY Q4		1,327,799		1,327,799
13	CY 2007		293,710	9,359,103	138,248	9,791,060
14		CY Q1		1,413,530		1,413,530
15		CY Q2		1,623,971		1,623,971
16		CY Q3	118,675	2,569,678	55,988	2,744,340
17		CY Q4	175,035	3,751,923	82,260	4,009,218
18	CY 2008		407,050	9,162,325	201,525	9,770,900
19		CY Q1	173,551	4,024,025	86,054	4,283,630
20		CY Q2	199,755	5,138,299	98,375	5,436,429
21		CY Q3	33,745		17,096	50,841
22	Grand Total		700,760	28,318,145	339,773	29,358,677

Figure 6-14 PivotTable Outline Form

The ***Blank Rows option*** inserts blank rows between the dimension groups which makes the tables more readable. Headers and banded effects are controlled by the ***Pivot Table Style Options*** command group.

Pivot Table Tools Options Tab

The left side of the Options tab is shown in Figure 6-15a and the right side in Figure 6-15b. The pivot table name can be changed in the ***PivotTable Name*** textbox on the left side. One reason to change the names from the default names of PivotTable 1, 2, 3, . . is to be able to refer to them more easily in VBA code.

Options in the PivotTable command group displays a menu list of Options, Show Report Filter Pages, and Generate GetPivot Data. ***Options*** allows you to manage a number of pivot table properties including alternative formatting for error values and empty cells. For example, some cells may display a divide by zero error (#DIV/0!). To change this to something else, say zero, check the For error values show option in the Pivot Table Options dialog box Layout & Format tab and enter zero in the textbox.

The ***Show Report Filter Pages*** creates a new worksheet for each value in a filter dimension. For example, using Report Filter Pages for the country filter in Figure 6-10 should create new worksheets for Australia, Canada, France, Germany, United Kingdom, and the United States with the values for the pivot table in those new worksheets limited to the individual country. However, if the pivot table data source is an OLAP cube, the show report filter pages option is disabled. I don't know why.

The ***Generate GetPivot Data*** switch turns that capability on and off. When you reference a pivot table cell in a formula in a cell outside of the pivot table by clicking on the cell in the pivot table after inserting the equal sign and if the switch is on, Excel will insert a GETPIVOTDATA function as shown below:

```
=GETPIVOTDATA("SalesAmount",$A$3,"Quarter",2,"Year",2
002,"ProductCategory","Bikes")
```

If the switch is off, the formula will just insert a cell reference as usual like =C8. The GetPivotData function references a location in the pivot table dimensional space instead of a cell in the worksheet. Thus, when pivot cell values change as data changes in the data source or pivot table dimensions change, the referenced value is adjusted to remain correct.

The ***Active Field*** textbox allows you to change the active field name. Note that the active field is the one that is currently selected. The ***Field Settings*** option brings up the field settings dialog box shown in Figure 6-16 which has slightly different forms for dimensions and values. Regardless, field properties can be changed there including the type of aggregate calculation for values described above. The ***Expand and Collapse Entire Field*** buttons on the right side of the Active Field command group do just that for the field selected if there are nested fields. If there are no nested field, the buttons have no effect.

The ***Group*** command group will group/ungroup values in a numerical dimension, i.e., it discretizes the data. For an example I created a pivot table for the data used in the beginning of this chapter showing internet sales by product category and date (Figure 6-17). To get the data dimension into usable intervals, months in this case, I used the Grouping dialog box (Figure 6-18) displayed by the Group Selection option on the tab to discretize the data as shown in Figure 6-19. In the dialog box I set the starting and ending values and the interval. Please be aware that the Group command may not work the same way with Analysis Services cubes.

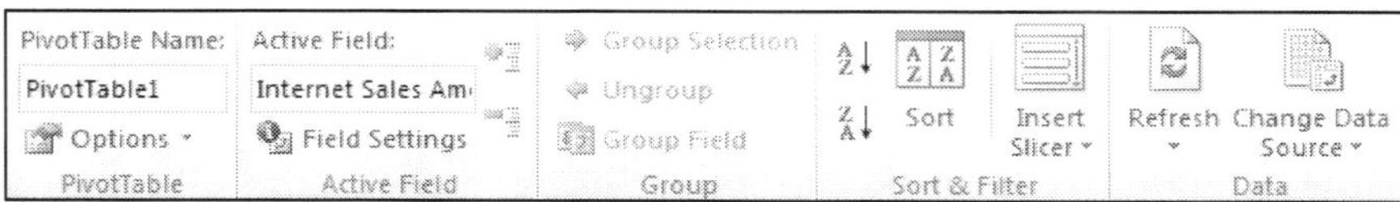

Figure 6-15a Options Tab - Left Side

Figure 6-15b Options Tab - Right Side

Figure 6--15 PivotTable Tool Options Tab

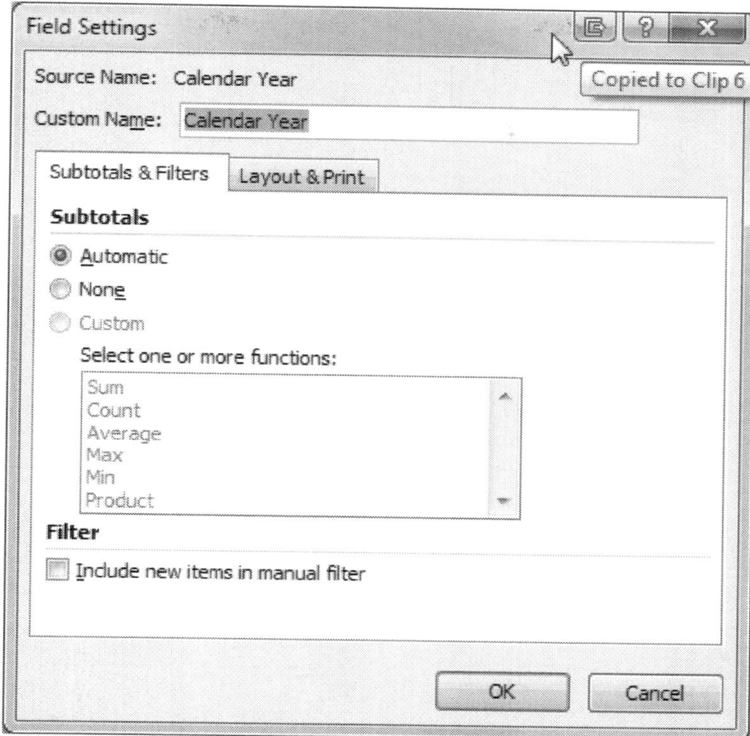

Figure 6-16 Field Settings Dialog Box

	A	B	C	D	E
4	Row Label:	Accessories	Bikes	Clothing	Grand Total
5	7/1/2005		14,477		14,477
6	7/2/2005		13,932		13,932
7	7/3/2005		15,012		15,012
8	7/4/2005		7,157		7,157
9	7/5/2005		15,012		15,012
10	7/6/2005		14,313		14,313
11	7/7/2005		7,856		7,856
12	7/8/2005		7,856		7,856

Figure 6-17 Internet Sales Pivot Table

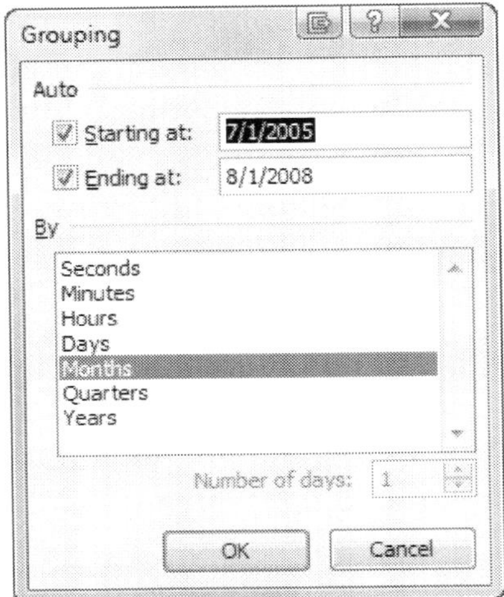

Figure 6-18 Groupings Dialog Box

	A	B	C	D	E
3	Sum of Sale Amount	Column Labels			
4	Row Labels	Accessories	Bikes	Clothing	Grand Total
5	Jan	56,457	2,290,180	29,220	2,375,857
6	Feb	56,996	2,417,326	28,065	2,502,387
7	Mar	60,098	2,521,748	28,769	2,610,615
8	Apr	62,674	2,684,140	32,028	2,778,842
9	May	71,880	3,011,626	31,140	3,114,646
10	Jun	65,201	3,080,517	35,206	3,180,924
11	Jul	48,213	1,839,446	23,604	1,911,263
12	Aug	52,057	1,824,215	23,335	1,899,607
13	Sep	52,150	1,756,374	26,144	1,834,668
14	Oct	54,595	1,928,649	25,926	2,009,169
15	Nov	54,832	1,995,709	25,528	2,076,070
16	Dec	65,608	2,968,215	30,807	3,064,630
17	Grand Total	700,760	28,318,145	339,773	29,358,677

Figure 6-19 Date Field Grouped

The ***Sort*** option in the Sort & Filter command group will display a Sort by Value dialog box were you may set sort options. The buttons to the left of the Sort button sort in descending and ascending order. ***Slicers*** are a new feature in Excel 2010 so I have addressed them separately below.

We talked about ***Refresh*** in Chapter 5. You probably won't use the Change Data Source option so we'll pass it by. The ***Clear*** option resets the entire pivot table (Clear All) or the filter(s) (Clear Filters). ***Select*** controls selecting cells, rows, or the entire pivot table. The menu options are Labels and Values, Values, Labels, Entire Pivot Table, and Enable Selection. When you try to select a row the first three menu items are disabled. To enable them click Enable Selection until the menu items are enabled. The ***Move Pivot Table*** option presents the Move Pivot Table dialog box where you may choose to move the pivot table to another location in the same worksheet or to a new one.

Summarize Values by in the Calculations command group displays a menu of aggregation and descriptive statistics options for the data values as in Figure 6-20a. For example, instead of the sum of internet sales shown in Figure 6-19 we could change it to Count to show the number of items ordered. Clicking More Options displays the Value Fields Settings box at the top of Figure 6-20b where you can do the same thing in the Summarize Values by tab. ***Show Values As*** is particularly useful for visually inspecting. More about Show Values As follows later in this chapter. The ***Fields, Items, & Sets*** included calculated fields that we will cover separately below.

The ***Pivot Chart*** option inserts a pivot chart into the worksheet. We will look at pivot charts in a bit and cover ***OLAP Tools*** items in a later chapter. ***What-if Analysis*** allows you to see the effects on the worksheet by changing a value, an advanced topic that we will also not cover here.

The ***Field List*** button shows/hides the Pivot Table Field List as on the right side of Figure 6-10. The ***+/- Buttons*** button shows/hides the +/- buttons on nested dimensions. And, the ***Field Headers*** button hides/shows the field headers, e.g., the Row Labels and Column Labels headings in Figure 6-10.

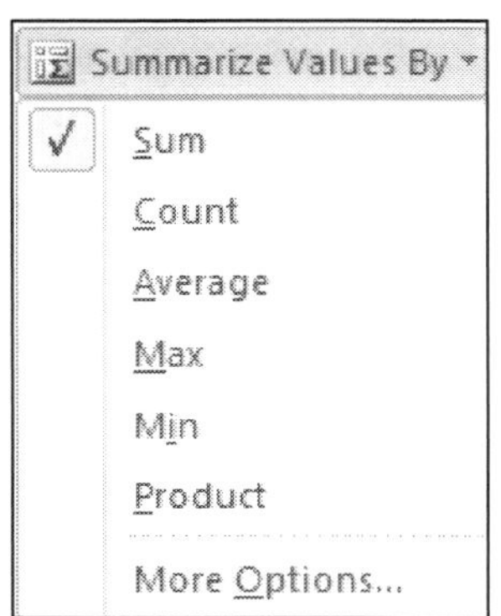

Figure 6-20a Summarize Values by

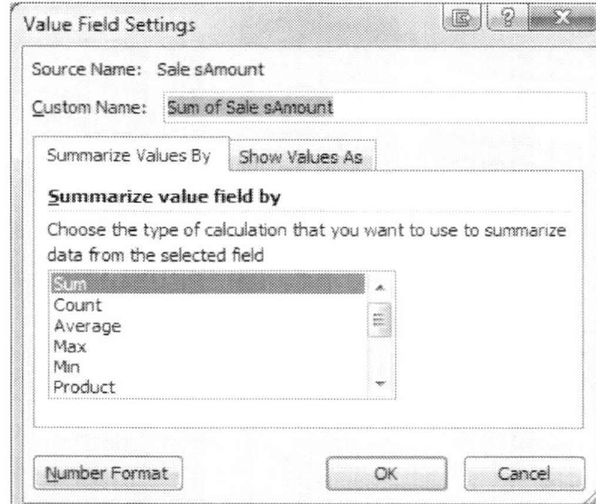

Figure 6-20b Field Value Settings

Figure 6-20 Summarize and Show Values

Slicers

Slicers, a wonderful addition to Excel 2010, expands the filter capability of pivot tables to allow you to easily filter the data on any dimension field. You may use multiple Slicers at the same time with the Slicers filtering each other. Figure 6-21 shows three Slicers—Product Category, customers' Occupation, customers' Country of Sale—for the data in Figure 6-10a. In this case the Slicers display internet sales for Road Bikes purchased by customers in management positions in the US.

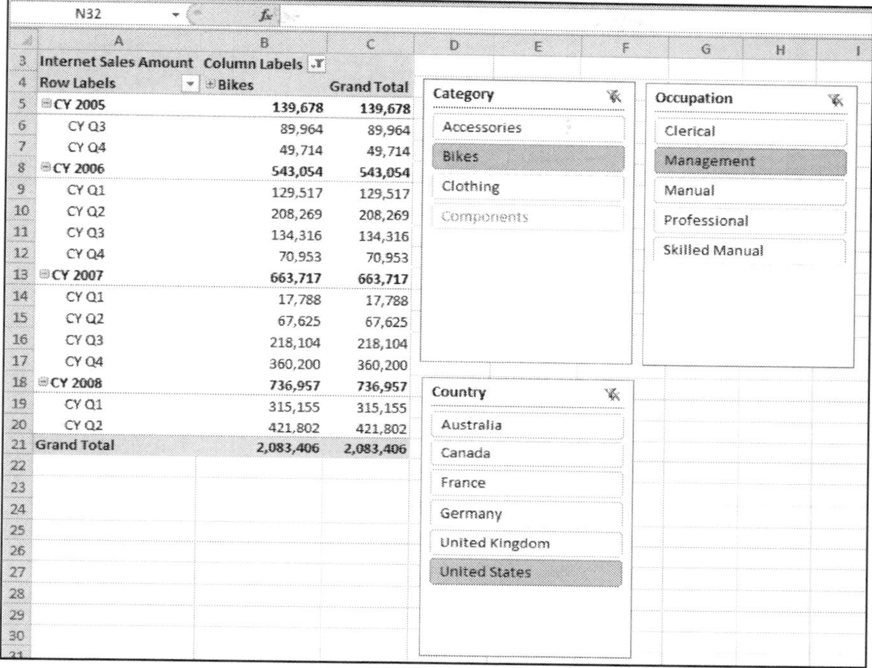

Figure 6-21 Slicers

Slicers are added to a worksheet by using the Insert Slicer command in the Sort & Filter group. This will display the Insert Slicers window (Figure 6-22) that lists the available dimensions. The dimensions that you check will appear individually in Slicer windows as the three in Figure 6-21. You may move the Slicer windows around in the worksheet and resize them. Click the icon in the upper right corner of the window to clear the filter selection, i.e., allow all values in the Slicer dimension. To delete a Slicer just select it and delete.

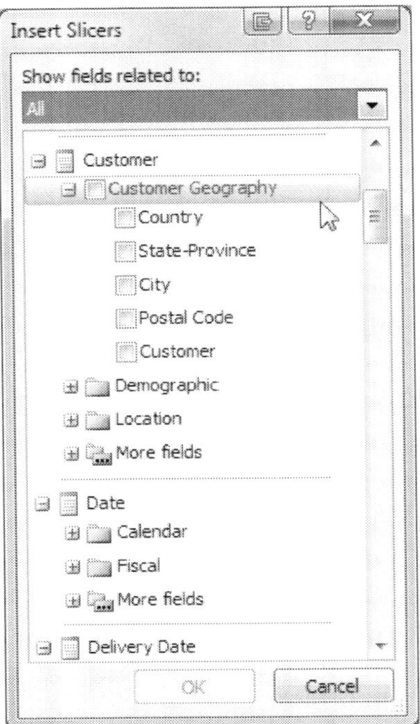

Figure 6-22 Insert Slicers Window

The Slicer Toolbar is shown in Figure 6-23 with the left side on top and the right side on the bottom. You may change the Slicer caption in the textbox on the left. The Slicer Setting button displays a dialog box (not shown) where you may also change the caption and set a few other properties such as the sorting order. PivotTable Connections just displays the name of the pivot table, and the Slicer Styles group that you are familiar with from Table Tools let you change colors for the selected dimension values within a Slicer.

The Bring Forward and Send Backward buttons affect the stacking order of the Slicer windows, e.g., if one window partially covers another you can control which is on top by using these buttons. The Selection and Visibility Pane display that window (not shown) where you hide and unhide the Slicer windows. Align displays a menu (not shown) to align and the Button and Size groups allow forma of the Slicer windows.

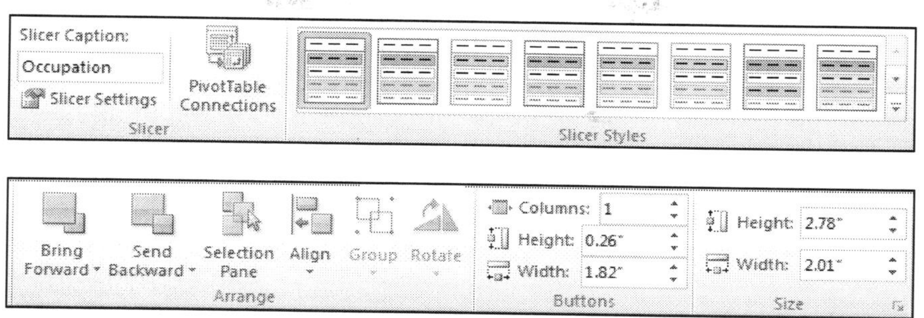

Figure 6-23 Slicer Toolbar

Calculated Fields and Calculated Items

Calculated fields, introduced earlier in chapter in the context of Excel tables, are added to the Pivot Table Field List by using the Calculated Field menu item in the Fields, Items, & Sets option in the Calculations group on the Pivot Table Tools Options Ribbon. This brings up the Insert Calculated Field dialog box (Figure 6-24) where you enter a name and formula for the new calculated field. Field1, Field2, . . . are the default field names. Fields used in formulas can be entered manually, by double clicking on a field in the Fields list, or by clicking the Insert Field button. A GrossMargin% calculated field is shown in Figure 6-25. After clicking the OK button, the new calculated field will appear in the Pivot Table Field List and in the cell value area of the pivot table. Figure 6-26 shows the GrossMargin% calculated values in a pivot table. Existing calculated fields may be edited or deleted by displaying the Insert Calculated Field dialog box and selecting the existing calculated field from the drop-down box at the right side of the Name text box. Please note that you cannot add calculated fields like this to Analysis Services pivot tables.

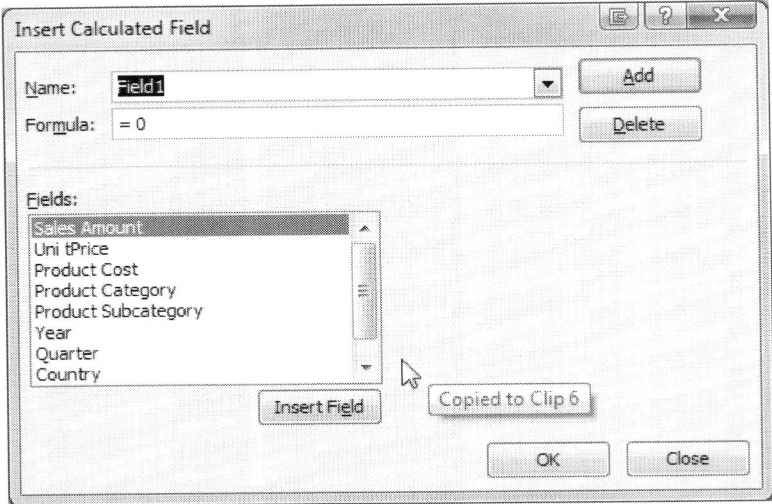

Figure 6-24 Insert Calculated Field Dialog Box

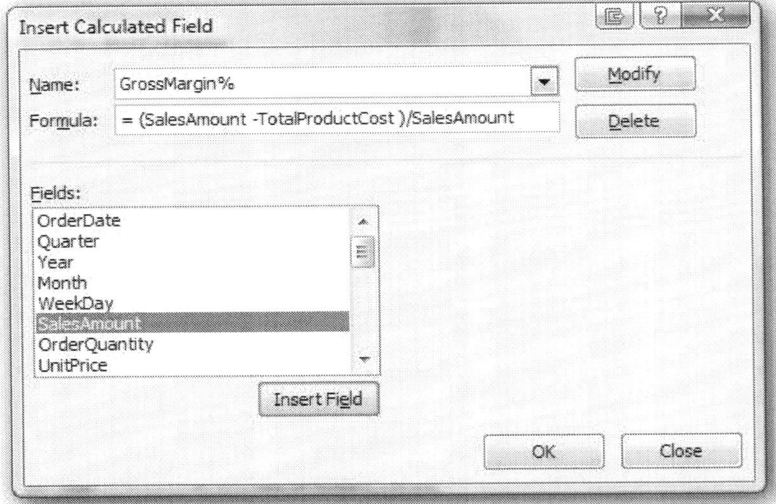

Figure 6-25 Calculated Field Dialog Box Example

	A	B	C	D	E
1	Country	(All)			
2					
3	Sum of GrossMargin%	Column Labels			
4	Row Labels	Accessories	Bikes	Clothing	Grand Total
5	⊞2005	0.00	0.40	0.00	0.40
6	⊞2006	0.00	0.41	0.00	0.41
7	⊞2007	0.63	0.41	0.40	0.42
8	⊟2008	0.63	0.41	0.40	0.41
9	1	0.63	0.41	0.40	0.41
10	2	0.63	0.41	0.40	0.41
11	3	0.63	0.00	0.42	0.56
12	Grand Total	0.63	0.41	0.40	0.41

Figure 6-26 Pivot Table Gross Margin % Calculated Field Example

Calculated items are a bit more confusing. The purpose of a calculated item is to add another row or column to a pivot table dimension based on existing values in the dimension. Calculated items are not relevant for measures. As an example of a calculated item, I could create a new product category (Not Bikes) that would contain all products except bicycles. To do that, I used the Insert Calculated Item dialog box (figure 6-27) accessed via the Fields, Items, & Sets option again when a dimension (row or column) is selected in the pivot table. There are Name and Formula textboxes in the dialog box like those for calculated fields. However, in this case the values to use in the formula are limited to the dimension's values displayed in the Items listbox.

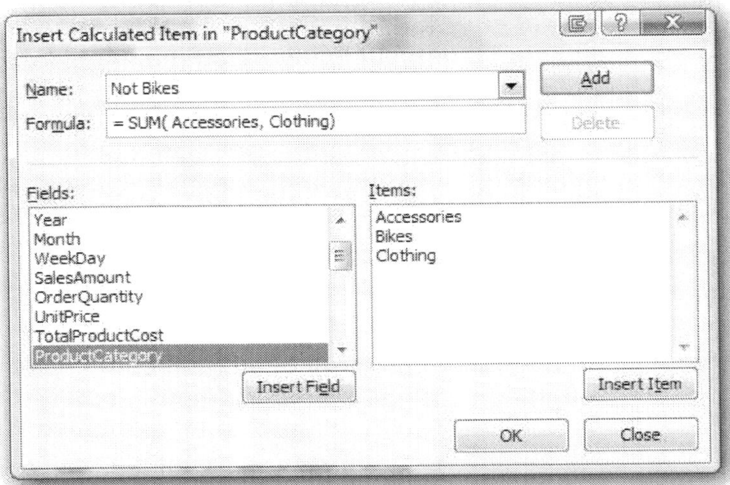

Figure 6-27 Calculated Item Dialog Box Example

Figure 6-28 shows a pivot table with three calculated items: the Not Bikes item in the ProductCategory columns as created above and Jan-June and July-Dec items in the Quarter rows. The Jan-June formula is: =SUM('1','2') and the July-Dec formula is =SUM('3','4'), i.e., sum quarter 1 and quarter 2 for the Jan-June item and quarter 3 and quarter 4 for the July-Dec item. Note that the subtotals and grand totals in Figure 6-28 do not match those in Figure 6-10 because the calculated items are now included in the subtotal and grand total calculations. The way to handle this is to hide grand and subtotals in pivot tables with calculated items. Calculated fields and items exist in the pivot cache only so the original data sources are not affected.

	A	B	C	D	E	F
1	Country	(All)				
2						
3	Sum of Sales Amount	Column Labels				
4	Row Labels	Accessories	Bikes	Clothing	Not Bikes	Grand Total
5	2005	0	6,532,747	0	0	6,532,747
6	2006	0	13,060,687	0	0	13,060,687
7	2007	587,419	18,718,205	276,496	863,915	20,446,036
8	2008	814,100	18,324,650	403,049	1,217,150	20,758,949
9	1	173,551	4,024,025	86,054	259,604	4,543,234
10	2	199,755	5,138,299	98,375	298,130	5,734,559
11	3	33,745		17,096	50,841	101,681
12	4				0	0
13	Jan-June	373,306	9,162,325	184,429	557,734	10,277,793
14	July-Dec	33,745	0	17,096	50,841	101,681
15	Grand Total	1,401,520	56,636,289	679,545	2,081,065	60,798,420

Figure 6-28 Calculated Item Example in the Pivot Table

Show Values As

So far in our examples the cell values area in the pivot tables have been set to no calculation as shown in the Field Settings dialog box in Figure 6-29a. However, there are 14 other values types as described in Table 6-1. You may select a Field Setting by using the Show Values As tab in the Value Field Settings window (Figure 6-29a) or the Show Values As command in the Calculations command group (Figure 6-29b) Selecting some of the Field Setting such as % of Grand Total will result in an immediate recalculation of the pivot table values. Selecting others will display the Value Field Settings window (Figure 6-30)where you select the Base field and item.

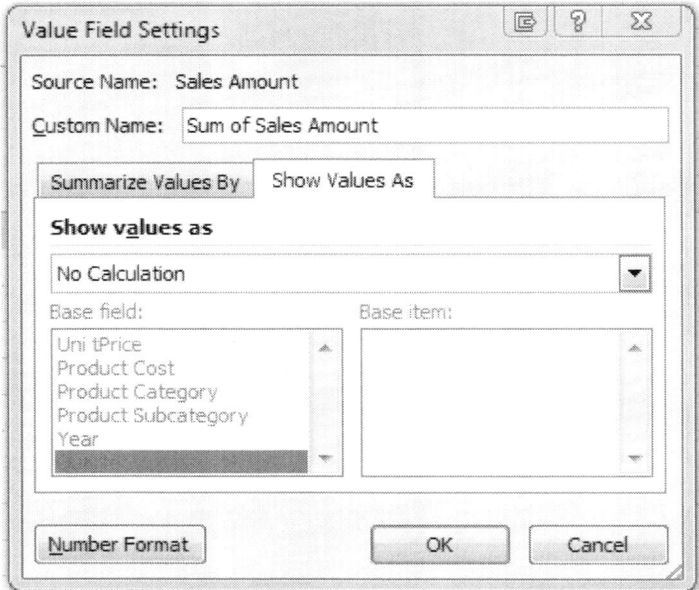

Figure 6-29a Value Field Settings

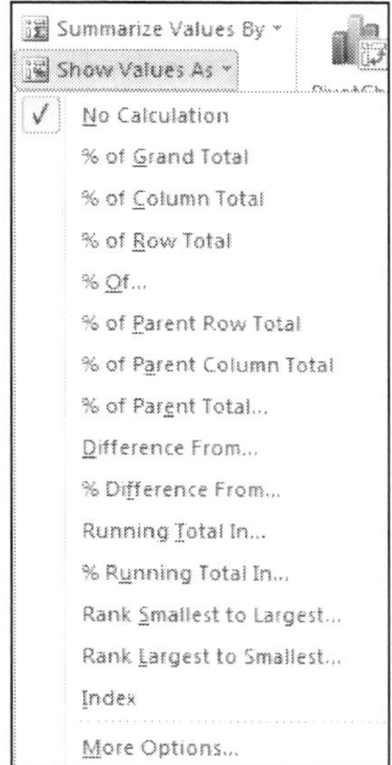

Figure 6-29a Calculations Group

Figure 6-29 Value Field Settings - Show Values As

Option	Description
% of Grand Total	Converts cell values into percentages of the grand total.
% of Column Total	Converts column values into percentages of the column total.
% of Row Total	Converts row values into percentages of the row total
% Of	Shows a percent calculation of the values to the Base item in the Base field
% Of Parent Row Total	Shows a percent calculation of the values to a selected item on a row.
% of Parent Column Total	Shows a percent calculation of the values to a selected item on a column.
% of Parent Total	Shows a percent calculation of the values to Parent item in the Base field.
Difference From	Calculates the difference form the value of the Base item in the Base field
% Difference From	Calculates the percentage difference form the value of the Base item in the Base field
Running Total in	Sums a running total, i.e., year to date.
%Running Total in	Displays a running total as a percentage
Rank Smallest to Largest	Show the ranks of the values with respect to the selected dimension
Rank Largest to Smallest	Show the ranks of the values with respect to the selected dimension
Index	Computes a comparative index (1, 2, 3, . . .) for each value.

Table 6-1 Show Values As Options

(For better viewing of this image, go to http://www.zerobits.info/bibook/bibookimages/)

The Base field in some of the descriptions in the table above is the field with which the calculation will be performed, and the Base item is the reference point for the calculation. In the example (Figure 6-30) with the base field as Quarter for the sum of sales amount aggregate calculation we could select the previous or next quarter as the reference point for a relative type of comparison or one of specific quarters as an absolute type of comparison. I selected previous to get a feel for the trend in sales. The resulting pivot table is shown in Figure 6-31. You can see that bike sales declined in Q3 and Q4 of 2003 and Q3 of 2004 but gained in other quarters. Note that there are no entries in the table for the first quarter in each year because the quarter dimension is nested within the year dimension. Given the results in Figure 6-31 I would explore the data to try to determine where the losses and gains occurred. For example, the pivot table in Figure 6-32 with countries as row headings, the product category filter set to Bikes, and the value field set to % Diff From Previous provides some insight into the gains and losses.

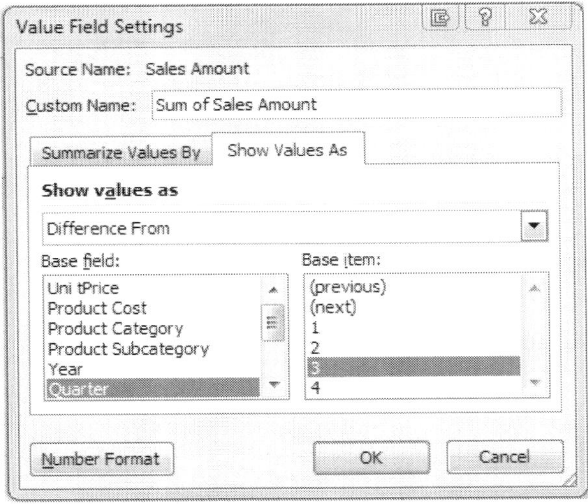

Figure 6-30 Show Values As - Base Field and Item

	A	B	C	D	E	F
1	Country	(All)				
2						
3	Sum of Sales Amount	Column Labels				
4	Row Labels	Accessories	Bikes	Clothing	Not Bikes	Grand Total
5	2005					
6	1					
7	2	0	0	0	0	0
8	3	0	1,453,523	0	0	1,453,523
9	4	0	359,328	0	0	359,328
10	2006					
11	1					
12	2	0	222,314	0	0	222,314
13	3	0	-617,179	0	0	-617,179
14	4	0	-69,034	0	0	-69,034
15	2007					
16	1					
17	2	0	210,441	0	0	210,441
18	3	118,675	945,707	55,988	174,662	1,295,032
19	4	56,361	1,182,245	26,273	82,633	1,347,511
20	2008					
21	1					
22	2	26,204	1,114,274	12,321	38,525	1,191,324
23	3	-166,010	-5,138,299	-81,279	-247,289	-5,632,878
24	4	-33,745	0	-17,096	-50,841	-101,681
25	Grand Total					

Figure 6-31 Pivot Table for Difference Between Quarters

	A	B	C	D	E	F	G	H
1	Product Category	Bikes						
2								
3	Sum of Sales Amount	Column Labels						
4	Row Labels	Australia	Canada	France	Germany	United Kingdom	United States	Grand Total
5	2005							
6	3							
7	4	15.95%	13.49%	-9.25%	41.33%	-11.54%	55.56%	24.72%
8	2006							
9	1							
10	2	3.22%	-27.51%	21.22%	33.71%	-32.50%	47.28%	12.41%
11	3	-37.95%	-23.70%	3.37%	-29.15%	51.94%	-42.79%	-30.64%
12	4	25.36%	-57.10%	12.51%	19.93%	9.84%	-31.71%	-4.94%
13	2007							
14	1							
15	2	3.26%	-22.78%	39.88%	24.28%	-5.31%	44.04%	14.89%
16	3	19.61%	184.46%	35.49%	53.91%	107.24%	95.34%	58.23%
17	4	38.03%	66.11%	28.50%	28.04%	41.85%	65.52%	46.01%
18	2008							
19	1							
20	2	14.24%	36.16%	31.80%	31.16%	19.75%	38.73%	27.69%
21	Grand Total							

Figure 6-32 Bike Sales Percent Difference Between Quarters

The Running Total in option has a Base field setting (not shown). If I selected quarter there, the pivot table would display cumulative totals down the quarter rows. Percent of row, column and total options are self-explanatory. The Index option calculates an index by weighting the cell values with the following formula:

((cell value) * (Grand Total of Grand Totals)) / ((Grand Row Total) * (Grand Column Total))

Figure 6-33a shows an example index pivot table for bike sales based on the sales data in Figure 6-33b. Notice the indexes for Canada and France in 2005. Although France had higher sales than Canada, the Canada index is higher than the France index because Canada's grand total sales is less than France's.

	A	B	C	D	E	F	G	H
1	Product Category	Bikes						
2								
3	Sum of Sales Amount	Column Labels						
4	Row Labels	Australia	Canada	France	Germany	United Kingdom	United States	Grand Total
5	2005	1.28	0.70	0.61	0.73	0.77	1.06	1.00
6	2006	1.06	1.48	0.87	0.80	0.78	1.02	1.00
7	2007	1.01	0.78	1.17	1.10	1.15	0.90	1.00
8	2008	0.85	0.99	1.05	1.13	1.08	1.06	1.00
9	Grand Total	1.00	1.00	1.00	1.00	1.00	1.00	1.00

Figure 6-33a Bike Sales Index

	A	B	C	D	E	F	G	H
1	Product Category	(All)						
2								
3	Sum of Sales Amount	Column Labels						
4	Row Labels	Australia	Canada	France	Germany	United Kingdom	United States	Grand Total
5	2005	1,309,047	146,830	180,572	237,785	291,591	1,100,549	3,266,374
6	2006	2,154,285	621,602	514,942	521,231	591,587	2,126,697	6,530,344
7	2007	3,033,784	535,784	1,026,325	1,058,406	1,298,249	2,838,512	9,791,060
8	2008	2,563,884	673,628	922,179	1,076,891	1,210,286	3,324,031	9,770,900
9	Grand Total	9,061,001	1,977,845	2,644,018	2,894,312	3,391,712	9,389,790	29,358,677

Figure 6-33b Bike Sales Index Data

Conditional Formatting

Of course, you may use conditional formatting in pivot tables as we described earlier for Excel tables.

Drill-Through

To drill-through a pivot table into the underlying data just double click on a cell in the value area. This will create a new worksheet with the underlying data presented as an Excel table.

Sparklines

In Chapter 4 we saw how to use sparklines in Report Builder so you probably know that Sparklines are small charts embedded in a cell. Sparklines, now available in Excel 2010 as well, make it easier to visually identify patterns in the data. In Excel three types of Sparklines are available: Line, Column, and Win/Loss. The latter are bar charts indicating if values are positive (win) or negative (loss). Figure 6-34 shows the three types in row 18: a Line Sparkline is in column B, Column Sparklines in columns C to E, and a Win/Loss in column F. I added column F to calculate the change of internet sales of Accessories from month to month. The Win/Loss Sparkline depicts the changes with sales growth bars above the line and losses below the line.

	A	B	C	D	E	F
3	Sum of Sale Amount	Column Labels				Accessories
4	Row Labels	Accessories	Bikes	Clothing	Grand Total	Change
5	Jan	56,457	2,290,180	29,220	2,375,857	
6	Feb	56,996	2,417,326	28,065	2,502,387	539
7	Mar	60,098	2,521,748	28,769	2,610,615	3,102
8	Apr	62,674	2,684,140	32,028	2,778,842	2,576
9	May	71,880	3,011,626	31,140	3,114,646	9,207
10	Jun	65,201	3,080,517	35,206	3,180,924	-6,680
11	Jul	48,213	1,839,446	23,604	1,911,263	-16,988
12	Aug	52,057	1,824,215	23,335	1,899,607	3,844
13	Sep	52,150	1,756,374	26,144	1,834,668	93
14	Oct	54,595	1,928,649	25,926	2,009,169	2,445
15	Nov	54,832	1,995,709	25,528	2,076,070	237
16	Dec	65,608	2,968,215	30,807	3,064,630	10,776
17	Grand Total	700,760	28,318,145	339,773	29,358,677	
18						

Figure 6-34 Sparklines

You add a Sparkline to a cell using the Sparkline command group on the Insert tab. After you have added the Sparkline and selected the Sparkline cell, a Sparklines Tools Design tab will appear on the Ribbon as shown in Figure 6-35. You may edit the range of the Sparkline data and its location with the Edit Data command, change the Sparkline type with the three buttons in the Type group, and show various points on the Sparkline with the check boxes in the Show group. We have seen Style scroll boxes before, e.g., PivotTable Styles, so we won't describe them here. The Sparkline Color button displays a color picker for the Sparkline, and Marker Color displays a drop-down menu were you specify the color for negative, high, low, first, and last points. The Axis command in the Group group displays the menu in Figure 6-36 where you may select options for the Axes.

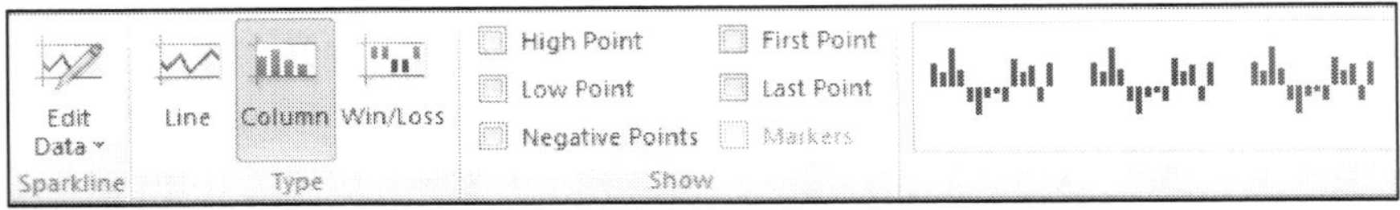

Figure 6-35 Sparkline Toolbar

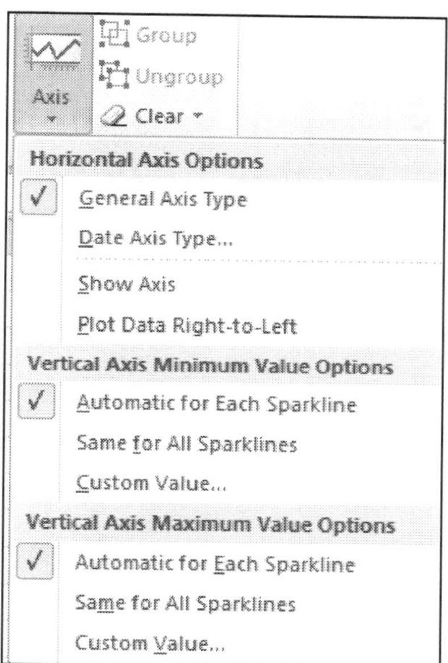

Figure 6-36 Sparkline Toolbar

When you insert Sparklines they will be grouped, meaning that a change in format in one will be changed in all. For example, when I added the first four Sparklines to the table in Figure 6-34 they were all columnar. To change the Sparkline in column B to a Line I first had to ungroup them using the Ungroup command. If you are going to use Sparklines, I recommend pursuing some of the many examples that are available on the Internet.

Pivot Charts

A pivot chart is just like an ordinary Excel chart except that the pivot chart is linked to the pivot table displaying the data shown in the pivot table. Since for this book we have assumed that you have some expertise in using Excel charts, we will not review chart basics here. Rather, we will focus on creating and using pivot charts.

A pivot chart is inserted into the worksheet either by selecting the Pivot Chart and Pivot Table Report option in the Import Data dialog box (Figure 6-11) or by clicking the PivotChart button on the Pivot Table tools Options Ribbon. If you use the former method, then an empty pivot chart and table will be inserted into the worksheet. Then, as you drag and drop fields into the drop zones for the pivot table those values will be reflected in the pivot chart. If you use the latter approach, then a familiar chart selection dialog box will be displayed as in Figure 6-37. After you select the chart type, the pivot chart will be inserted into the work sheet. As you change the design on the pivot table by moving fields in the drop zone the pivot chart will be updated accordingly.

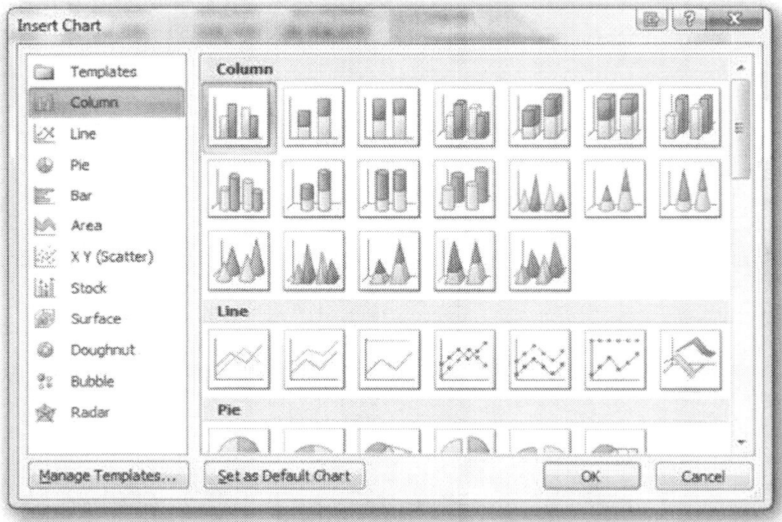

Figure 6-37 Chart Selection Dialog Box

An example pivot table and its companion Pivot chart for bike sales by country and year are shown in Figure 6-38a and b. In creating the chart I did nothing more than select the fields for the chart type and the fields for pivot table drop zones. Note that if Excel's automatic placement of the fields on the chart are incorrect, just exchange fields in the drop zones to get the correct configuration.

	A	B	C	D	E	F	G	H
2	Product Categories	Bikes						
3								
4	Internet Sales Amount	Column La						
5	Row Labels	Australia	Canada	France	Germany	United Kingdom	United States	Grand Total
6	CY 2005	1,309,047	146,830	180,572	237,785	291,591	1,100,549	3,266,374
7	CY 2006	2,154,285	621,602	514,942	521,231	591,587	2,126,697	6,530,344
8	CY 2007	2,947,789	471,445	987,840	1,023,610	1,251,080	2,677,338	9,359,103
9	CY 2008	2,440,928	581,425	870,222	1,025,889	1,148,586	3,095,275	9,162,325
10	Grand Total	8,852,050	1,821,302	2,553,576	2,808,514	3,282,843	8,999,860	28,318,145

Figure 6-38a Example Pivot Table

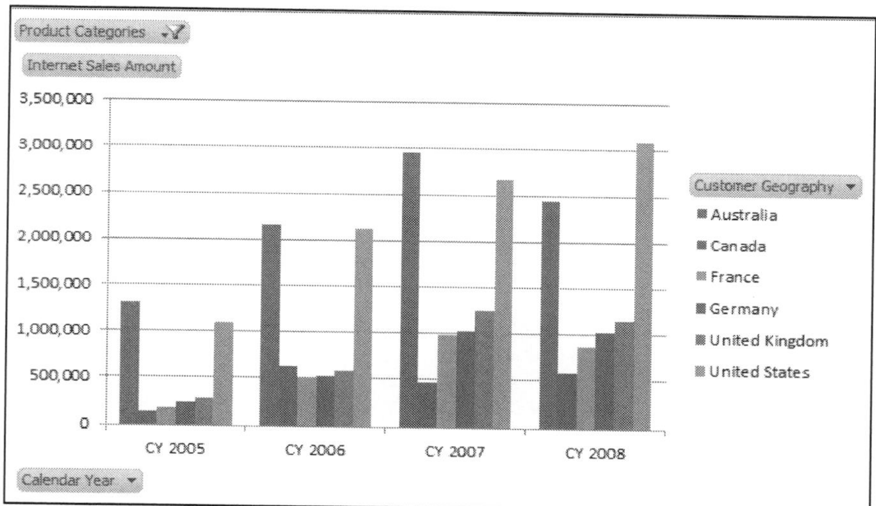

Figure 6-38b Example Pivot Chart with Dimension Selectors

When you click on the pivot chart, a Pivot Chart filter Pane and four tabs in the Pivot Chart Tool area on the Ribbon are displayed. The first three tabs (Design, Layout, and Format) are identical to the ones displayed for a regular Excel chart so we won't cover them here. The fourth tab, Analyze, in Figure 6-39 contains a few of the of options from the Pivot Tables Tools Options tab that we have already described. The button above the Field Buttons button toggles whether the dimension selectors, in this example Product categories, Calendar Year, and Customer Geography – are displayed on the chart. Figure 6-40 shows the chart without selectors. You may insert Slicers just like in pivot tables by clicking the Insert Slicers button. Figure 6-40 shows the pivot chart with hidden dimension selectors.

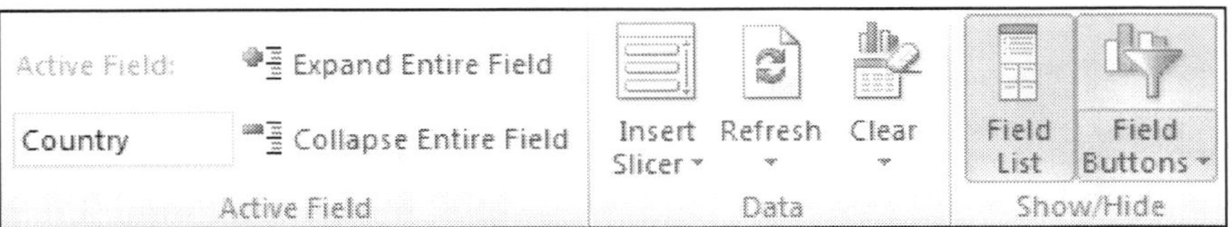

Figure 6-39 Pivot Chart Tools Analyze Tab

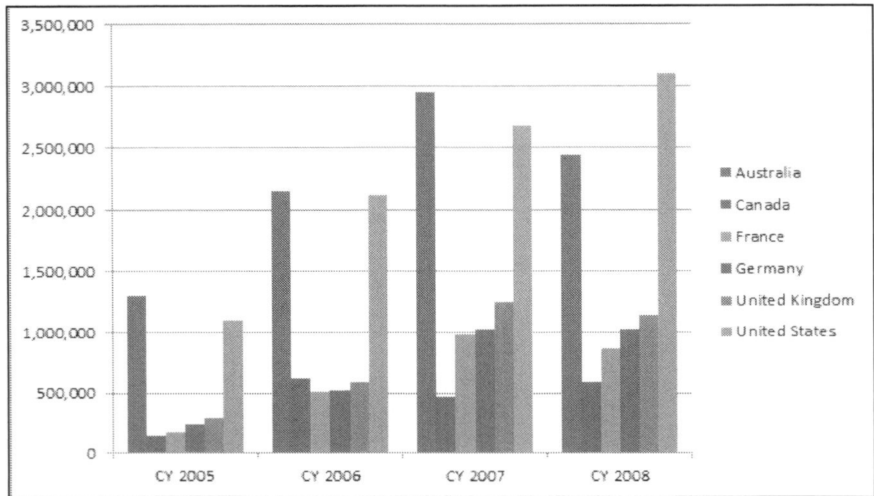

Figure 6-40 Example Pivot Chart without Dimension Selectors

Data Analysis With OLAP Cubes

As mentioned in the previous chapter connecting to an Analysis Services cube is similar to connecting to a SQL Server database. You select From Analysis Services on the From Other Sources menu on the Data tab and go on from there. We'll use the AdventureWorks DW SE sample as our example.

The pivot tables for the AdventureWorks2008DW database that we have been using such as in Figure 6-10 and an Analysis Services cube from AdventureWorks DW (Figure 6-41) that you have seen before are very similar although the database version is organized with tables and the cube version is organized with measures and dimensions. The cube version also contains calculated values and KPIs. You may drill-through to the underlying data in a cube pivot table the same way as a regular pivot table by double clicking on a cell in the value area.

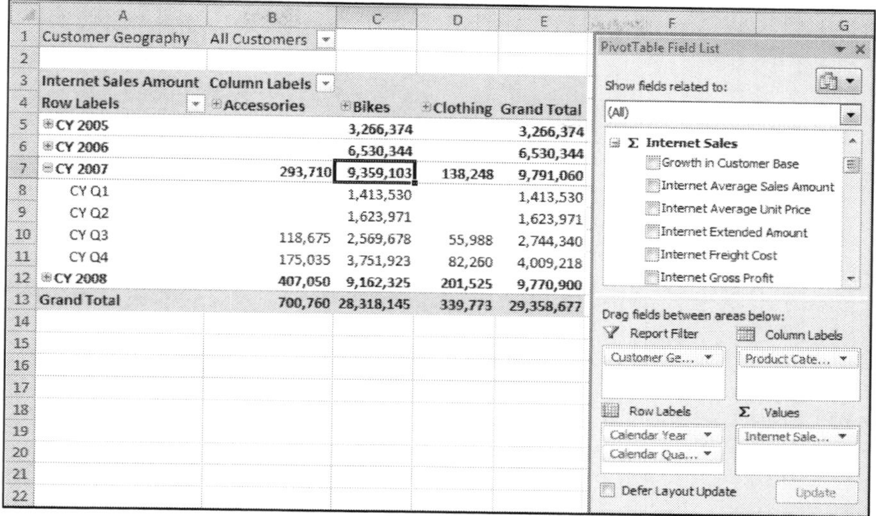

Figure 6-41 OLAP Cube Pivot Table Example

Offline Cube Files

Since OLAP cube pivot tables rely on Analysis Services to supply the data in real time and there is no local pivot cache, cube pivot tables do not have some of the features of regular Excel pivot tables. In particular, disconnection from Analysis Services results in the loss of pivot table functionality, i.e., the pivot table won't pivot anymore. So, if you want to use a cube when you cannot access Analysis Services or if the cube data is relatively static, you can create an offline cube, a file that acts like a pivot cache, by using the Offline OLAP menu item in the OLAP Tools option on the Pivot Table Tools Option tab to bring up the Offline OLAP Settings dialog box as in Figure 6-42. Clicking on the Create offline data file button will start a somewhat time consuming configuration process within which you must specify the dimension items and measures to include in the offline cube. The cube file will be saved in a location of your choice. To use the cube in another workbook open it with the Open option in the Excel Office button. You may copy the file to use elsewhere and send a copy for others to use.

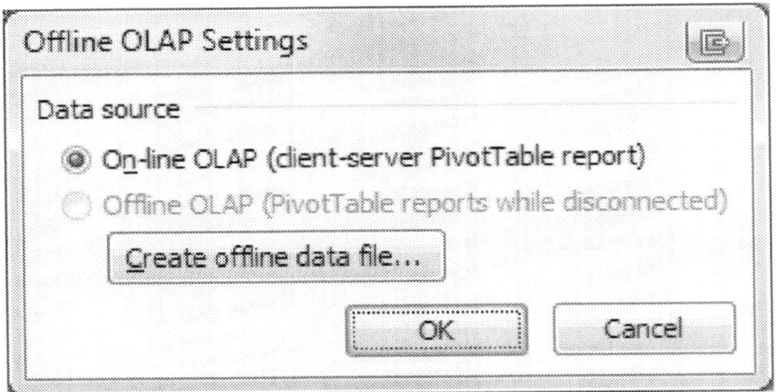

Figure 6-42 Offline OLAP Settings Dialog Box

Cube functions

Cube data presented in pivot table cells are produced by cube functions in each cell. The functions can be displayed by using the Convert to Formulas menu item on the OLAP Tools option. Doing that for the example in Figure 6-41 results in Figure 6-43 where the cube function for cell C10 is shown in the formula bar. Note that this resultant table is not a pivot table so the Pivot Table Field List pane no longer appears. Each cell in the pivot table will have a cube function. Some of the other cube functions in the example are listed in Table 6-2.

C10 =CUBEVALUE("AdventureWorks 2008 R2 Main Cube",$B$1,$A$3,$A10,C$4)

	A	B	C	D	E	F
1	Customer Geography	All Custo▾ rs				
2						
3	Internet Sales Amount	Column Labels				
4	Row Labels	Accessories	Bikes	Clothing	Grand Total	
5	CY 2005		3,266,374		3,266,374	
6	CY 2006		6,530,344		6,530,344	
7	CY 2007	293,710	9,359,103	138,248	9,791,060	
8	CY Q1		1,413,530		1,413,530	
9	CY Q2		1,623,971		1,623,971	
10	CY Q3	118,675	2,569,678	55,988	2,744,340	
11	CY Q4	175,035	3,751,923	82,260	4,009,218	
12	CY 2008	407,050	9,162,325	201,525	9,770,900	
13	Grand Total	700,760	28,318,145	339,773	29,358,677	

Figure 6-43 Cube Function Conversion

Cell	Cube Function
A3	=CUBEMEMBER("AdventureWorks 2008 R2 Main Cube","[Measures].[Internet Sales Amount]")
A10	=CUBEMEMBER("AdventureWorks 2008 R2 Main Cube","[Measures].[Internet Sales Amount]")
B7	=CUBEVALUE("AdventureWorks 2008 R2 Main Cube",$B$1,$A$3,$A7,B$4)
A13	=CUBEVALUE("AdventureWorks 2008 R2 Main Cube",$B$1,$A$3,$A7,B$4)
E13	=CUBEVALUE("AdventureWorks 2008 R2 Main Cube",$B$1,$A$3,$A7,B$4)

Table 6-2 Cube Function Examples

You can see from the pattern in the examples that the CUBEMEMBER function points to measures and dimensions and the CUBEVALUE function gets data from the cube based on cell references to the measures and dimensions. The available cube functions are briefly described in Table 6-3.

CUBEMEMBER (connection, member_expression,[caption]) Returns a member or tuple from the cube. Use to validate that the member or tuple exists in the cube.
CUBEVALUE (connection, [member_expression_1], [member_expression_2], …) Returns an aggregated value from the cube.
CUBESET (connection, set_expression, [caption], [sort_order], [sort_by]) Defines a calculated set of members or tuples by sending a set expression to the cube on the server, which creates the set, and then returns that set to Microsoft Office Excel.
CUBESETCOUNT (set) Returns the number of items in a set.
CUBERANKEDMEMBER (connection, set_expression, rank, [caption]) Returns the Nth item from a set.
CUBEMEMBERPROPERTY (connection, member_expression, property) Returns the value of a member property from the cube. Use to validate that a member name exists within the cube and to return the specified property for this member.
CUBEKPIMEMBER (connection, kpi_name, kpi_property, [caption]) Returns a key performance indicator (KPI) property and displays the KPI name in the cell.

Table 6-3 Cube Functions

You can move the cells with the cube functions to reorganize the data, and you can reference cells in a pivot table from cells outside the pivot table using cube functions. For example , I could insert the formula

=CUBEVALUE("AdventureWorks 2008 R2 Main Cube",$B$1,$A$3,$A5,C$4)

into a cell outside of the pivot table and it would return the correct value of 3,226,374. Thus, you can build custom tables with cube function. Note that you may need to convert the values to formulas for this to work. To do that use the Convert to Formulas command in OLAP Tools in the Tools group on the PivotTable Tools Options tab.

OLAP Pivot Table Extensions

OLAP PivotTable Extensions is an Excel 2007 and 2010 add-in that provides supplemental functionality to Excel when working with Analysis Services cubes. The additional features include adding local MDX calculations, i.e., calculated members; a calculations library; a pivot table MDX viewer; and changing pivot table defaults and searching capabilities. To use the OLAP extensions download the exe file from CodePlex and install it. An OLAP PivotTable Extensions options will be added to the list of menu items that are displayed when you right click anywhere in the pivot table. This will bring up the OLAP PivotTable Extensions dialog box shown in Figure 6-44.

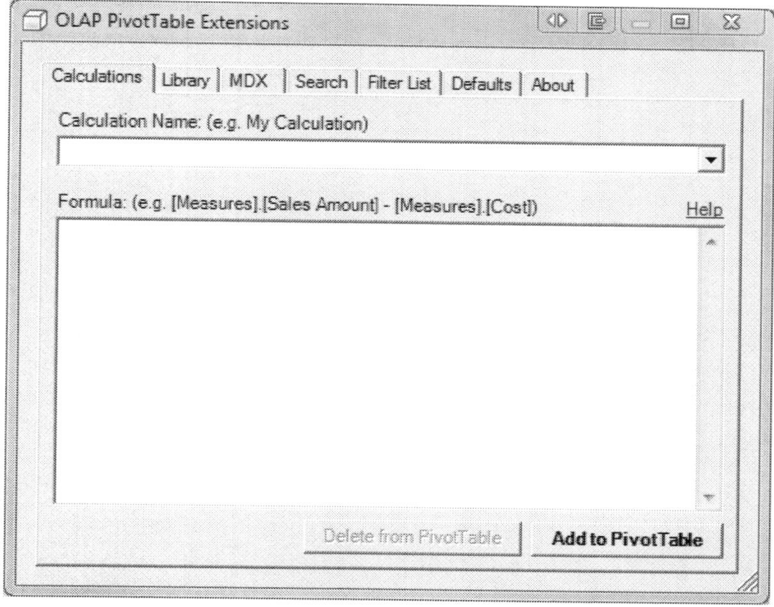

Figure 6-44 OLAP Pivot Table Extensions Dialog Box

Calculations (Calculated Members)

To me the most useful feature of the extensions add-in is the creation and management of local calculated members represented by the Calculations and Library tabs in the dialog box. As we mentioned in Chapters 3 and 4 calculated members are created with Multidimensional Expressions (MDX), a SQL type language for working with multidimensional databases. Since coverage of MDX is beyond the scope of this book, we will only look at a few examples.

Figure 6-45 shows the MDX expression for the calculated member Internet Gross Profit Margin which we introduced in Chapter 3. For illustrative purposes here I just copied and pasted it from BIDS. Clicking the Add to Pivot Table button will add the calculated member to the values area and to the Pivot Table Field list.

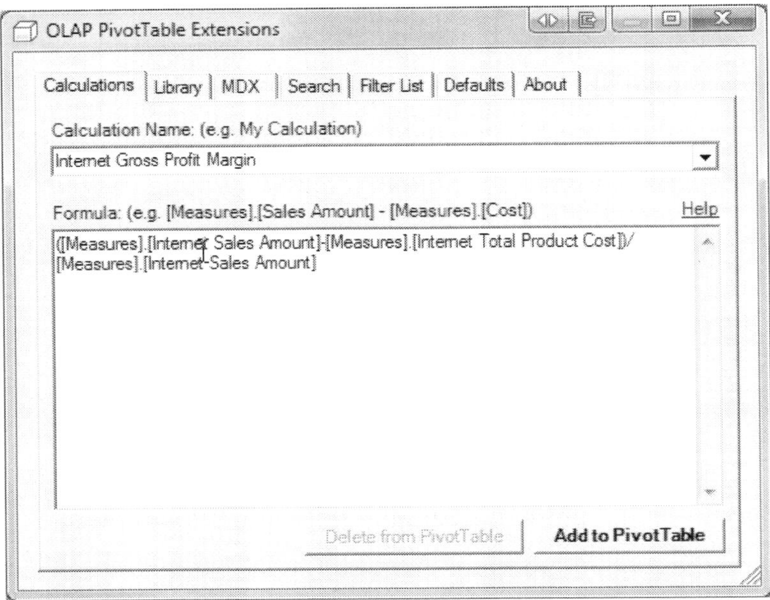

Figure 6-45 OLAP Pivot Table Extensions Calculations Tab

Clicking Help in the Calculations tab will take you to a CodePlex Web page that contains some additional information about MDX calculations and a few references.

Library

The Library tab in the dialog box shown in Figure 6-46 lists the calculated members in the local pivot table. As you can see I created two more, Internet Gross Profit and Internet Sales Average Sales Amount, by copying their MDX expressions from BIDS. The local calculated members are listed in the dialog box only if the Export to or Delete Calculations radio buttons are selected. You may export some or all of those calculated members to a xml file which you may use in other pivot tables or send a copy to others to use. To do that you must specify a file name and path in the textbox beside the Export radio button by either entering it directly or using the browse button to its right. Clicking the browse button will bring up the usual file finder window. Navigate to the directory where you want to save the xml file, enter a file name, and click open to return to the OLAP Pivot Table Extensions dialog box. Click the Execute button to have Excel save the file. Note that only calculated members with checks (✓) will be included in the xml file. Table 6-4 displays the XML for the calculated members in the example.

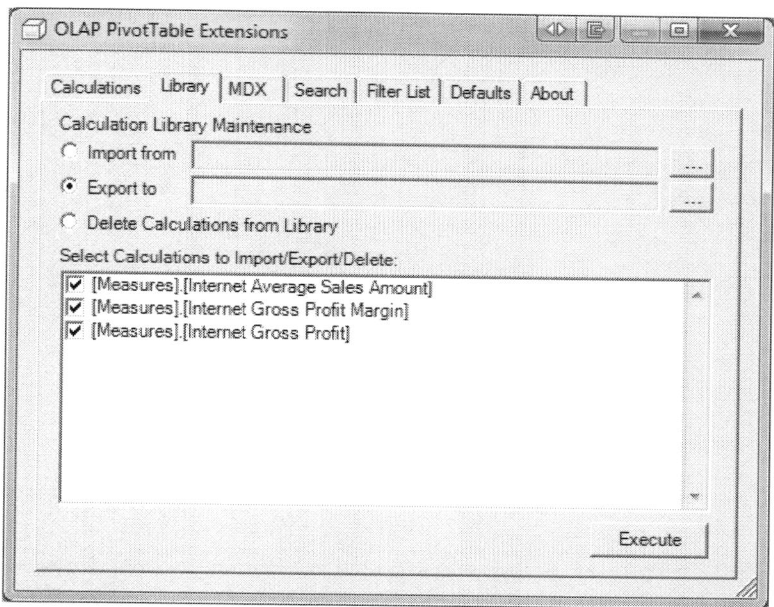

Figure 6-46 OLAP Pivot Table Extensions Library Tab

```
<?xml version="1.0" encoding="utf-8"?>
<CalculationsLibrary
xmlns:xsi="http://www.w3.org/2001/XMLSchema-instance"
xmlns:xsd="http://www.w3.org/2001/XMLSchema">
  <Calculations>
    <Calculation Name="[Measures].[Internet Average Sales
Amount]">
      <Formula>[Measures].[Internet Sales Amount]/
[Measures].[Internet Order Count]</Formula>
    </Calculation>
    <Calculation Name="[Measures].[Internet Gross Profit
Margin]">
      <Formula>([Measures].[Internet Sales Amount]-
[Measures].[Internet Total Product Cost])/
[Measures].[Internet Sales Amount]</Formula>
    </Calculation>
    <Calculation Name="[Measures].[Internet Gross Profit]">
      <Formula>[Measures].[Internet Sales Amount] -
 [Measures].[Internet Total Product Cost]
 </Formula>
    </Calculation>
  </Calculations>
</CalculationsLibrary>
```

Table 6-4 Calculated Members XML File

To import calculated members from a calculated members xml file select the Import from radio button, enter the file location or browse to it, and then click Execute. To delete one or more calculated members select the Delete Calculations radio button, check the calculated members to delete, and click Execute.

MDX, Search, and Default tabs

The MDX tab displays the query that Excel is using to get the pivot table data. The Search tab allows you to use a text search to find items in the Pivot Table Field List, in their descriptions, or in the cube's dimension members. The Default tab lets you enable the "Show calculated members from OLAP server" option without using the Excel Option on the Office button and to Turn on "Refresh data when opening the file" by default.

Distributing OLAP Pivot Tables

OLAP pivot tables can be distributed and used by others without the OLAP PivotTable Extensions except when other users want to reuse the private calculations of the creator.

Using Statistical Inference

It's doubtful that you will use classical statistical inference except correlation and regression directly unless you are involved with quality management or some kind of research. However, you may use it indirectly in interpreting results from data analysis algorithms. We review some basic concepts of statistical inference in Appendix B so we'll only briefly describe the statistical tests in the Analysis ToolPak add-in and go over one example which should be enough to make you skip to the next section. There are a few other tests available as Excel functions, e.g., chi square, which you can explore on your own.

The Analysis ToolPak contains three ANOVA tests, one freestanding F-test, three t-tests, and one z-test. ANOVA (Analysis of Variance) tests whether a factor(s) has a statistically significant impact on numerical results. For example, we could perform an analysis of variance on salary and categories of individuals' amount of education—say high school, college, and graduate degrees—to determine if education is a significant determinant of salary. The F-test allows comparison of two population variances. The t-tests and z-test assess differences between sample means: t-tests for small samples and the z-tests for large samples.

To demonstrate using the tests I created two random samples of sales from the AdventureWorks resellers data with twenty values each and tried the two sample equal variances t-test. Some of the data is shown on the left side for Figure 6-47. Since the samples were pulled from the same population I expected that the test should indicated that there is no statistically significant difference in the population means of the two samples. As mentioned previously the AnalysitToolPak tools are accessed by the Data Analysis option in the Analysis command group on the Data tab. After I selected the appropriate t-test and entered values in the dialog box, Excel generated the table of results on the right side of Figure 6-47.

	A	B	C	D	E	F
1	Sample 1	Sample 2		t-Test: Two-Sample Assuming Equal Variances		
2	1784.49	2770.164				
3	4293.924	323.994			*Sample 1*	*Sample 2*
4	3123.2728	818.883		Mean	1110.80834	1063.271235
5	424.845	298.062		Variance	1609472.7	975946.9086
6	404.664	1295.988		Observations	20	20
7	780.8182	2041.188		Pooled Variance	1292709.81	
8	20.746	627.768		Hypothesized Mean Difference	0	
9	939.588	2783.988		df	38	
10	149.676	202.332		t Stat	0.13221544	
11	3688.3767	194.364		P(T<=t) one-tail	0.44775575	
12	59.988	973.3581		t Critical one-tail	1.68595446	
13	647.988	735.7528		P(T<=t) two-tail	0.8955115	
14	1295.976	606.996		t Critical two-tail	2.02439415	
15	1943.952	838.9178				
16	111.762	1943.964				
17	129.576	140.904				
18	83.988	1200.525				
19	602.346	3274.8				
20	1430.442	63.9				
21	299.748	129.576				

Figure 6-47 Example t-Test

The t statistic is similar to the z statistic or z score which indicates how many standard deviations a value is away from the mean in a normal distribution. You may recall from your statistics course that Z ± 1 represents about 66 percent of a normal distribution, Z ± 2 about 95 percent, and Z ± 3 about 99 percent. The t statistic is similarly interpreted. In the example above the computed t value is .132 (cell E10) as compared with the critical value for a two-tail test of 2.02 (cell E14) which is determined by the alpha level parameter that you specify in the t-Test dialog box. I left the alpha level at its default value of .05 which is saying that I am willing to accept the risk of making a Type I error five percent of the time. (See Appendix B for a bit more about this.) So, since the computed t value is less than the critical value, I can accept the hypothesis that the means are equal which I knew anyway. Another way of looking at this is that to reject the null hypothesis that the means are equal the P(T<=t) two-tail value in cell E13 must be less than or equal to .05.

The importance of the example is that you can manage the risk that you are taking in making a decision where statistical inference is applicable by using the concept of statistical significance and confidence levels. This concept is also pertinent to regression analysis summarized in the next section.

Correlation and Regression

Correlation measures the strength of the linear association between two numeric variables, and regression constructs mathematical models of the relationship between a dependent variable and one or more independent variables.

Correlation

The strength of the linear correlation between two variables is measured by the correlation coefficient (r) which can take on values between -1 to +1, i.e., -1 <= r <= 1. Positive values for r indicate that the variables move together—as one rises so does the other, and negative values indicate that the variables move inversely—as one rises the other falls. The example in Figure 6-48 contains three data series on the left side and the correlation table showing the pair-wise correlations for them on the right. The cells on the diagonal show that each series is perfectly correlated with itself. Series one is perfectly inversely correlated with Series 2, and Series 3 has little correlation with either.

	A	B	C	D	E	F	G	H
1	Series 1	Series 2	Series 3		Correlations (r value)			
2	1	5	4			*Series 1*	*Series 2*	*Series 3*
3	2	4	1		Series 1	1		
4	3	3	5		Series 2	-1	1	
5	4	2	2		Series 3	-0.1	0.1	1

Figure 6-48 Correlation Example

The coefficient of determination (r^2), the square of the coefficient of correlation, gives the proportion of the variation in one variable explained by the other variable. For example, if two data series have a r value of -.78, then r^2 at .61 says that the variation in one variable explains 61 percent of the variation in the other.

Regression

The introduction to regression analysis presented in Chapter 3 in the context of Analysis Services data mining algorithms will not be repeated here. Rather, we will focus on using Excel's regression analysis tools. In that introduction we used an example of the relationship between General Electric's annual net income in millions of dollars and the Dow Jones Industrial Index (DJI) year-end value. Those data are shown in Figure 6-49a, the regression results in Figure 6-49b, and the scatter chart with a trend line in 6-49c. Note that the trend line was included in the scatter chart by right clicking on one of the data points and selecting Add Trendline from the menu.

	A	B	C
1	Year End	DJI	GE Net Income
2	1996	6,448	7,280
3	1997	7,908	8,203
4	1998	9,181	9,296
5	1999	11,497	10,717
6	2000	10,787	12,735
7	2001	10,022	13,684
8	2002	8,342	14,118
9	2003	10,454	15,518
10	2004	10,783	17,222
11	2005	10,718	16,720
12	2006	12,463	20,742
13	2007	13,265	22,208
14	2008	8,776	17,410
15	2009	10,428	11,025
16	2010	11,577	11,644

Figure 6-49a Regression Example Data

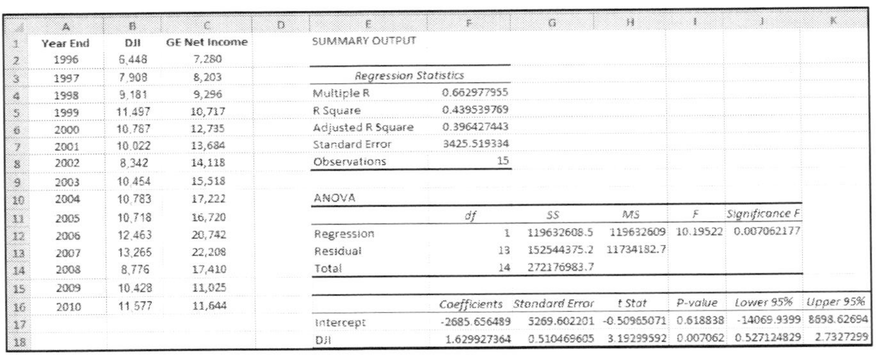

	A	B	C
1	Year End	DJI	GE Net Income
2	1996	6,448	7,280
3	1997	7,908	8,203
4	1998	9,181	9,296
5	1999	11,497	10,717
6	2000	10,787	12,735
7	2001	10,022	13,684
8	2002	8,342	14,118
9	2003	10,454	15,518
10	2004	10,783	17,222
11	2005	10,718	16,720
12	2006	12,463	20,742
13	2007	13,265	22,208
14	2008	8,776	17,410
15	2009	10,428	11,025
16	2010	11,577	11,644

SUMMARY OUTPUT

Regression Statistics	
Multiple R	0.662977955
R Square	0.439539769
Adjusted R Square	0.396427443
Standard Error	3425.519334
Observations	15

ANOVA

	df	*SS*	*MS*	*F*	*Significance F*
Regression	1	119632608.5	119632609	10.19522	0.007062177
Residual	13	152544375.2	11734182.7		
Total	14	272176983.7			

	Coefficients	*Standard Error*	*t Stat*	*P-value*	*Lower 95%*	*Upper 95%*
Intercept	-2685.656489	5269.602201	-0.50965071	0.618838	-14069.9399	8698.62694
DJI	1.629927364	0.510469605	3.19299592	0.007062	0.527124829	2.7327299

Figure 6-49b Regression Example Results

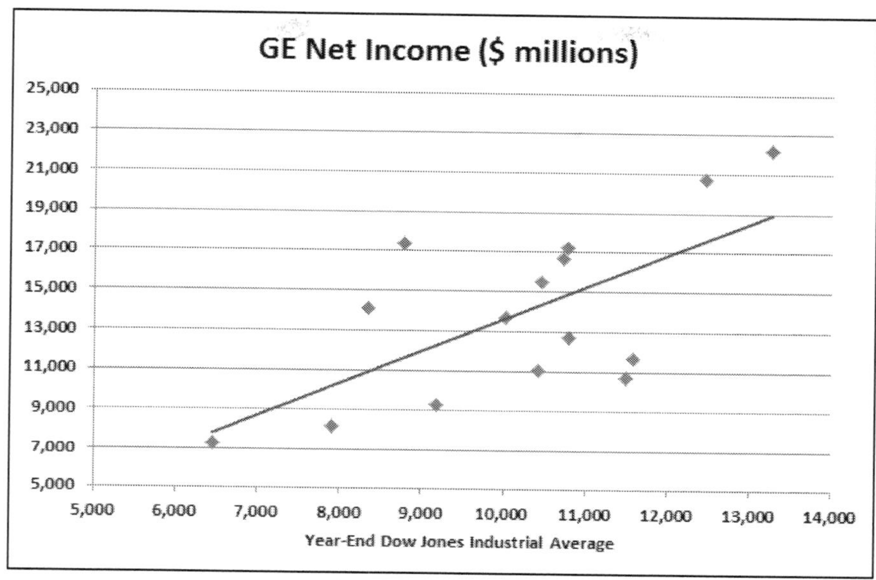

Figure 6-49c Regression Example Chart

Excel uses a linear regression algorithm, the most common type of regressions analysis, to formulate a model of the relationship between the DJI as the independent variable and GE's net income as the dependent variable by minimizing the sum of the squared errors between the linear model and the actual values, i.e., the algorithm finds the line of best fit. The general linear equation for the relationship is Y = a + bX where Y is the dependent variable, X is the independent variable, a is the Y-intercept (a constant), and b is the slope of the line. In this equation a and b are the model's parameters which are computed by the regression algorithm. For the GE data that we're using a = -2685.65 and b= 1.62992 shown in Figure 6-41b cells F17 and F18 respectively. So, the model turns out to be:

$$Y = -2685.65 + 1.62992X$$

or

$$\text{GE Net Income} = -2685.65 + 1.62992\ (\text{DJI})$$

The Summary Output for the model (Figure 6-49b) includes regression statistics, analysis of variance results to determine the statistical significance of the overall model, and information about the model's components. The Multiple R in this case is the correlation coefficient of the two series, and R Square is the coefficient of determination. The ANOVA section reports values for the sum of the square deviations from the mean, partitioning the values into that due to the model (Regression) and that not accounted for by the model (Residual). MS is the mean sum of squares deviations, and F is the ratio of the mean square values. In this case F = 10.19522 (119632609/11734183). You could look in a F distribution table for the significance of the F value but Excel provides it. In this case there is only a .007 probability that the coefficient computed for the DJI term in the model is equal to zero. So we can conclude that the model is statistically significant.

The regression coefficients section below the ANOVA section reports statistics for the model's parameters, the intercept and the DJI coefficient in this case. The important values in that section are the coefficient values, of course, and the t statistic and the corresponding P-values. The t statistic is the coefficient divided by the standard error and is interpreted similarly as in the t-test example above. The null hypothesis is that the coefficient (on DJI in this case) is equal to zero. Excel gives the probability of that occurring (the P-value) of .007 which says that it is very likely to be different than zero. Note that for this two variable example the P-value and the F Significance in the ANOVA section are the same. The P-value for the intercepts is quite high at .61 indicating that the intercept value is not significantly different than zero. So, you could easily rerun the analysis enabling the Constant is Zero feature.

The Lower 95% and Upper 95% columns present the values for the 95% confidence interval for each parameter. In the example the confidence interval for the DJI coefficient is 0..527 <= DJI <= 2.732 which says that you can be 95% confident that the DJI coefficient falls within that range. The confidence intervals for the Intercept and the 99% range can be interpreted in a similar manner.

This model differs somewhat from the one in Chapter 3 because I use all 15 rows of data for the analysis here. In Chapter 3 I left the 2010 data out of the analysis so that I could use the 2010 DJI to "predict" GE's 2010 net income. It's interesting to compare the regression results in Chapter 3 r=.717 with those here r= .663 . The difference is the effect of the addition of the 2010 outlier which you can see on the scatter chart.

To run a linear regression analysis with Excel select Regression from the Data Analysis option menu on the Data tab to bring up the Regression dialog box as in Figure 6-50. First, enter the data ranges for the dependent and independent variables. I do this by selecting the values in the worksheet. The other dialog box options are briefly described in Table 6-5. I normally don't use the residuals features.

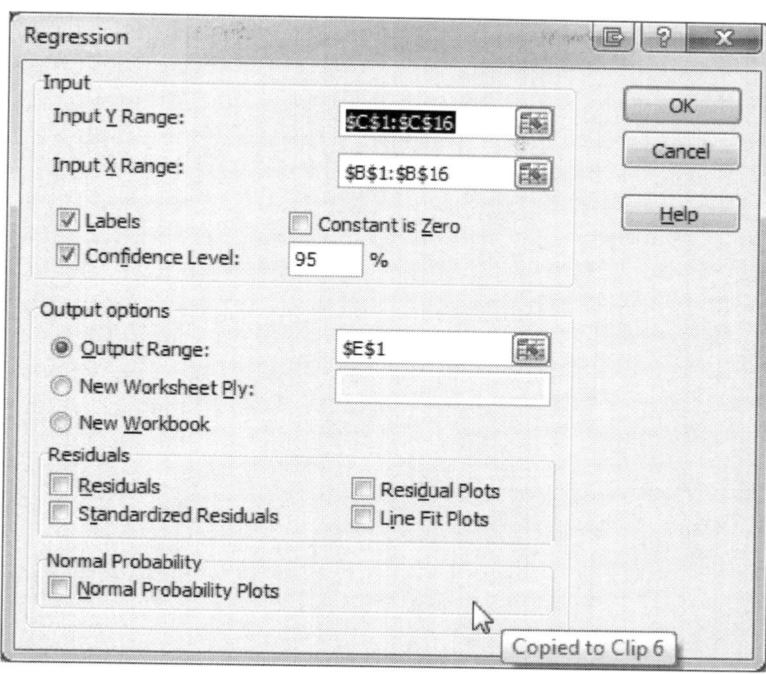

Figure 6-50 Regression Dialog Box

Option	Description
Labels	Used if labels appear in the first row of the series.
Constant is Zero	Forces the constant in the equation to zero. Thus, the trend line will intersect both axes at the zero point.
Confidence Level	A 95% confidence level is always returned with the results. To include another check the box and enter the value in the textbox.
Residuals	Provides the residuals, the difference between the value predicted by the model and the actual value, for each observation.
Standardized Residuals	Are standardized (normalized) residual values calculated by dividing the residual by standard deviation of the residuals which is not provided in the output. This gives a Z-score of the residual on a standard normal distribution.
Residual Plots	Produces a chart showing residuals on the vertical axis and each independent variable on the horizontal axis.
Line Plots	Creates a chart of predicted and actual values somewhat similar to similar to the one in Figure 6-41c. However, the default chart type is a column chart.
Normal probability Plots	Shows the degree to which the data are normally distributed. The straighter the upward sloping line the more normal the distribution.

Table 6-5 Regression Options

(For better viewing of this image, go to http://www.zerobits.info/bibook/bibookimages/)

Statisticians warn about violating the assumptions underlying linear regression such as multicollinearity and homoscedasticity. We won't cover them here but there are plenty of Web pages that address the issues. In practicality, users seem unconcerned about the assumptions and use regression models without checking for violations. The attitude appears to be if the model works, don't worry about it.

Regression analysis is commonly used in time-series forecasting where the independent variable in the model is time. We will postpone discussion of time-series forecasting until Chapter 8.

Multiple Regression

Multiple regression is identical to simple regression, the two variable case, described above except that there are two or more independent variables in the model which takes the form:

$$Y = a + b_1X_1 + b_2X_2 + b_3X_3 + \ldots + b_nX_n$$

where a is the Y-intercept and the bs are the coefficients on the n independent variables. (Purists please note that I have intentionally not included an error term at the end of the equation.) For an example I scrounged around on the Internet and found a number of economic data series partially shown in Figure 6-51a which I threw into the regression pot with Crude Oil Price as the dependent variable to see what happened. The resultant output is in Figure 6-51b.

Year	Crude Oil Price	GDP	U.S. Population	Coal - Short Tons	Gold - $ per oz.	Retail Sales	Crude Oil Production	Unemployment	S & P End	S & P 500 Return
1973	$22.73	1,382.70	211,908,788	562,583,603	$114.50	1,150,923	55.68	4.9	119.1	18.09%
1974	$40.29	1,500.00	213,853,928	558,401,800	$135.20	1,098,806	55.72	5.6	97.68	-29.81%
1975	$48.21	1,638.30	215,973,199	562,640,432	$150.80	1,090,363	52.83	8.5	70.23	28.42%
1976	$48.91	1,825.30	218,035,164	603,789,974	$145.10	1,146,353	57.34	7.7	90.9	18.22%
1977	$50.48	2,030.90	220,239,425	625,290,963	$179.20	1,187,544	59.71	7.1	107	-11.12%
1978	$48.71	2,294.70	222,584,545	625,224,827	$244.90	1,229,412	60.16	6.1	93.82	2.44%
1979	$71.44	2,563.30	225,055,487	680,524,248	$578.70	1,233,292	62.67	5.8	96.73	11.59%
1980	$97.47	2,789.50	227,224,681	702,729,735	$641.20	1,158,759	59.56	7.1	105.76	28.37%
1981	$83.54	3,128.40	229,465,714	732,626,833	$430.80	1,181,899	56.06	7.6	134.34	10.11%

Figure 6-51a Multiple Regression Data

M	N	O	P	Q	R	S	T	U
Multiple R	0.922088238							
R Square	0.850246718							
Adjusted R Square	0.796335537							
Standard Error	8.891109844							
Observations	35							
ANOVA								
	df	*SS*	*MS*	*F*	*Significance F*			
Regression	9	11220.71613	1246.746237	15.77124995	3.07207E-08			
Residual	25	1976.295856	79.05183425					
Total	34	13197.01199						
	Coefficients	*Standard Error*	*t Stat*	*P-value*	*Lower 95%*	*Upper 95%*	*Lower 99.0%*	*Upper 99.0%*
Intercept	573.2947724	209.265316	2.739559442	0.01118278	142.3047899	1004.284755	-10.01886222	1156.608407
GDP	0.011132269	0.006720917	1.656361675	0.110148248	-0.002709718	0.024974255	-0.007601855	0.029866392
U.S. Population	-4.0606E-06	1.24747E-06	-3.255071364	0.003245766	-6.62981E-06	-1.49139E-06	-7.53784E-06	-5.83361E-07
Coal - Short Tons	2.03746E-07	9.52602E-08	2.13883875	0.042403162	7.55415E-09	3.99938E-07	-6.17855E-08	4.69278E-07
Gold - $ per oz.	0.07332127	0.015981106	4.587997233	0.000108409	0.040407566	0.106234973	0.028774963	0.117867576
Retail Sales	-5.7217E-05	5.92314E-05	-0.965991759	0.343300707	-0.000179206	6.47723E-05	-0.000222321	0.000107887
Crude Oil Production	3.390839984	0.926377133	3.660323494	0.001178667	1.48293058	5.298749387	0.808623195	5.973056773
Unemployment	10.38427867	2.42858669	4.275852581	0.000243326	5.382510791	15.38604654	3.614749171	17.15380816
S & P End	0.043476122	0.013314558	3.265307167	0.003164944	0.016054277	0.070897968	0.006362646	0.080589598
S & P 500 Returns	5.686939845	10.56133859	0.538467714	0.59501665	-16.06454397	27.43842366	-23.7521135	35.12599319

Figure 6-51b Multiple Regression Output - All Variables

(For better viewing of this image, go to http://www.zerobits.info/bibook/bibookimages/)

The output is interpreted the same as the one above for the simple regression example. The correlation between the oil price and the independent variables together is quite high at .92 and the ANOVA result is highly significant. The P-values for the GDP, Retail Sales, and S & P 500 Returns are not significant so I deleted them from the data set and reran the regression. The Multiple R only declined to .91 and the ANOVA significance increased a bit. I looked at the correlation table (not shown) and noticed that some of the independent variables were highly intercorrelated. Since one of the assumptions underlying regression is an absence of high collinearity among independent variables, I deleted U. S. Population and S & P End and reran it again. The resulting output is shown in Figure 6-51c. The Multiple R has now dropped to .847 but I have pared five independent variable from the model and the ANOVA results are still highly significant as are the coefficient P-values. Using the principle of parsimony I am probably willing to lose a little multiple r to gain model simplicity.

H	I	J	K	L	M	N	O	P
Multiple R	0.84682727							
R Square	0.717116425							
Adjusted R Square	0.679398615							
Standard Error	11.15529461							
Observations	35							
ANOVA								
	df	*SS*	*MS*	*F*	*Significance F*			
Regression	4	9463.794053	2365.949	19.01267395	6.98881E-08			
Residual	30	3733.217935	124.4406					
Total	34	13197.01199						
	Coefficients	*Standard Error*	*t Stat*	*P-value*	*Lower 95%*	*Upper 95%*	*Lower 99.0%*	*Upper 99.0%*
Intercept	-89.9174676	40.41062276	-2.22509	0.033741127	-172.446969	-7.38796608	-201.046504	21.21156926
Coal - Short Tons	-1.026E-07	1.90384E-08	-5.3892	7.76195E-06	-1.4148E-07	-6.372E-08	-1.5496E-07	-5.0246E-08
Gold - $ per oz.	0.07858137	0.0146167	5.376136	8.05348E-06	0.048730086	0.108432655	0.038385508	0.118777233
Crude Oil Production	2.436030225	0.656420585	3.711081	0.000839127	1.095440549	3.776619901	0.63087647	4.241183979
Unemployment	6.691080354	2.047830543	3.267399	0.002720446	2.508852455	10.87330825	1.059555266	12.32260544

Figure 6-51c Multiple Regression Output - Trimmed Variables

(For better viewing of this image, go to http://www.zerobits.info/bibook/bibookimages/)

So, our final model is :

Crude Oil Price = -89.917 -1.026E-07 Coal + 0.0785 Gold + 2.436 Crude Production + 6.691 Unemployment

Although the coefficient on Coal - Short Tons is quite small, deleting it results in a decline of Multiple R to .666 (not shown) so I'll keep it in the model for now. If you wanted to see the charts plotting each independent variable against the dependent variable, you could enable the Line Fit Plots option in the Regressions dialog box. Note that this model is only useful for demonstrating how to use multiple regression and probably has no actual predictive or explanatory value. However, it does describe the linear relationships between the dependent and independent variables.

This is a good time to make a point about causality. In regression analysis we are only assessing if and how variable move together, i.e., we look at the relationships among the variables. This does not imply any causality between the independent and dependent variables. In the example above we should not conclude that higher unemployment causes higher crude oil prices. In fact, intuitively I would expect the opposite.

Other Types of Regression

Although linear regression is the most well-known and used form, there are other types of regression including nonlinear regression, log linear regression, logistic regression, etc. As far as I know Excel add-ins are not available for these, at least are free ones, but you could spring for more full-featured statistical analysis software, say SAS or SPSS, if you need to do advanced work. One useful algorithm is stepwise regression which builds the regression model in steps by either adding or subtracting variables one at a time based on their impact on the performance of the model.

Excel regression can be adapted, forced if you will, to accommodate non-linearity and categorical variables. In the case of the former the nonlinear independent variable(s) are converted to a near linear form and then the regression is run with the converted data. For example, in the concocted data in Figure 6-52a column B is obviously the exponential function 2^n as represented by the solid line in the chart (Figure 6-52b). That series can be transformed into a linear form by taking the log to the base 2 which is depicted by the dashed line in the chart. The log data would be used in the regression analysis.

	B	C
1	Data	Log
2	2	1
3	4	2
4	8	3
5	16	4
6	32	5
7	64	6
8	128	7
9	256	8
10	512	9
11	1024	10
12	2048	11
13	4096	12
14	8192	13
15	16384	14
16	32768	15

Figure 6-44a Data

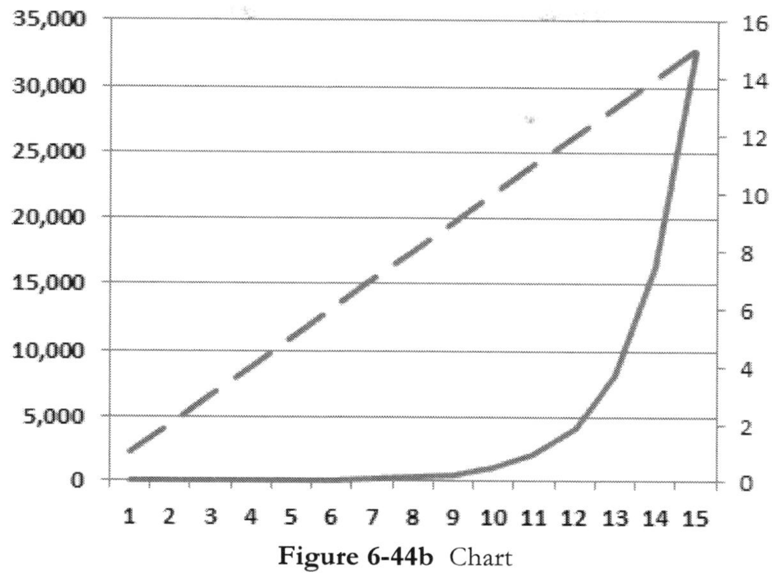

Figure 6-44b Chart

Figure 6-52 Non-Linear Data

(For better viewing of this image, go to http://www.zerobits.info/bibook/bibookimages/)

Categorical data can be accommodated in an Excel regression model by using dummy variables that take on the values zero or one. We'll wait until Chapter 8, time series forecasting, to show how to use them.

What's Next

Well, we've covered a lot of territory about using Excel's capabilities for data analysis in this and the previous chapter. However, we have not exhausted all of the possibilities but I hope that what we've explored will address most of you data analysis needs. If not, dig around in Excel and search on the Web—you'll probably find a solution.

In the next chapter we move on to Access 2010 to look at its data analysis capabilities and how it can complement and supplement Excel.

Chapter 7 - Data Analysis with Access 2010

We'll spend time in this chapter looking at Access 2010's features that are helpful and useful for your work in BI. It is in no way intended to be a comprehensive treatment. For more complete coverage of data analysis with Access please see other sources.

Preliminaries

As with Excel we assume a moderate level of expertise with Access, meaning that you should be comfortable creating and using Access databases with multiple tables, select queries, forms, and reports. Also, as with Excel if you need to jog your memory about Access basics, there is a short refresher in Appendix E.

Reasons for Using Access

In Chapter 5 we mentioned that although Excel is a near perfect mechanism for analyzing data, it has shortcomings with respect to database management. In my opinion, Microsoft Office Access 2010 (hereafter referred to as Access) is the easiest to use full-featured, single-user database management software available. In addition, at times data cleaning and transformation tasks are easier with Access, and it plays nice with Excel and other Microsoft products. To me an Access database is much easier to understand than a series of complex Excel worksheets

ACCDB File Format

Access 2007 introduced a new main file format, accdb (as in MyNewData.accdb), instead of the mdb format (as in the file MyOldData.mdb) in previous versions. This change was necessary to accommodate new features such as multi-valued lookup fields, the attachment data type, and integration with Windows SharePoint Services and Outlook 2007. Although Access 2010 can still use mdb files in compatibility mode, you may convert them to utilize the new features. However, be aware that the accdb format is not backwards compatible so if you are sharing an Access database with others who have not upgraded to the 2007 or 2010 versions, then use the mdb format.

Chapter Organization

I originally tried to organize this chapter similar to the preceding Excel chapters in the order of data analysis steps but that didn't work because of overlapping topics. So, we'll start with external data sources, then move on to queries, then database management, and finish with Access Data Projects. I choose not to address charting and graphing or producing reports with Access because the former is much easier to do in Excel and the latter is a lengthy topic not directly connected with data analysis. Both topics are covered much better in the many Access 2010 books available.

External Data Sources

Access can and is used for OLTP and multi-user applications which accept direct data input but that is not recommended, and since our focus is on data analysis, we won't cover direct data entry in Access, say via forms. Rather, we will focus on acquiring data from external sources as we did in the first Excel chapter. We will look at the usual sources such as Access itself, Excel, and ODBC but we'll skip less likely sources like dBase and Paradox files.

With many external data sources you have the option of importing into Access which creates identical copies of the source objects or linking to tables in the data source which does not move the data from the source. Note that you have access to all objects in the data source when importing, e.g., tables, queries, forms, etc. whereas access to some objects may be limited with linking.

From Access

Clicking Access in the Import & Link command group on the External Data tab displays the Get External Data - Access Database dialog box shown in Figure 7-1 where you identify the source file and select whether to import objects or link tables. Since we are working with other Access databases, the source file extension must be either mdb or accdb. The example we'll use here is the Northwind Traders sample database, and I have elected to import the data. Clicking the OK button brings up the Import Objects dialog box with multiple tabs as in Figure 7-2. You may select as many items that you want in each tab. If you want to import all of the items, it may be easier just to copy the database and give it a new name.

For our example I selected all of the tables and no other objects. Clicking OK will display a Save Import Steps dialog box (Figure 7-3) which will save the import information so that you can subsequently run the import without using the wizard just like using an existing connection in Excel. The saved import will be listed in the Manage Data Tasks dialog box which is accessed via the Saved Imports option on the External Data tab.

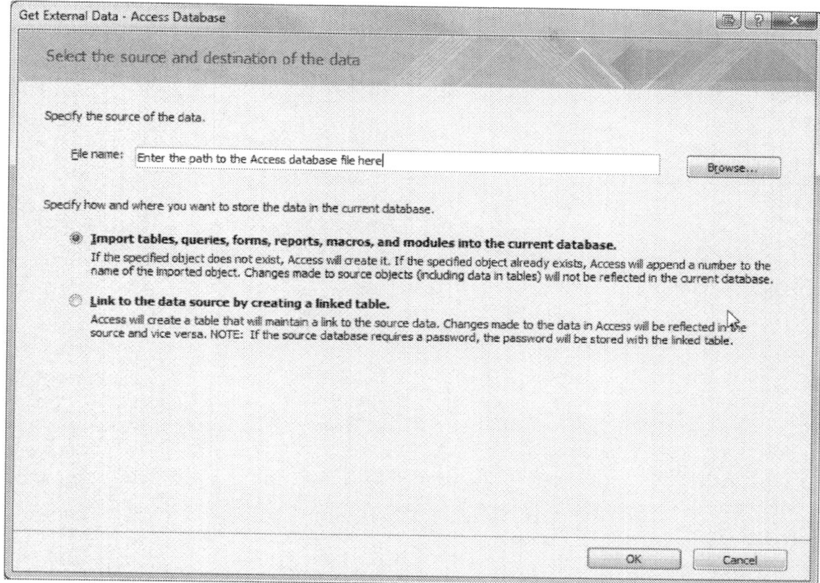

Figure 7-1 Get External Data - Access Database

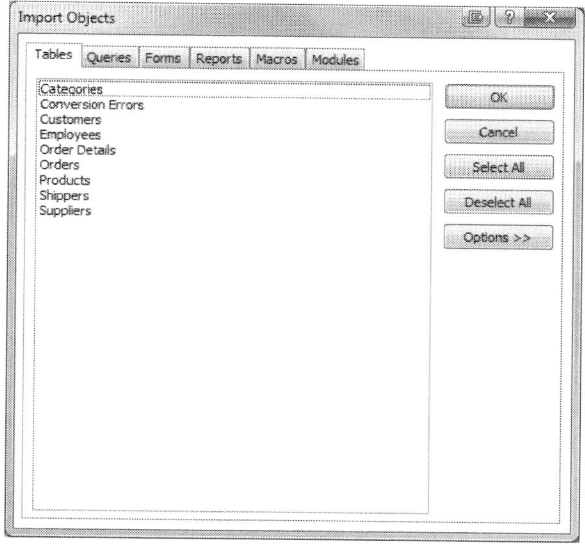

Figure 7-2 Import Objects Dialog Box

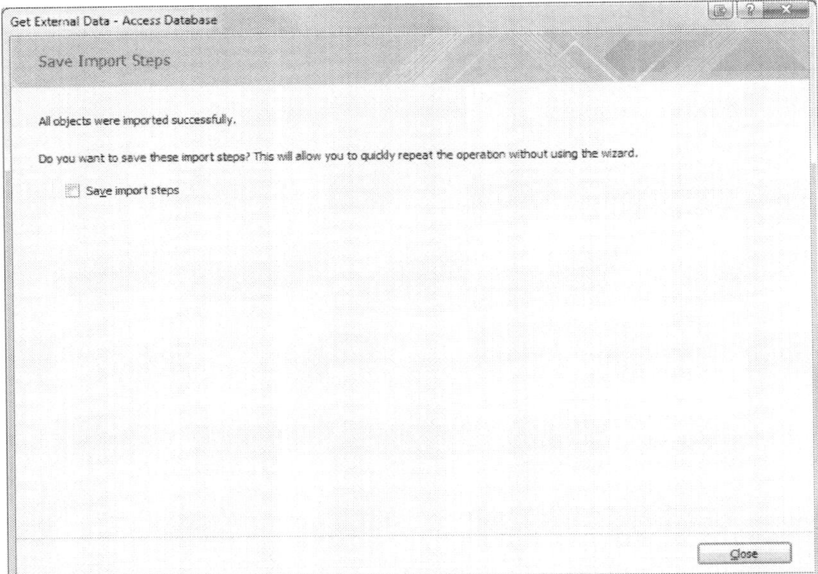

Figure 7-3 Save Import Steps Dialog Box

Selecting the link option in Figure 7-1 brings up a Link Tables dialog box (not shown) identical to Figure 7-2 except that there is only a Tables tab. Clicking the OK button after selecting tables to link will immediately insert the tables into the database without displaying the Save Import Steps dialog box (Figure 7-3). Figure 7-4 shows the navigation panes in Access for the database containing the imported tables on the left (Figure 7-4a) and linked tables on the right (Figure 7-4b). Note the arrows next to the table icons in Figure 7-4b which indicate that the tables are linked.

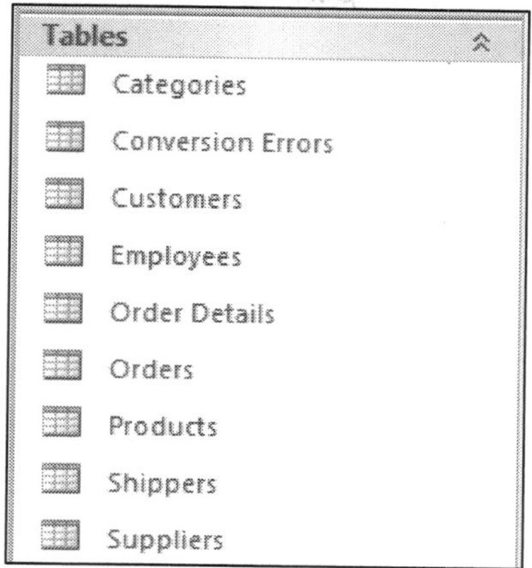

Figure 7-4a Import

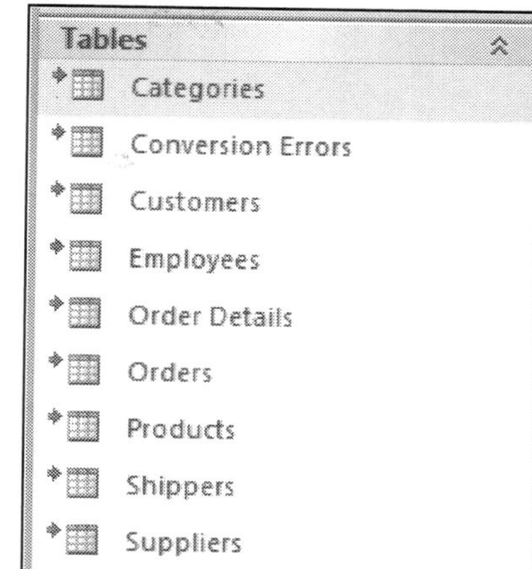

Figure 7-4b Linked Tables

Figure 7-4 Import and Linked Tables Navigation Panes

You may import and link objects from multiple Access databases into another one. For example, after creating the database shown in Figure 7-4a I could run the Import Access option again and link to the tables in the Pubs database so that the resultant database would contain tables from each. Note that the relationships (discussed later in this chapter) among the tables in the source databases are preserved in the resultant database.

To convert a linked table into a non-linked table first copy the linked table by right clicking on it and select copy from the menu or using the copy option on the Home tab. Then, right click on the navigation pane and select paste from the menu or use the Paste option on the Home tab to display the usual Paste Table As dialog box as in Figure 7-5. Rename the table if you prefer, select the paste type, and click the OK button.

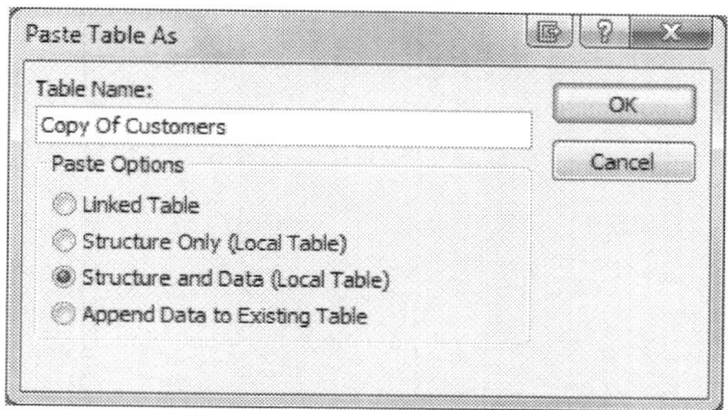

Figure 7-5 Paste Table As Dialog Box

From Excel

In Chapter 5 I confessed to inappropriately using Excel as a database manager more than once. In each of these cases the data became increasingly more difficult to manage in Excel, and I eventually moved to Access. It's easy to import data from Excel into Access by using the Excel option in the Import & Link command group on the External Data tab which displays a Get External Data - Excel Spreadsheet dialog box (not shown) identical to the one in Figure 7-1. Regardless of specifying import or link, the next dialog box begins the Import Spreadsheet Wizard as in Figure 7-6a where you select the worksheet or named range to import or link. The example in the figure is using an Excel workbook containing AdventureWorks2008 Internet sales data that we used previously. The next window (Figure 7-6b) asks about column heading in the first row, and since we are importing data from an Excel table the column headings are there.

The next window (Figure 7-6c) allows you to specify properties about each field, and the following window (Figure 7-6d) asks you to set the primary key. In the Internet sales example there is no acceptable primary key in the Excel table so I let Access add one, the highlighted ID field. Note that if you select to choose your own, you are limited to only one existing field as the primary key, i.e., you cannot specify a compound primary key here. However, you could proceed with no primary key and then edit the table structure later to create the compound key. In the final window (Figure 7-6e) you can give the new table a name and select if you want the table to be analyzed after importation. The latter option initiates the Table Analyzer Wizard (not shown) which will split the data into separate tables if necessary to avoid duplication and create relationships among the new tables. The Table Analyzer is discussed later in the chapter.

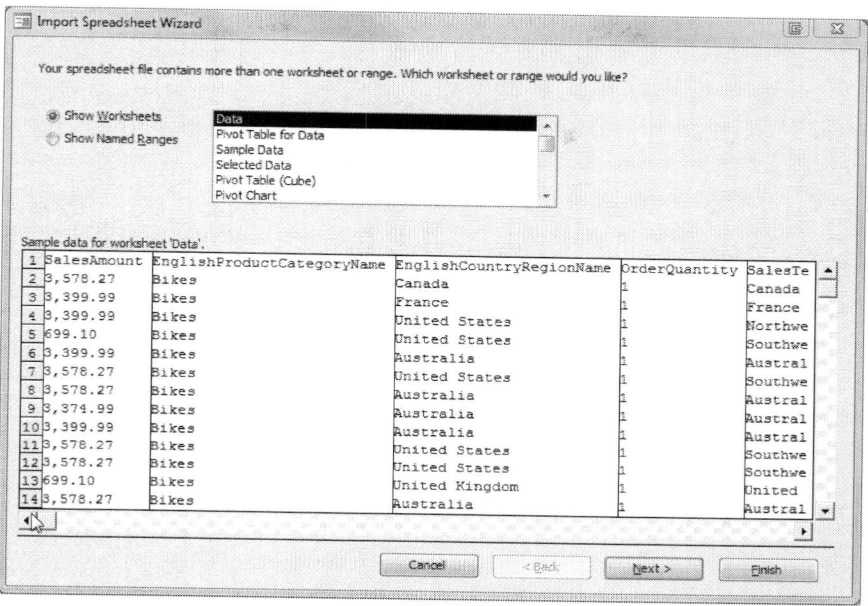

Figure 7-6a Import Spreadsheet Wizard - Step 1

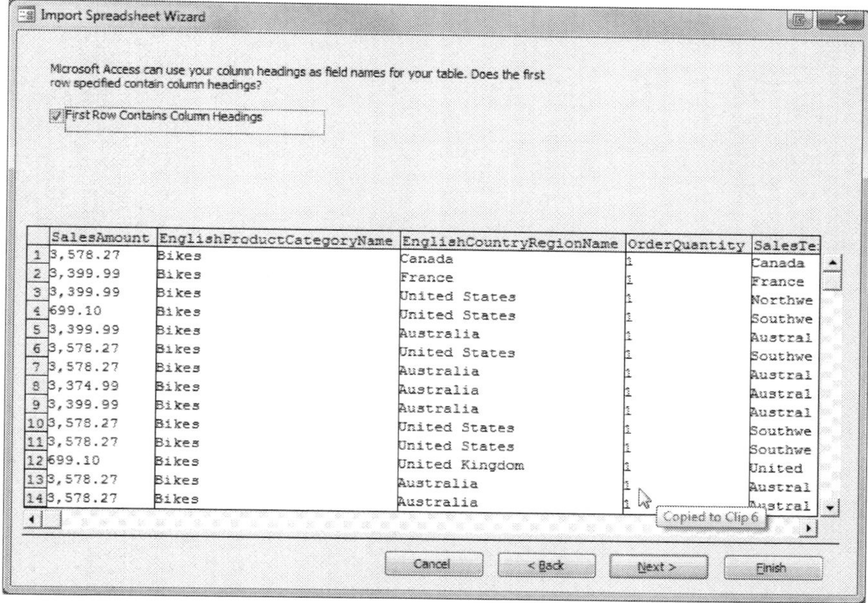

Figure 7-6b Import Spreadsheet Wizard - Step 2

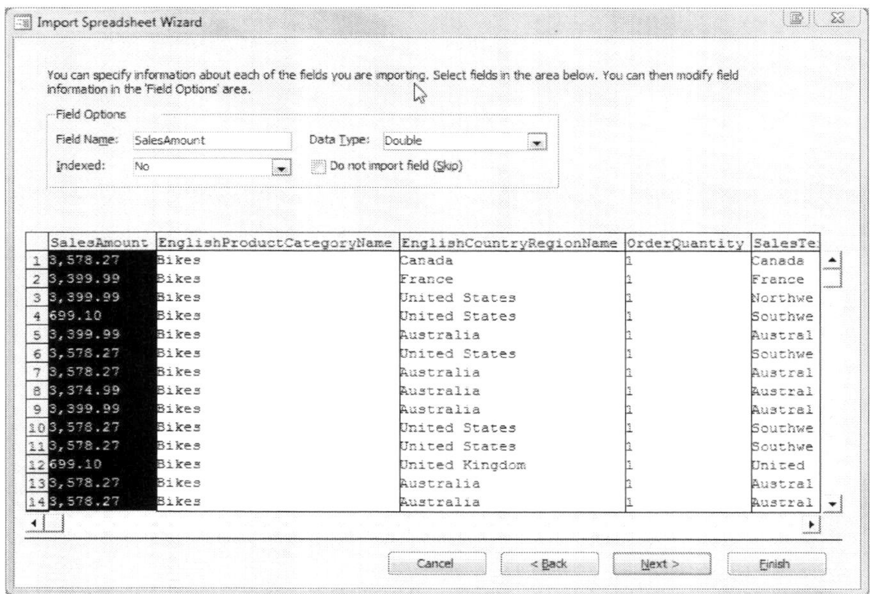

Figure 7-6c Import Spreadsheet Wizard - Step 3

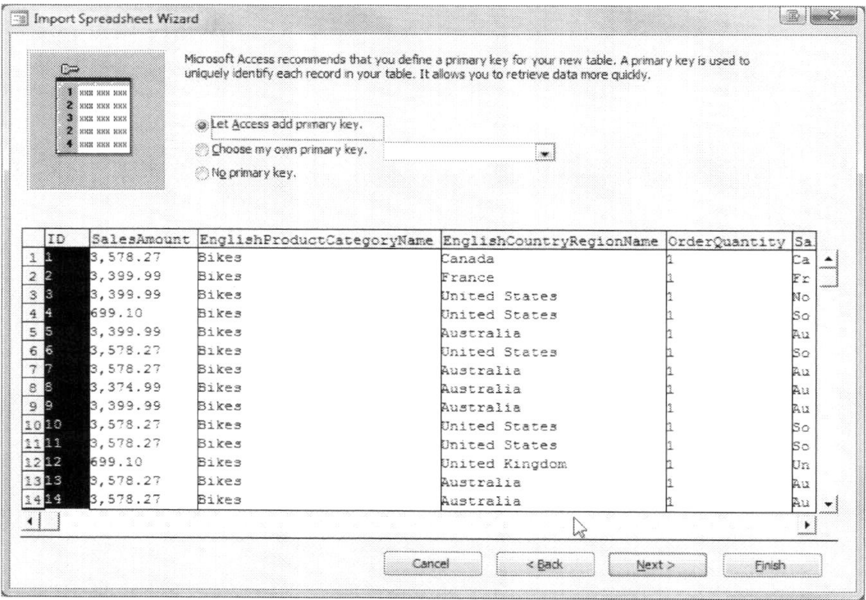

Figure 7-6d Import Spreadsheet Wizard - Step 4

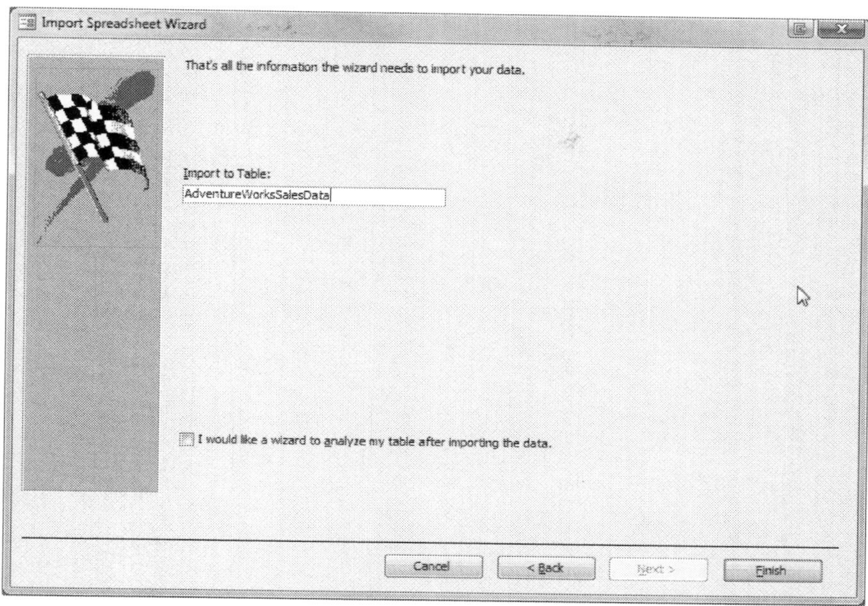

Figure 7-6e Import Spreadsheet Wizard - Step 5

From Text Files

Clicking on Text File in the Import & Link command group on the External Data tab brings up the Select source and destination of the data dialog box as in Figure 7-1 which allows you to specify whether to import or link to a source. Next window begins the Import Text Wizard (Figure 7-8a) and prompts you to specify whether the text file is delimited or not. You can see in the sample data presented by the Wizard that this text file is comma delimited. The next window in the Wizard (Figure 7-8b) allows you to choose the delimiter, designate if the first row contains field names, and set the text qualifier. The text qualifier is the character that specifies that the value surrounded by it should be formatted as text. If the data are in a fixed width format, the delimiters window is replaced by a field break window (not shown) where you set the fixed field widths.

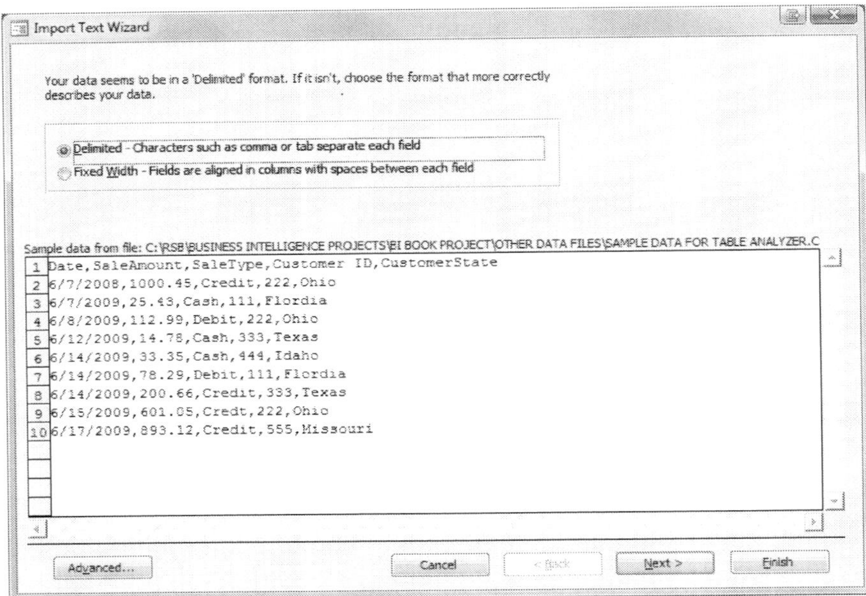

Figure 7-8a Import Text Wizard

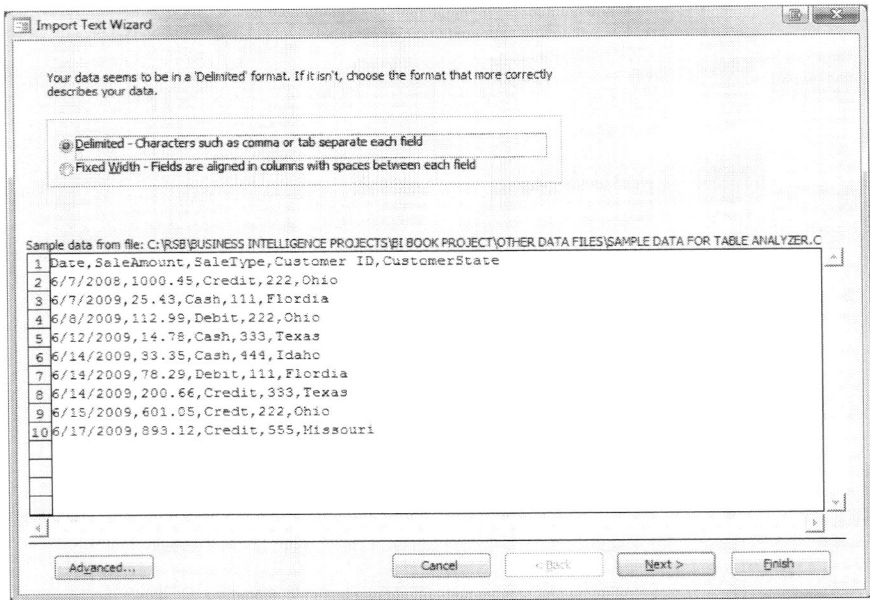

Figure 7-8b Import Text Wizard - Delimiters

The final three windows in the Wizard are identical to Figure 7-6c, d, and e which let you to set properties for the fields, configure primary keys, and name the imported table.

From XML Files

Selecting the XML option also displays the Select the source and destination of the data dialog box (Figure 7-1). In this case no options for importing or linking appear because xml data can only be imported. The Import XML dialog box (Figure 7-9) comes next which displays the structure of the data and lets you select an import option. The Transform button will lead to a dialog box (not shown) to add a XSLT file to transform the xml into a form that Access can use if that is necessary. The xml file in the example is a query in the Northwind Traders sample database that I converted into XML.

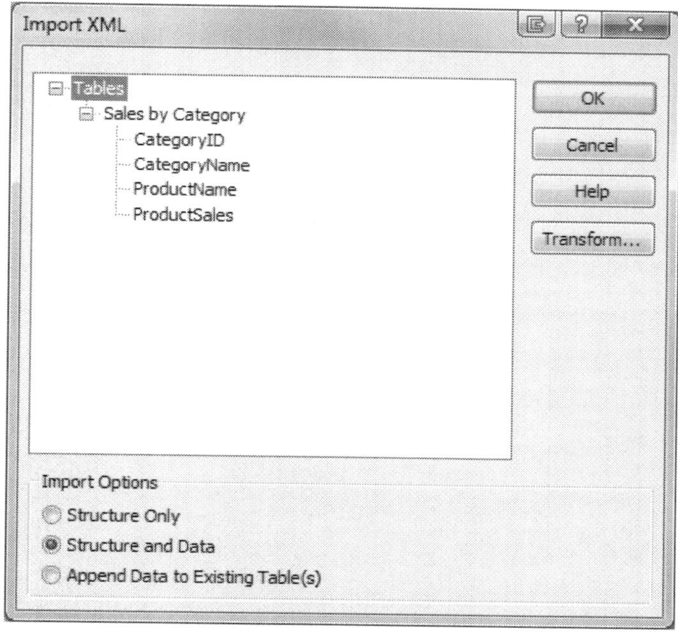

Figure 7-9 Import XML Dialog Box

From HTML

Importing data into Access from a HTML document is essentially the same process as outlined for XML above and uses similar dialog boxes so it's unnecessary to go through an example. You navigate to the HTML option by clicking on More in the Import & Link command group on the External Data tab. Access will do its best to identify the data in the document and then give you a chance to modify the structure.

From ODBC

We've discussed ODBC elsewhere, particularly in Appendix C, so we won't describe it again here. The ODBC source is available from the ODBC command in the Import & Link command group. The usual Select the source and destination dialog box is the first window followed by a Select Data Source dialog box as in Figure 7-10 which has two tabs: one for file data sources (Figure 7-10a) and one for one for machine data sources (Figure 7-10b). A data source name (DSN) is a specification that contains information about an OBDC data source There are three types of DSNs: file DSNs are text files with a dsn file extension and user and system DSNs store the information in the registry. User DSNs are limited to a specific user, and system DSNs can be used by any user on a specific machine. User and system DSNs are combined in the Machine Data Source tab in Figure 7-10b. Note that DSNs can be managed in Windows by using the ODBC Data Source Administrator accessed via Data Sources in Administrative Tools on the Start menu.

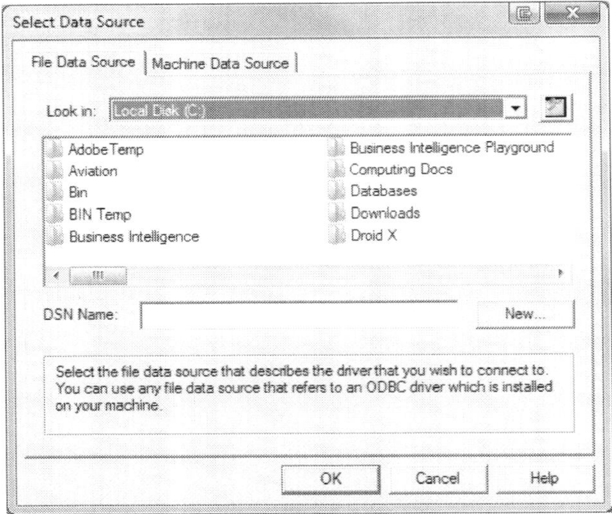

Figure 7-10a File Data Source

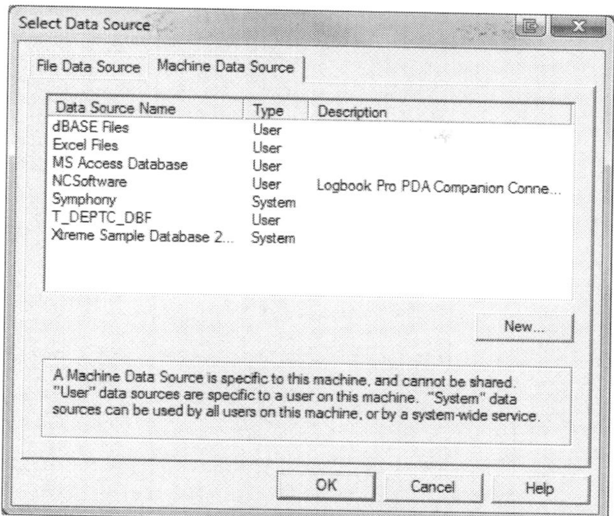

Figure 7-10b Machine Data Source

Figure 7-10 Select Data Source Dialog Box

If the ODBC data source is not in the list on either tab, then you can create a new one by clicking the New button on either tab. Using either will bring up the Create New Data source dialog box (Figure 7-11). If you create a new data source in the machine tab, then you must first designate the type of DSN: user or system. Remember, a user DSN is limited to a particular user but any user on the machine can access a system DSN. To create a new DSN you select a driver from the list. If the driver that you need is not on the list, it's likely that you can download it from the Internet. After you select the driver, the wizard will guide you through the steps to create the DSN and import the data into Access.

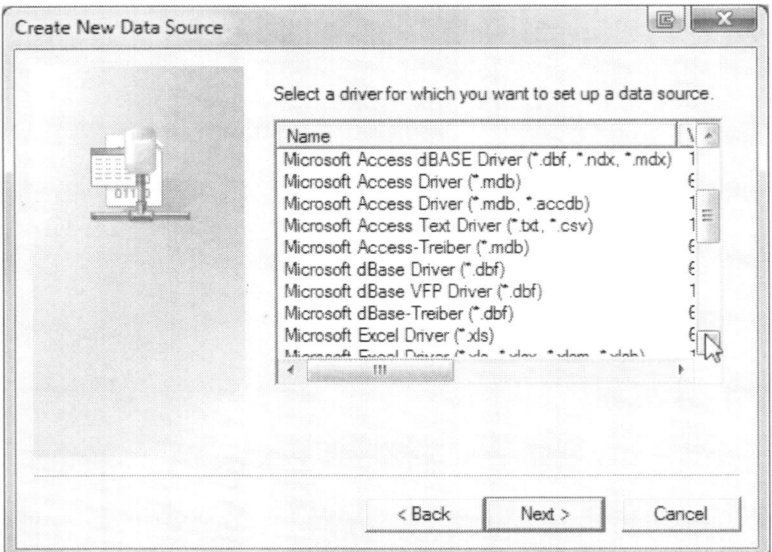

Figure 7-11 Create a New Data Source Dialog Box

From SQL Server

Access connects to SQL Server via ODBC. Note that you must have been granted appropriate permissions to connect to a SQL Server database. If a DSN is available. then use it. For the example one is not available so we'll have to create it. To do that I selected the SQL Server Native Client 10.0 driver from the Create New Data Source dialog box as in Figure 7-11 to connect to SQL Server 2008. (You can download this driver if it is not installed on your system.) In the next dialog box (Figure 7-12a) you enter a DSN name, an optional description, and a server name. This is followed by an authentication dialog box (Figure 7-12b) and a default database dialog box (Figure 7-12c) to select the database to use. In the latter the default database will be master so you should change it to the one that you want to use by checking Change the default database to box and selecting the database from listbox. In the example I selected the AdventureworksDW2008 database.

The next two dialog boxes allow you to select options (Figure 7-12d) and review the configuration (Figure 7-12e) where you may test the connection. Clicking OK will return you to the Select Data source dialog box as in Figure 7-10. Note the new DSN now appears in the list (Figure 7-12f).

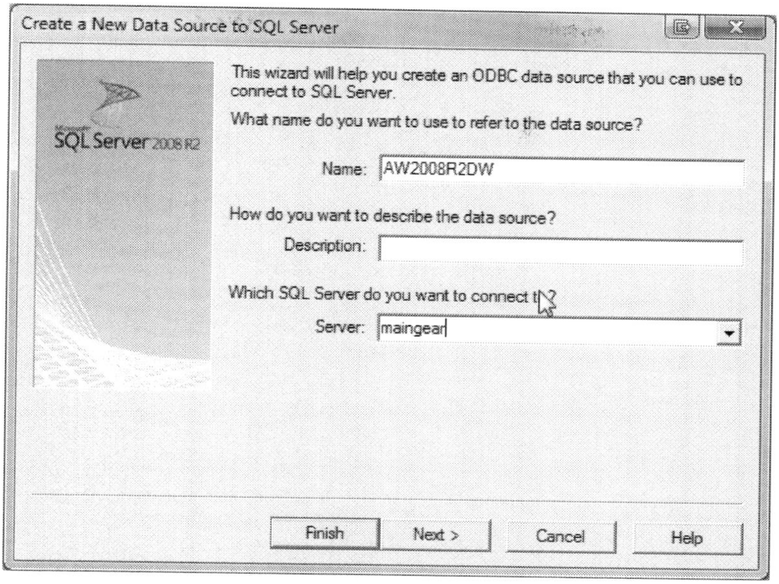

Figure 7-12a Create a New Data Source to SQL Server

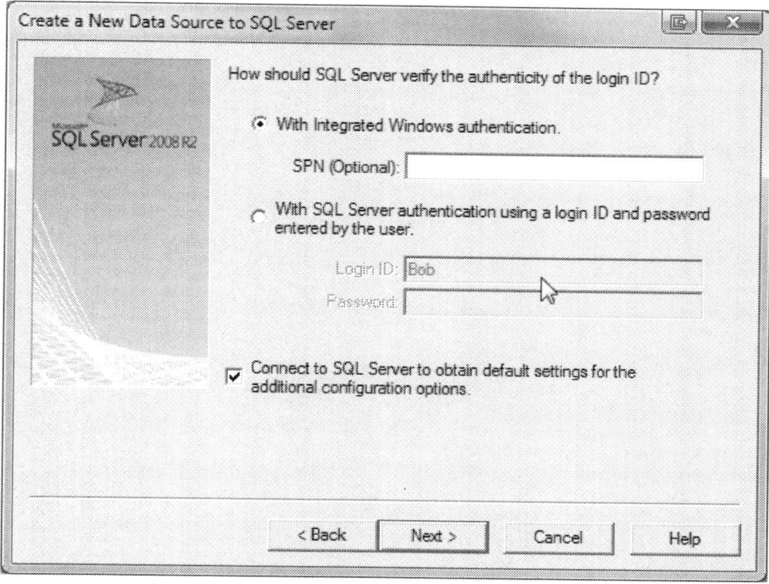

Figure 7-12b Create a New Data Source to SQL Server - Authentication

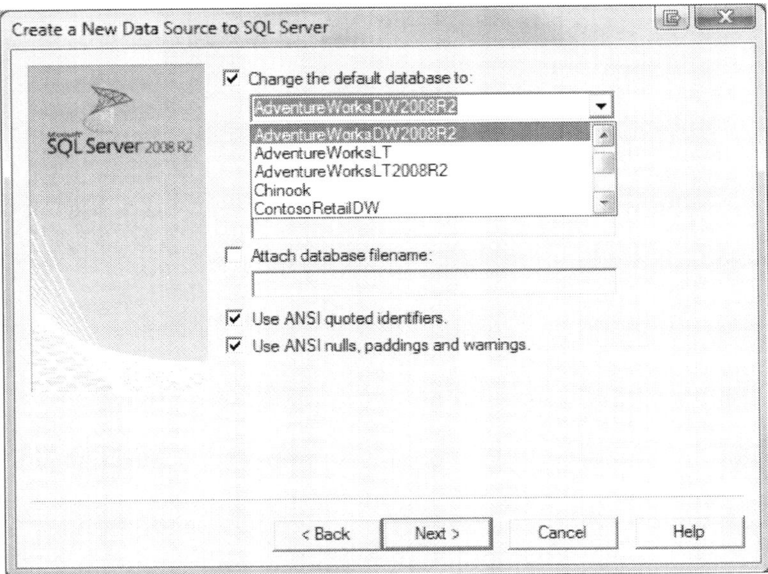

Figure 7-12c Create a New Data Source to SQL Server - Select Database

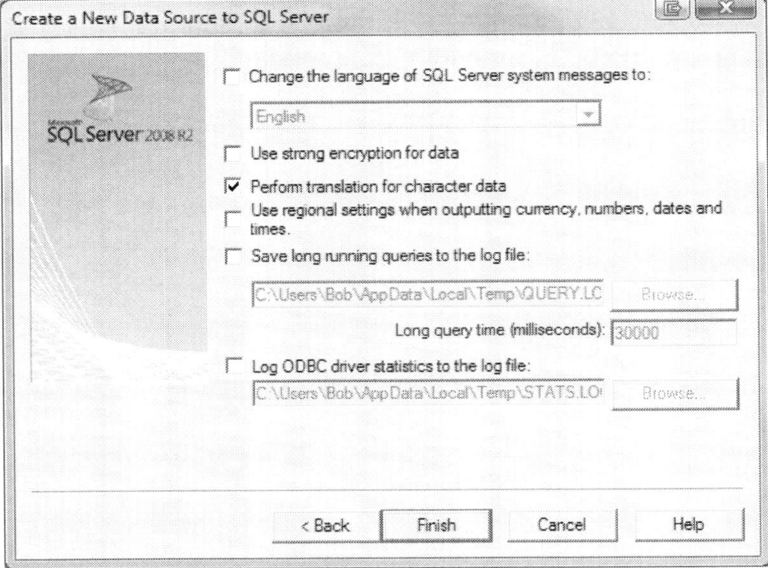

Figure 7-12d Create a New Data Source to SQL Server - Options

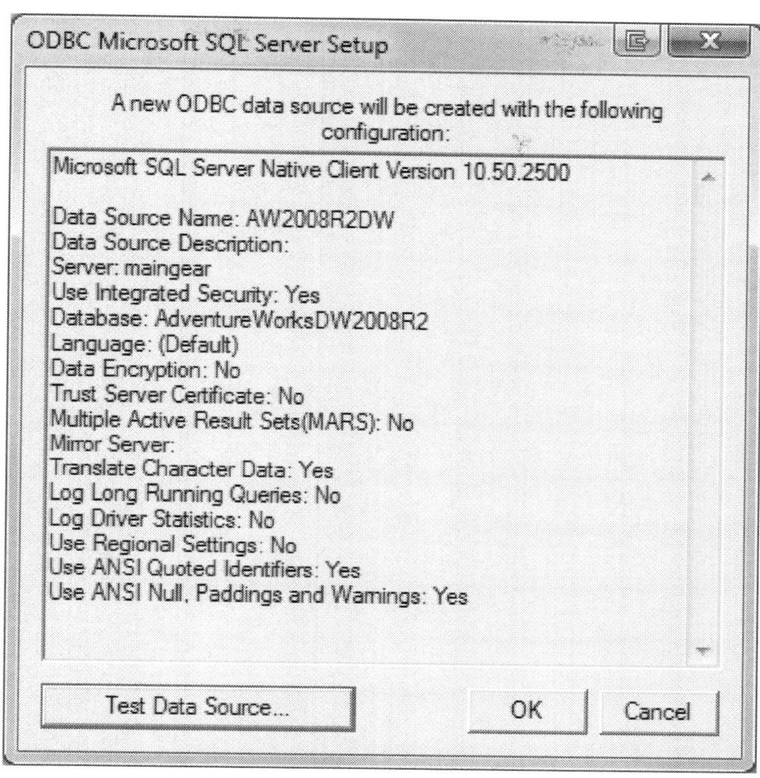

Figure 7-12e Create a New Data Source to SQL Server - Configuration

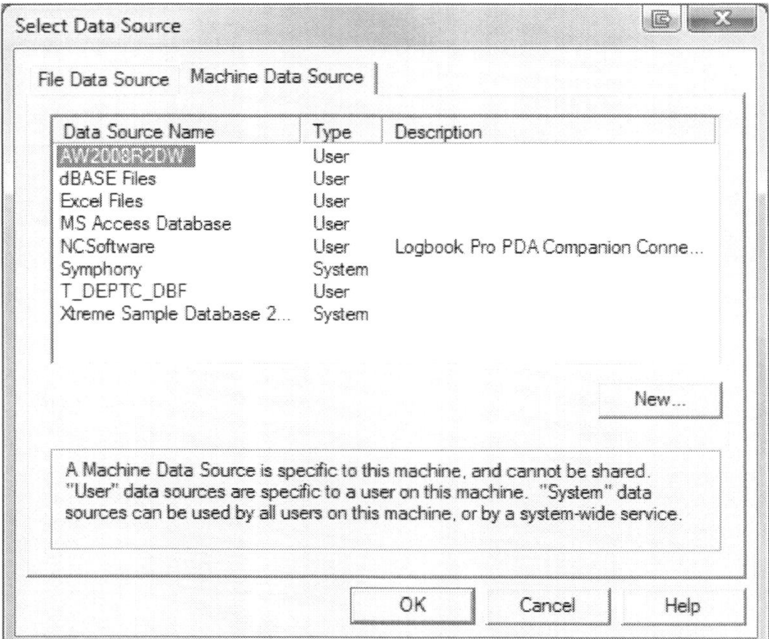

Figure 7-12f Select Data Source - AdventureWorks

Selecting the new DSN and clicking the OK button will bring up the Import Objects dialog box (Figure 7-13) where I selected a few tables, and clicking the OK button will import them into Access as you can see in Figure 7-14. When the data are imported, the Access database is disconnected from the SQL Server database so any modifications to the Access version will not appear in the SQL Server version. However, if you have appropriate permissions, changes in the Access tables of a linked version update the SQL version.

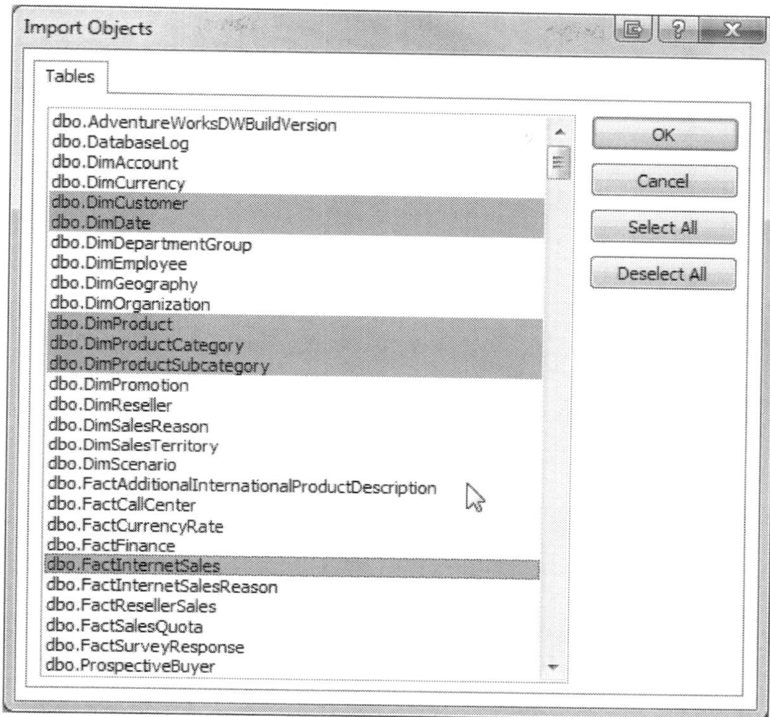

Figure 7-13 Import Objects

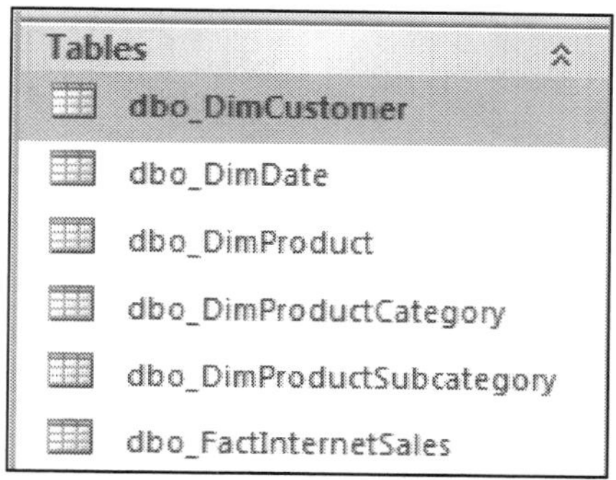

Figure 7-14 SQL Server Tables in Access

Queries

There are a number of types of queries in Access but we'll focus on those that are more helpful for data analysis and related tasks and only mention the others. Queries usually obtain data from more than one table or other query, and for multiple source queries to work correctly relationships must be established among those sources. For our purposes we will assume that the relationships for the data sources in the query have already been defined. Relationships are described in more detail later in this chapter.

Select Queries - Advanced features

Regardless of the type of query that I'm building I usually create a select query and then convert it to the other type. There are three ways to create a query: use the Query Wizard, write a SQL Statement, or use the Query Designer. All three are initiated by using options in the Other command group on the Create tab. The Query Wizard option starts the Query Wizard, and the Query Design option is used to access the Query Designer and with another step the SQL view. I find that the Query Wizard is more trouble than it's worth so I never use it and won't discuss it here. I also don't write SQL often enough to be proficient at it so I usually don't write SQL from scratch. I do all my query building in the Query Designer which is described in Appendix C. We'll use it here.

The Access Database that we'll use for example queries shown in Figure 7-15 is a pared down version of Internet sales data in the AdventureWorksDW2008 SQL Server dimensional database. There are seven tables: InternetSales from the original fact table and five dimension tables - Customer, Product, ProductSubcategory, ProductCategory, SalesTerritory, and Date.

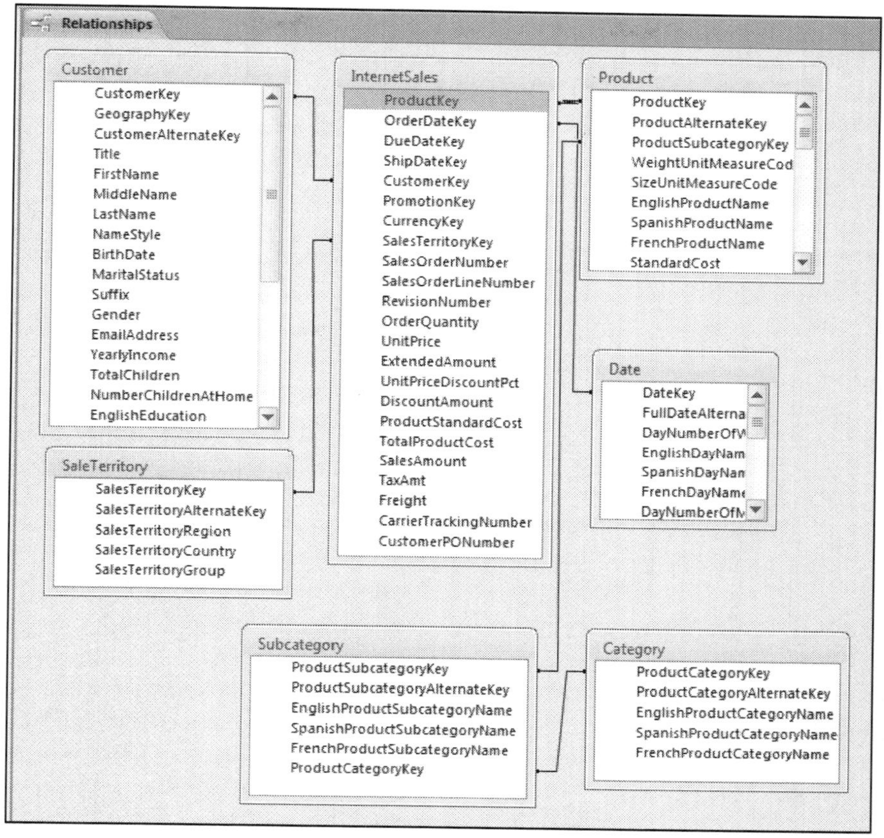

Figure 7-15 Example Database

(For better viewing of this image, go to http://www.zerobits.info/bibook/bibookimages/)

Calculated Fields

Creating calculated fields in Access is similar to that discussed in previous chapters and Appendix C. We'll create calculated fields for year, quarter, and gross profit margin as we have done elsewhere. I opened the Query Designer and added five tables to the design surface shown at the top of Figure 7-16 using the Show Table dialog box by right clicking on the design surface and selecting Show Table from the menu. I then added fields to the query by double clicking on a field or dragging and dropping fields onto the query design grid.

There are two "measures" in this query—SalesAmount and the gross profit margin percent (GPM%), a calculated field—and three "dimensions"—Category, Year, and Quarter with Year and Quarter being calculated fields. Note that the two tables on the design surface that are not used in the query—Product and Product Subcategory—are required to indirectly link the InternetSales table with the ProductCategory table through their primary keys.

Calculated fields are created by inserting an expression in the Field row on the query design grid. The form of the entry is FieldName: Expression. For Example, the expression for the Year calculated field is Year: Year(FullDateAlternateKey) which uses the Year date function to extract the year from the FullDateAlternateKey field. Similarly, the expression for the Quarter calculated field is Quarter: DatePart("q", [FullDateAlternateKey]) which uses the DatePart function to extract the quarter value. Note that you can use the FieldName component to rename a field in a query. For example, to rename the ProductCategoryName field to just Category add the new name as a prefix to the field name followed by a colon as in Category:EnglishProductCategoryName.

You may enter an expression directly into the Field area in a design grid column or use the Expression Builder as in Figure 7-17. The Expression Builder is accessed by first positioning the cursor in the Field area in the design grid, and then clicking on the Builder button in the Query Setup command group on the Design tab. The Expression Builder has two sections: the expression is constructed in the top pane, and the bottom panes present items such as table or query fields, functions, and constants that can be inserted into the expression.

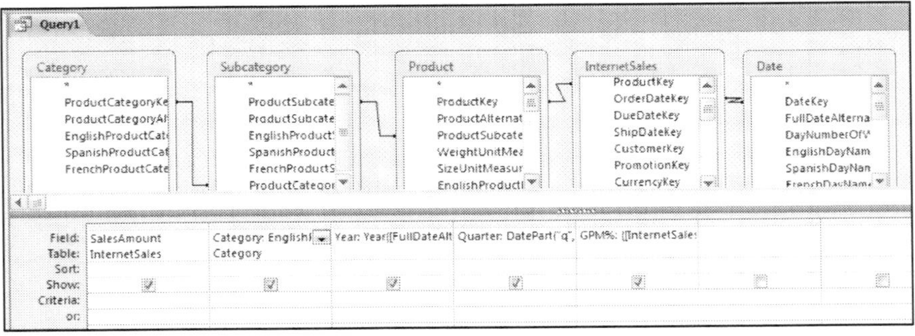

Figure 7-16 Access Query Designer

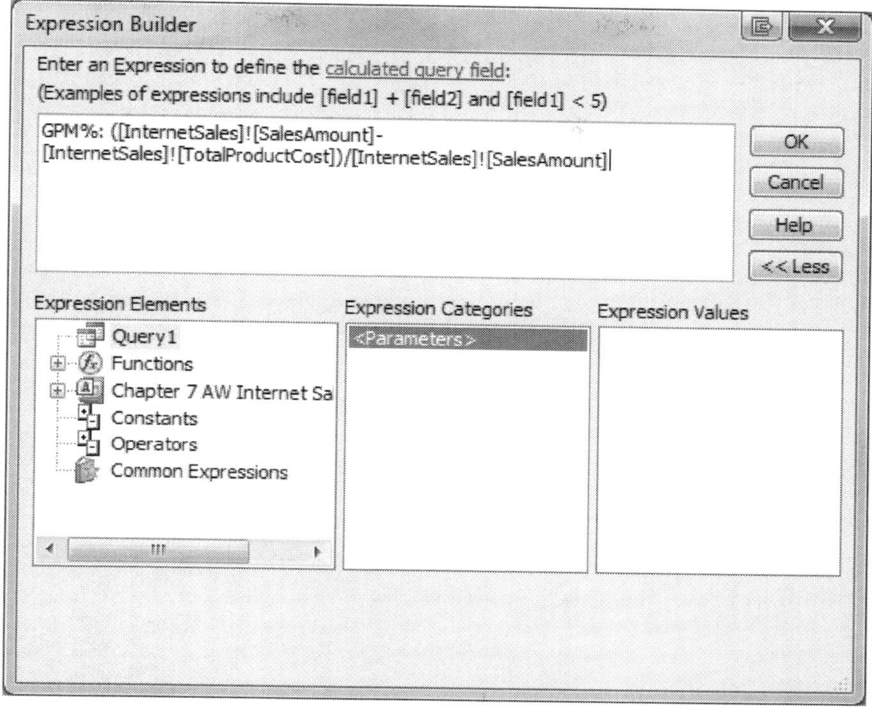

Figure 7-17 Expression Builder

The expression in Figure 7-17 calculates the gross profit margin percentage with the formula:

> GPM%: ([InternetSales]![SalesAmount]-
> [InternetSales]![TotalProductCost])/[InternetSales]![SalesAmount]

which says that the field named GPM% is calculated by dividing the difference between the InternetSales value and the TotalProductCost value by the InternetSales value. Fields in the expression take the form of [*Source Name*]![*Field Name*] where the Source Name is the name of a table or query on the design surface.

I formatted the GPM% field as a percent with two decimal places by using the Property Sheet (Figure 7-18) accessed by either clicking the Property Sheet button in the Show/Hide command group or right clicking on the column in the design grid and selecting Properties from the menu.

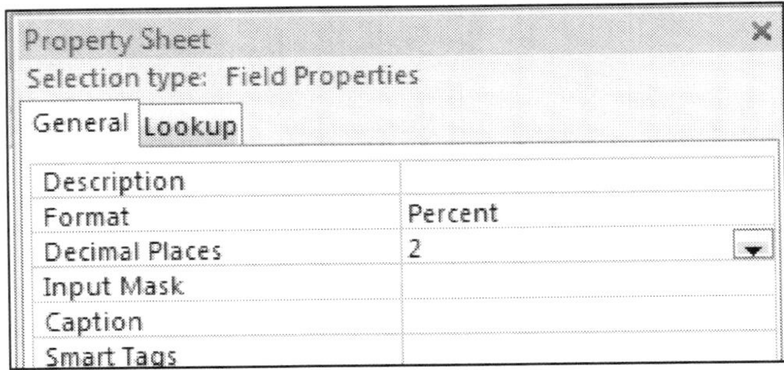

Figure 7-18 Query Field Property Sheet

There are three ways to run the query. The most obvious is to click the Run button (Figure 7-19a) in the Results command group. The other options are to click on the Datasheet View in either the menu presented by the View option in the Results command group (Figures 7-19 a and b) or the menu (Figure 7-19c) displayed when you right click on the tab at the top of the query panel that contains the query name. The latter two options also allow you to return to design view from the data sheet view or to go to the other views listed.

A partial screen shot of the resultant query is shown in Figure 7-20. You can filter and sort the query results in the usual manner by clicking on the down arrowhead at the top of a column or by using the Filter option in the Sort & Filter command group on the Home tab.

Figure 7-19a Run

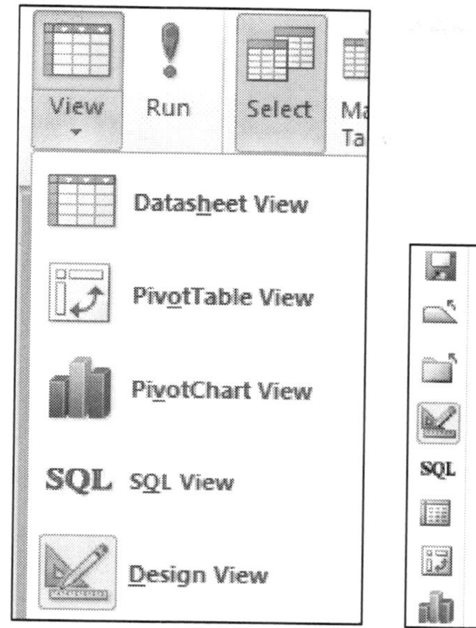

Figure 7-19b View menu

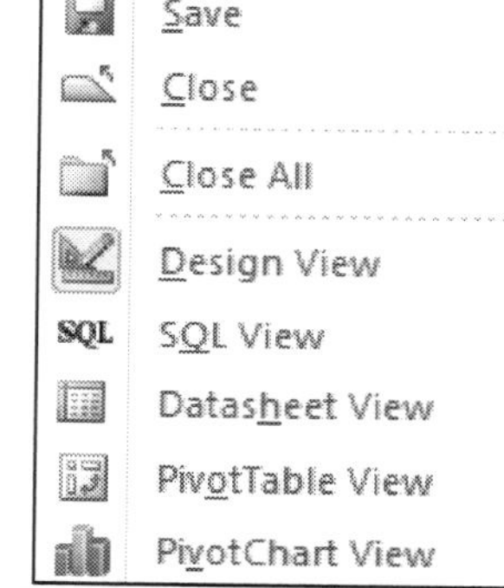

Figure 7-19c Right Click

Figure 7-19 Run query or Select Query View

Q_InternetSales

SalesAmour	Category	Year	Quarter	GPM%
$3,578.27	Bikes	2005	3	39.32%
$3,399.99	Bikes	2005	3	43.76%
$3,399.99	Bikes	2005	3	43.76%
$699.10	Bikes	2005	3	40.90%
$3,399.99	Bikes	2005	3	43.76%

Figure 7-19 Datasheet View (Run Query)

Aggregate Queries

A regular select query as in Figure 7-19 in itself isn't much use for data analysis. However, adding an aggregate calculation to the query can be quite useful. We've mentioned aggregate calculations elsewhere. In an Access query aggregate calculations are activated in design view by either the Totals (Σ) option in the Show/Hide command group on the Design tab or by right clicking a column. Initially Group By appears in all fields in the Total row as shown in Figure 7-20. The other options (Sum, Avg, Min, etc.) are shown in the drop-down list. The function of each of the options is briefly described in Table 7-1.

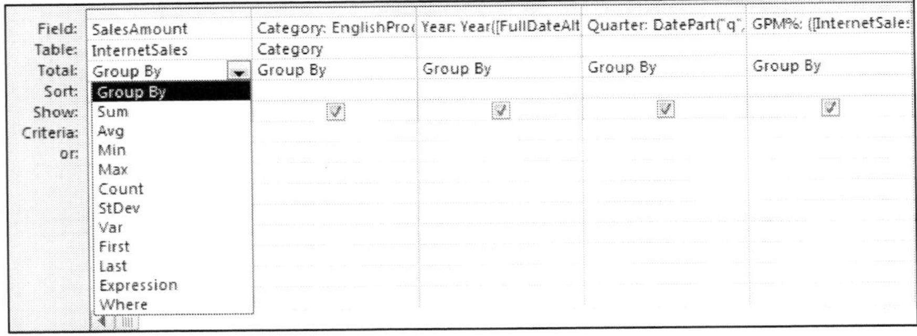

Figure 7-20 Aggregate Query - Totals Row

Function	Description
Group By	Groups the query results by the values in the field.
Sum	Sums all of the values for a Group By combination.
Avg	Calculates the mean of all of the values for a Group By combination.
Min	Displays the minimum value for a Group By combination.
Max	Displays the minimum value for a Group By combination.
Count	Counts the number of records in a Group By combination.
StDev	Calculates the standard deviation for a Group By combination.
Var	Calculates the variance for a Group By combination.
First	Displays the value in the first row Calculates the standard deviation for a Group By combination.
Last	Displays the value in the last row Calculates the standard deviation for a Group By combination.
Expressio n	Tells Access to perform the calculation located in the field.
Where	Uses the field as a filter. The filter expression is entered in the Criteria row.

Table 7-1 Access Aggregate Functions

The example of an aggregate query in Figure 7-21a displays the sum of the SalesAmount and the average of the GPM% for the first quarter only (note the Where function and the Criteria value in the Quarter field) categorized by product category and year. The results are shown in Figure 7-20b. In Figure 7-21b the SumOfSalesAmount column name can easily be changed to, say Total Sales, by adding that prefix to the SalesAmount field name in Figure 7-21a. We're finally producing some results usable for data analysis purposes by adding aggregate calculation to a select query. Note that in the results

Accessories and Clothing product categories had sales in the first quarter in 2008 only. And, also note again that the data can be sorted and filtered in the query datasheet view by using the Filter option or the drop-down arrow on the column heading.

Field:	SalesAmount	Category: EnglishProd	Year: Year([FullDateAlt	Quarter: DatePart("q",	GPM%: Avg(([Internet
Table:	InternetSales	Category			
Total:	Sum	Group By	Group By	Group By	Expression
Sort:					
Show:	✓	✓	✓	✓	✓
Criteria:				=1	

Figure 7-21a Aggregate Query Example - Design

Q_InternetSales - Aggregate

SumOfSales	Category	Year	Quarter	GPM%
$173,550.63	Accessories	2008	1	62.60%
$1,791,698.45	Bikes	2006	1	40.24%
$1,413,530.30	Bikes	2007	1	41.48%
$4,024,025.47	Bikes	2008	1	39.99%
$86,053.86	Clothing	2008	1	38.11%

Figure 7-21b Aggregate Query Example - Result

Parameter Queries

Parameter queries can enhance a select query even more. We describe parameter queries in Appendix C so we won't repeat that here—just keep in mind that parameter queries are like dynamic filters. In Access parameter queries are defined by an expression enclosed in brackets in the Criteria row of a field. The phrase in the brackets will appear in the parameter prompt. For example, the query directly above can be easily modified to prompt for a quarter upon which to base the calculations by the expression [Enter a Quarter Number] as shown in Figure 7-22a. Entering a quarter number in the resultant prompt (Figure 7-22b) will cause the query to use this value as a criteria when running the query.

Field:	SalesAmount	Category: EnglishProd	Year: Year([FullDateAlt	Quarter: DatePart("q",[FullD	GPM%: Avg(([Internet
Table:	InternetSales	Category			
Total:	Sum	Group By	Group By	Where	Expression
Sort:					
Show:	✓	✓	✓	☐	✓
Criteria:				[Enter a Quarter Number]	
or:					

Figure 7-22a Parameter Query Example - Design

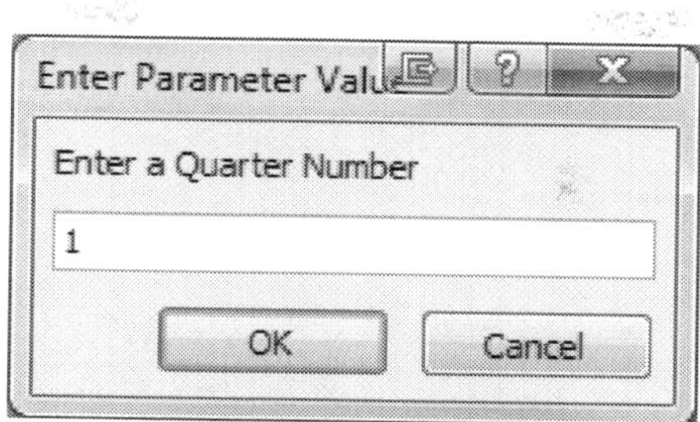

Figure 7-22b Parameter Query Example - Parameter Prompt

You can to some degree validate the entered parameter value by using the Query Parameters dialog box (Figure 7-23) with the data type drop-down list displayed. The dialog box is accessed via the Parameters option in the Show/Hide group on the Design tab. The parameter must be entered manually exactly as it appears in the Criteria row so I copy and paste it to make sure that it is correct. Then, you select the data type from the drop-down list. Now, if I run the query and enter something other than an integer, say a string of characters, Access will display a dialog box that says the value entered is not valid and gives me a chance to correct it.

Query Parameters

Parameter	Data Type
[Enter a Quarter number]	Text

Yes/No
Byte
Integer
Long Integer
Currency
Single
Double
Date/Time
Binary
Text
OLE Object
Memo
Replication ID
Decimal
Value

OK

Figure 7-22b Query Parameters Dialog Box

When more than one parameter is defined in a query, Access just displays a series of prompts, one for each parameter. For example, if you wanted to sum a field value between two dates, you could include one parameter for the start date and one for the end date. To specify the order of appearance of multiple prompts just arrange then in the order you prefer in the Query Parameters dialog box.

All of the criteria operators listed in Appendix C, Table C-5 such as equals, Like, Between, and so forth can be used as criteria with embedded parameters. For example, instead of using two date columns to sum a field between dates as described above, you could use the Between-And operator in one date criteria cell. The expression would look like: BETWEEN [Enter Start Date] AND [Enter End Date].

Crosstab Queries

Think of a crosstab query as a puny pivot table with one row, one column, and one value measure. The design of a crosstab query must contain at least three fields—one for each of those fields. It can contain other fields as filters. The example in Figure 7-23a has quarters for rows, product categories for columns, and Internet sales as the values. In addition, there is a parameter for year which is used as a filter. To convert a select query into a crosstabs query just select the Crosstabs option in the Query Type command group on the Design tab.

A crosstabs query design contains a Crosstabs row which specifies the function of the field in the query: row heading, column heading, or value as shown in the crosstabs row and drop-down list in the Figure 7-23a. The Total row is retained and is used as described above. In the example the Year column is used as a filter with the Crosstabs row having no entry. The result from the query with the Year parameter set to 2007 is shown in Figure 7-23b. Note that parameters in Crosstab queries must be explicitly declared using the Parameters command on the Ribbon.

Field:	Category: EnglishPro	Quarter: DatePart("q",	SalesAmount	Year([FullDateAlternat
Table:	Category		InternetSales	
Total:	Group By	Group By	Sum	Where
Crosstab:	Column Heading	Row Heading	Value	
Sort:			Row Heading	
Criteria:			Column Heading	[Enter a Year]
or:			Value	
			(not shown)	

Figure 7-23a Crosstabs Query - Design

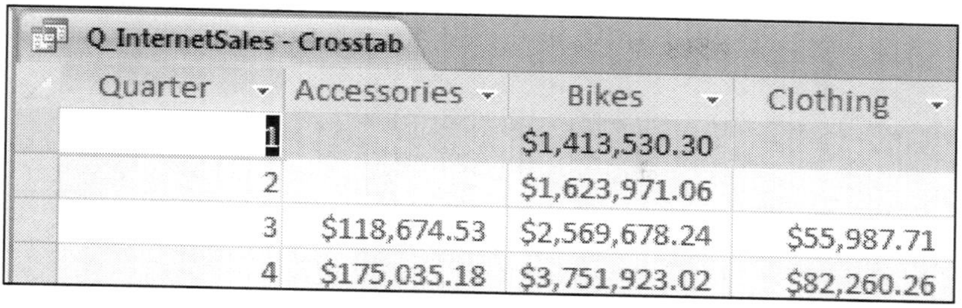

Q_InternetSales - Crosstab

Quarter	Accessories	Bikes	Clothing
1		$1,413,530.30	
2		$1,623,971.06	
3	$118,674.53	$2,569,678.24	$55,987.71
4	$175,035.18	$3,751,923.02	$82,260.26

Figure 7-23b Crosstabs Query - Results

To me the crosstabs query is even more useful than the aggregate select query for data analysis. But, it is still not as flexible as a pivot table.

Other Queries

The other types of queries that I use infrequently, if at all, are listed in Table 7-2. Please refer to one of the many books about Access or search the Internet for more information about them.

Query Type	Function
Make Table	Creates a new table based on the query design
Append	Adds rows to an existing table
Update	Updates one or more fields
Delete	Deleted records from a table
Union	Combines the results of several select queries. Requires writing SQL.
Pass-Through	Sends SQL statements directly to a back-end server, e.g., sending T-SQL to SQL Server.
Data Definition	Modifies the design of tables, constraints, indexes, and relationships via SQL. Note that it's much easier to do this in design view and the relationships window.
Subquery	Queries embedded in another query. Requires writing SQL. An advanced topic.

Table 7-2 Other Query Types

Pivot Tables and Charts

Pivot Tables

We worked with pivot tables and pivot charts in the previous chapter so we'll focus here on how to use them in Access. In a query to get to the pivot table view either click the View option in the Home tab or the Design tab and select PivotTable View from the menu (Figure 7-24) or right click on PivotTable View displayed when you right click on the tab at the top of the query panel that contains the query name. The pivot table view will be displayed as in Figure 7-25 which is different from the pivot table interface in Excel 2010 (Figure 6-10). The Access rendition is the dated pivot table display format used in previous versions of Excel where you drag and drop fields directly onto the pivot table instead of using the Pivot Table Field List. This is not a problem—it works fine.

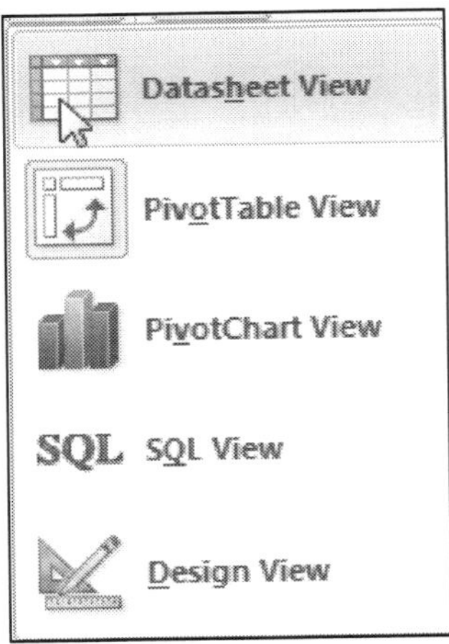

Figure 7-24 Query View Options

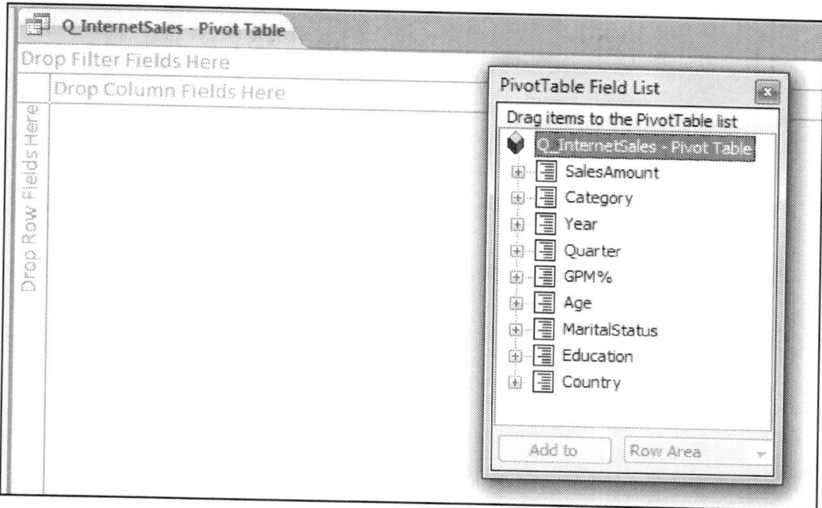

Figure 7-25 Pivot Table View

For an example I created another query and inserted a sampling of fields: Internet sales, product category, and customer marital status, gender, education and country. I also added four calculated fields: year, quarter, GPM%, and age calculated from the customer's birth date. I then converted it to an aggregate query. The fields are shown in the query design grid divided into two parts for ease of viewing them in Figure 7-26 and in the Access Pivot Table Field List in Figure 7-25.

To construct a pivot table switch to pivot table view and drag row and column dimensions and filter fields to the respective locations on the canvas. Value fields should be selected in the Field List and added to the pivot table by selecting Data Area from the drop-down list at the bottom of the field list (Figure 7-27) and then clicking the Add to button. If you try to drag and drop value fields directly onto the canvas, the aggregation (sum, average, count, etc.) will be ignored and the individual values in the field will appear in the table.

Field:	Year: Year([OrderDate]	Quarter: DatePart("q",	InternetSales: SalesAr	GPM%: Avg(([Internet:	ProductCategory: Pro
Table:			InternetSales		ProductCategory
Total:	Group By	Group By	Sum	Expression	Group By
Sort:					
Show:	☑	☑	☑	☑	☑
Criteria:					
or:					

Field:	Country: SalesTerritor	Age: Avg((DateDiff("m	MaritalStatus	Gender	Education
Table:	SalesTerritory		Customer	Customer	Customer
Total:	Group By	Expression	Group By	Group By	Group By
Sort:					
Show:	☑	☑	☑	☑	☑
Criteria:					
or:					

Figure 7-26 Query for Pivot Table Design

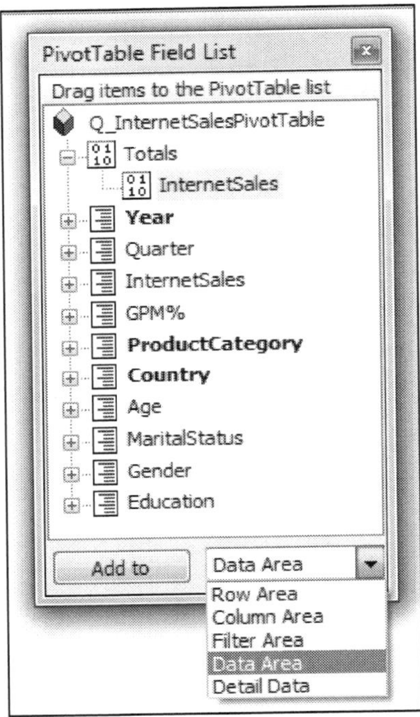

Figure 7-27 Assigning a Field to the Pivot Table Value Area

For the example pivot table in Figure 7-28 I dragged and dropped the Country field into the filter drop area, Year and Quarter into the row drop area, and ProductCategory into the column drop area and used the Pivot Table Field list to select InternetSales for the value area. As with an Excel pivot table you can drill-down and up using the Plus (+) and minus(-) buttons on the fields and filter the values by clicking on the drop-down arrows. To delete a field from a pivot table right click on its name in the pivot table and select remove from the menu.

Q_InternetSalesPivotTable

Country
All

Year	Quarter	ProductCategory: Accessories	Bikes	Clothing	Grand Total
		InternetSales	InternetSales	InternetSales	InternetSales
2005	3		$1,453,522.89		$1,453,522.89
	4		$1,812,850.77		$1,812,850.77
2006	1		$1,791,698.45		$1,791,698.45
	2		$2,014,012.13		$2,014,012.13
	3		$1,396,833.62		$1,396,833.62
	4		$1,327,799.32		$1,327,799.32
2007	1		$1,413,530.30		$1,413,530.30
	2		$1,623,971.06		$1,623,971.06
	3	$118,674.53	$2,569,678.24	$55,987.71	$2,744,340.48
	4	$175,035.18	$3,751,923.02	$82,260.26	$4,009,218.46
2008	1	$173,550.63	$4,024,025.47	$86,053.86	$4,283,629.96
	2	$199,754.98	$5,138,299.38	$98,374.79	$5,436,429.15
	3	$33,744.64		$17,095.99	$50,840.63
Grand Total		$700,759.96	$28,318,144.65	$339,772.61	$29,358,677.22

Figure 7-28 Access Pivot Table Example

Design Tab Options

The options for pivot tables on the Design tab are fairly straight forward but a few of them are worthy of additional comment. In pivot table view the Show top/bottom option in the Filter & Sort command group is somewhat similar to the top/bottom rules in Excel conditional formatting in that you can choose to display the top X or bottom X items where X is a number or percentage, e.g., top 10 items or bottom 25%. Clicking on the Export to Excel option in the Data command group immediately exports the pivot cache to a new Excel workbook and displays a pivot table in a worksheet. The Property Sheet option displays the Property dialog box (Figure 7-29) which displays the properties that can be set for the object selected in the pivot table. The example shows the property tabs for the InternetSales value field. Properties for any of the other fields in the current pivot table can be displayed by either clicking on one in the pivot table or selecting one from the Select drop-down listbox. The properties and tabs displayed will vary depending on the field selected.

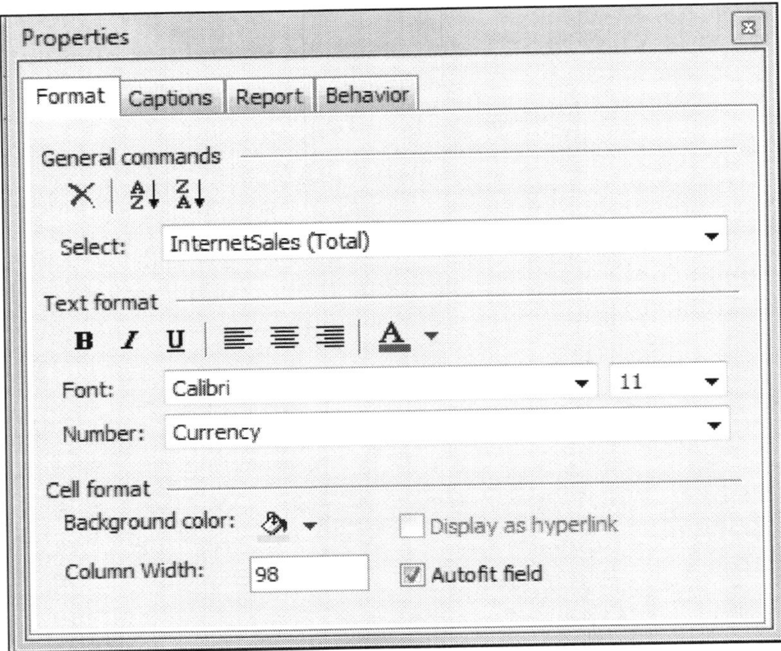

Figure 7-29 Access Pivot Table Property Sheet

Calculated Fields

We've discussed calculated fields in the two previous chapters. Calculated fields can also supposedly be inserted into Access pivot tables from the Formulas option in the Tools command group on the Design tab in pivot table view as in Figure 7-30 where the drop-down menu has two options: Create Calculated Total used for new value (measure) fields and Create Calculated Detail Field used for new dimensions (rows and columns).

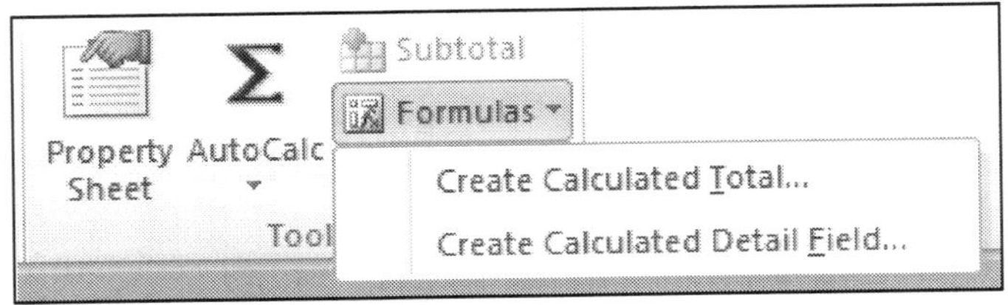

Figure 7-30 Calculated Fields Menu

An example would be an AgeGroup calculated value to discretize the age field into two categories: Seniors and Not Seniors based on the usual age 55 criteria. Clicking on the Create Calculated Detail Field button in Figure 7-30 brings up the version of the Properties dialog box in Figure 7-31 to create a new calculated value. I named it AgeGroup and used the Access IIF function which is similar to Excel's IF function to define the two categories. Clicking change will insert the new calculated field in to the Pivot Table Field List. You can use the listbox at the bottom of the dialog box to insert existing pivot table fields into the calculation expression. For example, instead of typing Age into the expression I could have selected it from the list and then clicked the Insert Reference to button. Before exiting the dialog box you can also use the other tabs to set the properties of the new calculated value.

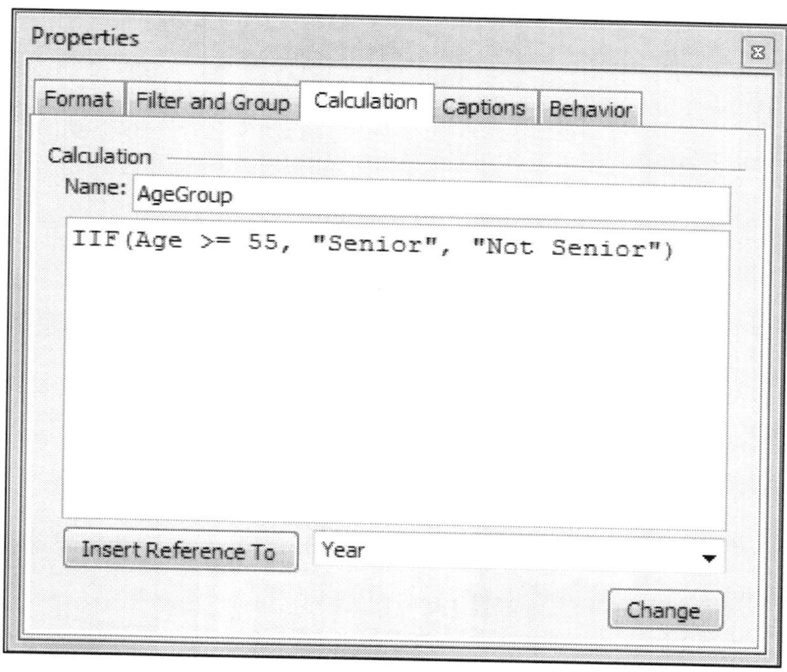

Figure 7-31 Calculated Fields Properties

Although this procedure worked in Access 2007 it fails in the 2010 version at least in my attempts to use it. So, to add a calculated field just insert it as a column in design view as described earlier in the chapter.

Grouping Attributes

You can rearrange dimension field values into custom subgroups by using the group capability. For example, to create a Not Bikes group containing accessories and clothing sales I selected those two columns in Figure 7-31, right clicked on the selection, and selected Group Items from the menu which displayed the new pivot table in Figure 7-32. Accessories and Clothing are now nested together in the new Group 1 category, and bikes is listed in the Other category. Note that a new column dimension, ProductCategory1, was added and is included in the Field List (Figure 7-33).

Q_InternetSalesPivotTable

Country
All

		ProductCategory1 / ProductCategory					
		Group1			Other		Grand Total
		Accessories	Clothing	Total	Bikes	Total	
Year	Quarter	InternetSales	InternetSales	InternetSales	InternetSales	InternetSales	InternetSales
2005	3				$1,453,522.89	$1,453,522.89	$1,453,522.89
	4				$1,812,850.77	$1,812,850.77	$1,812,850.77
2006	1				$1,791,698.45	$1,791,698.45	$1,791,698.45
	2				$2,014,012.13	$2,014,012.13	$2,014,012.13
	3				$1,396,833.62	$1,396,833.62	$1,396,833.62
	4				$1,327,799.32	$1,327,799.32	$1,327,799.32
2007	1				$1,413,530.30	$1,413,530.30	$1,413,530.30
	2				$1,623,971.06	$1,623,971.06	$1,623,971.06
	3	$118,674.53	$55,987.71	$174,662.24	$2,569,678.24	$2,569,678.24	$2,744,340.48
	4	$175,035.18	$82,260.26	$257,295.44	$3,751,923.02	$3,751,923.02	$4,009,218.46
2008	1	$173,550.63	$86,053.86	$259,604.49	$4,024,025.47	$4,024,025.47	$4,283,629.96
	2	$199,754.98	$98,374.79	$298,129.77	$5,138,299.38	$5,138,299.38	$5,436,429.15
	3	$33,744.64	$17,095.99	$50,840.63			$50,840.63
Grand Total		$700,759.96	$339,772.61	$1,040,532.57	$28,318,144.65	$28,318,144.65	$29,358,677.22

Figure 7-32 Grouping Dimension Values

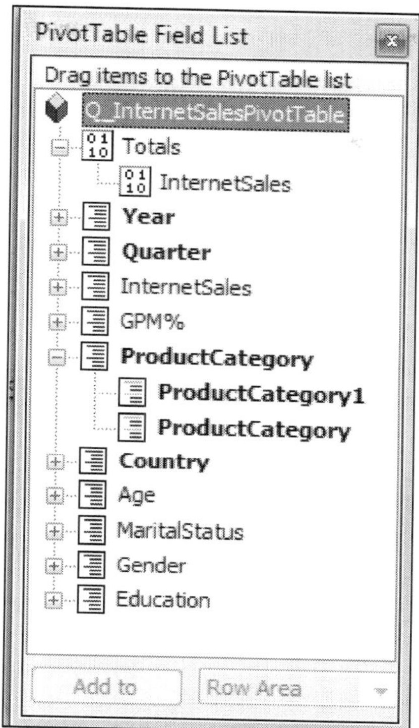

Figure 7-33 Field List with Group Name

The titles for the groups and the new column dimension can be changed by displaying the Properties dialog box for the item and then using the Caption textbox to modify the name as I did in Figure 7-34 to change the ProductCategory1 column dimension to "Bikes or Not." The new name will replace the previous on in the Field List. I also changed the title of Group 1 to "Not Bikes" and Other to "Bikes." The resultant pivot table is not shown.

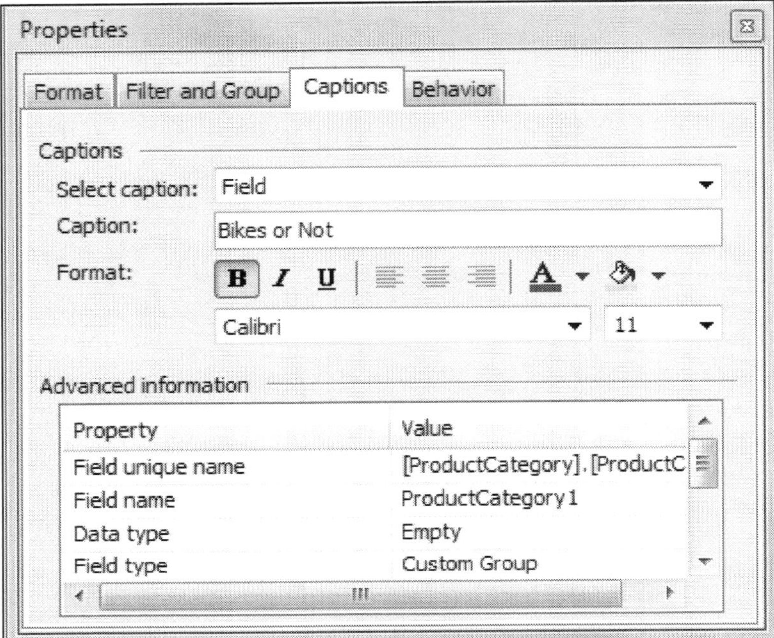

Figure 7-34 Properties Dialog Box to Rename a Grouping

Date Groups

If a field contains date values, Access will automatically create a data hierarchy in the Pivot Table Field List. For example, I created a new Access database from the AdventureWorksDW sample that includes the original date dimension table. Figure 7-35a shows a partial screen shot of a query with an OrderDate field. In pivot table view the Pivot Table Field List (Figure 7-35b) now includes a number of new date attributes that were created automatically. Using Years and Quarters from the field list as row headings, Product Category as the column heading, and InternetSales for the data area will reproduce the pivot table in Figure 7-28 only now using the automatically generated date attributes.

Q_InternetSalesPivotTable for Date Group

OrderDate	InternetSale	ProductCat	GPM%	Country
7/1/2005	$3,399.99	Bikes	43.76%	Australia
7/1/2005	$3,578.27	Bikes	39.32%	Canada
7/1/2005	$3,399.99	Bikes	43.76%	France
7/1/2005	$699.10	Bikes	40.90%	United States
7/1/2005	$3,399.99	Bikes	43.76%	United States
7/2/2005	$3,399.99	Bikes	43.76%	Australia
7/2/2005	$6,953.26	Bikes	41.54%	Australia

Figure 7-35a Query with Date Field

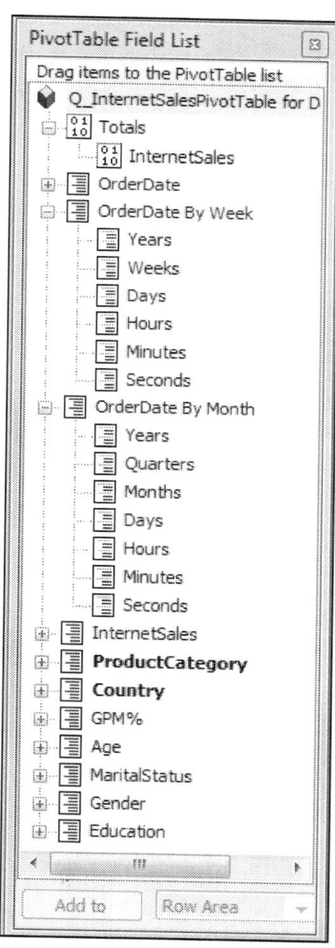

Figure 7-35b Field List with Expanded Date Attributes

Pivot Table Default View

By default queries, at least select and crosstabs queries, are presented in datasheet view. To change the initial presentation of the query to another view use the Property Sheet option in the Show/Hide command group on the Design tab in design view to bring up the Property Sheet for the query (Figure 7-36) and select the default view that you prefer from the listbox shown. Other properties can be set there as well.

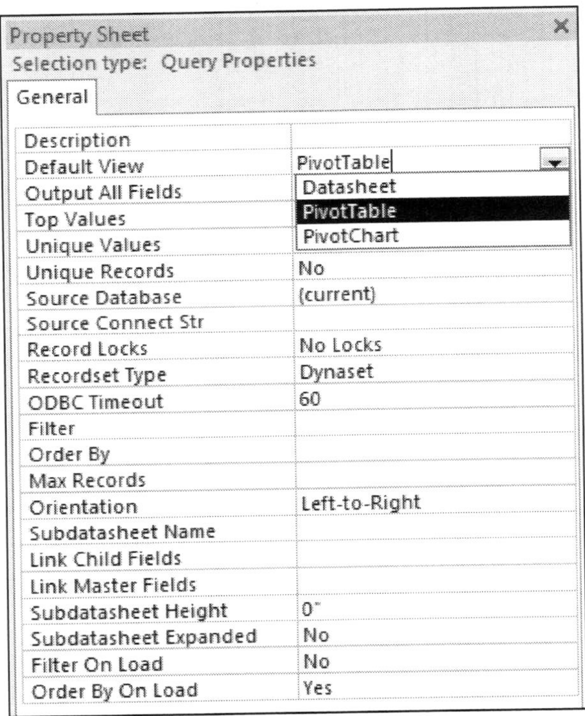

Figure 7-36 A Query Property Sheet

Pivot Charts

A pivot table has a pivot chart directly linked to it so changing the pivot table changes the pivot chart and conversely. To display a pivot chart just change to pivot chart view by either using the View option on the Ribbon or right clicking on the query name tab and selecting pivot chart view. The pivot chart for the Internet sales query in dollars is shown in Figure 7-37. The tall columns represent bike sales and the short ones on the right side are accessory and clothing sales.

You can rearrange the pivot chart just as in a pivot table by dragging and dropping a field from the Field List into one of the drop zones or using the Field List Add to button. Fields are removed from the pivot table by deleting them. You can adjust the filters as usual by selecting/deselecting values in the drop-down list boxes in the drop areas. Again, note that the changes that you make in the pivot chart view are reflected back to the pivot table view.

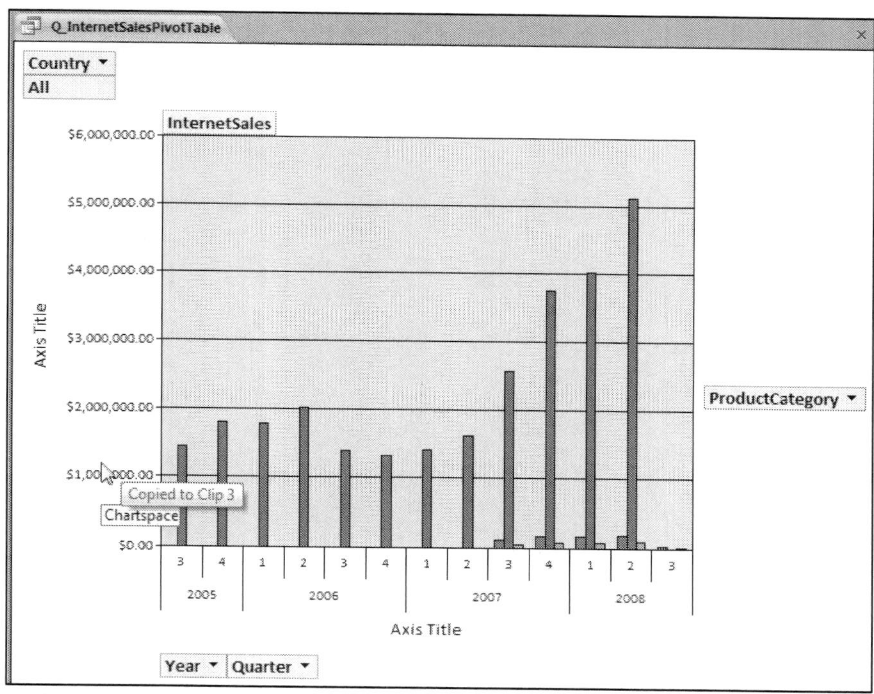

Figure 7-37 Pivot Chart Example

To modify the properties of the chart or objects in it either select the Property Sheet option in the Tools command group or right click anywhere on the chart and select Properties from the menu which will display the Properties dialog box as in Figure 7-38. Select the object from the listbox and go to it.

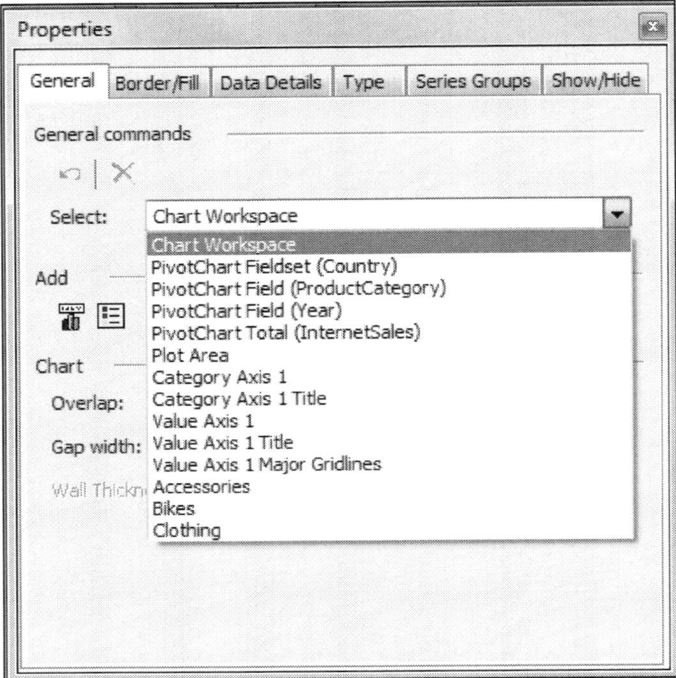

Figure 7-38 Pivot Chart Properties Dialog Box

Database Management

The Database Tools tab provides access to a number of database management mechanisms. We'll look at two of those that are more useful for data analysis purposes and also mention database compacting and repair and backup.

Relationships between Tables

As discussed in Appendix C relationships establish links between two tables via primary and foreign keys. In Access relationships are managed in the Relationships window which is displayed by selecting the Relationships option in the Relationships command group on the Database Tools tab. For an example I created a simple database to keep track of books in a library. The database has only three tables as shown in the Relationships window in Figure 7-39. To link the tables drag and drop a primary key field in one table into a foreign key field in another table. When you do that an Edit Relationships dialog box (Figure 7-40) will pop up. You can see there that I am linking the Author table by its primary key to the Book table by its Author_FK foreign key. Clicking the Create button at this point will establish the relationship as in Figure 7-41 where I also linked the Publisher and Book tables by their keys.

Now that the relationships are established we could create queries that would utilize data from all three tables.

Figure 7-39 Relationships Window

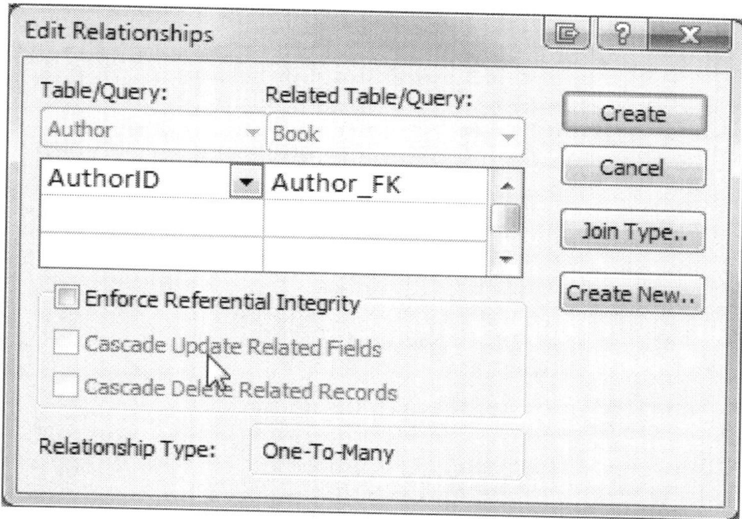

Figure 7-40 Edit Relationships Dialog Box

Figure 7-41 Linked Tables

There are some relationship options available regarding the join type and referential integrity. To get back to the Edit relationships dialog box (Figure 7-40) either double click on the link which will display the dialog box or right click on the link to display the menu in Figure 7-42a and select Edit Relationships. (Note: the latter approach is how to delete relationships between tables.) Either way will display the Edit Relationships dialog box as in Figure 7-40. Clicking the Join Type button presents the Join Properties dialog box in Figure 7-42b which lists the three types of joins (links) available: join 1 is called an inner join, 2 a left outer join, and join 3 a right outer join. Join 1, the default, is the one that you will usually use.

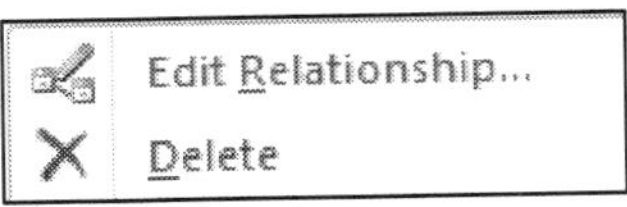

Figure 7-42a Link Menu

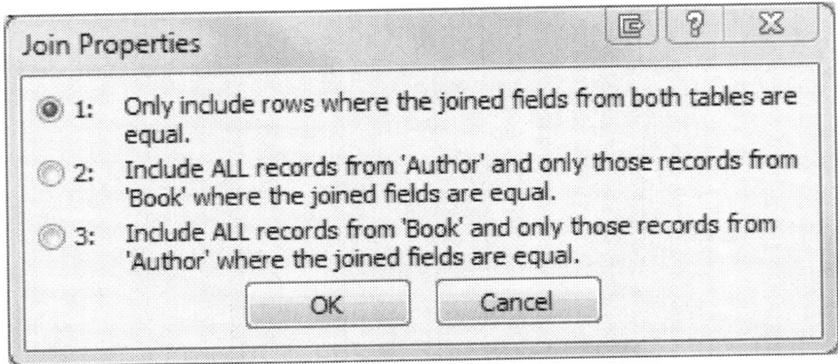

Figure 7-42b Join Properties

Figure 7-42 Relationship Options - Join Properties

Clicking the Enforce Referential Integrity box in Figure 7-40 will enable the Cascade Delete Related Records and Cascade Update Related Fields options. Enforcing referential integrity prevents orphan records and records that reference other records that were deleted. Cascade Update Related Fields automatically updates all fields affected by and update of the primary key. Similarly, Cascade Delete automatically deletes records that referenced a deleted primary key. Enforcing referential integrity is generally recommended.

Table Analyzer

The Table Analyzer examines an existing table or one being imported for duplicate data, then splits the data into more tables, if appropriate, and creates the relationships among those new tables. Its purpose is to try to normalize the data which you probably want for OLTP but not for OLAP. We'll use the concocted Excel data in Figure 7-43 to illustrate the use of the Analyzer. You can see that the data are not normalized with the repeating values of the customers' states which is not good database design because it would allow a customer to reside in more than one state which is a possibility but not one allowed in this database.

Sample Data for Table Analyzer

ID	Date	SaleAmount	SaleType	Customer ID	CustomerSt
1	6/7/2008	1000.45	Credit	222	Ohio
2	6/7/2009	25.43	Cash	111	Flordia
3	6/8/2009	112.99	Debit	222	Ohio
4	6/12/2009	14.78	Cash	333	Texas
5	6/14/2009	33.35	Cash	444	Idaho
6	6/14/2009	78.29	Debit	111	Flordia
7	6/14/2009	200.66	Credit	333	Texas
8	6/15/2009	601.05	Credt	222	Ohio
9	6/17/2009	893.12	Credit	555	Missouri
(New)					

Figure 7-43 Sample Data for Table Analyzer

The Table Analyzer is started in Access by selecting the Analyze Table option in the Analyze command group on the Database tools tab or by checking the analyze box on the Import Spreadsheet Wizard (Figure 7-6e). The first three windows in Wizard (not shown) are informative, and the fourth (Figure 7-44a) lets you elect to have the Wizard decide about the table structure or not. If you let the Wizard decide, the page in Figure 7-44b is displayed which shows the table structure determined by the Wizard. In this case the Wizard wants to create one new table for sales type (Table 2) instead of one for customer state which is more necessary to normalize the data. We'll keep the Table 2 and create another table for customer and customer state by dragging and dropping those fields from Table 1 onto an empty area on the canvass which will create a new table shown in Figure 7-44c. I changed the names of the tables by clicking on the button with the pencil character beside the button with the curvy arrow. The result is shown in Figure 7-44d.

If you elect to decide yourself about the table structure in Figure 7-44a, then the Analyzer will display a window similar to the one in Figure 7-44b where you can drag and drop fields onto the canvas to create new tables.

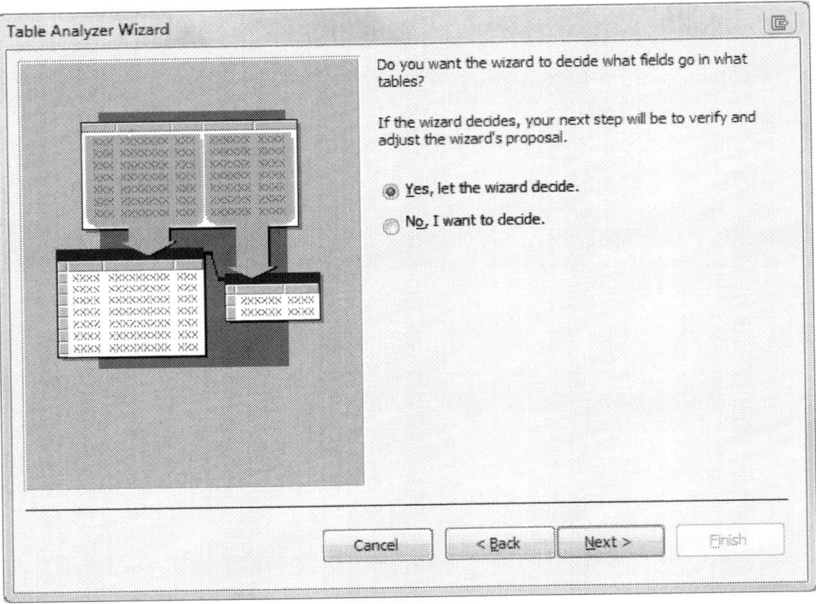

Figure 7-44a Table Analyzer Wizard - Page 3

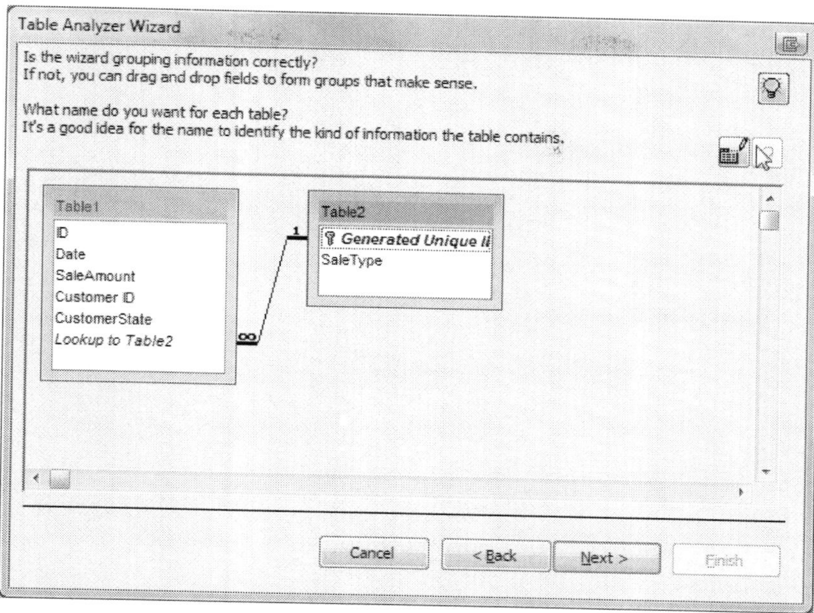

Figure 7-44b Table Analyzer Wizard - Proposed Structure

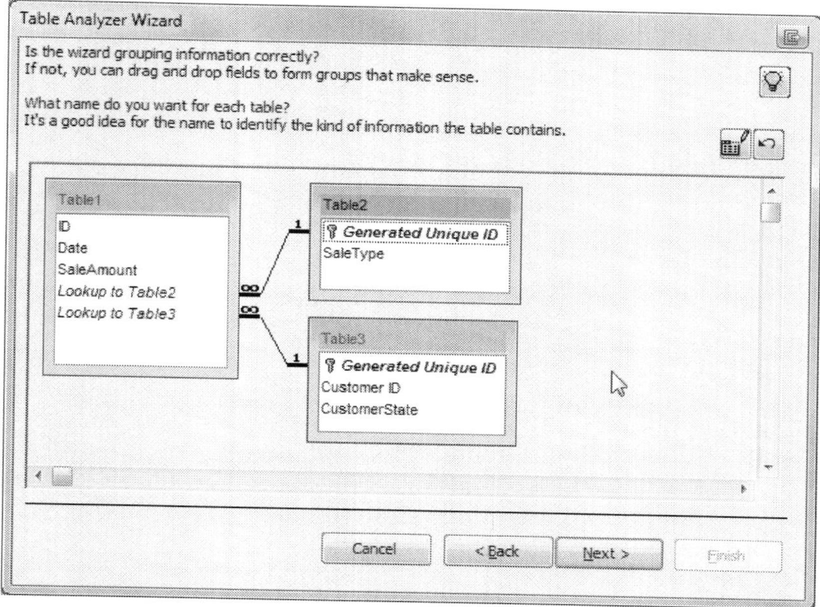

Figure 7-44c Table Analyzer Wizard - Modified Structure

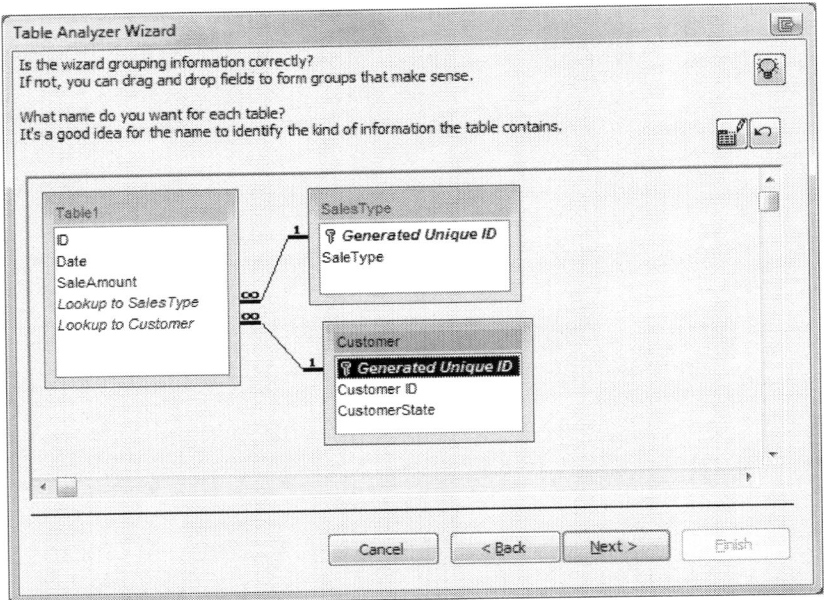

Figure 7-44d Table Analyzer Wizard - New Table Names

The next window in the Table Analyzer (not shown) asks about primary keys and allows you to add them if they are absent, and the one after that (not shown) gives you the opportunity to correct duplicate lookup values. The last window (Figure 7-44e) presents the option of creating a query to replace the original table that was analyzed. If you are constructing a new database as we are in the example or the table being analyzed is not used elsewhere in the database, say by a query, then it is not necessary to create this query. However, if the table is used elsewhere, then replacing the original table with the Analyzer versions will obfuscate references to it. The query will substitute for the original table in queries, forms, reports, etc. that reference it, and the objects should still function properly. Think of this replacement query as an alias for the original table.

The resultant table structure created by the Analyzer is shown in Figure 7-44f. I would change the field names of the keys in the SalesType and InternetSales tables to something more descriptive such as SalesTypeID and InternetSalesID.

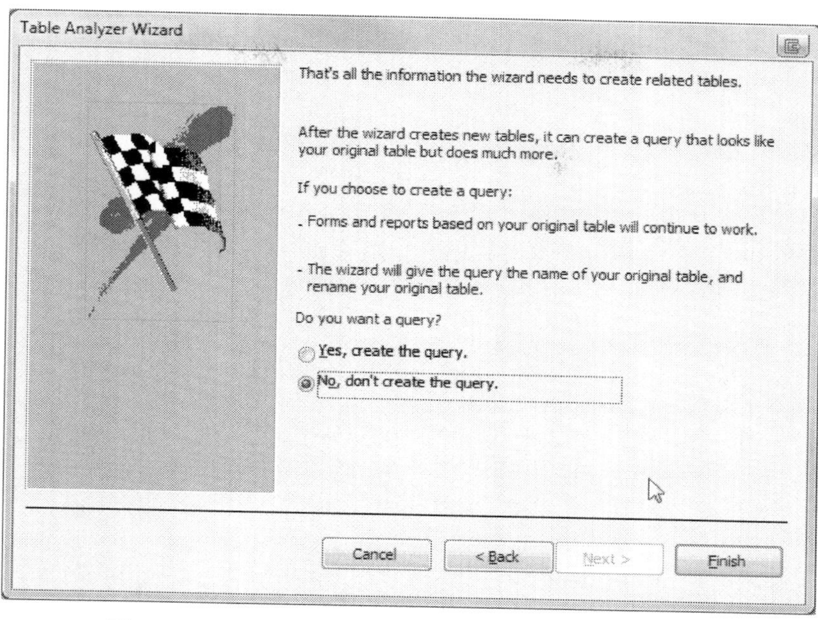

Figure 7-44e Table Analyzer Wizard - Create Query

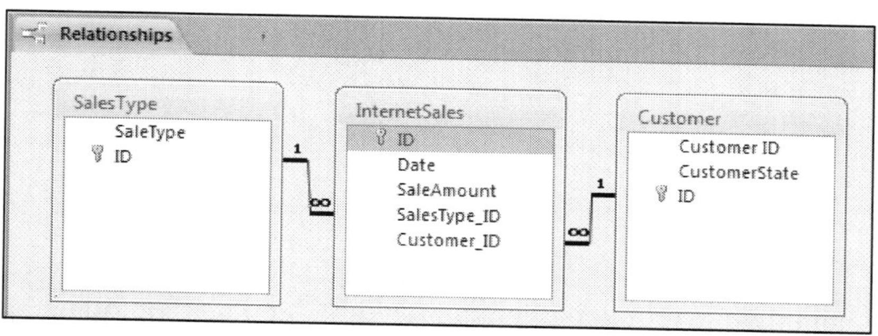

Figure 7-44f Table Analyzer Wizard - New Table Structure

Compact and Repair and Backup

An Access database can become fragmented and/or corrupted over time. To address these problems you can compact and repair it either manually or automatically. To manually compact and repair a database click the File (Office button) and then click Compact and Repair. If you check the file size of the database prior to compaction and compare it with the size after, there will usually be a significant reduction. To have the database automatically compacted click Options in the Office button menu and check the Compact on Close option on the Current Database page. Enabling automatic compaction is recommended unless the database is shared with others.

Access Data Projects

Access Data Projects (ADPs), now called Access Projects by Microsoft, provide direct links to SQL Server databases via OLE DB connections. Interestingly, some Access books claim that ADPs are no longer supported in Access 2010. I have not found that to be the case.

An ADP acts essentially as a front-end to a SQL Server Database and does not itself contain data or other database objects. You must have appropriate SQL Server permissions to utilize ADP capabilities. If you do, then ADPs offer a simpler and easier to use user interface for SQL Server databases relative to the SQL Server Management Studio. In addition, you may not have access to the SQL Server Management Studio—ADP is, in part, a surrogate for it.

To create a new ADP select New on the File (Access Office button) window which will display the Available Templates page with the Blank Database area on the right side. In that area click on the file folder button to the right of the File Name textbox to bring up a File New Database file finder (not shown). Navigate to the location that you want to store the database, give it a name, and select Microsoft Office Access Projects from the Save as type listbox (Figure 7-45). Clicking the OK button will return you to the Available Templates page with the new project listed in the area on the lower right (Figure 7-46).

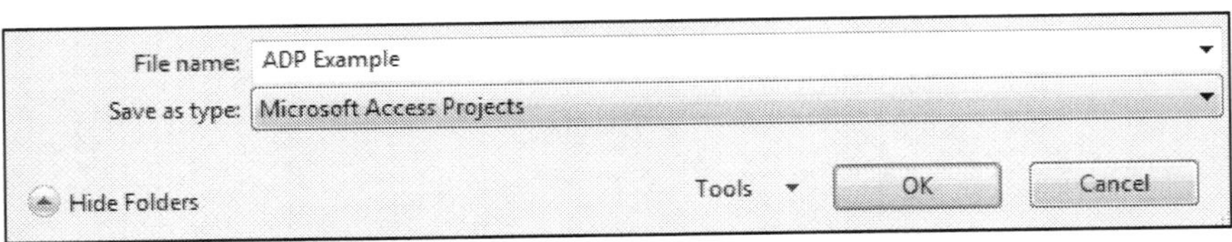

Figure 7-45 Table ADP File Type

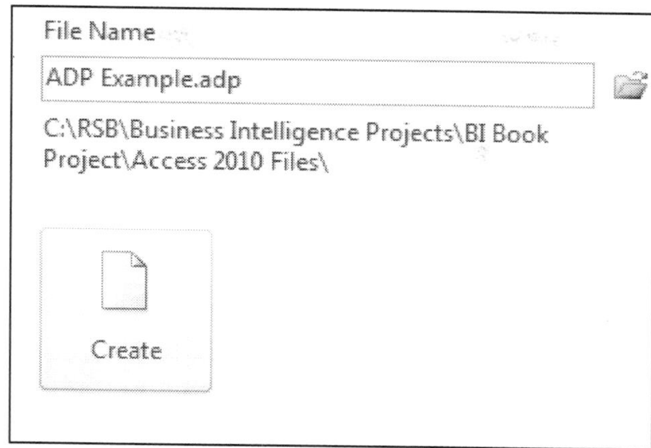

Figure 7-46 ADP New Project Area

Clicking the Create button will bring up a dialog box (not shown) that asks if you want to connect to an existing SQL Server database or create a new one. For our example we'll connect to AdventureWorksDW2008R2 on SQL Server 2008. In the next Data Link Properties dialog box (Figure 7-47) you identify the SQL Server instance, specify the type of security, and select the database to use from the drop-down listbox. Notice that you can also test the connection to the SQL Server instance. When you click the OK button, Access will grind away and eventually appear with all of the objects in the SQL Server database listed in the Navigation Pane (not shown) which will contain SQL Server tables in the Tables group; views, functions, and stored procedures in the Queries group; and database diagrams. The navigation pane may also list local Access forms and reports, and an ADP can include VBA code in modules or class modules. Figure 7-48 shows the navigation pane for the example where only the Queries group is expanded.

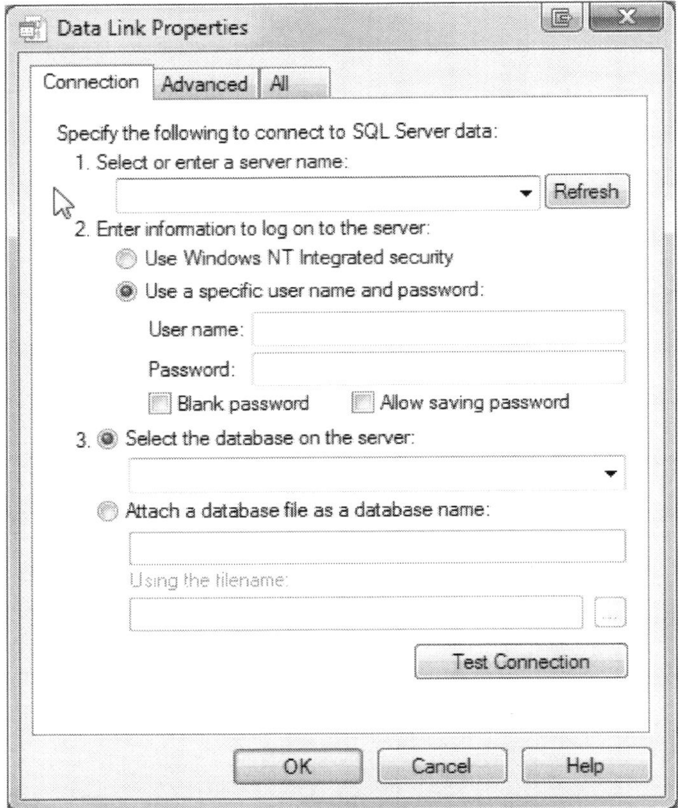

Figure 7-47 ADP Data Link Properties

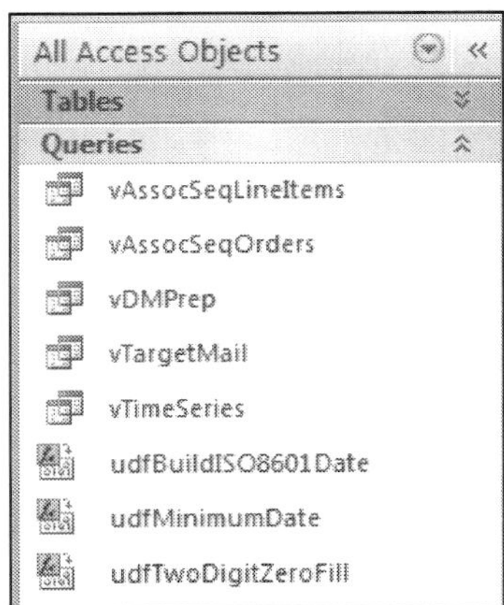

Figure 7-48 ADP Navigation Pane

ADPs use a Project Designer to create and modify tables, views, stored procedures, functions, and relationships. Figure 7-48 shows the Project Designer Table Design view and Figure 7-49 a View Design view which is more akin to the view designer in SQL Server. The View designer is also used for Stored Procedures and In-Line Functions. There are three panes in the View Designer: the top one displays the tables, views, and functions used in the design which you should be familiar with from our discussions of Access and query designers; the middle pane contains the grid view that lists the fields in the view where you can include an alias name for the field and specify sorts and filters; and the bottom pane displays the resultant T-SQL statement. Each of these panes can be hidden or unhidden by using the buttons in the Tools command group on the Design tab. As far as I know calculated fields can be only added to a view by inserting SQl expressions directly into the T-SQL statement. A type of aggregate query is available using the Group by option on the Output Operations command group.

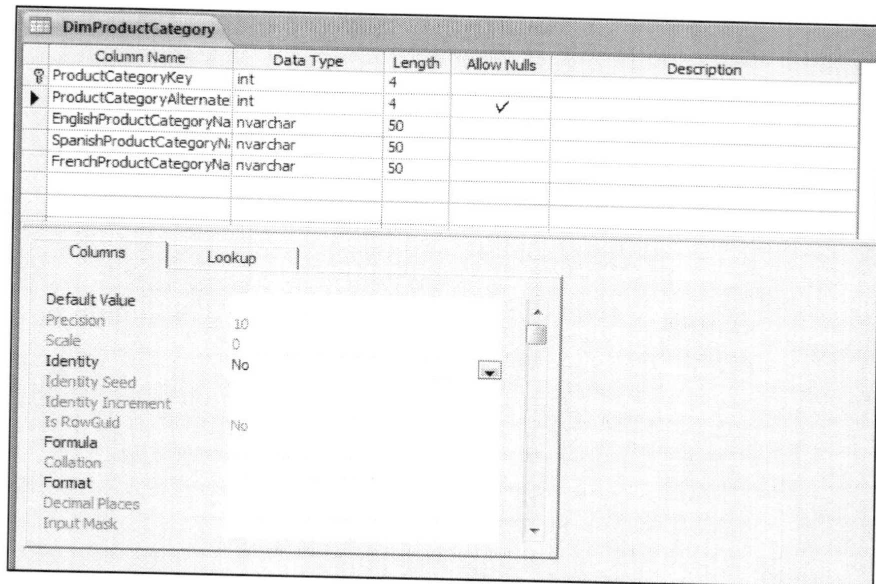

Figure 7-48 ADP Table Design View

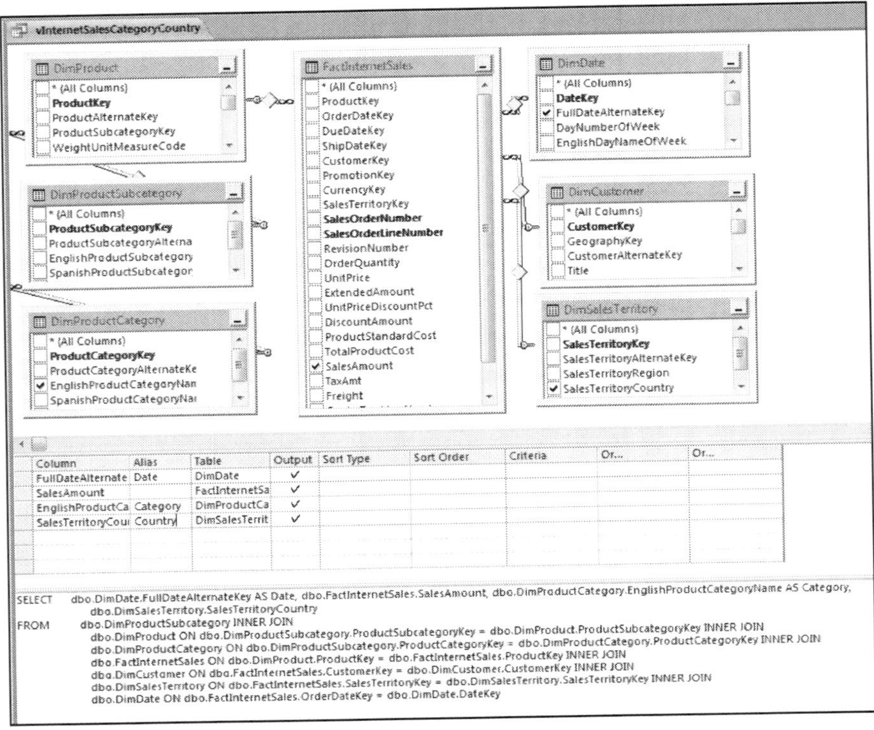

Figure 7-49 ADP View Design View

(For better viewing of this image, go to http://www.zerobits.info/bibook/bibookimages/)

Views (queries), stored procedures, etc. are created by clicking on the Query Wizard command in the Create tab that displays the New Query window in Figure 7-50. Thereafter choosing a type of query you design a new one in a Project designer as in Figure 7-51 for a stored procedure I created for Reseller sales. The resultant view is shown in Figure 7-52.

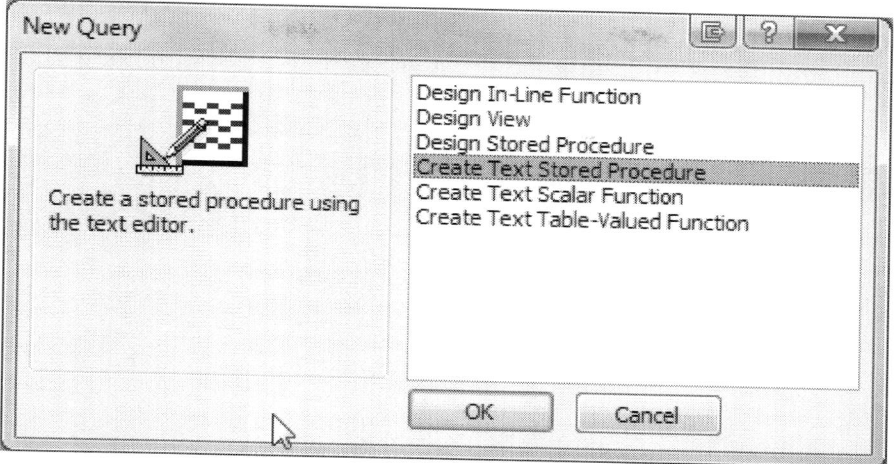

Figure 7-50 Query Wizard – New Query

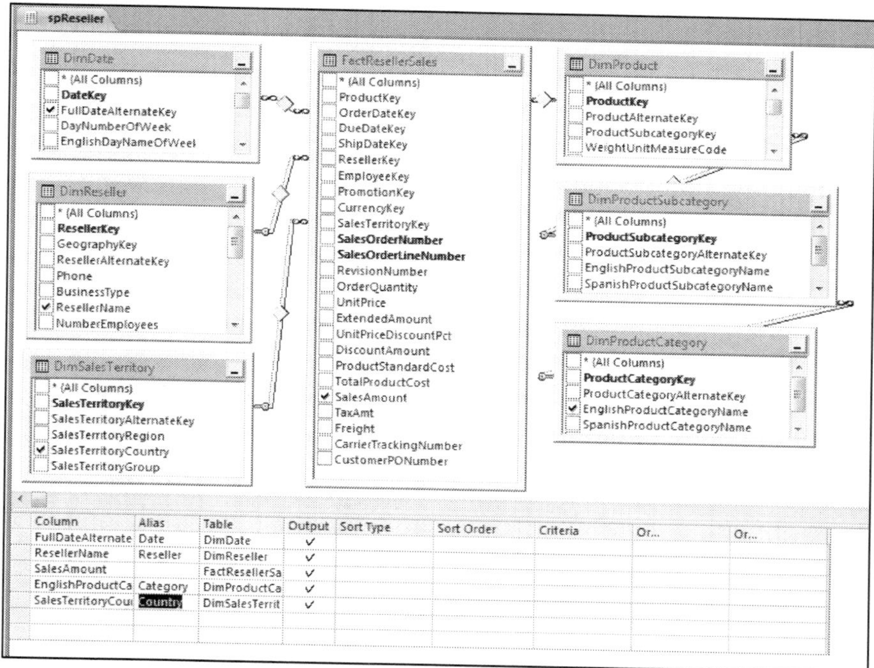

Figure 7-51 Stored Procedure Design

(For better viewing of this image, go to http://www.zerobits.info/bibook/bibookimages/)

Date	Reseller	SalesAmount	Category	Country
2005-07-01	Pedals Warehouse	$419.46	Bikes	United States
2005-07-01	Pedals Warehouse	$874.79	Bikes	United States
2005-07-01	Original Bicycle Supply Company	$809.76	Components	Canada
2005-07-01	Original Bicycle Supply Company	$714.70	Components	Canada
2005-07-01	Original Bicycle Supply Company	$1,429.41	Components	Canada
2005-07-01	Original Bicycle Supply Company	$20.75	Clothing	Canada
2005-07-01	Original Bicycle Supply Company	$115.36	Clothing	Canada
2005-07-01	Original Bicycle Supply Company	$1,445.19	Components	Canada
2005-07-01	Original Bicycle Supply Company	$6,074.98	Bikes	Canada
2005-07-01	Original Bicycle Supply Company	$4,049.99	Bikes	Canada

Figure 7-52 Stored Procedure View

The Create tab also includes form, report, and macro and code tools. Pivot tables and pivot charts are available for tables and queries in the usual manner by right clicking on the tab that contains the object's name. Stored procedures can be changed into make-table, append, update, and delete queries by using the options in Query Type command group on the Design tab. And, there are also ways to run parameter queries.

Access databases can be upsized to SQL Server databases by using the Upsizing Wizard initiated by selecting the SQL Server option in the Move Data command group on the Database Tools tab in an existing Access database (not in an ADP). This is not a foolproof process, and you can expect to do quite a bit of tinkering, especially if the original database is a complex one. Please refer to other sources that provides details about upsizing. An alternative is to use a SQL Server Migration Assistant for Access . Downloads are available—just search the Internet for SQL Server Migration Assistant for Access.

A number of server and database management functions are available from the Manage server information for the database window in Figure 7-53 displayed via the Server option on the File (Office button) menu. These functions are self-explanatory.

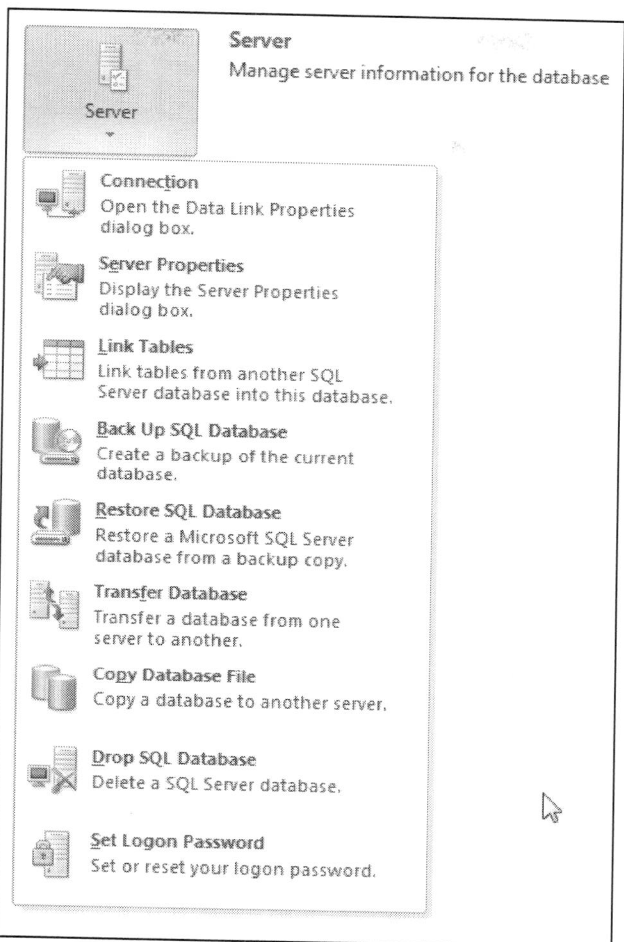

Figure 7-53 Server and Database Management Window

An ADP is a powerful tool for using SQL Server and its databases. Although it does not have all of the features of the SQL Server Management Studio, everything that I want to do in a database for data analysis is there except for KPIs and data mining. Keep in mind that with an ADP you have the capability to modify objects and data in the SQL Server instance itself, and that you can do irreparable harm to a database even if you know what you're doing. It's unlikely that analysts and power users like us will be granted permissions to connect to a production server with an ADP but, perhaps you can talk your DBA into letting you play with an offline copy on SQL Server Express.

What's Next

Although we've covered a lot of Access territory in this chapter, there remains much more to learn to become truly proficient with it. But, that is not the purpose of this book so we leave Access for now with the hope that what we've covered will help you with your data analysis tasks.

In the next chapter we move on the time series forecasting with Excel using approaches that range from simple moving averages to sophisticated data mining algorithms.

Chapter 8 - Time Series Forecasting with Excel 2010

There are many types of forecasting approaches: qualitative and quantitative, exploratory and predictive, and causal and time series just to name a few. In this chapter we focus on time series forecasting because time series data are ubiquitous in organizations. In addition, we already looked at associative-type models, albeit briefly, in our discussion of regression analysis in Chapter 6.

Preliminaries

Forecasting, even when limited to time series forecasting, is a lengthy, complex topic, and we have no intention of covering it all here. We'll try to keep the presentation practical with a minimum of scary wigglies (mathematical notation) and avoid esoteric topics.

Time Series Fundamentals

Data values vary. If they didn't, then there would be no need for forecasting. These variations in values derive from two sources: systematic variation and random variation. The purpose of quantitative forecasting is to identify the pattern(s) in the systematic variation and use that pattern to predict future values. Time series data depict the values of a variable(s) over time, usually in equally spaced intervals such as years, quarters, months, days, hours, etc. There are no cause and effect relationships implied, i.e., there are generally no independent variables other than time that impact the value of the dependent variable as there is in the regression example in Figure 6-42.

The systematic variation in time series data is usually ascribed to three types of patterns: trend, cyclical, and seasonal components. Trend is defined as a long-term inclination of the data, i.e., whether the values are increasing or decreasing over the long-term as represented by the straight line in Figure 8-1. However, I think of trend more as the fundamental pattern in the data, linear or otherwise, like the concave line in the figure.

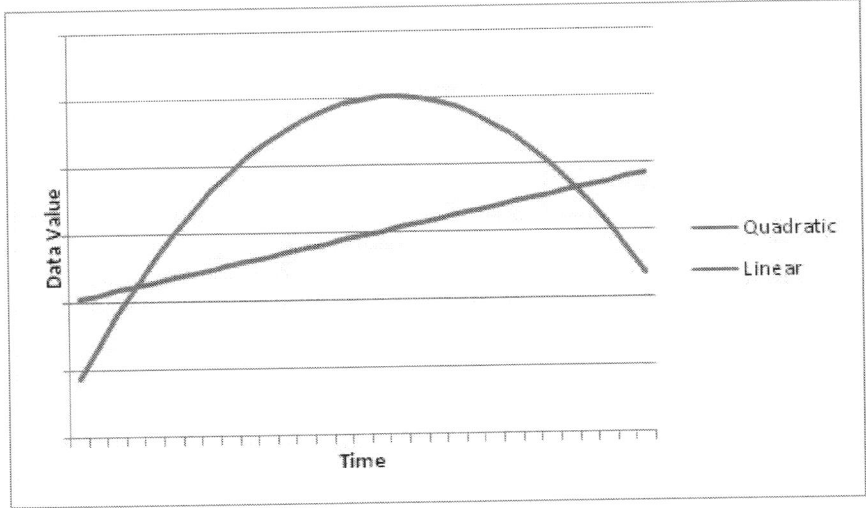

Figure 8-1 Trend Component

Cyclical patterns are long-term variations usually illustrated as sinusoidal waves. The business cycle is a prime example. Seasonal patterns are like cyclical ones only with a much shorter periodicity usually within one year, e.g., spring, summer, fall, and winter or the four quarters. Some time series data may display all of these patterns and some only one or even none when the data are entirely random.

It's sometime difficult to visually discern a pattern. In the contrived time series data in Figure 8-2a it looks to me like there may be as slight concave curve. Figure 8-2b shows the components that I used to construct the pattern with the straight line as the trend, the gentle sinusoidal curve as the cycle, and the more volatile sinusoidal component as the seasonal part. The patterns are overlaid with the seasonality imposed on the cyclical part which follows the trend, i.e., I first generated the trend data, added the cycle to it, and then appended the seasonal component. I produced the final data set in Figure 8-2a by adding a random component shown with the triangle marker in Figure 8-2c. Interestingly, a simple time series regression analysis (not shown) on the data in Figure 8-2a picks up very little pattern with an r^2 of less than .05

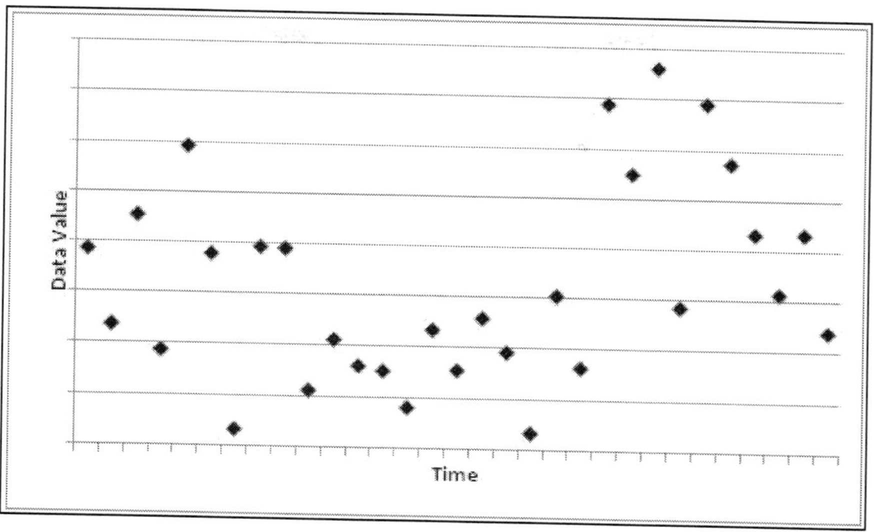

Figure 8-2a Example Time Series Data

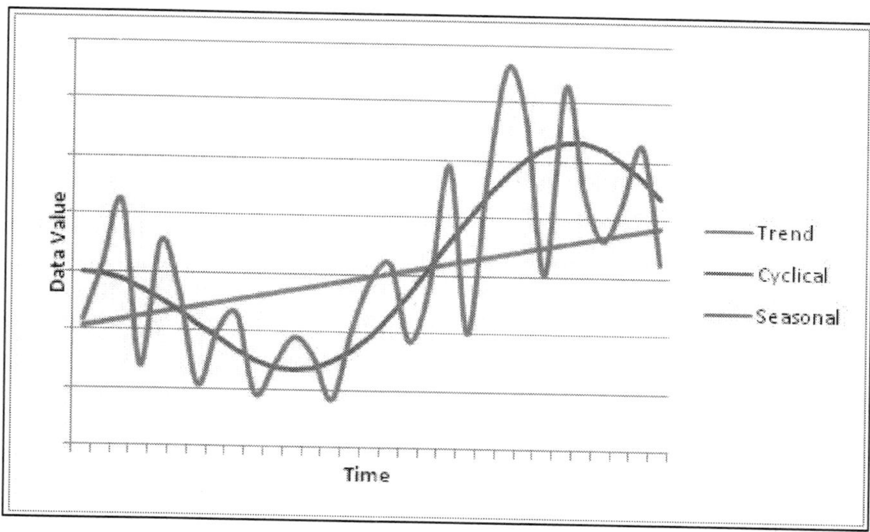

Figure 8-2b Systematic Patterns

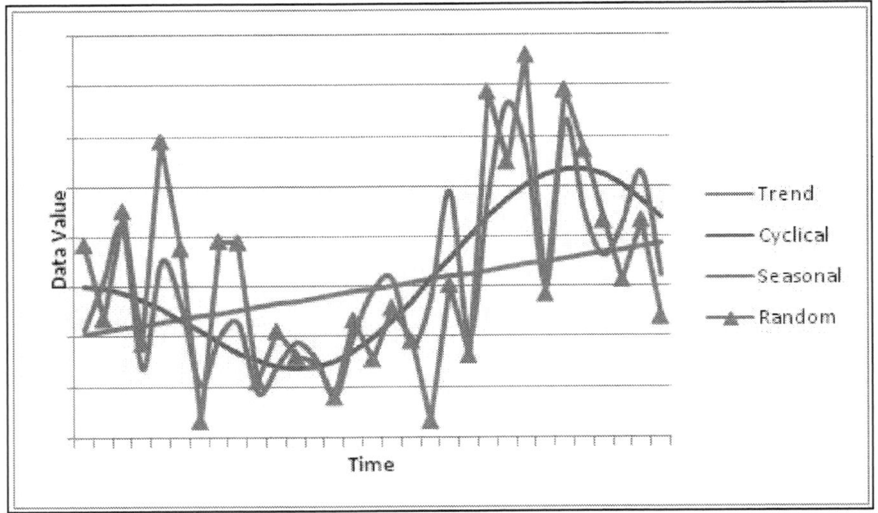

Figure 8-2c Random Variation Added

Planning Horizon

Planning horizons are conventionally classified as short-term, defined as less than one year but usually no more than a few months; intermediate-term as one to three years; and long-term as beyond three years. The length of the planning horizon in part determines the type of forecasting method to use. As the planning horizon lengthen quantitative forecasting methods become less accurate because they make projections based on the assumption that patterns discerned in past data will continue into the future. Of course, patterns are more likely to deviate from the past in the long-term.

In addition, each forecasting method is better suited for one of the planning horizon categories. For example, linear regression may not be applicable to day-to-day forecasting for production runs but smoothing methods are, and smoothing methods would not be appropriate to model the business cycle but decomposition would.

Forecasting Performance

The objective of forecasting is to predict future values of a variable(s) with high accuracy. However, the degree to which this can be accomplished is constrained by the amount of random variation. If random variation is high relative to systematic variation, then forecasts will be inaccurate regardless of the accuracy inherent in the method. The more frequently used quantitative forecasting accuracy measures are mean error, mean absolute deviation (MAD), and mean squared error (MSE) as explained below.

The small data set in Figure 8-3 includes sales data for twelve months, a forecast for ten months, and calculations of error, absolute error and squared error with accuracy measures presented at the bottom. Mean error is not a useful accuracy measure because positive and negative errors cancel each other out as you can see in the figure. But, it is a good indicator of bias—the property of the forecast to have a propensity to forecast high or low. In this case there is a positive bias, i.e., the forecast is low on the average.

	A	B	C	D	E	F
1					Absolute	Squared
2	Month	Sales	Forecast	Error	Error	Error
3	1	11				
4	2	14				
5	3	13	12.5	0.50	0.50	0.25
6	4	17	13.5	3.50	3.50	12.25
7	5	20	15.0	5.00	5.00	25.00
8	6	24	18.5	5.50	5.50	30.25
9	7	25	22.0	3.00	3.00	9.00
10	8	29	24.5	4.50	4.50	20.25
11	9	30	27.0	3.00	3.00	9.00
12	10	17	29.5	-12.50	12.50	156.25
13	11	14	23.5	-9.50	9.50	90.25
14	12	17	15.5	1.50	1.50	2.25
15		Mean Error (Bias) =		4.50		
16		Mean Absolute Deviation =			4.85	
17				Mean Squared Error =		35.48

Figure 8-3 Accuracy Measures

MAD and MSE take care of the positive-negative error offset problem. The difference is that MSE emphasizes larger errors because of squaring. For example, compare an error of 5 and an error of 10 which is double that of 5. The former results in a squared error of 25 and the latter quadruple that at 100. MSE is traditional in conventional statistics. MAD is used more frequently in forecasting. Although there are other forecasting accuracy measures such as mean absolute percentage error, the three described above are sufficient for our purposes. Computationally as Excel pseudo-formulas they are:

MAD = AVERAGE of ABS(Error)
MSE = AVERAGE of Error^2
Bias = AVERAGE(Error)
where: Error = Actual-Forecast

Another approach to evaluating accuracy in forecasting it to divide the data into two parts: one part is used to build the model and the other to test it. There is an Excel data mining tools to split a data set into two parts randomly for this purpose.

Chapter Organization

We first look at easy to use smoothing methods both moving averages and exponential smoothing, then see how linear regression can be used with time series data. After that we move on to decomposition to deal with seasonality, then briefly touch on autoregression and ARIMA in preparation for a description of the Microsoft Time Series Algorithm used in Analysis Services and Excel's Forecast Table Tools and Data Mining tools.

Smoothing

Smoothing forecasting methods which include moving averages and exponential smoothing are non- statistical techniques, i.e., they are not based on statistical theory as in, say, regression analysis. However, they are widely used; perform well in the right circumstances; and are easy to understand and calculate. Smoothing methods use previous values to forecast the next period, and, consequently, they are more appropriate for short-term forecasts.

All smoothing methods dampen fluctuations in the data in an attempt to control random variation. The degree of dampening is determined by a parameter(s): the number of periods in moving averages and a smoothing constant(s) in exponential smoothing. In setting the values for parameters there is a trade-off between dampening and responsiveness, that is, more dampening results in less responsiveness to current values and conversely. More on this shortly.

Moving Averages

Simple Moving Average

Moving averages use an average of previous actual values for the forecast of the next period. There are two types: the simple moving average and the weighted moving average. The simple moving average places equal weights on the previous values in the average. A simple moving average (MA) as an Excel pseudo-formula is:

MA = SUM(data values in the previous n periods)/n
or
MA = AVERAGE(data values in the previous n periods)

The formula says use the arithmetic mean of the last n values as the forecast for the next period. The number of periods used in the average (n) is the parameter for the formula. The forecast (Column C) in Figure 8-3 is a two period moving average so the first two cells in the forecast column are empty because the formula needs two values to compute the mean. Figure 8-4 shows the formulas for the worksheet in Figure 8-3.

	A	B	C	D	E	F
1						
2	Month	Sales	Forecast	Error	Absolute Error	Squared Error
3	1	11				
4	2	14				
5	3	13	=AVERAGE(B3:B4)	=B5-C5	=ABS(D5)	=D5^2
6	4	17	=AVERAGE(B4:B5)	=B6-C6	=ABS(D6)	=D6^2
7	5	20	=AVERAGE(B5:B6)	=B7-C7	=ABS(D7)	=D7^2
8	6	24	=AVERAGE(B6:B7)	=B8-C8	=ABS(D8)	=D8^2
9	7	25	=AVERAGE(B7:B8)	=B9-C9	=ABS(D9)	=D9^2
10	8	29	=AVERAGE(B8:B9)	=B10-C10	=ABS(D10)	=D10^2
11	9	30	=AVERAGE(B9:B10)	=B11-C11	=ABS(D11)	=D11^2
12	10	17	=AVERAGE(B10:B11)	=B12-C12	=ABS(D12)	=D12^2
13	11	14	=AVERAGE(B11:B12)	=B13-C13	=ABS(D13)	=D13^2
14	12	17	=AVERAGE(B12:B13)	=B14-C14	=ABS(D14)	=D14^2
15			Mean Error (Bias) =	=SUM(D5:D14)		
16				Absolute Deviation =	=AVERAGE(E5:E14)	
17					Mean Squared Error =	=AVERAGE(F5:F14)

Figure 8-4 2-Period Moving Average Formulas

As the number of periods in the mean increase, say from two to five, there will be more dampening (smoothing) and less responsiveness. This is demonstrated in the contrived example in Figure 8-5 which shows actual data as the solid line and forecasts with dashed lines. As you can see the forecast with n = 5 is much smoother and less responsive than the one for n = 2.

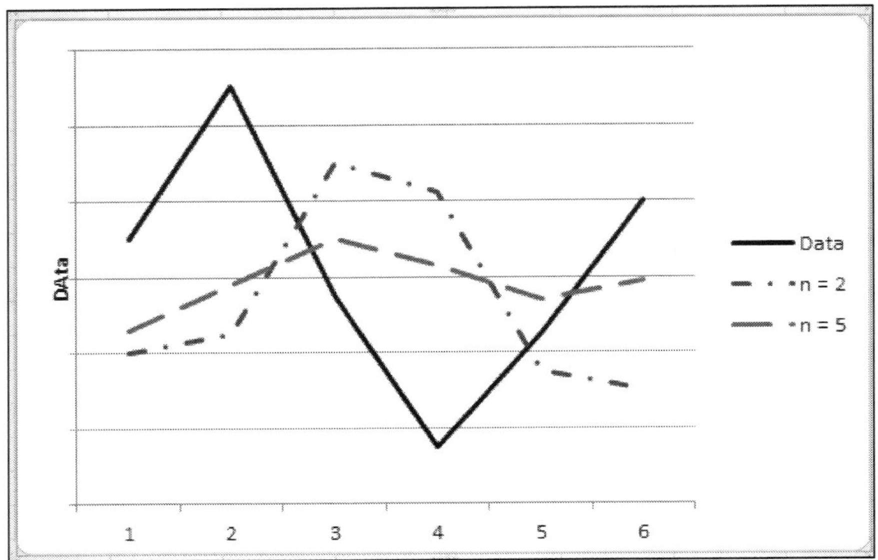

Figure 8-5 Smoothing as a Function of N

Well then, what is the best value for n? That depends on the data, of course. Practically, you would set n at the value that maximizes accuracy of the forecasted historical data values, i.e., the value that minimizes an accuracy measure such as MAD or MSE, and you would do that probably by trial and error. However, it is possible to write a VBA procedure that would automate the process.

When there is a trend or seasonal pattern (non-stationarity) in the data, the simple moving average forecast will usually lag the actual values as shown in Figure 8-5. There are variations on the simple moving average such as a double moving average that will compensate for trend, and you could extract seasonal variation by decomposition (see below) before computing the moving average and then re-seasonalizing the forecasted values. These advanced topics are beyond the scope of this book, and essentially irrelevant given the availability of better, more advanced methods like the Microsoft Time Series Algorithm.

To make using the moving average easier, a moving average tool is included in Excel's Analysis ToolPak add-in accessible via the Data Analysis option in the Analysis command group on the Data tab.

Weighted Moving Average

The weighted moving average (WMA) places a weight on each of the periods used in the average as in:

WMA = SUM(Weight*Data Value) for n periods/Sum(Weights)

The weights usually sum to one so in that case the denominator can be ignored. The example three-period weighted moving average in Figure 8-6 uses weights of .6, .3, and .1 as shown in the gray parameter area in the upper right corner. This model has better accuracy in terms of MAD than the simple moving average used above even when the previous forecast is adjusted to nine forecasted periods as in the WMA. This occurs as mentioned above because data series is not stationary so the forecasts lag. The WMA places more weight on the most recent period which reduces the lag.

	A	B	C	D	E	F	G	H
1					Absolute		Period	Weight
2	Month	Sales	Forecast	Error	Error		t - 1	0.6
3	1	11					t - 2	0.3
4	2	14					t - 3	0.1
5	3	13					Sum	1.0
6	4	17	13.1	3.90	3.90			
7	5	20	15.5	4.50	4.50			
8	6	24	18.4	5.60	5.60			
9	7	25	22.1	2.90	2.90			
10	8	29	24.2	4.80	4.80			
11	9	30	27.3	2.70	2.70			
12	10	17	29.2	-12.20	12.20			
13	11	14	22.1	-8.10	8.10			
14	12	17	16.5	0.50	0.50			
15			Bias =	4.60				
16				MAD =	5.02			

Figure 8-6 3-Period Weighted Moving Average Example

Different weight configurations can easily be tested by changing the values in Column H. For example, weights of 0.5, 0.5, and 0.0 turn the model into the simple 2-period moving average used above. In fact, the simple moving average is just a special case of the weighted moving average where the weights are equal. For this data series a minimum MAD will occur with the weights set at 1.0, 0.0, and 0.0, i.e., the forecast will be the most current actual value, because of the lag. Figure 8-7 shows the formulas for the worksheet in Figure 8-6.

	A	B	C	D	E	F	G
1					Absolute	Period	Weight
2	Month	Sales	Forecast	Error	Error	t - 1	0.6
3	1	11				t - 2	0.3
4	2	14				t - 3	0.1
5	3	13				Sum	=SUM(G2:G4)
6	4	17	=SUM(B5*$G$2,B4*$G$3,B3*$G$4)	=B6-C6	=ABS(D6)		
7	5	20	=SUM(B6*$G$2,B5*$G$3,B4*$G$4)	=B7-C7	=ABS(D7)		
8	6	24	=SUM(B7*$G$2,B6*$G$3,B5*$G$4)	=B8-C8	=ABS(D8)		
9	7	25	=SUM(B8*$G$2,B7*$G$3,B6*$G$4)	=B9-C9	=ABS(D9)		
10	8	29	=SUM(B9*$G$2,B8*$G$3,B7*$G$4)	=B10-C10	=ABS(D10)		
11	9	30	=SUM(B10*$G$2,B9*$G$3,B8*$G$4)	=B11-C11	=ABS(D11)		
12	10	17	=SUM(B11*$G$2,B10*$G$3,B9*$G$4)	=B12-C12	=ABS(D12)		
13	11	14	=SUM(B12*$G$2,B11*$G$3,B10*$G$4)	=B13-C13	=ABS(D13)		
14	12	17	=SUM(B13*$G$2,B12*$G$3,B11*$G$4)	=B14-C14	=ABS(D14)		
15			Bias =	=SUM(D5:D14)			
16				MAD =	=AVERAGE(E5:E14)		

Figure 8-7 3-Period Moving Average Formulas

Exponential Smoothing

Exponential smoothing is similar to weighted moving averages except that the weights exponentially decline, and all of the previous actual data points are used to the compute the forecast. Exponential smoothing is the easiest to use quantitative forecasting method because of its computational simplicity. We'll get to that shortly but first let's look at the general equation for single exponential smoothing (SES):

$$F_{t+1} = \alpha X_t + \alpha(1-\alpha)X_{t-1} + \alpha(1-\alpha)^2 X_{t-2} + \ldots + \alpha(1-\alpha)^{n-1} X_{t-(n-1)}$$

where: ***F*** = Forecasted value
X = Actual values
t = The most current time period
n = The number of actual values
α = The smoothing constant where $0 <= \alpha <= 1$

In the equation you can see that the actual values are weighted by the factor $\alpha(1-\alpha)^n$ where n starts at zero on the first term. Thus, the weights on later periods decrease exponentially. As shown in Figure 8-8 higher values of α, the single parameter in the model, more heavily weight current periods and therefore will be more responsive to current variations than smaller values that dampen or smooth out the variation. So, higher values of α result in more responsiveness and less smoothing and conversely. Note that the values for α range between 0 and 1.

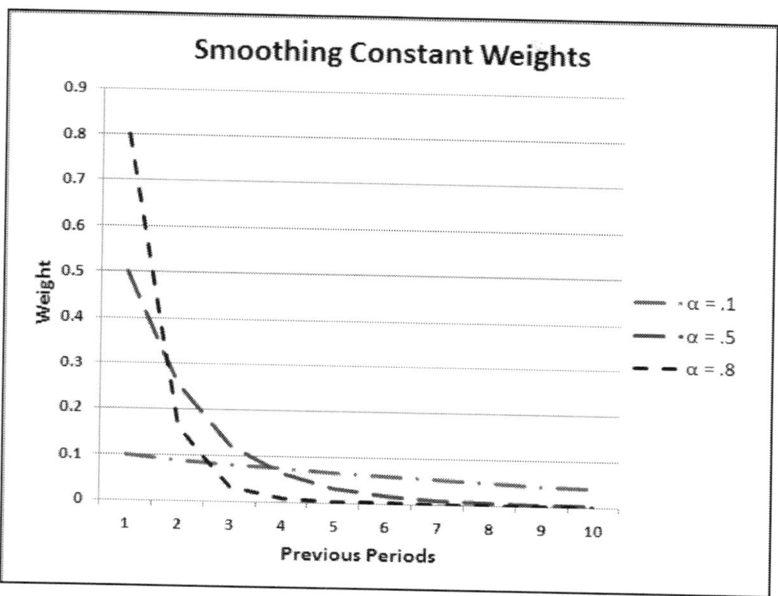

Figure 8-8 α Value Effect on Data Weights

A single exponential forecast is calculated as:

$$F_{t+1} = F_t + \alpha(X_t - F_t)$$

As compared with the general equation above you just need three values to calculate the forecast: the forecast for the current period, the actual value of the current period, and the smoothing constant. Using this formula and the same data as before the results for a SES model are presented in Figure 8-9 with α at 0.5 as highlighted in the shaded parameter area.

The exponential smoothing forecast must be initialized for the first period because there is no forecast for the previous period. There are two ways to select that initial value: use the actual value for the first period, 11 in this case, or use a guesstimate like I did in the example shown in the crosshatched cell. Regardless of the initialization method, the model will stabilize after a few periods. Figure 8-10 displays the formulas for the worksheet in Figure 8-9.

	A	B	C	D	E	F	G
1					Absolute		
2	Month	Sales	Forecast	Error	Error	α =	0.5
3	1	11	10				
4	2	14	10.5				
5	3	13	12.3				
6	4	17	12.6	4.38	4.38		
7	5	20	14.8	5.19	5.19		
8	6	24	17.4	6.59	6.59		
9	7	25	20.7	4.30	4.30		
10	8	29	22.9	6.15	6.15		
11	9	30	25.9	4.07	4.07		
12	10	17	28.0	-10.96	10.96		
13	11	14	22.5	-8.48	8.48		
14	12	17	18.2	-1.24	1.24		
15			Bias =	9.99			
16				MAD =	5.71		

Figure 8-9 Single Exponential Smoothing Example

	A	B	C	D	E	F	G
1					Absolute		
2	Month	Sales	Forecast	Error	Error	α =	0.5
3	1	11	10				
4	2	14	=C3+$G$2*(B3-C3)				
5	3	13	=C4+$G$2*(B4-C4)				
6	4	17	=C5+$G$2*(B5-C5)	=B6-C6	=ABS(D6)		
7	5	20	=C6+$G$2*(B6-C6)	=B7-C7	=ABS(D7)		
8	6	24	=C7+$G$2*(B7-C7)	=B8-C8	=ABS(D8)		
9	7	25	=C8+$G$2*(B8-C8)	=B9-C9	=ABS(D9)		
10	8	29	=C9+$G$2*(B9-C9)	=B10-C10	=ABS(D10)		
11	9	30	=C10+$G$2*(B10-C10)	=B11-C11	=ABS(D11)		
12	10	17	=C11+$G$2*(B11-C11)	=B12-C12	=ABS(D12)		
13	11	14	=C12+$G$2*(B12-C12)	=B13-C13	=ABS(D13)		
14	12	17	=C13+$G$2*(B13-C13)	=B14-C14	=ABS(D14)		
15			Bias =	=SUM(D5:D14)			
16				MAD =	=AVERAGE(E5:E14)		

Figure 8-10 3-Period Moving Average Formulas

In the parameter area you can easily try different values for α to minimize MAD by trial and error. Because SES lags similarly to moving averages, higher α values will be more accurate as shown in Figure 8-11 for the example data. The figure also illustrates the responsiveness-smoothing tradeoff for the different α values.

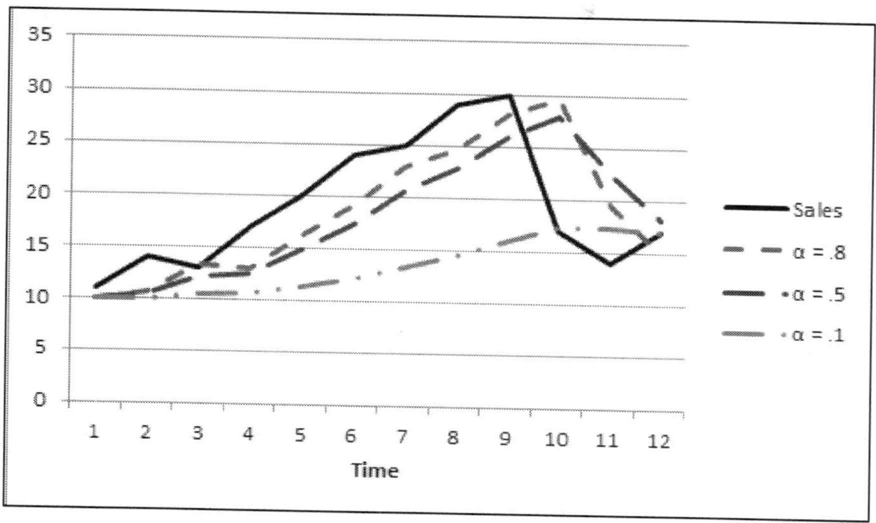

Figure 8-11 Forecasts for Different α Values

Another way to optimize the α value is to use Excel's Solver. (We won't go into detail about the Solver here, so if you are unfamiliar with it just skip this part.) The Solver Parameter dialog box (Figure 8-11) for the worksheet in Figure 8-9 minimizes MAD, the target cell, by changing values of α in cell G2 subject to the constraint that α must be between 0 and 1. Of course, because of the lag the optimal result is that α =1 minimizes MAD.

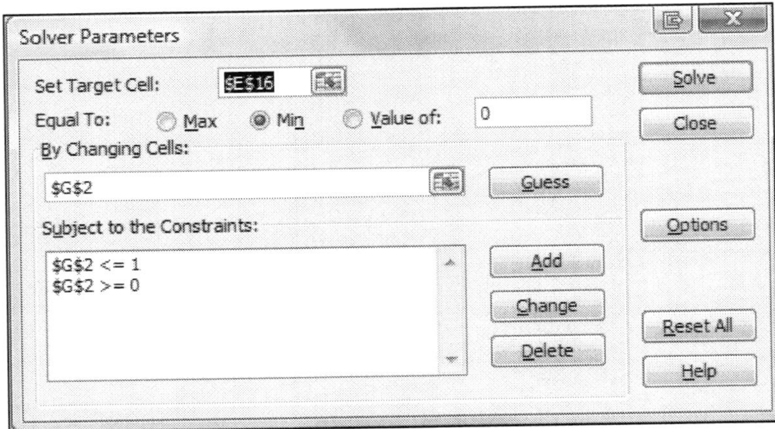

Figure 8-12 Solver Parameters Dialog Box to Optimize α

As with the moving average an exponential smoothing tool is included in the Analysis ToolPak add-in accessible via the Data Analysis option in the Analysis command group on the Data tab.

A number of enhanced exponential smoothing models are available. Some like the Adaptive Response Rate model allow the smoothing constant to vary to pick up changing patterns in the data. Others use double smoothing to accommodate trend patterns. And, there is even one, Winters' Method, that deals with trend and seasonality. We will not cover these advanced models here so please see Books on forecasting for details.

Time Series Linear Regression

Time series linear regression uses regression analysis described in Chapter 6 to create a linear model for a dependent variable such as sales or demand as it varies with time as an independent variable as shown below:

$F_t = a + bt$ where: Ft = Forecast for period t
a = Y intercept
b = slope

The example data in Figure 8-13a obviously has a trend component which is shown by the trend line in Figure 8-13b. Note that trend lines can be superimposed on data in a chart by using the Trendline option in the analysis command group on the Chart Tools Layout tab. Trendlines are available for exponential, linear, logarithmic, polynomial, power, and moving average functions.

M30		
	A	B
1	Period	Sales
2	1	81
3	2	116
4	3	148
5	4	127
6	5	104
7	6	137
8	7	181
9	8	144
10	9	130
11	10	147
12	11	202
13	12	160

Figure 8-13a Data

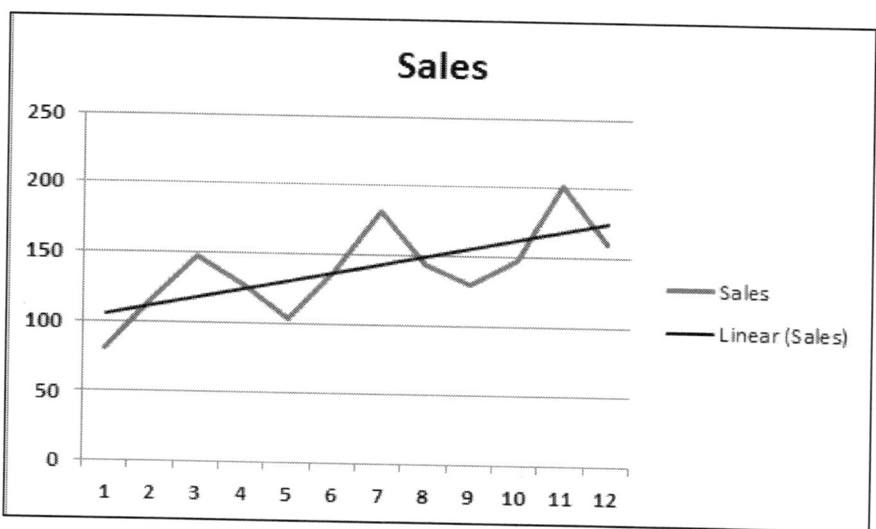

Figure 8-13b Chart with Trendline

Figure 8-13 Time Series Data Example

I ran a regression analysis on these data by selecting Regression from the Data Analysis option menu on the Data tab to bring up the Regression dialog box (Figure 8-14a) which produced the regression summary table in Figure 8-14b. Note that the Sales data is the Input Y Range and Period (time) is the Input X range. The resultant regression model has a r^2 of 0.49 with statistical significance for both the constant and period components. The model is:

$$\text{Sales in period t} = 98.5 + 6.34615(t)$$

where 98.5 is the value for the constant (Cell G17) and 6.346 is the value for the slope (Cell G18). Forecasted sales for any time period may be computed by inserting the period value in the formula. For example, the forecast for period 15 is 193.7 (98.5 + 6.34615*15).

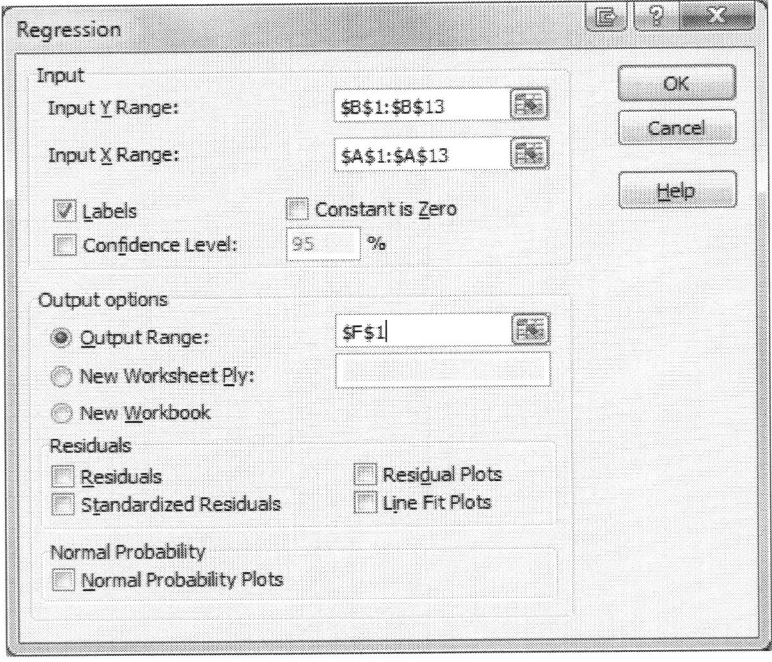

Figure 8-14a Regression Dialog Box for Example Data

	F	G	H	I	J	K	L
1	SUMMARY OUTPUT						
2							
3	*Regression Statistics*						
4	Multiple R	0.7020664					
5	R Square	0.4928972					
6	Adjusted R Square	0.442187					
7	Standard Error	24.34156					
8	Observations	12					
9							
10	ANOVA						
11		*df*	*SS*	*MS*	*F*	*Significance F*	
12	Regression	1	5759.134615	5759.135	9.719869	0.01091718	
13	Residual	10	5925.115385	592.5115			
14	Total	11	11684.25				
15							
16		*Coefficients*	*Standard Error*	*t Stat*	*P-value*	*Lower 95%*	*Upper 95%*
17	Intercept	98.5	14.98119451	6.57491	6.27E-05	65.11981862	131.8801814
18	Period	6.3461538	2.035543498	3.11767	0.010917	1.810680313	10.88162738

Figure 8-14b Regression Analysis Results

I used the regression formula to calculated forecasted values for the next eight periods (periods 13 through 20) as shown in the shaded area of Figure 8-15a with formulas in Figure 8-15b. In addition to forecasting sales in Column B I included 95% lower and upper limit values. These limits establish a confidence interval around the forecasted values where, if the historical pattern holds into the future, the forecasted values should fall within the confidence interval 95 percent of the time. For example, the forecasted value for Period 13 should fall between 122 and 240 95 out of 100 times.

	A	B	C	D
1	Period	Sales	Lower Limit	Upper Limit
2	1	81		
3	2	116		
4	3	148		
5	4	127		
6	5	104		
7	6	137		
8	7	181		
9	8	144		
10	9	130		
11	10	147		
12	11	202		
13	12	160		
14	13	181.0	122.0	240.0
15	14	187.3	123.8	250.8
16	15	193.7	125.7	261.7
17	16	200.0	127.5	272.6
18	17	206.4	129.3	283.5
19	18	212.7	131.1	294.4
20	19	219.1	132.9	305.3
21	20	225.4	134.7	316.1

Figure 8-15a Forecasted Values

	A	B	C	D
1	Period	Sales	Lower Limit	Upper Limit
14	13	=\$G\$17+\$G\$18*\$A14	=\$G\$17+\$K\$18*\$A14	=\$G\$17+\$L\$18*\$A14
15	14	=\$G\$17+\$G\$18*\$A15	=\$G\$17+\$K\$18*\$A15	=\$G\$17+\$L\$18*\$A15
16	15	=\$G\$17+\$G\$18*\$A16	=\$G\$17+\$K\$18*\$A16	=\$G\$17+\$L\$18*\$A16
17	16	=\$G\$17+\$G\$18*\$A17	=\$G\$17+\$K\$18*\$A17	=\$G\$17+\$L\$18*\$A17
18	17	=\$G\$17+\$G\$18*\$A18	=\$G\$17+\$K\$18*\$A18	=\$G\$17+\$L\$18*\$A18
19	18	=\$G\$17+\$G\$18*\$A19	=\$G\$17+\$K\$18*\$A19	=\$G\$17+\$L\$18*\$A19
20	19	=\$G\$17+\$G\$18*\$A20	=\$G\$17+\$K\$18*\$A20	=\$G\$17+\$L\$18*\$A20
21	20	=\$G\$17+\$G\$18*\$A21	=\$G\$17+\$K\$18*\$A21	=\$G\$17+\$L\$18*\$A21

Figure 8-15b Forecasted Values - Formulas

The chart for the actual and forecasted values is shown in Figure 8-15c where the lines beyond the vertical dashed line are the forecasted values. The dashed lines are the upper and lower limits.

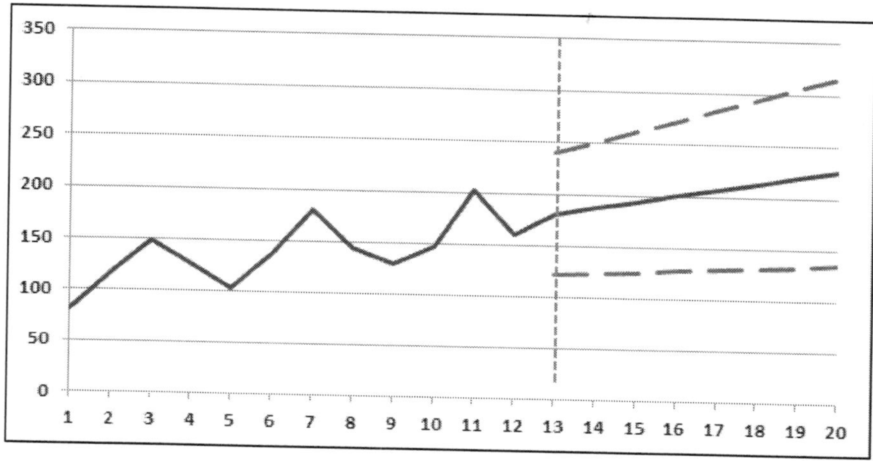

Figure 8-15c Forecasted Value Formulas

Decomposition - Seasonality

As opposed to smoothing methods which make no attempt to identify patterns in the time series data, at least in the simpler models, decomposition methods seek to identify seasonal, trend, and/or cyclical factors. These methods have been around for a long time, and although they are not founded in statistical theory, they, like smoothing methods, have been used successfully. Furthermore, it is possible to use decomposition along with other methods to improve forecast accuracy.

The standard decomposition model considers a time series data value to be composed of four parts: a seasonal component, a trend component, and cyclical component, and an error component (randomness). The U. S. Census Bureau developed software programs, X11 and more recently X12, to perform decomposition, and these approaches are sometimes embedded in statistical software applications. As far as I know they are not available as add-ins to Excel. Using this software is beyond the scope of this book so we will limit our discussion to a few basic approaches to deal with seasonality.

Deseasonalization

The data in the preceding example seem to have a seasonal component in addition to trend. Consider that the periods in those data are quarters in a year so there are three years of data in the twelve value series. We can estimate the seasonal effects by calculating seasonal indexes. To do that I reorganized the data into rows and columns (Figure 8-16) by using a pivot table and calculated the mean (average) value for each quarter in Row 25. Seasonal indexes in the shaded row are computed by dividing the quarter mean by the overall mean, e.g., the index for Quarter 1 (0.75) is calculated by dividing the mean (Cell B25) by the overall mean (Cell F25). So, a seasonal index represents the degree to which a season's mean value deviates from the overall mean.

	A	B	C	D	E	F
19	Actual Data					
20			Quarter			
21	Year	1	2	3	4	Mean
22	1	81	116	148	127	
23	2	104	137	181	144	
24	3	130	147	202	160	
25	Mean	105.00	133.33	177.00	143.67	139.75
26	Index	0.75	0.95	1.27	1.03	

Figure 8-16 Seasonal Indexes

Now what we need is a way to produce forecasted values without a seasonal component, and then we can incorporate seasonality with the seasonal indexes. We'll do that in the next section.

Seasonality and Trend

We know that the sales data series in the example has a trend component from the earlier regression analysis and a seasonal component from the seasonal indexes above. There are different ways to deal with seasonality and trend. One is to combine the approaches above to produce forecasts that incorporate both patterns. The first step is to deseasonalize the original data as in Figure 8-17a by dividing each of the actual values by the appropriate seasonal index. For example, the value in Cell B31 is calculated by dividing 81 by 0.75, the index for the first quarter in Cell B26 above. (Note that the seasonal indexes have more significant digits than shown so the result of the calculation described above is slightly different that 81/.75.)

	A	B	C	D	E
29			Quarter		
30	Year	1	2	3	4
31	1	107.8	121.6	116.9	123.5
32	2	138.4	143.6	142.9	140.1
33	3	173.0	154.1	159.5	155.6

Figure 8-17a Deseasonalized Data

The second step is to perform a regression analysis on the deseasonalized data as in Figure 8-17b which produced a much higher r^2 than the regression analysis (Figure 8-14b) on the original data. The regression model changes to:

Sales in period t = 108.3 + 4.8235(t)

	F	G	H	I	J	K	L	M
35	SUMMARY OUTPUT	- Desesaonalized Data						
36								
37	*Regression Statistics*							
38	Multiple R	0.898817						
39	R Square	0.807871						
40	Adjusted R Square	0.788659						
41	Standard Error	8.895411						
42	Observations	12						
43								
44	ANOVA							
45		*df*	*SS*	*MS*	*F*		*Significance F*	
46	Regression	1	3327.22794	3327.23	42.0485		7.03253E-05	
47	Residual	10	791.28345	79.1283				
48	Total	11	4118.51139					
49								
50		*Coefficient*	*tandard Errc*	*t Stat*	*P-value*		*Lower 95%*	*Upper 95%*
51	Intercept	108.3965	5.4747473	19.7994	2.37E-09		96.19796055	120.5949548
52	Period	4.823622	0.74387168	6.48448	7.03E-05		3.166172525	6.481071275

Figure 8-17b Regression Analysis on Deseasonalized Data

The final step is to use these results by seasonalizing the forecasts from the regression model as in Figure 8-17c with the formulas in Figure 8-17d.

	A	B	C	D
74		Regression	Seasonal	
75	Period	Projection	Index	Forecast
76	13	171.1	0.75	128.6
77	14	175.9	0.95	167.8
78	15	180.8	1.27	228.9
79	16	185.6	1.03	190.8
80	17	190.4	0.75	143.1
81	18	195.2	0.95	186.3
82	19	200.0	1.27	253.4
83	20	204.9	1.03	210.6

Figure 8-17c Seasonalized Regression Forecast

	A	B	C	D
74		Regression	Seasonal	
75	Period	Projection	Index	Forecast
76	13	=$G$51+$G$52*A76	0.75134168157424	=B76*C76
77	14	=$G$51+$G$52*A77	0.954084675014908	=B77*C77
78	15	=$G$51+$G$52*A78	1.26654740608229	=B78*C78
79	16	=$G$51+$G$52*A79	1.02802623732856	=B79*C79
80	17	=$G$51+$G$52*A80	0.75134168157424	=B80*C80
81	18	=$G$51+$G$52*A81	0.954084675014908	=B81*C81
82	19	=$G$51+$G$52*A82	1.26654740608229	=B82*C82
83	20	=$G$51+$G$52*A83	1.02802623732856	=B83*C83

Figure 8-17d Seasonalized Regression Forecast Formulas

To evaluate the model's performance I calculated forecasts for the first twelve periods and compared them with the original values. In Figure 8-17e Column H contains the forecasted values, Column I the original values from Figure 8-13a, Column J the difference between those two values (error), and Column K the percentage of the error to the original value. The mean percent error is only 4.4 which is good. But, it looks even better when considering the amount of random error included in the original values (Column L) which absorbs 3.3 percent (Cell M88) of that error. Wow!

	G	H	I	J	K	L	M
74					Percent	Random	Random
75	Period	Forecast	Original	Error	Error	Component	% Error
76	1	85.1	81	-4.1	5.0%	-4	4.9%
77	2	112.6	116	3.4	2.9%	6	5.2%
78	3	155.6	148	-7.6	5.1%	-7	4.7%
79	4	131.3	127	-4.3	3.4%	4	3.1%
80	5	99.6	104	4.4	4.3%	-1	1.0%
81	6	131.0	137	6.0	4.4%	7	5.1%
82	7	180.1	181	0.9	0.5%	6	3.3%
83	8	151.1	144	-7.1	4.9%	1	0.7%
84	9	114.1	130	15.9	12.3%	5	3.8%
85	10	149.4	147	-2.4	1.7%	-3	2.0%
86	11	204.5	202	-2.5	1.2%	7	3.5%
87	12	170.9	160	-10.9	6.8%	-3	1.9%
88				Mean =	4.4%	Mean =	3.3%

Figure 8-17d Seasonalized Regression Forecast Accuracy

Figure 8-17e shows how I contrived the original data. Trend was calculated as 95 + 5t; the seasonal component has a fixed pattern of -15, 5, 45, and 8; and the random component was generated by the Excel RANDBETWEEN function with limits of plus/minus 7. The time series regression model was not very accurate in estimating the Y intercept (108 vs. 95 actual) but quite accurate in estimating the slope (4.8 vs. 5 actual). The seasonal adjustment error is about eight percent (calculations not shown), and much of this may be due to using a multiplicative decomposition model whereas the seasonal factor is additive, i.e., a constant seasonal value is added to the increasing trend value. But that's a technicality we need not be concerned with here. Overall, the model performs well.

	A	B	C	D	E
2	Period	Trend	Seasonal	Random	Total
3	1	100	-15	-4	81
4	2	105	5	6	116
5	3	110	45	-7	148
6	4	115	8	4	127
7	5	120	-15	-1	104
8	6	125	5	7	137
9	7	130	45	6	181
10	8	135	8	1	144
11	9	140	-15	5	130
12	10	145	5	-3	147
13	11	150	45	7	202
14	12	155	8	-3	160

Figure 8-17e Composition of Original Data

Linear Regression with Dummy Variables

In Chapter 6 we mentioned that it was possible to use dummy variables in linear regression to incorporated categorical data. The example in this section applies them to designate seasons in a regression model. Binary variables represent the absence or presence of a category in a data series row. If there are n categories, then you need n-1 binary variables—you can think of this as degrees for freedom. In Figure 8-18a I coded three binary valued columns to tag Quarters 1 through 3. Quarter 4 is coded with all zeroes. It does not make any difference which categories have which coding. Note that I placed the dummy variable columns beside the Period column because Excel's regression function requires the independent variable columns to be contiguous. The regression results are shown in Figure 8-18b.

	A	B	C	D	E
1	Dummy Variables				
2	Q1	Q2	Q3	Period	Sales
3	1	0	0	1	81
4	0	1	0	2	116
5	0	0	1	3	148
6	0	0	0	4	127
7	1	0	0	5	104
8	0	1	0	6	137
9	0	0	1	7	181
10	0	0	0	8	144
11	1	0	0	9	130
12	0	1	0	10	147
13	0	0	1	11	202
14	0	0	0	12	160

Figure 8-18a Time Series Data with Dummy Variables

	G	H	I	J	K	L	M
1	SUMMARY OUTPUT						
2							
3	*Regression Statistics*						
4	Multiple R	0.9895377					
5	R Square	0.9791849					
6	Adjusted R Square	0.9672906					
7	Standard Error	5.8944082					
8	Observations	12					
9							
10	ANOVA						
11		*df*	*SS*	*MS*	*F*	*Significance F*	
12	Regression	4	11441.04167	2860.26	82.32375	5.7603E-06	
13	Residual	7	243.2083333	34.74405			
14	Total	11	11684.25				
15							
16		*Coefficients*	*Standard Error*	*t Stat*	*P-value*	*Lower 95%*	*Upper 95%*
17	Intercept	101.91667	5.380833859	18.94068	2.84E-07	89.1930164	114.640317
18	Q1	-23.01042	5.060201504	-4.54733	0.002644	-34.975892	-11.044941
19	Q2	0.1041667	4.92427151	0.021154	0.983713	-11.539885	11.7482185
20	Q3	38.552083	4.840881767	7.963856	9.38E-05	27.1052169	49.9989498
21	Period	5.21875	0.520996998	10.01685	2.12E-05	3.98678786	6.45071214

Figure 8-18b Time Series Data with Dummy Variables Results

The model (shown below) has a very high r^2 of .98 and all of the components have significant t-statistics except for Q_2 which you would expect because its coefficient is so close to zero. The model was used to generate the forecasted values in Figure 8-18c.

$$\text{Sales in period t} = 101.91 + 5.209(t) - 23.01Q_1 + .104Q_2 + 38.55Q_3$$

	A	B	C	D	E
2	Q1	Q2	Q3	Period	Sales
15	1	0	0	13	146.8
16	0	1	0	14	175.1
17	0	0	1	15	218.8
18	0	0	0	16	185.4
19	1	0	0	17	167.6
20	0	1	0	18	196.0
21	0	0	1	19	239.6
22	0	0	0	20	206.3

Figure 8-18c Time Series with Dummy Variables Forecasts

How does the performance of this model (Model 2) compare with the seasonally adjusted trend model immediately above (Model 1)? In Figure 8-18d Model 2 had about a 30 percent lower MAD than Model 1 although they are both fairly accurate. However, this is not meant to imply that the dummy variable model is necessarily superior to the seasonally adjusted model in all circumstances—it will depend upon the patterns in the data.

	A	B	C	D	E	F
24					Model 1	Model 2
25	Period	Sales	Model 1	Model 2	Error	Error
26	1	81	85.1	84.1	4.1	3.1
27	2	116	112.6	112.5	3.4	3.5
28	3	148	155.6	156.1	7.6	8.1
29	4	127	131.3	122.8	4.3	4.2
30	5	104	99.6	105.0	4.4	1.0
31	6	137	131.0	133.3	6.0	3.7
32	7	181	180.1	177.0	0.9	4.0
33	8	144	151.1	143.7	7.1	0.3
34	9	130	114.1	125.9	15.9	4.1
35	10	147	149.4	154.2	2.4	7.2
36	11	202	204.5	197.9	2.5	4.1
37	12	160	170.9	164.5	10.9	4.5
38				MAD =	5.8	4.0

Figure 8-18c Time Series with Dummy Variables Forecasts

Autoregression

Autoregression uses previous values of the dependent variable as independent variables. Figure 8-19a shows a worksheet set up to perform an autoregression analysis on the data from our previous example. Notice that each data series to the right of Column B is offset one row downward and that the values are identical on the diagonal. Only four periods are used as previous values here but there is no constraint on how far back we can go. The principle of autoregression is to determine the degree to which values of the data series in previous periods are related to the value of the current period . We do this by running a regression analysis starting with the first row that has a full set of values, Row 46 (Period 5) in this case. Please be aware that I extended this data set to 36 rows (nine years) to have ample data for the analysis. The first four rows are not used in the analysis because the data are incomplete as you can see in Figure 8-19a. The results are shown in Figure 8-19b.

	A	B	C	D	E	F
41	**Period**	**Sales t**	**Sales t-1**	**Sales t-2**	**Sales t-3**	**Sales t-4**
42	1	81				
43	2	116	81			
44	3	148	116	81		
45	4	127	148	116	81	
46	5	104	**127**	148	116	81
47	6	137	104	**127**	148	116
48	7	181	137	104	**127**	148
49	8	144	181	137	104	**127**
50	9	130	144	181	137	104
51	10	147	130	144	181	137
52	11	202	147	130	144	181
53	12	160	202	147	130	144

Figure 8-19a Autoregression Example Data

	M	N	O	P	Q	R	S
5	SUMMARY OUTPUT						
6							
7	*Regression Statistics*						
8	Multiple R	0.99240438					
9	R Square	0.98486645					
10	Adjusted R Square	0.98262444					
11	Standard Error	6.879203					
12	Observations	32					
13							
14	ANOVA						
15		*df*	*SS*	*MS*	*F*	*Significance F*	
16	Regression	4	83152.73603	20788.18	439.2789	3.84066E-24	
17	Residual	27	1277.732716	47.32343			
18	Total	31	84430.46875				
19							
20		*Coefficients*	*Standard Error*	*t Stat*	*P-value*	*Lower 95%*	*Upper 95%*
21	Intercept	20.6520318	5.527655723	3.736128	0.000886	9.310219194	31.9938443
22	Sales t-1	0.06004132	0.080628883	0.744663	0.462908	-0.105395477	0.22547813
23	Sales t-2	-0.0696973	0.08144271	-0.85578	0.399649	-0.236803895	0.09740938
24	Sales t-3	0.08394723	0.081670576	1.027876	0.313129	-0.083626947	0.25152141
25	Sales t-4	0.91918524	0.081106621	11.33305	9.08E-12	0.7527682	1.08560228

Figure 8-19b Autoregression Example Regression Results

This model with an even higher r^2 than the linear regression with dummy variables example is:

Sales t = 20.65 + .06(Sales t-1) - .07(Sales t-2) + .08(Sales t-3) + .02(Sales t-4)
However, notice that the coefficients for Sales t-1, t-2, and t-3 are not statistically significant meaning that they could just as well be zero. This result is not unexpected since we know that the series has a four-period seasonality component. So, let's try a simplified model with only Sales t-4 in it. The results in Figure 8-19c indicate that we lost essentially nothing in r^2 by dropping the three sales variable and gained simplicity. To use this model all you need is the sales data from one year ago.

	M	N	O	P	Q	R	S
37	SUMMARY OUTPUT						
38							
39	*Regression Statistics*						
40	Multiple R	0.99210534					
41	R Square	0.98427301					
42	Adjusted R Square	0.98374877					
43	Standard Error	6.65291287					
44	Observations	32					
45							
46	ANOVA						
47		*df*	*SS*	*MS*	*F*	*Significance F*	
48	Regression	1	83102.63126	83102.63	1877.548	1.2962E-28	
49	Residual	30	1327.837488	44.26125			
50	Total	31	84430.46875				
51							
52		*Coefficients*	*Standard Error*	*t Stat*	*P-value*	*Lower 95%*	*Upper 95%*
53	Intercept	21.8997761	4.468997976	4.900377	3.09E-05	12.77286461	31.0266875
54	Sales t-4	0.99026125	0.02285358	43.33068	1.3E-28	0.943588014	1.03693449

Figure 8-19c Simplified Model Regression Results

ARIMA

ARIMA, Autoregressive Integrated Moving Average, known as Box-Jenkins analysis and named after the early developers of the methodology, adds two other components to an autoregressive model (the AR part): a differencing or integration component (I) and a moving average of error component (MA). ARIMA models are specified as ARIMA(p,d,q) where p, d, and q stand for the number of lags, i.e., previous values, for the AR part, the differencing part, and the MA part, respectively. The ARIMA methodology gets very complicated very quickly so we'll only mention a few basic concepts here. This is OK because the Microsoft Time Series Algorithm discussed next takes care of all of the details.

The AR component specifies the number of lags used in autoregression. An ARIMA(1,0,0) model uses only one previous value and has no differencing or MA components. The basic idea of the MA part which is not the same as the moving average approach discussed in the Smoothing section is a relationship between the dependent variable and successive error terms where, as before, error is the difference between the actual and forecasted values. So, the MA part which deals with random shocks in the series is something like:

$$F_t = a + b_1 e_{t-1} + b_2 e_{t-2} + b_3 e_{t-3} + \ldots + b_i e_{t-i} + e_t$$

That is, the forecast is composed of a constant term and previous error terms multiplied by their respective coefficients. An ARIMA(0,0,1) model uses only one error term and has no AR or differencing components.

The AR and MA components assume that the series is stationary, e.g., that the mean of the series does not change over time as would occur if a trend is present. If the series is not stationary, then differencing is used make it so. A difference is just the value in one time period less the value of the series in the previous time period. The equations below represent a first difference where D is the difference and X is the value of the series.

$$D_t = X_t - X_{t-1}$$

An ARIMA model with first differencing without AR and MA components would be specified as ARIMA(0,1,0). Higher orders of differencing indicate a differencing of differences if you can comprehend that. AIRMA models can be extended to incorporate seasonality as well. The p, d, q parameters are determined by examining patterns in the data manually by using charts such as correlograms (not shown) or automatically as in the Microsoft Time Series Algorithm which comes up next.

Microsoft Time Series Algorithm

The time series forecasting procedure included in SQL Server 2008 Analysis Services combines the results from two different algorithms: Autoregressive Tree with Cross Prediction (ARTxp), the only time series algorithm used in SQL Server 2005, and ARIMA. ARTxp is better suited for short-term predictions and ARIMA for longer-term. The ARTxp algorithm may split the data into segments in a decision tree framework with branches for each predictable attribute and for each segment of linearity, i.e., a split will occur when there is a change in the trend pattern. The ARIMA algorithm divides the data based on periodicity, a repeating pattern in the data. In the time series algorithm the ARTxp and ARIMA results are blended to optimize a forecast.

In addition, the ARTxp algorithm supports cross-prediction in which data from other time series are used as predictors for another series. For example, in the AdventureWorks sample data from other bicycle models may be used by ARTxp to forecast sales for a particular bicycle model. The Forecast tools in both Excel's Table Tools and Data Mining Tools utilize the Time Series Algorithm with the Data Mining option offering more customization and information about the results. Because these tools employ the Time Series Algorithm in Analysis Services, note again that an instance of SQL Server 2008 must be running and available to utilize them.

Forecast - Table Tools

In the first example we'll use the 36 periods of sales data from the Autoregression section above and the Forecast option in the Table Tools Analyze tab. Remember that the Table Analysis Tools require the data to be in an Excel table format.

Clicking Forecast displays a SQL Server Data Mining—Forecast dialog box (Figure 8-20a) where you specify values and a few parameters for the forecasting model. In the example I checked Sales to be forecasted, left the forecasting horizon to the five period default, selected Period as the time stamp, and accepted detect periodicity automatically, the default. The other values in the Periodicity listbox are Hourly, Daily, Weekly, Monthly, Quarterly, and Yearly. Clicking the Run button produces a Forecasting Report worksheet as in Figure 8-20b where the forecast is represented by the dashed line. The forecasted values are inserted at the bottom of the data table as in Figure 8-20c. That's all the output there is for this tool, quick and dirty. However, by eyeball it appears that the algorithm identified the pattern quite well.

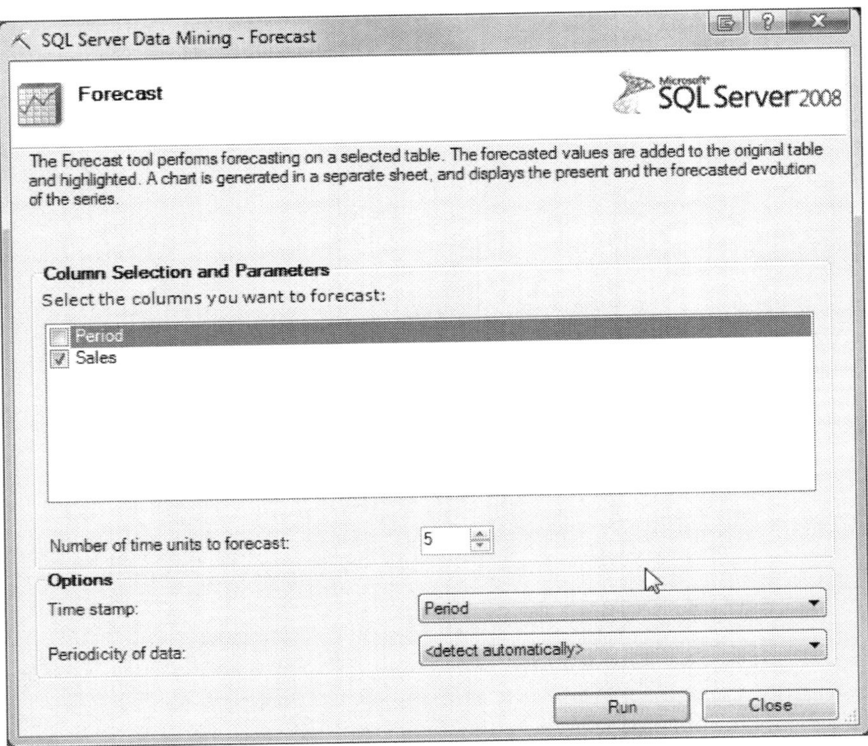

Figure 8-20a Table Tools Forecast Dialog Box

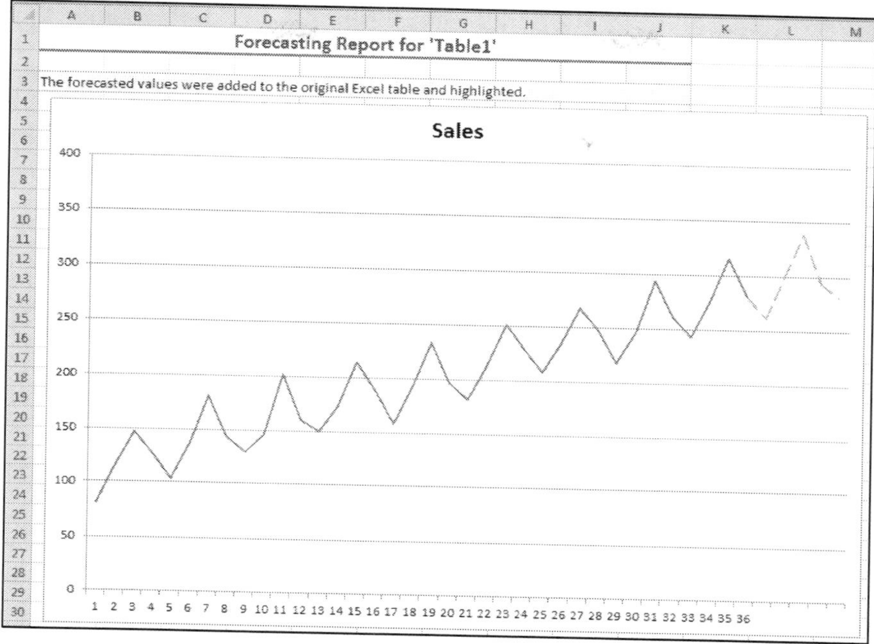

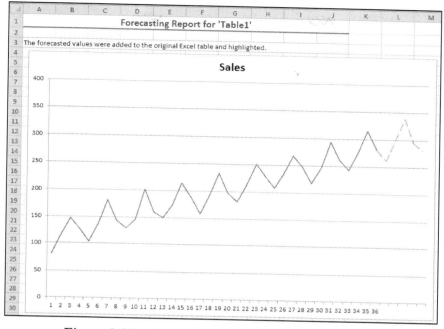

Figure 8-20b Table Tools Forecast Report Worksheet

	A	B
1	Period	Sales
33	32	261
34	33	243
35	34	276
36	35	315
37	36	280
38		261
39		300
40		339
41		294
42		281

Figure 8-20c Table Tools Forecast Series Projections

Forecast - Data Mining

Basics

A Forecast tool is also available on the Data Mining tab which uses a Forecast Wizard that provides access to Analysis Services data mining features. The Select Source Data dialog box (Figure 8-21a) is displayed after getting past the welcome page (not shown) where I selected a data table for the source. The Time stamp and Input Columns (data series to forecast) are specified in the next dialog box (Figure 8-21b). We'll leave the Parameters button there alone for now and come back to it shortly. The Finish dialog box (Figure8-21c) allows you to modify the names and descriptions and select options. You may create a "permanent" model for future use, the default, or a temporary model for the session by checking the Use Temporary model checkbox. Permanent models are stored in Analysis Services

The Browse model and Enable drill-through options must be enabled to display the Microsoft Time Series Viewer, the same as the BIDS Mining Model Viewer, which presents the forecasting results (Figure 8-21d). The Viewer is displayed in a new window (titled Browse) on the Taskbar, not in an Excel worksheet. If you created a permanent model, you may later display the viewer by using the Model Usage and Management options on the Data Mining tab. More on that in Chapter 10.

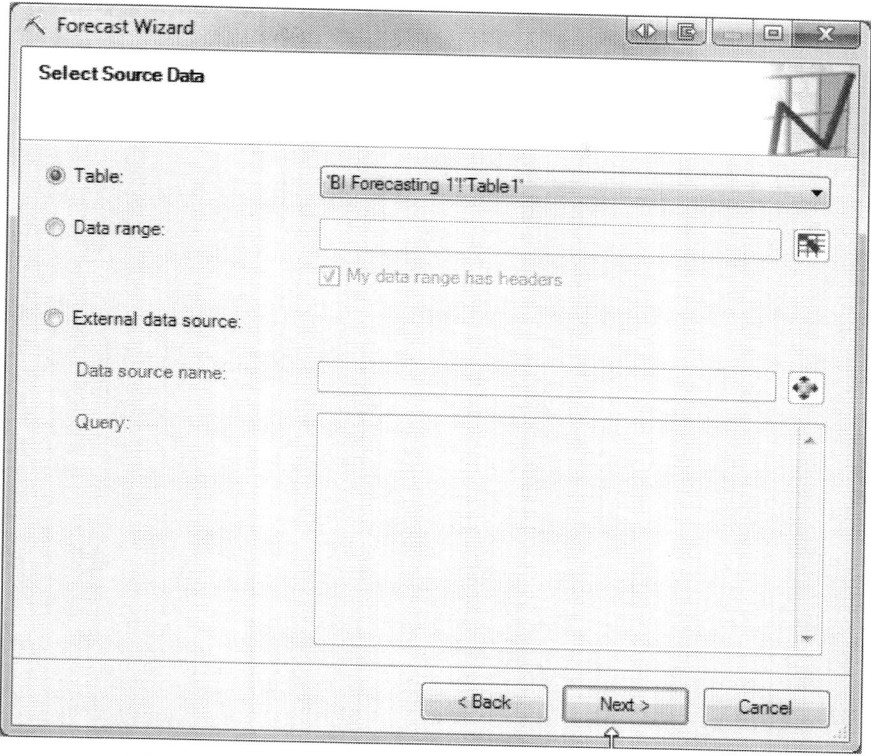

Figure 8-21a Data Mining Forecast Wizard - Page 2

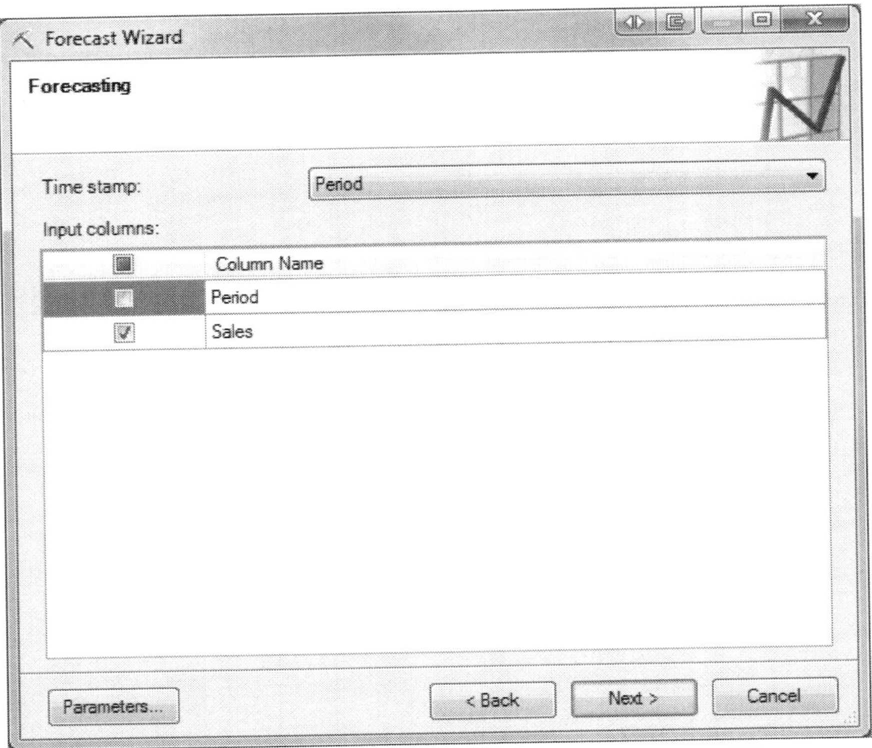

Figure 8-21b Data Mining Forecast Wizard - Page 3

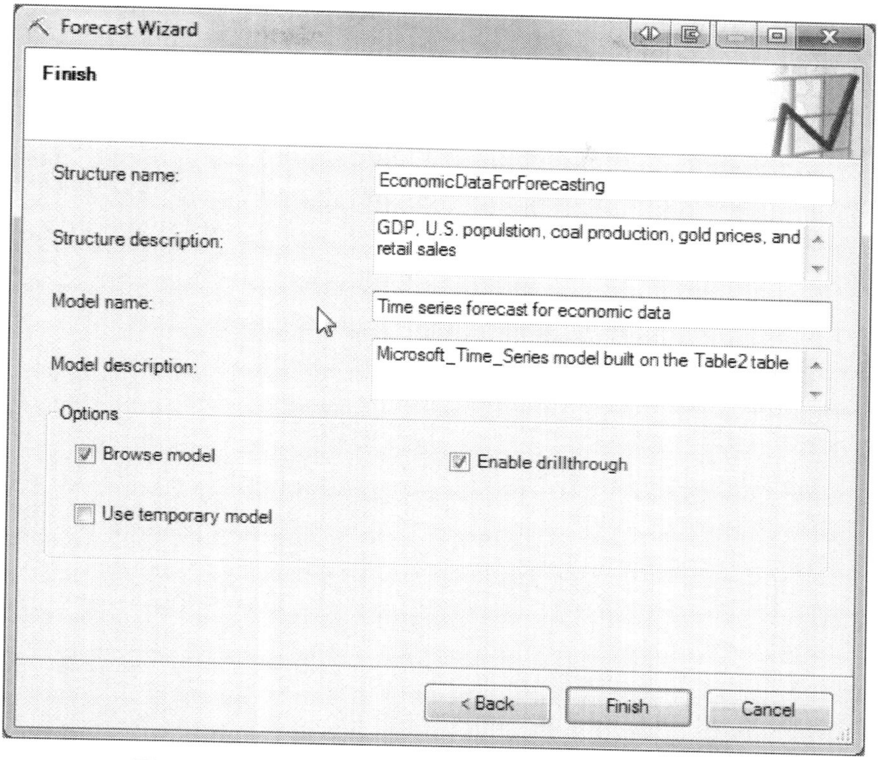

Forecast Wizard

Finish

Structure name: EconomicDataForForecasting

Structure description: GDP, U.S. populstion, coal production, gold prices, and retail sales

Model name: Time series forecast for economic data

Model description: Microsoft_Time_Series model built on the Table2 table

Options

Browse model

Enable drillthrough

Use temporary model

< Back | Finish | Cancel

Figure 8-21c Data Mining Forecast Wizard - Page 4

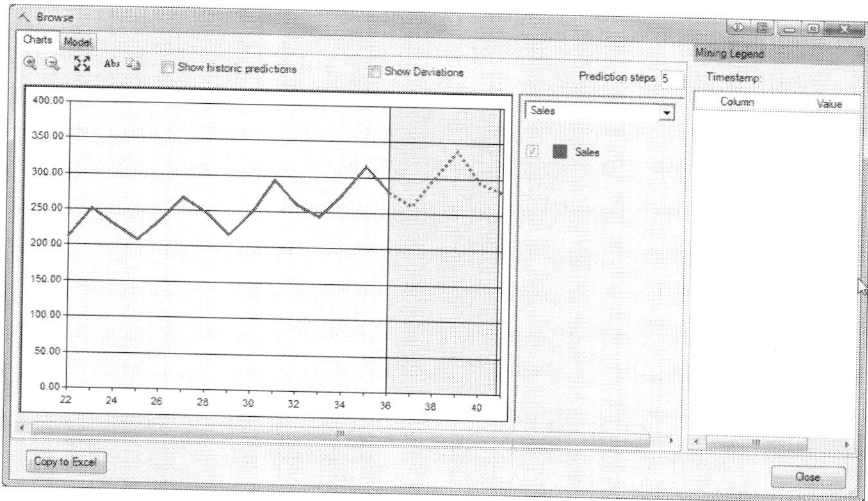

Figure 8-21d Time Series Viewer - Charts Tab

The Viewer has two tabs: Charts and Model. The Charts tab presents a graph of the data series including the forecasted values shown by the dashed line in the shaded section of the chart. The plus (+) and minus (-) buttons in the upper left zoom the chart in and out, and the multi-arrow button scales the chart to fit the window. The Abs button toggles between absolute and relative curves which is used when displaying multiple data series on the chart. If the series scales are considerably different, some of the lines will appear squashed at the bottom of the chart. Switching to the relative view changes the vertical axis scale to percent which will better display the pattern in each series. More on how this works shortly. The two-page icon button copies the chart to the clipboard as in Figure 8-21e.

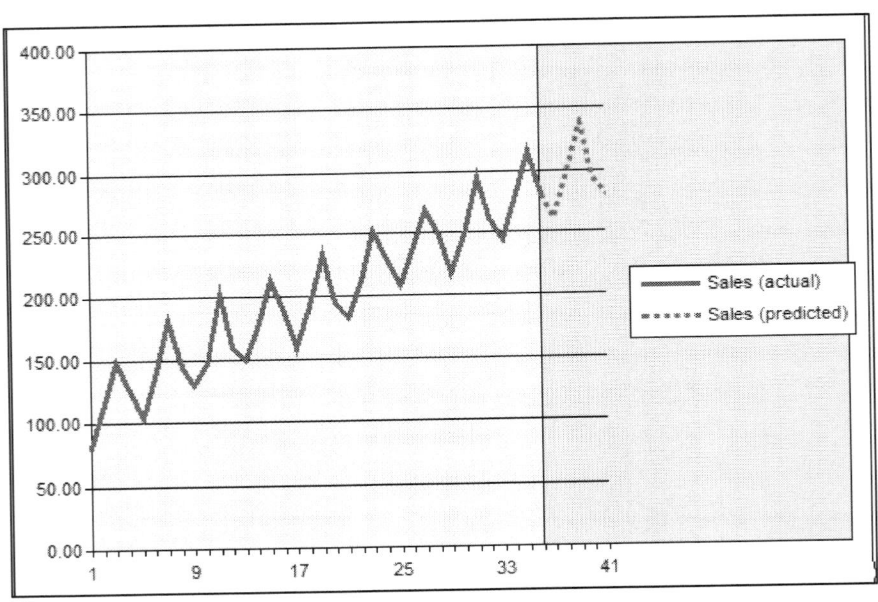

Figure 8-21e Chart copied to the Clipboard

The Show historic predictions checkbox enables a plot of the actual data series on the chart. In the example I had to zoom in to make the actual data values visible as in Figure 8-21f. The Show Deviations checkbox places vertical bars on the predicted values to represent the standard deviations. Longer bars indicate greater variance in the forecasts and, of course, a larger confidence interval. In our example, the bars are too short to show up in a figure. The Predictions steps combo box allows you to set the number of periods to forecast. The appropriate number of steps depends on the nature of the data series and its underlying time dimension. If the data series is well behaved and stable as in the current example, then projecting out many periods may be useful. Similarly, if the underlying time scale, the time differences between rows in the series, are short such as hours, days, and weeks, then projecting a large number of steps may be OK, e.g., forecasting for the next 52 weeks. However, forecasting for the next 52 years may not be advisable.

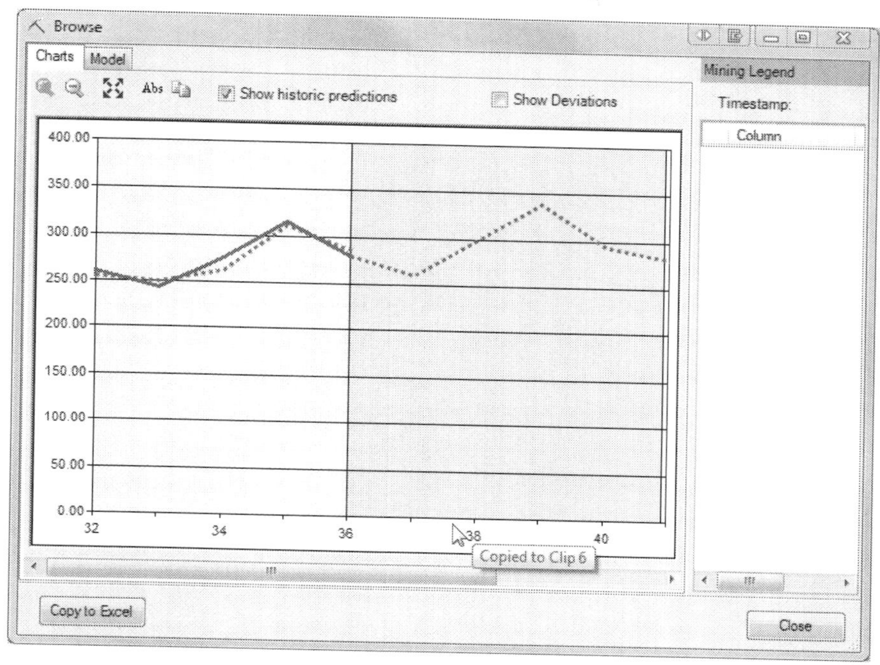

Figure 8-21f Show Historic Predictions

The listbox below the Prediction steps combo box is used to select the series to appear in the chart. In this example there is only one, Sales. More on this shortly too. The Time Series Viewer does not copy forecasted values back into the Excel table as does the Table Tools Forecast option as in Figure 8-20c. However, the values at any point will be shown in a pop up box by mousing over the plotted line. Or, you can show the predicted values in the Mining Legend pane on the right side of the Viewer window by clicking on the chart which will insert a vertical line from one of the time values on the horizontal axis. Figure 8-21g has the time indicator line at period 38. The value of the series for that period is 300, shown in the Mining Legend pane.

You can zoom in to a particular time segment anywhere in the historical or forecasted areas clicking on the chart at a time segment boundary, dragging the line to the other boundary, and then clicking inside the boundary area to zoom in. For example, in Figure 8-21h I clicked somewhere above period 25 and dragged the line to period 13 to set he boundaries. When I click inside the segment, the chart will zoom in to that section (not shown). To reset the view use the plus and minus buttons.

The copy to Excel button at the bottom left does just that—it copies the chart like the one in Figure 8-21e into a new Excel worksheet. Note that the chart is inserted as an image and is not a true Excel chart that you can format and customize. The chart is copied exactly as it appears in the Viewer so if you change the view and copy it, another chart will be inserted into Excel.

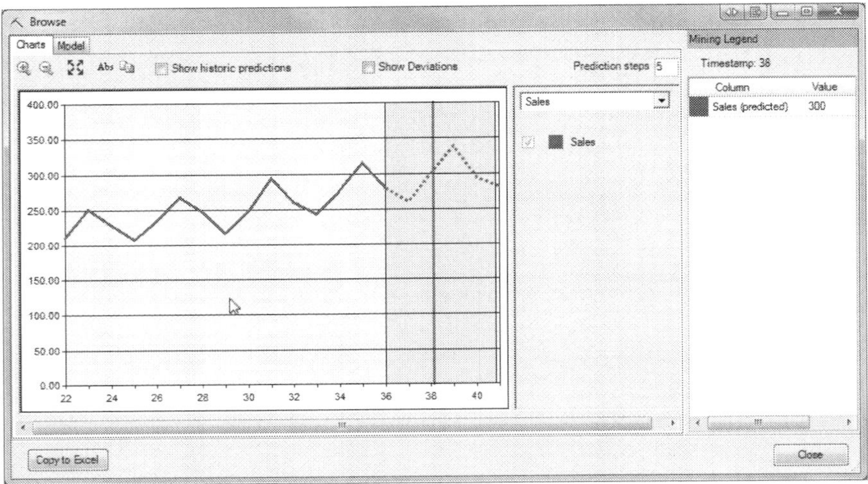

Figure 8-21g Historic and Forecasted Data Series Values

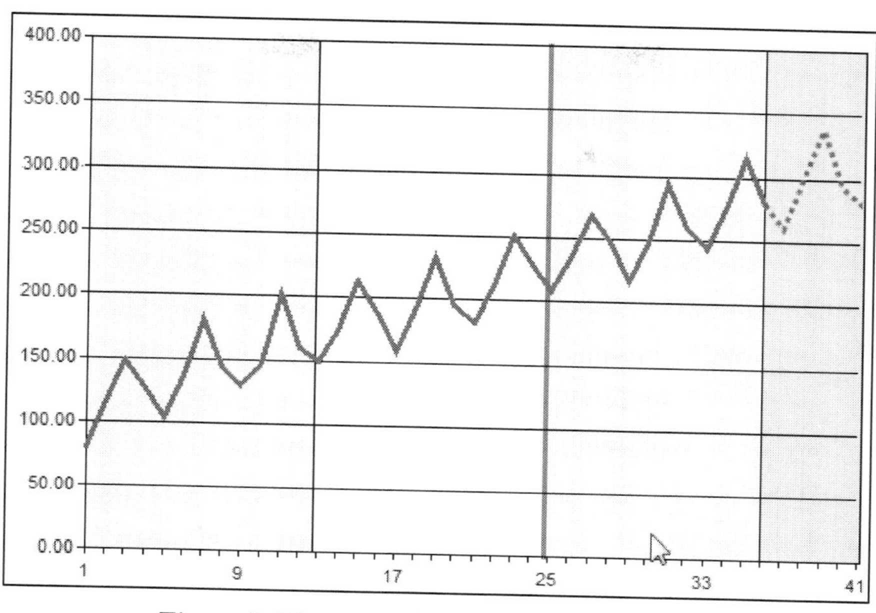

Figure 8-21h Setting Time Segment Boundaries

We will discuss the Model tab in greater length below so for now note that the equations for the model in our example are displayed in the Model tab Mining Legend pane as in Figure 8-21i. This is a blended ARTxp and ARIMA model with the ARTxp part including three lags, one for four quarters back, one for eight back, and one for twelve back. The default blending is a 0.5 weight on each model for the first forecasted period but the weight of ARTxp declines and AIRMA increases as the forecast horizon extends. More on this in the parameters section below. The coefficients on the ARTxp model components are in the middle section of the pane and the expressions for the models are shown at the bottom. I'll attempt to explain the ARIMA equation format shortly.

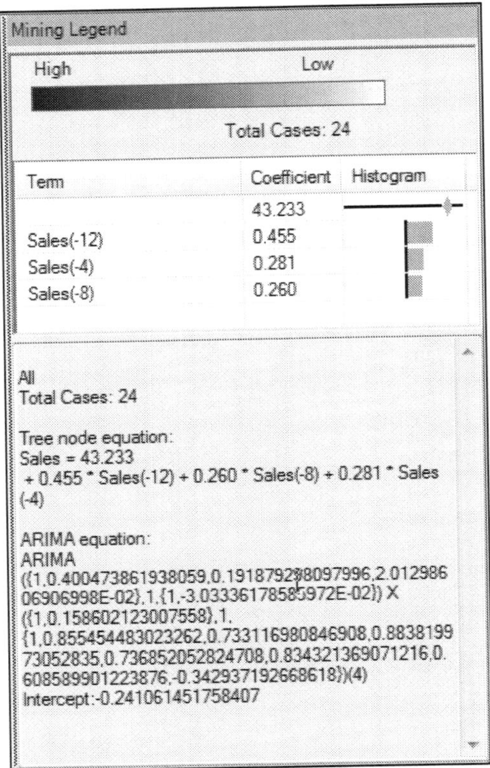

Figure 8-21i Model Equations in the Model Tab

Multiple Time Series

The data series in the multiple regression section in Chapter 6 (Figure 6-42a) provides a richer example to illustrate forecasting multiple time series with the Time Series Algorithm. To recap, that data set contains annual data on crude oil prices and production, GDP, U. S. population, coal production, gold prices, and retail sales from 1971 to 2007. Using the Forecasting Wizard as we did above the forecasting results are shown in Figure 8-22a for the Chart tab. This is the absolute scale view so all series except coal production and U. S. Population are squashed at the bottom of the chart. Switching to relative view by clicking on the Abs button changes the vertical axis to percent (Figure 8-22b) which is cluttered but we can see the patterns in the individual series.

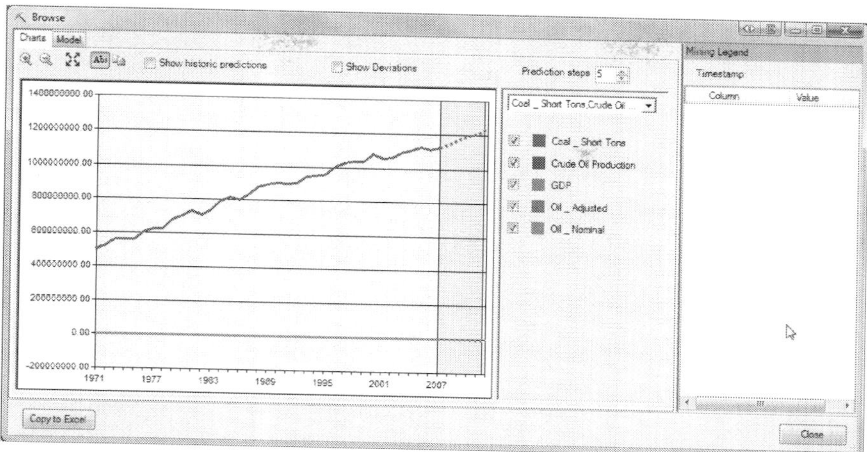

Figure 8-22a Multiple Time Series Example - Absolute View

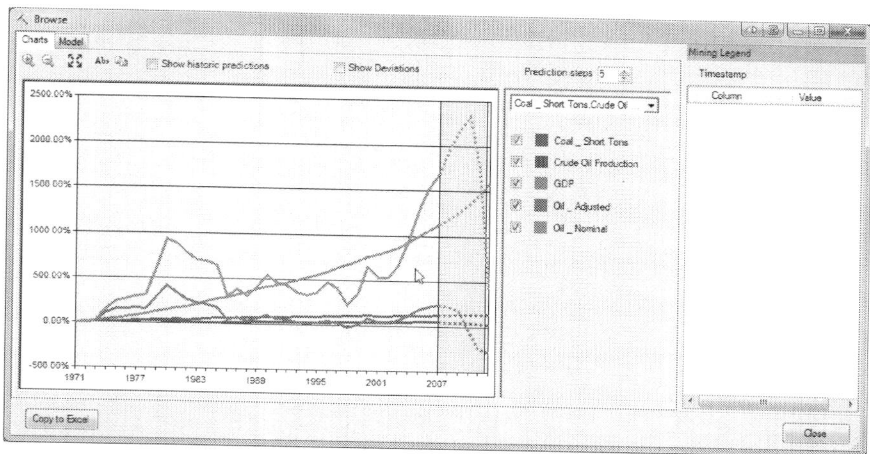

Figure 8-22b Multiple Time Series Example - Relative View

For an even better view the series to display on the chart can be selected with the check boxes in the series legend below Prediction steps .For example, the chart in Figure 8-22c displays only crude oil production, the smoother line, in millions of barrels per day and inflation adjusted crude oil prices per barrel. Note that the forecasted values for 2009 are listed in the Mining Legend pane. To identify which series to show/hide you can use the series legend color or mouse over a line plot.

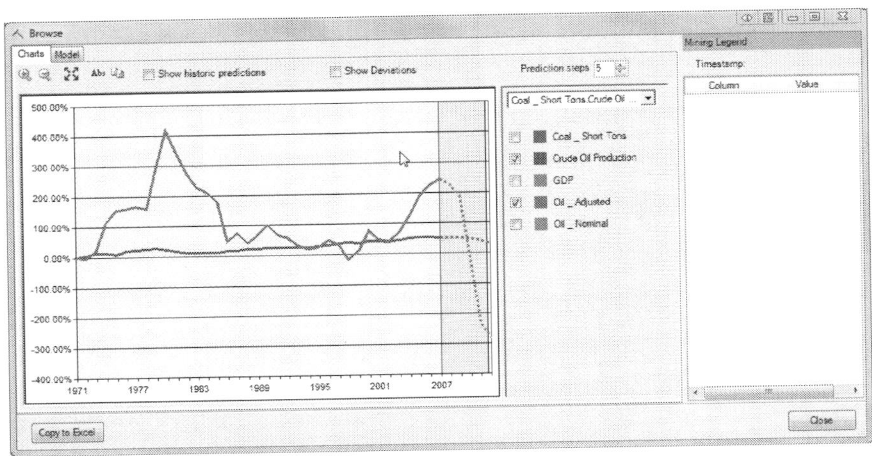

Figure 8-22c Multiple Time Series Example - Selected Series

Model Tab

The Viewer Model tab contains a tree pane on the left and the Mining Legend pane that we introduced above on the right. The tree shows partitions of the series, if there are any, to the right of the All node which represents all of the cases in the historical data. The ARTxp algorithm splits the data when it finds significant differences. In Figure 8-23a which shows the tree diagram for the inflation adjusted oil price series the algorithm found a significant difference in the data series patterns in segments that occurred before and after the gold series price of $309.303 per ounce. That is, the algorithm created two different ARTxp models for the oil price based on the gold price.

We can view each of these models in the Mining Legend pane by clicking on a node in the tree view. Figure 8-23b shows the Mining Legend for the gold >= 309.303 partition and Figure 8=23c the gold < 309.303 partition. You can see that the ARTxp model equations in the panels differ. Note that the ARTxp models contain autoregression components, e.g., Oil_Adjusted(-2) where (-2) indicates the lag, and cross prediction components, e.g., Gold__per oz_(-6) where (-6) indicates the lag, which incorporates data from other series into the model somewhat like we discussed in the multiple regression section in Chapter 6. Note that the ARIMA model is the same for both partitions and is identical to the one in Figure 8-23a which has the All tree node selected, i.e., the ARIMA model does not change. The models at each node may also be viewed by mousing over the node in the tree view.

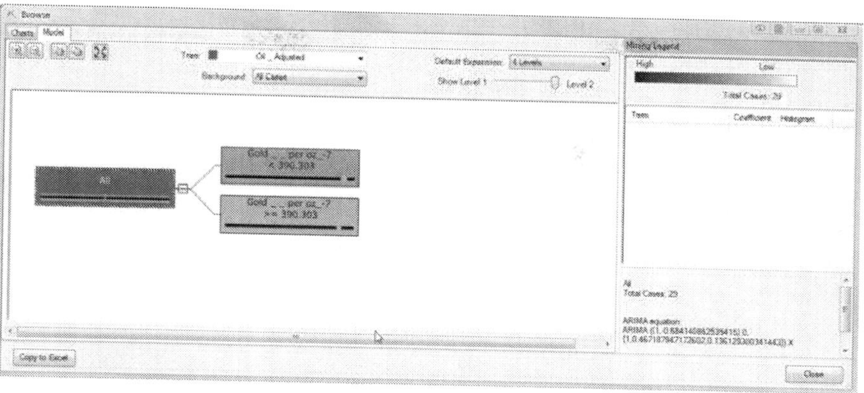

Figure 8-23a Time Series Viewer - Model Tab

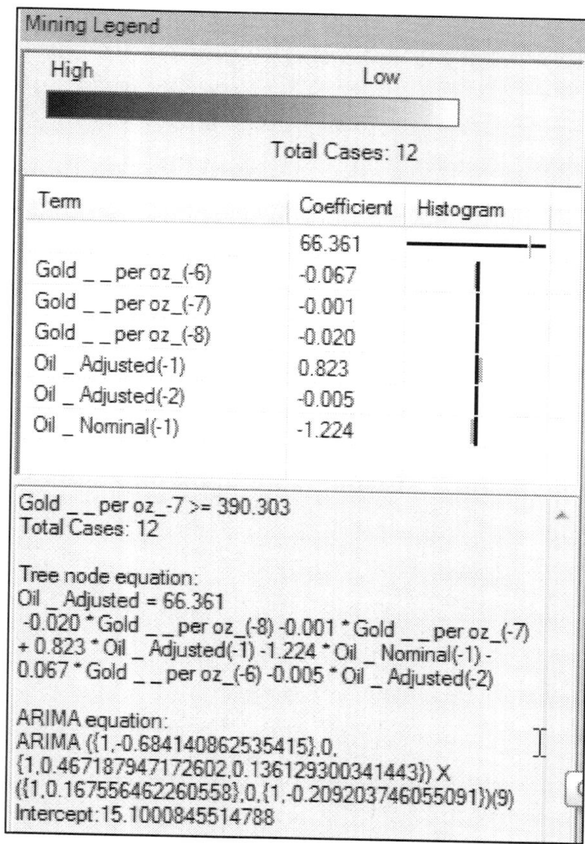

Figure 8-23b Gold >= $309.303 per oz.

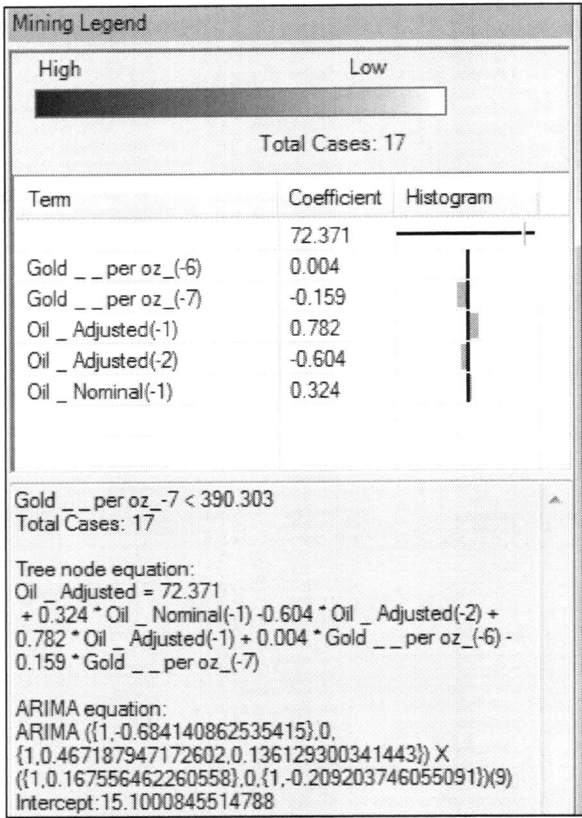

Figure 8-23c Gold < $309.303 per oz.

Figure 8-23 6.34615(t)

You select the series to display in the tree viewer by using the Tree listbox at the top. We already described the buttons on the top left. The Default Expansion listbox lets you set the maximum levels in the tree to display, and the Show Level slider lets you expand or contract the tree.

The background shading on the tree nodes indicates the relative number of cases at that node. The All node will always be the darkest. The number of cases is displayed in the tool tip when you mouse over a node and in the Mining Legend for each node: 29 cases in total in the All node, 12 cases in the higher gold price partition, and 17 cases in the lower gold price partition.

A diamond chart is also presented on a tree node. The position of the diamond indicates the mean for the node and the width represents the variance. Thinner diamonds suggest more accurate predictions because of lower variance.

The crude oil nominal price is the only other series in the data set that has partitions to the right of the All node. In the crude oil case there are three levels as shown in Figure 8-23d with Crude Oil Production as the second level and GDP as the third level. The Mining Legend in the figure lists the information about the bottom GDP node, GDP-1 >= 4088.320. Note that that node only has an ARIMA component because it is partitioned by Crude Oil Procuction. ARTxp components only appear in the last node of a branch. But, if there are no branches, i.e., there is only an All node, then an ARTxp component may appear there as in Figure 8-23e for crude oil production.

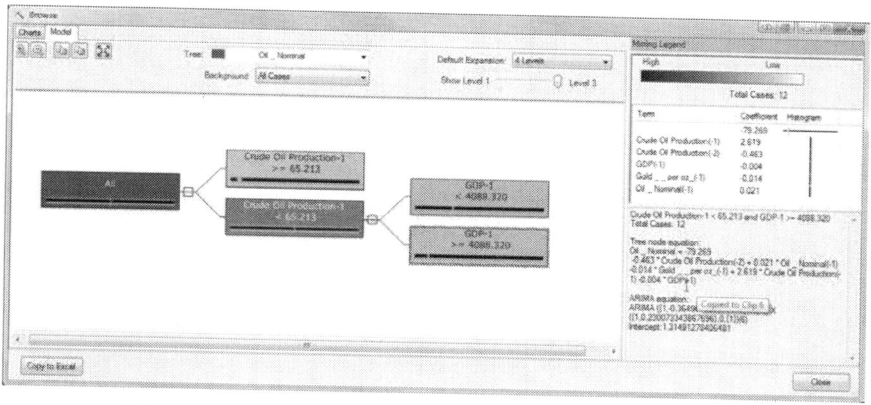

Figure 8-23d Time Series Viewer - Gold $ per ounce

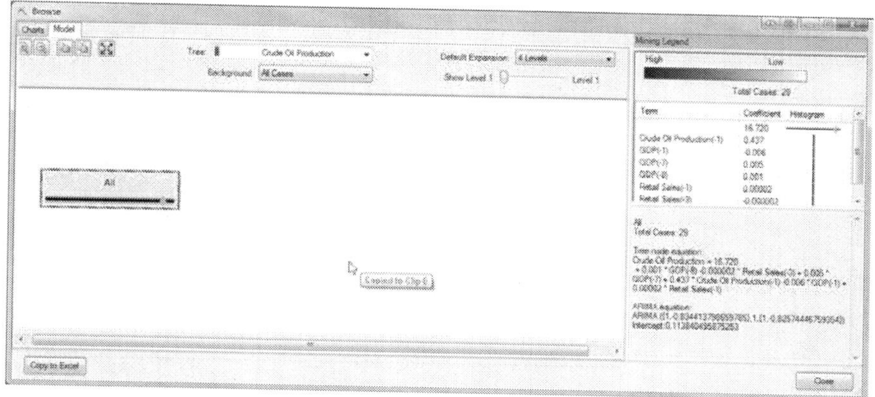

Figure 8-23d Time Series Viewer - Crude Oil Production

ARIMA equations take the form:

Short Form: (Auto Regressive Order, Difference Order, Moving Average Order}(s)

Long Form: ({Auto Regressive Coefficients}, Difference Order, {Moving Average Coefficients})(s)

where (s) is the periodicity. Combining the two forms deciphers our ARIMA equations. For example the ARIMA equation in Figure 8-23d:

ARIMA ({1,-0.83441,3798659785},1,{1,-0.82574446759354})
Intercept:0.113840495875253

indicates that this is an ARIMA(1,1,1) model with a coefficient of -0.834 on the autoregressive term and -0.825 on the moving average term. The intercept is 0.113. There is only first differencing and no periodicity because a value for s is absent. On the other hand the ARIMA model for the gold price series in Figure 8-23c has a periodicity of 4:

ARIMA ({1},1,{1,0.293353218920748}) X ({1},1,{1, -0.908525907507911,9.97173293538021E-02})(4)
Intercept:9.73125064373016

From what I can determine the segment of the ARIMA equation that comes after the multiplication symbol (X) is the seasonal part of the model. Indeed, a seasonal ARIMA model has the form ARIMA (p,d,1)X(P,D,Q) where P, D, and Q are the seasonal terms. Note that the ARIMA equation for the first example (Figure 8-21i) also has a seasonal component.

Parameters

The Parameters button on Page 2 of the Forecast Wizard (Figure 8-21b) brings up the Algorithm Parameters dialog box (Figure 8-24) that gives access to all of the parameters available in Analysis Services for the Time Series Algorithm. Table 8-1 briefly describes each parameter. The dialog box provides descriptions as well. You change parameter values by entering a value in the Value field. Note that the parameters values specified in the dialog box apply to all series selected as input columns. Buttons at the bottom allow you to add and remove parameters. We won't get into that here. See SQL Server 2008 Books Online for details.

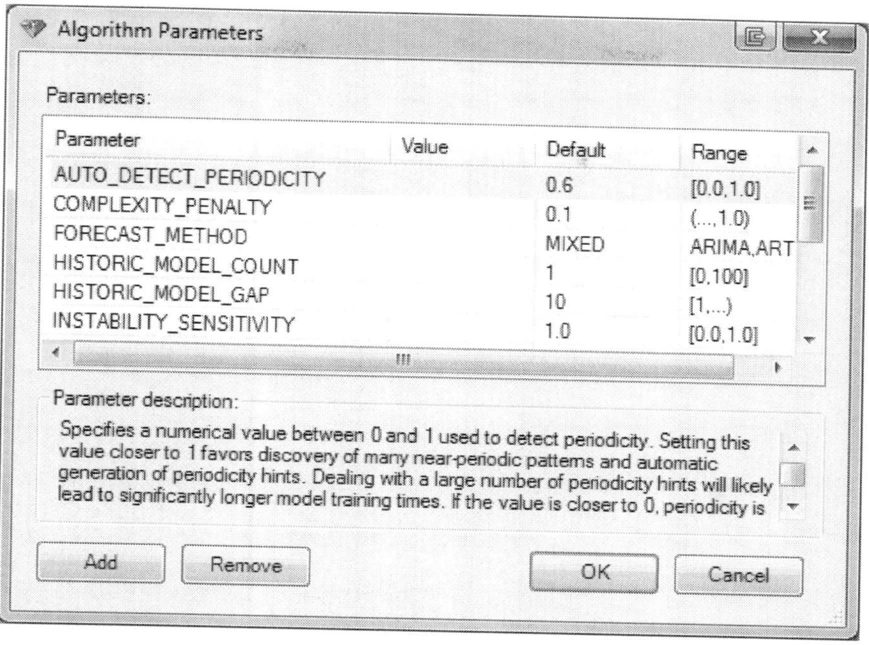

Figure 8-24 Time Series Algorithm Parameters Dialog Box

Parameter	Description
Auto Detect Periodicity	Specifies the degree that periodicity is detected. The parameter value ranges between 0 and 1 with 0.6 as the default. Values closer to one result in many more periodicities being detected.
Complexity Penalty	Controls the chance of a split with higher values decreasing the chance.
Forecast Method	Selects the algorithm used: ARTxp, ARIMA, or Mixed.
Historic Model Count and Historic Model Gap	Related to the assessment of model accuracy.
Instability Sensitivity	Used only for ARTxp only models for instability detection.
Maximum and Minimum Series Value	Sets the range of predictions. For example, predicted sales may be limited to a minimum of zero.
Minimum Support	Specifies the minimum number of time slices to create a split.
Missing Value Substitution	Determines how missing data in a series it treated.
Periodicity Hint	Suggests a periodicity.
Prediction Smoothing	Sets the ARTxp and ARIMA model blend. See below.

Table 8-1 Time Series Algorithm Parameters

The Prediction Smoothing parameter warrants some additional explanation. As mentioned earlier, in a blended model the ARTxp influence on the forecast declines and the ARIMA influence increases as the time horizon lengthens. The Prediction Smoothing parameter controls how quickly the model switches from ARTxp to ARIMA. If the parameter is set to zero, then the model is ARTxp only. Conversely, if it is set to one, then the model is ARIMA only. SQL Server 2008 Books Online recommends using an ARTxp model (setting the parameter to zero) for predictions up to five periods. For longer predictions I suppose you would increase the parameter value to bring in more

ARIMA. Please search the Internet for the "Microsoft Time Series Algorithm Technical Reference" for more information.

What's Next

Although we've covered a lot territory, there is much more to learn to become proficient with forecasting. However, what we covered here is more than the basics so you should feel comfortable tackling some real world data. Because of its accuracy and sophistication, my recommendation is to utilize the Microsoft Time Series Algorithm for your forecasting projects. However, remember to explore and understand your data before getting into number crunching.

In the next chapter we'll look at the other data mining methods available in Excel's Table Analysis Tools.

Chapter 9 - Data Mining with Excel 2010: Table Analysis Tools

Some usual definitions of data mining say that it is used to find patterns in data. Well, so do many other analytical techniques. Also, how is data mining different from statistical analysis? The answer is that it really isn't—it is a subset or special type of statistical analysis to find patterns in complex data.

Most of the data mining methods are not new. However, over the years the methods have been improved and made easier to use with advancements in the technology and computing so that they are accessible and usable by us normal humans and no longer limited to the purview of statisticians.

You can consider the Table Analysis Tools in the Table Tools Analyze tab as a subset of the data mining tools available on the Data Mining tab described in the next chapter. The Table Analysis Tools are designed for quick and dirty analyses providing no frills methods with few customization options. They create temporary models in Analysis Services that vanish when Excel is closed as opposed to models created with Excel's data mining tools which may be stored for later use.

Each of the Table Analysis Tools is described below except for the Fill From Example and Highlight Exceptions tools which were discussed in Chapter 6 and the Forecast tool in Chapter 8. The Help command in the Table Tools analyze tab provides a help file for the Data Mining Add-Ins for Office, a Getting Started Wizard, and a link to the Data Mining Add-Ins for Office 2007 Web page where a number of videos are available. The algorithms used by the Tools are described in Chapter 10.

As examples we'll use the Table Analysis Tools and Associate worksheets in the Sample Data Excel file from the Data Mining Add-Ins for Office download that provides AdventureWorks sample data in an easy to use format. The Table Analysis Tools data set of 1,000 records contains eleven of the customer fields such as gender, marital status, and yearly income and a yes-no Purchased Bike field indicating if the customer bought a bicycle or not. The Associate worksheet contains 32,265 records of purchasing pairs of items that we will use for Shopping Basket Analysis.

Another reminder: these tools rely on Analysis Services so an instance of SQL Server 2008 must be running and available.

Analyze Key Influencers

Consider key influencers as a type of correlation analysis that identifies a set of factors that are related to the factor of interest (the target). A prime example is relating customer characteristics with buying behavior. i.e., finding customer characteristics that correlate or don't correlate with buying a product(s). Analyze Key Influencers uses the Naive Bayes algorithm.

Clicking on the Analyze Key Influencers command in the Table Tools Analyze tab displays the Analyze Key Influencers dialog box in Figure 9-1a where you select the "column to analyze" (target), in this case Purchased Bike. You may also select the fields to relate to the target by clicking on the "Choose columns to be used for analysis" button which will bring up the Advanced Columns Selection (Figure 9-1b) where I deselected ID and Purchased Bike (not shown) fields. Returning to the previous dialog box and clicking the Run button creates a new worksheet titled "Influencers for Purchased Bikes" and displays a Discrimination Reporting dialog box (Figure 9-1c) where you may insert discrimination tables into the report worksheet for pairs of influencers. In this case the Purchased Bike field is dichotomous so only one discrimination report is necessary to represent the two values. However, if the target has more than two values, then you could insert more than one table representing other combinations.

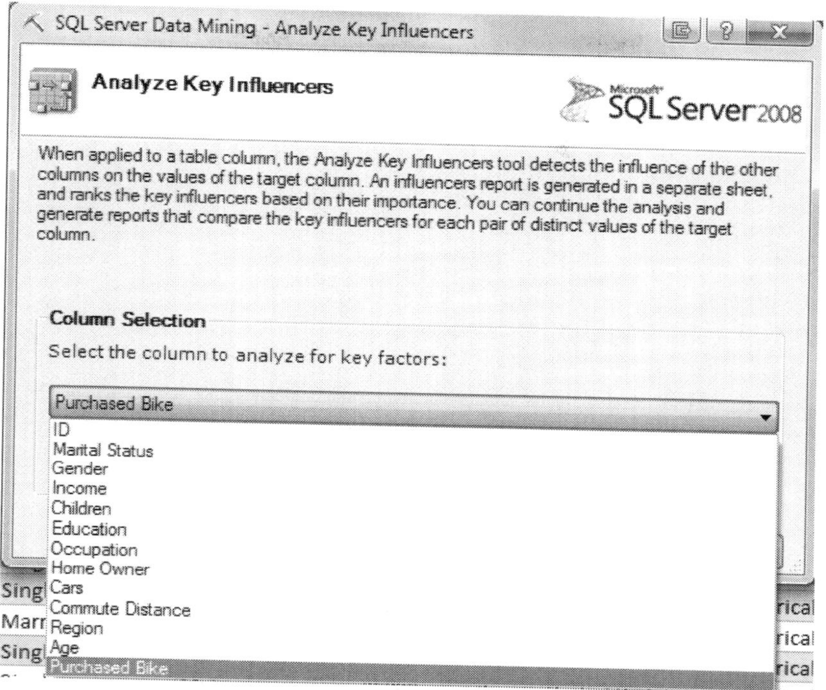

Figure 9-1a Analyze Key Influencers Dialog Box

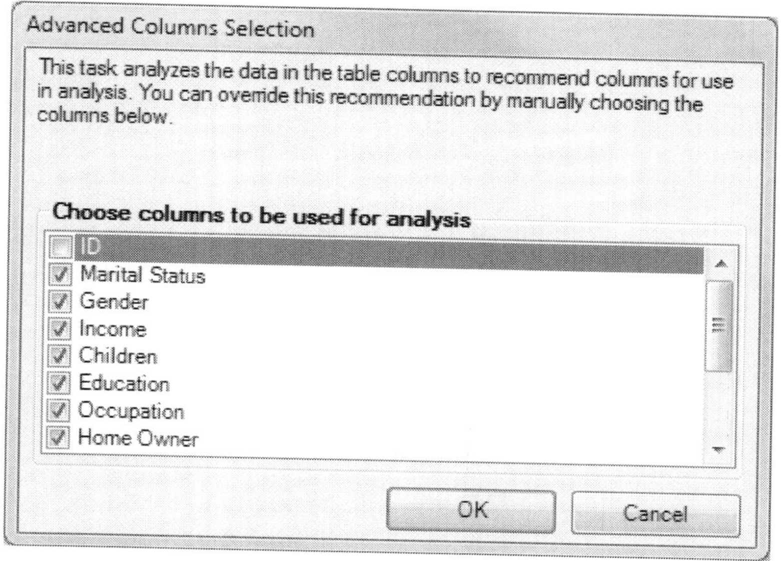

Figure 9-1b Advanced Columns Selection Dialog Box

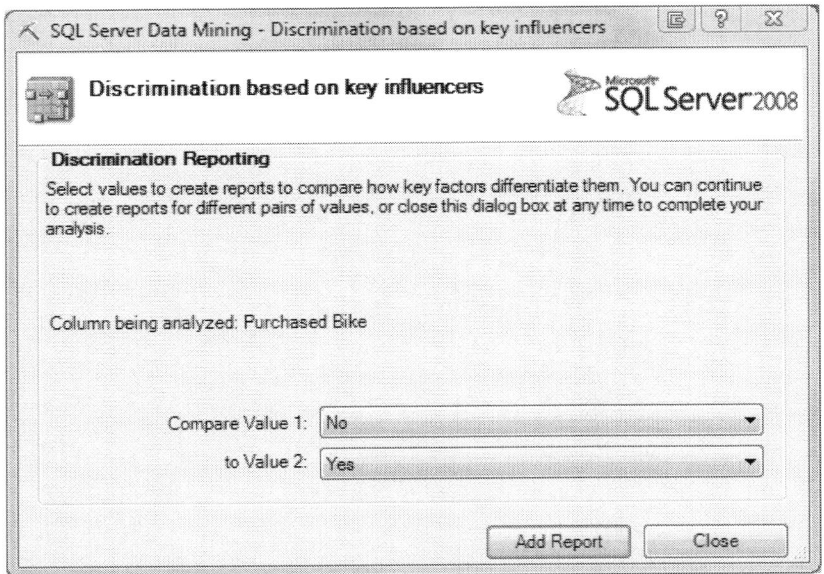

Figure 9-1c Discrimination Reporting Dialog Box

The "Influencers for Purchased Bikes" worksheet shown in Figure 9-1d presents a key influencers table at the top and the discrimination table at the bottom. The key influencers table lists the key factors that are "correlated" with bicycle purchasing behavior. In this case it identified three factors—car ownership, marital status, and region—as key influencers out of the eleven possible fields. The columns in the table are fairly self-explanatory: Column identifies the field, Value shows the specific value for the field, Favors indicates the value for the target that the influencer impacts, and Relative Impact displays a bar representing the relative strength of the association for a particular Favors value. The length of the bars in one Favors section, say the No value in this case, should not be compared with the bars in another Favors section, say the Yes value.

Key Influencers Report for 'Purchased Bike'

Key Influencers and their impact over the values of 'Purchased Bike'

Filter by 'Column' or 'Favors' to see how various columns influence 'Purchased Bike'

Column	Value	Favors	Relative Impact
Cars	2	No	
Marital Status	Married	No	
Region	North America	No	
Cars	0	Yes	
Marital Status	Single	Yes	
Cars	1	Yes	
Region	Pacific	Yes	

Discrimination between factors leading to 'No' and 'Yes'

Filter by 'Column' to see how different values favor 'No' or 'Yes'

Column	Value	Favors No	Favors Yes
Cars	2		
Cars	0		
Marital Status	Married		
Marital Status	Single		
Cars	1		
Region	Pacific		
Region	North America		

Figure 9-1d Discrimination Reporting Dialog Box

The discrimination table at the bottom of Figure 9-1c displays a different view of the results with the two Favors values in each row. The rows in the tables can, of course, be filtered by using the usual down arrowhead buttons on the columns. Note that factors with continuous values like income in this example will be automatically discretized.

My no brainer interpretation of the results is that married North American customers with two cars tend not to buy bicycles whereas single customers with less than two cars living in the Pacific region do. This could be useful information for the marketing folks.

Detect Categories

Detect Categories is a segmentation tool (see Chapter 3) using the Microsoft Clustering algorithm to assign records with similar characteristics to a group. The only dialog box for the Detect Categories tool is shown in Figure 9-2a where you select the fields to include in the categorization process. You can specify the maximum number of categories in the drop-down combo box (the listed values range from 2 to 10); you can enter the number of categories directly into box; or you can let the algorithm try to detect the natural number of categories with Auto-detect. Checking "Append a Category column to the original Excel table" will tag the rows in the data table with the appropriate category identifier. Click the Run button and a new worksheet titled "Categories Report" will be inserted into the workbook.

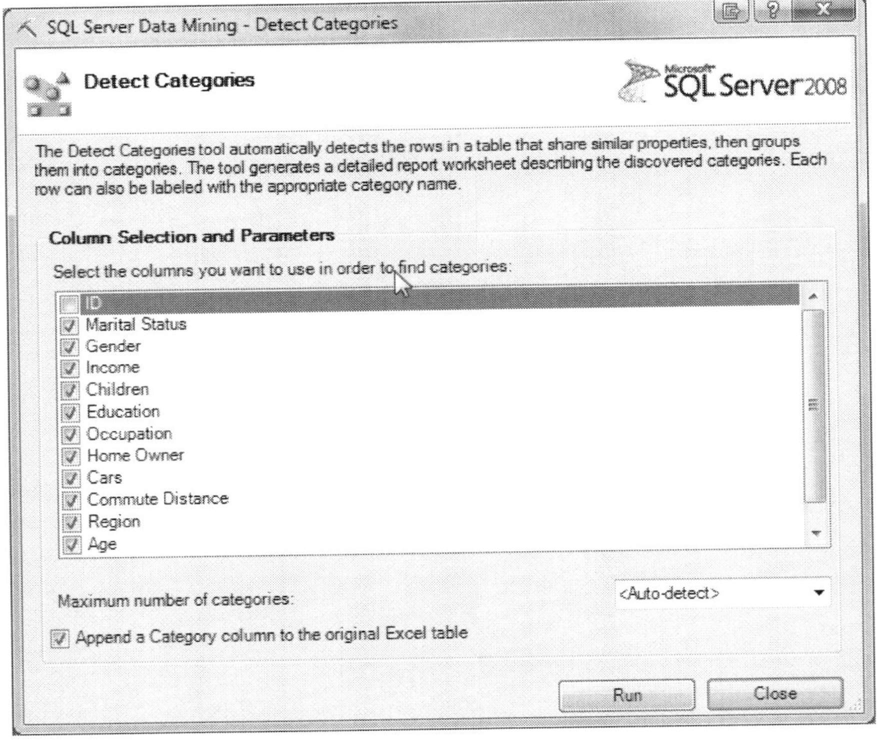

Figure 9-2a Detect Categories Dialog Box

Two tables and a pivot chart are displayed in the new worksheet. The first table (Figure 9-2b) lists the categories detected and the number of records in each. The categories can be renamed by entering new names in the category name cells. We will return to this shortly. The second table (Figure 9-2c) displays the profile for one category with bars representing the relative frequency of appearance of each attribute that define the category, e.g., Very Low Income will appear most frequently in those cases (rows) identified as Category 1. Use the filter button at the top of the Category column to switch to another category or to show all categories. Note again that the algorithm discretizes fields with continuous values like income and age. It also tags the discretized categories with a range name such as very low, low, etc.

	A	B	C	D
1	7 categories were detected			
2				
3	To rename a category, edit the 'Category Name' below.			
4	('Category Name' changes are visible in the 'Category' column of the source Excel table)			
5	Category Name	Row Count		
6	Category 1	189		
7	Category 2	141		
8	Category 3	158		
9	Category 4	149		
10	Category 5	126		
11	Category 6	129		
12	Category 7	108		

Figure 9-2b Categories Detected

	A	B	C	D
15			Category Characteristics	
16	Filter the table by 'Category' to see the characteristics of different categories.			
17	Category	Column	Value	Relative Importance
18	Category 1	Income	Very Low:< 39050	
19	Category 1	Region	Europe	
20	Category 1	Occupation	Manual	
21	Category 1	Occupation	Clerical	
22	Category 1	Commute Distance	0-1 Miles	
23	Category 1	Cars	0	
24	Category 1	Children	2	
25	Category 1	Children	1	
26	Category 1	Education	Partial High School	
27	Category 1	Education	High School	
28	Category 1	Children	3	

Figure 9-2c Category Profile

The default pivot chart view in Figure 9-2d displays the percentage of cases in each range of a particular characteristic by category as a stacked bar chart. In this case it shows the age distributions. For example, Category 3 has the highest percentage of young customers and Category 4 the highest percentage of older customers. As described in Chapter 6 clicking on the pivot chart will enable the Pivot Chart Tool tab with tools to manipulate, edit, and format the chart. Use the Field List command in the Analyze tab to display the Pivot Table Field List (Figure 9-2e) with which you should be familiar. In the top panel of the Field List click on the Column field and use the down arrowhead to display the listbox (Figure 9-2f) to select the characteristics to display in the chart. In this case the Age discretized field was selected to be displayed by default. You may select more than one characteristic to be displayed in the chart. However, showing more than one characteristic at a time makes the chart hard to interpret so I advise against it.

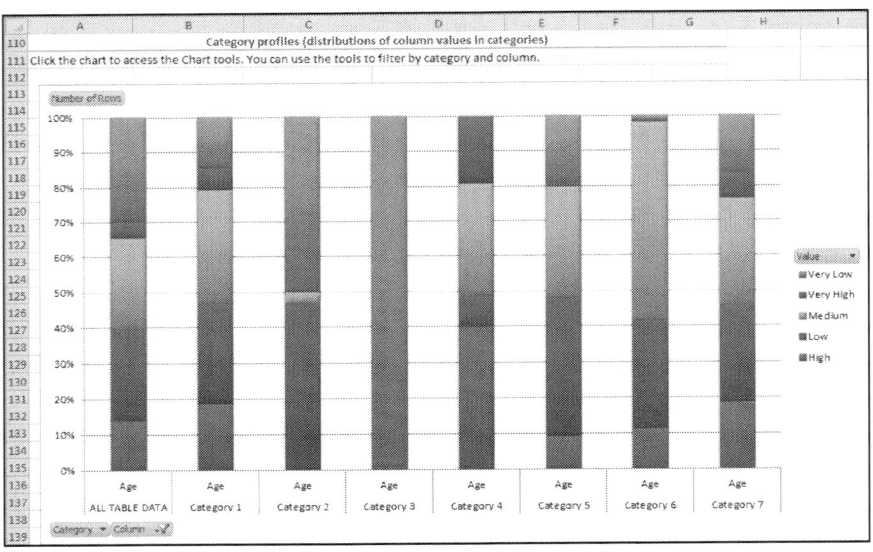

Figure 9-2d Category Profile Pivot Chart

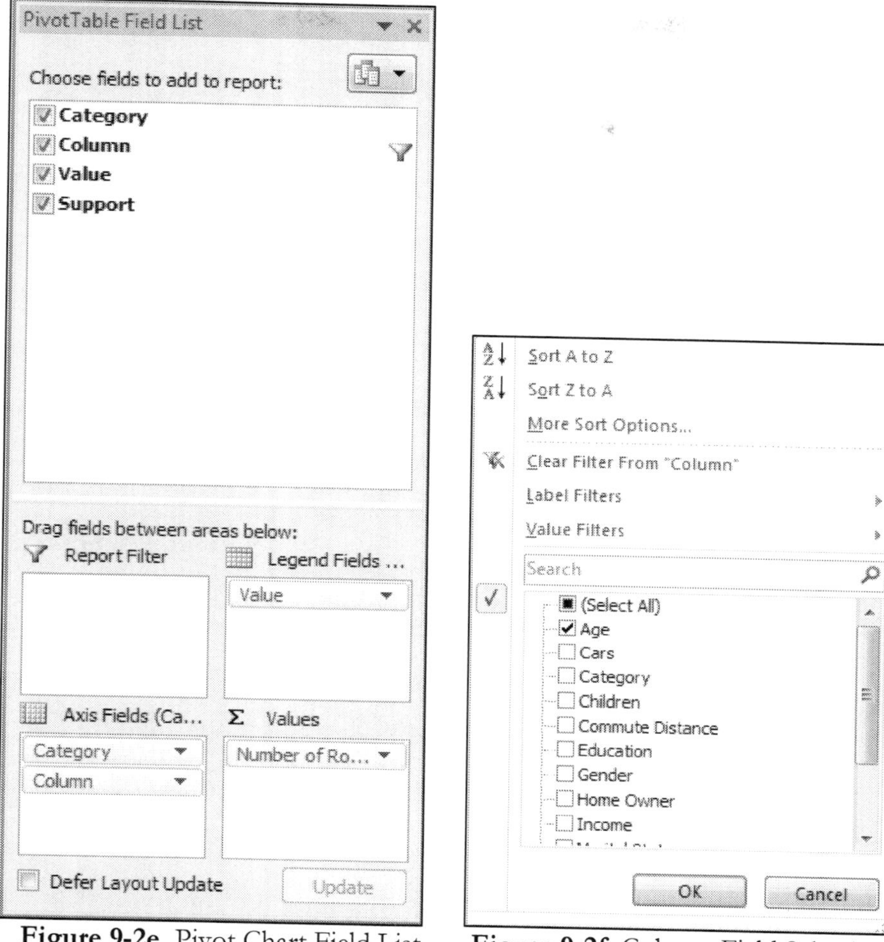

Figure 9-2e Pivot Chart Field List **Figure 9-2f** Column Field Selection

Figure 9-2e-f Pivot Chart Field List

The profile table and pivot chart are useful for renaming categories. For example, we'll rename Category 1 to European, low income as in Figure 9-2g. The partial screen shot of the refreshed Table Analysis Tools Sample worksheet in Figure 9-2h shows that the new name was replicated in the Category field so you can sort and filter on the new name as usual. The a new name for a category does not automatically show up in the pivot chart. To replicate the name there press the control-alt-F5 keys.

	A	B
5	Category Name	Row Count
6	European Low Income	189
7	Category 2	141
8	Category 3	158
9	Category 4	149
10	Category 5	126
11	Category 6	129
12	Category 7	108

Figure 9-2g Renaming a Category

	A	D	K	L	M	N
3	ID	Income	Region	Age	Purchased Bike	Column1
4	12496	40000	Europe	42	No	Category 2
5	24107	30000	Europe	43	No	European Low Income
6	14177	80000	Europe	60	No	Category 5
7	24381	70000	Pacific	41	Yes	Category 5
8	25597	30000	Europe	36	Yes	European Low Income
9	13507	10000	Europe	50	No	European Low Income
10	27974	160000	Pacific	33	Yes	Category 7

Figure 9-2h Original Data Table

Scenario Analysis

Scenario Analysis is a tool with two different interfaces that determines the likelihood of achieving a specified state in a target attribute by changing the value of another attribute, usually for a particular row in the data table. For example, I may explore the possibility of switching a particular non bicycle buyer to a buyer by increasing the income attribute. All of work is done within the Scenario Analysis window—a new worksheet is not inserted into the workbook. The Scenario Analysis tool uses the Microsoft Logistic Regression algorithm, a subset of the Microsoft Neural Network algorithm. Clicking on Scenario Analysis presents two options: Goal Seek and What-IF.

The Goal Seek option in the Scenario Analysis tool determines a value for an attribute to achieve a particular value for the target attribute. As an example I clicked anywhere on the row for customer number 20619 in the sample data table and then selected Goal Seek from the Scenario Analysis menu to display the window in Figure 9-3a which has four sections. In the first, Goal to seek, you select the target attribute and the value to achieve. If the attribute is categorical, then the Exactly option will be enabled with the listbox showing the options available. In the case of Purchased Bike there are only two options: Yes and No. I selected Yes because I'm interested in how to change customer 20619 into a buyer. If the attribute values are continuous, then Percentage and In range options will be enabled allowing you to select one or the other as value targets. For example, for this customer with an income of $8,000 if I selected Income as the target and 150 percent as the goal, then the tool would try to find a value of the other attribute that would create an income greater than or equal to $12,000. In the range option you specify a minimum and maximum value for the target.

In the second section you select an attribute to change to try to achieve the goal, and you may also select the columns (fields) to use in the analysis. The third section lets you choose to perform the analysis only on the row you selected, the customer 20619 row in this case, or expand it to all rows in the table. If you select the latter option, two new columns will be inserted into the data table: one for the goal value and one for the attribute value as is Figure 9-3b.

The last section in Figure 9-3a presents the results. The tool will display the solution, if there is one, showing the value for the changed attribute, in this case Commute Distance would have to be 0-1 miles for this customer to be a bicycle buyer, and a statement and bar indicating the likelihood for this result. Note that you can change the target and other attribute or even select a different row in the data table while the window is open and then click the Run button to get results for a different combination or row.

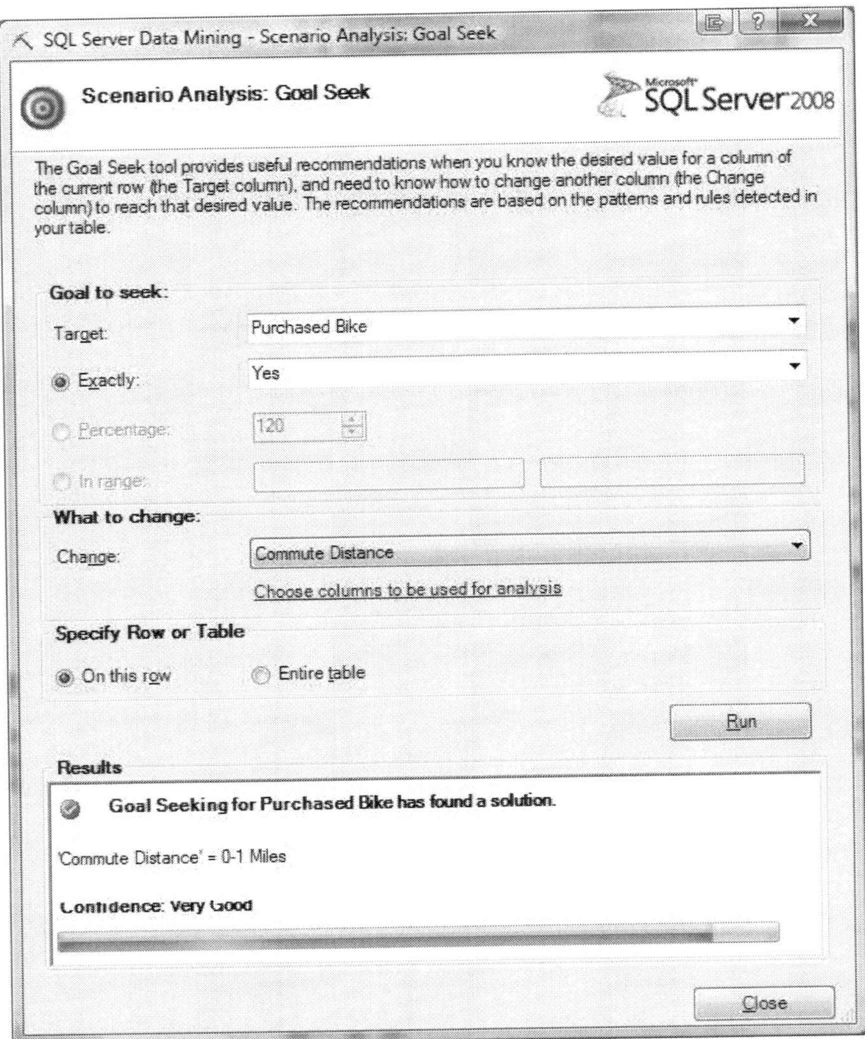

Figure 9-3a Scenario Analysis - Goal Seek

(For better viewing of this image, go to http://www.zerobits.info/bibook/bibookimages/)

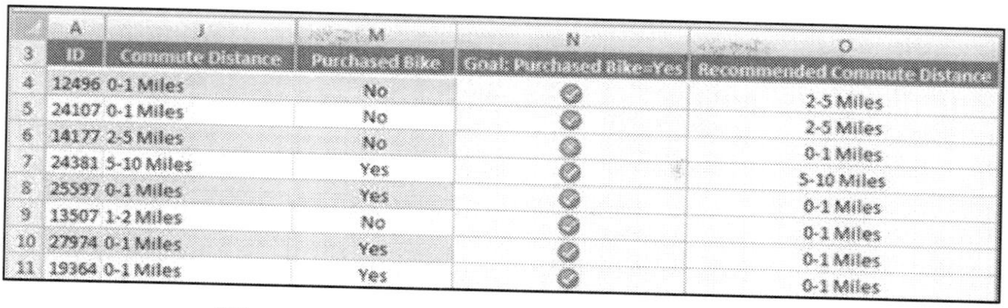

	A	J	M	N	O
3	ID	Commute Distance	Purchased Bike	Goal: Purchased Bike=Yes	Recommended Commute Distance
4	12496	0-1 Miles	No	✓	2-5 Miles
5	24107	0-1 Miles	No	✓	2-5 Miles
6	14177	2-5 Miles	No	✓	0-1 Miles
7	24381	5-10 Miles	Yes	✓	5-10 Miles
8	25597	0-1 Miles	Yes	✓	0-1 Miles
9	13507	1-2 Miles	No	✓	0-1 Miles
10	27974	0-1 Miles	Yes	✓	0-1 Miles
11	19364	0-1 Miles	Yes	✓	0-1 Miles

Figure 9-3b Scenario Analysis - Goal Seek

The What If option in the Scenario Analysis tool determines the effect on the target of changing the value of another attribute. The section in the What If window are similar to the ones above. For the example (Figure 9-3c) the tool found that it's highly likely that if the commute distance was reduced to 2-5 miles for someone like customer 20619, then that customer would buy a bicycle.

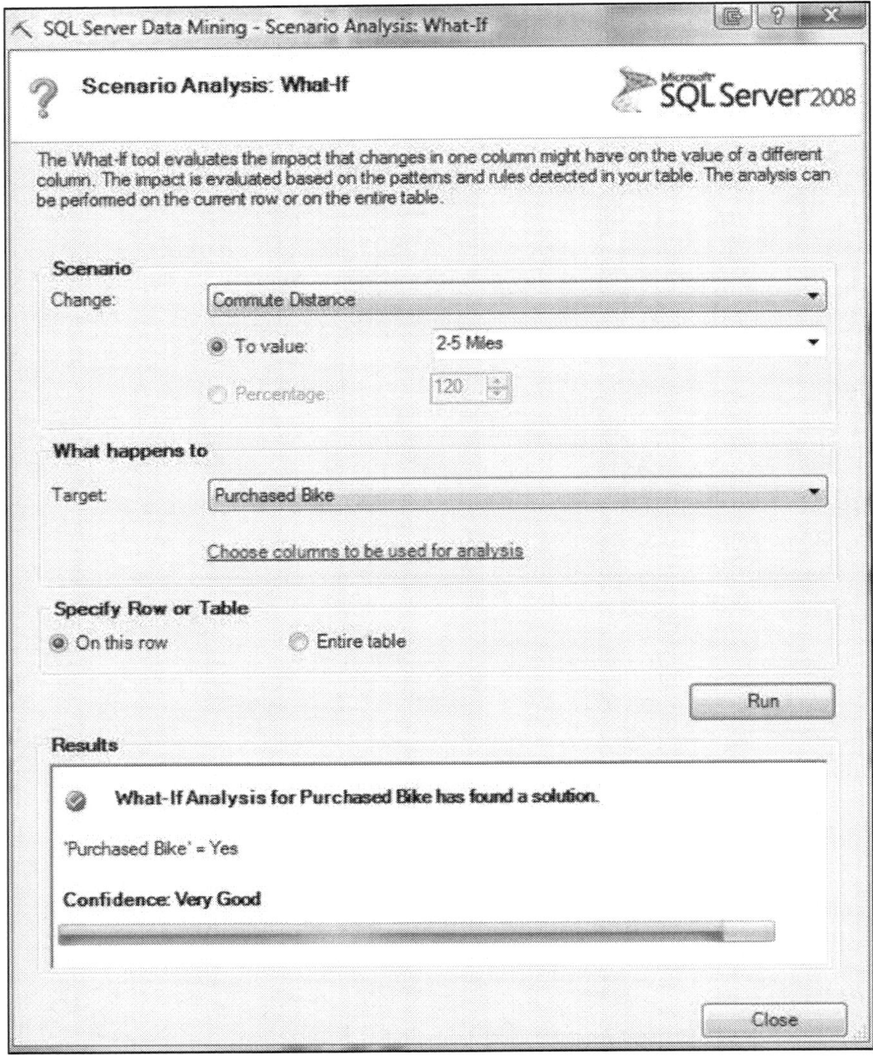

Figure 9-3c Scenario Analysis - What If

(For better viewing of this image, go to http://www.zerobits.info/bibook/bibookimages/)

Prediction Calculator

The Prediction Calculator scores entities, customers in our case, on various attributes and then uses those scores to predict the value of a target attribute, say buying a bicycle. The Calculator is an enhanced computerized equivalent of a decision making scorecard where you numerically score an object on a number of characteristics and set a minimum score required to take some action. For example, a college may score applicants on factors such as SAT score, high school rank, extracurricular activities, voluntarism and so forth and set a minimum cumulative cut-off score required for admission. The Prediction calculator uses the Microsoft Logistic Regression algorithm and makes only dichotomous predictions such as yes—no or it is in a category or it isn't.

The Prediction Calculator dialog box (Figure 9-4a), displayed by the Prediction Calculator command in Table Analysis Tools, is similar to the ones described for the Scenario Analysis tool above except for the Output Options. The Calculator inserts up to three new worksheets in the workbook: Prediction Report, Prediction Calculator, and Printable Calculator worksheets. The latter two are optional and controlled by the dialog box Output Options.

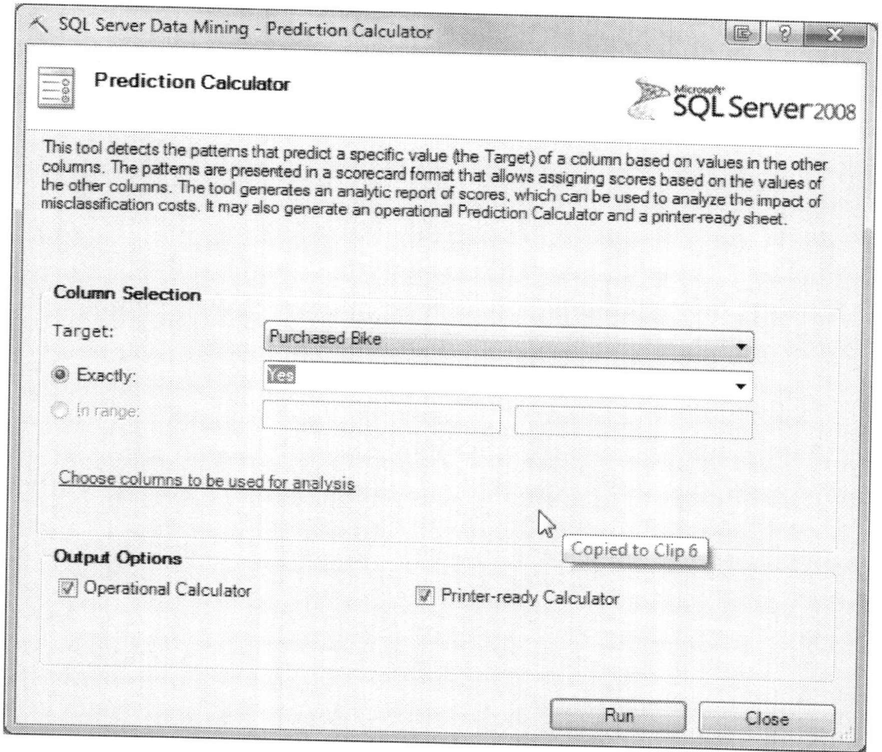

Figure 9-4a Prediction Calculator Dialog Box

Prediction Report Worksheet

The example "Prediction Calculator Report for the 'YES' state of 'Purchased Bike'" worksheet not shown in its entirety contains one worksheet range to enter costs and profits, two Excel tables, and two charts. In the worksheet range that I'll call the Cost/Profit Parameter Area you enter the costs and profits of decision making outcomes. These outcomes shown in Table 9-1 are essentially the same as the those for Statistical Decision Making in Appendix B, Table B-2. The Calculator uses the costs and profit values to assess the financial impact of the predictions and produces a cut-off score to maximize profit, 572 in this case. This means that with the given cost and profit parameters you should accept those predictions with a score greater than or equal to 523 to maximize profit.

	A	B	C
3	*Specify the costs and profits associated with correctly and incorrectly predicting*		
4	*'Yes'. These costs/profits are needed to compute the optimum score threshold for*		
5	*the calculator.*		
6	False Positive Cost	10	
7	False Negative Cost	0	
8	True Positive Profit	10	
9	True Negative Profit	0	
10			
11	Suggested Threshold to maximize profit:	572	
12			

Figure 9-4b Prediction Calculator Report - Cost/Profit Parameter Area

	Actual	
Predict	No	Yes
No	True Negative	FalseNegative Type II Error
Yes	False Positive Type I Error	True Positive

Table 9-1 Prediction Outcomes

A true positive prediction should produce a positive return (profit or some measure of benefit). A true negative prediction usually should have no effect on the net return. A false positive prediction may involve some cost, e.g., the expense of promotion to the customer. And, a false negative may represent an opportunity cost.

The chart in the upper right on the worksheet (Figure 9-4c) plots the predicted profit return at various threshold scores. The vertical line that I inserted designating the maximum profit threshold score of 572 is the high point on the plot. The plot is linked to the Cost/Profit Parameter Area and will change as the parameters are changed.

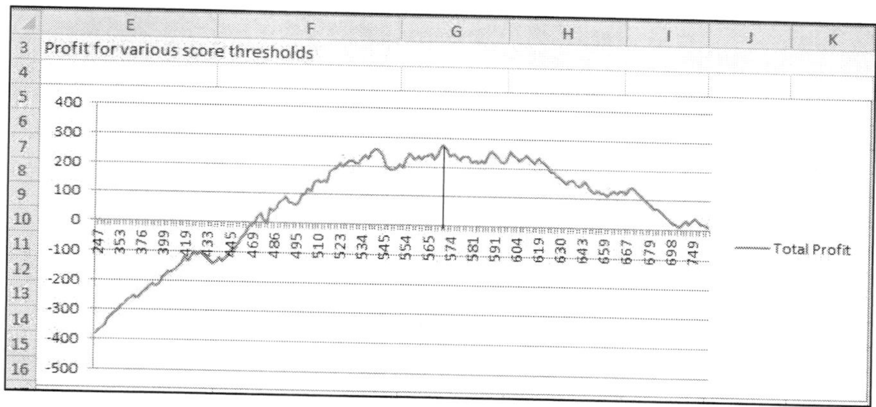

Figure 9-4c Prediction Score Profit Chart

The Score Breakdown table below the Cost/Profit Parameter Area in the worksheet lists the relative impact the model assigned to the values of each attribute. Figure 9-4d shows part of the Score Breakdown table for our example. From what I can determine the relative impact value is a probability expressed like a baseball batting average where the value ranges between 0 and 1,000 to represent a percentage. For example, the Relative Impact for Marital Status—Single is really a probability of 0.040 which means that a married customer has a 0.040 higher probability of buying a bicycle than a single customer. And, the probabilities are additive. For example, a married male has a 0.059 higher probability of buying a bicycle than a single female.

The relative impact is also used as the score for that attribute value. In this case a single customer gets 40 points, someone with three children gets 141 points, and so on. The points from all the attributes are summed to get the total score which would be compared to the threshold score to predict if the customer would buy a bicycle.

	A	B	C
13	**Score Breakdown**		
14	*Individual scores for each state of each analysed column*		
15			
16	Attribute	Value	Relative Impact
17	Marital Status	Married	0
18	Marital Status	Single	40
19	Gender	Female	0
20	Gender	Male	19
21	Income	< 39050	0
22	Income	39050 - 71062	84
23	Income	71062 - 97111	89
24	Income	97111 - 127371	161
25	Income	>= 127371	150
26	Children	0	74
27	Children	1	90
28	Children	2	41
29	Children	3	141
30	Children	4	77
31	Children	5	0

Figure 9-4d Score Breakdown Table

The second chart (Figure 9-4e) to the right of the Score Breakdown table and below the Prediction Score Profit chart displays the "Cumulative misclassification cost for various score thresholds. If we change the False negative cost in the Cost/Profit Parameter Area to 10 from 0 (not shown), the Cumulative Misclassification Cost chart appears as in Figure 9-4e and the revised Prediction Score Profit Chart in Figure 9-4f.

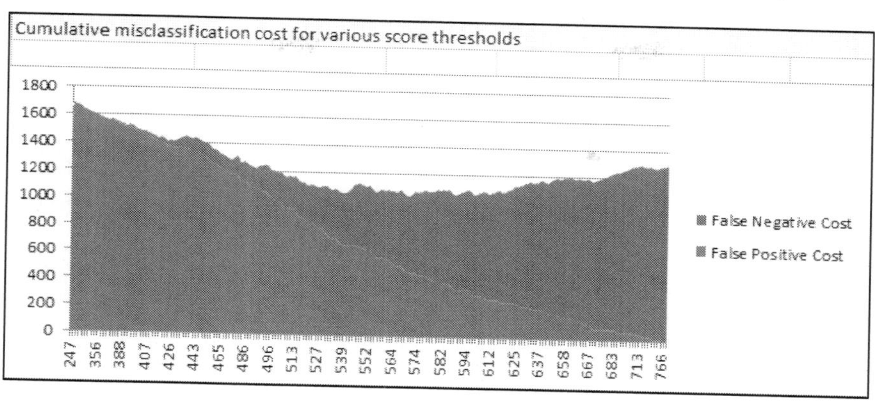

Figure 9-4e Cumulative Misclassification Cost

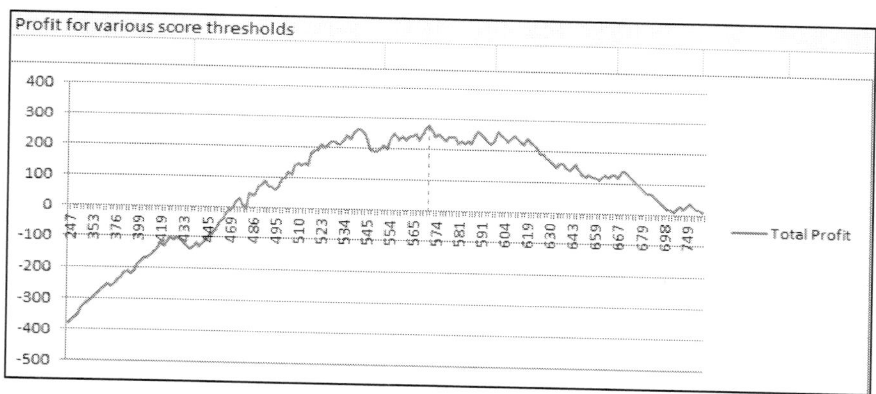

Figure 9-4f Revised Prediction Score Profit Chart

The table at the bottom of the worksheet (not shown) contains calculations and values for the two charts listing Total Profit and Score for the Predictions Score Profit chart and False Positive and False Negative costs for the Cumulative Misclassification Cost chart. The scores in the table range between 247 and 863 which are similarly shown on the chart in Figure 9-4c on the horizontal axis. If I'm interpreting the meaning of the scores correctly, the chart in the figure shows the minimum probability of likelihood of buying a bicycle at 0.247 to a maximum probability of .863.

As a somewhat more realistic example consider the Cost/Profit Parameter values for bicycle purchase predictions in Figure 9-4g. I calculated the mean price of an AdventureWorks bicycle sold on the Internet as $1,862. Assuming a 20 percent net margin, the True Positive Profit would average about $375. I guesstimated an opportunity cost on a false negative at $100, and a minimal selling charge for a false positive of $5. This configuration substantially lowers the threshold from 523 to 363, the minimum value, saying essentially that AdventureWorks should market to anyone. Figure 9-4h shows the resultant Prediction Score Profit Chart.

	A	B	C
3	*Specify the costs and profits associated with correctly and incorrectly predicting*		
4	*'Yes'. These costs/profits are needed to compute the optimum score threshold for*		
5	*the calculator.*		
6	False Positive Cost	5	
7	False Negative Cost	100	
8	True Positive Profit	375	
9	True Negative Profit	0	
10			
11	Suggested Threshold to maximize profit:	363	

Figure 9-4g Cost/Profit Parameter Area - New Scenario

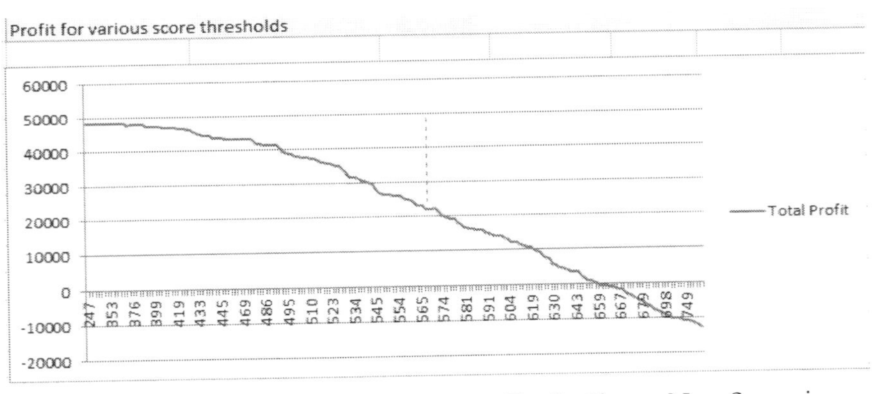

Figure 9-4h Revised Prediction Score Profit Chart - New Scenario

Prediction Calculator Worksheet

The Prediction Calculator worksheet contains two tables: the calculator (Figures 9-5a and b) and a copy of the Score Breakdown table from the Prediction Report worksheet (not shown). The Calculator in Figure 9-5a is set to its initial values for the attributes resulting in a total score of 516. This suggests that a customer with these demographics is not likely to purchase a bicycle because that score is below the 572 cut-off shown in the upper right corner. You can change any of the values of the attributes by using the drop-down listboxes in the Value column as shown for the Commute Distance attribute in Figure 9-5b. When I changed the parameters (not shown) to married European male with a high income the score increase to 614 indication a yes prediction for buying a bike.

	A	B	C
3	Suggested Threshold to maximize profit:		572
4			
5	Select or type a value in the Value column of the table belowto see how it affects the score.		
6	Attribute	Value	Relative Impact
7	Marital Status	Married	0
8	Gender	Female	0
9	Income	39050 - 71062	84
10	Children	0	74
11	Education	Bachelors	36
12	Occupation	Professional	65
13	Home Owner	Yes	9
14	Cars	2	71
15	Commute Distance	0-1 Miles	82
16	Region	North America	0
17	Age	37 - 46	95
18	Total		516
19			
20	Prediction for 'Yes'		FALSE

Figure 9-5a Prediction Calculator - Initial Parameters

	A	B	C
3	Suggested Threshold to maximize profit:		572
4			
5	*Select or type a value in the Value column of the table belowto see how it affects the score.*		
6	**Attribute**	**Value**	**Relative Impact**
7	Marital Status	Married	0
8	Gender	Female	0
9	Income	39050 - 71062	84
10	Children	0	74
11	Education	Bachelors	36
12	Occupation	Professional	65
13	Home Owner	Yes	9
14	Cars	2	71
15	Commute Distance	0-1 Miles	82
16	Region		0
17	Age		95
18	Total		516
19			
20	Prediction for 'Yes'		FALSE

0-1 Miles
10+ Miles
1-2 Miles
2-5 Miles
5-10 Miles

Figure 9-5b Prediction Calculator - Revised Parameters

Of course, the scores in the Prediction Calculator are updated when you change values in the Cost/Profit Parameters Area of the Prediction Report worksheet.

Printable Calculator Worksheet

The Printable Calculator worksheet (Figure 9-6) contains a scoring sheet to printout for manual scoring, say for sales representative to use on site. Much of the scoring sheet is not shown in the figure because of its length—the seven missing attributes are represented by the hatched area. The sheet is used by checking on box in an attribute row, entering the points in the Score column, summing the scores, and then comparing the total with the criteria at the bottom.

	A	B	C	D	E	F	G	H
1	Prediction Calculator for the 'Yes' state of 'Purchased Bike'							
2								
3	*Check one value per attribute.*							
4	*Enter the associated points into the 'Score' box.*							
5	*Sum the scores for all attributes to determine the total score.*							
6								
7								
8	Attribute	Value	Points		Score			
9	Marital Status							
10		Married	0	❑				
11		Single	40	❑				
12	Gender							
13		Female	0	❑				
14		Male	19	❑				
15	Income							
16		< 39050	0	❑				
17		39050 - 71062	84	❑				
18		71062 - 97111	89	❑				
19		97111 - 127371	161	❑				
20		>= 127371	150	❑				
59								
60								
61	Age							
62		< 37	112	❑				
63		37 - 46	95	❑				
64		46 - 55	134	❑				
65		55 - 65	33	❑				
66		>= 65	0	❑				
67			Total					
68								
69	*Result:*	*at least 572*	*'Yes'*					
70		*less than 572*	*Other than 'Yes'*					

Figure 9-6 Printable Prediction Calculator
(For better viewing of this image, go to
http://www.zerobits.info/bibook/bibookimages/)

Shopping Basket Analysis

Shopping Basket Analysis, aka Market Basket Analysis, uses the Microsoft Association Rules algorithm that we briefly described in Chapter 3 to identify items that occur together such as products that are purchased together in a retail transaction. Shopping basket analysis results can be used in recommendation engines that implement suggestive selling. You may have experienced it if you have shopped on Amazon.com.

The Shopping Basket Analysis tool requires transaction data like that provided in the Associate worksheet in the Sample Data Excel file from the Data Mining Add-Ins for Office. A segment of the Excel table on that worksheet is shown in Figure 9-7a. Each row identifies a product purchased in a transaction along with its transaction (Order) number and optionally its price. There may be multiple entries (rows) for a specific transaction number meaning the multiple products were purchased at the same time showing what was in the "shopping basket." In the example the first customer listed (Order Number SO61277) bought a jersey and cap with a mountain bike; the second a bottle and cage and a jersey with a road bike; and so on.

	A	B	C	D
3	Order Number	Category	Product	Product Price
17	SO61277	Mountain Bikes	Mountain-500	539.99
18	SO61277	Jerseys	Short-Sleeve Classic Jersey	539.99
19	SO61277	Caps	Cycling Cap	8.99
20	SO61278	Road Bikes	Road-350-W	2443.35
21	SO61278	Bottles and Cages	Road Bottle Cage	8.99
22	SO61278	Bottles and Cages	Water Bottle	4.99
23	SO61278	Jerseys	Short-Sleeve Classic Jersey	539.99
24	SO61279	Mountain Bikes	Mountain-200	2319.99
25	SO61279	Fenders	Fender Set - Mountain	21.98
26	SO61280	Helmets	Sport-100	53.99

Figure 9-7a Transactions Table

Figure 9-7b shows the main dialog box for the Shopping Basket Analysis tool where you specify a Transaction ID field and the Item field to track in the shopping basket. The Item listbox (not shown) will list all of the fields in the table—Order Number, Category, Product, and Product Price in our case. Our choices are Category for a more general association or product for a more specific association. We'll leave the default as is. Specifying an Item Value is optional—use it if there is one.

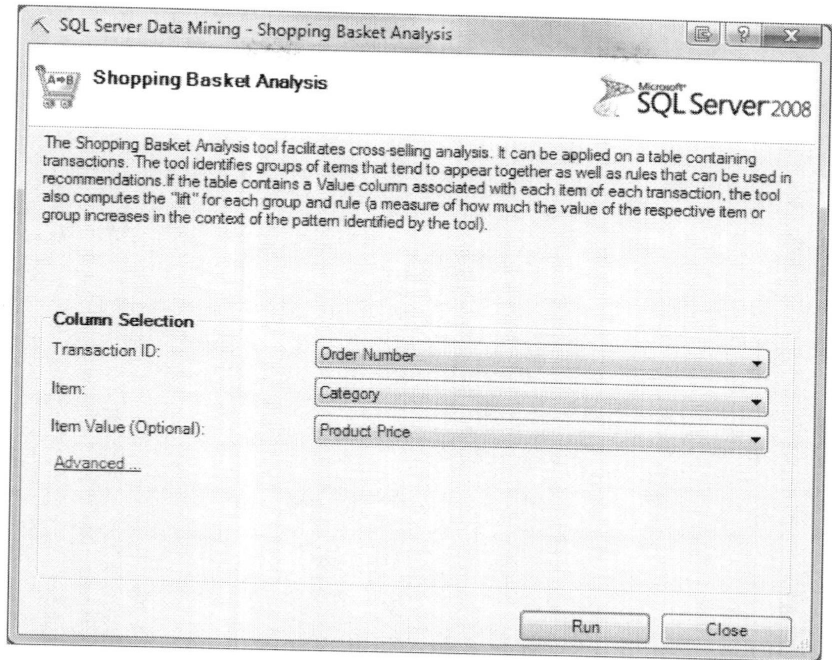

Figure 9-7b Shopping Basket Analysis Dialog Box

Clicking the Advanced button brings up the Advanced parameters Setting dialog box (Figure 9-7c). The Minimum Support parameter specifies the number of transactions that contain a specific bundle of items that must occur in the data set before that bundle is included in the analysis. This may be specified as a percent of the number of transactions or a specific number of transactions. The default shown here is 10 transactions.

The Minimum Probability Rule parameter specifies the minimum proportion of bundles containing a specific item that must occur in that bundle with another item. An example will explain this better. Suppose we're looking at shopping baskets that contain hot dogs and hot dog buns. If the Minimum Probability is set at the default value, 40 percent, then hot dog buns would have to be purchased with hot dogs in at least 40 percent of the bundles that contain hot dogs before the Shopping Basket Analysis tool will make a recommendation about the bundle of hot dog buns with hot dogs. The converse bundle, hot dogs with hot dog buns, is treated as a separate bundle, i.e., saying that hot dog buns are usually purchased with hot dogs does not necessarily imply that hot dogs are usually purchased with hot dog buns although for this pair, it is probably the case.

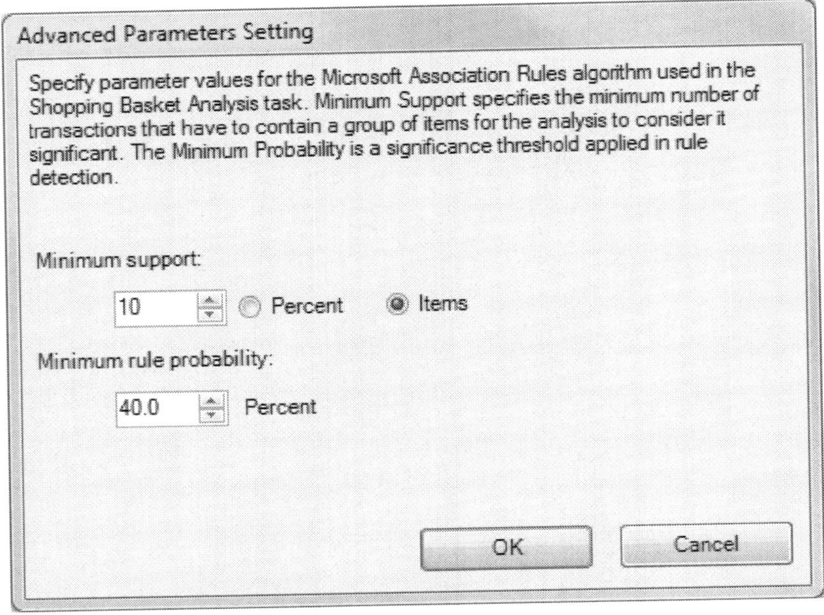

Figure 9-7c Advanced Parameters Setting Dialog Box

Running the analysis produces two new worksheets. The partial screen shot of the Shopping Basket Bundled Items worksheet in Figure 9-7d lists pairs of items that frequently occur together in descending order of overall value where overall value is based on the Item Value field, if one was available, in the Shopping Basket dialog box . Bundle size, Number of sales, and Average value per sale data are also provided.

Shopping Basket Bundled Items

Bundle of items	Bundle size	Number of sales	Average Value Per Sale	Overall value of Bundle
Road Bikes, Helmets	2	805	1570.228025	1264033.56
Mountain Bikes, Tires and Tubes	2	569	2208.067434	1256390.37
Fenders, Mountain Bikes	2	539	2022.477421	1090115.33
Mountain Bikes, Bottles and Cages	2	563	1923.73222	1083061.24
Mountain Bikes, Helmets	2	537	1966.57311	1056049.76
Jerseys, Road Bikes	2	480	2183.375083	1048020.04
Touring Bikes, Helmets	2	536	1925.792761	1032224.92
Road Bikes, Tires and Tubes	2	486	1541.535514	749186.26
Road Bikes, Bottles and Cages	2	552	1157.4025	638886.18
Touring Bikes, Bottles and Cages	2	351	1819.513846	638649.36

Figure 9-7d Shopping Basket Bundled Items Worksheet

The Shopping Basket Recommendations worksheet (Figure 9-7e) displays the items that the tool deems important to recommend. The first column in the table lists the items purchased; the second column the item to recommend; the third, Sales of Selected Items, reports the number of transactions that contained the Selected Item; and the fourth shows the number of those transaction that contained the recommended item. The last column reports the total value of the bundle, e.g., the 539 transactions that contained Fenders and Mountain Bikes produced $1M plus sales. The next to the last column is the Overall Value divided by the Sales of Selected Items. For example, for the first row $1,078,268.11 divided by 1,238 equals $870.98.

Recommendations may penalize popular products. For example, inspection of the complete Shopping Basket Bundled Items table Figure 9-7d shows that Bottles and Cages are very frequently purchase with bicycles. However, that bundle does not appear in the recommendations list because the popularity of Bottles and Cages suggests that Bottles and Cages don't have to be recommended because customers have a high likelihood of buying them anyway.

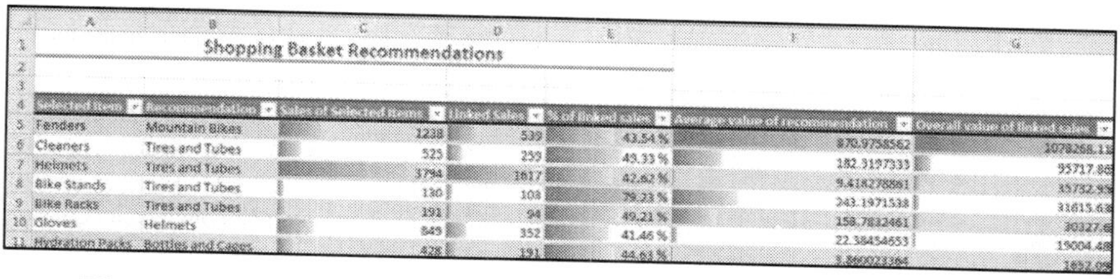

Shopping Basket Recommendations

Selected Item	Recommendation	Sales of Selected Items	Linked Sales	% of linked sales	Average value of recommendation	Overall value of linked sales
Fenders	Mountain Bikes	1238	539	43.54 %	870.9758562	1078268.11
Cleaners	Tires and Tubes	525	259	49.33 %	182.3197333	95717.88
Helmets	Tires and Tubes	3794	1617	42.62 %	9.418278861	35732.95
Bike Stands	Tires and Tubes	130	103	79.23 %	243.1971538	31615.63
Bike Racks	Tires and Tubes	191	94	49.21 %	158.7832461	30327.6
Gloves	Helmets	849	352	41.46 %	22.38454653	19004.48
Hydration Packs	Bottles and Cages	428	191	44.63 %	3.860023364	1652.09

Figure 9-7e Shopping Basket Recommendations Worksheet

Of course, both tables can be filtered and sorted using the usual down arrow on the column headings. If a Value Items is not included in the Shopping Basket Analysis dialog box (Figure 9-7b), then the value columns in Shopping Basket Bundled Items table are not shown and the Average value and overall value columns in the Shopping Basket Recommendations table are replaced by an Importance score.

What's Next

In this chapter we've looked at five relatively easy to use data analysis tools that utilize Microsoft's data mining algorithms. In the next and final chapter we'll explore the true data mining tools available in Excel and briefly describe their underlying algorithms.

Chapter 10 - Data Mining with Excel 2010: Data Mining Tools

This is a long chapter because the Data Mining Client in SQL Server 2008 Data Mining for Microsoft Office 2007 and 2010 provides access to most of the data mining functionality in Analysis Services and, thus, we have much material to cover. After some preliminaries, we'll describe the Microsoft data mining algorithms and how they are used in Excel's data mining tools. This is followed by a discussion of accuracy and validation of data mining models and how to use the models.

Preliminaries

Select Data Source

The five data mining tools—Classify, Estimate, Cluster, Associate, and Forecast—in the Data Modeling command group all utilize variations of the Data Mining Wizard which begins with a Getting Started window (not shown) that can be turned off. This is followed by a Select Source Data dialog box that we have seen in previous chapters which with the exception of the Associate tool appears as in Figure 10-1a. The Associate tool dialog box does not have the External data source section. If you have clicked on one cell in an Excel table before using a tool, then the Table source will be automatically selected. If you have selected a range of cells in a worksheet, the Data range source will be chosen. Use the External data source section if you want to access an external data source without importing the data into Excel.

If you elect to use an external data source, you must click on the Data Source button to the right of the Data source name textbox to bring up the Data Source Query Editor (Figure 10-1b) where a current data source connection may be displayed. If you want to utilize data from that source, then select the fields for the query as usual. Note that the Data Source Query Editor limits access in the query to one table or view so you cannot build queries that contain multiple tables with the designer. However, you can enter a SQL statement containing multiple tables and views directly into the Query textbox at the bottom of the Query Editor. For example, in the Data Source Query in Figure 10-1c I copied a multiple table T-SQL statement from a query that I designed in the SQL Server Management Studio to produce a list of transactions that could be used as a data source for the Shopping Basket

Analysis tool in Chapter 9 or the Associate Data Mining tool. Click OK to return to the Select Data Source dialog box.

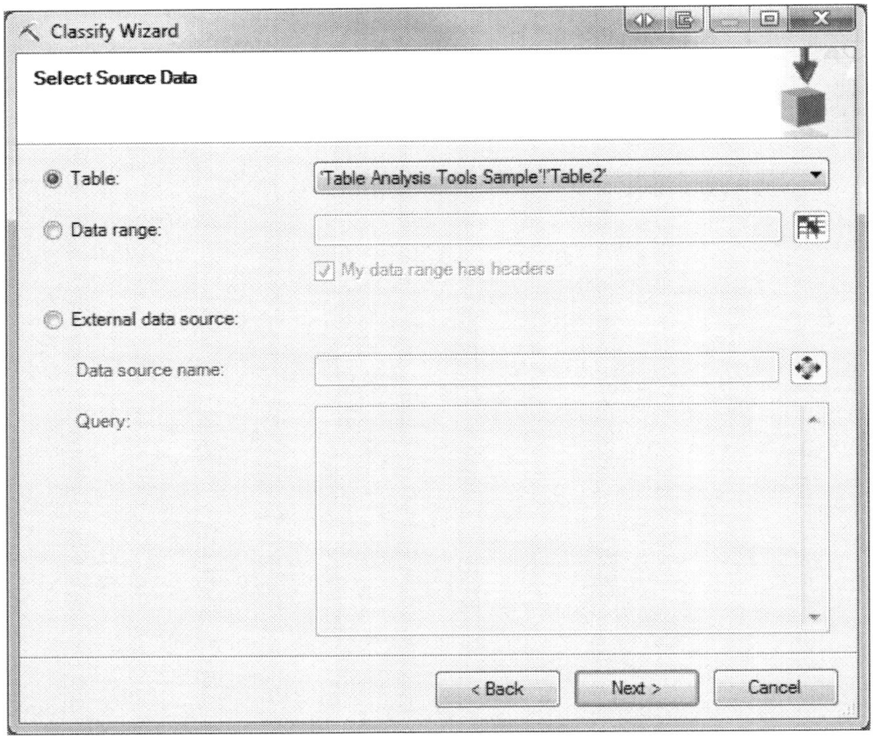

Figure 10-1a Select Source Data Dialog Box

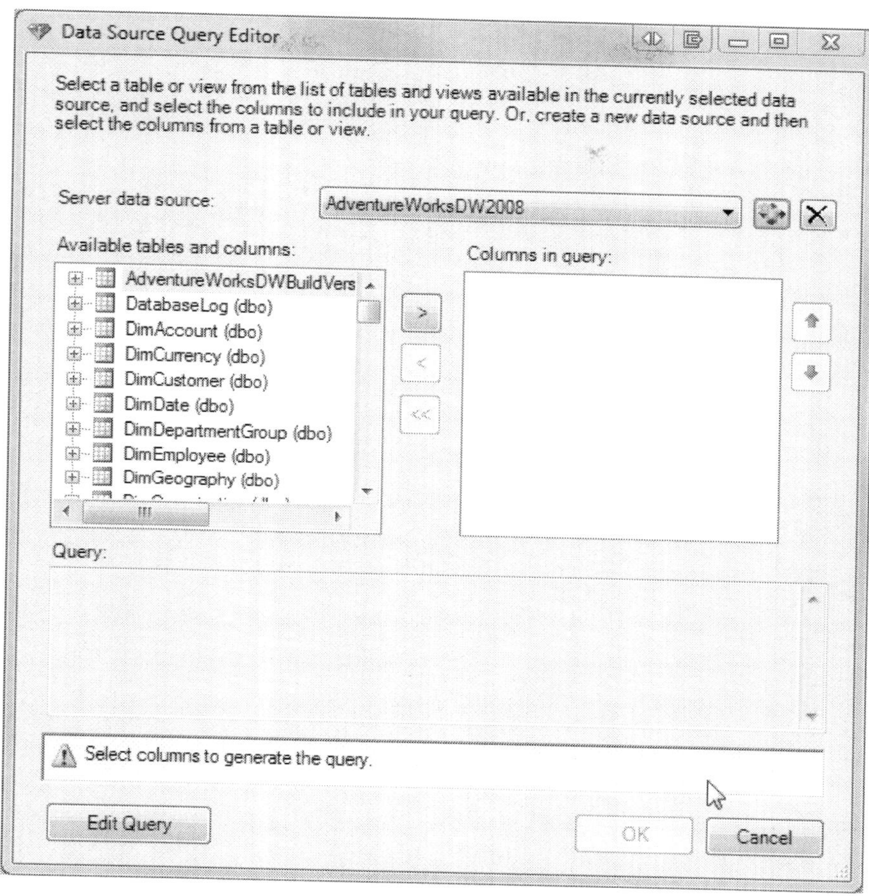

Figure 10-1b Initial Data Source Query Editor

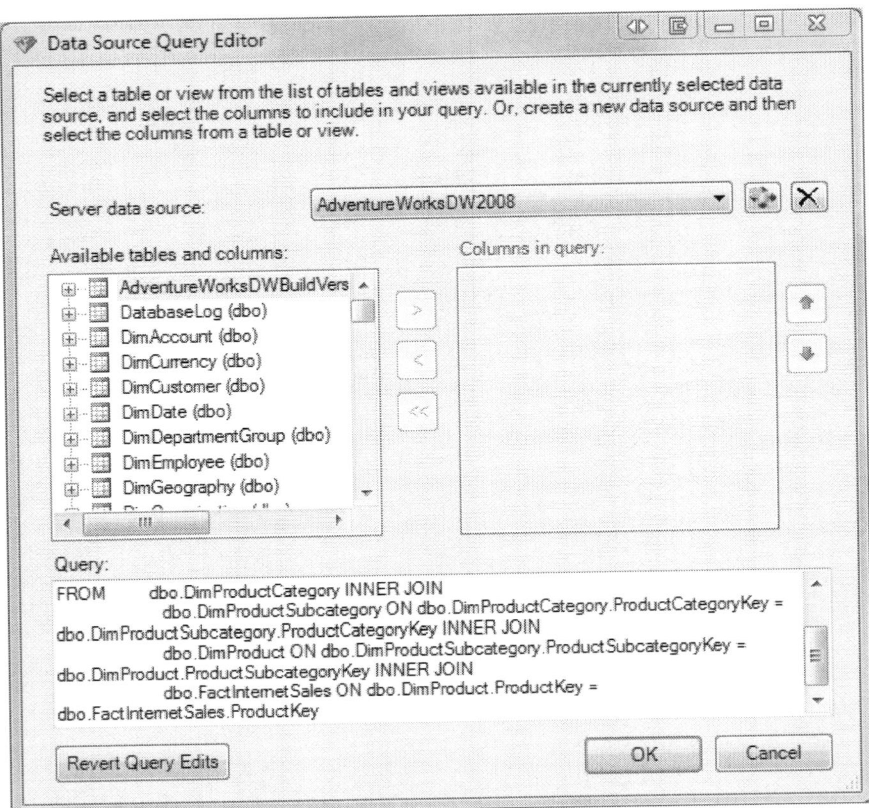

Figure 10-1c Multiple Table Query as a Data Source

If you prefer to use a different data source, click on the New Data source button to the right of the Server data source textbox to display the New Analysis Services data source dialog box (Figure 10-1d) to specify data source, server, and catalog names. First enter the name of your server instance, and select the database to use from the Catalog name drop-down listbox. Then, provide a name for the connection and test it if you want to. Clicking OK will return you the Data Source Query Editor

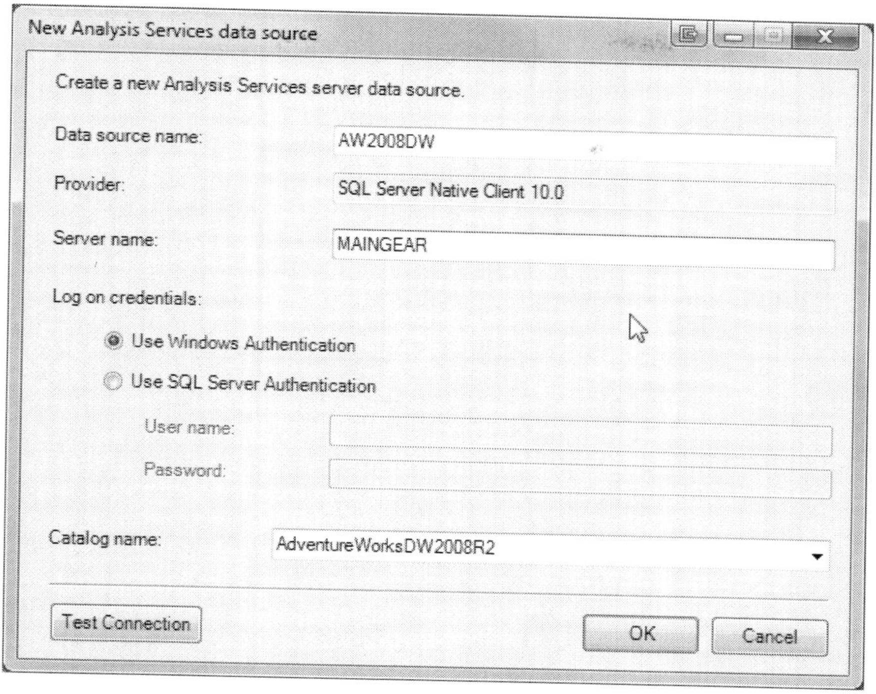

Figure 10-1d New Data Source Dialog Box

Proceeding from the Select source Data dialog box will display Wizard windows that differ depending on the data mining tool selected. We will describe those windows in the section for each tool later in this chapter.

Sample Data Tool

There are a number of reasons for taking a sample of your data. One is when importing data into Excel and the data source exceeds Excel's maximum capacity you can pare the data set to an acceptable size. Another is when you want to partition the data into a set to use for training and a set for testing. Regardless of the reason, the Sample Data tool makes it easy and simple. In the Select Sampling Type (Figure 10-2a), the next dialog box in the Sample Data Wizard after Select Source Data, you specify either Random Sampling or Oversample. By definition random sampling should produce a representative sample. Oversampling is used to balance representation of attributes in the sample regardless of the distribution in the original data set. The Wizard description uses an example of balancing the number of males and female in the sample.

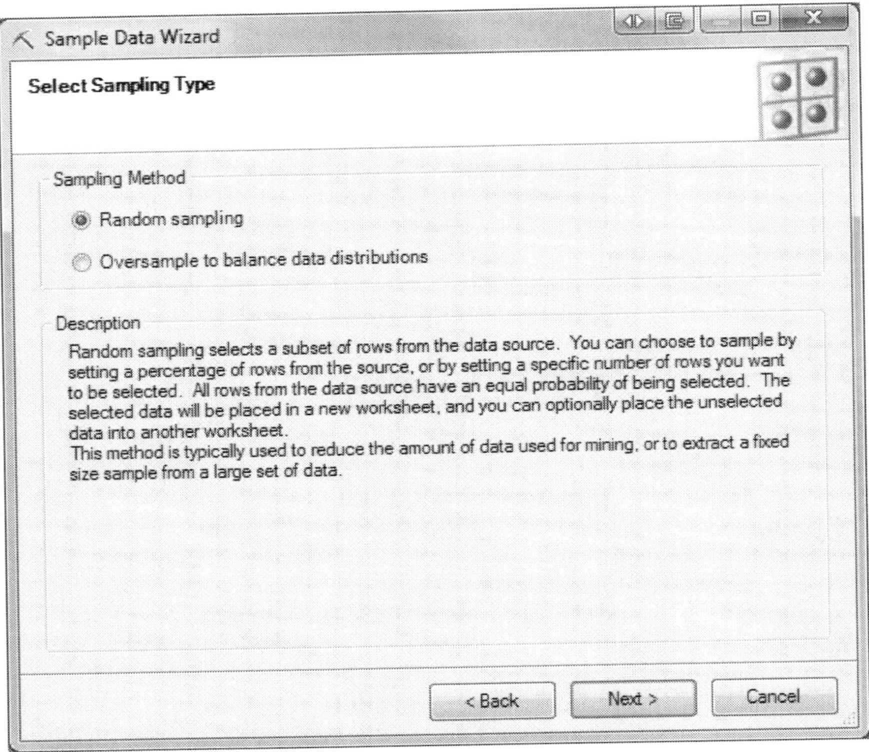

Figure 10-2a Select Sampling Type Dialog Box

If you select random sampling, in the next dialog box (Figure 10-2b) you set the sample size by either a percentage of the rows in the data source or a specific row count. If you select oversampling, in the next dialog box (Figure 10-2c) you identify the attribute (field) to balance, the target state (value) to which the Target percentage applies, and specify the sample size. In the example, the sample will contain 600 records with gender as female and 400 records as male. In the final dialog box (not shown) you specify the name for the new worksheet that will be inserted into the workbook, and, if using random sampling, specify whether to create a worksheet for the unselected data which is useful for creating training and test data sets.

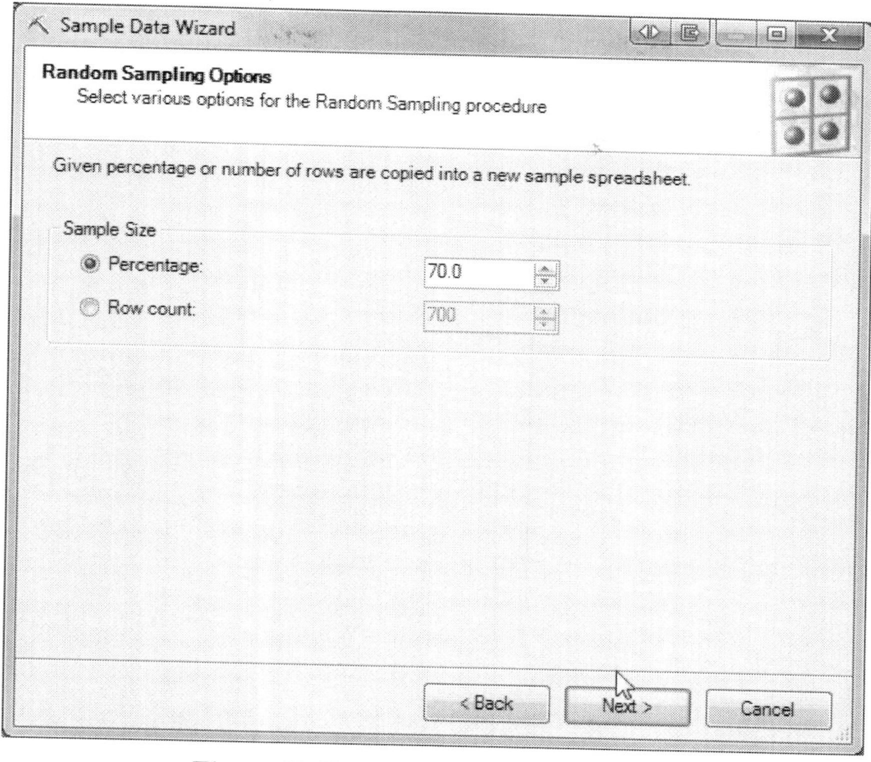

Figure 10-2b Random Sampling Options

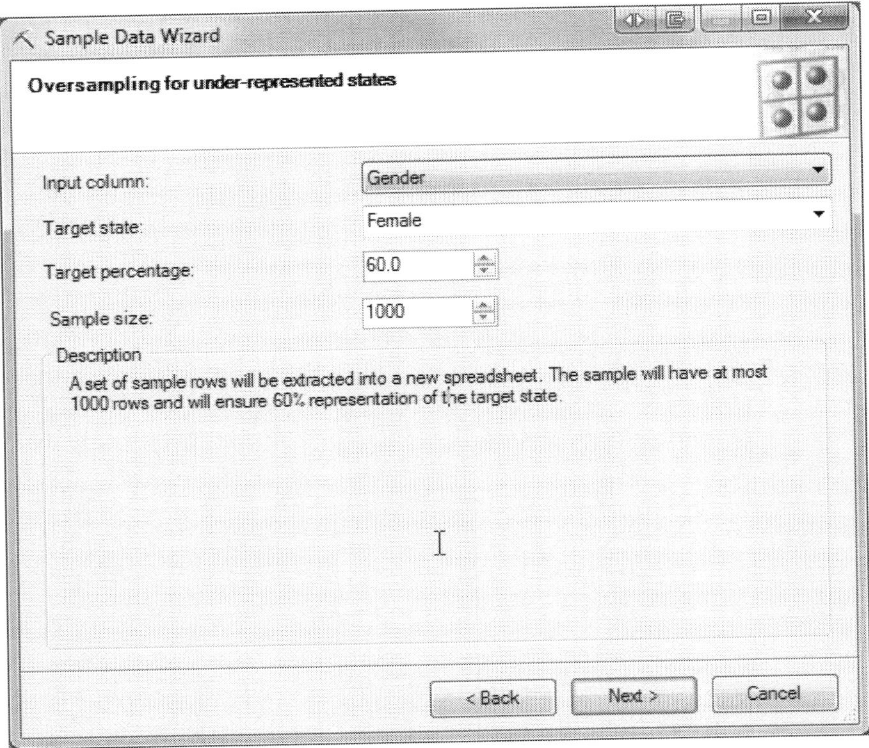

Figure 10-2 Oversampling Sampling Options

The Viewer

In Chapter 8 the Data Mining Forecast tool displayed results in a BIDS mining model viewer. The other Data Modeling tools also use variations of the viewer to present their results but what the viewer displays depends on the particular tool. For example, we saw that the viewer for the Forecast tool contains Chart and Model tabs whereas, as we'll see shortly, the Classify tool uses Decision Tree and Dependency Network tabs.

You may recall from Chapter 8 that the you can copy the contents of a viewer tab to an Excel worksheet. If the view is a graphic, say a chart, then the display in the tab will be copied into the worksheet as a bitmap image. However, when the viewer tab contains tabular data like a cluster profile, a table corresponding to the one in the viewer that can be filtered, sorted, and otherwise manipulated will be inserted into the worksheet.

Models and Structures

In simple terms, the data mining structure defines the data and the model specifies the algorithm and how it is applied to those data. Using BIDS for Analysis Services a developer can create a mining structure independent from a mining model or a structure and model together and also add another model to an existing structure. Fortunately, in Excel the Data Mining Wizard takes care of creating the structures and models for us. But, as we shall see we can construct them manually for Excel as well. Please see SQL Server 2008 Books Online for a more complete description of models and structures.

The Analysis Services Connection

We already know that Excel's data mining tools rely on Analysis Services for processing. To accomplish this Excel connects to an existing Analysis Services database where it stores its mining structures and models. The current connection name is displayed in the Connection command group on the Data Mining tab. Clicking on the current connection name displays the Analysis Services connections dialog box (Figure 10-3a) that lists the current connection and others that are immediately available. To make one of the other connection current just double click on it or select it and click the Make Current button.

You may add an existing Analysis Services database to the connection list by clicking the New button which will bring up a Connect to Analysis Services dialog box as in Figure 10-3b where you first enter the SQL Server instance name and then use the Catalog name listbox to specify the existing Analysis Services database to use. You may also enter a friendly name and test the connection. Clicking the Close button will insert the new connection into the list in Figure 10-3a. The DMAddinsDB was created during the installation of the Data Mining Add-ins for Microsoft Office. Note that data mining structures and models stored in Analysis Services can be accessed and manipulated by others who have access to the SQL Server instance.

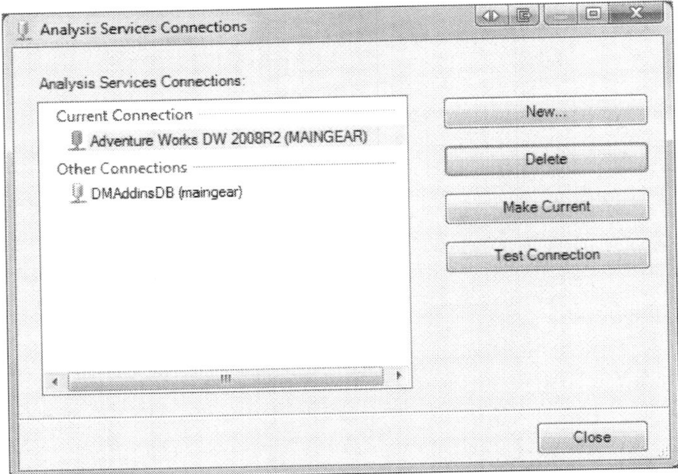

Figure 10-3a Analysis Services Connections Dialog Box

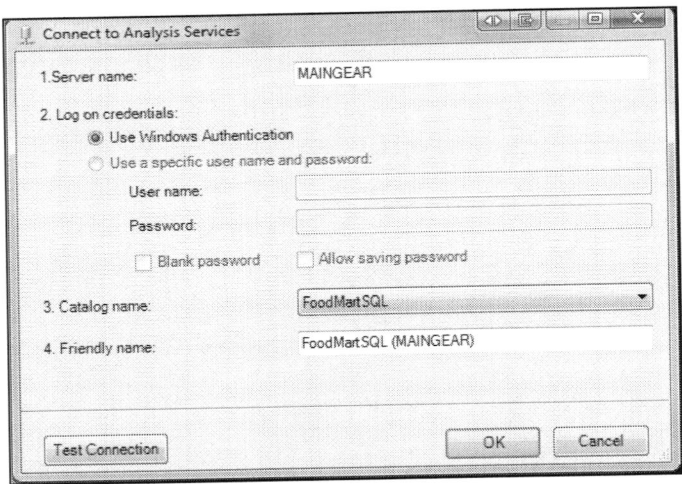

Figure 10-3b Connect to Analysis Services Dialog Box

The Trace command in the Connection command group displays a Tracer that displays all of the commands sent to Analysis Services by the Data Mining Add-in during the current Excel session. For example, Figure 10-3c displays a section that created a mining model from the Classify tool. Like a log file you may edit, copy, or delete all or parts of the command list.

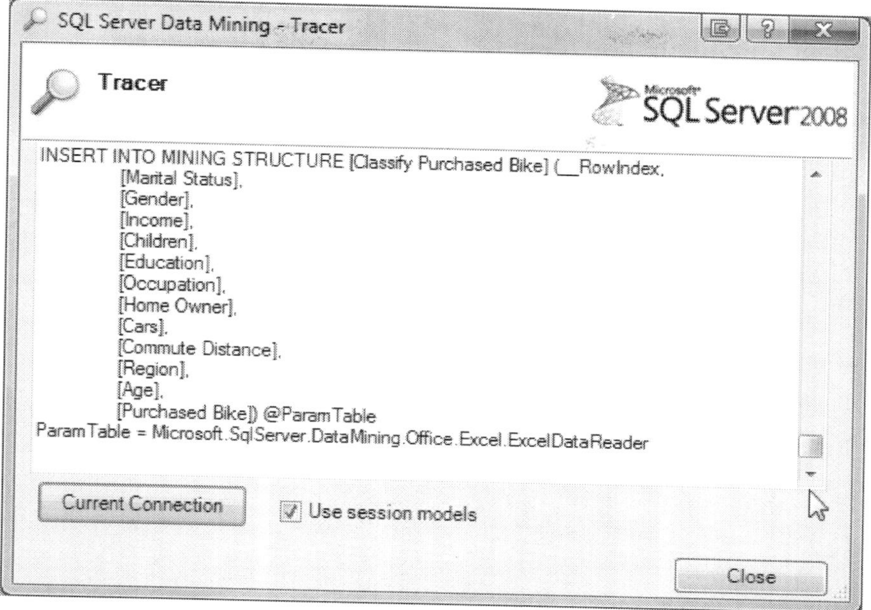
SQL Server Data Mining - Tracer
Tracer
Microsoft SQL Server 2008
INSERT INTO MINING STRUCTURE [Classify Purchased Bike] (_RowIndex,
[Marital Status],
[Gender],
[Income],
[Children],
[Education],
[Occupation],
[Home Owner],
[Cars],
[Commute Distance],
[Region],
[Age],
[Purchased Bike]) @ParamTable
ParamTable = Microsoft.SqlServer.DataMining.Office.Excel.ExcelDataReader
Current Connection
Use session models
Close

Figure 10-3c The Tracer

Model Usage and Management

The Data Mining add-in provides tools to directly manage mining models in Excel given appropriate permissions without having to work within BIDS. The Browse tool in the Model Usage command group initiates the viewer to display mining models that were saved in the Analysis Services database for the active connection; the Document Model tool provides properties and information about a model; and the Query tool utilizes the Data Mining Query Wizard to create Data Mining Extension (DMX) language queries to make predictions with existing models, modify them, or even create new mining structures and models. Using the Query tool to make predictions is described at the end of this chapter whereas more advanced topics related mining structures and models are introduced in Appendix F.

Browse

Figure 10-4a shows the Browse dialog box for the AdventureWorks DW connection on my machine. You select a model in the list and click the Next button to open the model in the viewer. Note that in the left panel the models are the indented entities nested within a structure. For example, there is a structure named Customer Mining that contains two models: Customer Clusters and Subcategory Associations.

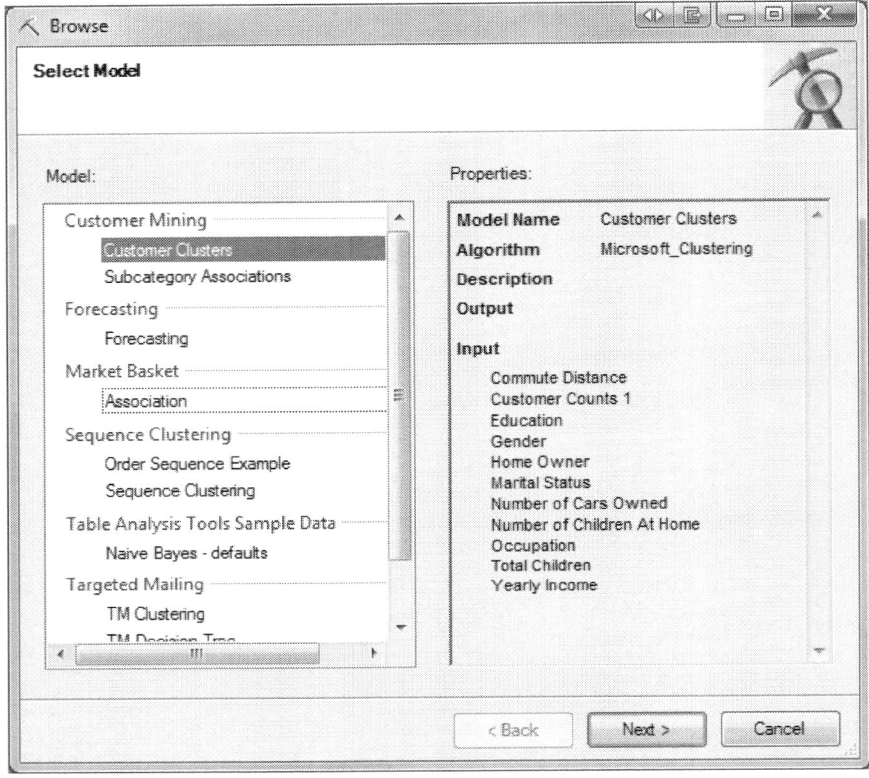

Figure 10-4a Select Model Dialog Box

Document Model

Clicking the Document Model command first brings up a Select Model dialog identical to the one above, and after selecting a model, it displays a Select documentation details dialog box (not shown) where you may select complete or summary information. Selecting summary information will create a new worksheet named Model Documentation that will contain the model name, description, algorithm used, and last processed date. Selecting complete information will also create a new worksheet named Model Documentation with considerably more information. For example, Figure 10-4b shows the complete information worksheet for a forecasting model in the AdventureWorks sample database. Note in particular that the model parameter values are listed at the bottom.

	A	B	C	D	E
1	**Mining Model Documentation for Forecasting**				
2					
3	**Model Information**				
4	Model Name	Forecasting			
5	Model Description				
6	Algorithm	Microsoft Time Series			
7	Last Processed	7/30/2011 17:14			
8					
9	**Output Column Information for 'Amount'**				
10	Content Type	Continuous			
11	Mean	204045.2673			
12	Min	2097.2946			
13	Max	405993.24			
14					
15	**Output Column Information for 'Quantity'**				
16	Content Type	Continuous			
17	Mean	89			
18	Min	2			
19	Max	176			
20					
21	**Mining Model Columns**				
22	**Column Name**	**Usage**	**Data Type**	**Content Type**	**Values**
23	Amount	Input and Predict	Double	Continuous	2097.2946 - 405993.24
24	Model Region	Input	Text	Key	
25	Quantity	Input and Predict	Long	Continuous	2 - 176
26	Time Index		Long	Key Time	
27					
28	**Algorithm Parameters**				
29	**Name**	**Value**			
30	AUTO_DETECT_PERIODICITY	1E-15			
31	COMPLEXITY_PENALTY	0.1			
32	FORECAST_METHOD	MIXED			
33	HISTORIC_MODEL_COUNT	0			
34	HISTORIC_MODEL_GAP	10			
35	INSTABILITY_SENSITIVITY	1			
36	MAXIMUM_SERIES_VALUE	1E+308			
37	MINIMUM_SERIES_VALUE	-1E+308			
38	MINIMUM_SUPPORT	10			
39	MISSING_VALUE_SUBSTITUTION	None			
40	PERIODICITY_HINT	{1,12}			
41	PREDICTION_SMOOTHING	0.5			

Figure 10-4b Complete Model Information Worksheet

(For better viewing of this image, go to http://www.zerobits.info/bibook/bibookimages/)

Model Management

We'll hold the discussion of the Query command until later in the chapter and in Appendix F and move on to model management. Clicking the Manage Models command displays the Manage Mining Structures and Model dialog box as in Figures 10-5 where the top right pane lists the tasks that can be performed on the structure or model. These tasks differ depending on whether you are working on a structure or a model as in Figure 10-5a for a structure and Figure 10-5b for a model. As an example I could rename the Forecast model by selecting that model and clicking Rename this mining model. A Rename Mining Model dialog box (not shown) would pop up where I could change the name to something more descriptive.

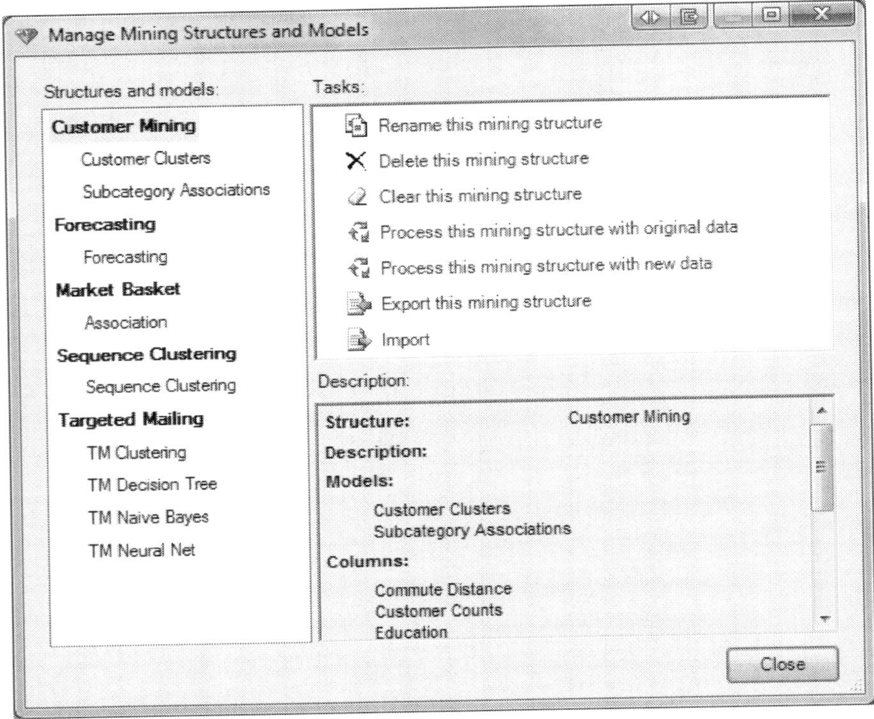

Figure 10-5a Manage Mining Structures and Models Dialog Box for Structures

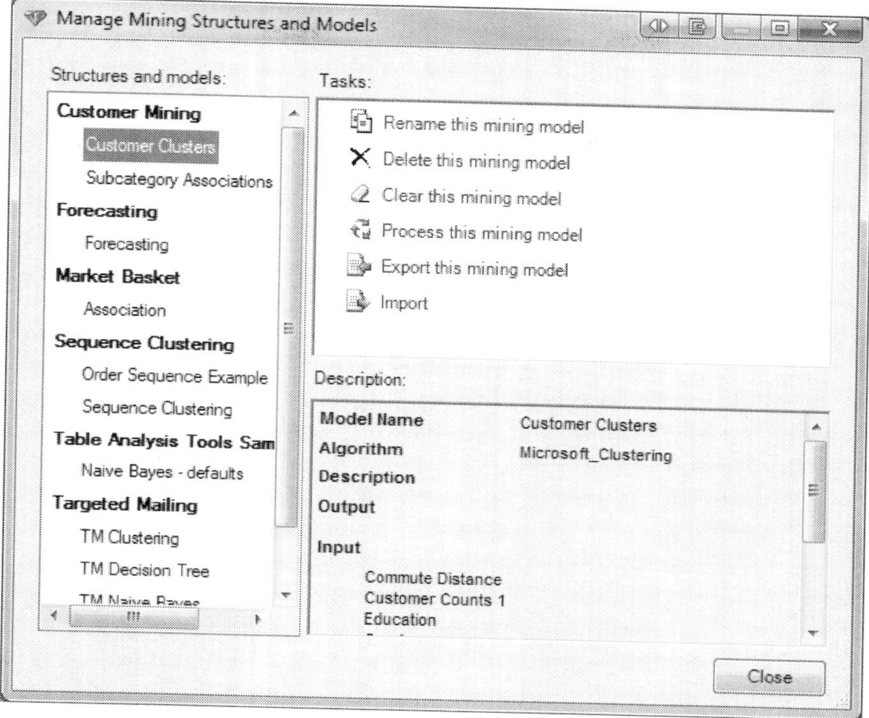

Figure 10-5b Manage Mining Structures and Models Dialog Box for Models

Now we can better understand the Forecast Wizard Finish window in Figure 10-6, first shown in Figure 8-21c. The Structure and Model names and descriptions in the Finish window are used in the Browse and Manage Mining Structures and Model dialog boxes, and the Model name and Model description appear in the Model Documentation worksheet. The Browse model checkbox initiates the viewer after the Finish button is clicked. If it is not checked, you can, of course, bring up the viewer with the Browse command. The Enable drill-through does just that for those algorithms that support drill-through. And, as mentioned above, checking the Use temporary model checkbox will prevent the model being saved via the current Analysis Services database connection.

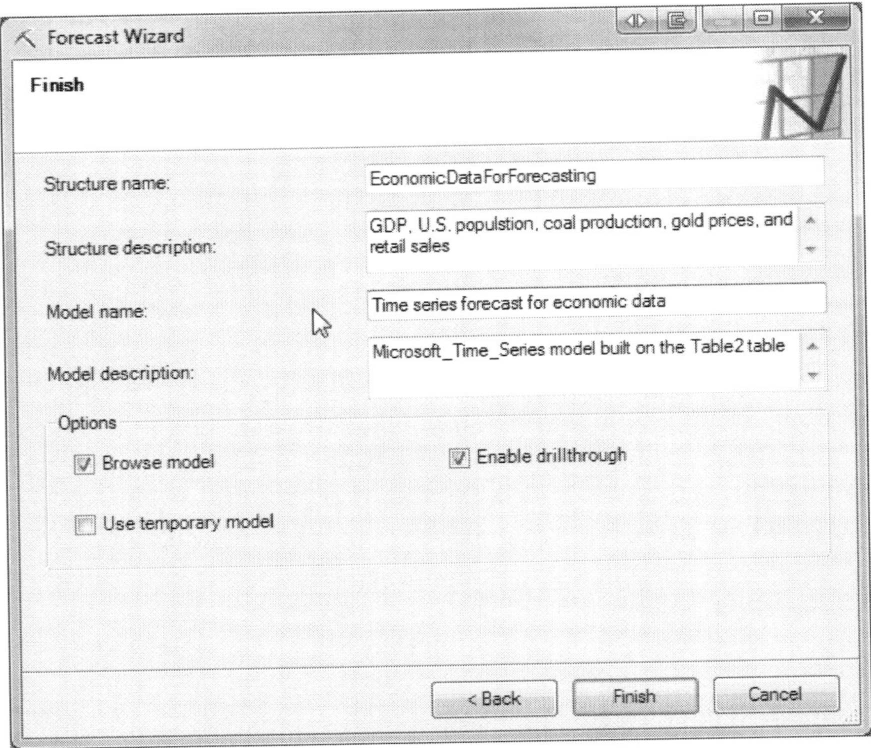

Figure 10-6 Forecast Wizard Finish Window

Feature selection reduces the variety that some of the data mining algorithms have to deal with, i.e., it simplifies the modeling process, may increase performance, and may improve results Feature selection may be used input and predictable attributes or on the number of states depending on the algorithm.

Microsoft Data Mining Algorithms

In this section we'll briefly describe seven of the nine Microsoft data mining algorithms. We already discussed linear regression in Chapter 6 and the Time Series algorithm in Chapter 8. A list of parameters for each algorithm is also included for each algorithm. They are displayed along with a description of each in the Algorithm Parameters dialog box that is accessible from the Parameters button on a data mining tool's wizard as we saw in Chapter 8. For ease of reference Figure 10-7 shows an example of an Algorithm Parameters dialog box.

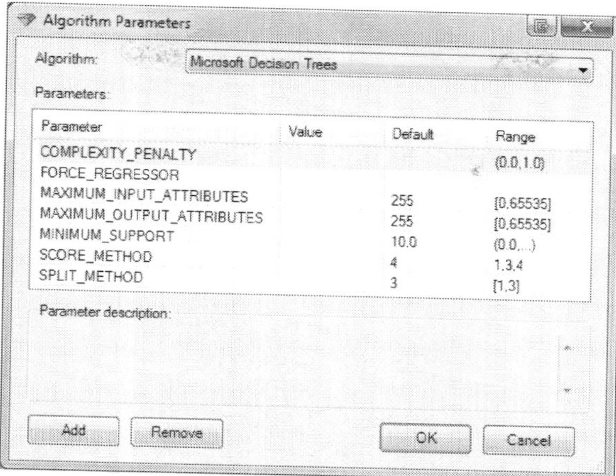

Figure 10-7 Forecast Algorithm Parameters Dialog Box

I relied on SQL Server Books Online for writing the descriptions. If you want to know more about the algorithms, in addition to SQL Server Books Online, there are books and Internet sources available that provide explanations of each in considerable detail.

Association

We've already used the Association algorithm in the Shopping Basket Analysis in the last chapter so you know that it identifies items that appear together (itemsets) and creates rules about these associations. The Association algorithm is an implementation of the Apriori algorithm which counts occurrences of items in an itemset and identifies itemsets that occur frequently. It begins with an itemset size of one, e.g., single products, to find frequently occurring items, then incrementally increases the itemset size searching for itemsets with multiple items until there are no longer combinations that meet criteria specified by parameters. The algorithm then generates association rules based on other parameters.

The Association algorithm parameters are:

- Maximum Itemset Count
- Maximum Itemset Size
- Maximum Support
- Minimum Importance
- Minimum Itemset Size
- Minimum Probability
- Minimum Support

Clustering

We saw an example of the Clustering algorithm when we used the Detect Categories tool in Chapter 9. A clustering algorithm identifies groups of items that have similar characteristics by measuring the "distance" between them and assigning ones with shorter distances to the same group. The diagram in Figure 10-8 illustrates this concept in a two dimensional space. The items that are close together would be identified as a group (cluster).

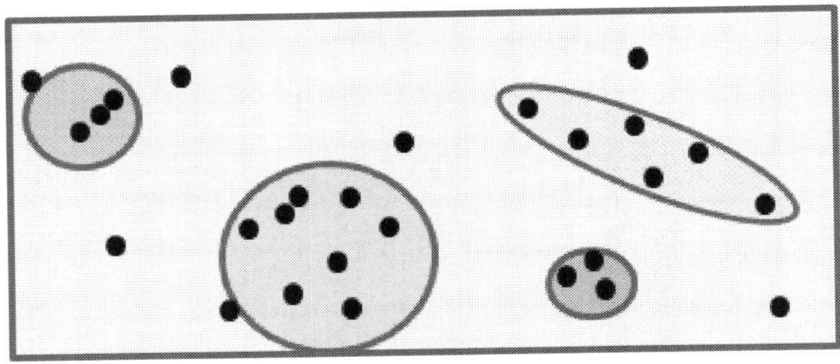

Figure 10-8 Cluster Diagram

The Microsoft Clustering algorithm has two methods for identifying clusters. The K-means method permits an item to be a member of only one group whereas the Expectation Maximization method (EM), the default, allows items to belong to multiple groups. SQL Server Books Online says that the EM method is preferable. The EM method provides scalable and non-scalable options for how it uses the data. The scalable approach which uses a subset of the data for an initial scan and only accesses additional records if necessary, is the preferable approach because it's faster. The non-scalable option uses all of the available data. The method and option to use for a particular clustering model are specified by parameters.

The Clustering algorithm parameters are:

- Cluster Count
- Cluster Seed
- Clustering Method
- Maximum Input Attributes

Decision Trees

We saw an example of a decision tree structure when we used the Data Mining Forecast tool in Chapter 8, specifically in Figure 8-23. A decision tree branches from a parent node containing all of the data into separate trees for each predictable attribute. (In the Chapter 9 example there are multiple predictable attribute with each attribute having its own tree.) The algorithm determines correlations between the input columns (fields) and the target (the to be predicted field) and uses the highest correlation to create branches in the tree. This is done recursively until no more splits are possible. When the target field has discrete values, say like purchase a bicycle or not, then the trees branch on discrete attributes. To predict continuous valued fields the algorithm uses linear regression to create the branches by making splits when there is non-linearity as we saw in the forecasting example. The Decision Tree algorithm can be used for classification or estimation.

The Decision Tree algorithm parameters are:

- Complexity Penalty
- Forced Regressor
- Maximum Input Attributes
- Maximum Output Attributes
- Minimum Support
- Score Method
- Split Method

Logistic Regression

Logistic regression predicts the probability of a value of a categorical dependent variable based on patterns in the relationship between the dependent variable and a set of categorical or discretized continuous independent variables. For example, we can use logistic regression in classification analysis to examine the relationship between customer attributes such as gender, age, and income and the probability of buying a bicycle.

"Logistic" in the name of the method derives from its use of the logistic function as in Figure 10-9 whose functional form is something like:

$$P(X) = \frac{1}{1 + e^{-X}}$$

The function is useful because it returns values between zero and one (like probabilities) regardless of the values of the independent variables which can be negative or positive. In addition, its shape favors the zero and one points on the graph which is useful for representing discrete attributes like purchased a bicycle or not where 1 = yes and 0 = no.

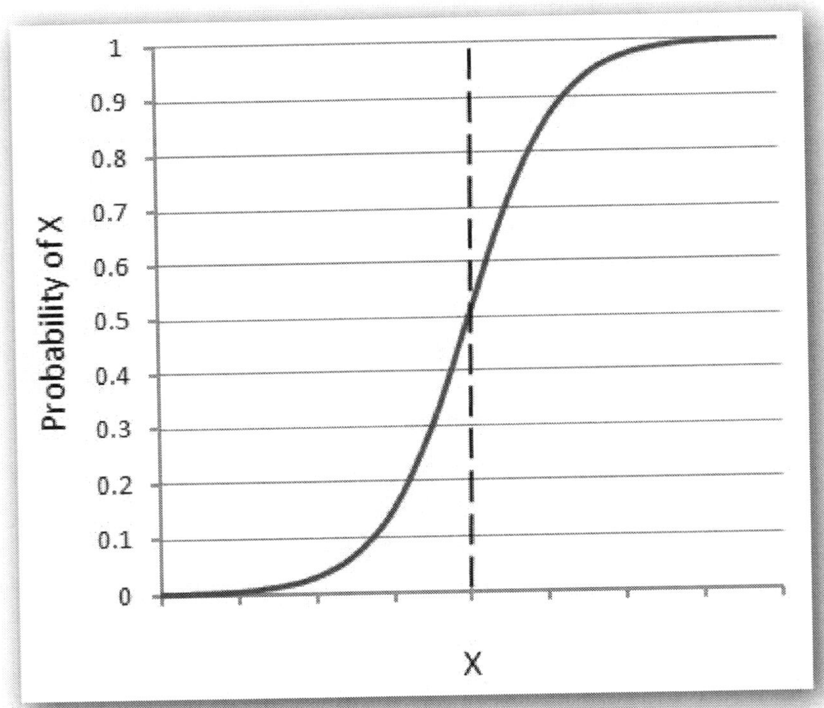

Figure 10-9 Logistic Function

The Microsoft data mining version of logistic regression uses its Neural Network algorithm (see below) without a hidden layer. The output in the Browser allows you to explore the strength of the association between dichotomous values of the target field and various attributes such as the likelihood that an attribute, say commute distance, favors buying a bicycle or not.

The Logistic Regression algorithm parameters are:

- Holdout Percentage
- Holdout Seed
- Maximum Input Attributes
- Maximum Output Attributes
- Maximum States
- Sample Size

Naive Bayes

Bayes Theorem, postulated by Reverend Thomas Bayes and published posthumously in 1764, describes the relationship between conditional and marginal probabilities of events and is stated as:

$$P(A|B) = \frac{P(B|A)P(A)}{P(B)}$$

or computationally

$$P(A|B) = \frac{\mathrm{P(B|A)P(A)}}{\mathrm{P(B|A)P(A) + \ P(B|not\ A)P(not\ B)}}$$

This says that the probability of event A occurring given that event B occurred is equal to the probability of B given A multiplied by the probability of A occurring by itself, all divided by the probability of B occurring by itself. A common example is the probability of having a disease given the results of a test for it where the test is not definitive. For the example let event A be having the disease and event B a positive result from the test for the disease. Suppose that data shows that 10 out of 1,000 people have the disease (the probability of A, i.e., P(A) = .01) and that there is a .90 probability of having the disease if the test is positive. Then, the probability of a person having the disease given a positive test result is:

$$P(\text{Disease given a positive test}) = \frac{.9 * .01}{.9 * .01 + \ .1 * .999} = \ .0833$$

So, what does this have to do with data mining? Well, suppose event A is purchasing a bicycle and event B is being married. Using Bayes Theorem the probability of purchasing a bicycle given a customer is married can be calculated because in our database we can compute the proportion (probability) of married customers who purchased bicycles P(B|A) and the proportion of customers in general who bought bicycles P(A).

Naive Bayes analysis is used to describe how each one of a set of attributes predicts a target. The "Naive" part of Naive Bayes relates to the requirement that a set of input attributes should be independent, or in practicality somewhat independent, meaning that one attribute is naive about the others. If attributes are substantially dependent, e.g., are significantly correlated, then probability estimates can be distorted. Naive Bayes is particularly useful for exploring data as we saw with the Analyze Key Influencers tool in Chapter 9. It is fast but in some circumstances may be less accurate that other methods. More on that later.

The Naïve Bayes algorithm parameters are:

- Maximum Input Attributes
- Maximum Output Attributes
- Minimum Dependency Probability
- Maximum States

Neural Network

An artificial neural network (ANN) is a simplified, abstract representation of a biological neural network which is a collection of biological neurons that have inputs that can be modified by synapses and outputs. In an ANN as in Figure 10-10 the neurons are processing elements (PEs) that transform one or many inputs into one output. Weights can be assigned to the inputs somewhat like a weighted moving average that we described in Chapter 8 except that the weights may take on negative as well as positive values. Negative values inhibit the neuron and positive values excite the it. The ANN can learn by varying the weights to minimize error. A PE uses some kind of transfer function to covert inputs into an output, and in an ANN one or more hidden layers (see the figure) can occur between the input and output layers.

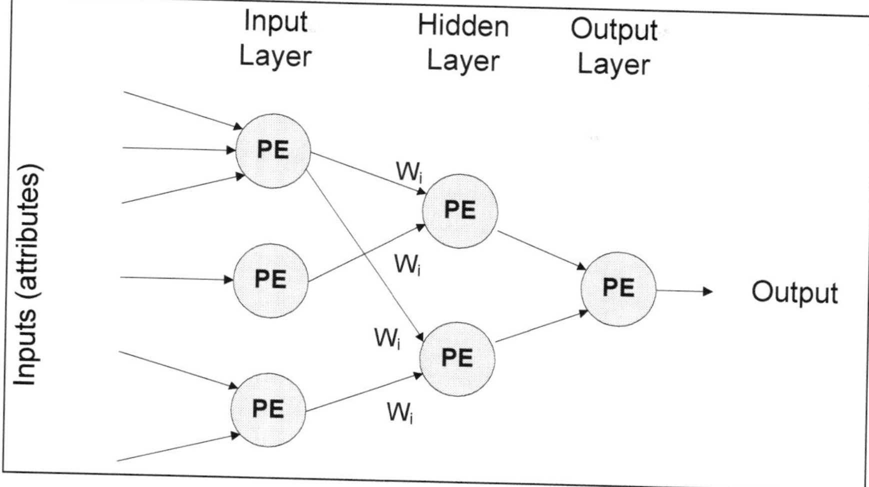

Figure 10-10 Artificial Neural Network

The algorithm uses three layers as in the figure above. The input PEs represent the attribute values and their probabilities; the hidden layer assigns weights to the probabilities to represent the importance of the input; and the output layer represents predictable attribute values. The algorithm reserves a portion of the training data, called holdout data, to assess the accuracy of the network and then iteratively builds the network evaluating it after each iteration. Training is discontinued when accuracy stabilizes.

The Neural Network algorithm parameters are:

- Hidden Node Ratio
- Holdout Percentage
- Holdout Seed
- Maximum Input Attributes
- Maximum Output Attributes
- Maximum States
- Sample Size

Sequence Clustering

Sequencing algorithms model how a multiple state system moves from state to state. A common example is clickstream analysis that describing how users of a Web site navigate from page to page. The Microsoft Sequence Clustering algorithm combines sequencing with clustering described earlier in the chapter

to also divide the cases into groups that display similar sequence patterns. For example, Web site shopping patterns may differ by gender.
The Sequence Clustering algorithm is a hybrid of the Clustering algorithm and Markov chains. In a Markov chain, named after Andrey Markov a Russian mathematician, at any given time an item will be in one of a finite number of states. For example, in selling a house the house may be listed, under contract, sold, or listing expired. We can represent this as a first-order Markov process where the transition to another state is only dependent on its current state. In second-order Markov process the transition depends on the previous two states. And so on. The example in Figure 10-11 shows contrived probabilities in a state transition matrix of moving from one state to another in a given month for the house selling example. If the house is listed at the beginning of the month, there is a .75 probability that it will remain listed at the end of the month, a .10 probability that it will be under contract, and so forth. The 1.00 probabilities in the Sold and Listing Expired rows are called absorbing states, i.e., once you get there you don't leave. Note that the row marginal totals must be equal to one. You can do calculations on the Markov table to determine system states after multiple time periods, for example, but we won't go into that here.

	To				
From	Listed	Under contract	Sold	Listing Expired	Marginal Total
Listed	0.75	0.10	0.05	0.10	1.00
Under contract	0.20	0.29	0.50	0.01	1.00
Sold	0.00	0.00	1.00	0.00	1.00
Listing Expired	0.00	0.00	0.00	1.00	1.00

Figure 10-11 Markov State Transition Matrix

The Sequence Clustering algorithm parameters are:

- Cluster count
- Maximum Sequence States
- Maximum States
- Minimum Support

Excel Data Modeling Tools

In this section we'll look at five of the six tools in the Data Modeling command group. The Forecast tool was described in Chapter 8. We'll continue using the AdventureWorks data in the Sample Data Excel file from the Data

Mining Add-Ins for Office download for our examples: the Table Analysis Tools Sample data worksheet for the Classify, Estimate, and Cluster tools and the Associate data worksheet for the Associate tool. Note that wizards for the four tools described here all begin with the Select Source Data dialog box described earlier in this chapter so we will not repeat the description again. In addition, if on the Split data into training and testing sets page of the tool Wizard, e.g., the Estimate Wizard, you elect to create a testing set which is the default setting, then the results from instance to instance of applying the tool will vary. For example, the parameters on the ARIMA function in the Estimate tool example (see Figure 10-17b) will be different each time you run the tool with the split data option because records are assigned to the training and test sets randomly. Thus, each time the tool runs it will have slightly different data as input. So, if you try data mining in the Table Analysis Tools Sample data worksheet, your results will likely differ from those below.

Classify

Classification algorithms model the relationship between one or more discrete target variables and a number of predictor attributes. The Analyze Key Influencers tool described in Chapter 9 is an example of classification analysis.

The Classification dialog box (Figure 10-11a) is used to specify the target field, the one to be predicted, in the Column to analyze listbox and the predictor variables, the Input Columns. The Classify tool applies one of four algorithms—Decision Trees, Logistic Regression, Naive Bayes, or Neural Network—which can be specified in the algorithm Parameters dialog box as in Figure 10-11b. Decision Trees is the default. We'll examine the output from each of these algorithms below. All parameters will be left at their default values except as otherwise noted.

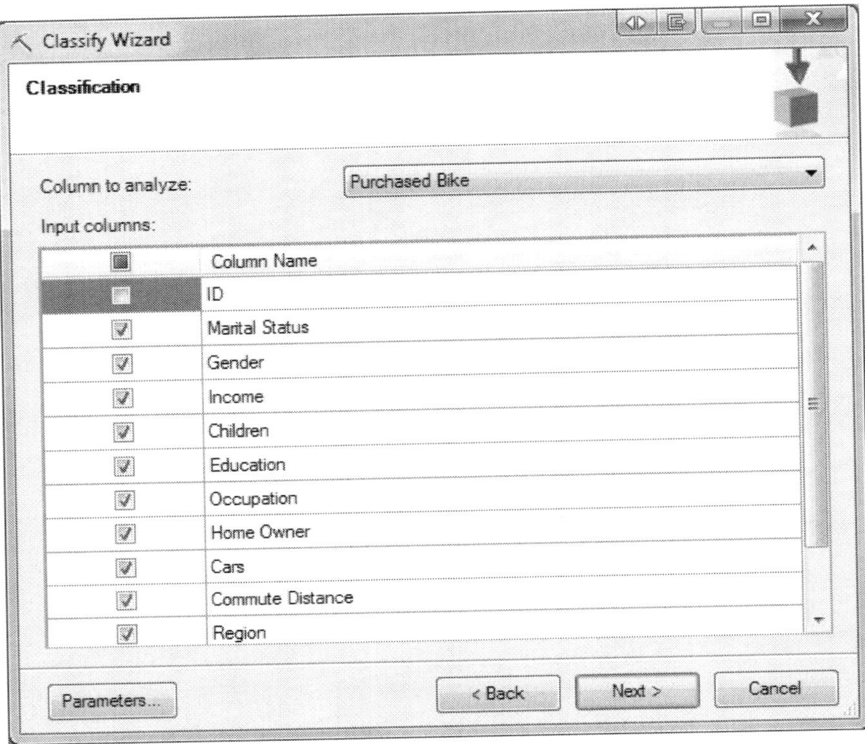

Figure 10-11a Classification Dialog Box

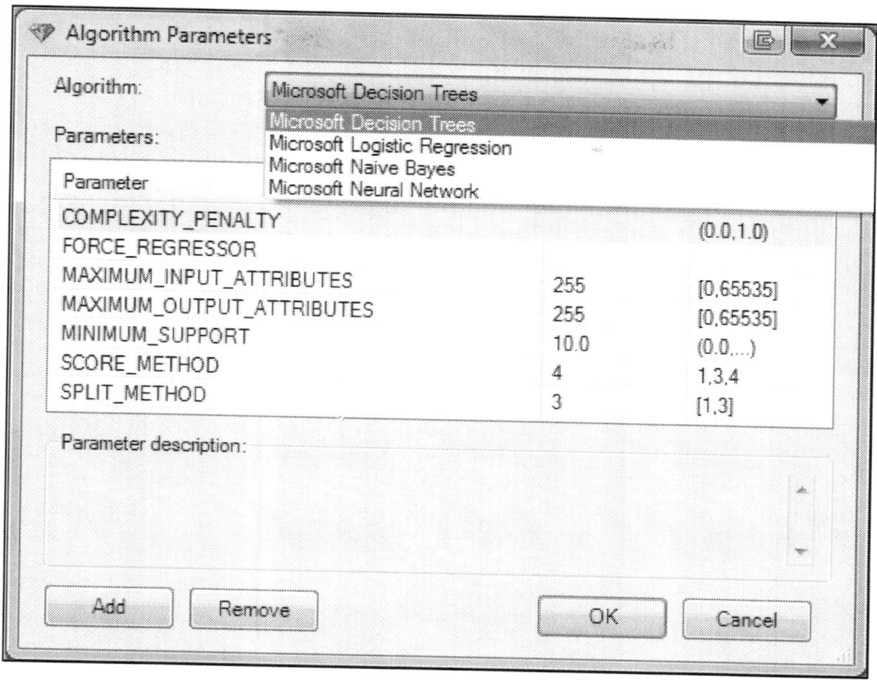

Figure 10-11b Classify Tool Algorithm Options

Decision Trees Algorithm

The Decision Tree tab in the Viewer (Figure 10-12a) is similar to the ones in the Viewer Model tabs in Chapter 8 that displayed results for the time series forecasting example. There is a tree pane on the left and a Mining Legend pane on the right. The tree diagram shows partitions of the target values based on the most significant attributes. In this case the root node containing all of the target field data is split by a dichotomous discretized Age attribute (between 32 and 39 or not), and then the not 32 to 39 age node is split further by the Marital Status attribute. The buttons, listboxes, and slider in the tree pane are identical to those described in Chapter 8. In this model the Complexity Penalty parameter is set to 0.9.

The Background listbox is useful for exploring values for the target variable. By default the shade of the background color represents the relative number of cases in a node. Nodes with darker shades contain more cases than those with lighter shades as shown in the color bar at the top of the Mining Legend pane. Of course, the All node is the darkest because it contains all 700 cases, and the not 32 to 39 age group in next darkest with 553 cases. And so on. You can use the listbox to have the tree node background reflect specific values of the target variable—Yes, No, or missing in this case. When you do that the background color represents probabilities of the value selected. For example, Figure 10-12b displays the tree for Purchased Bike = Yes indicating that the 32 to 39 age group has the highest probability of buying bicycles. Using that information AdventureWorks Marketing Department may elect to focus more sales effort to the 32 to 39 group or, conversely, try to increase the frequency of bike buying of prospective customers outside of this age group.

Similar information is presented in the Mining Legend pane for the node selected in the tree along with a histogram to visually display the probabilities. Hovering the mouse over a node will pop up a box with the case count for that node.

Right clicking on the All node will display the menu in Figure 10-12c. Right clicking on subordinate nodes will display a similar menu (not shown) with fewer options. Selecting the Drill-through Structure or Model Columns options will insert a Drill-through worksheet (not shown) into the workbook that lists all of the cases in that node. Hide Legend will hide the Mining Legend pane.

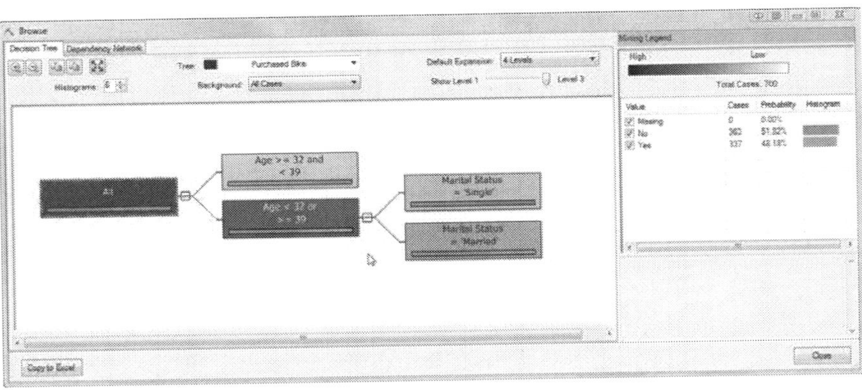

Figure 10-12a Classify Decision Tree Tab

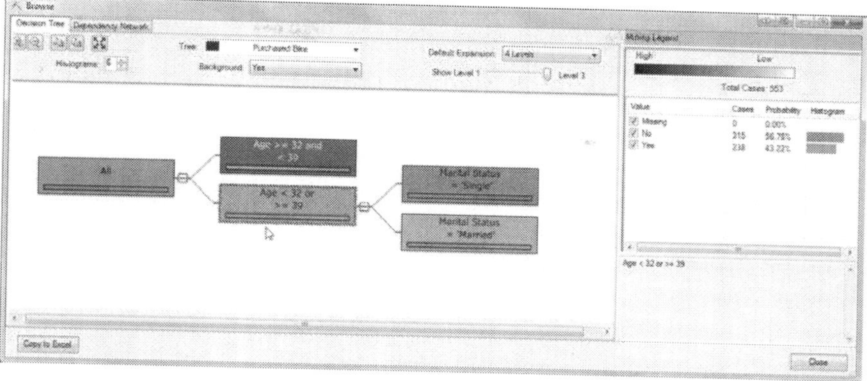

Figure 10-12b Tree with Background Set to Yes

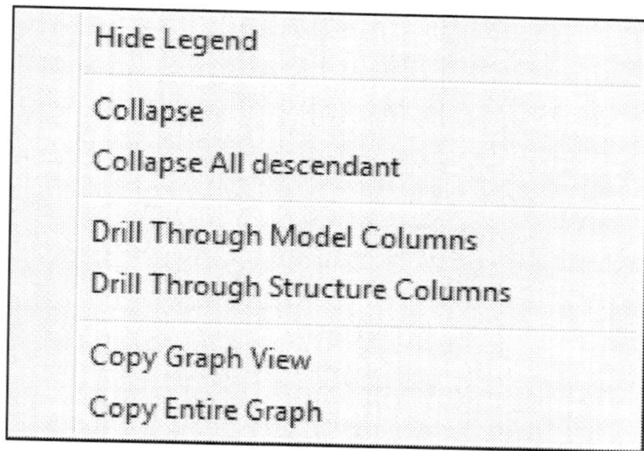

Figure 10-12c Classify Decision Tree Tab Right Click Menu

The Dependency Network tab (Figure 10-12d) displays the relationships in the model as a dependency network where the nodes represent attributes and the arrows (called arcs or edges) represent the relationship. Thicker arcs represent stronger relationships. The vertical links slider on the left side controls how many arcs are visible. If I move the slider down to the middle, the arc between Marital Status and Purchased Bike disappears indicating that it is a weaker predictor than Age. You may click on a node to highlight its dependencies as in Figure 10-12e. When I clicked on Purchased Bike the notes and arcs are color coded as per the legend at the bottom of the chart. The Dependency Network diagram is particularly helpful for exploring complex networks.

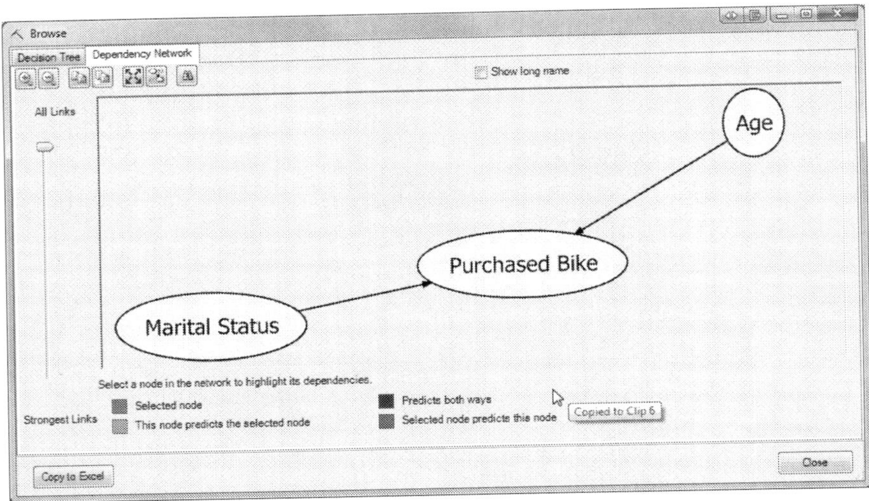

Figure 10-12d Classify Dependency Network View

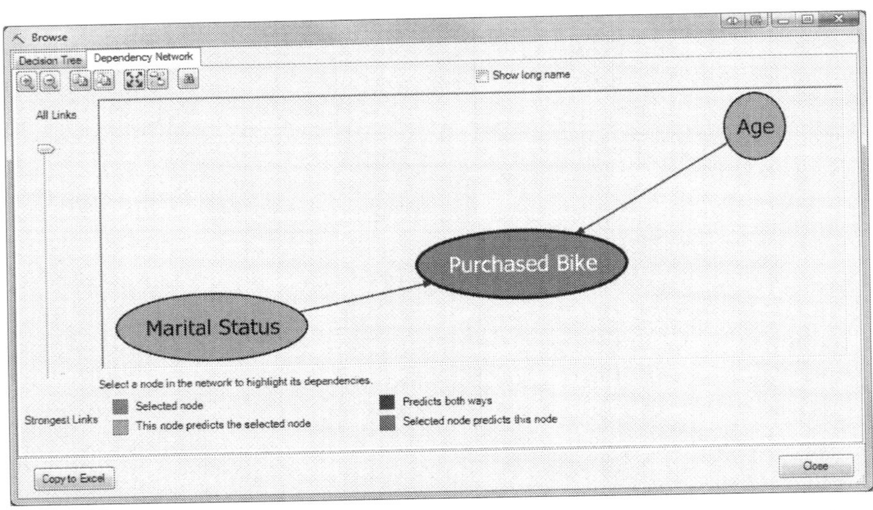

Figure 10-12e Classify Dependency Network View with Highlighted Dependencies

Figure 10-12f shows the Decision Tree when the Complexity Penalty parameter is set to 0.1 meaning that the algorithm will create more splits. In this case there are seven attributes in the tree—Age, Commute Distance, Children, Education, Cars, Income, and Occupation—that appear in multiple branches at different levels. Continuous attributes may be discretized differently in different branches.

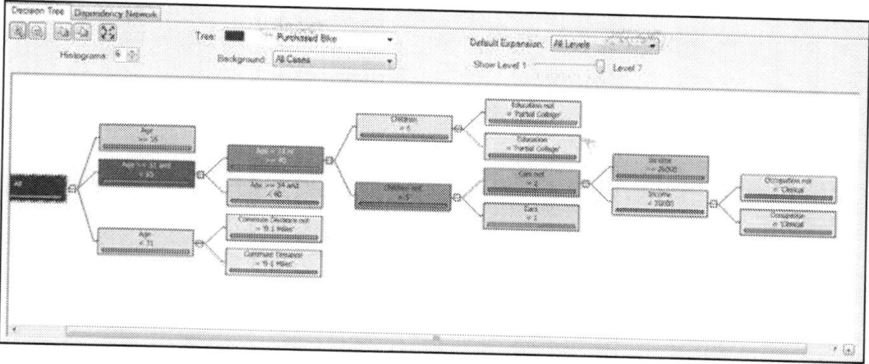

Figure 10-12f Complexity Penalty set at 0.1

Logistic Regression Algorithm

The results from the Logistic Regression algorithm are shown in a Neural Network Viewer as in Figure 10-13a which displays the relative impact of the value of an attribute on two values of the target via histograms. In the example the strongest relationship is that customers with 5 children, with a 10+ miles commute distance, or with 4 cars are not likely to purchase bicycles. You select the two states to view (the Favors columns) by using the Value 1 and Value 2 listboxes.

The Input panel at the top left is used to set specific values for attributes so that the Viewer shows the strength of the relationship of other attributes given the values of the specified attributes as in Figure 10-13b with the Children attribute set to 1 and Education set to Bachelors.

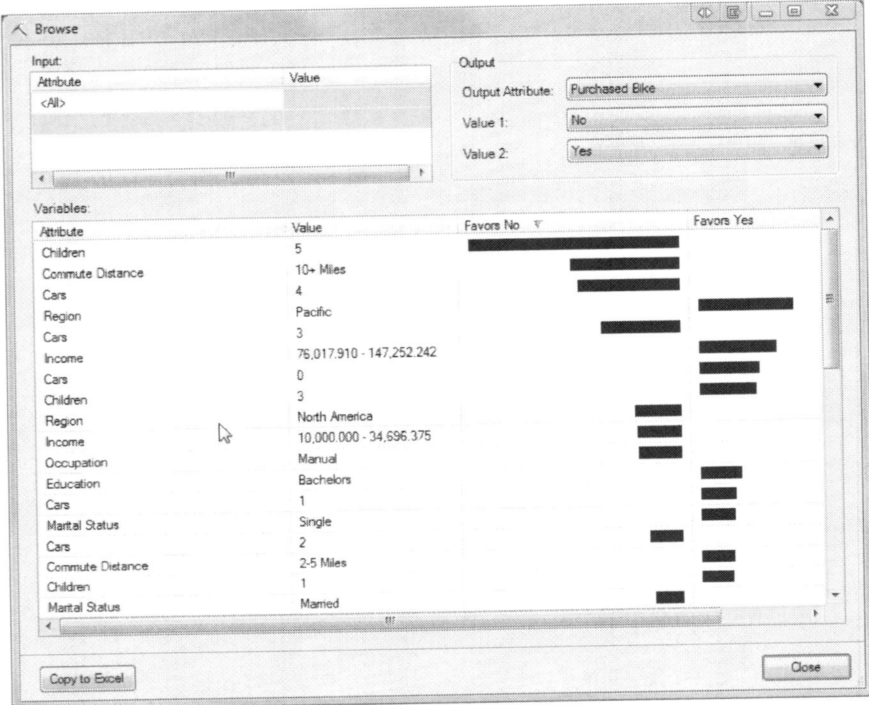

Figure 10-13a Neural Network Viewer for Logistic Regression

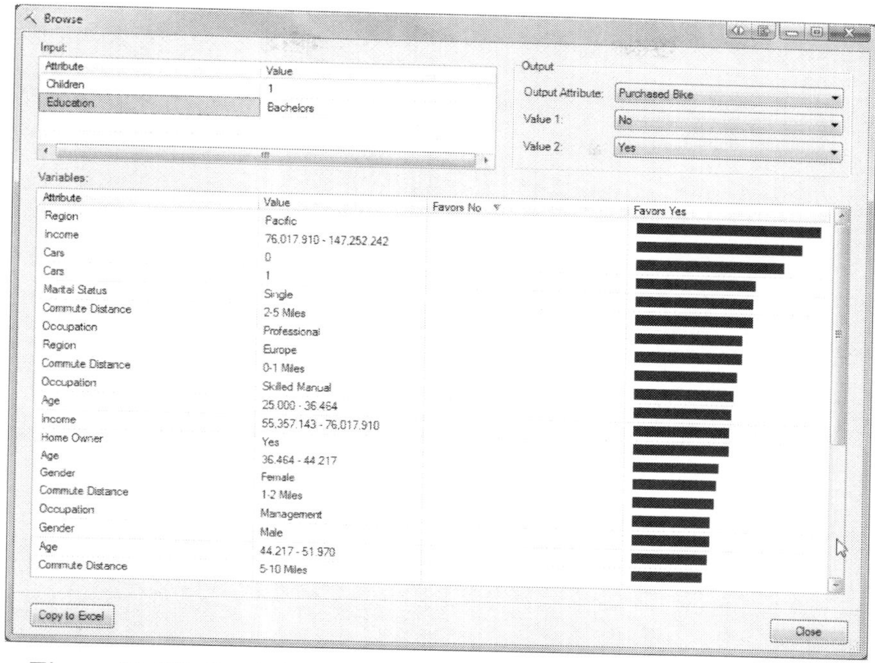

Figure 10-13b Logistic Regression Viewer with Constrained Attributes

Naive Bayes Algorithm

The Naive Bayes Viewer has four tabs: Dependency Network, Attribute Profiles, Attribute Characteristics, and Attribute Dimensions. The Dependency Network tab in Figure 10-14a is identical to the one for the Decision Tree algorithm in Figure 10-12d except that Cars is identified as a significant attribute instead of Age. Note that I had to set the Minimum Dependency Probability parameter to 0.005 because the model with the default value of 0.5 returned no associated attributes, i.e., the Dependency Network diagram for the 0.5 parameter contained only the Purchased Bike node.

The Attribute Profiles tab (Figure 10-14b) presents color coded histograms showing frequency counts for the values of the attributes. It shows, for example, that in the population of 700 cases married and single customers are approximately equally represented, that there are slightly more single customers who purchased a bicycle, and that considerably more married customers did not purchase a bicycle. You can rearrange the columns containing the histogram by dragging and dropping. Clicking on an attribute in the Attributes column or on a histogram will display a related vertical bar chart in the Mining Legend pane.

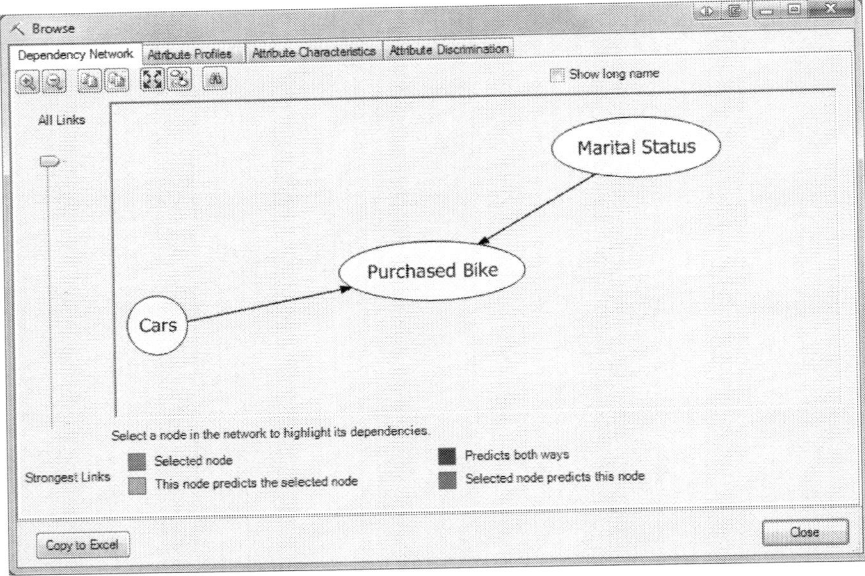

Figure 10-14a Naive Bayes Dependency Network

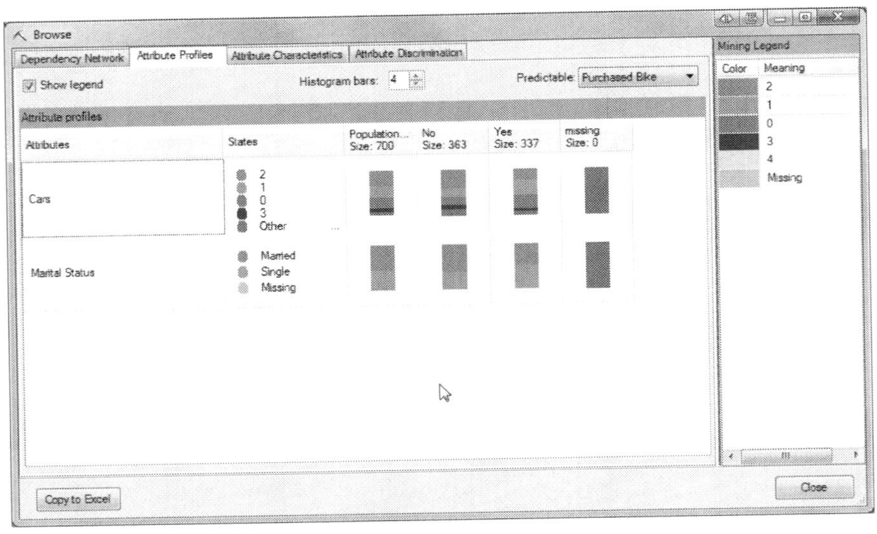

Figure 10-14b Naive Bayes Attribute Profiles

The Attribute Characteristics tab (Figure 10-14c) shows the relative frequency of cases (probability) related to a target attribute value for the input attributes selected by the algorithm. The Attribute Discrimination tab ((Figure 10-14d) compares how attribute values favor two of the target attribute values, set in the Value 1 (Yes to a bike purchase) and Value 2 (All other states) listboxes. The Mining Legend lists the case count for the row selected in the Discrimination pane.

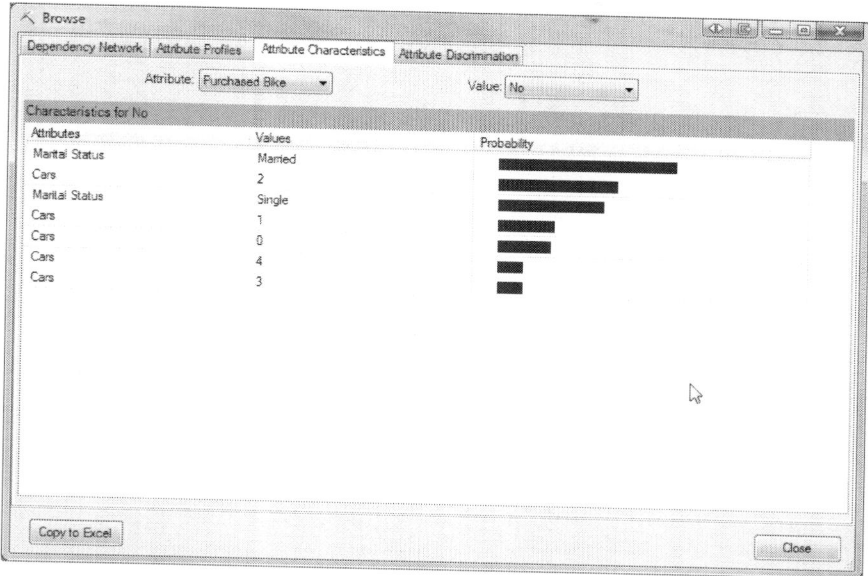

Figure 10-14c Naive Bayes Attribute Characteristics

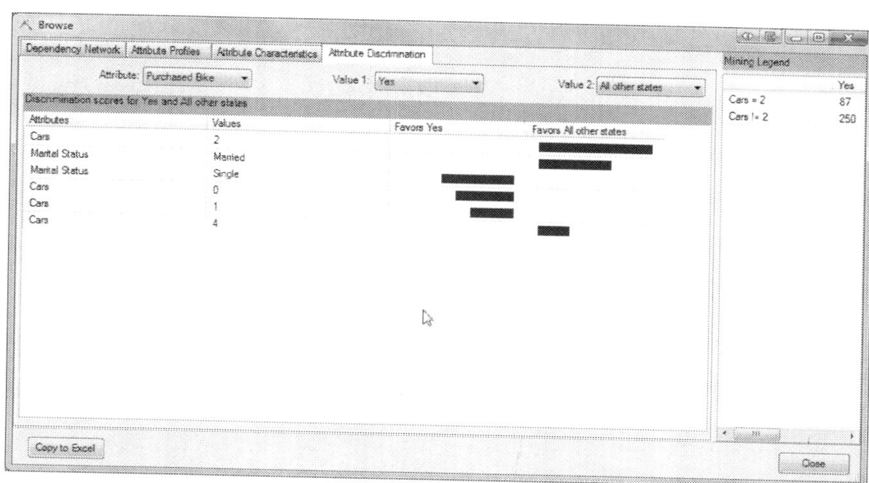

Figure 10-14d Naive Bayes Attribute Discrimination

Neural Network Algorithm

The Viewer for the Neural Network algorithm (Figure 10-15) is identical to that for Logistic Regression (Figure 10-13a), and the Input panel on the top left is used as described for Logistic Regression. Reminder: the Neural Network algorithm is the general case of the Logistic Regression algorithm in which there may be a hidden layer.

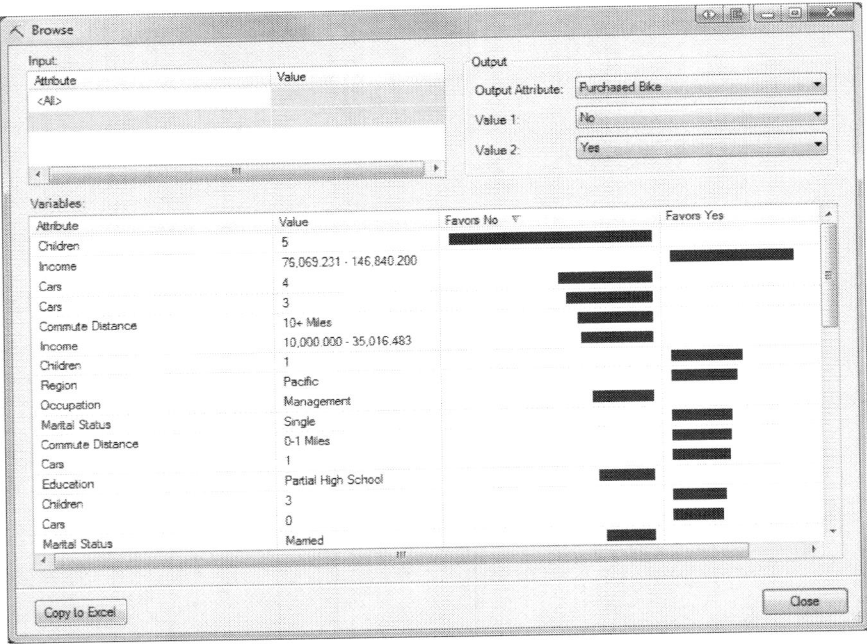

Figure 10-15 Neural Network Algorithm Viewer

Estimate

The Estimate tool creates models to predict values for a continuous dependent variable based on patterns of input attributes by applying one of four algorithms: Decision Trees, Linear Regression, Logistic Regression, and Neural Networks. The Column to analyze listbox in the Estimation dialog box (Figure 10-16) lists the fields with continuous values that are eligible as dependent variables, and you select the Input columns (independent variables) by using the check boxes. As before, you may select the algorithm to use by clicking the Parameters button. For illustration purposes I selected Income as the dependent variable in the examples below. I doubt that AdventureWorks would need to predict their customers' number of children as in Figure 10-16.

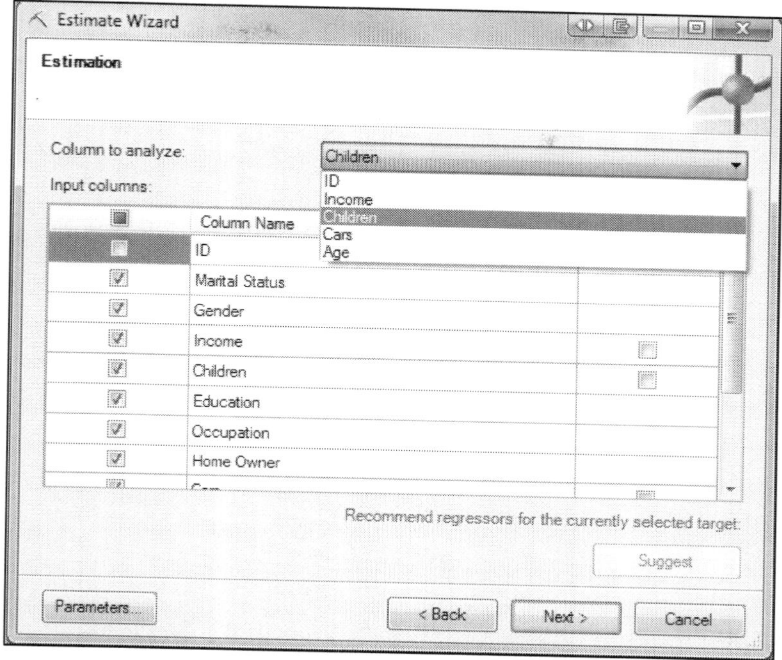

Figure 10-16 Estimation Dialog Box

Decision Trees

The Estimation dialog box for the Decision Tree algorithm (Figure 10-17a) has an additional column, Regressor, which is used to identify the independent variables for linear regression models within the decision tree and a Suggest button which recommends the regressors to use. For this example, I picked regressors manually. Only continuous valued attributes are eligible as regressors.

I selected all of the fields as Input columns except ID, Income, and Purchased Bike; Children, Cars, and Age as regressors; and proceeded using the default parameter values. However, that configuration produced a humongous decision tree (not shown) so for illustration purposes I set the Minimum Support parameter to 50 cases which produced the substantially pared decision tree in Figure 10-17b and the dependency network in Figure 10-17c where Occupation, Education, and Region appear as nodes and Age, Cars, and Children are used as independent variables in the linear regression models. Recall that you may click on a node to highlight its dependencies as in shown previously in Figure 10-12e. The Mining Legend panel in the Decision Tree tab again provides information about the selected node. In the example the All node is selected in Figure 10-17b showing the regression equation for that node as:

> Income = 57,088.113+2,228.455*(Children-1.961)+11,742*(Cars-1.446)

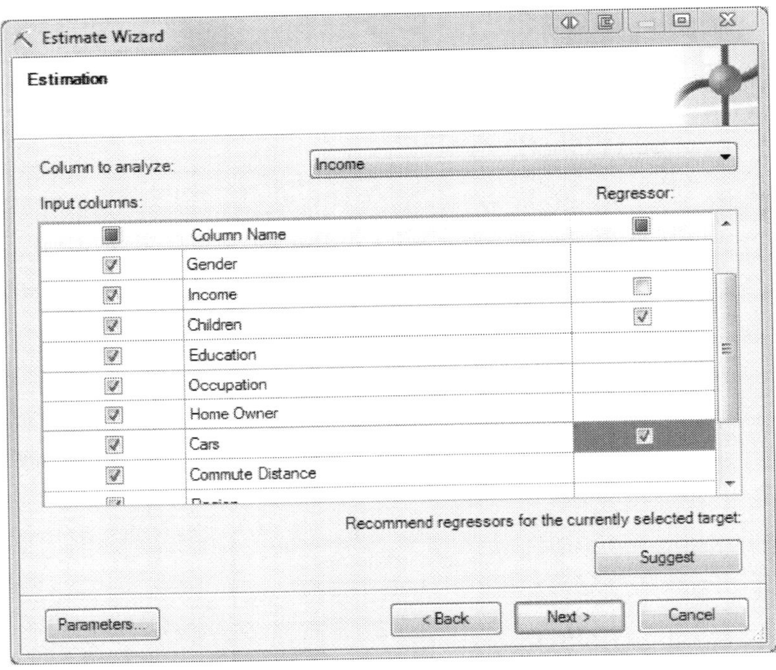

Figure 10-17a Estimation Dialog Box for Decision Trees

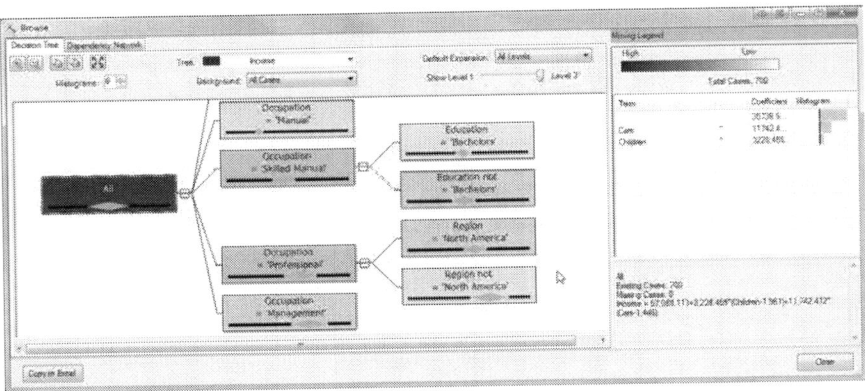

Figure 10-17b Decision Tree Tab

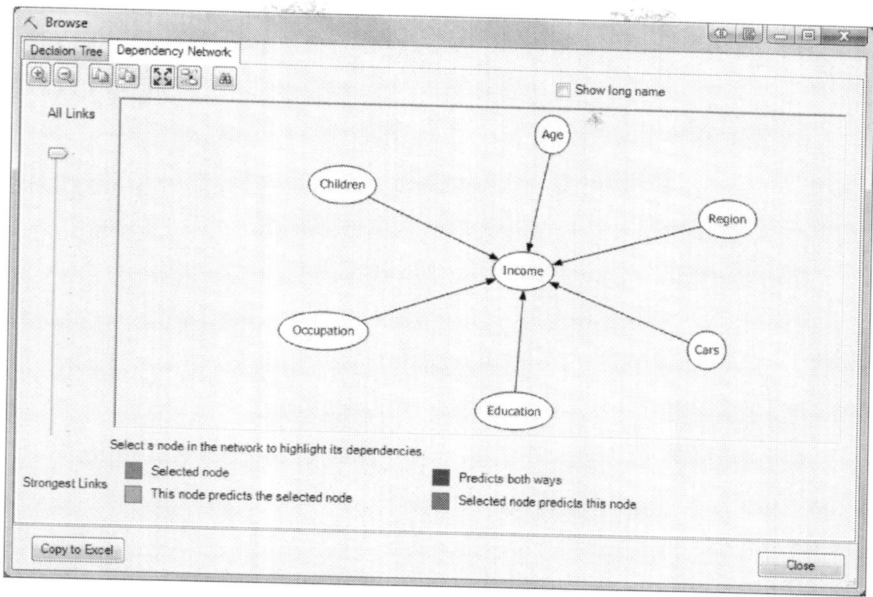

Figure 10-17c Dependency Network Tab

Linear Regression

As you know from Chapter 8 the basic linear regression model deals with continuous dependent and independent variables. Consequently, only the continuous valued fields (Input columns) are enabled in the Linear Regression version of the Estimation dialog box (not shown) which prevents you from selecting categorical fields even though they remain visible. Figure 10-18 shows the Decision Tree tab for the Estimate tool using the Linear Regression algorithm for Income as the dependent variable and Age, Cars, and Children as independent variables. The decision tree for the Linear Regression algorithm has only one node for the regression model. For our example the model which is similar to the one for the All node for the Decision Tree algorithm above is:

> Income = 55,546.757+10,944.783*(Cars-1.436)+2,702.391*(Children-1.936)

Interestingly, although I selected Age as an independent variable it does not appear in the equation probably because it lacks statistical significance. To support that contention the Correlation tool in the Analysis Tool Pak (not shown) found only a 0.17 correlation (r) between income and Age. You can force the model to include Age as an independent variable by inserting Age into the Force Regressor parameter. If you do that, the resultant model becomes:

> Income = 54,695.662+11,207.342*(Cars-1.444)-15.072*(Age-44.286)+2,591.801*(Children-1.931)

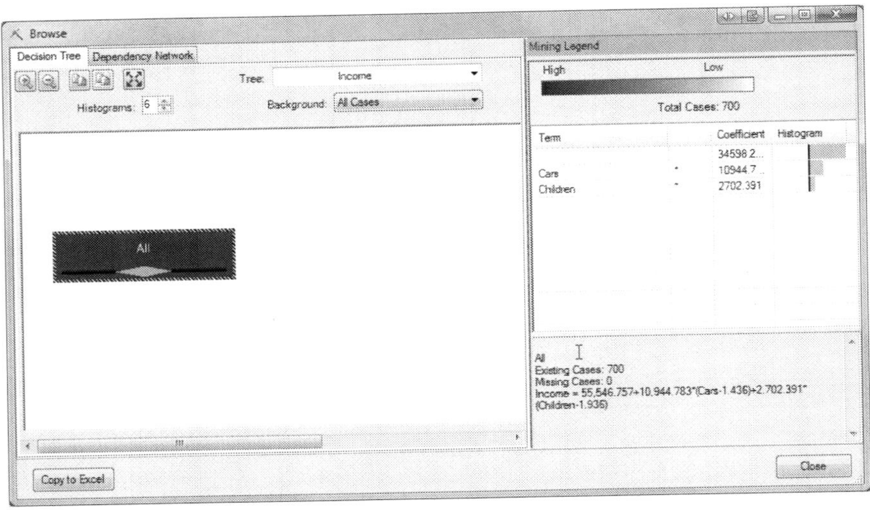

Figure 10-18 Linear Regression Decision Tree Tab

The Dependency Network tab in the Viewer for the Estimate Linear Regression algorithm (not shown) just displays the variables that appear in the regression equations.

Logistic Regression

Recall that every continuous valued attribute in Logistic Regression is discretized so as we've seen before the Logistic Regression Viewer displays the strength of the relationship between two values of the target variable with a value of an attribute category as in Figure 10-19. Of course, you may change the values to compare by using the Value 1 and Value 2 listboxes.

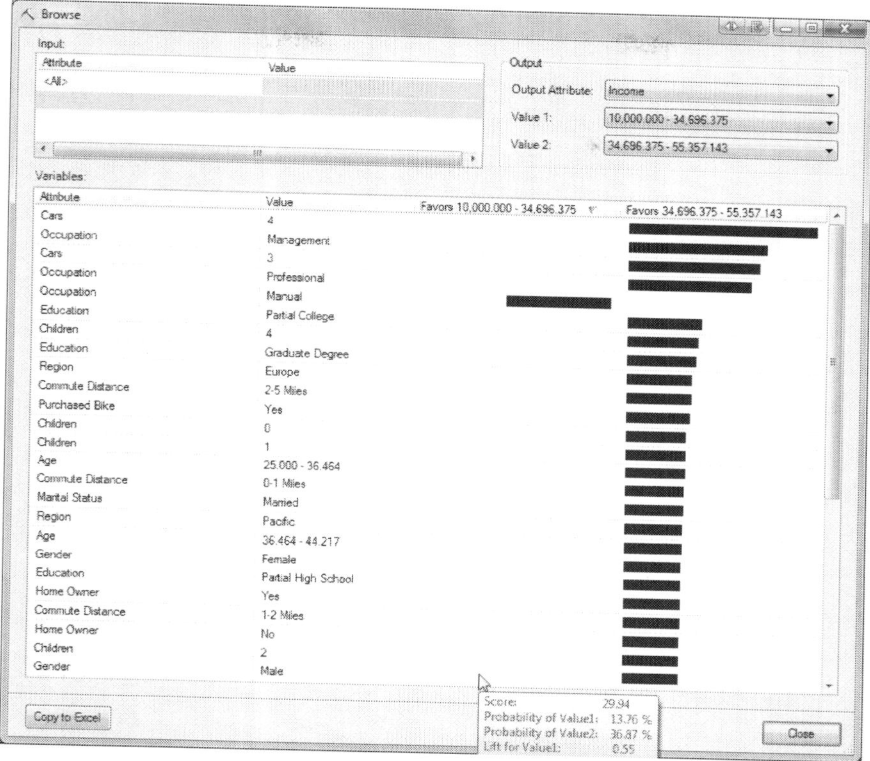

Figure 10-19 Logistic Regression Viewer

Neural Network

The Viewer for the final algorithm (Figure 10-20) that can be used in the Estimate tool, Neural Network, as we've seen before differs slightly from the one for Logistic Regression directly above probably because of the hidden layer.

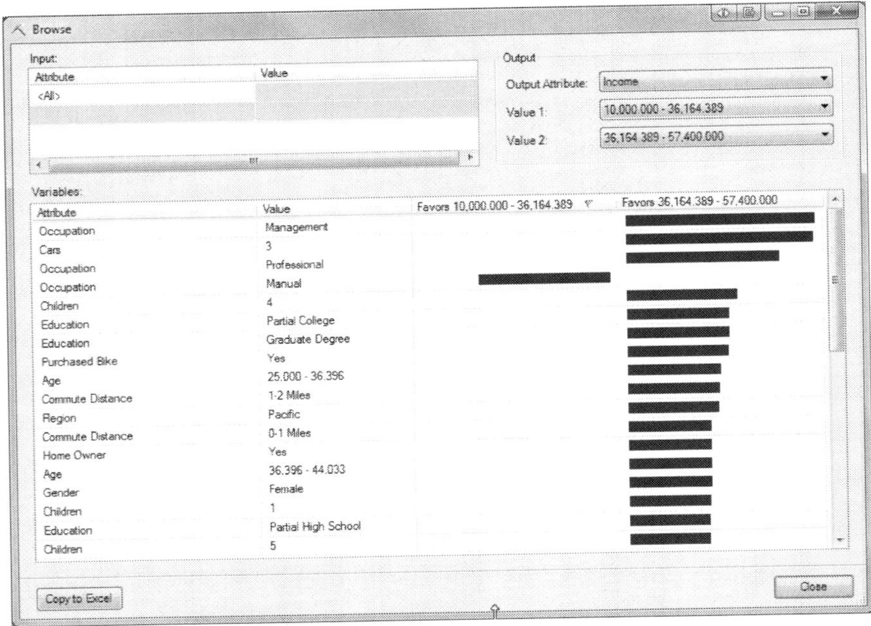

Figure 10-20 Neural Networks - Estimate

Cluster

The Cluster tool, of course, is an implementation of the Clustering algorithm which we've already used in the Detect Categories tool in Chapter 9. The attributes to analyze are selected in the Clustering dialog box (Figure 10-21a). As with the Detect Categories tool you can let the algorithm automatically detect the number of segments (clusters) or specify a target value. I used ten clusters in this example. The cluster tool does not have the option of appending a category column to the original Excel table as does the Detect Categories tool.

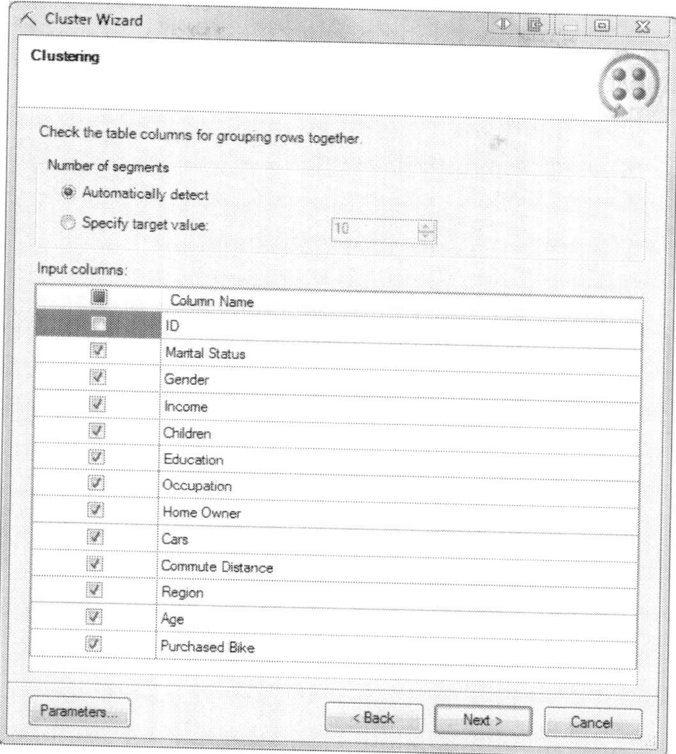

Figure 10-21a Clustering Dialog Box

The Cluster tool Viewer contains four tabs—Cluster Diagram, Custer Profiles, Cluster Characteristics, and Cluster Discrimination—that contain similar but more extensive information than that from the Detect Categories tool.

Cluster Diagram

The Cluster Diagram tab (Figure 10-21b) displays the ten clusters that the algorithm detected in the example data with the strength of the similarity of clusters represented by the thickness of the arcs (the lines connecting them), i.e., clusters with darker lines between them are more similar. The shading of a cluster denotes the distribution of the attribute selected in the Shading Variable listbox shown in the figure in the drop-down position. A darker shade represents more cases of that attribute in the cluster. Figure 10-21c shows a cluster diagram for Purchased Bike = Yes where Clusters 3, 4, 7, 8, and 10 contain more bicycle purchasers. You can click on a cluster to highlight the arcs between other clusters with which it is most similar. The slider on the left controls how many arcs are displayed. Moving it toward the bottom, Strongest Links, displays fewer links, toward the top, All Links, displays more.

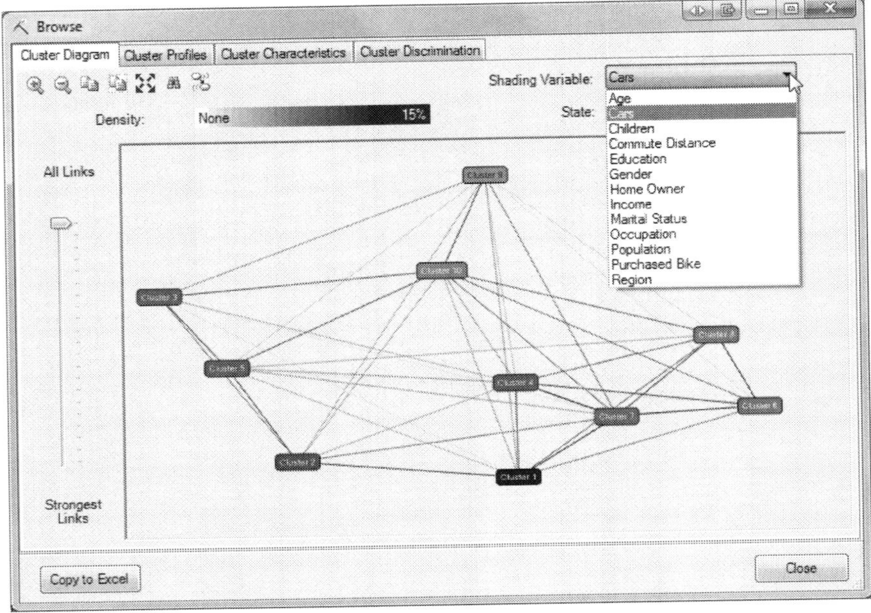

Figure 10-21b Cluster Diagram

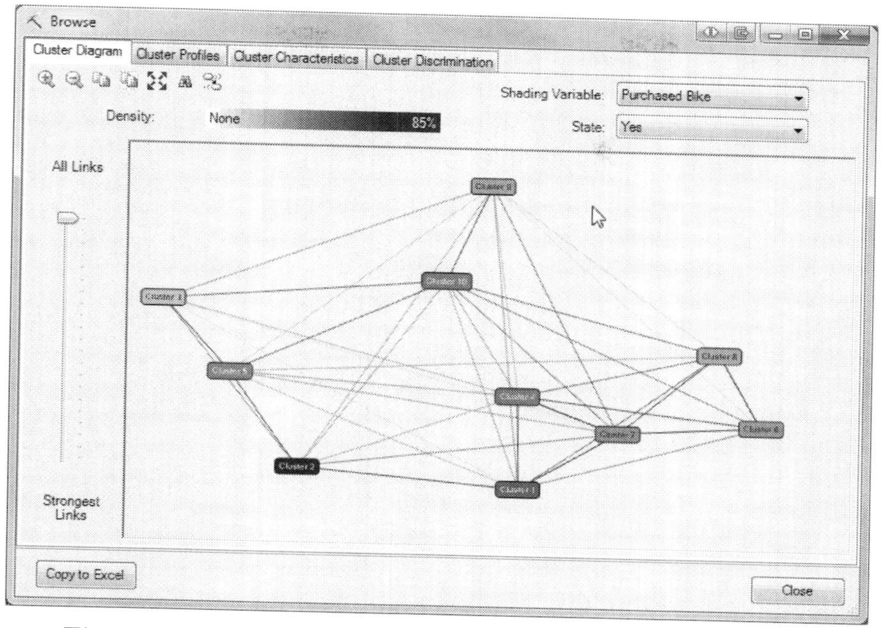

Figure 10-21b Cluster Diagram with Shading for Purchased Bike

Cluster Profiles

The Cluster Profiles tab (Figure 10-21c) shows how the attribute values are represented in each cluster. Continuous attributes, e.g., Age, are represented by a diamond chart where the location of the diamond designates its mean and the width of the diamond its standard deviation. Stacked vertical bars (histograms) show how the categories in categorical attributes are distributed in the cluster as in the Cars row in the figure. The Histogram bars listbox at the top controls the maximum number of attributes displayed in each histogram. Note that because of space limitations the figure displays only four of the ten clusters.

The Mining Legend contains one or two panes depending on the object selected. Selecting a variable or state displays only one pane that contains descriptive statistics for continuous variables and a histogram legend for categorical variables. Selecting a cell at the intersection of an attribute row and a cluster column displays two panes in the Legend with the top pane providing either descriptive statistics for continuous variables or a histogram for categorical variables. The bottom pane lists the characteristics for the cluster. In the figure the cell at the intersection of the Age attribute row and the Cluster 4 column is selected so the top panel in the Legend shows descriptive statistics for age in that cluster, e.g., the mean age in Cluster 4 is 43.55. The bottom pane lists all of the attribute values for the cluster, e.g., Education = Bachelors, Region = Pacific, etc.

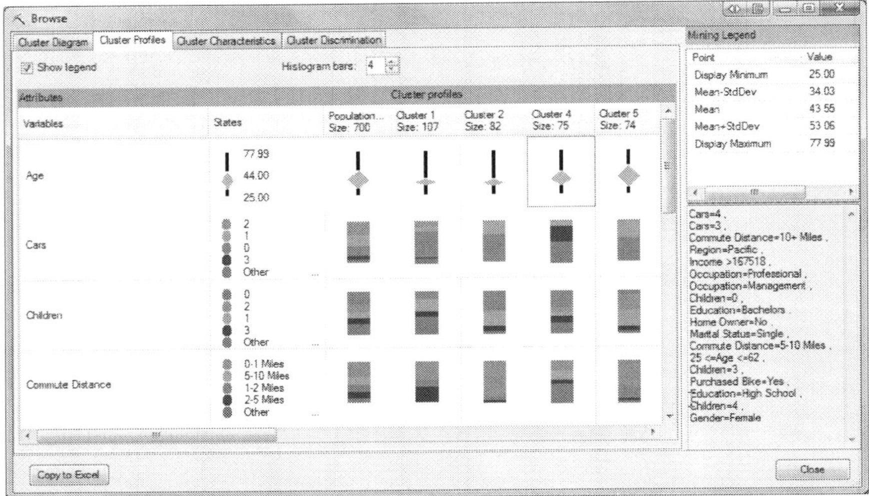

Figure 10-21c Cluster Profiles View

Hovering the cursor over a cluster column name displays a tip with the number of cases in the cluster, and hovering over a profile cell will display a tip that displays distribution statistics for the attribute values in the cell. You can change the sort order for the rows by clicking the Variables or Population column headings to switch back and forth between ascending and descending sorts. Clicking on a cluster column heading sorts the attributes in order of importance as distinguishing characteristics. For example, in Figure 10-21d when I clicked on the Cluster 2 column heading the rows were sorted in descending order showing the Commute Distance attribute at the top as most important followed by Age, Income, and so forth. When I clicked the heading again the view changed to that in Figure 10-21e listing the attributes in ascending order with Gender identified as the least significant attribute for the cluster.

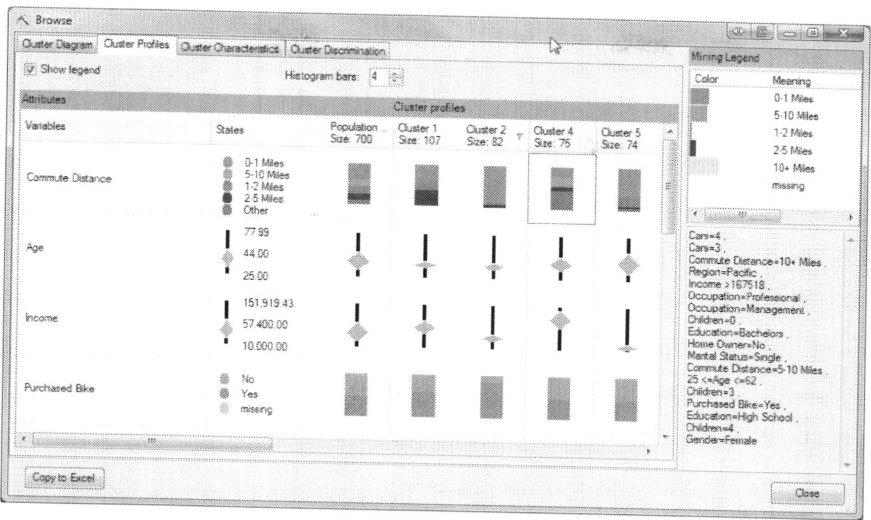

Figure 10-21d Cluster Profiles View Sorted on Cluster 8 in Descending Order

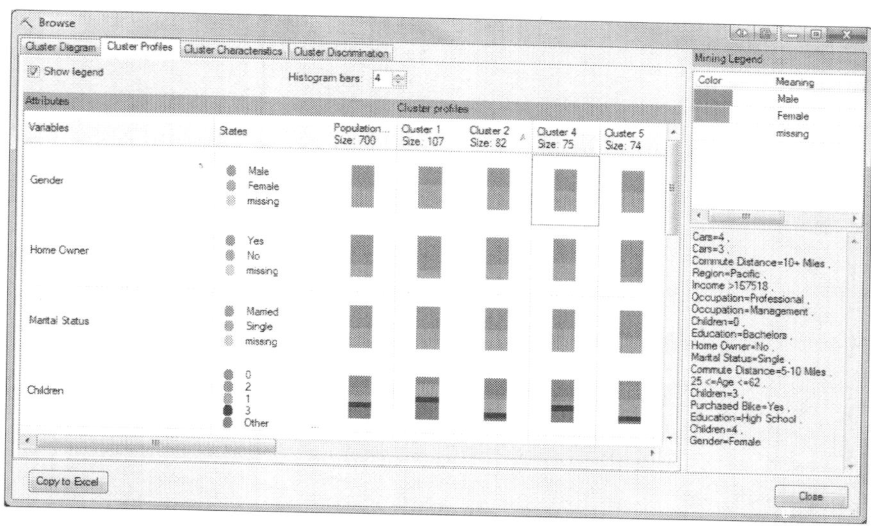

Figure 10-21e Cluster Profiles View Sorted on Cluster 8 in Ascending Order

You may rename a cluster by right clicking on the cluster's column heading which will display a menu that includes a Rename cluster option.

Cluster Characteristics

The cluster Characteristics tab (Figure 10-22) lists all attribute values for a specific cluster in descending order. The Probability column displays the percentage composition that the attribute value has in the attribute for the cluster. For example, the tool tip hanging below the Purchased Bike probability bar in the figure shows that 84.722% of the cases did so.

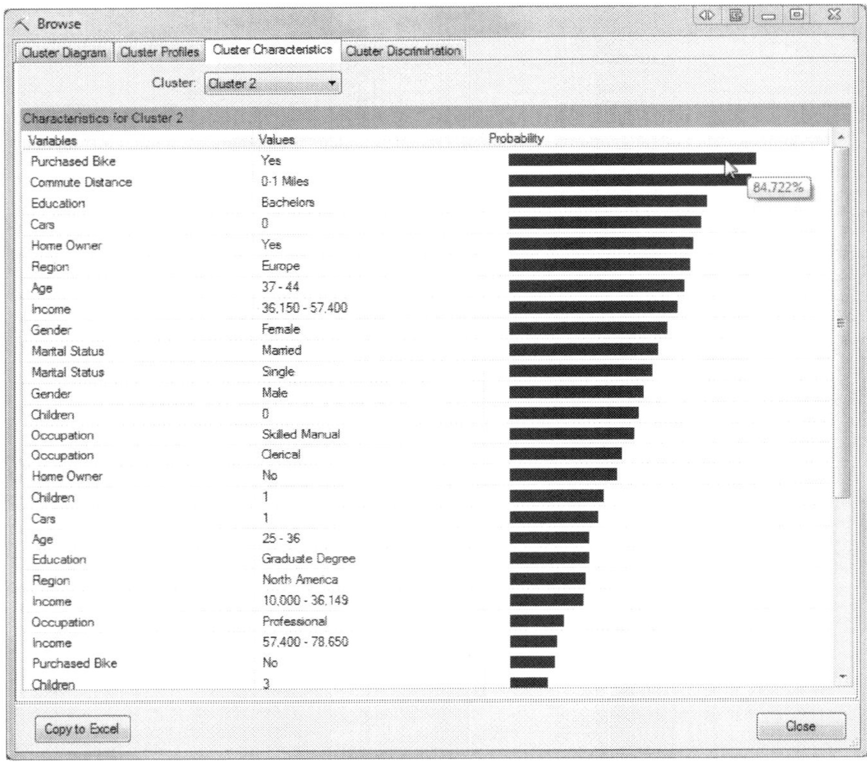

Figure 10-22 Cluster Characteristics View

Cluster Discrimination

In the Cluster Discrimination view you can compare the composition of one cluster with another cluster or the complement of itself which is all records not in the cluster. Figure 10-23a compares Cluster 2 with Cluster 3 and Figure 10-23b compares Cluster 8 with its complement.

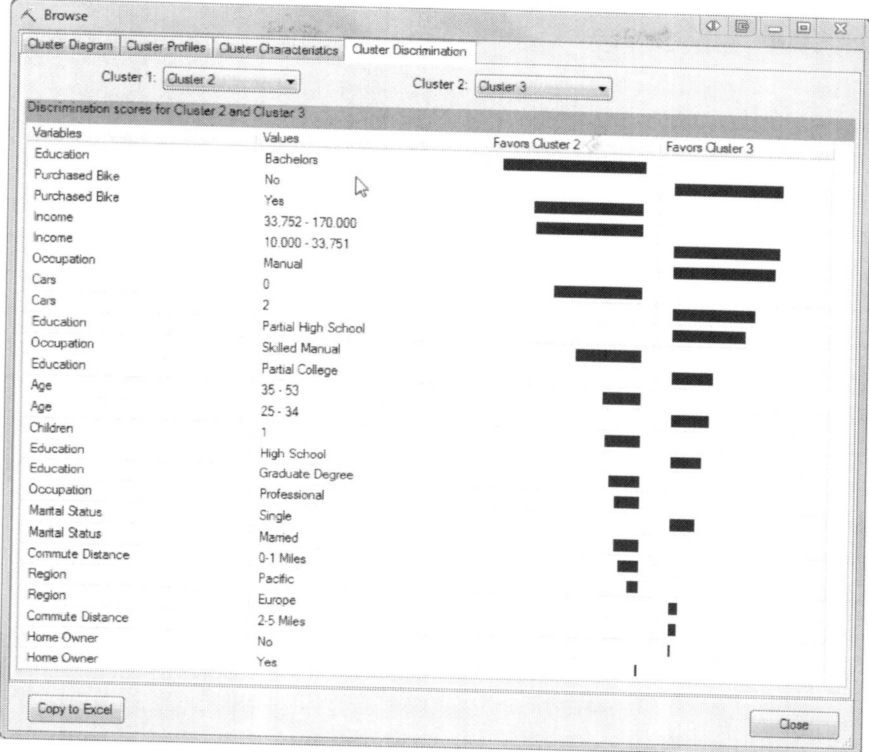

Figure 10-23a Cluster Discrimination - Cluster 8 with Cluster 9

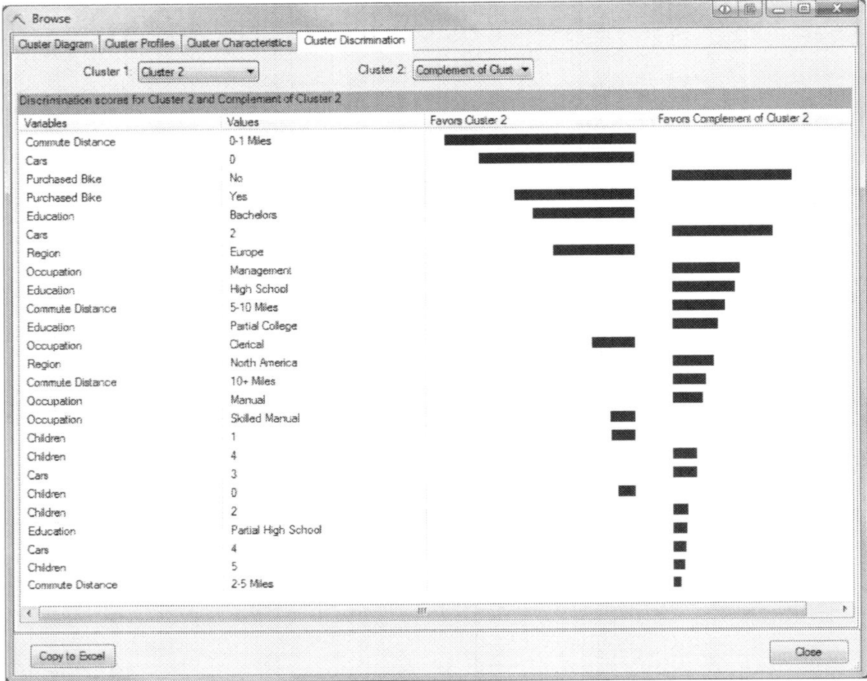

Figure 10-23b Cluster Discrimination - Cluster 8 with its Complement

One use of clustering is market segmentation. Market segmentation divides a market into customer groups with similar characteristics so as to tailor marketing to specific groups or to develop pricing strategies among others. The clusters identified could provide valuable information to AdventureWorks management to devise marketing and operational strategies.

Associate

We've already seen an example of the Associate tool in the Shopping Basket Analysis example in Chapter 9 so you know that it identifies items that occur together as in a shopping basket. A s we did in the Chapter 9 we'll use the data in the Associate worksheet from the Sample Data Excel file from the Data Mining Add-Ins for Office for our example.

You may recall from Chapter 9 that the Association algorithm requires that the data must be structured with a transaction identification field such as an order number and one or more item fields. A subset of the example data is shown again in Figure 10-24a for convenience. You select transaction and item fields in the Association dialog box as in Figure 10-24b. Our choices for the Item listbox (list not shown) as in Chapter 9 are Category for a more general association, Product for a more specific association, or Product Price. We'll leave Category, the default, as is. The Item Value optional field in the Shopping Basket Tool in Chapter 9 is not available in the Associate tool. As we shall see you can increase the values for the Minimum support and Minimum rule probability parameters in the Viewer above the minimums set in the dialog box but you cannot reduce the values in the Viewer below the minimums. So, set those values to the lowest values in which you may be interested.

	A	B	C	D
17	SO61277	Mountain Bikes	Mountain-500	539.99
18	SO61277	Jerseys	Short-Sleeve Classic Jersey	539.99
19	SO61277	Caps	Cycling Cap	8.99
20	SO61278	Road Bikes	Road-350-W	2443.35
21	SO61278	Bottles and Cages	Road Bottle Cage	8.99
22	SO61278	Bottles and Cages	Water Bottle	4.99
23	SO61278	Jerseys	Short-Sleeve Classic Jersey	539.99
24	SO61279	Mountain Bikes	Mountain-200	2319.99
25	SO61279	Fenders	Fender Set - Mountain	21.98
26	SO61280	Helmets	Sport-100	53.99

Figure 10-24a Transactions Table

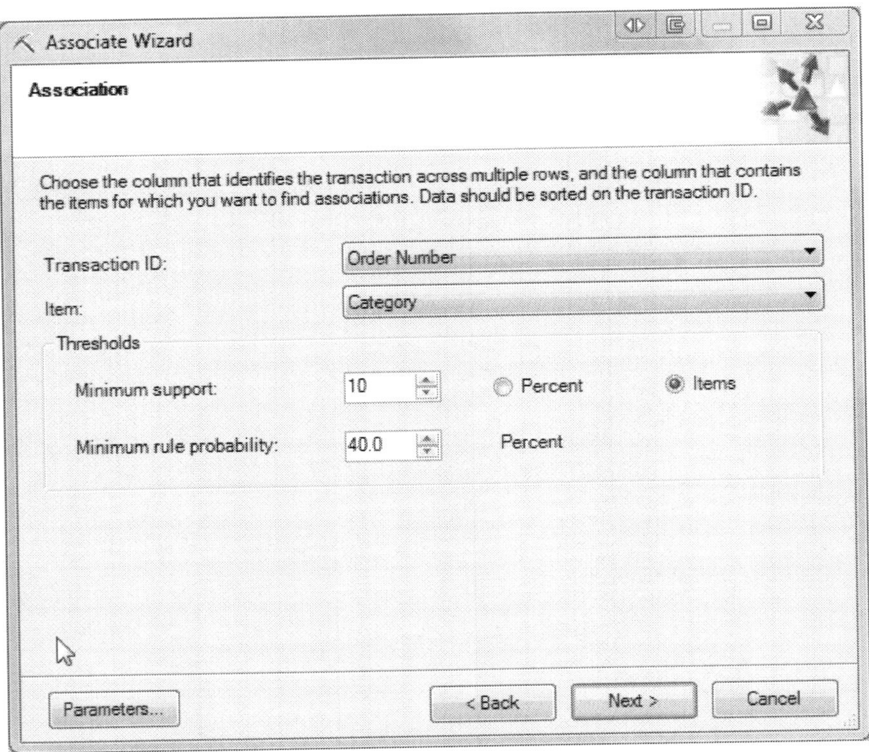

Figure 10-24b Association Dialog Box

Itemsets View

The Associate tool Viewer in Figure 10-24c has three tabs: Rules, Itemsets, and Dependency Network. In the figure the Viewer is set to the Itemsets tab that lists itemsets in descending order of the frequency of occurrence (the Support column). The Size column reports the number of items in the Itemset. So in the figure the first itemset in the list, the product category Tires and Tubes, occurred by itself in 4,019 out of the 32,265 rows in the dataset. Note that Tires and Tubes occurs by itself or with other categories in 8,787 rows (count not shown). The highlighted itemset, Helmets with Tires and Tubes, has, of course two items in it, and occurs 1129 times. You can sort the itemset table by clicking on the column headings.

In this view you can change the Minimum Support parameter, the Minimum itemset size, and the Maximum rows to display in the table. In Chapter 9 we described the Minimum Support parameter as "the number of transactions that contain a specific bundle of items that must occur in the data set before that bundle is included in the analysis. This may be specified as a percent of the number of transactions or a specific number of transactions. The default shown here is 10 transactions." If the Minimum itemset size of 2 was specified, then itemsets with two or more items will be displayed leaving out the single item itemsets which is probably what you want to do for market basket analysis. The number of itemsets displayed (rows in the table) is shown at the bottom above the Copy to Excel button.

If the Filter Itemset combo box is populated, you may select an itemset upon which to filter the table. If it is empty as in the example, then you can enter an itemset directly. In Figure 10-24d the itemsets are filtered by "Bikes" so only itemsets that include Bikes are listed. The Show listbox presents the options of Show attribute name and value, Show attribute value only, and Show attribute name only. The attribute value can take on the values of Missing or Existing. The Show long name checkbox just prefaces the item name with its location as in "Category_Table(Tires and Tubes) = Existing" for the long name for the first entry in the table.

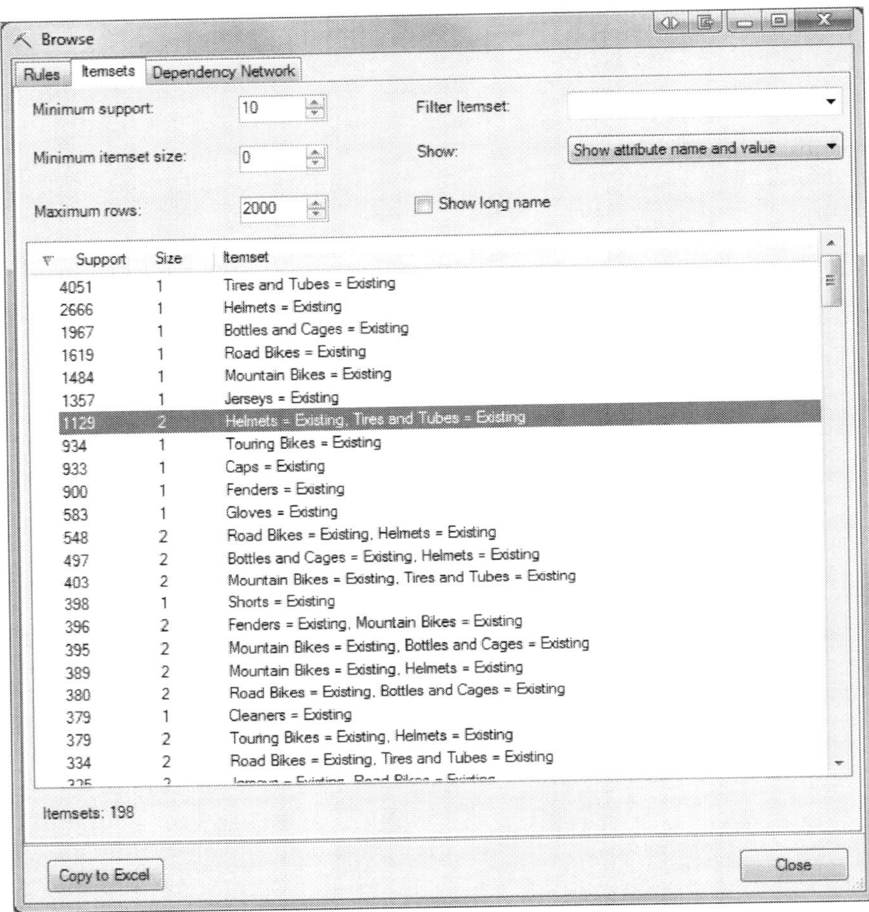

Figure 10-24c Associate Itemsets View

(For better viewing of this image, go to http://www.zerobits.info/bibook/bibookimages/)

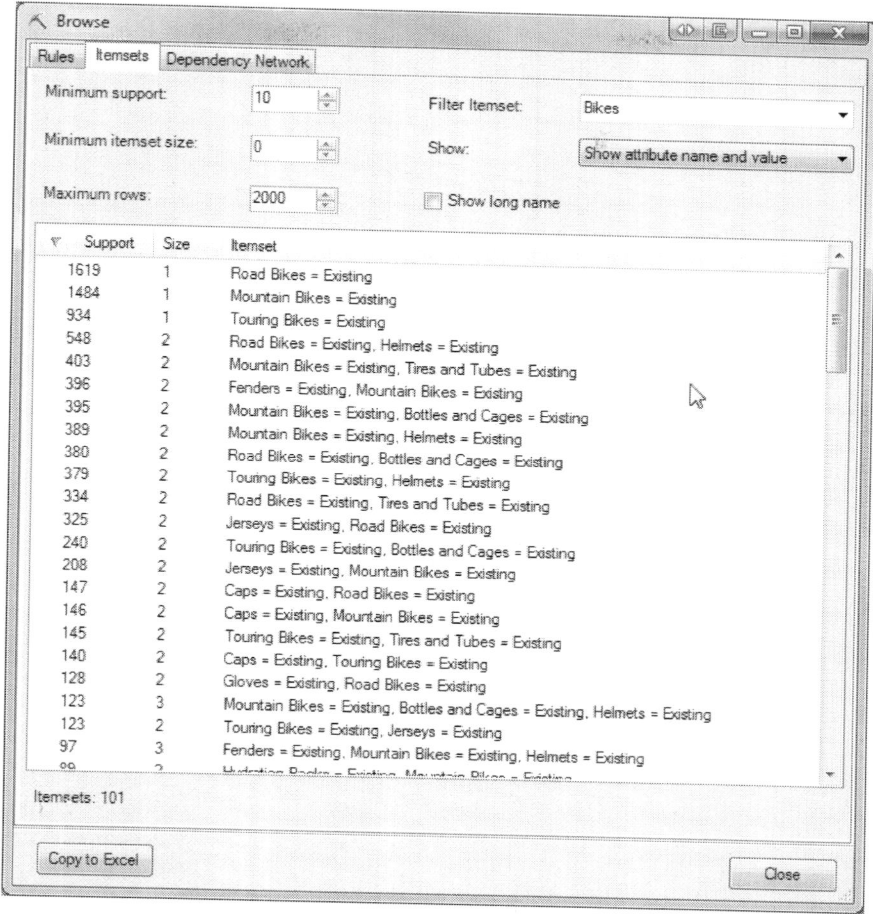

Figure 10-24d Itemsets View Filtered by Bikes

(For better viewing of this image, go to http://www.zerobits.info/bibook/bibookimages/)

Rules View

An association rule is a statement about what item(s) accompanies items occurring together, e.g., hot dog buns occurring with hot dogs. A rule is denoted with a -> symbol as in the rule highlighted in Figure 10-24e:

Socks = Existing, Mountain Bikes = Existing -> Fenders = Existing

where Socks and Mountain Bikes (A) occurring together predicts Fenders (B) occurring in the same itemset or symbolically A -> B The likelihood of this occurring is a conditional probability of the form P(B|A), the probability of B given A, or for the example the probability of Fenders (B) occurring with Socks and Mountain Bikes together (A). The probability can be computed as:

$$P(B|A) = \frac{P(A, B)}{P(A)}$$

which says that the conditional probability is equal to the joint probability of A and B divided by the probability of A. For the example, the conditional probability is equal to the probability of Socks, Mountain Bikes, and Fenders occurring together divided by the probability of Socks and Mountain Bikes occurring. In the dataset the itemset Socks and Mountain Bikes (A) occurs 31 times and the itemset Socks, Mountain Bikes, and Fenders occurs 20 times. Thus, the Rule Probability (conditional probability) is 20 divided by 31 or 0.645 which is the probability displayed in the Rules Viewer below. You can change the Minimum (Rule) probability parameter in the Itemset view as shown. If I changed it to 0.70, then only two itemsets would be listed in the table.

In a rule IF A THEN B the importance score is somewhat like a correlation coefficient in that a positive value means that the likelihood of B rises when A occurs, and a negative value means that the likelihood of B falls when A occurs. An importance score of zero indicates that there is no association between A and B. So, meaningful rules are those with higher probabilities and higher importance scores. Probability measures the likelihood of the event occurring and the importance score the usefulness of the rule. For example, if an item is contained in most market baskets, its it will be relatively useless in the model.

Thus, the second rule in Figure 10-24e is not very useful even though it has a .781 probability of occurrence because it has a low importance score. You can adjust the Minimum probability and Minimum importance with the listboxes in the Viewer. And, you can sort the rules table by clicking on the column headings.

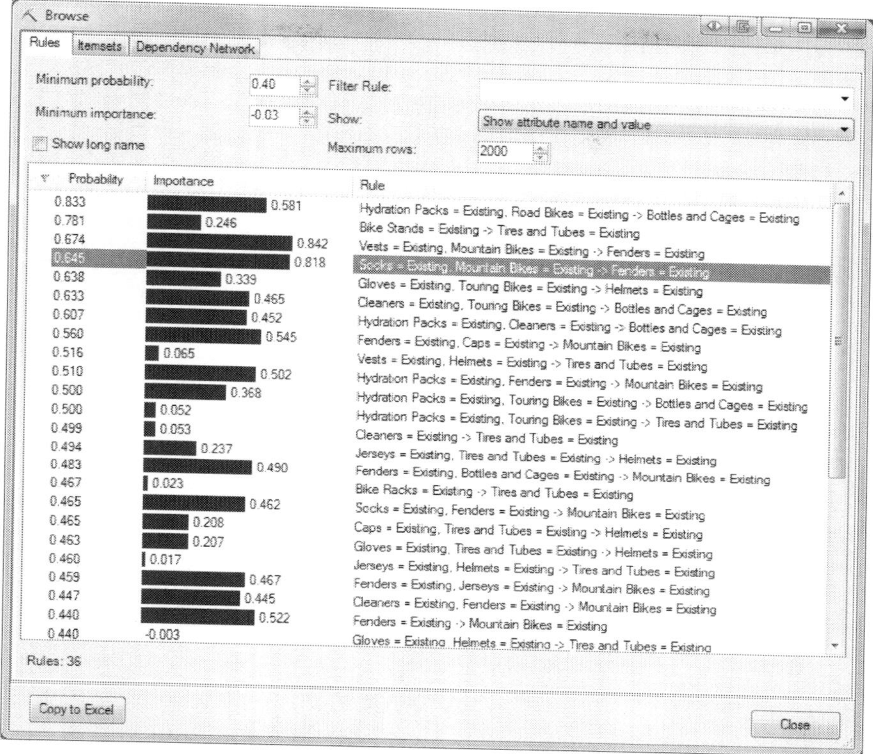

Figure 10-24e Associate Rules View

(For better viewing of this image, go to http://www.zerobits.info/bibook/bibookimages/)

Dependency Network View

We've seen a dependency network a few times earlier in the chapter. For the Associate tool it seems to display the itemsets for the individual items that occur most frequently. The arrows indicate the prediction direction. For example, Helmets, Bike Stands, Cleaners, and Bike Racks all predict Tires and Tubes. The slider on the left adjusts an importance score where moving the slider toward the bottom increases the importance score required to display an item in the diagram so fewer nodes will be shown.

Recall that you may click on a node to highlight its dependencies as in shown previously in Figure 10-12e, and you can rearrange the network by dragging nodes around the canvas. Hidden nodes can be added to the view by using the Find Node dialog box (Figure 10-24g) displayed by clicking the binocular icon at the top of the Dependency Network view. The dialog box on the left in

Figure 10-24g lists the nodes displayed in the original Dependency Network (Figure 10-24f) whereas the one on the right with the Show hidden nodes box checked lists all of the nodes available which in this case is the complete set of product categories in the data set. Double click on a hidden node to insert it into the Dependency Network diagram.

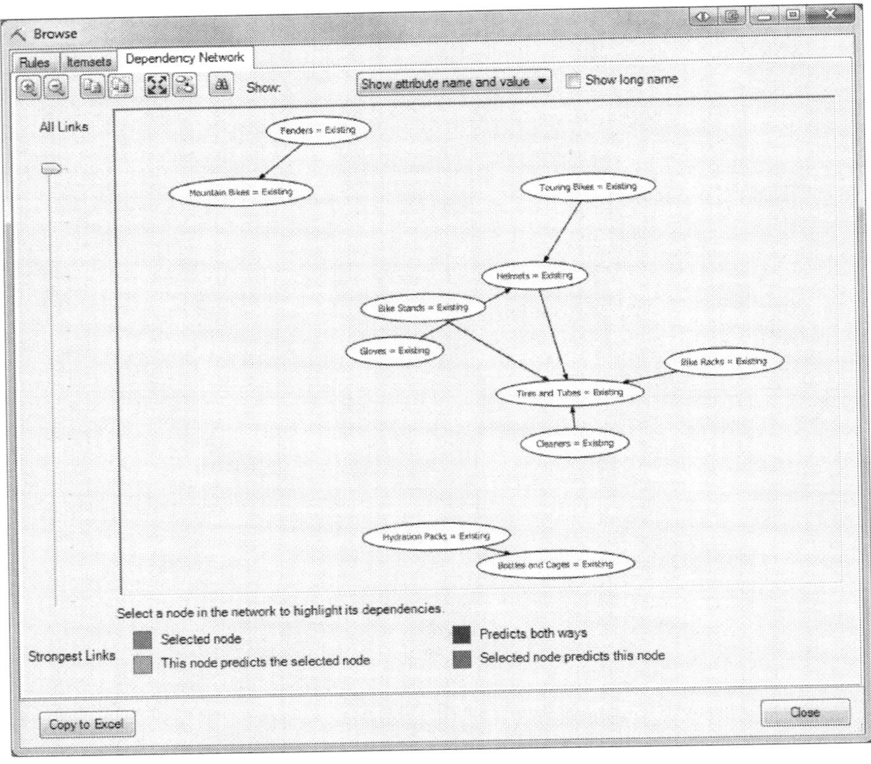

Figure 10-24f Associate Dependency Network View
(For better viewing of this image, go to http://www.zerobits.info/bibook/bibookimages/)

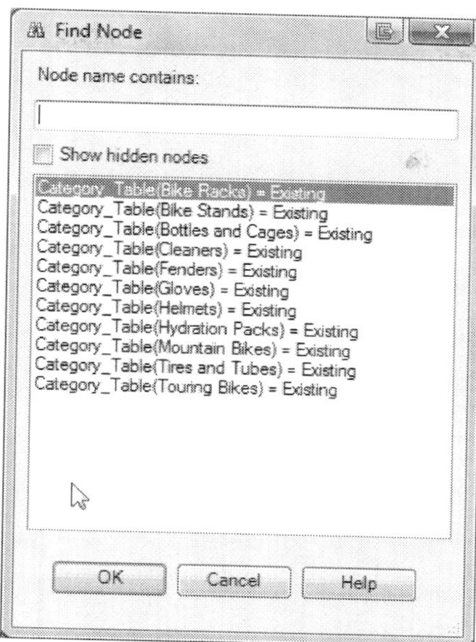

Without Hidden Nodes

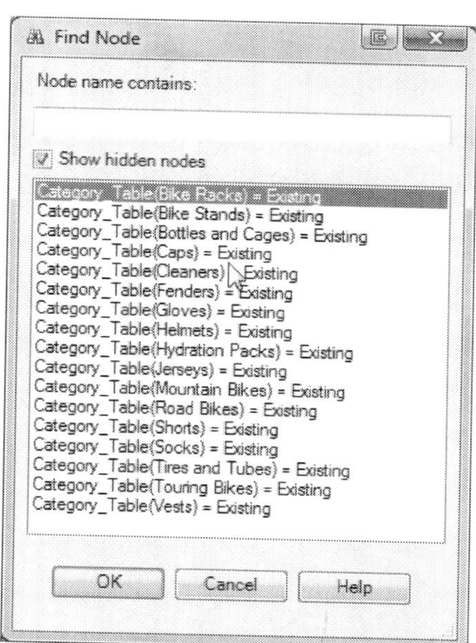

With Hidden Nodes

Figure 10-24g Dependency Network Find Node Dialog Box

Advanced

The Advanced tool in the Data Modeling command group allows you to create new data mining structures and to add new data mining models to existing structures. Clicking on the Advanced button will display a menu (not shown) listing these options. Using the Create Mining Structure option will start the Create Mining Structure Wizard that will display the dialog boxes such as Select Source Data with which we are familiar to create the new structure.

Selecting the Add Model to Structure option displays the Select Structure or Model dialog box in the Add Model to Structure Wizard as in Figure 10-25a which is similar to the one in Figure 10-4a. For this example I changed the current connection to the AdventureWorks DW Analysis Services database by using the Connection command on the Data Mining tab so the dialog box lists the mining structures and models that were originally included in that sample database plus a new mining structure, Table Analysis Tools Sample Data, that I added. For illustration purposes let's create a new Naive Bayes model in the Table Analysis Tools Sample Data structure. Selecting it and clicking Next displays the Select Mining Algorithm dialog box (Figure 10-25b). After that, the next dialog box in the Wizard (Figure 10-25c) is used to select the columns for analysis and their purpose: input, Predict only, etc. In this case I set the Purchased Bike field to Predict only as usual. In the last dialog box (Figure 10-25d) you can rename the new model and edit its description as we have seen before. Clicking the Finish button will insert the new model into the AdventureWorks2008DW Analysis Services database as shown in the Browse dialog box in Figure 10-25e.

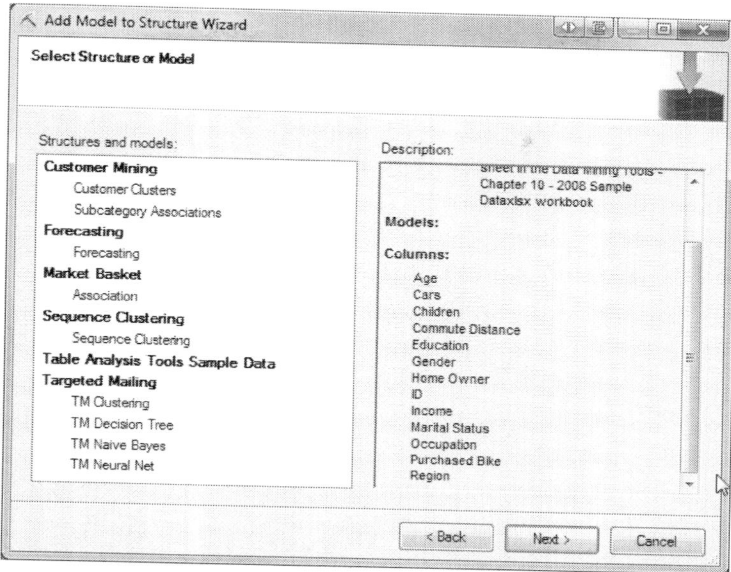

Figure 10-25a Select Structure or Model Dialog Box

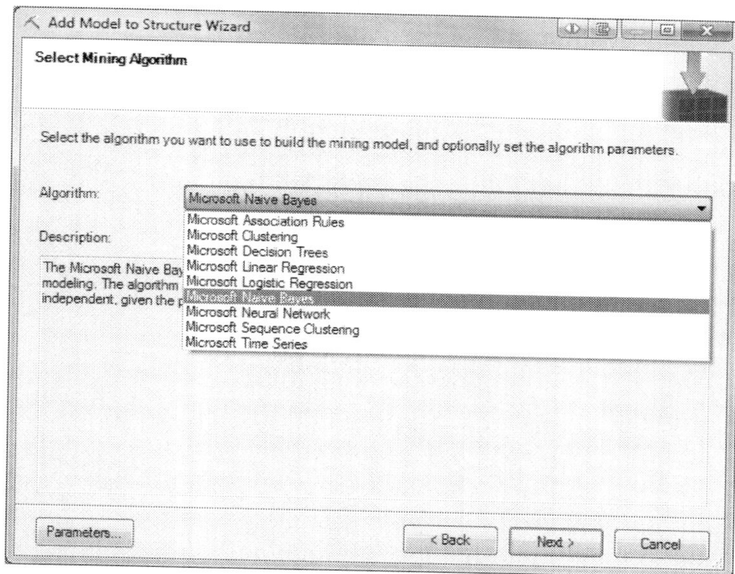

Figure 10-25b Select Mining Model Dialog Box

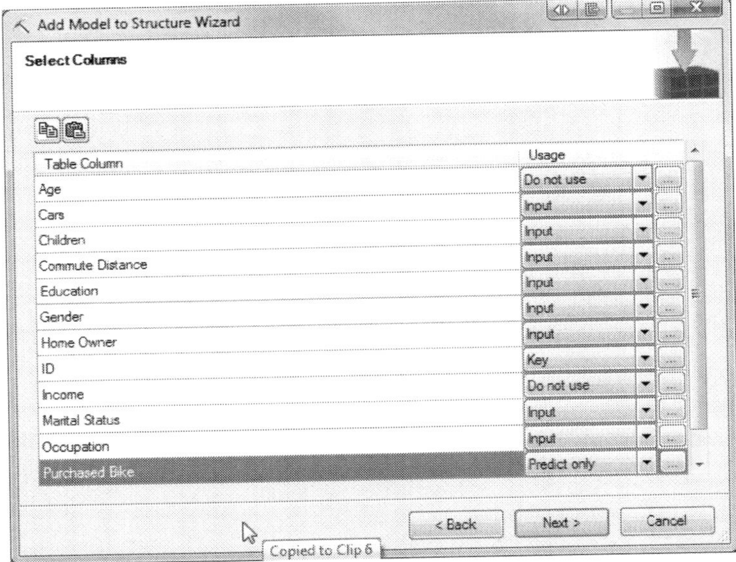

Figure 10-25c Select Columns Dialog Box

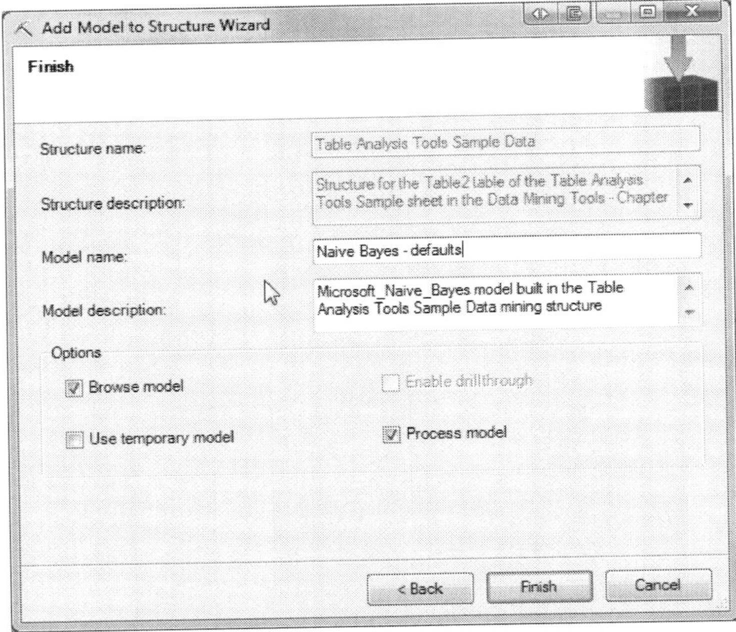

Figure 10-25d Finish Dialog Box

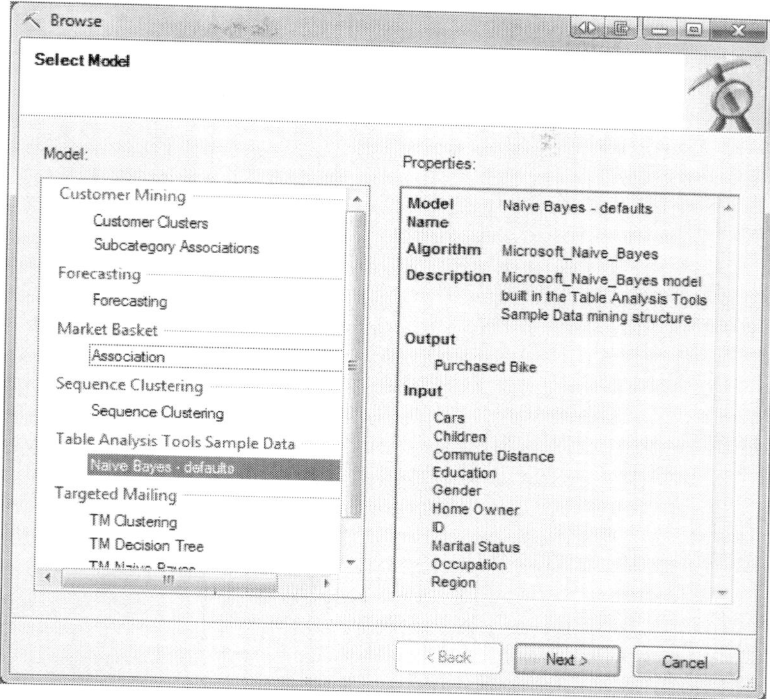

Figure 10-25e Browse Dialog Box

Sequence Clustering

The Sequence Clustering algorithm is not represented in the set of Data Modeling tool in the Data Analysis tab probably because the algorithm requires the sequence data to be stored in a nested table that cannot be easily created in Excel. This is an advanced topic that we'll address in Appendix F. In the mean time we'll use the sequence clustering mining structure in the AdventureWorks DW Analysis Services database to create a model.

In addition to clickstream analysis that we mentioned earlier another application for sequence clustering is customer purchase analysis for modeling how customers sequence items in an order. Figure 10-26a shows a segment of order sequence data from a AdventureWorks2008DWR2 database view where Line Number represents the sequence in which items (Model column) were added to the order (OrderNumber column).

	A	B	C
1	OrderNumber	LineNumbe	Model
2	SO51184	1	Mountain-200
3	SO51184	2	HL Mountain Tire
4	SO51184	3	Mountain Tire Tube
5	SO51184	4	Sport-100
6	SO51185	1	Touring-3000
7	SO51185	2	Touring Tire
8	SO51185	3	Touring Tire Tube
9	SO51192	1	Mountain-200
10	SO51192	2	Sport-100

Figure 10-26a Order Sequence Data

Using the Add Model to Structure option in the Advanced command I selected the Sequence Clustering mining structure (see Figure 10-25e) and the Sequence Clustering algorithm in the Select Mining algorithm dialog box (not shown). In the next dialog box (Figure 10-26b) you can see that the Line Number field is designated as a Key Sequence. In the Finish dialog box (not shown) I named the model "Order Sequence Example" which created the model described below. We could have used the Sequence Clustering model that already exists in the structure but I wanted to create a new one to make sure that it worked.

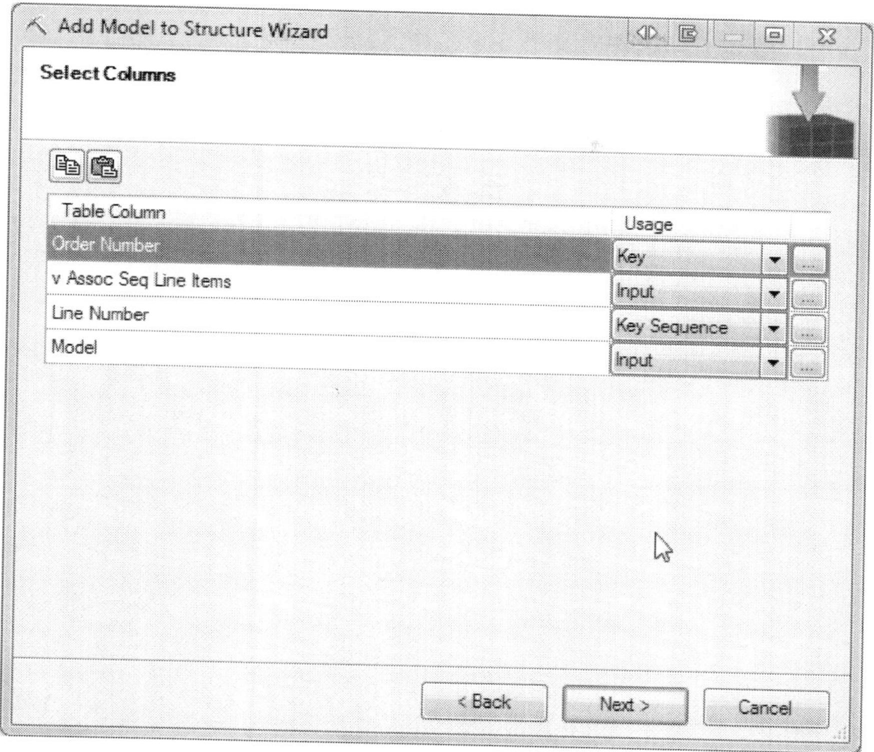

Figure 10-26b Select Columns Dialog Box for Sequence Data

Cluster Diagram

We've described cluster diagrams earlier in the description of the Cluster tool. The busy one in Figure 10-26c displays the fifteen clusters that the algorithm found in the AdventureWorks order sequence data. Clusters that are closer together have more similar characteristics. As before, the shading of the clusters represent the number of cases in the cluster for the Shading Variable selected in that listbox, Population in this case. You can display the cluster diagram for a particular item by selecting the field name in the Shading Variable listbox and then the item in the State listbox. In our case in Figure 10-26d the field name is Model (the model column in Figure 10-26a) with the State listbox superimposed on the cluster diagram for the Classic Vest. Clicking on a cluster will highlight arcs (edges) to related clusters. As usual you can hide or expose links by using the slider on the left.

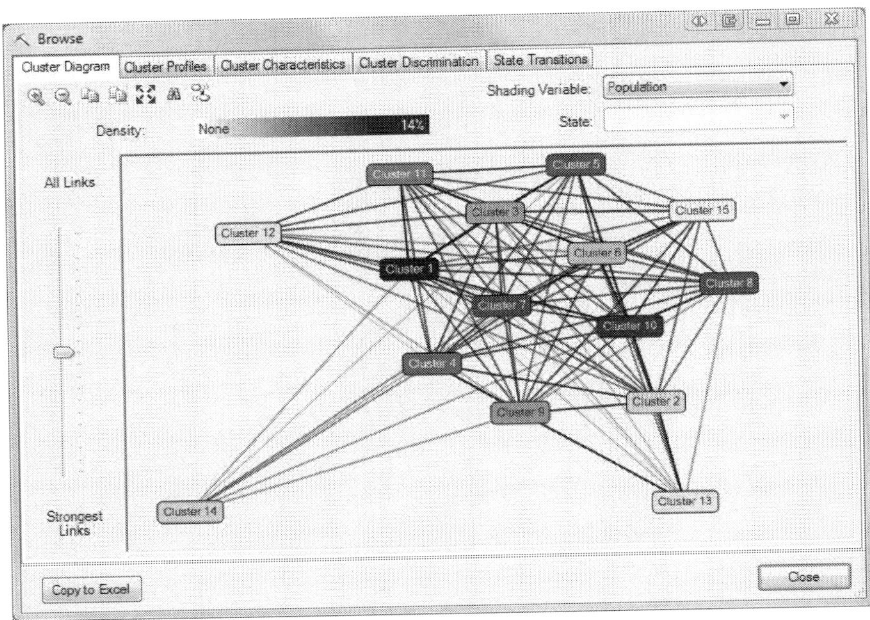

Figure 10-26c Sequence Clustering Cluster Diagram

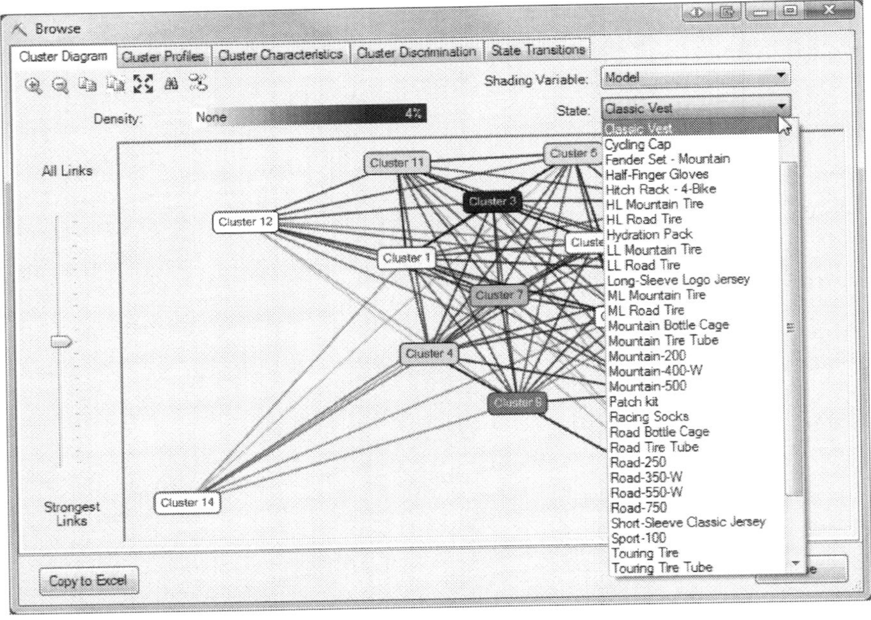

Figure 10-26d Sequence Clustering Cluster Diagram

Cluster Profiles

The Cluster Profiles tab displays the composition of the clusters in two rows. The top row, Attribute.samples, in our case Model.samples, row shows a sample of sequences that occur in each cluster as in Figure 10-26e. The bottom row , Attribute, in our case Model, row lists the items in the cluster and their distribution as in Figure 10-26f. Of course, the figures here only display a few of the clusters because of space limitations. The States column lists the more frequently occurring items. The Mining Legend pane presents a better view of the object selected in the table. For example, the Mining Legend in Figure 10-26e and enlarged on the left in Figure 10-26g lists item names along with the color coded sequences for Cluster 10. The first row there shows the sequence of LL Mountain Tire => Mountain Tire Tube => Patch Kit. You can scroll the list to see all of the sequences. Notice from the color coded bars or the list in the Mining Legend the greater frequency of occurrence of LL and ML Mountain tires being first in the list which indicates that customers in this cluster usually put those in their shopping carts first. Clicking on the frame in the States column will list the color codes for all of the items in the Mining Legend (not shown).

The stacked histogram in the Model row shows the more frequently occurring items in the cluster, and the Mining Legend lists the relative frequency distribution for all items in the cluster. For example, in Figure 10-26f the Sport-1 bicycle is at the top of the histogram for Cluster 10, and has a relative frequency (probability) of .0169 in the Mining Legend on the right side of Figure 1026g which is higher than any other item in the cluster. Note that as with the Cluster tool you may rename a cluster by right clicking on its column heading.

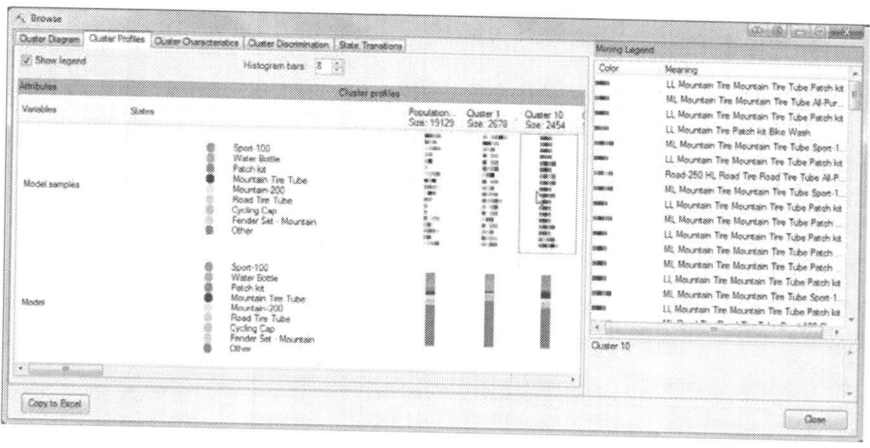

Figure 10-26e Cluster Profiles Samples View

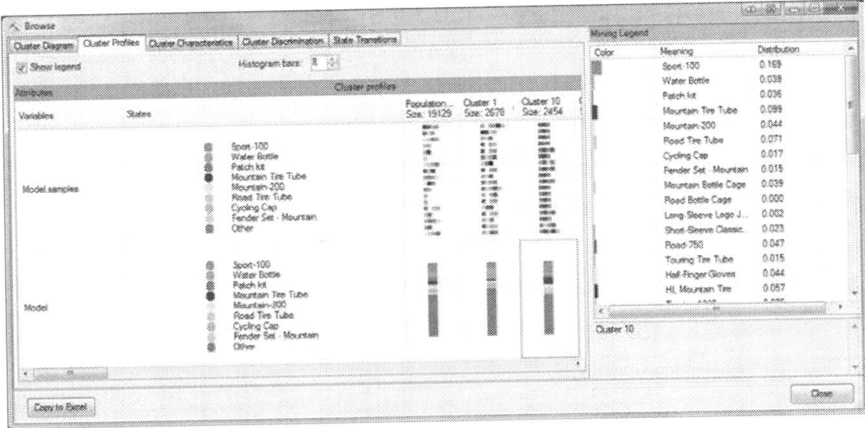

Figure 10-26f Cluster Profiles Attribute View

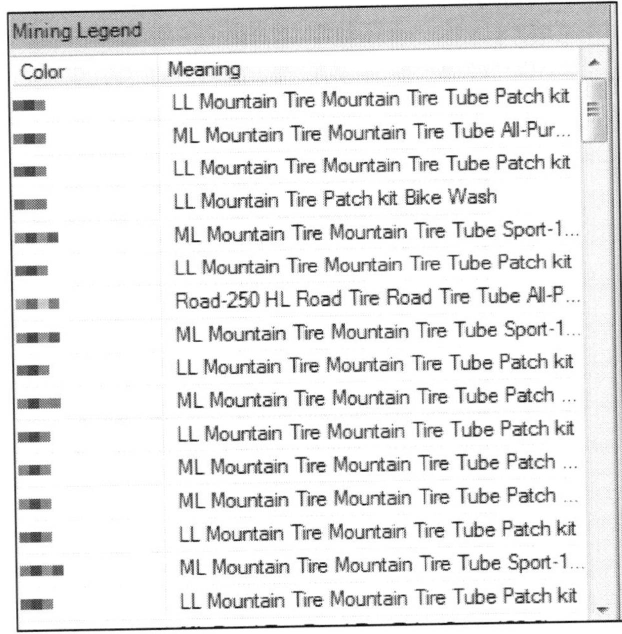

Model.samples Legend

Mining Legend

Color	Meaning	Distribution
	Sport-100	0.169
	Water Bottle	0.039
	Patch kit	0.036
	Mountain Tire Tube	0.099
	Mountain-200	0.044
	Road Tire Tube	0.071
	Cycling Cap	0.017
	Fender Set - Mountain	0.015
	Mountain Bottle Cage	0.039
	Road Bottle Cage	0.000
	Long-Sleeve Logo J...	0.002
	Short-Sleeve Classic...	0.023
	Road-750	0.047
	Touring Tire Tube	0.015
	Half-Finger Gloves	0.044
	HL Mountain Tire	0.057
	Touring-1000	0.025

Model Legend

Figure 10-26g Mining Legends

It's interesting and informative to compare clusters. For example, as we've seen Cluster 10 has many items in it and a number of sequences. However, Cluster 12 (not shown) contains only two items: Water Bottle with a relative frequency of 0.896 and Cycling Cap at 0.104, and the only sequence in the cluster is Cycling Cap => Water Bottle which occurs much less frequently than a single Water Bottle Order (Mining Legends not shown).

Cluster Characteristics

The Cluster Characteristics tab lists the items and sequences in descending order of occurrence in the cluster. For example, Figure 10-26h shows the Sport-100 as the most frequently occurring item in Cluster 10 as we knew from above. It also displays sequences, rows with Attribute.Transitions Variable column values, including Start and End events which equate to the first and last items placed in the shopping cart. The second row, [Start] -> Road-750 says that customers in this cluster have a higher probability of starting an order with the Road-750 bicycle. And so on.

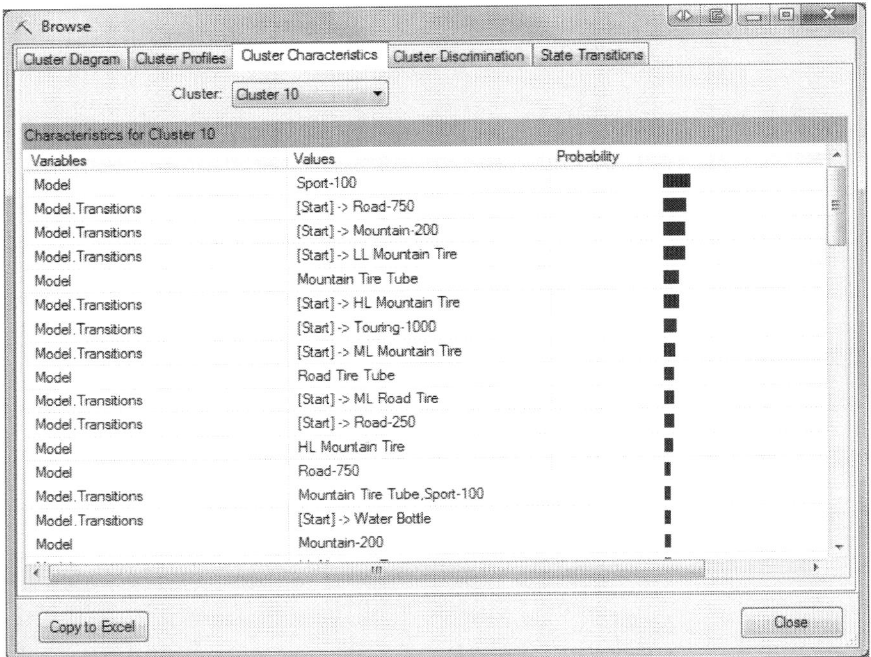

Figure 10-26h Cluster Characteristics Tab

Cluster Discrimination

The Cluster Discriminations tab lets you compare two clusters or one cluster with its complement, i.e., everything that's not in the cluster. Figure 10-26 compares Cluster 12 with Cluster 14. Cluster 12 customers more frequently start an order with a Water Bottle and Cluster 14 customers with Women's Mountain Shorts. Cluster 12 customers may end an order with Women's Mountain Shorts whereas Cluster 14 customers frequently end with a Cycling Cap.

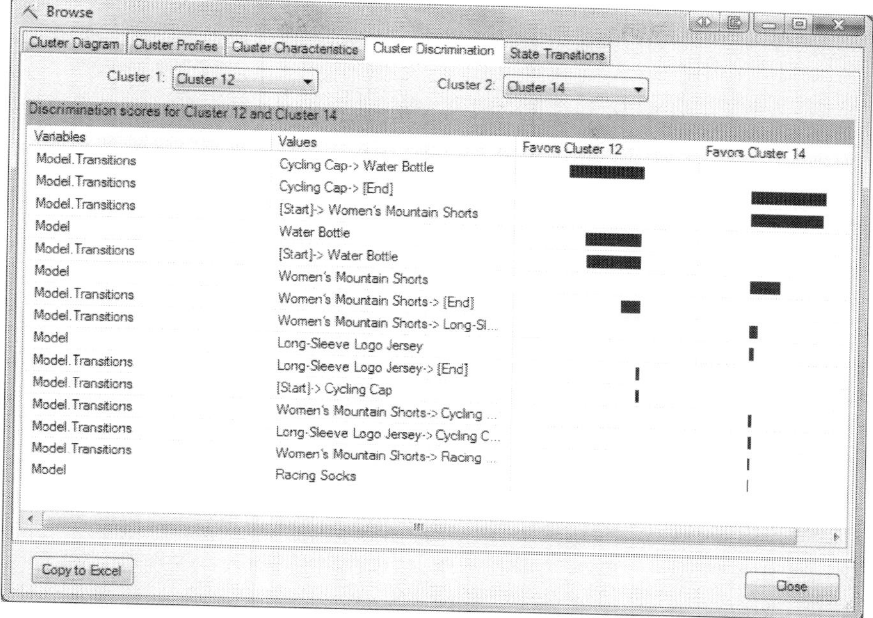

Figure 10-26i Cluster Discrimination Tab

State Transitions

In the State Transitions tab view the nodes represent items in a cluster and the arcs represent transitions. Using the cluster listbox as before you can select a cluster or the population to view. Figure 10-26i presents the state transition diagram for Cluster 10. As usual the shading on the nodes indicates the relative frequency of that item occurring in the cluster, and the slider hides or exposes links. The values on the arcs are the probabilities of the transition from one item to another. clicking on a node will highlight the higher probability transitions.

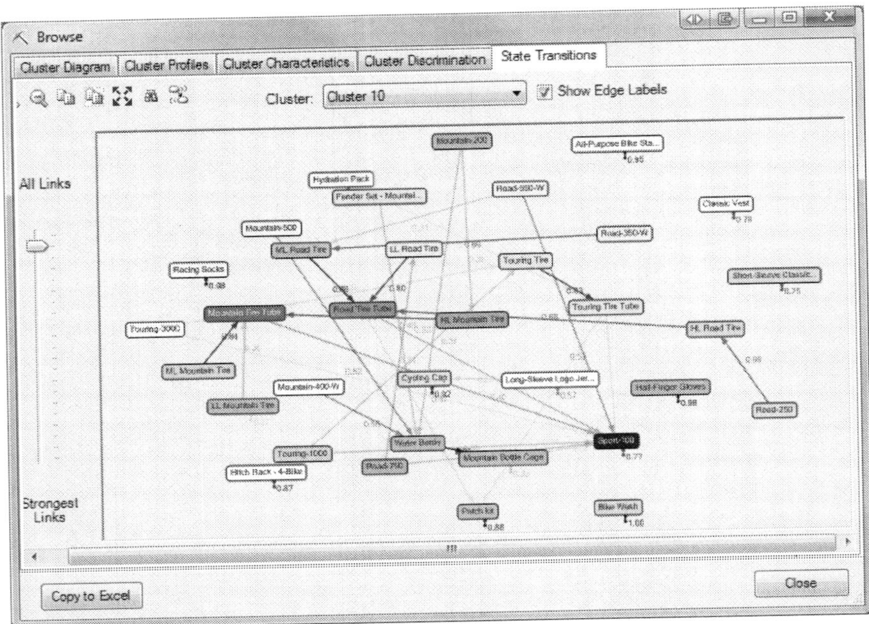

Figure 10-26j Cluster 10 State Transitions

It's interesting to compare clusters here as well. The diagram for Cluster 12 in Figure 10-26k is remarkably different from the one for Cluster 10 above reflecting the few items in Cluster 12 as compared with Cluster 10.

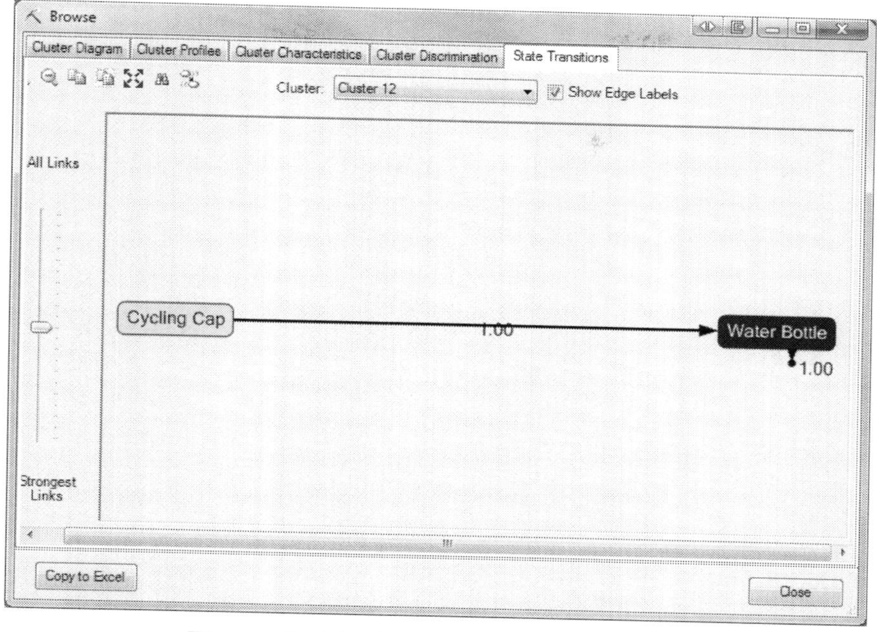

Figure 10-26k Cluster 12 State Transitions

Accuracy and Validation

The Data Mining tools also provide access to Analysis Services accuracy charts and cross-validation measures via the Accuracy and Validation command group. The Accuracy Chart assesses the accuracy of a model(s); the Classification Matrix provides data about correct and incorrect predictions; the Profit Chart attaches revenue and costs to mining model results; and Cross-Validation produces statistics about the accuracy of models in a mining structure. Accuracy and Validation tools are not available for all types of data mining structures and models. For example, Time Series Forecasting and Association models and other models without a predictable fields such as clustering do not provide accuracy and validation information.

Accuracy Chart

The Accuracy Chart tool tests the accuracy, of course, of a model or set of models using a specified dataset. The test data are usually separate from the data used to train the model either from a holdout from the original dataset or other external data, say new data received after the model was created. The reason for using a different dataset for testing is that if you use training data, there is a good chance that the tests will overstate accuracy. So, it's common practice to split the data into training and testing partitions prior to model building.

The Wizard for some of the Data Modeling tools described above includes a Split Data dialog box as in Figure 10-27a where you specify the number or percentage of rows to be set aside for testing purposes. In addition, the Logistic Regression and Neural Network algorithms have holdout percentage parameters which default to 30 percent.

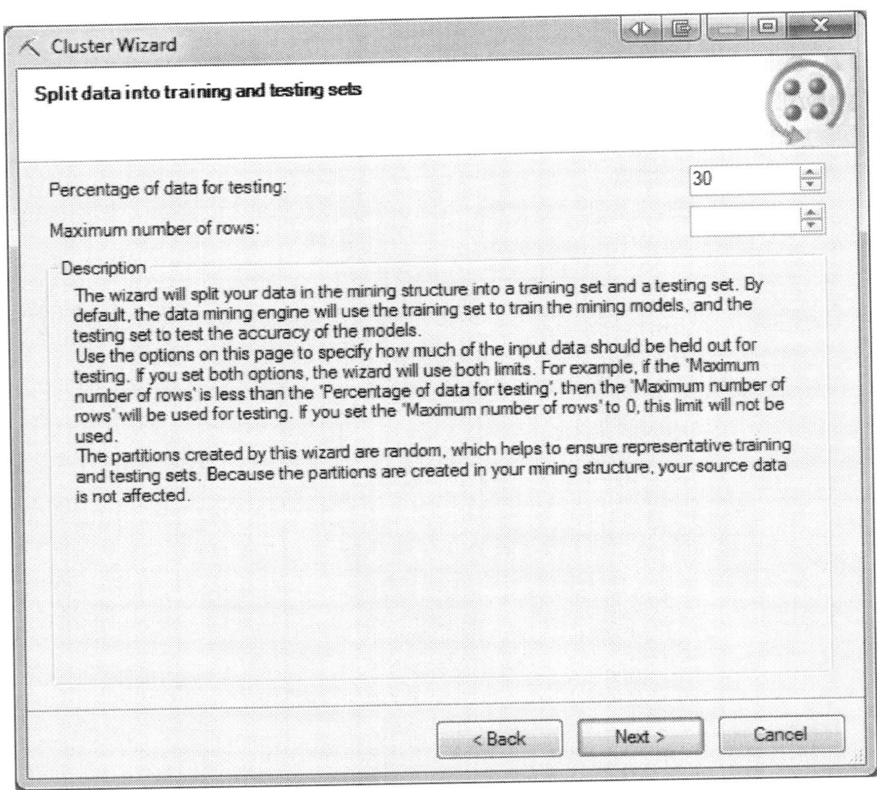

Figure 10-27a Split Data Dialog Box

The Lift Chart

The Accuracy Chart tool displays one of two charts depending on the type of model: a lift chart for models with discrete target values and a scatter chart for models with continuous target fields. A Lift Chart displays line plots showing what percentage of the cases that contain the predicted characteristic versus the number of cases that the model used to make the prediction. Figure 10-27b shows the Lift Chart for models in the Table Analysis Tools - Purchase Bike mining structure for the Classify tool described earlier in this chapter. The horizontal axis on the chart represents the percent of the overall population that the model used in the test set, and the vertical axis represents the percentage of the predicted target attribute that is correct. In the example the target attribute is Purchase Bike - Yes so a value of say 40 percent on the horizontal axis and 60 percent on the vertical axis means that the model used 40 percent of the test cases to identify 60 percent of the bike buyers correctly.

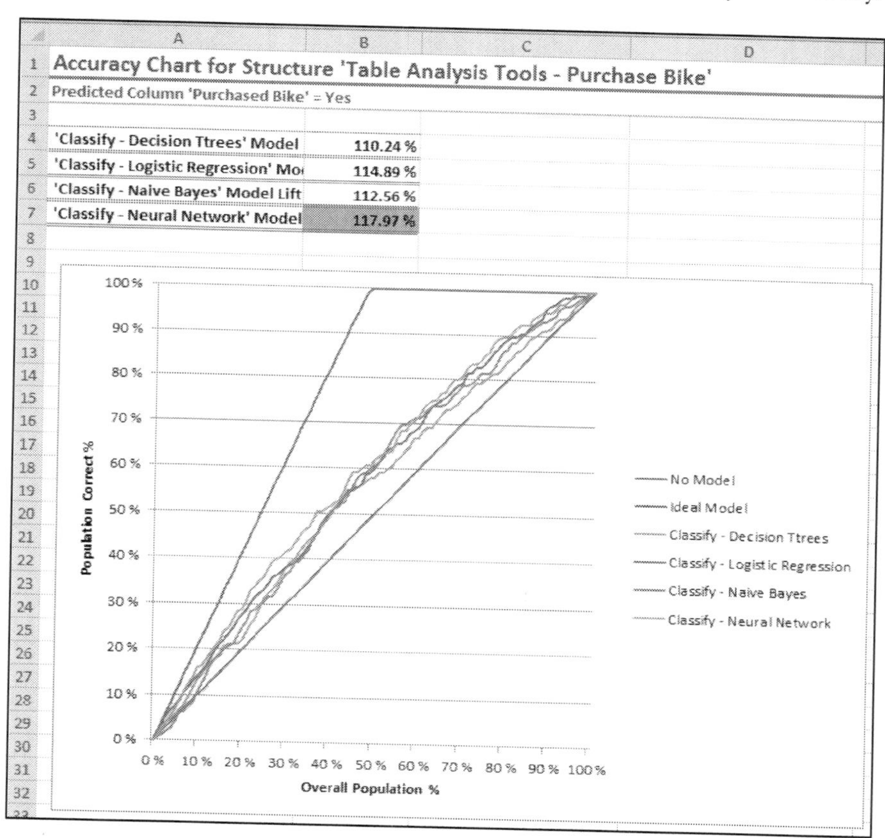

Figure 10-27b Accuracy Lift Chart

There are two boundary lines on the chart. The lower line represents a random guess model (the No Model line in the chart) as a line with a 45 degree angle (slope = 1) where using a percentage of the population will identify the same percentage correct. For example, a No Model using 50 percent of the population will correctly identify 50 percent of the bike buyers because with the discrete target attribute there is a 50-50 chance of being correct. The higher straight line represents an ideal model using all of the available information for prediction. The models produced by the algorithms should lie between the two lines with higher lines representing more accurate models. "Lift" is the degree to which a mining model lifts predictive accuracy above the random guess model.

For illustration purposes I've included the lift chart (Figure 10-27b) for the Targeted Marketing mining structure in the AdventureWorksDW2008 Analysis Services sample database in Figure 10-27c which shows fairly clear distinctions among the mining models. You can see the worst performing model, Clustering, predicts 60 percent correctly using 50 percent of the population compared with the most accurate model, a Decision Tree, with over 70 percent correct.

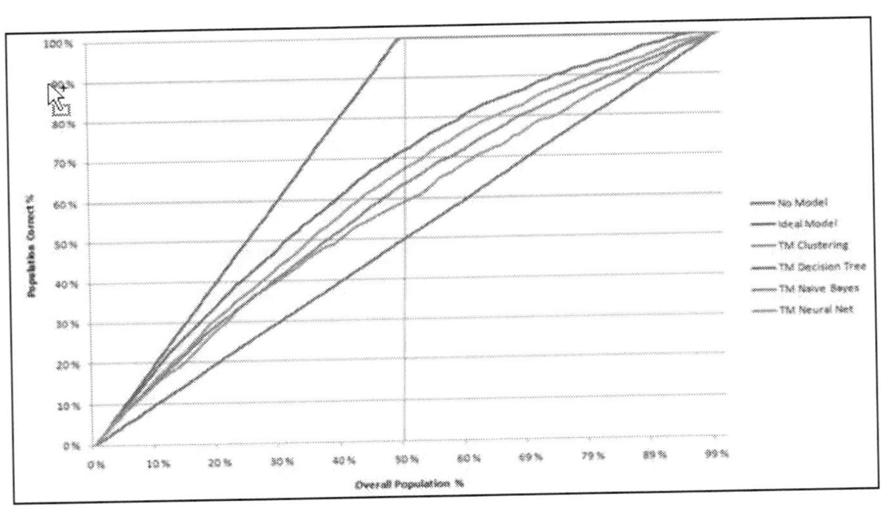

Figure 10-27c Lift Chart for Targeted Mailing Mining Structure

Clicking the Accuracy Chart option in the Accuracy and Validation command group starts the Accuracy Chart Wizard. After selecting a model or structure in the Select Structure or Model dialog box as in Figure 10-27d where I selected the Classify tool structure, you enter the column and value to predict the next dialog box (Figure 10-27e), Purchased Bike - Yes in our case. You specify the test data source in the final dialog box (Figure 10-27f) where you may choose among test data, a table or range in an Excel worksheet, or an external data source. We're using the holdout data from when the structure was created. Clicking finish will insert a new worksheet named Accuracy Chart into the workbook as in Figure 10-27a above.

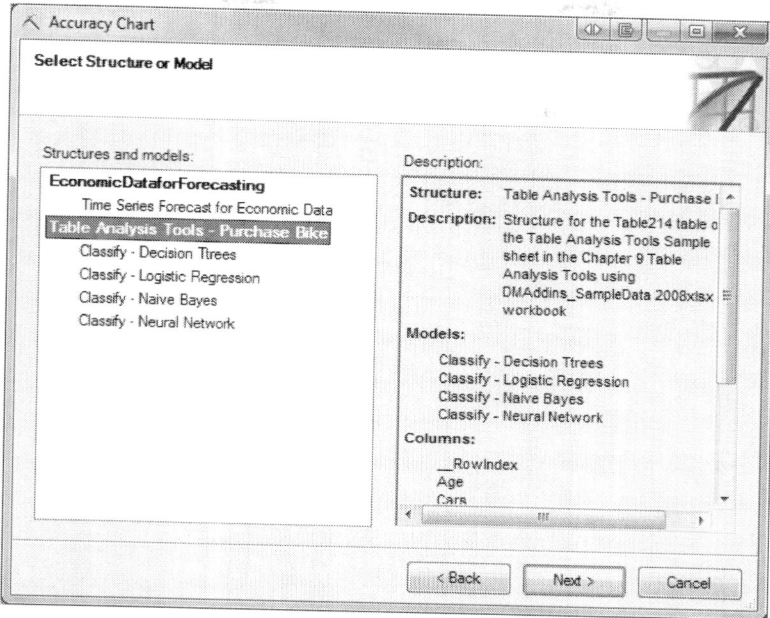

Figure 10-27d Select Structure or Model Dialog Box

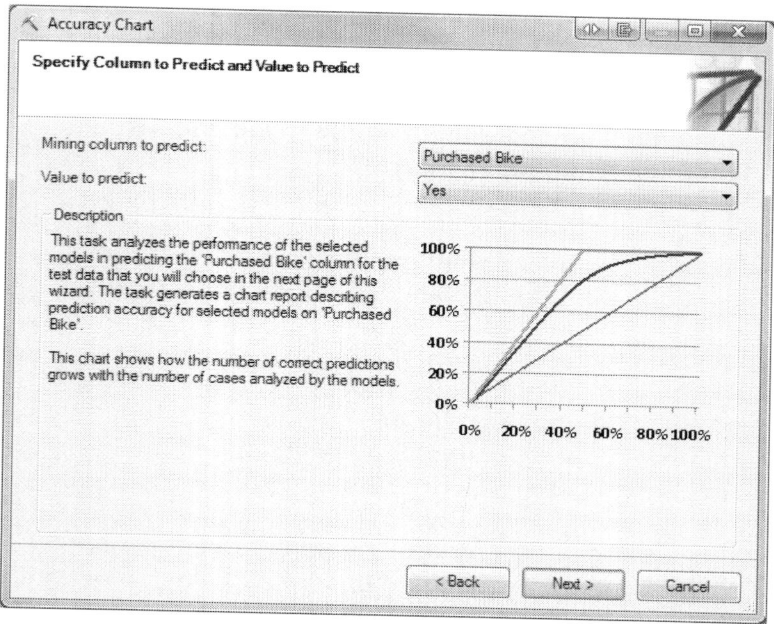

Figure 10-27e Select Column and Value to Predict Dialog Box

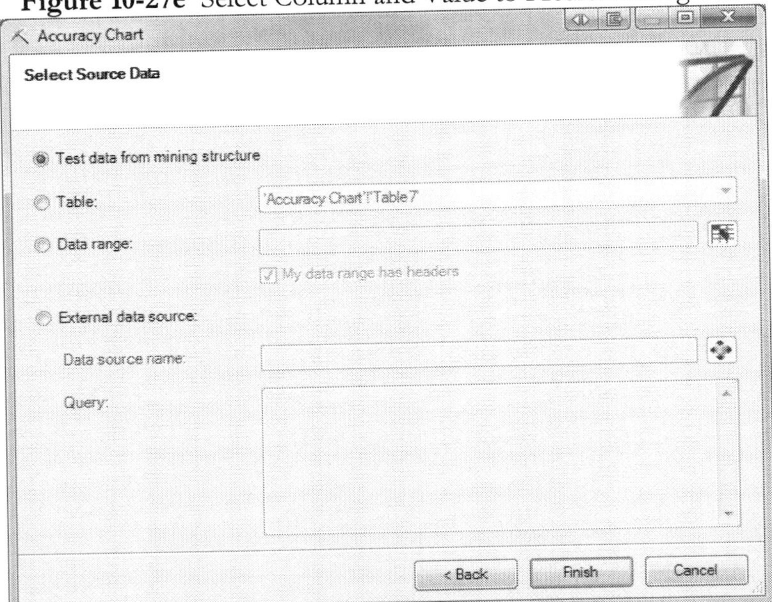

Figure 10-27f Select Source Data Dialog Box

The new worksheet contains a table with accuracy indexes at the top, a lift chart in the middle, and an accuracy data table at the bottom. Figure 10-27g shows a section of the accuracy data table hidden below the accuracy chart in Figure 10-27b with the middle rows of the table hidden. The first column, Percentile, lists the percentage of the overall population, i.e., the horizontal axis in Figure 10-27b, and the remaining columns provide the percent correct values on the vertical axis for the various models. For example, using 10 percent of the population the Decision Tree model identified 13.10 percent of bike buyers correctly. This is the same data that is displayed in the chart.

I added a SUM function in row 141 to sum the percentages in each column, e.g., =SUM(A39:A141) for cell A141, and a ratio computation of the percentage a model sum is of the Percentile sum, i.e., the Accuracy improvement row is the model sum in row 141 divided by the Percentile sum. For example, the formula in cell B141 is =B141/$A$141. The Accuracy Improvement row then becomes a measure of the accuracy lift of a model above the random guess model because the Percentile column values are a surrogate for the No Model population correct values. For example, the accuracy improvement for an Ideal Model is 151.15 percent (7633/5050), for Decision Trees 110.24 percent (5567/5050), and so on. These are the same values reported in the table at the top of the worksheet in Figure 10-27b where you can see that the Neural Network model is the most accurate with the highest lift.

	A	B	C	D	E	F
38	Percentile	Ideal Model	Decision Trees	Logistic Regression	Naive Bayes	Neural Network
39	0 %	0.00 %	0.00 %	0.00 %	0.00 %	0.00 %
40	1 %	2.07 %	2.07 %	2.07 %	0.69 %	1.38 %
41	2 %	4.14 %	2.07 %	3.45 %	1.38 %	2.76 %
42	3 %	6.21 %	4.14 %	5.52 %	2.07 %	4.14 %
43	4 %	8.28 %	4.83 %	6.90 %	2.76 %	5.52 %
44	5 %	10.34 %	5.52 %	7.59 %	4.14 %	6.90 %
45	6 %	12.41 %	6.90 %	8.97 %	6.21 %	8.97 %
46	7 %	14.48 %	7.59 %	10.34 %	6.21 %	10.34 %
47	8 %	16.55 %	9.66 %	11.72 %	7.59 %	12.41 %
48	9 %	18.62 %	11.72 %	13.10 %	8.28 %	13.79 %
49	10 %	20.69 %	13.10 %	13.79 %	10.34 %	15.86 %
135	96 %	100.00 %	97.24 %	99.31 %	97.93 %	100.00 %
136	97 %	100.00 %	97.93 %	99.31 %	98.62 %	100.00 %
137	98 %	100.00 %	99.31 %	99.31 %	98.62 %	100.00 %
138	99 %	100.00 %	100.00 %	100.00 %	100.00 %	100.00 %
139	100 %	100.00 %	100.00 %	100.00 %	100.00 %	100.00 %
140						
141	5050 %	7633 %	5567 %	5802 %	5684 %	5957 %
142	Accuracy Improvement	151.15%	110.24%	114.89%	112.56%	117.97%

Figure 10-27g Accuracy Data Table

The Scatter Chart

A Scatter Chart replaces the Lift Chart if the target attribute has continuous values like our earlier estimate income example that we'll use here. The Scatter Chart (Figure 10-27g) uses actual value - predicted value coordinates to plot points on the chart with actual values on the horizontal axis and predicted values on the vertical axis. The 45 degree line represents the ideal model where actual and predicted values are always equal. Models with higher accuracy will have plotted points closer to the ideal model line. Figure 10-27h is an enlargement of a section of the scatter chart where you may be able see the plots more clearly using the legend in Figure 10-27i. However, even with the enlargement I cannot determine which model has the tightest dispersion around the ideal model line.

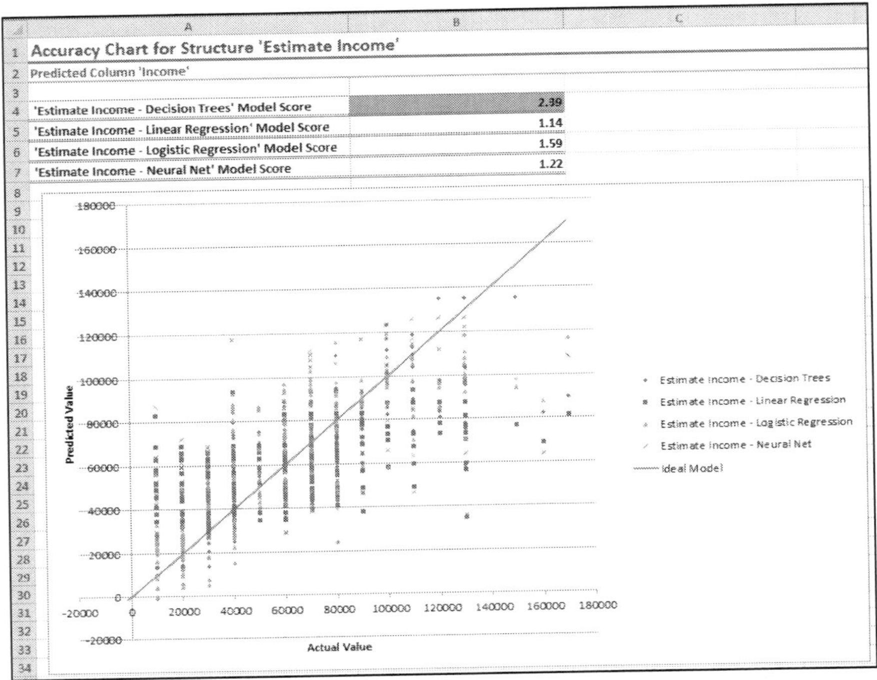

Figure 10-27g Accuracy Scatter Chart

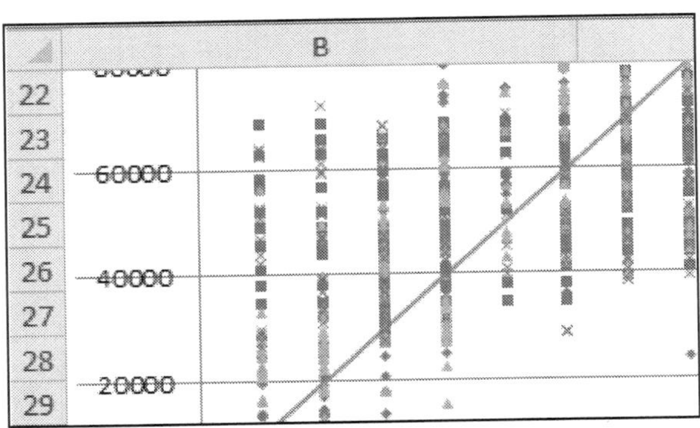

Figure 10-27h Accuracy Scatter Chart Enlargement

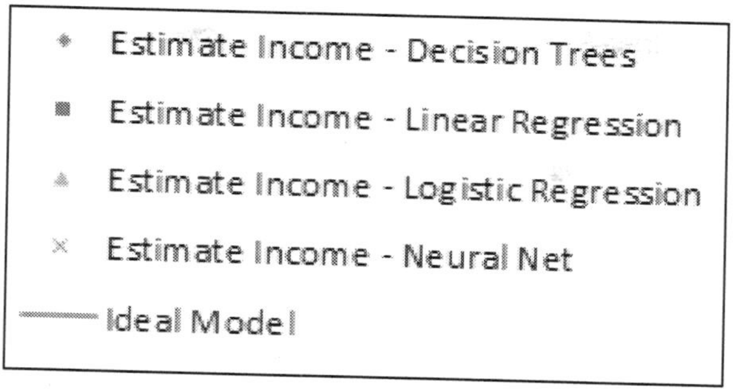

- Estimate Income - Decision Trees
- Estimate Income - Linear Regression
- Estimate Income - Logistic Regression
- Estimate Income - Neural Net
- Ideal Model

Figure 10-27i Accuracy Scatter Chart Legend

The Model Scores at the top of the worksheet in Figure 10-27g are equivalent to the Lift Scores in Figure 10-27b. This seems to mean that the score is a measure of how much better a model predicts the actual values than the mean of the actual values. The scores indicate that the Decision Trees model is the most accurate with a score of 2.39 The Scatter Chart worksheet also has a table at the bottom (not shown) that lists the actual values and predicted values used in the chart.

Classification Matrix

The Classification Matrix tool inserts a new worksheet that contains statistics about correct and incorrect predictions. Figure 10-28 shows a section of the Classification Matrix worksheet for Classify models for Purchase Bike that we have been using all along: Decision Trees, Logistic Regression, Naive Bayes, and Neural Network. Row 7 and 8 provide percentage and frequency counts for correct and incorrect predictions or classifications for each model. I hid the columns for the Logistic Regression and Naive Bayes models. The Decision Tree and Naïve Bayes models (not shown) had the best and identical performance

Below that summary data in columns A through C are two tables for each model comparing correct and incorrect predictions or classifications for the states of the target attribute, Purchase Bike Yes and No in our case. This is a similar framework as discussed about statistical errors in Appendix B. The Predict No - Actual Yes cell is like a Type II error, the Predict Yes - Actual No cell like a Type I error. Assigning costs to the errors, may help you decide which model to use.

	A	B	C	H	I
1	Counts of correct/incorrect classification for structure 'Classify'				
2	Predicted Column 'Purchased Bike'				
3	Columns correspond to actual values				
4	Rows correspond to predicted values				
5					
6	Model name:	Classify - Decision Trees	Classify - Decision Trees	Classify - Neural Network	Classify - Neural Network
7	Total correct:	63.00 %	189	61.00 %	183
8	Total misclassified:	37.00 %	111	39.00 %	117
9					
10	Results as Percentages for Model 'Classify - Decision Trees'				
11		No(Actual)	Yes(Actual)		
12	No	84.02 %	64.12 %		
13	Yes	15.98 %	35.88 %		
14					
15	Correct	84.02 %	35.88 %		
16	Misclassified	15.98 %	64.12 %		
17					
18	Results as Counts for Model 'Classify - Decision Trees'				
19		No(Actual)	Yes(Actual)		
20	No	142	84		
21	Yes	27	47		
22					
23	Correct	142	47		
24	Misclassified	27	84		

Figure 10-28 Accuracy Classification Matrix

Profit Chart

A profit chart is somewhat like the Prediction Calculator in Chapter 9 in that it calculates a monetary return from using a model for predictions based on cost and revenue parameters. A frequently mentioned example for using a profit chart is a marketing campaign where you can identify the size of the target population, the fixed cost of designing and implementing the campaign, the variable cost for each prospective customer contacted, and the revenue for each sale. The parameter values are entered in the Profit Chart Parameters dialog box as in Figure 10-29a for our Classify - Purchased Bike example. For illustration purposes I left the parameters set at their default values.

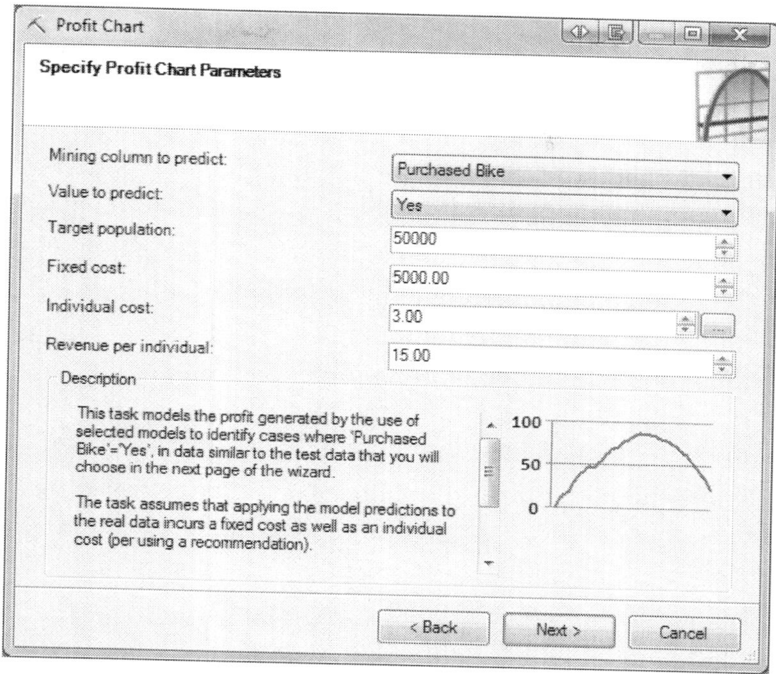

Figure 10-29a Profit Chart Parameters

The Profit Chart (Figure 10-29b) contains four sections: a table at the top listing the parameter values, a summary table below it, the profit chart, and a data table at the bottom. Row 10 of the summary table shows the maximum profit for using each model to predict bicycle buyers. The value for the Naïve Bayes model is highlighted because it maximizes profit. The probability threshold, as I understand it, specifies the probability cut-off value for marketing to a new customer. For example, if we were using the Decision Tree model to classify potential customers, we would not market to anyone with a Purchase Bike prediction probability of less than 44.20 percent.

The Profit Chart plots the net profit for each of the models as a function of the percentage of the overall population, 50,000 in this case. The 45 degree line at the bottom is once again a plot of the random guess model If you could see the legend colors on the chart, you could tell that the Naïve Bayes profit line is on top from the 35 percent population point, the Decision Trees line is on the bottom in the bottom of the chart, and the Logistic Regression line is on the bottom in the middle part of the chart.

I added identifiers for three points on the chart: at Point A if you could only market to approximately 10 percent of the population you would use the Logistic Regression model because it's predicted to return the highest profit at that point; at Point B at about 30 percent of the population you would prefer the Neural Network model; and Point C identifies the maximum profit for the Naïve Bayes model as displayed in the summary table, $175,500.

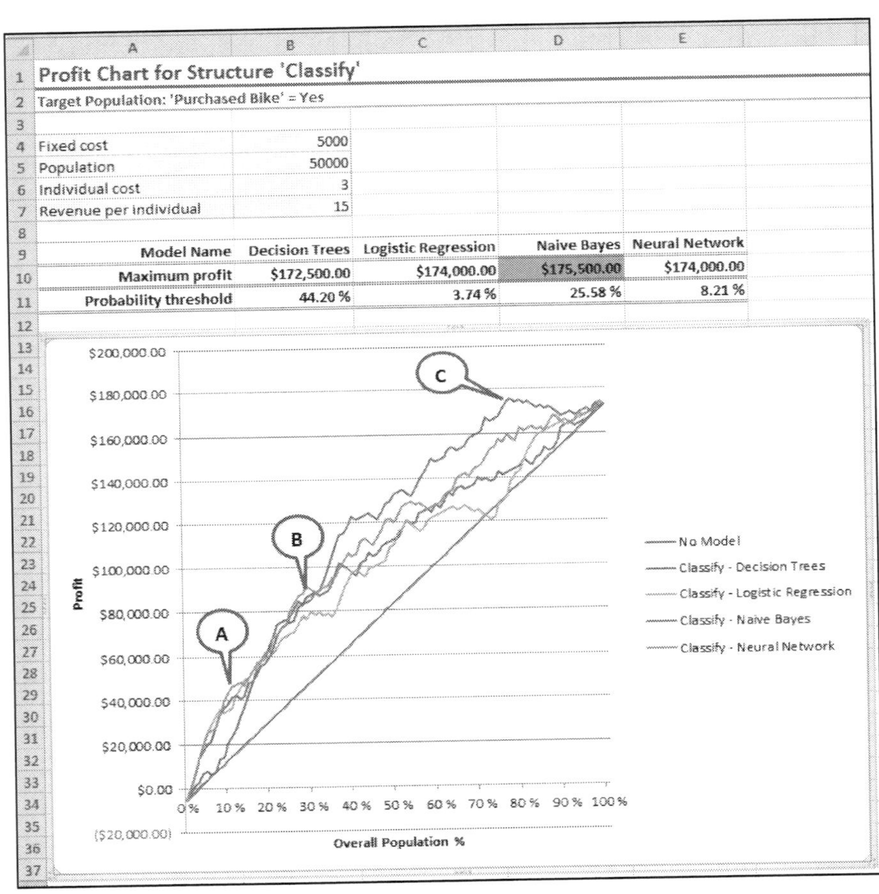

Profit Chart for Structure 'Classify'

Target Population: 'Purchased Bike' = Yes

Fixed cost	5000
Population	50000
Individual cost	3
Revenue per individual	15

Model Name	Decision Trees	Logistic Regression	Naive Bayes	Neural Network
Maximum profit	$172,500.00	$174,000.00	$175,500.00	$174,000.00
Probability threshold	44.20 %	3.74 %	25.58 %	8.21 %

Figure 10-29b Profit Chart

(For better viewing of this image, go to http://www.zerobits.info/bibook/bibookimages/)

Figure 10-29c shows a section of the data table (just the data for the Decision Trees model) at the bottom of the Profit Chart worksheet. The plot points in the chart above come from the Percentile (column A) and the Profit (column

D) columns. For example, at five percent of the population the Decision Tree model will produce $7,500 in profit. Note that the Decision Trees Probability (column E) declines to 44.20 percent which is the Probability Threshold for the Decision Tree model in the summary table above. It remains at that value up to the 100 percentile.

	A	B	C	D	E
42	Percentile	Random Guess Profit	Decision Trees Population Correct %	Decision Trees Profit	Decision Trees Probability
43	0 %	($5,000.00)	0.00 %	($5,000.00)	100.00 %
44	1 %	($3,225.00)	1.53 %	($1,500.00)	70.85 %
45	2 %	($1,450.00)	3.05 %	$2,000.00	70.85 %
46	3 %	$325.00	3.82 %	$3,000.00	70.85 %
47	4 %	$2,100.00	5.34 %	$6,500.00	70.85 %
48	5 %	$3,875.00	6.11 %	$7,500.00	70.85 %
49	6 %	$5,650.00	6.11 %	$6,000.00	70.85 %
96	53 %	$89,075.00	62.60 %	$120,500.00	44.20 %
97	54 %	$90,850.00	62.60 %	$119,000.00	44.20 %
98	55 %	$92,625.00	63.36 %	$120,000.00	44.20 %
99	56 %	$94,400.00	64.89 %	$123,500.00	44.20 %
100	57 %	$96,175.00	65.65 %	$124,500.00	44.20 %
101	58 %	$97,950.00	66.41 %	$125,500.00	44.20 %

Figure 10-29c Profit Chart Data Table

Cross-Validation

The Cross-Validation tool splits the data into a number of folds (separate test data set partitions); for each fold it trains a model using the data not in the fold and tests its accuracy using multiple measures on the data in the fold; it iterates this process through all folds and all models and then produces statistics for each model - measure combination. If the statistics are relative stable, then you can be more confident that the model is generalizable. Note that the accuracy measures used by the tool vary with the type of mining structure. We will not describe all of them here so see SQL Server 2008 Books Online for the details.

The parameters for the cross-validation process are specified in the Cross-Validation Parameters dialog box as in Figure 10-30a for our usual example, the Cluster data mining structure. The maximum value for the Fold Count parameter is 10. Cross-validation uses the training data for its analysis, and if the Maximum Rows parameter is set to zero, then all of the training data will be used in cross-validation. Setting Maximum Rows to a number will limit the Cross-Validation data set to that size. For example, our Table Analysis Tools Sample worksheet contains 1,000 rows of data. In creating the Classify mining structure we accepted the default testing holdout of 30 percent leaving 70 percent or 700 rows for training. If Maximum Rows is set to zero, then all 700 rows will be used in cross-Validation. If Maximum Rows is set to 500, then Cross-Validation would use only 500 rows. You might restrict the number of rows and/or the number of folds in very large datasets to reduce long processing times. As we will see shortly with 10 folds and 700 rows each fold will contain 70 rows, i.e., each model will be built 10 times and tested with 70 different rows of data.

There are three other parameters: Target Attribute, Target State and Target Threshold. You will have options for Target Attribute only if you defined more than one target attribute in the mining structure. In our case there is only one, Purchased Bike. The Target State is set using the listbox where our options are Yes and No. the Target (Accuracy) Threshold sets a probability value above which a prediction is counted as correct. Higher values indicate stronger levels of confidence in the predictions. The default value of NULL uses the predicted state with the highest value.

In our example with four models the predict Bike Buyer the value we want to predict it 1 – buy a bike. If you set the Target Threshold to .20 and the four models returned values of .10, .14, .21, and .27, then the last two are counted as correct. If the NULL value is used, the most probable prediction is counted as correct. Are you confused yet?

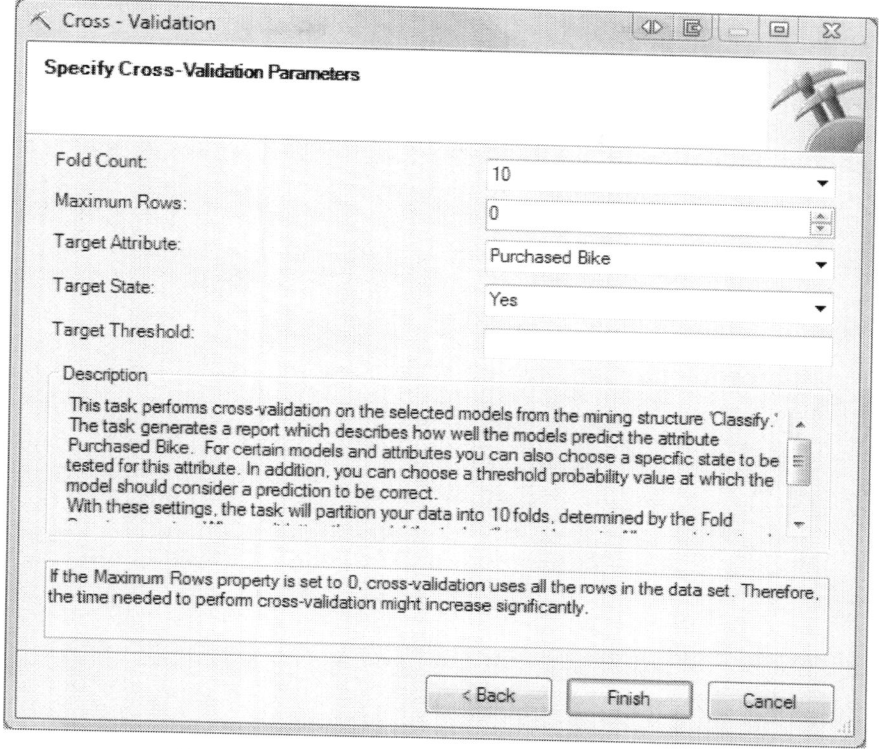

Figure 10-30a Cross-Validation Dialog Box

The Cross-Validation worksheet created when you run the analysis contains three sections: a recap of the parameters at the top (Figure 10-30b), a set of Cross-Validation Summary tables (Figure 10-30c), and a Cross-Validation Details table at the bottom (Figure 10-30d). We'll look at the Details table first because it helps explain the Summary tables. For this mining structure there are seven different validation measure used—True Positives, False Positives, True Negatives, False Negatives, Log Score, Lift, and Root Mean Square Error—for four mining models making a total of 28 segments in the Details table. The True - False, Positives - Negatives framework which counts the cases that meet the condition is similar to the Type I and Type II statistical error paradigm described in Appendix B. Please see SQL Server 2008 Books Online for descriptions of Log Score, Lift, and Root Mean Square Error.

The section of the Details table in Figure 10-30d shows only 2 of the 7 segments for the Decision Trees model only. .The first segment in the table (rows 62-73) presents data about true positives. The first 10 rows lists the frequency of true positives for each of the partition (fold) trials. For example, the model for the Partition 1 found 1 true positives out of 70 cases (rows) which doesn't really mean much by itself. What is bothersome is the inconsistency of the true positive count which range from 8 to 35 across the partitions. This produces a high standard deviation of 9.94 compared with the mean of 16.2. Also, of concern is the number of false positives and the very high standard deviation in the bottom section in the figure.

I don't have the space or the patience to describe each of the detail measures for each of the models but I hope that you get a feel for the process of examining these data to assess the accuracy and validity of the models.

	A	B	C	D	E
1	Cross-Validation Report for 'Classify'				
2	For Target 'Purchased Bike = Yes'				
3					
4	Models	Decision Trees, Logistic Regression, Naive Bayes, Neural Network			
5	Fold Count	10			
6	Maximum Rows	0			
7	Rows Used	700			
8	Target Attribute	Purchased Bike			
9	Target State	Yes			

Figure 10-30b Cross-Validation Report Parameters

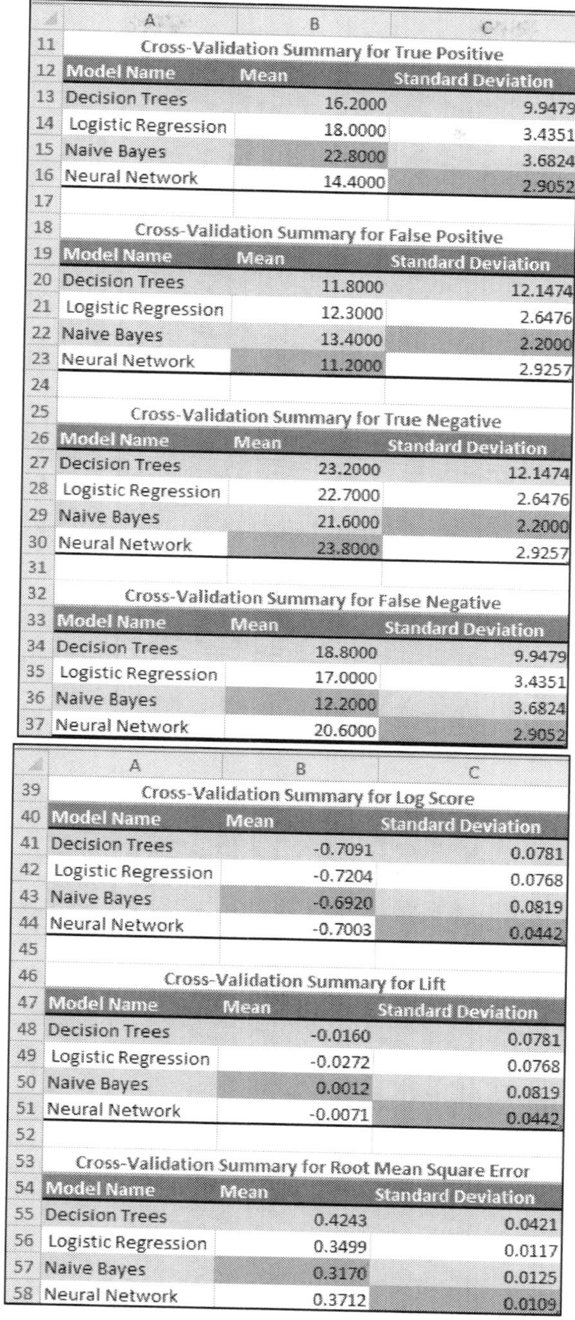

Cross-Validation Summary for True Positive		
Model Name	Mean	Standard Deviation
Decision Trees	16.2000	9.9479
Logistic Regression	18.0000	3.4351
Naive Bayes	22.8000	3.6824
Neural Network	14.4000	2.9052

Cross-Validation Summary for False Positive		
Model Name	Mean	Standard Deviation
Decision Trees	11.8000	12.1474
Logistic Regression	12.3000	2.6476
Naive Bayes	13.4000	2.2000
Neural Network	11.2000	2.9257

Cross-Validation Summary for True Negative		
Model Name	Mean	Standard Deviation
Decision Trees	23.2000	12.1474
Logistic Regression	22.7000	2.6476
Naive Bayes	21.6000	2.2000
Neural Network	23.8000	2.9257

Cross-Validation Summary for False Negative		
Model Name	Mean	Standard Deviation
Decision Trees	18.8000	9.9479
Logistic Regression	17.0000	3.4351
Naive Bayes	12.2000	3.6824
Neural Network	20.6000	2.9052

Cross-Validation Summary for Log Score		
Model Name	Mean	Standard Deviation
Decision Trees	-0.7091	0.0781
Logistic Regression	-0.7204	0.0768
Naive Bayes	-0.6920	0.0819
Neural Network	-0.7003	0.0442

Cross-Validation Summary for Lift		
Model Name	Mean	Standard Deviation
Decision Trees	-0.0160	0.0781
Logistic Regression	-0.0272	0.0768
Naive Bayes	0.0012	0.0819
Neural Network	-0.0071	0.0442

Cross-Validation Summary for Root Mean Square Error		
Model Name	Mean	Standard Deviation
Decision Trees	0.4243	0.0421
Logistic Regression	0.3499	0.0117
Naive Bayes	0.3170	0.0125
Neural Network	0.3712	0.0109

Figure 10-30c Cross-Validation Summary Tables

	A	B	C	D	E
60	Cross-Validation Details				
61	Model Name	Partition Index	Partition Size	Measure	Value
62	Decision Trees	1	70	True Positive	11
63	Decision Trees	2	70	True Positive	10
64	Decision Trees	3	70	True Positive	11
65	Decision Trees	4	70	True Positive	35
66	Decision Trees	5	70	True Positive	35
67	Decision Trees	6	70	True Positive	14
68	Decision Trees	7	70	True Positive	9
69	Decision Trees	8	70	True Positive	9
70	Decision Trees	9	70	True Positive	20
71	Decision Trees	10	70	True Positive	8
72	Decision Trees	All	700	Mean (True Positi	16.2000
73	Decision Trees	All	700	Standard Deviatic	9.9479
74	Decision Trees	1	70	False Positive	3
75	Decision Trees	2	70	False Positive	3
76	Decision Trees	3	70	False Positive	8
77	Decision Trees	4	70	False Positive	35
78	Decision Trees	5	70	False Positive	35
79	Decision Trees	6	70	False Positive	2
80	Decision Trees	7	70	False Positive	7
81	Decision Trees	8	70	False Positive	3
82	Decision Trees	9	70	False Positive	15
83	Decision Trees	10	70	False Positive	7
84	Decision Trees	All	700	Mean (False Posil	11.8000
85	Decision Trees	All	700	Standard Deviatic	12.1474
86	Decision Trees	1	70	True Negative	32

Figure 10-30d Cross-Validation Details

The Summary tables in Figure 10-30c contain the means and standard deviations from the Details table. For example, cell B13 in Figure 10-30c holds a cell reference to cell E72 in Figure 10-30d, the mean for the true positive partitions for the Decision Trees model. The Cross-Validation tool automatically highlights the best value in each column of the summary so in the second table, False Positives, the Neural Network model had the best (lowest) false positives mean and the Naïve Bayes model the lowest standard deviation. To me the data in the Summary tables indicates that the Neural Network and Naive Bayes models are better than Decision Trees and Logistic Regression. However, all of the standard deviations are high which may indicate that the sample size (70) may be too small.

To confirm this suspicion I ran the Cross-Validation tool on the AdventureWorksDW2008 Analysis Services Targeted Mailing mining structure which is the same structure as in the Table Analysis Tools Sample worksheet but with 18484 rows and the addition of a Clustering model. The Summary tables for this analysis are shown in Figure 10-30e. Each partition contains about 1,848 rows, a substantial increase over the 70 rows in the analysis above, and, consequently, the standard deviations dropped significantly in relation to the means. A quick scan of the tables suggests that the Decision tree model may be the best.

	A	B	C
12	**Model Name**	**Mean**	**Standard Deviation**
13	TM Decision Tree	675.6987	16.1609
14	TM Clustering	401.0933	21.4550
15	TM Naive Bayes	562.9983	6.6185
16	TM Neural Net	623.5955	14.0543
17			
18	**Cross-Validation Summary for False Positive**		
19	**Model Name**	**Mean**	**Standard Deviation**
20	TM Decision Tree	233.1015	17.2815
21	TM Clustering	203.9969	13.9384
22	TM Naive Bayes	313.1976	11.5141
23	TM Neural Net	291.7958	15.6714
24			
25	**Cross-Validation Summary for True Negative**		
26	**Model Name**	**Mean**	**Standard Deviation**
27	TM Decision Tree	702.0986	17.1420
28	TM Clustering	731.2033	14.1154
29	TM Naive Bayes	622.0025	11.6368
30	TM Neural Net	643.4043	15.9021
31			
32	**Cross-Validation Summary for False Negative**		
33	**Model Name**	**Mean**	**Standard Deviation**
34	TM Decision Tree	237.5014	16.2239
35	TM Clustering	512.1068	21.6685
36	TM Naive Bayes	350.2018	6.9113
37	TM Neural Net	289.6046	14.3222

	A	B	C
39	Cross-Validation Summary for Log Score		
40	Model Name	Mean	Standard Deviation
41	TM Decision Tree	-0.5274	0.0116
42	TM Clustering	-0.6615	0.0044
43	TM Naive Bayes	-0.6760	0.0115
44	TM Neural Net	-0.6044	0.0049
45			
46	Cross-Validation Summary for Lift		
47	Model Name	Mean	Standard Deviation
48	TM Decision Tree	0.1656	0.0116
49	TM Clustering	0.0316	0.0044
50	TM Naive Bayes	0.0171	0.0115
51	TM Neural Net	0.0887	0.0049
52			
53	Cross-Validation Summary for Root Mean Square Error		
54	Model Name	Mean	Standard Deviation
55	TM Decision Tree	0.2783	0.0062
56	TM Clustering	0.3941	0.0039
57	TM Naive Bayes	0.2942	0.0024
58	TM Neural Net	0.3562	0.0030

Figure 10-30e Cross-Validation Summary Tables for AdventureWorks Data

In evaluating the results we should look at the cross-validation statistics and also examine the cross-validation details for consistency. The results for the Table Analysis Tools sample does not fare well, but the results from the AdventureWorks database with the much larger number of case looks good.

Prediction Queries

The data mining tools that we've looked at so far help us to explore the copious and complex data in today's large databases and data warehouses. However, perhaps an even greater benefit is using mining models for prediction. We've already done that in forecasting, and the Query tool lets us perform predictions with other models as well.

The Data Mining Query Wizard, accessed with the Query option in the Model Usage command group, first displays a Select Model dialog box similar to the one in Figure 10-27c except that it has an Advanced button at the bottom to bring up the Data Mining Advanced Query Editor. We'll skip the advanced features here and cover them in Appendix F. After choosing the model you want to use for prediction, we'll use the Decision Trees model from our Classify example, the Wizard displays the usual Select Data Source dialog box where you may specify an Excel table, data range, or an external source for the data to use for prediction. We'll use the New Customers table in the New Customers worksheet from the Sample Data Excel file from the Data Mining

Add-Ins which contains 78 rows of customer data with attributes identical to those in the Table Analysis Tools Sample worksheet with which the mining models were developed. Our intention is to identify the new customers who are potential bicycle buyers.

In the next dialog box you map the relationships between the mining model columns and the table columns, the columns (fields) in the New Customers table, as in Figure 10-31a. Note that all of the columns matched except Income and Purchased Bike, and both of their names in the Table Columns were initially blank. The Income column in the mining structure is named Yearly Income in the New Customers table so I changed it with the listbox. The Purchased Bike column is the one that we want to predict and is specified in the next dialog box (Figure 10-31b).

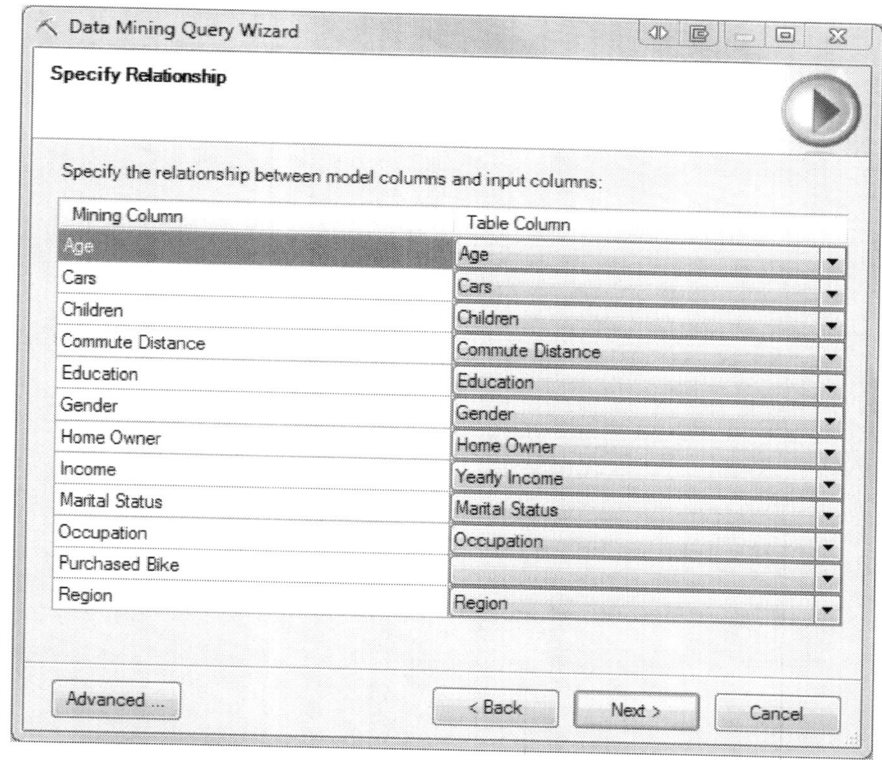

Figure 10-31a Specify Relationships Dialog Box

Initially, the middle panel in the Choose Output dialog box is blank—in our case it did not have the Purchase Bike Prediction and Probability Yes rows. To inset those you click the Add Output button to display the Add Output dialog box (Figure 10-31c) where you select a Column to predict and one of the Column Functions. Note that I checked the show Advanced functions and Parameters box so that you could see all available Column Functions. The Predict option will tag a new customer with a purchase bike Yes - No value. You can add only one output at a time so after returning to the Choose Output dialog box, I repeated the add output process to insert the Probability Yes function.

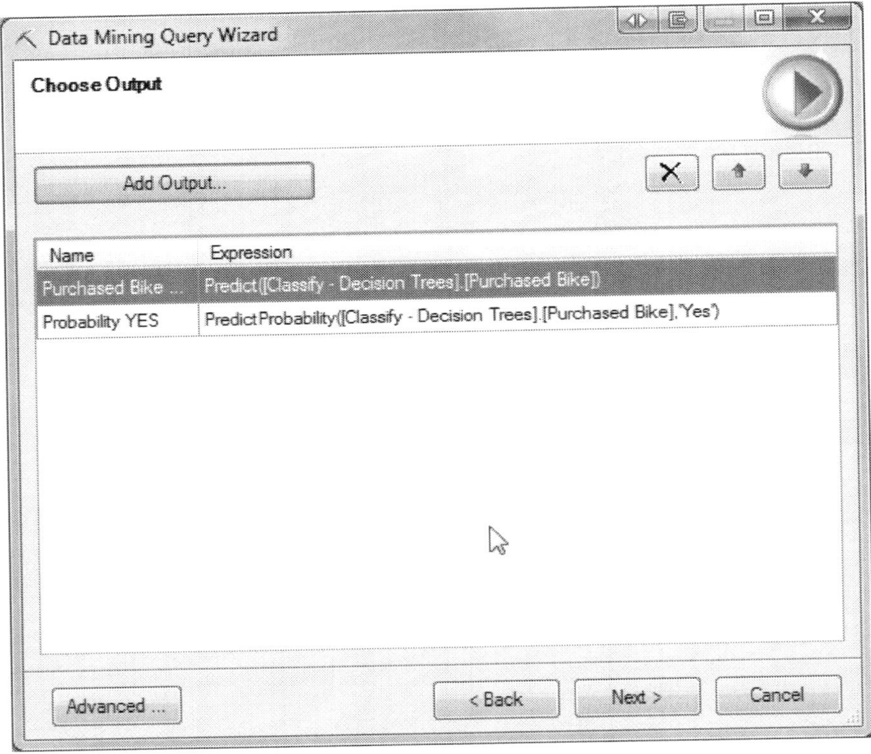

Figure 10-31b Choose Output Dialog Box

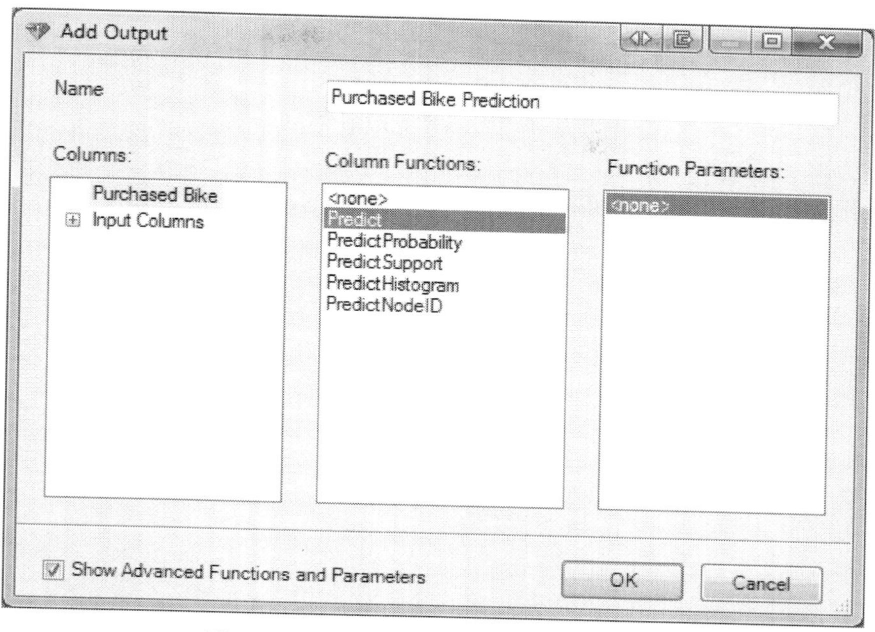

Figure 10-31c Add Output Dialog Box

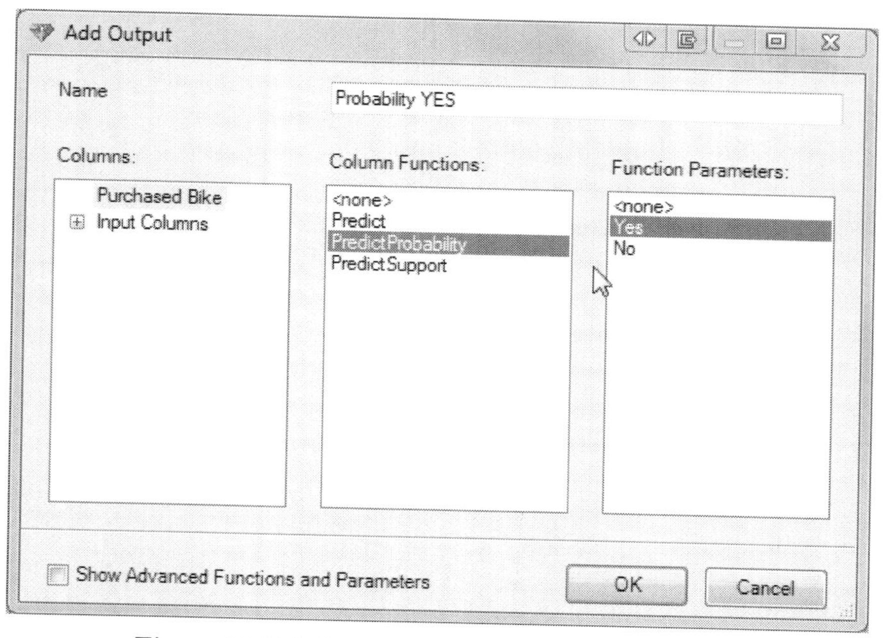

Figure 10-31d Output Dialog Box – Probability Yes

The final dialog box (not shown) presents options for the destination of the results: Append to the input data, New worksheet, or Existing worksheet. I choose to append. Figure 10-31e shows the two new columns appended to the New Customers table in rows R and S. The AdventureWorks Marketing Department could use the results to focus a promotion on those customers with a higher likelihood of purchasing a bicycle.

	A	D	E	P	Q	R	S
3	ID	Marital Status	Gender	Region	Age	Purchased Bike Prediction	Probability YES
4	11000	Married	Male	Pacific	40	No	0.441977237
5	11001	Single	Male	Pacific	41	No	0.441977237
6	11002	Married	Male	Pacific	41	No	0.441977237
7	11003	Single	Female	Pacific	38	Yes	0.708500401
8	11004	Single	Female	Pacific	38	Yes	0.708500401
9	11005	Single	Male	Pacific	41	No	0.441977237
10	11006	Single	Female	Pacific	40	No	0.441977237
11	11007	Married	Male	Pacific	42	No	0.441977237
12	11008	Single	Female	Pacific	42	No	0.441977237
13	11009	Single	Male	Pacific	42	No	0.441977237
14	11010	Single	Female	Pacific	42	No	0.441977237

Figure 10-31e Prediction Results

Data Mining Cell Functions

The Data Mining Add-In includes three undocumented Data Mining Cell Functions: DMPREDICT, DMPREDICTTABLEROW, and DMCONTENTQUERY which when inserted into an Excel cell will return values from an existing mining model. DMPREDICT returns a prediction based on values of input columns. The form of the function is:

=DMPREDICT(<Analysis Services Connection>, <Mining Model>, <Prediction Function (Prediction Entity)>, <Input Column Values and Names>)

For example:

=DMPREDICT("ExcelDataMining (maingear) ","Classify - Decision Trees","Predict ([Purchased Bike]) ", "Male", "Gender")

predicts if a male customer will purchase a bicycle using the Classify - Decision Trees model that we developed above. The cell value returned by the function for this example was "No," i.e., the single attribute, male, does not predict buying a bicycle. The function arguments are described in Table 10-2 below.

Argument	Example	Description
Analysis Services Connection	"ExcelDataMining (maingear)"	Existing data mining connections are listed by the Connections command. Use double quotes ("") to specify the current connection.
Mining Model	"Classify - Decision Trees"	Name of the mining model as listed in Browse or Manage Models commands.
Prediction Function and Entity	"Predict ([Purchased Bike])"	Use a prediction function Shown in Figure 10-31c , e.g., Predict or PredictProbability, and a predictable characteristic for the entity
Input Column Values and Names	"Male", "Gender")	Input column value, Input column name.

Table 10-2 Data Mining Cell Function Arguments

The function will accept up to 32 pairs of input columns values and names. The following example has 2 pairs.

=DMPREDICT("ExcelDataMining (maingear) ","Classify - Decision Trees","Predict([Purchased Bike]) ", "Yes", "Home Owner", "0-1 Miles", "Commute Distance")

The DMPREDICTTABLEROW function uses a table row for its input columns as in the following example:

=DMPREDICTTABLEROW("ExcelDataMining (maingear) ","Classify - Decision Trees","Predict([Purchased Bike]) ",G10:L10)

where the range G10:L10 refers to the Occupation (Management), Home Owner (Yes), Cars (4), Commute Distance (0-1 Miles), Region (Pacific), and Age (33) columns in row 10. This combination of attributes predicted YES.

The DMCONTENTQUERY function that obtains other information from a mining model is beyond the scope of this book..

What's Next

Well we've completed our tour of Microsoft business intelligence tools for us analysts and power users. I hope that you have found at least some of what we've covered useful and perhaps interesting at times. After immersing myself in SQL Server 2008, Excel, Access, etc. for months while writing this book, I remain amazed with and enthused about Microsoft's BI offerings.

Although this is the end of the main part of the book, I've provided a few appendixes with background material for, extensions of, and refreshers about the main topics.

Appendixes

Appendix A - Acronyms, Abbreviations, and Definitions

ADP
Access Data Project, alias Access Project—a Microsoft Access front-end for SQL Server databases.

Algorithm
A procedure for solving a problem in a series of steps.

ANN
Artificial neural network

ARIMA
Autoregressive Integrated Moving Average—a time series forecasting method.

ATP
Analysis Tool Pack – an Excel add-in containing data analysis tools

Autoregression
In time series forecasting using the data series offset by one or more time periods as an independent variable(s).

BI
Business Intelligence

BIDS
Business Intelligence Development Studio—Microsoft's add-in to Visual Studio to create and manage BI applications. It includes Integration, Analysis, and Reporting Services.

Bucket
A range of values for an interval of multi-valued data, e.g., 0-9, 10-19, etc. Buckets are used in discretizing data.

Cube
A data structure with multiple attributes for dimensions and measures (facts) as the cell values. Cubes are created in OLAP.

DBA
Database Administrator

DBMS
Database management System

DDL
Data definition language—SQL for creating and managing database objects

Discretization
Partitioning data into discrete ranges

DML
Data manipulation language—SQL for accessing and managing data in database objects.

DMX
Data Mining Extensions—a query language for data mining structures and models similar to SQL.

DSN
Data Source Name—a file that contains information about an OBDC data source.

DW
Data Warehouse as in AdventureWorks DW.

ETL
Extract, transform, and load. Designed in Integration Services.

Flat Table
Columnar data presented in a rudimentary sequential form.

GUI
Graphical user interface

FK
Foreign Key

HOPAP
Hybrid OLAP, a combination of ROLAP and MOLAP, stores the structure and aggregates in the cube but not the fact values.

KPI
Key performance indicator

IDE
Integrated development environment

MA
Moving average—a time series forecasting method.

MAD
Mean absolute deviation—a forecasting accuracy measure.

MDX
Multidimensional Expressions, the query language for OLAP multidimensional databases.

MOLAP
Multidimensional OLAP storage where the database structure, fact values, and aggregations are stored in the cube.

MSE
Mean squared error—a forecasting accuracy measure that emphasizes larger errors.

ODBC
Open Database Connectivity—an interface that allows interconnectivity between a variety of data sources with a variety of data consumers.

OLAP
Online Analytical Processing

OLE DB
Object Linking and Embedding—Database: a successor of and improvement on ODBC.

OLTP
Online Transaction Processing

RB3
Report Builder 3.0

PK
Primary Key

RDL
Report Definition Language

ROLAP
Relational OLAP storage where only the database structure is stored in the cube.

SES
Single exponential smoothing—a time series forecasting method.

SQL
Structured Query Language

SSMS
SQL Server Management Studio

T-SQL
Transact-SQL, SQL Server's version of structured query language.

URL
Uniform Resource Locator—the address of an Internet location.

VBA
Visual Basic for Applications—a programming language to write code in Microsoft Office applications.

WMA
Weighted moving average—a time series forecasting method.

Appendix B - Some Notes about Data Analysis Concepts

I've hidden these notes in an appendix for fear of driving readers away if they were included in the main part of the book. Admittedly, concepts like these are dry and boring to most of us so we avoid them as much as possible. However, over the years the concepts described here have stood me in good stead in my career. I find that they guide my thinking about data and its analysis and synthesis.

Data and Information

A number of places on the Internet define data as facts but this seems rather ambiguous to me, especially in the context of data analysis. Is the statement "the Earth is round" a fact? Sure, but is it data? Well, maybe. For data analysis purposes my thinking is that data are symbols—numbers, alphabetic characters, images, etc.—that attempt to represent facts. I use the word "attempt" here because the generally accepted definition of fact is something that is true. Data do not necessarily represent truth. We hope they do but many times we are disappointed to find that they don't.

Most of us incorrectly use the terms data and information interchangeably. We could go on here about the technical meaning of information in the communication theory sense as it is related to entropy but for our purposes it's sufficient to say that information is data that has meaning. Data is the raw material used to produce information.

The Value of Information

Data and information are resources (assets) that have value and require time, energy, and/or money to acquire, process, store, manage, and distribute. Too often data are considered as a free commodity or, perhaps, an under-valued one. Before we set out to collect data we should consider what we're going to do with it. In my consulting work a frequent approach to a problem or a decision is to "get more information." I usually then ask what will happen when you get this information. How does it resolve the problem or help you make the decision? What is its value to you and how much will it cost to get it? The point here is to determine the cost-benefit of getting additional information.

Appendix B

I find the concept of the value of perfect information in decision theory from Management Science to be helpful in considering the value of additional information. Without getting into a technical presentation of decision theory, the value of perfect information is the additional value to you by a decision made under complete certainty versus the value of the decision made under less sure conditions. Complete certainty means that you know exactly what the future outcome will be. For example, consider a book publisher faced with a decision about how many books of a particular title to publish as represented in Table B-1. To simplify the example I limited the publisher's alternatives to three lot sizes and the unknown future demand levels for the book to two. The publisher must print the books prior to knowing what the demand will be for it. However, the publisher knows what the profit or loss will be for each combination of lot size and demand as represented by the cell values.

	Future Demand for the Book	
Lot Size Decision	Low Demand	High Demand
Large	-$100,000	$200,00
Medium	-$10,000	$75,000
Small	$50,000	$50,000

Table B-1 Decision Theory Example

So, what lot size should the publisher print? Well that depends on how much more you know about the situation than is presented in the table and about the publisher's risk preference. For example, the publisher could improve its chances for a better return if the probability of the future demand states could be determined, say from market research. Better yet, would be knowing in advance of printing the book what would be the actual demand, i.e., under conditions of perfect information. In this case, to maximize profit if demand was to be low, the publisher would print a small lot and if demand was to be high, a large lot. Somewhat inaccurately stated, the value of perfect information to the publisher is the difference in the average return under perfect information less the average return under a less than certain conditions. The publisher should be willing to pay up to the value of perfect information for a 100 percent certain forecast.

The principle here is that there is a limit to the value of additional data or information, and that at times you will be better off not trying to acquire that data or information because it costs too much. So, before you scramble to get additional data for analysis consider in advance what value it will have to you.

Data Management

From my days in business school long ago I learned that management is the process of planning, organizing, and controlling an organization (POC). It is a proactive activity. Data management should involve the same functions for an organization's data. However, experience suggests that data systems are usually not necessarily well managed. Rather, data accumulate naturally just like the junk in your attic or basement or mini-warehouse or wherever. In fact, there is a bone fide principle in management that explains this phenomenon, Parkinson's Law published by C. Northcote Parkinson in 1958. Parkinson observed that in a bureaucracy work expands to fill the time available just like data on my hard drive expands to fill the space available. This happens in data systems too. Yes, there is some POC of data in organizations but clearly not enough. Going back to the point made above about data as a resource, it needs to be managed as a valuable one.

Fortunately, there is a discipline dedicated to data management. In fact, I learned in writing this that there is an association devoted to it—Data Management International—which is "dedicated to advancing the concepts and practices for data resource management and enterprise information."

Data Quality

First, note that the term "quality" is an attribute or property of an object and that it can take on different values, e.g., high quality, low quality, etc. In casual conversation I know that "quality" means "high quality" but as an attribute of data the minimum acceptable quality needs to be specified. If the quality objective is specified, then actual quality can be determined, a step that we commonly skip assuming we are dealing with "good" data. A saying that comes to mind that seems quite relevant to data quality is that if you measure something, it becomes important; and if it's important, you should measure it.

Data quality should be a moot point if you are using a well-designed and managed data warehouse as your source. Quality problems will be taken care of in the ETL process. But, if you are working directly with raw data sources, you need to deal with the data quality issue.

Data quality is really a set of properties including general properties like accuracy, precision, reliability, and validity and specific properties like the percent of duplicate records, the number of null values, the number of incorrect entries, and so on. We'll touch briefly on the general ones here.

Accuracy and precision go together. Accuracy is the degree to which a measure represents the actual value. Precision is the degree to which repeated measures of a property agree - it is a measure of the amount of variation. A bullseye target is a commonly used analogy for accuracy and precision. The upper left image in Figure B-1 represents fairly high accuracy but low precision; the bottom left high precision but low accuracy; the upper right low accuracy and low precision; and the lower right high accuracy and high precision with all bullets in the bullseye. For our purposes reliability is the same as precision.

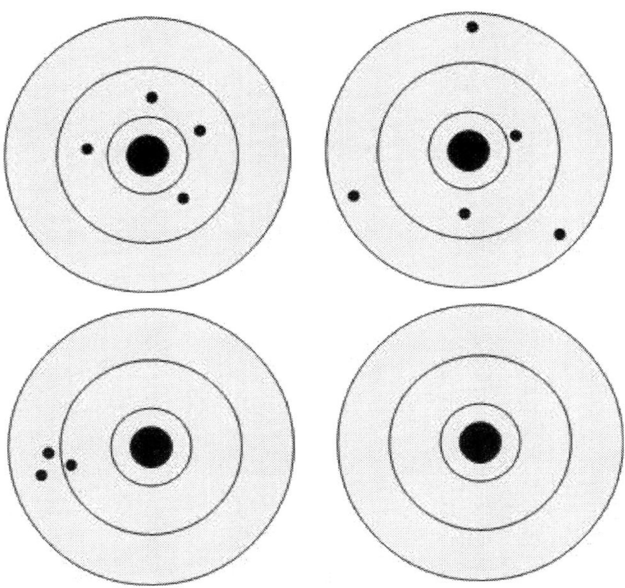

Figure B-1 Accuracy and Precision

In scientific inquiry validity is the degree to which a measure measures what it purports to measure. (Lots of measures here.) Validity is particularly important in research. For example, suppose a psychological instrument is designed to measure intelligence. The degree to which it does that is its validity. In the social sciences there are different types of validity. We won't get into them here.

In data processing (yes, I know that that is an archaic term) validation is the process of insuring that the data are correct and accurate. Validation usually should take place when data are first entered or imported. For example, suppose you have a Visual Basic application that records sales transactions via a form. Some, if not all, of the fields on the form should have a validation rule that checks that the data are entered correctly. Validation rules may check the data type (numerical, logical, or string); the format, e.g., if a Social Security number has nine digits; the range to determine if the value falls within minimum and maximum values; duplication, e.g., checking a database to determine if a customer is already in it; and so on. In the BI world much, if not all, of the data validation and repair should occur during ETL—this is one of the reasons why ETL is difficult and time consuming.

What do you do about post-import data quality assurance? Unacceptable data quality may occur after the fact for a variety of reasons including that the data were not validated at entry or during import, the data files became corrupted, or someone vandalized the database. There are a number of options that you may use to check and clean up data if you are uncertain about its quality. We'll only mention a few approaches here as examples. You could:

- Explore the data by producing descriptive statistics and charts. In Chapter 5 we'll see that Microsoft SQL Server 2008 Data Mining Add-in for Excel 2010 can help with this.
- Look for outliers. The Microsoft SQL Server 2008 Data Mining Add-in helps here too.
- 100% inspect a sample of the data.
- Write queries to find incorrect values.
- Re-import the data into a different table or database application with validation rules in place.
- Check and transform the data is a computer program, e.g., Visual Basic for Applications or Visual Basic .Net

Of course, your goal is high accuracy and high precision data but that may be costly or impossible to achieve so it's important determine how much error you can afford and how much you can tolerate.

Data Analysis Steps

For me there are two types of data analysis: directed and exploratory. Directed data analysis seeks answers to specific questions, e.g., why is profit down in the third quarter; what is the relationship between sales volume and store location; or how effective was the advertising campaign? Exploratory data analysis looks at the data to identify questions to ask. Exploratory data analysis has become increasingly more important as the data available has grown in volume and complexity.

Some of the data analysis methods that we consider in this book are particularly suited for directed analysis. Those methods based on statistical inference and forecasting are prime examples. Others are more useful in exploratory data analysis—examples that come to mind are descriptive statistics and charting. But many are useful for both—here I'm thinking about pivot tables and data mining as examples.

Regardless of the underlying purpose there are a number of common steps in the data analysis process: acquisition, inspection, cleaning and repair, transformation, analysis and modeling, testing and validation, deployment and presentation, and monitoring and maintenance. Comments about each follows.

Acquisition

The purpose of acquisition it to get the data that you need, in a form that you can use, to a place (application) where you can use it. This initial step can range from simple and quick to complex and time consuming. It may involve no more than connecting to an existing query or using data in an existing spreadsheet. Or it may require hours of work to create a computer program to parse the data from an oddball source or to amalgamate data from disparate sources. We address data acquisition in many places in the book.

Inspection

This is the operationalization of data quality management discussed above. We look at a number of methods to identify data errors, particularly with Excel and Access 2010.

Cleaning and Repair

Dirty data are identified and corrected by modifying, replacing, or removing it.

Transformation

After acquisition some data may not be in usable form or in less than desirable form. In some cases it may be more efficient to transform it in advance of analysis than to use it as is. For example, converting Imperial measures into metric measure (or the converse) in advance of analysis may be more efficient and reduce the chance of interpreting results in the wrong scale.

Analysis and Modeling

In this step we utilize a variety of analytical method to identify patterns and relationships in the data. Approaches may range from simple tabulation to using complex data mining algorithms. Although analysis and modeling is the crux of BI, the previous and subsequent steps are necessary to support it. In this book we spend considerable time on analysis and modeling.

Testing and Validation

It's important to test and validate the outcome from an analysis or a resultant model on data that was not part of the analysis, especially when dealing with sample data. The reason for this is that limiting confirmation of say a model to the dataset upon which it was constructed limits the generalizability of the model, i.e., the patterns and relationships found in it may not generalize beyond that set. There are two ways to test a model with different data: partition the dataset into subsets that will be used separately for model development and testing or use the entire available dataset for model development and collect a new sample for testing.

Deployment and Presentation

To be useful data analysis results must be made available to whomever or whatever will use it. So, results may be deployed to the Report Manager for user access or to an application that uses the resultant model for a procedure or function, or just presented to managers for decision making purposes.

Monitoring and Maintenance

Data analysis results that are used recurrently should be reviewed periodically for their continued currency and validity. Some analyses and models will last for long time periods while others must be updated frequently.

The steps above are neither all necessary nor must be followed in a rigid sequence for a given data analysis project. For example, when using a trusted data source, say one created by a well-designed ETL process, you may forgo inspection and possibly transformation. If you are using data in an existing spreadsheet that you created, you may skip directly to analysis and modeling. If you are the only one using the results for a one-shot analysis, you might bypass deployment and maintenance. The first five steps may be particularly intertwined. For example, it's not possible to suppress exploration as you import, inspect, clean and repair, transform, and analyze data. While focusing on one of these function, you are probably doing some of the other as well.

Compared to What

The second banana asks "how's your spouse," the top banana replies "compared to what." Sometimes data in itself has little meaning for all intents and purposes or can be easily misinterpreted when examining it myopically. In those cases, and perhaps in all cases, we should compare the data with something else. We do this automatically all of the time in everyday life but sometimes forget to when we're up to our ears in data. For our purposes here we'll call data analysis without comparison intrinsic and with comparison extrinsic. There are at least two concerns here: the innate risk of intrinsic data analysis and selecting appropriate and useful comparisons in extrinsic data analysis.

Extrinsic comparisons can be to data either internal or external to the organization. Internal sources include goals and previous values over time. Key performance indicators (KPIs) discussed in Chapter 3 and elsewhere in the book are examples of both. A KPI compares a measure (fact) with a goal to compute a status value and compares a previous value of a measure to the current value to compute a trend indicator value. Other internal sources for comparisons include comparative financial statements, operating results among departments and divisions, top ten performers with bottom ten performers, etc.

Industry statistics and norms and benchmarks are examples of extrinsic external comparison data. Industry statistics including means, medians, quartile, and decile may be available from governments, trade associations, and private data providers among others. An example is the Risk Management Association's Annual Statement Studies (previously Robert Morris Associates) that provides comparative financial data organized by North American Industry Classification System codes. So if you want to compare your financial ratios with others in your particular line of business, the RMA is one source to do that. Benchmarking, the process of using best practices in a line of business or the practices of the best organization in a line of business, is another source for extrinsic external data.

Extrinsic internal and external comparisons are complementary so it's wise to use both. For example, a convenience store operator may find its 11 cents per gallon fuel gross margin this year as compared to the 9 cents it achieved last year (an internal comparison) to indicate good performance. However, this would be a false conclusion if the industry average was 15 cents.

Models

Models are abstract representations of the real world. A model always leaves stuff out that is present in reality. An organization chart is a model of the relationships among people in an organization. However, it only represents the basic formal structure of the organization ignoring much of the complexity of organizational life. There are different types of models—iconic, analog, and mathematical come to mind. The models that we usually deal with in data analysis are graphical, mathematical and statistical, and spreadsheet in form. The latter two are characterized by three elements: parameters, variables, and relationships. A parameter is a fixed characteristic for a specific instance of the model whereas variables can take on different values for a given instance. Variables are of two types: independent variables that take on values outside of the model and dependent whose values are determined by the model via the relationships among parameters and variables specified in it. The linear equation below is a simple example of a model where a and b are parameters, X is the independent variable, and Y is the dependent variable. The specific instance of the model below specifies parameters values and relationships among the parameters and independent variables with the plus operator and multiplication of X by 2. Spreadsheets use a similar forms for their cell assignment statements.

$$Y = a + bX$$

example: $$Y = 5 + 2X$$

Two characteristic of models are worthwhile to mention here: whether they involve probabilities or time as a variable. Probabilistic models incorporate randomness in the value of the independent variables whereas in deterministic models independent variables take on specific (determined) values for each set of conditions without any variation. Dynamic models incorporate time as an independent variable, static models do not. The model above is a static, deterministic model.

Measurement Scales

In social science, particularly psychology, measurement scales are categorized into four types: nominal, ordinal, interval, and ratio. The scales have increasing "discriminationability" moving from the nominal scale to the ratio scale. Nominal scales just categorize objects, attributes or events and the categories cannot be ordered. Examples include gender, product categories, and music genre. In ordinal scales objects, attributes, or events can be rank ordered but the intervals between the scales values are indefinite. For example, categories on the Likert scale—strongly disagree, disagree . . . . strongly agree—are ordered but the intervals between the categories cannot be defined, e.g., we cannot say anything about how much more disagreeable strongly disagree is than disagree. The measures are just ordered.

The interval and ratio scales are what we commonly think of as true measures in that the scales have numerical values with equal intervals between them. In some fields these are called cardinal measures. Examples include temperature, length, and income. The difference between interval and ratio scales is whether the scale has an absolute zero point—the interval scale doesn't and ratio scale does. Temperature in degrees Fahrenheit is an interval scale because its zero point is arbitrary. Temperature can be below zero. Thus, we cannot say that 40 degrees Fahrenheit is twice as warm as 20 degrees Fahrenheit. However, in ratio scales like length and income the ratios remain constant, e.g., an annual income of $50K is twice that of $25K.

Why be concerned about this? There are at least two reasons. One is that fewer mathematical and statistical operations are permitted or make sense as we move from ratio to nominal measures. All mathematical and statistical operations can be performed on ratio measures and few on nominal measures. Another reason to bring this up is the operation of discretization which is the process of converting interval and ratio measures into ordinal or nominal measures. An example of discretization is converting family annual income into income categories such as $0 to $20,000, $21,000 to $40,000, etc. This is especially useful in data mining where categorization of dimensional data is common. In fact. some data mining algorithms require categorical data.

Statistics

The dreaded word "statistics"—attention dwindles, eyes glaze, and heads nod. I saved this one for last because I knew that you would enjoy it so much. Regardless of its reputation I think that a few comments about statistics are appropriate because statistics and its nomenclature are used extensively in data analysis and BI.

Statistics deals with two types of data: populations and samples. A population, sometimes called a universe, is the entirety of data that exists about whatever is the focus of attention. A sample is a subset of population data. A characteristic of a population like its mean is called a parameter, and a characteristic of a sample is called a statistic. In BI we are usually dealing with sample data because time is one of the dimensions of our data, i.e., we have samples of populations of data that extend back into the past or forward into the future.

There are two types of statistics: descriptive and inferential. Descriptive statistics present summary characteristics of a collection of data. Examples include measures of central tendency like the mean and measures of variability like the variance and range. Inferential statistics deals with sample data and attempts to infer characteristics about the population based on sample evidence, i.e., we try to determine values of parameters based on knowledge about sample statistics.

A major theme in statistics as a discipline is variation or variability where individual items of data take on different values. This variation is due to either some systematic pattern in the data, say normal seasonal vacillations in sales, or to random fluctuations that cannot be explained or accounted for by a model.

Generally, the less random variation the better. A major purpose of statistics (and data analysis as well) is to identify systematic data patterns and to determine their strength compared with the random variation present. That's what statistical models do.

In inferential statistics we infer something about a population by testing the truth of a statement about it or by making statements about the confidence we have in that statement or the degree to which the pattern in a model represents the pattern in the population. The former approach is called hypothesis testing and the latter deals with confidence intervals. Simplifying quite a bit, in hypothesis testing we usually test a statement about a parameter being equal to some value or that parameters from different population are equal, that is that there is no difference in the populations with respect to that parameter. This no difference statement is called the null hypothesis and we either accept it as true or reject it as false when we test it with data. If we reject it, we accept the alternative hypothesis. The null hypothesis and the alternative hypothesis together exhaustively represent all outcomes. For example, either the population mean is equal to 50 (null hypothesis) or it isn't (alternative hypothesis). Or the proportion of defects in a lot is less than or equal to 3 percent (null hypothesis) or it is greater than 3 percent (alternative hypothesis).

In this context there are two types of statistical errors: either we conclude that the null hypothesis is false when it really isn't or that the null hypothesis is true when it isn't. Hopefully, the diagram in Figure B-2 will "demuddle" this. The two main rows in the table represent what your decision will be given the data that you have, that the null hypothesis is either true of false. The two columns on the right show the true condition in the population—what is actually true. Thus, there are four outcomes: two for correct decisions and two for incorrect ones (errors). The outcome in row 2 column1 is called a Type I error, and the probability of it occurring is called alpha which can be specified by the investigator who says I will accept a X probability of making a Type I error for this test (where X is usually .05, .01, or .001). Since the column probabilities must sum to 1.0, then the probability of making a correct decision in row 1 column1 is one minus alpha (called the confidence level). Similarly, beta is the probability of making a Type II error in row 1 column 2 with the probability of making a correct decision when the alternative hypothesis is true is one minus beta (called the power of the test). Whew!

	True in the Population (actual)	
Decide from Sample Evidence	Null Hypothesis True	Alternative Hypothesis True
Null Hypothesis True	Correct 1 - α = P(Correct) Confidence Level **(Cell 1-1)**	Type II error β = P(Incorrect) **(Cell 1-2)**
Alternative Hypothesis True	Type I error α = P(Incorrect) **(Cell 2-1)**	Correct 1 - β = P(Correct) Power **(Cell 2-2)**
Sum of Column Probabilities	1.0	1.0

Figure B-2 Statistical Decision Making

Why is this important? Because you want to know or control the risk of error involved in using statistical inference results in making decision. For example, in last few years there have been a number of food recalls due to contamination from harmful organisms. If you are a food producer, I expect that you would like to ship a safe product (at least I hope that you would). Usually you test samples of the product because you can't do 100 percent inspection for legitimate reasons, say because inspection involves destructive testing. When tests for harmful contamination are conducted, the null hypothesis is that the lot (the population in this case) is Ok, and the alternative hypothesis is that the lot is contaminated. In this case you should be much more concerned with a Type II error where you would ship a bad lot based on the sample evidence. There are ways statistically of control the probability of Type I and Type II errors.

One of the reasons that we can make statements about the probability of making these errors is due to the Central Limit Theorem which says the distribution of sample means is normally distributed. Because we know the characteristics of the normal distribution from its probability density function, we can use it to determine or control the error probabilities. Going further with this topic, e.g., Z-scores, t values, and confidence limits, is getting way beyond the scope of the this brief explanation so I'll stop with this topic and mention just one more important data analysis issue.

Mark Twain supposedly popularize the expression that there are "lies, dammed lies, and statistics." Lying with statistics is leading someone to accept a false fact or conclusion by misrepresenting the data. I still have on my bookshelf the copy of How to Lie with Statistics by Darrell Huff that was required for an undergraduate required statistic course years ago. The book is still in print! I won't detail any of Huff's points about how people inadvertently or intentionally misrepresent facts. But I will say that you should be cautious about statistics and visualizations of them (charts and graphs) and make sure that you are not guilty of misrepresentation yourself. It's easy to do. For example, just changing the vertical scale on a chart can dramatically affect how the numbers are interpreted. Although it's dated, I recommend Huff's book for a quick, fun, and useful read.

Appendix C - Up to Speed with Queries

Queries are used extensively in BI and, of course, in this book. Some readers may be inexperienced with queries or are query challenged so this appendix covers the basics concepts and operations. It is far from a comprehensive treatment of the topic, and it intentionally avoids teaching structured query language (SQL), which for our purposes is unnecessary because of the availability of query designers.

In this appendix we will focus on using queries with databases although elsewhere in the book we will use queries-like processes to acquire data from other sources. Databases use SQL to create and managed database objects using a data definition language (DDL) and to access and manipulate data in them with a data manipulation language DML. Queries are the primary instruments for employing DML.

There are different types of queries that define different actions on data. For example, Microsoft Access 2010 offers select, make table, append, update, crosstab, delete, union, pass-through, and data definition queries (although the latter is a DDL-type table creation and modification mechanism). SQL Server does not classify queries like Microsoft Access because its interface is more DDL and DML statement oriented, i.e., you write more SQL statements in SQL Server than in Access where a query designer does most of the work. However, SQL Server has similar query actions such as INSERT, UPDATE, and DELETE. (Note that SQL Server has a query designer that can be used in creating stored queries called views.) Select queries are most useful for BI purposes so we will use that type for examples here.

Select queries acquire data from data sources in the form of transient tables with rows for records and columns as fields via a query language, usually a dialect of SQL, that is compatible with the data source. Data do not persist in queries as they do in database tables. When a select query is run, it displays the specified data or provides it to the application requesting the data. It does not persist. To refresh the query it must be run again. The basic form of a SQL select query is shown in Table C-1.

SQL Format	Example
SELECT <data fields>	SELECT CompanyName, Country, City
FROM <data source(s)>	FROM Customers
WHERE <filter statement>	WHERE (((Country)="USA")) OR (((Country)="Canada"))
ORDER BY <sort statement>;	ORDER BY Country, City;

Table C-1 Simple Select Query SQL

In the example from the Microsoft sample database Northwind Traders the fields CompanyName, Country, and City from the Customers table for customers located in the USA and Canada are selected with the data sorted by Country and City. The results returned by the query appear in Figure C-1.

Example Query

Company Name	Country	City
Mère Paillarde	Canada	Montréal
Bottom-Dollar Markets	Canada	Tsawassen
Laughing Bacchus Wine Cellars	Canada	Vancouver
Rattlesnake Canyon Grocery	USA	Albuquerque
Old World Delicatessen	USA	Anchorage
Save-a-lot Markets	USA	Boise
The Cracker Box	USA	Butte
Hungry Coyote Import Store	USA	Elgin
Great Lakes Food Market	USA	Eugene
Trail's Head Gourmet Provisioners	USA	Kirkland
Split Rail Beer & Ale	USA	Lander
The Big Cheese	USA	Portland
Lonesome Pine Restaurant	USA	Portland
Let's Stop N Shop	USA	San Francisco
White Clover Markets	USA	Seattle
Lazy K Kountry Store	USA	Walla Walla

Figure C-1 Simple Select Query Results

Query Designers

The query above was created with a query designer, in this case in Access 2010, that uses a graphical user interface to drag and drop data fields onto a query grid. Query designers vary slightly in form among applications but the basic functions are the same. So, if you know how to use one query designer, you can easily find your way around others. The first step in using a query designer is to specify a data source. However, if you are creating a query within a database open in the application, say Microsoft Access or SQL Server, then specification of a data source via a connection is unnecessary. (We'll get to connections shortly.) The next step is to use the designer to build the query. We'll use the Access 2010 designer for the example.

Some applications like Microsoft Access have query wizards available to build simple queries. The wizard will ask you to select the tables and/or existing queries to use as data sources and to specify the data fields to use from them. I find it easier and quicker to skip the wizard and go directly to the query designer. We'll do that here.

A query designer will have a design surface with at least two panels: one that contains the data source(s) and one for a query design grid that lists the fields to be in the query and specifies some properties about them. In addition, there is usually a properties window available to show properties for the objects used in the query and some way to preview the query. The query designer from Access 2010 for the example query in Figure C-1 is shown in Figure C-2.

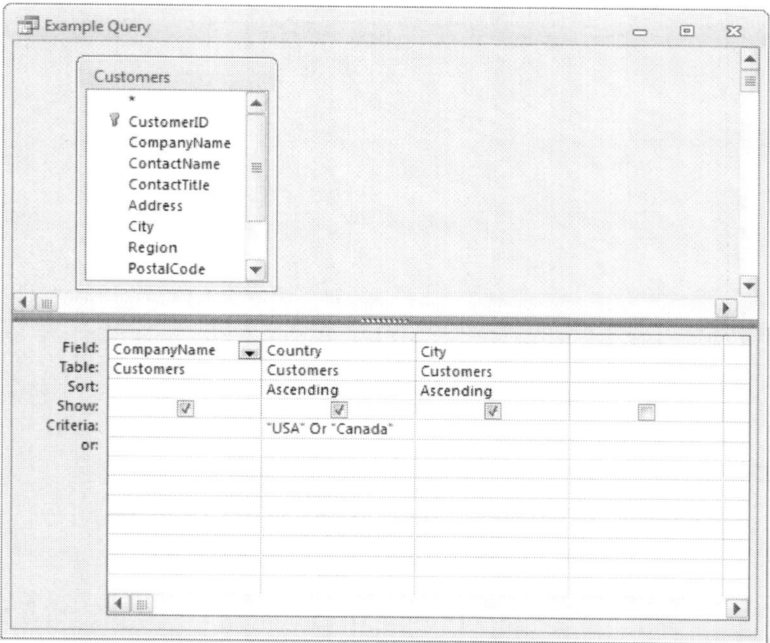

Figure C-2 Query Designer Example

When I first opened the query designer to build this query it was blank, i.e., the customers table was not there and , of course, neither were there fields in the designer grid. The first thing to do with a new query is to insert tables or existing queries as data sources, usually done by bringing up a Show Table (or Add Table) dialog box by right clicking on the design surface. Figure C-3a shows the one from Access 2010. Here I selected the Customers table and clicked the Add button to insert it onto the design surface. You can also just double click a table to add it or select multiple tables and then click the button. Note that you can view/select both tables and existing queries to add to the surface as indicated by the tabs. Tables and queries selected as data sources appear on the design surface with their available fields shown in a list. Unwanted tables and queries are easily removed by right clicking on them and selecting Remove Table from the menu. The Property Sheet as in Figure C-3b will show the properties for whatever object is selected on the design surface or in the grid. In this case it is showing the properties for the query itself.

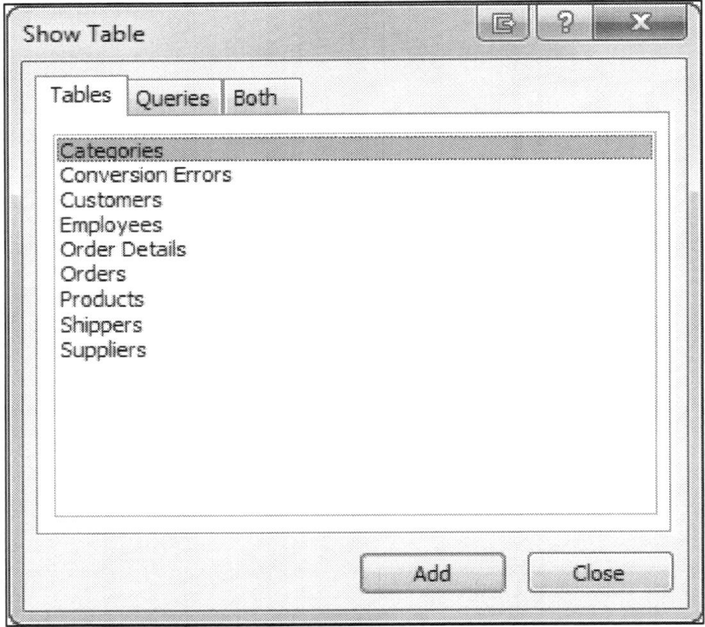

Figure C-3a Show Table Dialog Box

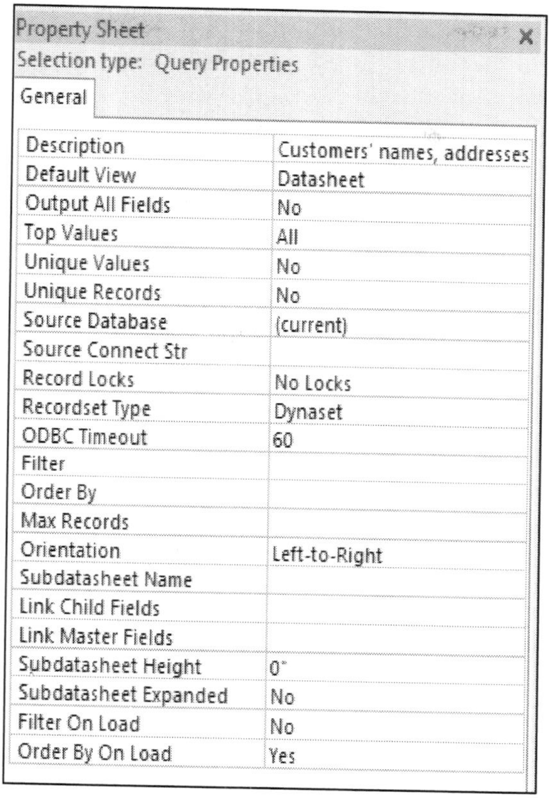

Property Sheet

Selection type: Query Properties

General

Description	Customers' names, addresses
Default View	Datasheet
Output All Fields	No
Top Values	All
Unique Values	No
Unique Records	No
Source Database	(current)
Source Connect Str	
Record Locks	No Locks
Recordset Type	Dynaset
ODBC Timeout	60
Filter	
Order By	
Max Records	
Orientation	Left-to-Right
Subdatasheet Name	
Link Child Fields	
Link Master Fields	
Subdatasheet Height	0"
Subdatasheet Expanded	No
Filter On Load	No
Order By On Load	Yes

Figure C-3b Properties Window

Figure C-3 Query Designer Example Continued

After specifying the data source(s) you may proceed to choose the data fields to include in the query by either double clicking on a field which will insert it into the grid or dragging and dropping it onto the grid. You may also select multiple fields in the table or query and then drag and drop them as a group. I dropped CompanyName, Country, and City fields onto the grid for this simple query. Then, I defined a filter (SQL keyword WHERE)—an expression that limits the records to be returned in the query—in the criteria row of the query grid and specified sorting (SQL keyword ORDER BY) for the Country and City fields. The check boxes in the Show row in the grid indicate that those fields will be displayed when the query is rendered. (There are times when you do not want to show all fields in a query.)

As opposed to the simple one-table query in the example most queries use multiple tables or multiple existing queries as data sources which somewhat complicates query design. As we mentioned in Chapter 2 relational databases establish relationships among tables to facilitate querying data by using keys, unique identifier fields that are common to two or more tables. This allows a query to find appropriate rows in the multiple tables to display together. There are different types of relationships between two tables called joins because they join tables together into a single query result. The most common type is an inner join where only the rows that have matching values in the tables are shown in the query.

In Figure C-4 I added the Orders and Order Details tables to construct a query that will list the quantity sold and the total sales amount for each customer. For your information although the Orders table does not contain any data used in the query, it is required to link the Customers table with the Orders Details table where the sales data are recorded. Without the Orders table there is no way to connect a customer with its sales. (The Orders table in this case is called an associative entity.)

The lines connecting the tables show the relationships between each pair. The connection between the Customers table and the Orders table shows that the CustomerID field (foreign key) in the Orders table is linked with the CustomerID field (primary key) in the Customers table. While it is not necessary for the linked fields to share the same name as in this example, they do have to have the same properties such as data type. The 1 and infinity symbol on the link indicates the type of relationship between the two tables. The 1 indicates one and the infinity symbol indicates many. So, the relationship between the Customers table and the Orders table is one-to-many meaning that only one specific customer number may appear in the customers table but that it may be use many times in the Orders table, i.e., a customer may place many orders but an order may only have one customer.

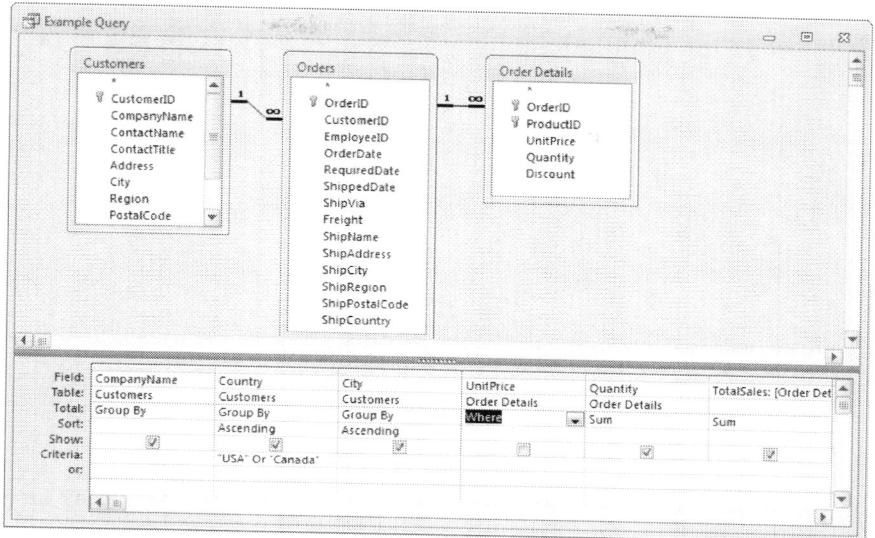

Figure C-4 Multiple Table Query Design

To construct this query I added the UnitPrice and Quantity fields from the Order Details table to the query grid. In addition I added the column on the right to calculate the amount of a sale. Following relational database principles the database table design intentionally does not include a sales amount field because it would be redundant, i.e., it can be calculated by multiplying UnitPrice and Quantity. The expression for the sales amount field (TotalSales) is shown below:

TotalSales: [Order Details]![UnitPrice]*[Order Details]![Quantity]

This says that a field to be called TotalSales is calculated by multiplying UnitPrice in the Order Details table by Quantity in the Order Details table. I elected not to show the UnitPrice field in the query by unchecking the Show box, and I enabled the Total row in the grid to allow for summing the quantity and sales amounts to calculate total units sold and total sales for each customer. I also took the opportunity to format the new TotalSales field in a currency format with no decimal places by using the Property Sheet. The result from running the query is shown in Figure C-5.

Company Name	Country	City	SumOfQuan	TotalSales
Mère Paillarde	Canada	Montréal	966	$32,204
Bottom-Dollar Markets	Canada	Tsawassen	956	$22,608
Laughing Bacchus Wine Cellars	Canada	Vancouver	62	$523
Rattlesnake Canyon Grocery	USA	Albuquerque	1383	$52,246
Old World Delicatessen	USA	Anchorage	603	$16,325
Save-a-lot Markets	USA	Boise	4958	$115,673
The Cracker Box	USA	Butte	59	$1,947
Hungry Coyote Import Store	USA	Elgin	122	$3,063
Great Lakes Food Market	USA	Eugene	345	$19,711
Trail's Head Gourmet Provisioners	USA	Kirkland	89	$1,571
Split Rail Beer & Ale	USA	Lander	327	$12,490
Lonesome Pine Restaurant	USA	Portland	134	$4,259
The Big Cheese	USA	Portland	46	$3,361
Let's Stop N Shop	USA	San Francisco	181	$3,490
White Clover Markets	USA	Seattle	1063	$29,073
Lazy K Kountry Store	USA	Walla Walla	20	$357

Example Query — Record: 1 of 16 — No Filter — Search

Figure C-5 Multiple Table Query Design

I avoid writing SQL statement and rely on query designers as much as possible for two reasons. First, query designers are easy to use, and second, I do not write SQL statement often enough to remember the correct syntax. However, at times when composing SQL statements is unavoidable, say to insert a SQL string into a Visual Basic program to access a database, I will, if at all possible, still use the query designer in the data source application to rough out the SQL statement and then copy it to the program. For example, to use Microsoft Access data in a Visual Basic program I would first create a query to the data in Access itself and then copy the SQL string statement into the Visual Basic code. Others much more proficient with SQL can write SQL statements from scratch.

Connections

Connections and queries are closely related. Connections link a query with its data source. A query requires a connection but a connection does not necessarily require a query because a connection can be used for other tasks. Connections can be explicit or implicit. An explicit connection specifies a link to a data source external to the application in which the query is used. For example, using data from SQL Server in Microsoft Excel requires establishing a connection to the SQL Server instance prior to querying the database for data. Implicit connections occur when using queries inside the application in which the data are stored. For example, creating a query within a Microsoft Access database (or SQL Server for that matter) to tables or existing queries in that database usually do not require specification of a connection—the connection to the database itself is implied.

Explicit connections require providers/drivers to serve as intermediaries between the data source application, say a SQL Server database, and the application using the connection, say an Excel workbook. Think of the providers/drivers as interpreters that allow the data consumer and data provider to communicate. There are a bunch of provider/drivers available in Microsoft BI tools. Some provide connections to specific applications only, say SQL Server, and other establish connections to a variety of application types. Examples of the latter are Microsoft's Open Database Connectivity (ODBC) and Object Linking and Embedding, Database (OLE DB). Generally, it's preferable to use a specific provider/driver if one is available.

As an example, we'll use Excel 2010 to connect to SQL Server data source. Figure C-6 shows the Get External Data and Connections command groups in the Excel 2010 Data tab. To access data in Excel from Microsoft Access, the Web, or from a text file click on one of those buttons to display a dialog box or wizard that will assist in creating the connection and selecting the data to access. Clicking the Existing Connections button provides a list of stored previously used connections saved as Office Data Connection (ODC) files which may be located by default in C:\My Documents\My Data Sources. From what I can understand, ODC files are primarily used by Excel and not by other Office applications. Clicking Connections in the Connections command group will open the Workbook Connections dialog box where connections local to the current workbook are listed. Connections saved in a workbook and not as an ODC file are not available in other workbooks. In the figure I had also clicked the From Other Sources button to display the drop-down menu for other data sources.

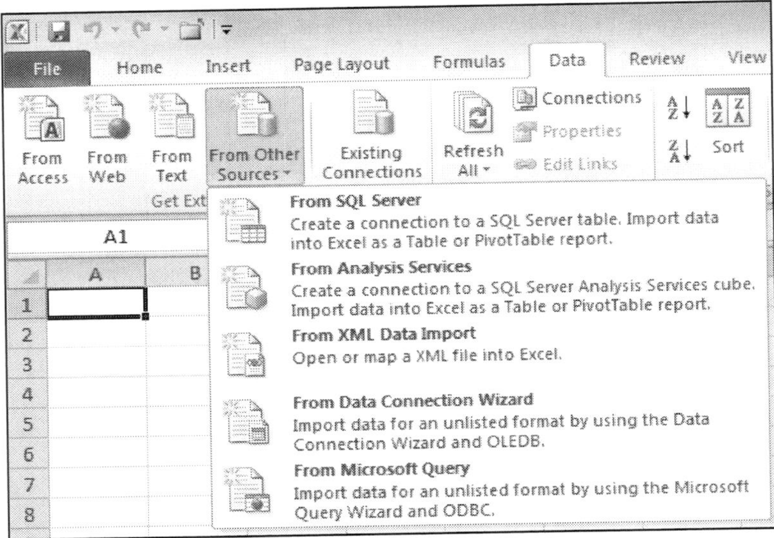

Figure C-6 Multiple Table Query Design

Selecting From SQL Server or From Analysis Services will bring up a Data Connection Wizard like the one shown in Figure C-7 where you must enter the name of the SQL Server instance and specify an authentication option. Clicking Next will display the Select Database and Table dialog box as in Figure C-8 which is for a SQL Server connection. Clicking on the down arrowhead will display a listbox to choose the database that you want to use. In this case I choose the AdventureWorks2008DW database. If the Connect to a specific table check box is checked, then a list of tables and views is presented in the list below from which you select one to use. If you do not want to limit the connection to only one table, then unclick the box. Either way click next to proceed to the Save Data Connection File and Finish dialog box shown in Figure C-9.

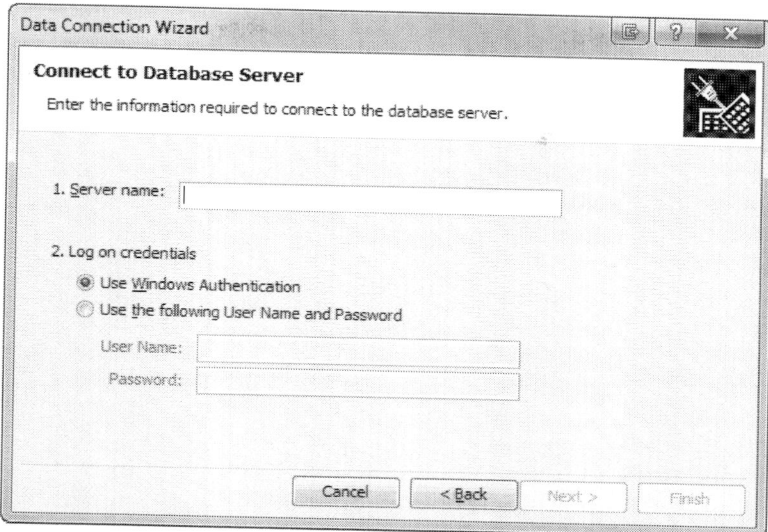

Figure C-7 Data connection Wizard

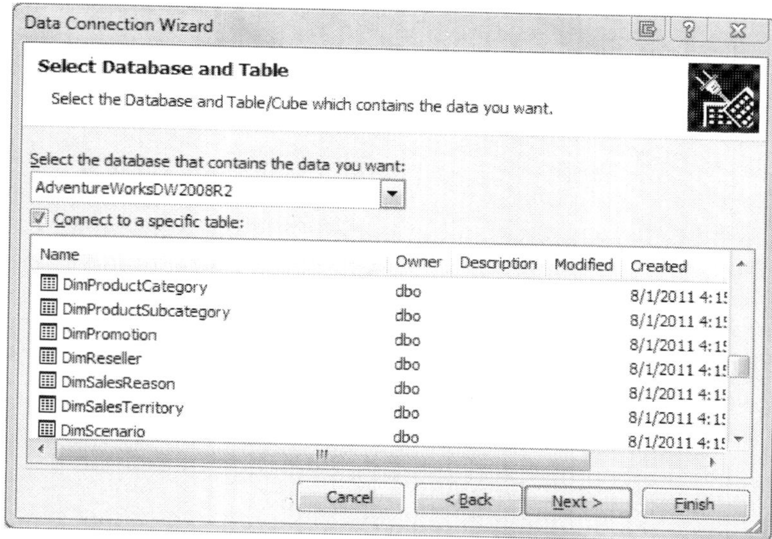

Figure C-8 Select Database and Table Dialog Box

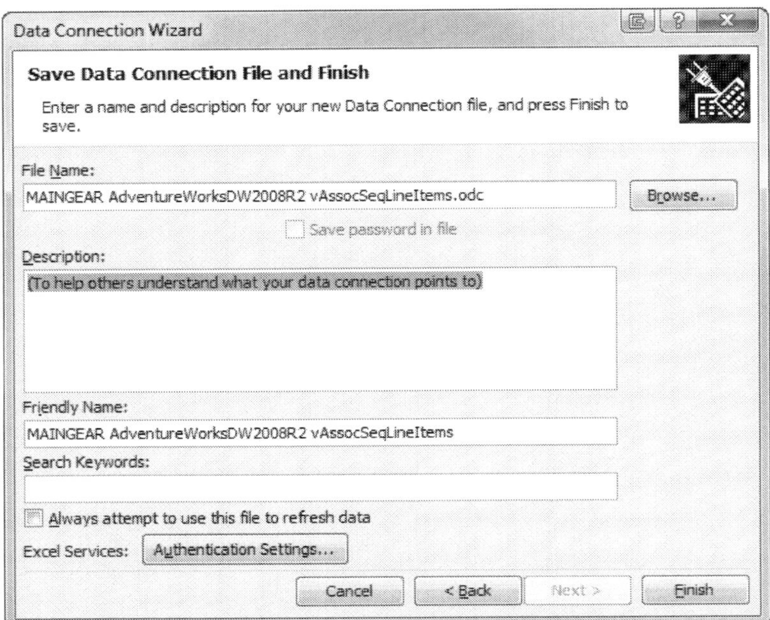

Figure C-9 Save Data Connection File Dialog Box

Note that the connection will be saved as an ODC file. Click the Browse button to bring up the standard File Save dialog box if you prefer to change the folder location. You may also change the name of the ODC file, insert a description, attach a friendly name, and insert keywords. I would not mess with the authentication settings. If you did not select a table or view to use earlier, when you click Finish a Select Table dialog box will appear where you must select one table or view to use in a current or new worksheet. So, keep in mind that the SQL Server connection allows connection to only one table or view. This constraint may be avoided by using Microsoft Query.

Selecting the From XML Data Import option in Figure C-6 will display a Select Data Source (File Open-type) dialog box from which you may select the XML file. (See Excel 2010 Help for instructions about importing XML data.) Selection of the From Data Connection Wizard option displays the Data Connection Wizard as in Figure C-10. Selecting SQL Server or Analysis Services from the list of data sources takes you on the same sequence of steps as described above. Selecting ODBC DSN (Data Source Name) takes you to a list of defined data sources on your machine. DSNs are managed via Control Panel > Administrative Tools > Data Sources (ODBC). The OLE DB Provider for Oracle does just that. Clicking the Other/Advanced option in

Figure C-10 displays a Data Link Properties dialog box as in Figure C-11 which lists a variety of connection providers/drivers in the Provider tab including the SQL Server Native Client 10.0 for SQL Server 2008. The Connection tab allows selection of a DSN like the ODBC DSN option or writing a connection string. The Other/Advanced option is a more flexible way to establish a data source connection of the ones we've covered so far.

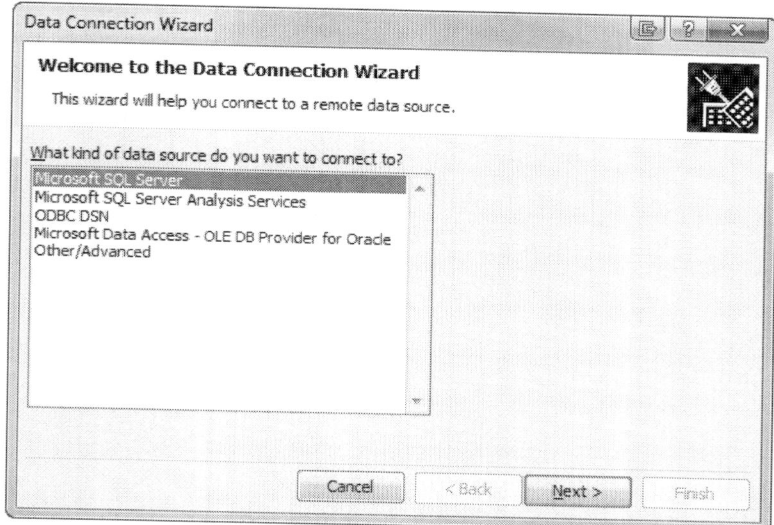

Figure C-10 Data Connection Wizard

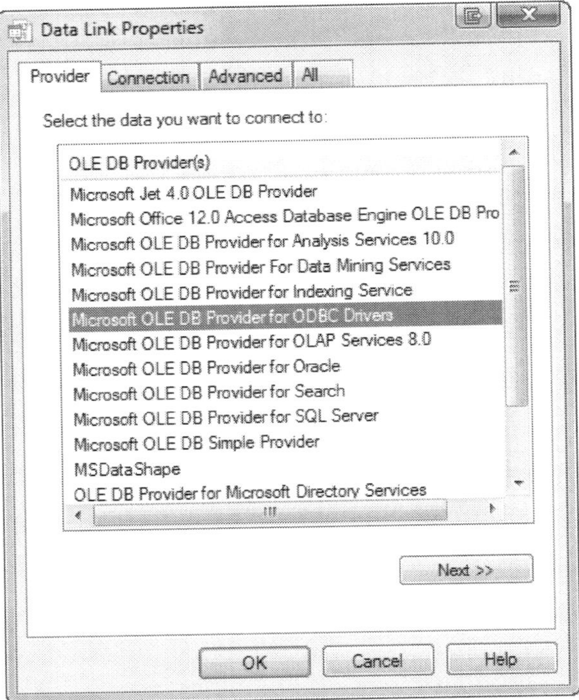

Figure C-10 Data Connection Wizard

Microsoft Query

Last but not least the From Microsoft Query option in Figure C-6 may be the most useful of all of the options because it incorporates a query designer so you can select fields from different tables and views for the query. If Microsoft Query was not installed with Office, do so now by rerunning Office setup and select Microsoft Query from the Database Tools options.

Figure C-11 shows the Choose Data Source dialog box displayed after clicking the Microsoft Query Option. The tabs lists previously saved connections from the three types of data sources: databases, queries, and OLAP cubes. Clicking the <New Data Source> connection in the Databases tab or in the OLAP Cubes tab brings up the Create New Data Source dialog box as in Figure C-12. The New Data Source dialog box will initially appear with blank textboxes. For the example, I entered the name and selected the ODBC driver from the list that appears by clicking the down arrowhead. The next step is to click Connect.... to display the SQL Server Login dialog box as in Figure C-13 where you enter the name of the SQL Server instance and specify the type of authentication. (I selected Trusted because I use Windows not SQL Server authentication.)

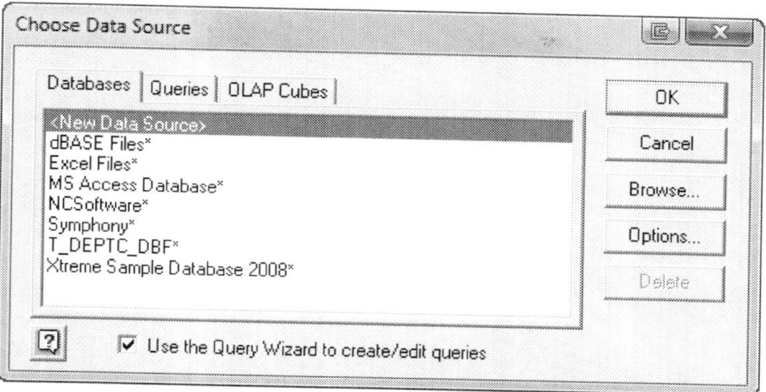

Figure C-11 Data Connection Wizard

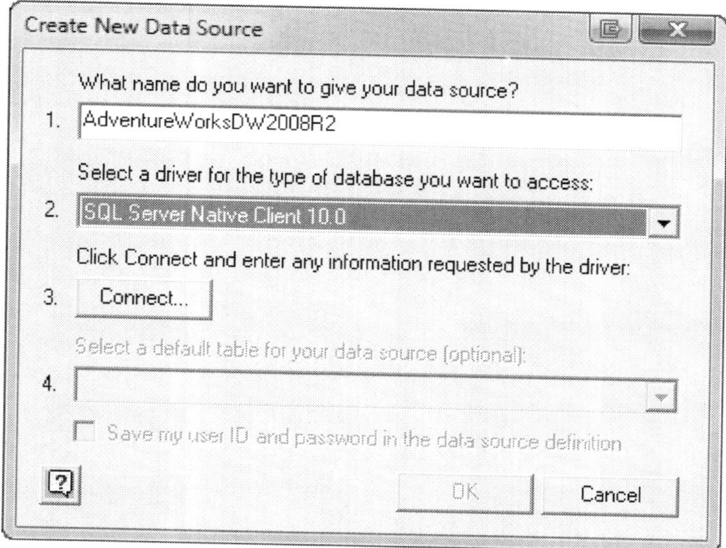

Figure C-12 Data Connection Wizard

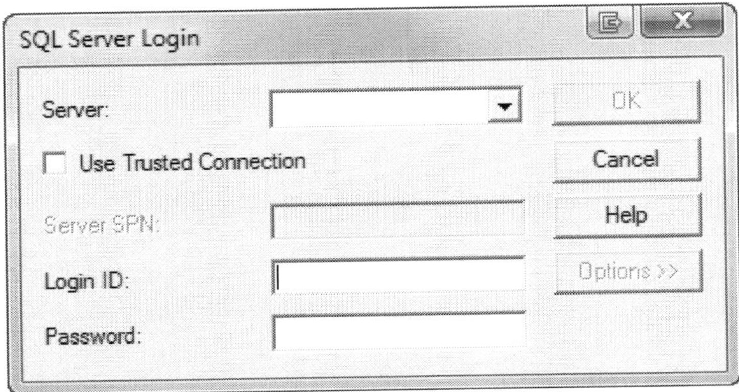

Figure C-13 SQL Server Login Dialog Box

With that accomplished the Options button will be enabled. Clicking it makes visible the Options frame at the bottom of the dialog box shown in Figure C-14 where you select the database to use from the drop-down listbox. Note that selecting a different driver in Figure C-12 will result in working with different types of connection dialog boxes. For example, selecting a Microsoft Access driver will lead to a ODBC Microsoft Access Setup dialog box where you can select an existing Access database file or create a new one.

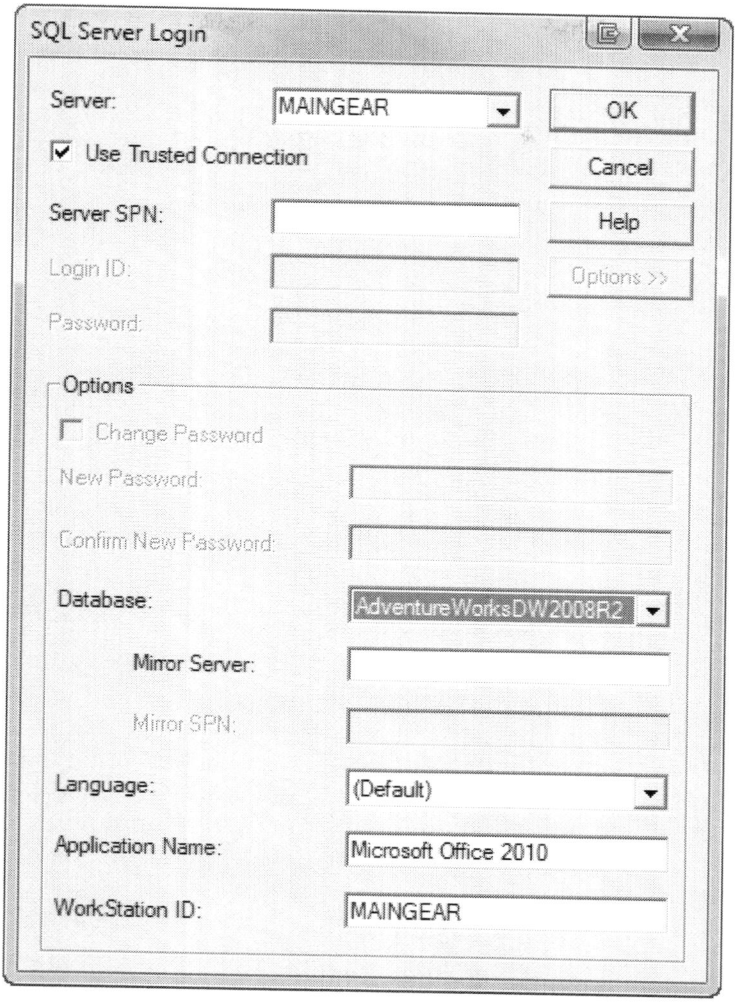

Figure C-14 Expanded SQL Server Login Dialog Box

With the connection definition complete I clicked OK repeatedly until I got to the Query wizard - Choose Columns dialog box in Figure C-15. Use the left panel to select the tables, views, and data fields (columns) to use in the query. Note that the panel may contain many irrelevant data objects as well as tables and views in which you may be interested so carefully browse the list. Selections are moved in and out of the Columns in your query list in the right panel by using the move buttons. All fields in a table or view may be inserted into the query all at once by selecting the table or view and using move button or fields may be selected and moved individually.

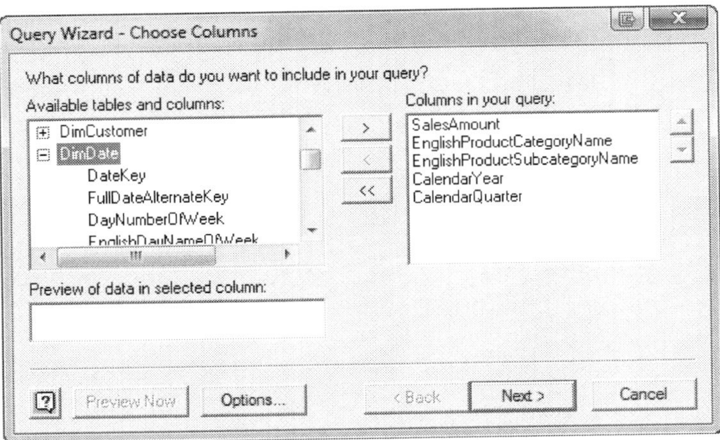

Figure C-15 Query Wizard - Choose Columns

Clicking next may trigger a warning about the tables not being joined. If that is the case, then click OK to proceed to the Microsoft Query Designer window shown in Figure C-16 to clean up the query. For this example there were two problems. First, I had forgotten to include the Product table which is necessary to link the InternetSales table with the ProductSubcategory table. When I added the Product table by selecting Add Table from the Table menu the relations between the tables were automatically connected. Second, the Date table was not linked to the InternetSales table so I dragged the DateKey from the InternetSales table and dropped it on the OrderDataKey in the InternetSales table to establish the relationship. I then saved the query which by default is stored in the C:\Users\<User Name>\AppData\Roaming \Microsoft\Queries directory as a DQY file. DQY stands for database query. An OQY file in that directory is a OLAP query file, and an IQY is an Internet query file used in Excel to acquire data form a table(s) on a Web page.

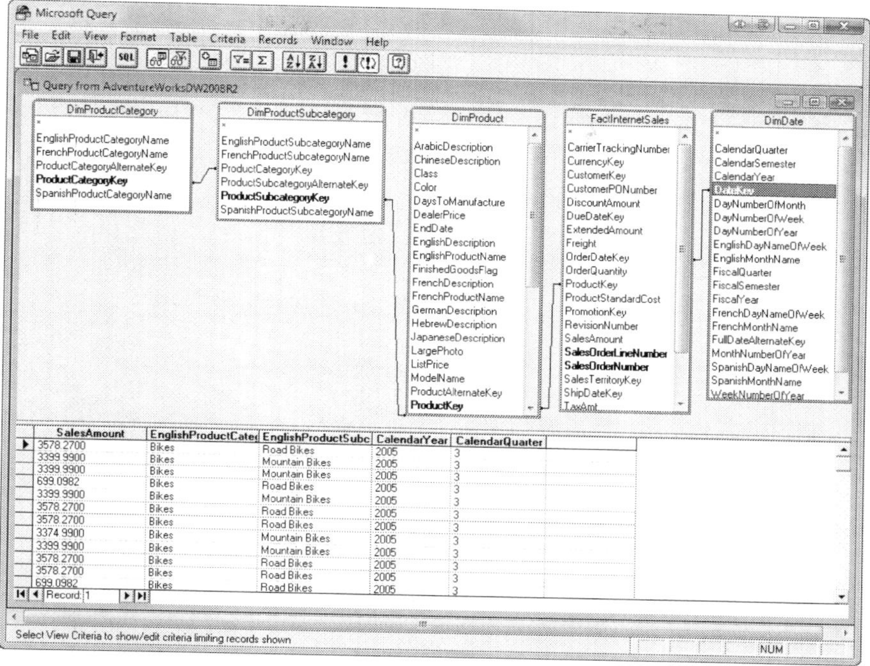

Figure C-16 Microsoft Query Designer - Example 1
(For better viewing of this image, go to
http://www.zerobits.info/bibook/bibookimages/)

To use this query in Excel, select the query from the Existing Connections option in the Data Ribbon This will bring the data into Excel. Note if you double clicked open or click on the DQY file itself, it will open Excel with the data in a worksheet. Is this tedious or What? Wait, there's more!

If there was no error warning, clicking Next in Figure C-15 will bring up a Filter Data dialog box where you may specify a filter to limit the records appearing in the query. In Figure C-17 I specified a filter of calendar years beyond 2005. You may specify sort properties in the next dialog box, and in the final dialog box shown in Figure C-18 you may choose to either Return the data to Excel,View the data or edit the query in Microsoft Query, or Save the Query using the button. I recommend saving it to make sure that it is available to you again.

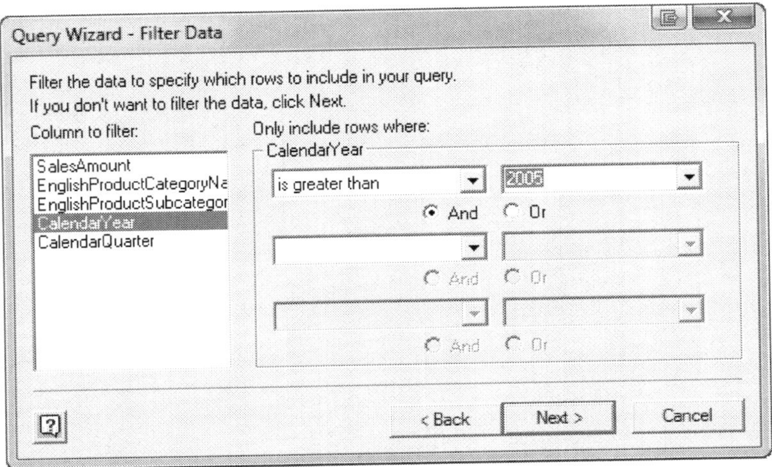

Figure C-17 Microsoft Query Wizard - Filter Data

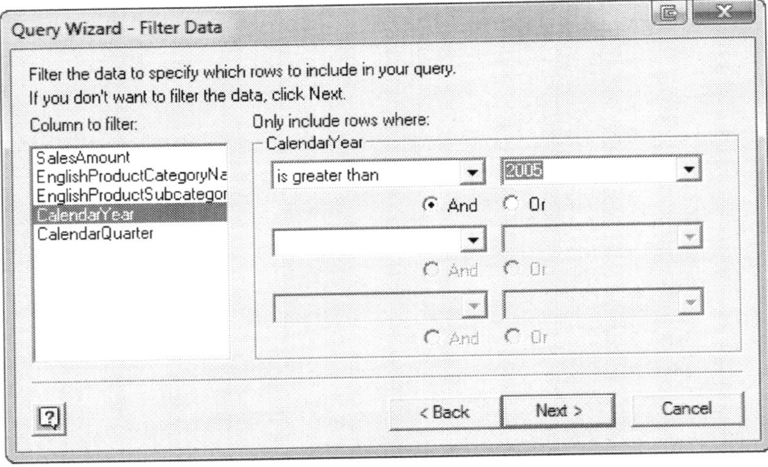

Figure C-18 Microsoft Query Wizard - Finish

Microsoft Query Designer

We'll use the query from the AdventureWorks2008DW database is shown in Figure C-19 using the Customer, ProductCategory, and InternetSales tables to exercise the Query Designer. The fields selected from these tables are listed in Table C-2. Note that the Product and ProductSubcategory tables are included only to create a link from InternetSales to ProductCategory. The purpose of the query is to explore what customer attributes are related to purchasing merchandise from AdventureWorks.

The default presentation of the Designer contains two panels: one showing data sources (tables and views or queries) and another with the results of the query which includes the field name at the top of each column. The query file name appears directly above the data source panel—in this case the query name is "Query from AdventureWorksDW2008R2—Internet Sales Customer Attributes." Microsoft Query has the traditional Windows menu interface since it has not yet been updated to the Ribbon. Table C-3 lists menu items that are unique to the Query Designer, i.e., it does not include usual Windows or Microsoft Office menu items; Figure C-20 shows an enlargement of the toolbar; and Table C-4 describes the functions of the toolbar buttons. The menu functions and toolbar buttons are cross referenced in Table C-3. The Criteria Panel in the center of Figure C-19 is displayed by clicking button 7 in Figure C-20. I recommend that you study Tables C-3 and C-4 to become familiar with the functionality of the Microsoft Query Designer.

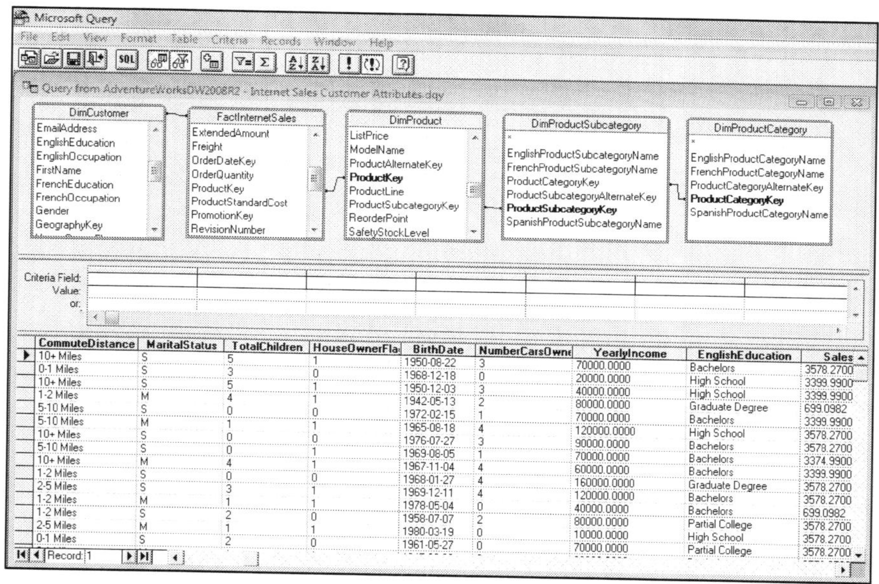

Figure C-19 Microsoft Query Designer - Example 2 (For better viewing of this image, go to http://www.zerobits.info/bibook/bibookimages/)

DimCustomer	DimProduct Category	FactInternetSales
BirthDate	English ProductCategory	SalesAmount
CommuteDistance		OrderQuantity
EnglishEducation [level]		
Gender		
HouseOwnerFlag		
MaritalStatus		
NumberCars Owned		
TotalChildren		
YearlyIncome		

Table C-2 Query Fields

Menu	Menu Item	Function
File	Table Definition	Opens the Choose Data Source dialog box.
	Execute SQL	Execute a SQL statement or stored procedure. (13)
View	Tables	Toggles the display of the data sources panel(Tables) on and off. (6)
	Criteria	Toggles the display of the criteria panel on and off. (7)
	Query Properties	Unique values only—hides exact duplicate records. Group Records—sorts all columns.
	SQL	Displays the SQL statement for the query. (5)
Format	Show/Hide Columns	Shows or hides columns.
Table	Add Table	Displays the Add Table Dialog box to Add tables into the query panel. (8)
	Remove Table	Removes the selected table from the query.
	Joins	Lists the joins between tables in the query and allows their modification. Do not modify the joins unless you know what you are doing!
Criteria	Add Criteria	Displays the Add Criteria Dialog box.
	Remove All Criteria	Removes all criteria (filters) from the Criteria Panel.
Records	Add Column	Displays the Add column Dialog box to add a column to the query from the available fields. Also can enter a column heading and select a total option.

Menu	Menu Item	Function
	Sort	Displays the Sort dialog box to sort the results by the column selected. Also can specify ascending or descending order. (11 & 12)
	Go to	Move to the Nth record in the result set.
	Query Now	Execute the query. (13)
	Automatic Query	Toggles auto query on and off. (14)

Note: Numbers in parenthesis () refer to equivalent actions via button numbers in Table C-4.

Table C-3 Useful Microsoft Query Menu Items
(For better viewing of this image, go to
http://www.zerobits.info/bibook/bibookimages/)

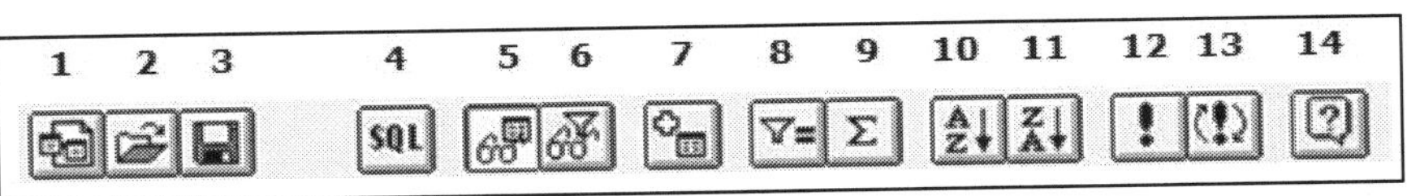

Figure C-20 Microsoft Query Toolbar

Button (Icon)	Tool Tip	Function
1	New Query	Create a new query.
2	Open Query	Open an existing query.
3	Save File —	Save the query as a dqy or qry file.
4	View SQL	Show the SQL statement for the query.
5	Show/Hide Tables	Toggles the tables panel.
6	Show/Hide Criteria	Toggles the Criteria panel.
7	Add Table(s)	Add a table(s) to the table panel.

Button (Icon)	Tool Tip	Function
8	Criteria Equals	Inserts the value of a selected cell in the Results panel as a filter into the Criteria panel.
9	Cycle Through Totals	Cycles through the selected column total options: sum, average, count, minimum, and maximum
10	Sort Ascending	Sorts the selected column in ascending order.
11	Sort Descending	Sorts the selected column in descending order.
12	Query Now	Execute the query.
13	Auto Query	Toggles auto query on and off. Auto query on initiates a refresh after every change to the query. This can result in long delays with large data sets.
14	Help	Displays Microsoft Query Help.

Table C-4 Microsoft Query Toolbar Functions
(For better viewing of this image, go to
http://www.zerobits.info/bibook/bibookimages/)

Criteria Panel

A better name for the Criteria panel would probably be the filter panel because this is where filters are defined. As mentioned earlier a filter is an expression that limits the records to be returned in the query. To create a filter insert the field name into the Criteria Field row by either dragging and dropping it from the Table panel; clicking on an empty Criteria Field and using the down arrowhead to bring up the list box of available fields; selecting an individual cell in the Results panel and click on the Criteria Equals button (13) on the tool bar; or using the Add Criteria menu item in the Criteria menu to display the Add Criteria dialog box. The latter two options also allow you to specify the attributes of the filter as well.

Figure C-21a shows the Add Criteria dialog box with the MaritalStatus field selected, and equals operator, and M as the value. This means that the query records will be filtered to only include those with customers who are married.

Use the down arrowhead on the field listbox to see the list of available fields and the down arrowhead on the operator list box to view the list of available operators. Click the Values button to bring up the Select Value(s) dialog box which lists the available values. Note that you may just enter the value(s) into the Value box without using the dialog box. Click Add to add the criteria to the Criteria panel. We'll discuss the Total listbox shortly.

Figure C-21b shows a criteria specification that requires two values so both must be selected, i.e., the expression will read "Not Between 1 And 3" to limit the query results to those records with the number of children equal to zero or above three. This is only for the example – you probably would not use this criteria.

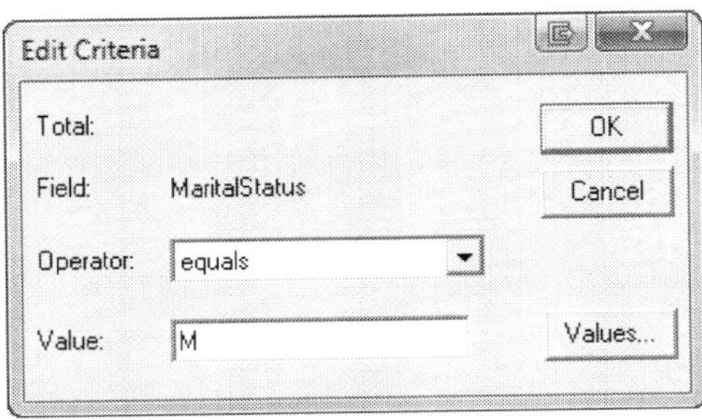

Figure C-21a Single Values

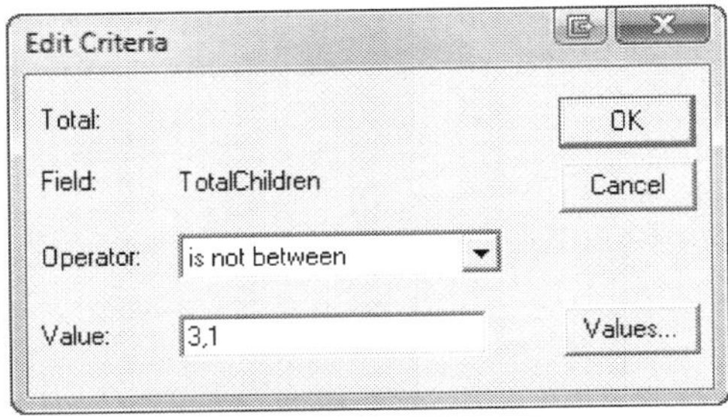

Figure C-21b Multiple Values

Figure C-21 Add Criteria Dialog Box

The available operators are listed in Table C-5 along with the symbol or expression used for the operator in the Value box in the Criteria panel and an example use of the criteria with the Criteria field listed in one column and the example expression in the other. You may avoid the Add Criteria dialog box by entering criteria values manually in the Value box in the Criteria panel using the symbols/expressions in the second column of Table C-5.

Operator	Symbol or Expression*	Example Field	Example Expression*
equals	=	Date	= #7/1/2001#
does not equal	<>	ProductCategory	<> 'Bikes’
is greater than	>	TotalChildren	> 2
is greater than or equal to	>=	TotalChildren	>= 2
is less than	<	TotalChildren	< 2
is less than or equal to	<=	TotalChildren	<= 2
is one of	In	ProductCategory	In ('Bikes')
is not one of	Not In	ProductCategory	Not In ('Bikes')
is between	Between X AND Y	TotalChildren	Between 1 And 3
is not between	Not Between X AND Y	TotalChildren	Not Between 1 And 3
begins with	Like 'X%'	ProductCategory	Like 'B%'
does not begin with	Not Like 'X%'	ProductCategory	Not Like 'B%'
ends with	Like '%X'	ProductCategory	Like '%B'
does not end with	Not Like '%X'	ProductCategory	Not Like '%B'
contains	Like '%X%'	ProductCategory	Like '%ik%'
does not contain	<>	ProductCategory	Not Like '%ik%'

Operator	Symbol or Expression*	Example Field	Example Expression*
like	Like <expression>	ProductCateg ory	Like 'Bi'
not like	Not Like <expression>	ProductCateg ory	Like 'Bi'
is Null	Is Null	Any field	Is Null
is Not Null	Is Not Null	Any field	Is Not Null

*Note: the % wildcard character matches zero or more characters.

Table C-5 Microsoft Criteria (Filter) Operators
(For better viewing of this image, go to
http://www.zerobits.info/bibook/bibookimages/)

A few filter examples in the Criteria panel are shown in Figure C-22. Note that the listbox in the fifth column of the Criteria panel is expanded to show the list of available fields and that the query results displayed in the bottom panel have been substantially filtered. The first two filters are described above. The third uses the "like" operator on the English Product Category Name to find all records that have "Bi" in that field. The syntax is like 'Bi%' with the % symbol as a wildcard. For these data this will display all Bike records that meet the other criteria. The fourth filter displays records with Yearly Income less than greater than $50,000 and less than $100,000.

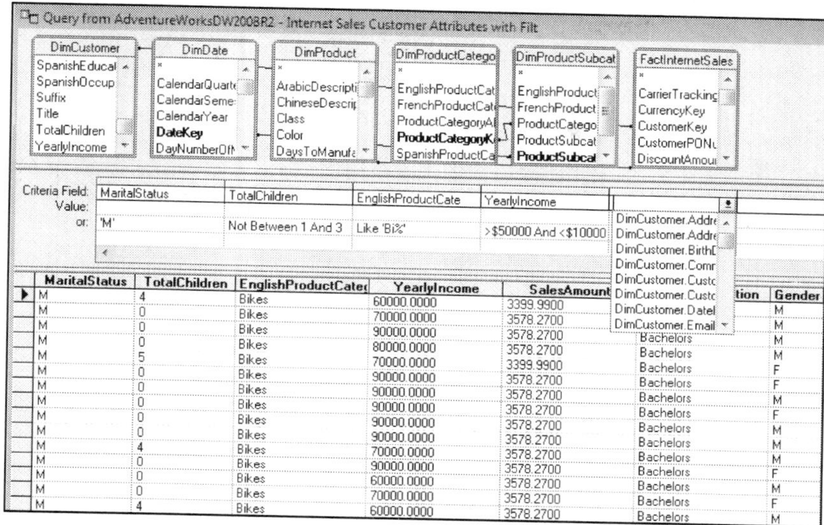

Figure C-22 Microsoft Query Designer - Criteria (Filter) Examples

To remove a criteria from the panel click on the border above the Criteria Field to select it and then press the Delete key. Similarly, to delete a field from the result set select the column and press the delete key or select the item and use the menus.

Aggregate Functions (Totals)

Aggregate functions include sum, average, count, minimum, and maximum values, but only some of them may be usable for a particular data type. An aggregate function performs the operation of its name on the specified query field (column). For example, the query in Figure C-23 provides the total sales amount (Sum), the number of sales transactions (Count), the mean sale amount (Avg), and the maximum sales amount (Max) for each product category. To insert an aggregate function, first insert the field into the query. For example, I dragged Sales Amount from the FactInternetSales table into the second column of the query and then double clicked in that column header to display the Edit Column dialog box shown on the right. There I entered a name for the column, Total Sales, and selected Sum for the operator.

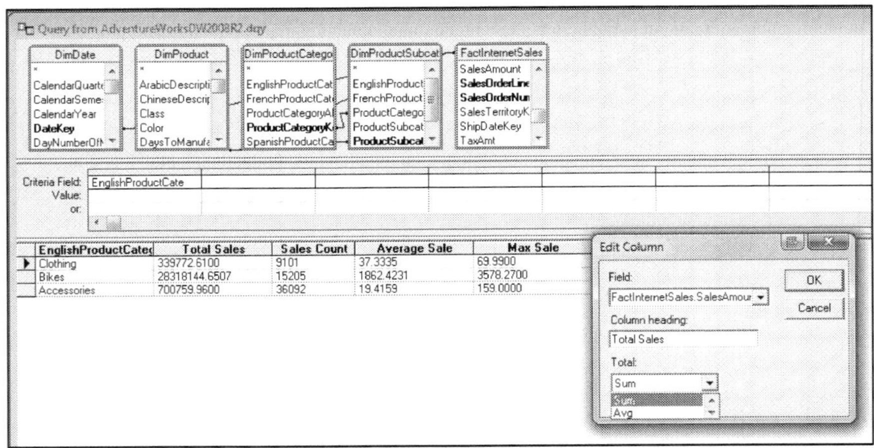

Figure C-23 Using Aggregate Functions

Calculated Values and Column Names

As described elsewhere calculated values use expressions or built-in functions to compute new fields from existing field values. There are two calculated values in Figure C-24a: Gross Profit Margin and Year. Gross Profit Margin is computed as:

(SalesAmount - ProductStandardCost)/ SalesAmount

Year is returned by the built-in function Year(DimDate.FullDatealternative Key). There are two ways to create a calculated value. One is to enter the expression for the calculated value in the header (column name) of an empty column. For example, to create the Gross Profit Margin calculated value you would enter the formula above in an empty column header. The other approach is to double click on the header of an occupied column to display the Edit Column dialog box as in Figure C-24b and enter the expression for the calculated value in the Field box as is shown for the Gross Profit margin in Figure C-24a and Year in Figure C-24c. The Edit Column dialog box also allows you to create an alias (a display name) for a field by entering the name in the Column Heading box. I entered an alias for all three fields in this query including the EnglishProductCategoryName field which is not a calculated value. Note that functions used in a calculated values expression have to be consistent with those in the data source. For example, you must the DATEDIFF with two Fs with a SQL Server database and not the DATEDIF with one F from Excel.

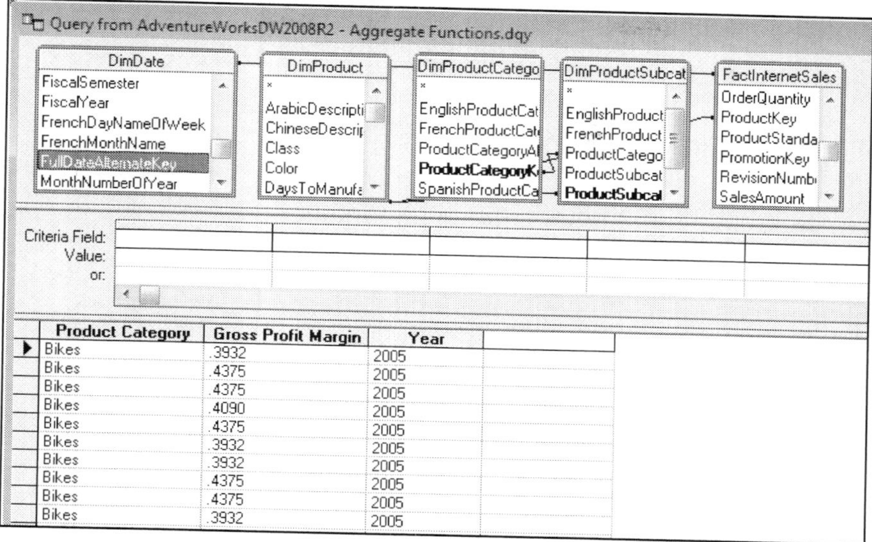

Product Category	Gross Profit Margin	Year
Bikes	.3932	2005
Bikes	.4375	2005
Bikes	.4375	2005
Bikes	.4090	2005
Bikes	.4375	2005
Bikes	.3932	2005
Bikes	.3932	2005
Bikes	.4375	2005
Bikes	.4375	2005
Bikes	.3932	2005

Figure C-24a Microsoft Query Designer - Calculated Values

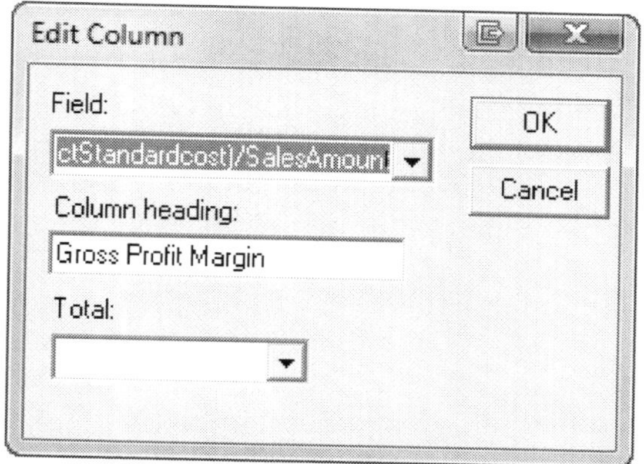

Figure C-24b Gross Profit Margin %

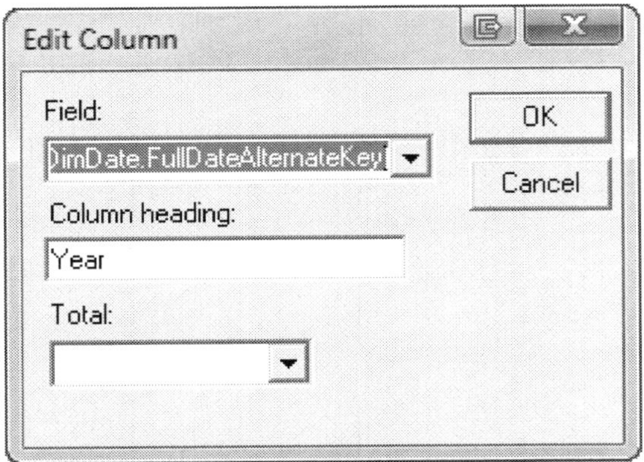

Figure C-24c Year

Figure C-24 Edit Column Dialog Boxes

Parameter Queries

Microsoft Query has a provision to create Microsoft Access-like parameter queries which are select queries that allow passing a parameter(s) to the query to specify a subset of the data to return, something like a dynamic filter. When a parameter query is executed, an Enter Parameter Value input box is displayed to prompt the user for the parameter value. For example, the input box in Figure C-25 requests an entry for the product category. I entered "Clothing," and, if this is a valid category name, then the query will be limited to records with only Clothing as the product category.

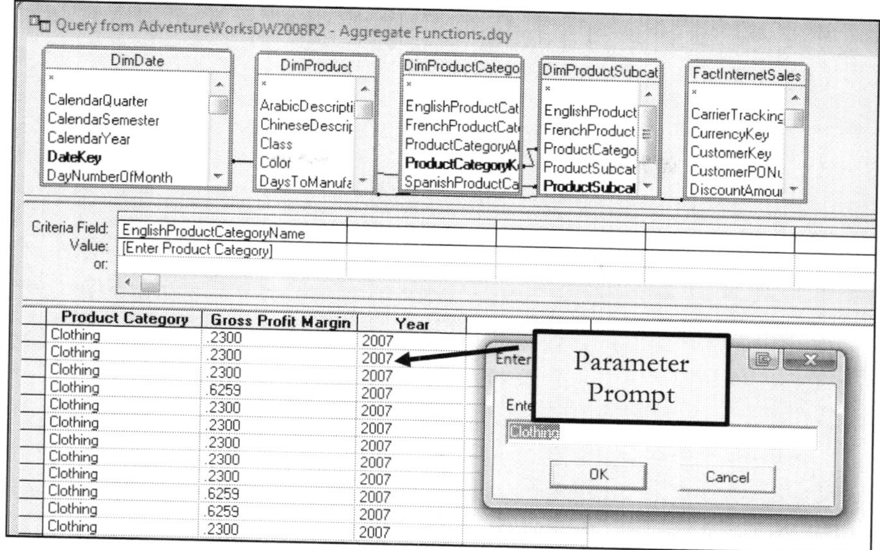

Figure C-25 Parameter Query Example

Parameter queries are created by enclosing a prompt in square brackets in the Criteria panel Value box. For example, for the query in Figure C-25 the Value box entry for the prompt is [Enter Product Category]. You may use multiple parameters in a query by entering multiple prompts in the Criteria panel, and you may also insert parameters into filter expressions with operators. Table C-6 provided a few examples of the latter. Note that the conventional ampersand (&) concatenation operator does not work in Microsoft Query but that the legacy plus concatenation operator (+) does as in the Like example in Table C-6. As discussed in Chapter 5 the parameter values may be embedded in an Excel worksheet to avoid using the inputbox.

Criteria Value Expression	Example Criteria Field	Results Returned
>=[Enter greater than or equal to Amount]	Internet Sales	Records with Internet sales greater than or equal to the amount entered.
Between [Start Date] And [End Date]	Order Date	Records with order date between Start Date and End Date
Like '%'+[Find What?]+'%'	Customer Last Name	Records that contain the Find What pattern in the customer's last name.

Table C-6 Examples of Using Parameters in Criteria Expressions

Parameter queries are implemented in SQL with the WHERE key word. The example SQL statement below retrieves Internet Sales Amount and Customer Marital Status from the AdventureWorks2008DW database with a parameter for Marital Status (S= single, M= married) via the SQL phrase ((DimCustomer.MaritalStatus=?)). The resulting Enter Parameter Value input box is shown in Figure C-26.

```
SELECT  FactInternetSales.SalesAmount, DimCustomer.MaritalStatus
FROM    AdventureWorksDW2008.dbo.DimCustomer
DimCustomer,
        AdventureWorksDW2008.dbo.FactInternetSales
FactInternetSales
WHERE   DimCustomer.CustomerKey                                    =
FactInternetSales.CustomerKey AND
        ((DimCustomer.MaritalStatus=?))
```

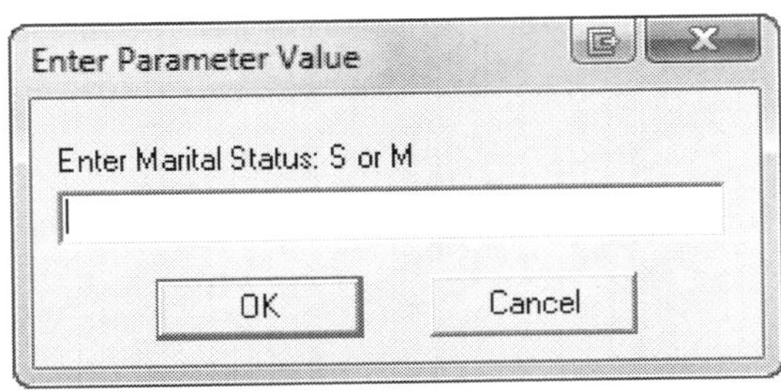

Figure C-26 Input Box for Parameter SQL Example

Editing a Query

To edit an existing query select it from the list in the Query tab of the Choose Data Source dialog box (Figure C-11) using the From Microsoft Query type in the From Other Sources option in the Data Ribbon (Figure C-6). If you have saved queries to other than the default directory, click the Browse button and navigate to the directory containing the query. Select the query in the Browse Data Sources window, click Open to return to the Choose Data Source window and Open again to bring it in to Microsoft Query. If the warning dialog box as in Figure C-27 appears, just click OK and proceed. (This seems to be a bug in the Query Designer.)

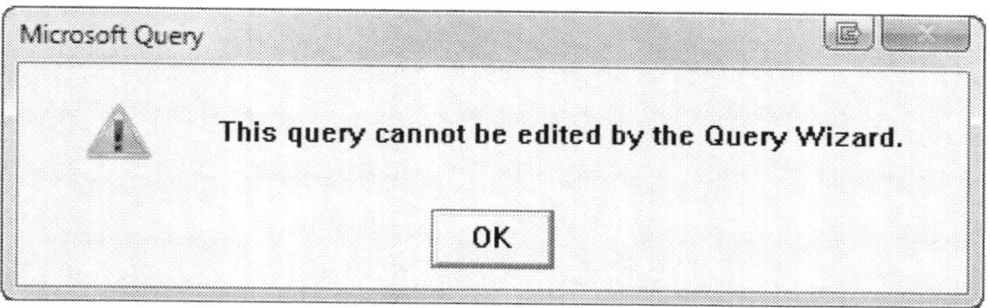

Figure C-27 Microsoft Query Toolbar

An existing query can also be edited outside of Excel by starting Microsoft Query as an independent application (see below).

Microsoft Query as an Independent Program

Microsoft Query can be used as an independent application outside of Excel to create a new query or to edit an existing one. The Microsoft Query executable file should be located in C:\Program Files (x86)\Microsoft Office\Office14\MSQRY32.EXE for Office 2010 32-bit in Windows 7. To start it navigate to that location in a file explorer and double click it or enter the directory path into a Windows Run box. If you plan to use Microsoft Query as an independent application frequently, then create a shortcut to it. Note that queries created or edited in Microsoft Query as an independent application are not returned directly to Excel. To access them in Excel use the Existing Connections options on the Data tab.

For SQL Server databases it is probably easier to create a query (View) in SQL Server and then establish a connection to it in from the application that will use it instead of using Microsoft Query. However, if you do not have permissions to create SQL Server database objects, particularly to create views, then you must use another approach like Microsoft Query.

Well, that's enough about queries for now. We use then extensively in the main part of the book..

Appendix D - Up to Speed with Excel 2010

This is a brief review of a few of Excel 2010's features for people with previous spreadsheet experience. It is not intended as a tutorial for the beginning spreadsheet user. Features described elsewhere in the book are not repeated here, and working with charts and graphs is not covered.

Workbooks and Worksheets

Work in Excel is done in a worksheet, essentially a two-dimensional table with rows and columns. An Excel workbook contain one or more worksheets as in Figure D-1 that has three: Sheet1, Sheet2, and Sheet3. You move among worksheets by clicking on the sheet tabs at the bottom of the worksheet and add worksheets by clicking on the Add worksheet button to the right of the last worksheet tab. Right clicking on a worksheet tab will display a worksheet menu (Figure D-2a) with which you may also insert a new worksheet or perform other worksheet related tasks such as renaming a worksheet. Note that I minimized the Office Ribbon for display purposes for this figure by right clicking on the hat button (^) beside the question mark button (?) on the far right of top bar. Click again to maximize the Ribbon.

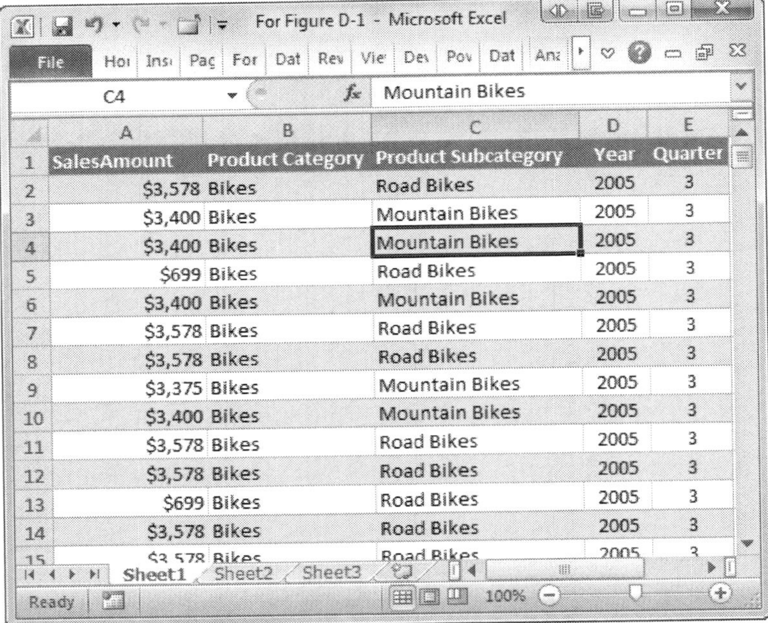

	A	B	C	D	E
1	SalesAmount	Product Category	Product Subcategory	Year	Quarter
2	$3,578	Bikes	Road Bikes	2005	3
3	$3,400	Bikes	Mountain Bikes	2005	3
4	$3,400	Bikes	Mountain Bikes	2005	3
5	$699	Bikes	Road Bikes	2005	3
6	$3,400	Bikes	Mountain Bikes	2005	3
7	$3,578	Bikes	Road Bikes	2005	3
8	$3,578	Bikes	Road Bikes	2005	3
9	$3,375	Bikes	Mountain Bikes	2005	3
10	$3,400	Bikes	Mountain Bikes	2005	3
11	$3,578	Bikes	Road Bikes	2005	3
12	$3,578	Bikes	Road Bikes	2005	3
13	$699	Bikes	Road Bikes	2005	3
14	$3,578	Bikes	Road Bikes	2005	3
15	$3,578	Bikes	Road Bikes	2005	3

Figure D-1 Excel Window

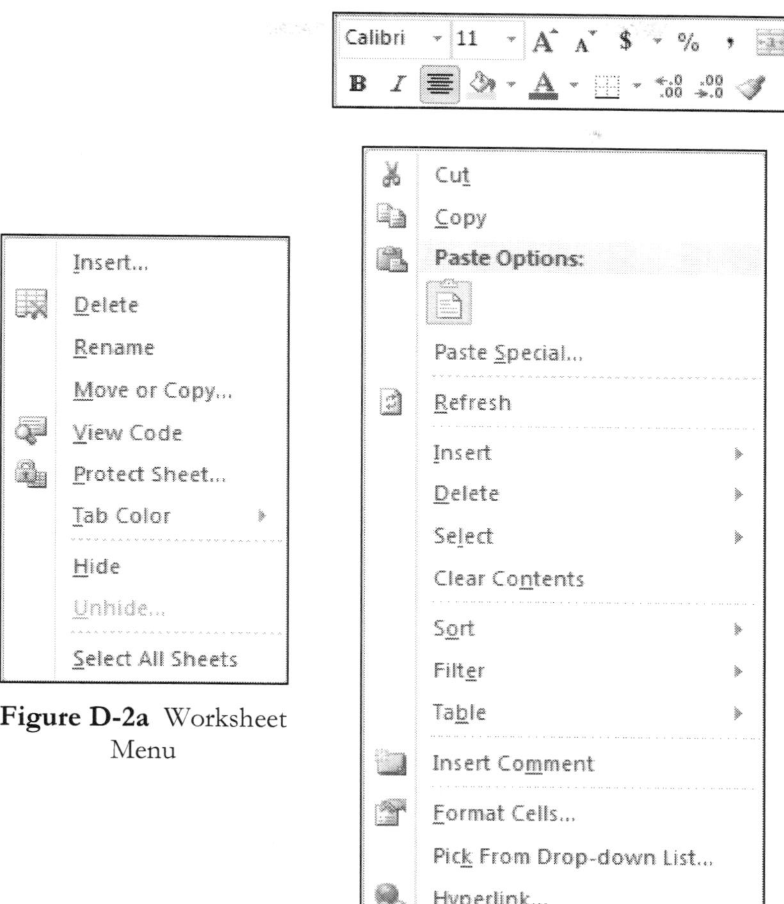

Figure D-2a Worksheet Menu

Figure D-2b Cell Menu

Figure D-2 Right Click Menus

The Ribbon

Excel's Ribbon initially contains seven tabs plus the Developer tab mentioned earlier. In addition, in this book we utilize Data Mining and Table Tools tabs as described in Chapter 1. The initial tabs and command groups within each are listed in Table D-1. The Home tab has a number of frequently used commands mostly related to formatting. The Insert tab is used to insert, of course, tables, charts, etc. into a worksheet. The Page Layout tab does just that. The Formula tab contains the Function Library and Defined names command groups as described earlier along with Formula Auditing and Calculation management.

We use the Data tab extensively in the book to access external data and manage data in a worksheet. You use the commands in the Review tab for proofing and working with others on a worksheet. And the Views tab manages workbook and window views.

Home	Insert	Page Layout	Formulas
Clipboard	Tables	Themes	Function Library
Font	Illustrations	Page Setup	Defined names
Alignment	Charts	Scale to Fit	Formula Auditing
Number	Sparklines	Sheet Options	Calculation
Styles	Filter	Arrange	
Cells	Links		
Editing	Text		
	Symbols		

Data	Review	View
Get External Data	Proofing	Workbook Views
Connections	Comments	Show
Sort & Filter	Changes	Zoom
Data Tools		Window
Outline		macros
Analysis		

Table D-1 Ribbon Tabs and Command Groups

Cell Indexes

The cells at the intersections of rows and columns contain either data or formulas that define what will be presented in the cell. Cells are identified by column and row identifiers which are of two types: the default A1 format and the R1C1 format. The A1 format identifies a columns with an alphabetic character followed by a row with a number as in cell C4 selected in the Figure D-1. The selected cell or upper left corner cell of a selected range of cells is displayed in the name textbox on the Formula Bar directly below the home tab in the figure. The R1C1 format denotes a cell by R<row number>C<column number> where both rows and columns are identified by numbers. To switch to a different cell identifier format select the Excel Options button near the bottom of the Office button menu to display the Excel Options window. Then, check or uncheck the R1C1 reference style check box in the Formulas window. The A1 format is used in this book.

Cell Entries

Entries are made in a cell by selecting it and entering data or formulas directly into it or doing the same in the textbox to the right of the *fx* label on the Formula bar which displays the contents of the selected cell or the upper left corner cell of a selected range of cells. Formulas, assignment statements that are prefixed with an equal symbol, may contain data, arithmetic and text concatenation operators, and/or functions. The result of the formula is assigned to the cell as its value. Formulas begin with an equal symbol (=). A few examples of formulas are provided in Table D-2 below.

Formula	Description/Result
=A4	Assigns the value of cell A4 to the cell
=A4/C2	Assigns the quotient of the value in cell A4 divided by the value in cell C2
= "This is " & " concatenation."	Assigns the text "This is concatenation." to the cell
=SUM(C2:C16)	Sums the values in cells C2 to C16

Table D-2 Example Formulas

To remove an entry from a cell just select it and press delete or right click on the cell and select delete. Right clicking on a cell displays the menu and tool bar in Figure D-2b which provides quick access to a variety of cell formatting and manipulation options.

Cell References

Cell references in formulas can be relative or absolute. A relative cell reference is just an offset from the target cell. For example, if cell B4 containing the formula =D5 is copied to cell B6, then the formula in it changes to =D6, i.e., the cell reference retains its relative position to the containing cell. On the other hand, an absolute cell reference, designated with $ prefixes to the row and column identifiers retains the original cell reference. For example, if cell B4 which contains the formula =$D$5 is copied to cell B6, then the formula in B6 stays the same. Cell references can be mixed, e.g., the formula =$B7 freezes the reference to the B column but allows the row reference to perform as an offset. A truly absolute cell reference will have the $ preceding both the column and row identifiers as in =$D$5. You can toggle the type of cell reference by using the F4 function key while the cursor is placed on the reference. The easiest way to insert a cell reference in a formula is to click on the cell to be referenced at the position in the formula that you want the reference inserted. For example, if I wanted a cell to contain the formula =124+D26, I would enter =124+ in the cell, click on cell D26, and then press the enter key or click on the formula bar.

References to cells in other worksheet are prefixed by the worksheet name with the bang operator (!) separating the worksheet name and cell reference as in =Sheet2!F14 which references cell F14 in worksheet Sheet2. The easiest way to enter a cell reference in another worksheet it to follow the procedure in the paragraph above. Just move to other sheet, click on the cell to be inserted, and press enter.

Arithmetic Operator Precedence

Excel uses the same arithmetic operator precedence as in Visual Basic for applications. In a formula with multiple arithmetic operators exponentiation will be performed first followed by multiplication and division and then addition and subtraction. For example, the formula = 4+12/4 will return 7. However, you may override the default precedence with parentheses as in the formula =(4+12)/4 which will return 4. Operations with the same precedence level are performed left to right.

Copy and Paste

When you copy a cell or range of cells, the selected cells will be surrounded by "moving ants." To get rid of the moving ants press the Escape key which cancels the copy. If you copy and paste a cell or cell range directly, all properties of the copied cell will be duplicated in the pasted to cell. However, you may select the properties to be pasted by using the Paste button in the Home tab Clipboard command group (Figure D-3a) or by right clicking the cell to which you are pasting to bring up the cell menu (Figure D-2b) or by selecting Paste Special to display the menu in Figure D-3b.

Figure D-3a Paste Button

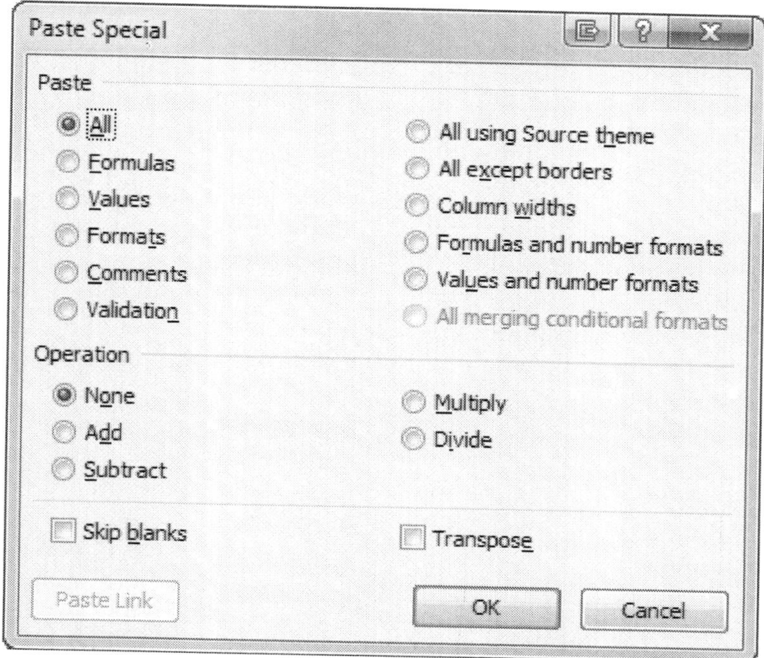

Figure D-3b Paste Special Menu

Figure D-3 Copy and Paste Menus

Most of the options in Figure D-3b are self-explanatory but two warrant additional comment. Transpose reverses or flips the rows and columns. The bottom section in Figure D-4a is the transposition of the top section. To do that I selected the range A1-E5, clicked on cell A8, right clicked and selected Paste Special, checked the transpose box, and clicked OK.

	A	B	C	D	E
1	Year	Accessories	Bikes	Clothing	Grand Total
2	2005		3,266,374		3,266,374
3	2006		6,530,344		6,530,344
4	2007	293,710	9,359,103	138,248	9,791,060
5	2008	407,050	9,162,325	201,525	9,770,900
6					
7	Year	2005	2006	2007	2008
8	Accessories			293,710	407,050
9	Bikes	3,266,374	6,530,344	9,359,103	9,162,325
10	Clothing			138,248	201,525
11	Grand Total	3,266,374	6,530,344	9,791,060	9,770,900

Figure D-4a Transpose Example

The Paste Link button at the bottom of Figure D-3b copies an absolute cell reference to the target cell or range of cells. In Figure D-4b I copied cell A1 to cell A2 normally and to cell A3 using the Paste Link button. If I click on cell A2, the formula bar will show the contents as 274.67. However, if I select cell A3, the contents there are =$A$1, a cell reference. To show the effect I reproduced the A column cells in the B column and changed the value in cell B1 to 3. As you can see cell B3 reflected the change in value but cell B2 didn't.

	A	B
1	274.67	3
2	274.67	274.67
3	274.67	3

Figure D-4b Paste Link Example

Moving Cells

You may move a cell or a range of cells by either cutting and pasting or by selecting the cell or range and dragging the upper right corner of the selection where the mouse pointer will turn into an arrow with a compass shape at the end to the new location. Figure D-5 shows the range A14:B17 selected with the mouse pointer and compass shape.

	A	B
12	Period	Sales
13	1	81
14	2	116
15	3	148
16	4	127
17	5	104
18	6	137
19	7	181
20	8	144
21	9	130
22	10	147

Figure D-5 Paste Selection with Mouse Pointer and Compass Shape

AutoFill

Excel can autofill cells based on a pattern in selected cells. To use this feature select a cell or range contiguous to the cells that you want to autofill and drag the bottom right corner where the mouse pointer will turn into a plus (+) shape as in Figure D-6a. In figure D-6b I dragged the corner downward to autofill five cells. As I did that an index (not shown) appeared alongside the bottom cell indicating the autofill value for the cell. When I release the mouse button, the autofill options button was displayed as in Figure D-6b to the right and below cell A27. Clicking on the plus symbol there will display the Autofill options list as shown. Figure D-6c shows the completed series. Excel will correctly autofill simple number sequences as in the example, dates, days of the week, and others. You may create custom lists for Autofill to use by clicking on the Edit Custom Lists button in the Popular tab Excel Options accessible via the Office Button.

A18

	A	B
12	Period	Sales
13	1	81
14	2	116
15	3	148
16	4	127
17	5	104
18	6	137
19	7	181
20	8	144
21	9	130
22	10	147
23		

Figure D-6a AutoFill Plus Shape

	A	B	C	D
12	Period	Sales		
13	1	81		
14	2	116		
15	3	148		
16	4	127		
17	5	104		
18	6	137		
19	7	181		
20	8	144		
21	9	130		
22	10	147		
23	11			
24	12			
25	13			
26	14			
27	15			
28				
29				
30				
31				
32				
33				

- Copy Cells
- Fill Series
- Fill Formatting Only
- Fill Without Formatting

Figure D-6b AutoFill with Options

	A	B
12	Period	Sales
13	1	81
14	2	116
15	3	148
16	4	127
17	5	104
18	6	137
19	7	181
20	8	144
21	9	130
22	10	147
23	11	
24	12	
25	13	
26	14	
27	15	

Figure D-6ac AutoFill Completed

Figure D-6 AutoFill Example
(For better viewing of this image, go to
http://www.zerobits.info/bibook/bibookimages/)

Named Ranges

Naming a cell or range of cells makes it easier to refer to them in formulas and functions. For example, if I named cells A2:A16 in Figure D-1 "SalesAmounts," then I could use the name to substitute for the cell range as in =SUM(SalesAmounts) which would return the sales total of $39,842.77. To name a cell or cell range you click on Defined Names in the Defined Names command group in the Formula tab. Doing so will display the New Name dialog box in Figure D-7a where the Scope listbox is shown dropped down. To define a named range you enter a name which cannot contain blanks, specify the scope, add a comment if you like, and define the range in the Refers to textbox. If you want to separate words in the name, use the underscore character instead of a space as in Sales_Amount. If you want to change the range, just select the entry in the Refers to textbox and then select the range in the worksheet. Note that you may name rows or columns as well by selecting them and then proceeding with the New Name dialog box.

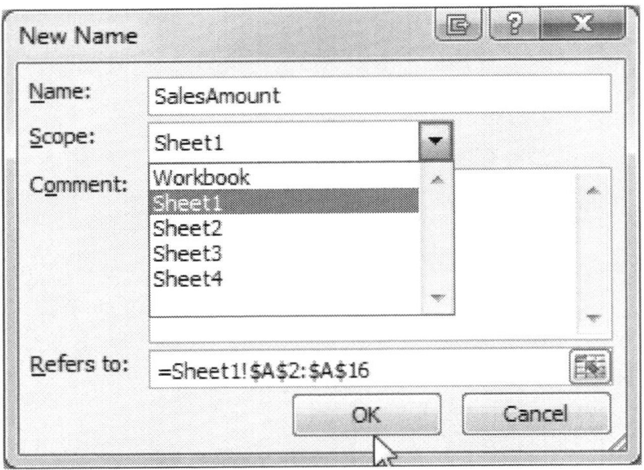

Figure D-7a Define a Name Dialog Box

The Defined Names command group in the Formulas tab contains four commands. The Name Manager bring up the Name Manager dialog box as in Figure D-7b which displays all defined names and tables that meet the filter conditions. You can see that the workbook has three named ranges including SalesAmount created above and one Excel table, Table 1. With the buttons at the top you can create a new named range, edit an existing entry, or delete one or more entries. The Filter button displays the filter menu as in Figure D-7c where you may select one or more options. In the example, only those names with a workbook scope and without errors would be shown in the list. The Clear Filter option is used to display all named ranges and tables.

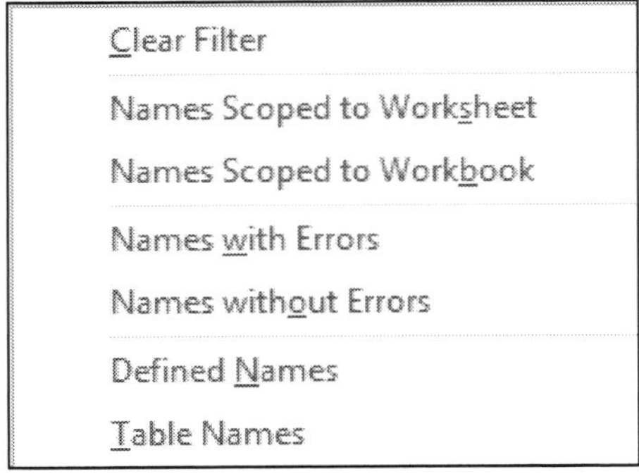

Figure D-7b Name Manager

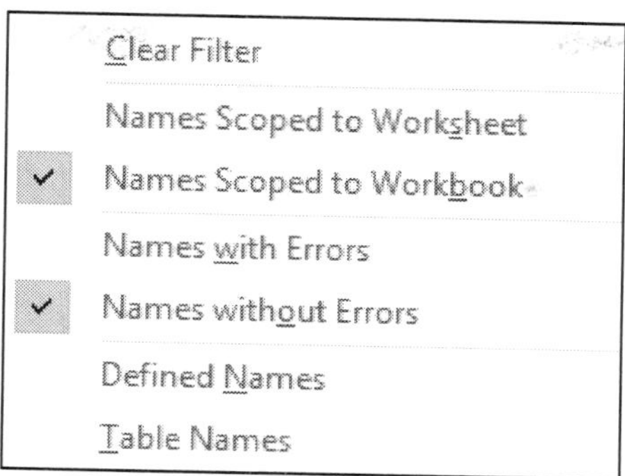

Figure D-7c Filter Menu

Back on the Defined Names command group clicking on the drop-down arrow on the Define Name button in the Defined Names command group brings up a menu with Define name and Apply name options. Define Name does as explained above. The Apply name assigns range names created after the range is used in the worksheet to the range. (Excel doesn't do this automatically.) The Use in Formula command display a list of existing range names to insert into a formula. And the Create from Selection command create a new named range with the name taken from a value specified in a dialog box.

Functions

Excel functions are predesigned procedures used in formulas that perform some kind of action, usually a computation, and return values. For example, the SUM function returns the total of a set of values. Excel has many built-in functions and others are available from the Internet and other sources. You can even create your own functions using Visual Basic for Applications. A function name is followed by parentheses that contain arguments which specify the values and properties to be used in the function. Some function have no arguments like NOW() that returns the current date and time, and others may require multiple arguments. Some arguments are required, others are optional.

If you know the name of the function that you want to use or an approximation of it, then just begin typing it in a cell with a formula, i.e., a cell with a leading equal symbol (=), and Excel will list possible candidates as shown in Figure D-7a where when I entered "av," Excel displayed a list of possibilities from which I could select the one that I wanted, AVERAGE in this case.

	A	B	C	D	E
28	=345.67+av				
29		AVEDEV			
30		AVERAGE	Returns the average (arithmetic mean) of its arguments,		
31		AVERAGEA			
32		AVERAGEIF			
33		AVERAGEIFS			

Figure D-7a Function Auto Complete Example

Excel offers other convenient ways to insert functions. The Function Library command group on the Formulas tab has seven buttons that display built-in functions by type: financial, Logical, etc. The Recently Used button displays recently used functions. The AutoSum button inserts the SUM function into the selected cell. If the cell is close to other cells with numerical values, Excel will guess about the cells to sum by identifying those cells with moving ants and inserting the range reference as arguments as in Figure D-7b. If Excel incorrectly identifies the range, just select the right range and Excel will correct the function. If Excel cannot automatically identify a range to sum, then =SUM() will be inserted into the cell for you to complete.

	A	B	C	D
12	Period	Sales		
13	1	81		
14	2	116		
15	3	148		
16	4	127		
17		=SUM(B13:B16)		
18		SUM(**number1**, [number2], ...)		
19				

Figure D-7b Automatic AutoSum

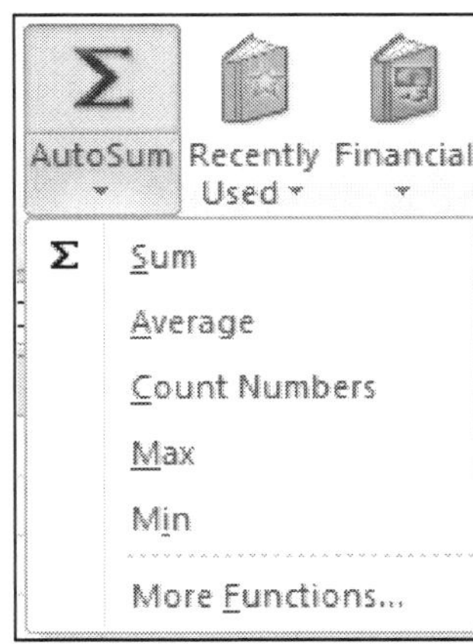

Figure D-7c AutoSum Menu

Figure D-7a-b AutoSum Examples

Clicking the down arrowhead on the AutoSum button will display the AutoSum menu (Figure D-7c) where you may select the function to use in the cell. For example, clicking Average will insert =AVERAGE() into the cell. The Insert Function button on the left side of the Ribbon displays the Insert Function dialog box (Figure D-7d) where you enter a description of a function in the Search for a function textbox, and Excel will list candidates in the Select a function textbox. Or you may select a category from the Select a category listbox to have Excel present a list of all functions in a category. Selecting a function in the list will display a brief description of the function below the Select a function textbox. Note that all of the other nine buttons in the Function Library command group include a link to the Insert Function dialog box by either a More Functions or an Insert function menu option.

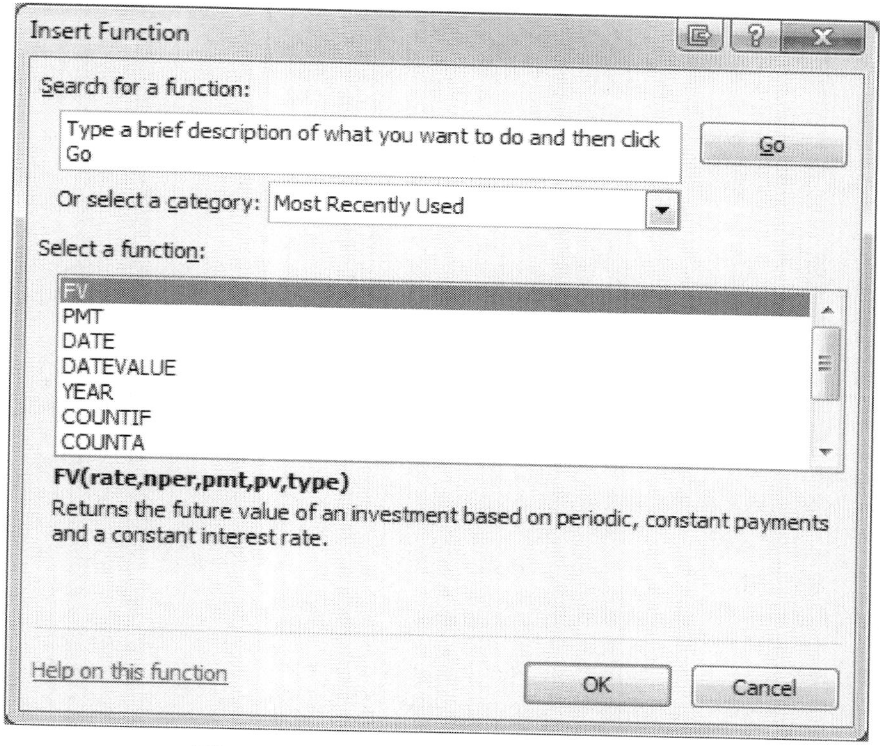

Figure D-7d Insert Function Dialog Box

Double clicking a function name or clicking the OK button after a function is selected will display the Function Arguments dialog box (Figure D-7e) with textboxes for all of the function's arguments in the top section. The middle section contains a brief description of the function with a description of the active argument displayed below it. The formula result will be presented in the bottom section. Figure D-7f shows a completed example.

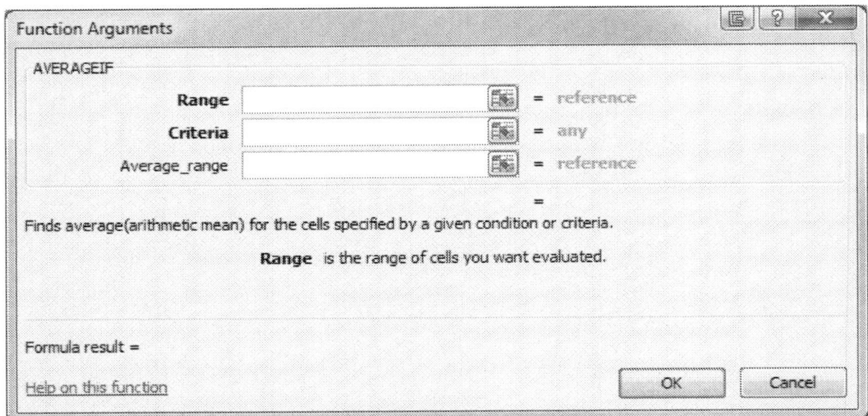

Figure D-7e Function Arguments Dialog Box

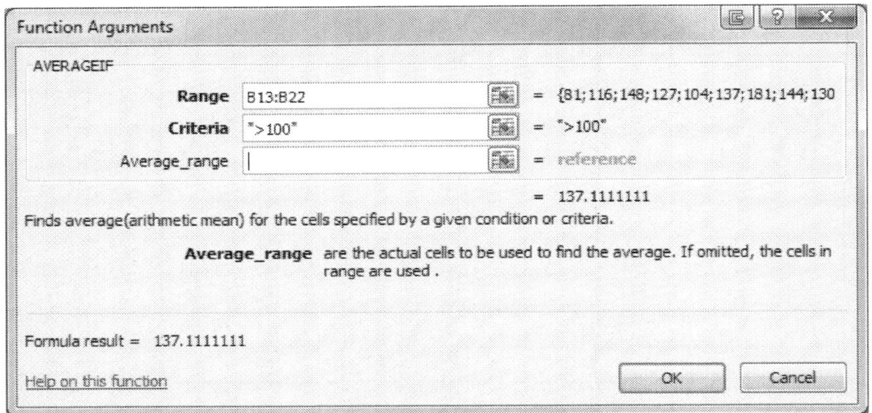

Figure D-7f Function Arguments Dialog Box Example

Macros

For the purposes of this appendix we'll say that macros allow you to record a set of Excel actions so that you may use the set over again by running the macro. However, macros are really Visual Basic for Applications sub procedures. To utilize macros the Developer tab must be available on the Ribbon as described in Chapter 1. To record a macro click the Record Macro button in the Code command group to display the Record Macro dialog box as in Figure D-8 where you enter a macro name and a shortcut key if you desire, select the storage location, and provide a description. Clicking Ok will return you to the worksheet where all of your actions will be recorded until you click Stop Recording in the Code command group. To run a macro click the Macros button to display the Macro dialog box (not shown), select a macro from the list, and click the Run button. Note that you must save a workbook containing macros as an Excel Macro-Enabled Workbook, an option in the Save As dialog box accessed from the Office Button.

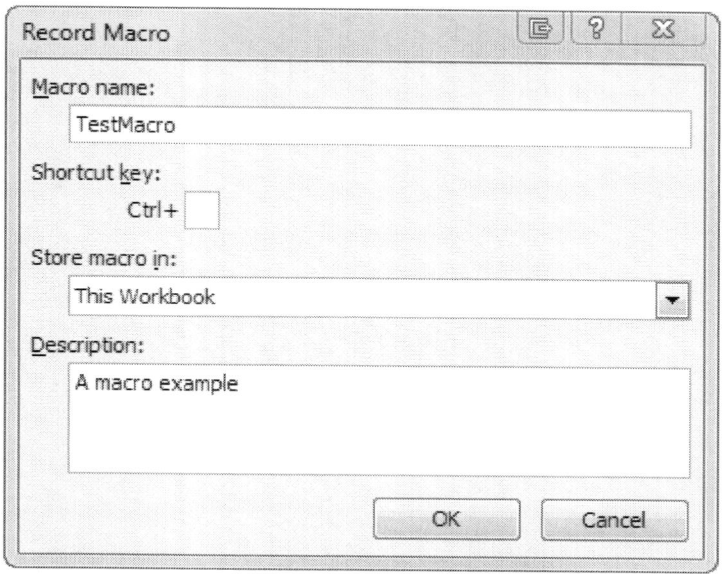

Figure D-8 Record Macro Dialog Box

Mange Rows and Columns

You can manage rows or columns by selecting one or more of them on their respective indexes as in Figure D-9a for four rows and then right clicking the selection to bring up the menu and tool bar as in Figure D-9b. The menu for columns is similar except the Row Height option is replaced with Column Width.

The tool bar provides quick access to frequently used formatting options. Most of the menu options are self-explanatory but three merit additional comment. Insert will insert the number of rows or columns selected, in this case four rows, above the selection for rows and to the left of the selection for columns. The Hide option hides the selected rows or columns. Figure D-10 shows columns B and C hidden. You unhide rows or columns by selecting at least the rows or columns contiguous to the hidden ones and clicking the unhide option in the menu. You may unhide everything by selecting the entire worksheet using the Select All button in the upper left corner of the worksheet index boundary and then right clicking on the row and column indexes in sequence to display the menu.

	A	B	C
1	Period	Sales	
2	1	81	
3	2	116	
4	3	148	
5	4	127	
6	5	104	
7	6	137	
8	7	181	
9	8	144	
10	9	130	
11	10	147	

Figure D-9a Select Rows

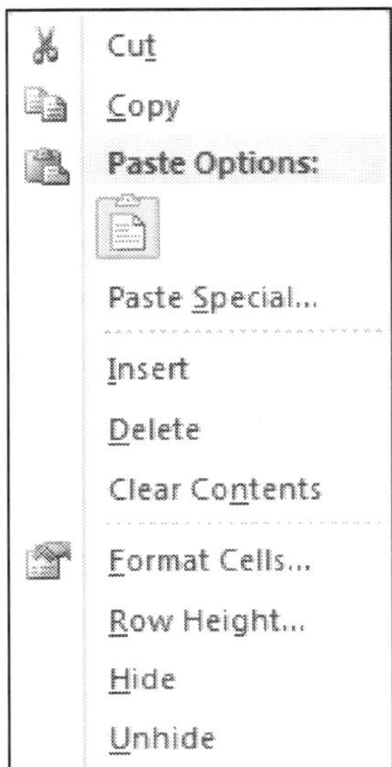

Figure D-9b Rows Menu and Tool Bar

Figure D-9 Record Insert and Delete Rows and Columns

	A	D	E
1	SalesAmount	Year	Quarter
2	$3,578	2005	3
3	$3,400	2005	3
4	$3,400	2005	3
5	$699	2005	3
6	$3,400	2005	3
7	$3,578	2005	3
8	$3,578	2005	3
9	$3,375	2005	3

Figure D-10 Hidden Columns

Well, that it for a brief refresher on Excel. If you are comfortable with the basic features described in this appendix, you should have no trouble with material in the chapters.

Appendix E - Up to Speed with Access 2010

As in Appendix D for Excel this is a brief review of a few of Access 2010's features for people with previous Microsoft Access experience. It is not intended as a beginner's tutorial, and features described elsewhere in the book are not repeated here. Please see in particular the discussion of tables and relations in the Chapter 2 section on Relational vs. Dimensional Database Architectures and queries in Appendix C.

Preliminaries

Access 2010 (hereafter referred to as Access) does not include sample databases as did previous versions nor does Microsoft provide any for download as far as I can determine. So, we'll use the old Northwind Traders database for our examples. You can download it from the Access 2000 tutorial page at http://www.microsoft.com/downloads/details.aspx?FamilyID=C6661372-8DBE-422B-8676-C632D66C529C&displaylang=en. When you initially open Northwind, Access displays the dialog box in Figure E-1a that asks about converting the database which has a mdb file extension to the Access 2010 format with a accdb file extension. Click the Yes button to proceed with the upgrade. When the upgrade is completed, Access may present the message box in Figure E-1b to alert you that an error was encountered and that information about the error(s) are available in a new table named Conversion Errors. The error description therein should relate to Access no longer supporting user-level security. You can disregard it and delete the Conversion Errors table.

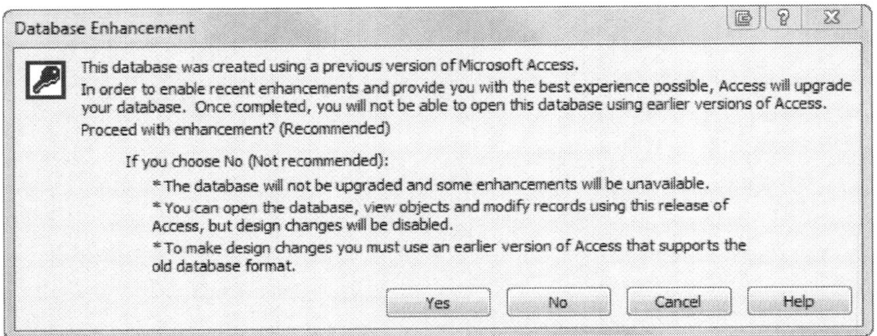

Figure E-1a Access Upgrade Dialog Box

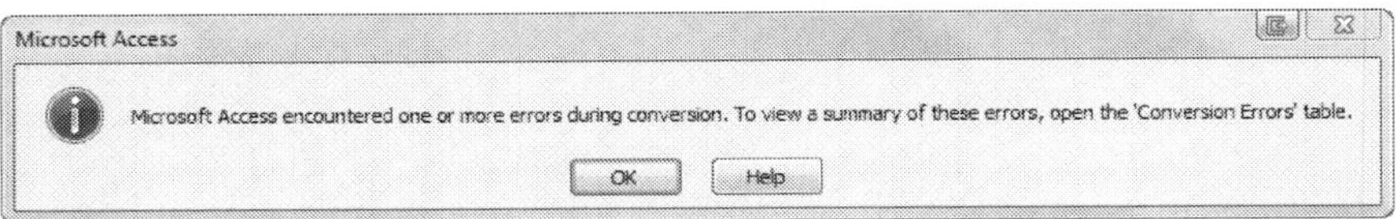

Figure E-1b Access Upgrade Error Message Box

Access User Interface

The Access user interface (window) in Figure E-2a has three main sections: the Ribbon at the top (not shown) with tabs that organize tools and commands in related groups, the Navigation Pane on the left where you view and access objects, and an area on the right where objects are displayed.

The Navigation Pane

You can open or collapse the Navigation Pane by clicking the Shutter Bar button, the square button with << at the top right of the Navigation Pane. Clicking the down arrowhead to the left of the Shutter Bar button displays the object category list as shown in the figure. The list has two sections. The Navigate to Category section lists the five types of object categories, and the Filter by Group section lists the types of objects within the category selected. In the example we are viewing the Access objects by their type with those types listed below the Filter by Group divider. When you click on one of the groups, the category list retract unhiding the underlying category view as in Figure E-2b where the list of tables in the database is displayed.

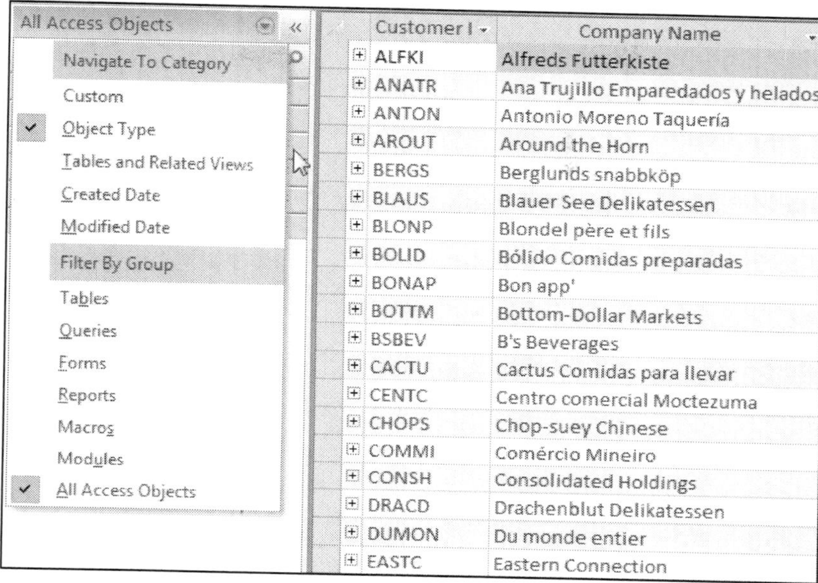

Figure E-2a Access Window

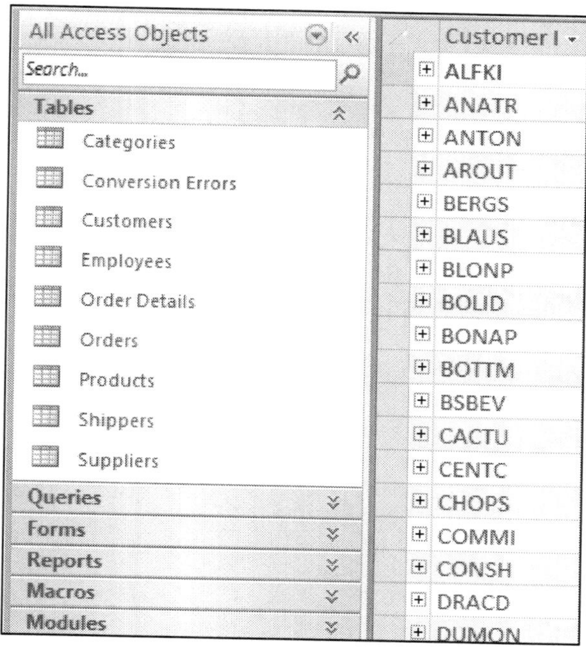

Figure E-2b Category View

Object Views

Left clicking on an object in Figure E-2b will open the object as shown by the Customers table that's open in the tab. Right clicking an object will display the menu in Figure E-2c. There are two object view options: the tabbed view as shown in the example and the overlapping windows view used in previous windows versions. New databases created in Access 2010 default to the tabbed view but databases created in previous versions default to the overlapping windows view. The views are database specific, i.e., you cannot globally specify a view to be used for all Access databases. To set the view for the current database go to Access Options via the Office button in the upper left corner of the Access window, click Current Database, and select either the Overlapping Windows or Tabbed Documents radio button (not shown). To close a tab either click the Close (X) button at the top right of the window containing the tab that you want to close or right click on the tab name which will open the menu in Figure E-2d. These same actions apply to the Overlapping Windows as well.

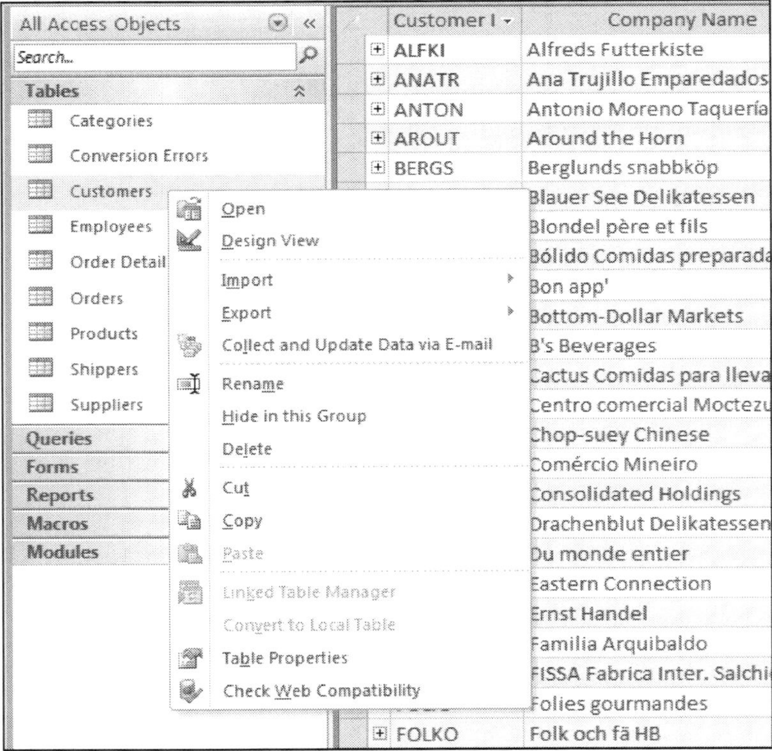

Figure E-2c Object Menu

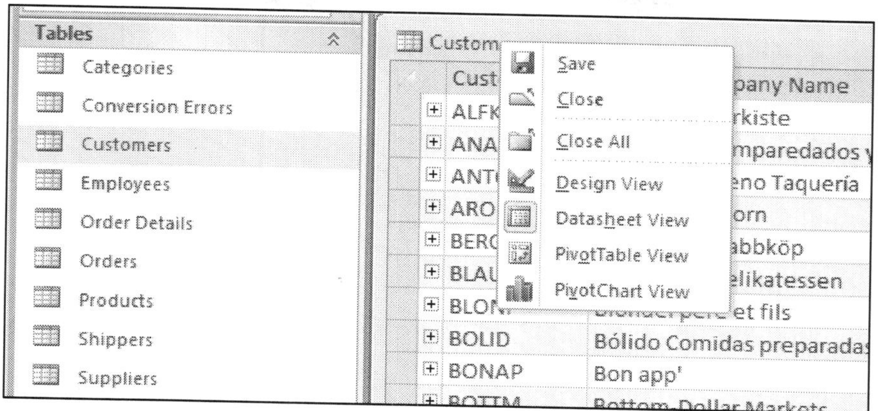

Figure E-2d Tab Menu

The Ribbon

Access' Ribbon initially contains five tabs but another tab may be included as appropriate for a particular view. The initial tabs and command groups within each are listed in Table E-1 with the exception of the Add-Ins tab because it only contains one command group, Custom Toolbars, which is initially empty. The Home tab has a number of frequently used commands related to formatting and records. The Create tab provides commands to quickly create objects such as a table, form, or report. The External Data tab contains commands to import and export data. And the Database Tools tab includes a variety of tools to manage the database and access Visual Basic for Applications.

Home	Create	External Data	Database Tools
Views	Templates	Import & Link	Tools
Clipboard	Tables	Export	Macro
Sort & Filter	Queries	Collect Data	Relationships
Records	Forms	Web Linked Lists	Analyze
Find	Reports		Move Data
Window	Macros & Code		Add-ins
Text Formatting			

Table E-1 Ribbon Tabs and Command Groups

Tables

Datasheet View

As mentioned in Chapter 2 a table, the fundamental entity in a database, is composed of columns which are its attributes (fields) and rows (records) which represent individual items. Only tables contain data in an Access database. Figure E-3a shows a partial screen shot of the datasheet view of the first four fields for the Northwind Orders table which has has 830 rows and 14 columns. There are four view options for tables: the datasheet view as in the figure that lists the data records, the design view that is used to create and modify the table structure, and the pivot table and pivot chart views. The latter two are described in Chapter 7.

Orders

	Order I	Customer	Employee	Order Date
+	10263	Ernst Handel	Dodsworth, Anne	23-Aug-94
+	10264	Folk och fä HB	Suyama, Michael	24-Aug-94
+	10265	Blondel père et fils	Fuller, Andrew	25-Aug-94
+	10266	Wartian Herkku	Leverling, Janet	26-Aug-94
+	10267	Frankenversand	Peacock, Margaret	29-Aug-94
+	10268	GROSELLA-Restaurante	Callahan, Laura	30-Aug-94
+	10269	White Clover Markets	Buchanan, Steven	31-Aug-94
+	10270	Wartian Herkku	Davolio, Nancy	01-Sep-94

Figure E-3a Orders Table Datasheet View

You can filter and sort the records in datasheet view as usual by either clicking on the down-arrowhead in a column header or using the Sort & Filter commands on the Home tab. You can select one or more contiguous records by using the record selection buttons on the left side of the table. The selected record(s) will be shaded as in Figure 3a for the three records that I selected. Right clicking on a record selector or a selected set of records will display a menu (not shown) with which you may insert, delete, cut, or copy records.

In the Datasheet view the Ribbon exposes the Table Tools Fields and Table tabs (Figure E-3b) where you have easy access to frequently used table related commands. For example, the View command lets you switch among the various view types, and the relationships command displays the Relationships tab.

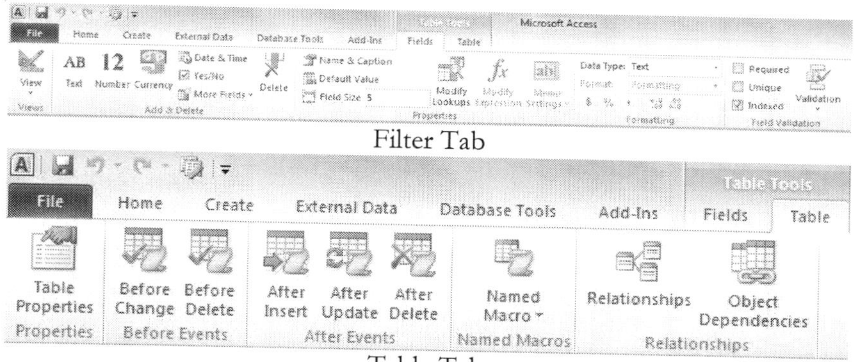

Filter Tab

Table Tab

Figure E-3b Table Tools Fields and Table Tabs

Design View

The design view (Figure E-3c) has two sections: the table design at the top with three columns --Field Name on the left, Data Type in the middle, and Description on the right—and field properties at the bottom. It is accepted practice not to use spaces in field names so all of the fields listed are without them. The data type of a field is specified by clicking on a field which exposes a down arrowhead button and then clicking on that button to display the listbox as in Figure E-3d. You usually use the AutoNumber data type for primary keys (described in Chapter 2) and Number as a long integer for foreign keys. Primary keys are designated by either selecting a field(s) and using the Primary Key command in the Table Tools Design tab or right clicking a field and clicking primary key on the menu.

Field properties for the selected field are listed in the bottom section. You set or edit a property by clicking on it and then either entering a value, e.g., Order ID for the Caption property, selecting a value from a drop-down list, or using the Expression builder to, say, define a validation rule.

Orders

Field Name	Data Type	Description
OrderID	AutoNumber	Unique order number.
CustomerID	Text	Same entry as in Customers table.
EmployeeID	Number	Same entry as in Employees table.
OrderDate	Date/Time	
RequiredDate	Date/Time	
ShippedDate	Date/Time	
ShipVia	Number	Same as Shipper ID in Shippers table.
Freight	Currency	
ShipName	Text	Name of person or company to receive the shipment.
ShipAddress	Text	Street address only -- no post-office box allowed.
ShipCity	Text	
ShipRegion	Text	State or province.
ShipPostalCode	Text	
ShipCountry	Text	

Field Properties

General | Lookup

Field Size	Long Integer
New Values	Increment
Format	
Caption	Order ID
Indexed	Yes (No Duplicates)
Smart Tags	
Text Align	General

Figure E-3c Table Design View

Orders

Field Name
OrderID
CustomerID
EmployeeID
OrderDate
RequiredDate
ShippedDate
ShipVia
Freight
ShipName
ShipAddress
ShipCity
ShipRegion
ShipPostalCode

Data Type: AutoNumber

Text
Memo
Number
Date/Time
Currency
AutoNumber
Yes/No
OLE Object
Hyperlink
Attachment
Calculated
Lookup Wizard...

Figure E-3d Design View Data Type Menu

In the Design view the Ribbon exposes the Table Tools Design tab (Figure E-3e) where you have easy access to frequently used design-related commands. For example, the View command is available here too, clicking the Property Sheet command button will display the property sheet for the table.

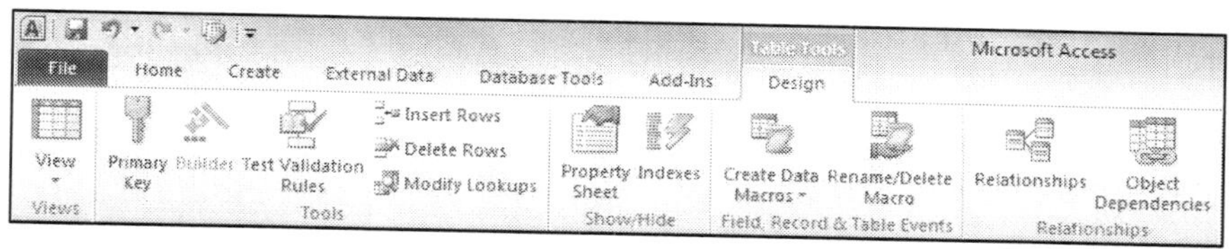

Figure E-3e Table Tools Design Tab

Subdatasheets

You may have noticed the expand indicators (the + symbols) in the second column of Figure E-3a. Clicking one as in Figure E-3f will display a subdatasheet with related data from another table or query. In the example the subdatasheet is showing the items in the Victuailles en stock order from the Order Details table. For tables with a one-to-one relationship or on the one side of a one-to-many relationship Access automatically creates a subdatasheet as in the Northwind database if the SubdatasheetName property of the table is set to Auto. You may override Auto in the Property Sheet to specify the table or query to show as the subdatasheet.

Orders

	Order I	Customer	Employee	Order Date	Required Dat
⊞	10248	Vins et alcools Chevalier	Buchanan, Steven	04-Aug-94	01-Sep-94
⊞	10249	Toms Spezialitäten	Suyama, Michael	05-Aug-94	16-Sep-94
⊞	10250	Hanari Carnes	Peacock, Margaret	08-Aug-94	05-Sep-94
⊟	10251	Victuailles en stock	Leverling, Janet	08-Aug-94	05-Sep-94

	Product	Unit Price	Quantit	Discount	Click to Add
	Gustaf's Knäckebröd	$16.80	6	5%	
	Ravioli Angelo	$15.60	15	5%	
	Louisiana Fiery Hot Pepper Sauce	$16.80	20	0%	
*		$0.00	1	0%	

	Order I	Customer	Employee	Order Date	Required Dat
⊞	10252	Suprêmes délices	Peacock, Margaret	09-Aug-94	06-Sep-94

Figure E-3f Table Subdatasheet

Relationships

Tables are linked by relationships using primary and foreign keys (see Chapters 2 and 7 and Appendix C). A relationship diagram (Figure E-3g) is displayed by using the relationships command in the Database Tools or Table Tools Table tab. Most relationships are one-to-many, meaning one record in table may be linked to many records in another table. For example, one employee will be linked to many orders. Sometimes the relationship is one-to-one where a record in one table is linked to only one record in another table. For example a manager usually only manages a single department and a department has only one manager. Many-to-many relationships are problematic for building queries because references are ambiguous so we handle many to many relationships by dividing them into two one-to-many relationships connected with an associative entity which has the many side relationship with two tables such as the Order Details table in the example. By using the Order Details table we are able to identify the products in a particular order.

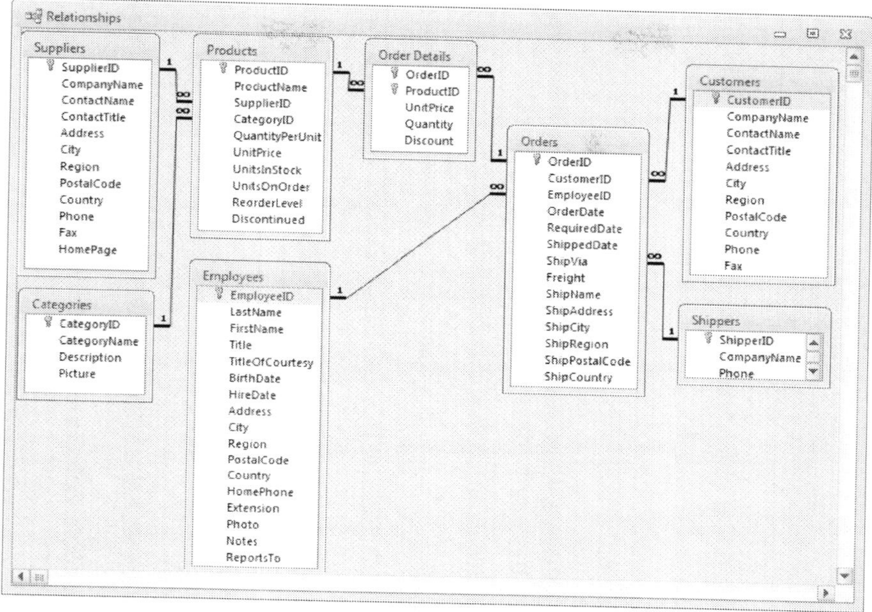

Figure E-3g Relationships
(For better viewing of this image, go to
http://www.zerobits.info/bibook/bibookimages/)

You create relationships between tables by dragging a field (usually a key) from one table to a field on another table. Creating and editing relationships is described in Chapter 7.

Create Tab

The Create tab includes groups for creating tables, queries, forms, and reports and a group for macros and code as shown in Figure E-4a.

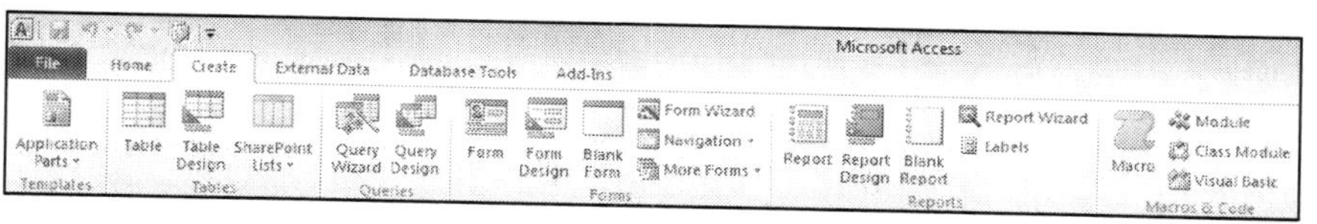

Figure E-4a Query Tools Design Tab

Tables

The Table button will insert a blank table and open it in datasheet view; the Table Design button opens a new table in design view; and the SharePoint Lists button displays the menu in Figure E-4b.

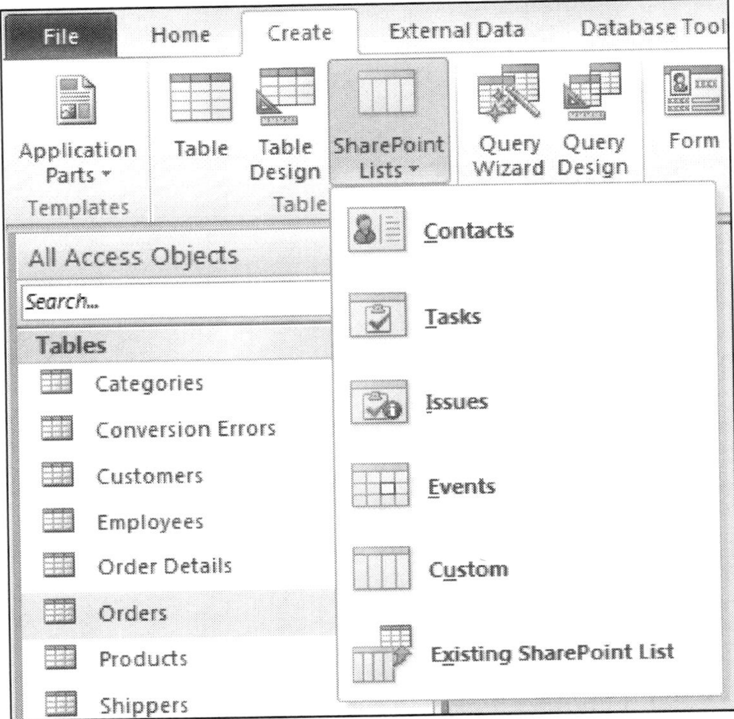

Figure E-4b SharePoint List Menu

Queries

Queries are described in detail in Appendix C. The Queries group has a button for the Query Wizard which will lead you through building a query and one for Query Design which will bring up a query designer.

Forms

Since we do not use forms in this book and forms are not directly useful for BI, we give only cursory mention of them here. The usual uses for forms are to input data into a table(s) and to display and edit data. However, you can use forms for other purposes such as containers for charts and graphs, as switchboards, and as a user interface for Visual Basic for Applications code.

Existing forms can be modified by selecting Design View from the menus displayed by right clicking on either a form name in the Navigation Pane or in Design view on the tab or on an empty area of the form. New forms are created by using one of the form commands in the Forms command group. For example, if I select the Customers table in the Navigation Pane and then click Form on the Create tab, then the form in Figure E-4c is created and displayed in form view. Note that the subdatasheet is automatically included in the form. Clicking Form Design will create a blank form as in Figure E-4d with a Field List to use for dragging and dropping fields onto the form. The Blank Form command displays an empty form in Layout view.

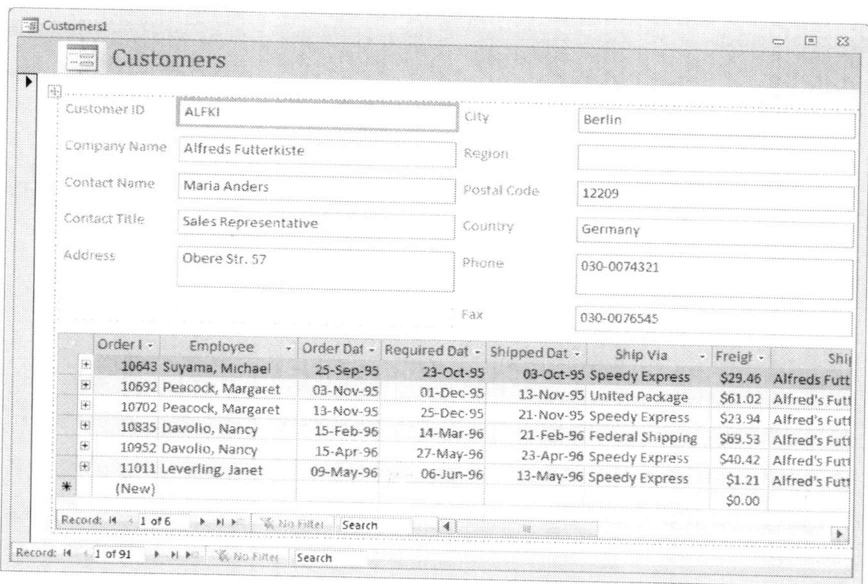

Figure E-4c New Form Example

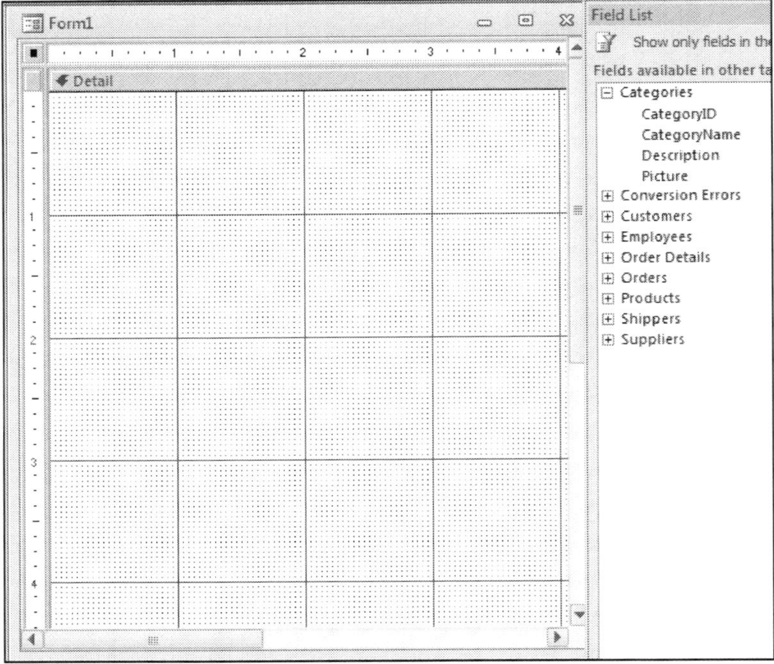

Figure E-4d New Form Example

Split Form and Multiple Items shown in the More Forms button's drop-down menu (Figure 4e) are just design variations. Split Form provides both form and datasheet views on the same form as in Figure E-4c, and Multiple Items presents a table-like continuous list of the records. The Pivot Chart command displays an empty pivot chart in design view for the object that was selected in the Navigation Pane. To complete the pivot chart you display the Field List and drag and drop fields into the appropriate drop zones. Pivot charts are described in detail in Chapters 6 and 7. The More Forms menu also has commands for a Datasheet view form, a form as a Modal Dialog Box, and a form containing a Pivot Table.

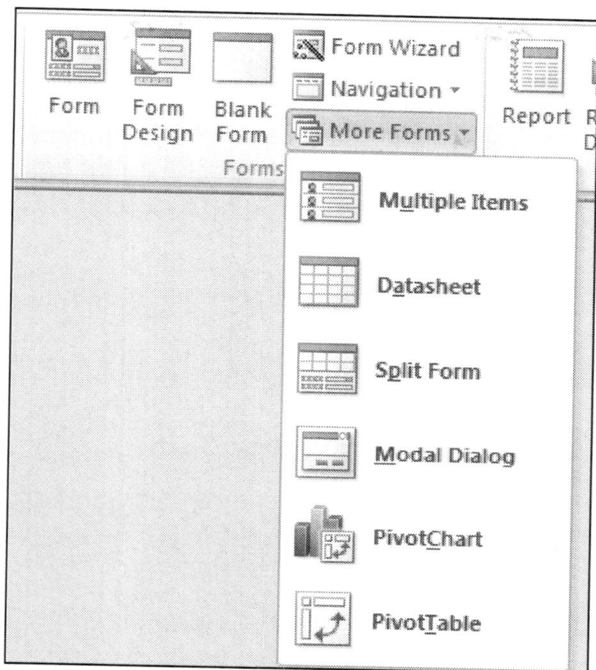

Figure E-4e More Forms Menu

Figure E-5e New Blank Form in Design View

Reports

Reports are generally used to present data from tables and queries in printed form. We have not used Access reports in this book and have intentionally avoided describing how to produce printed output . Please refer to one of the many Access books for information about creating reports in Access.

Macros

We briefly described using Excel macros in Appendix D. Access macros are a bit different in that you cannot record them in Access as you do in Excel, and they are not included in Visual Basic for Applications code. However, they are similar in that both allow you to "program" a set of actions to use over and over again.

A macro is created by using the Macro Builder (Figure E-5a) accessed by using the Macro command in the Macros & Code command group on the Create tab. When you do that Access also inserts the Macro Tools Design tab as shown. A new macro it will have a default name something like "Macro1."

When you close or run the macro for the first time you will be prompted to provide a name as I did for the Example Macro, and as shown it will be included in the Macro collection in the Navigation Pane. Example Macro has three actions: it opens the Current Product List query, it beeps, and then moves the cursor in the query to the first record.

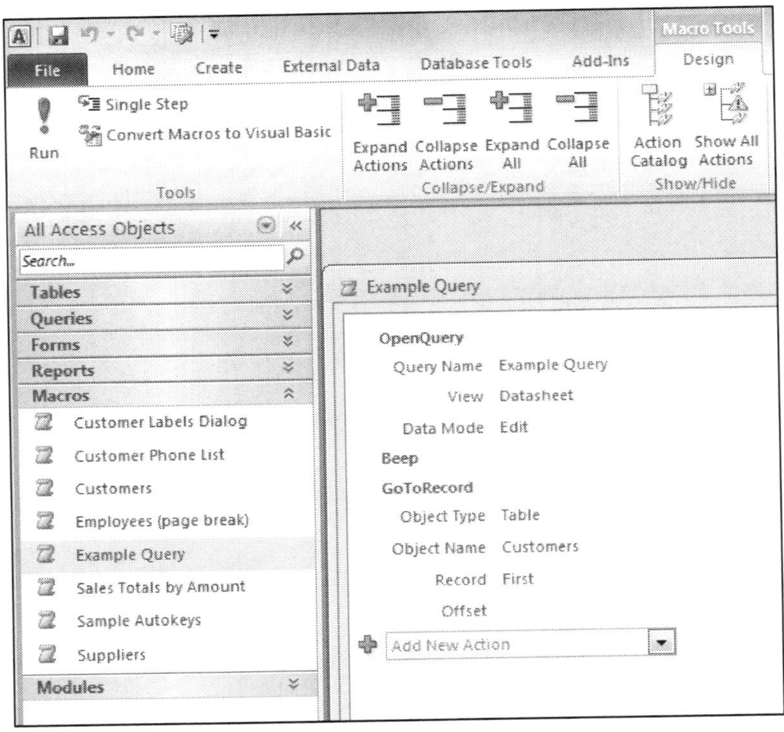

Figure E-5a Macro Builder

You "program" a macro by specifying Actions, Arguments, and Conditions. The latter is not shown in the figure but can be by clicking the Conditions button in the Show/Hide command group. Actions are selected from a listbox partially shown in Figure E-5b, and Arguments and Conditions are inserted into the textboxes on the form that is displayed after selecting the action as in Figure E-5c. The type and number of arguments will vary depending on the action selected. For example the Beep action has no arguments. To run a macro just double click the macro name in the Navigation Pane Macros list. Note that some actions are prevented from running if the database is not trusted.

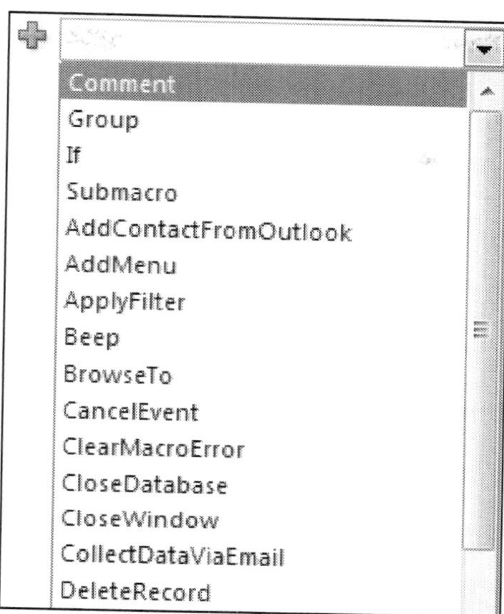

Figure E-5b Macro Builder Actions Listbox

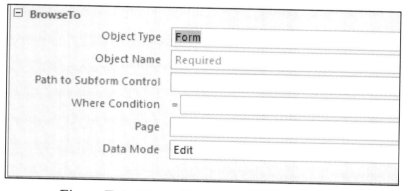

BrowseTo
Object Type: Form
Object Name: Required
Path to Subform Control
Where Condition =
Page
Data Mode: Edit

Figure E-5c Macro Builder Arguments Example

You can embed macros in event properties of forms, reports, or controls so that the macro will run when the event occurs by opening a form or report in design or layout view, displaying the Property Sheet for an object on the form or report, selecting the ... button on the event in the Property Sheet to which you want to attach a macro, choosing Macro Builder from the Choose Builder dialog box that pops up, and then proceeding to create the macro as described above. For example, we could put a command button on a form to print it by selecting the Macro Builder for the command button On Click event, and then setting the action in the Macro Builder to print.

Appendix F - The Data Mining Advanced Query Editor and DMX

In Chapter 10 we used the Data Mining Query tool to create and run prediction queries with the Data Mining Query Wizard. At that time we deferred discussion about the Data Mining Advanced Query Editor which is accessed with the Advanced button on any of the Data Mining Query Wizard's dialog boxes except Getting Started. The Data Mining Advanced Query Editor is a query designer for the data mining extensions (DMX) to the SQL language, a declarative language similar to SQL that is used by Analysis Services to create, manage, and process data mining structures and models.

Although exploring DMX in detail is beyond the scope of this book, we'll look at two uses for the Query Editor that overcome limitations of the mining structure and model tools provided by the Advanced and Manage Models commands in Excel's Data Mining tab: filtering and nested tables. But first, we need to know a few basics about DMX.

DMX Basics

Similar to SQL, DMX has data definition statements and data manipulation statements. DMX data definition statements are used to create, alter, import and export, and remove mining structures and models. The example below, a slightly altered version of one in SQL Server 2008 Books Online, creates a new mining structure named New Mailing that contains four columns (fields) with each field name followed by its data type and context type. The columns are separated by commas, and names with spaces are enclosed in brackets. The last statement specifies a 20 percent holdout for testing purposes.

```
CREATE MINING STRUCTURE [New Mailing]
(
   CustomerKey LONG KEY,
   Gender TEXT DISCRETE,
   [Number Cars Owned] LONG DISCRETE,
   [Bike Buyer] LONG DISCRETE )
    WITH HOLDOUT (20 PERCENT)
```

All the CREATE statement does is construct an empty structure, i.e., no data are defined for the structure so you cannot use it for processing at this point.

The data types are TEXT, LONG, BOOLEAN, DOUBLE, and DATE. Table F-1 lists the context types.

Content Type	Description
Discrete	The field contains values as individual parts as in gender, education, or cars owned.
Continuous	Field values are on a continuous scale like temperature and income. Continuous values may have decimal fractions.
Discretized	The values derive from discretizing a continuous filed, e.g., low, medium, and high income.
Key	A row identifier
Key Sequence	This field indicates a row's sequence in a series of events. We used this in Sequence Clustering in Chapter 10
Table	This indicates that nested tables are contained in the field, i.e., that there are fields within this field.
Cyclical	The field contains values in an ordered set like the days of the week.
Ordered	Similar to the key sequence type but the values are on an ordinal scale (see Appendix B).
Classified	Allows specifying as data type contains data about another field. The types are probability, variance, standard deviation, probability variance, probability standard deviation, and support.

Table F-1 DMX content Types

DMX data manipulation statements are used to work on existing models. One of those, the INSERT statement, binds data to a structure as in the following:

```
INSERT INTO [New Mailing] (CustomerKey, Gender, [Number Cars Owned],
   [Bike Buyer])
OPENQUERY([Adventure Works DW],'Select CustomerKey, Gender,
   [NumberCarsOwned], [BikeBuyer] FROM [vTargetMail]')
```

Here the data from a view [vTargetMail] in the Adventure Works 2008 DW database is bound to the New Mailing structure. A mining model is added to a structure with the ALTER MINING STRUCTURE statement as below:

```
ALTER MINING STRUCTURE [New Mailing]
ADD MINING MODEL [Naive Bayes]
(
  CustomerKey,
  Gender,
  [Number Cars Owned],
  [Bike Buyer] PREDICT
)
USING Microsoft_Naive_Bayes (MAXIMUM_STATES = 50)
WITH FILTER(Gender = 'M' AND Age <50)
```

This statement adds a Naive Bayes model into the New Mailing Structure created above and filters the data to include only males (M) less than 50. Finally, the PREDICTION JOIN statement is used to make prediction queries on a model as this example from SQL Server 2008 Books Online demonstrates:

```
SELECT
  [TM Decision Tree].[Bike Buyer],
  PredictHistogram([Bike Buyer])
FROM
  [TM Decision Tree]
NATURAL PREDICTION JOIN
(SELECT 35 AS [Age],
  '5-10 Miles' AS [Commute Distance],
  '1' AS [House Owner Flag],
  2 AS [Number Cars Owned],
  2 AS [Total Children]) AS t
```

This query predicts if a customer with specific characteristics such as age 35, two children, etc. will be a bike buyer using the model TM Decision Tree and presents the result as a histogram.

With this brief look at DMX we can move on to the Query Editor.

The Data Mining Advance Query Editor

As noted above the Data Mining Query Editor is accessed by using the Advanced button on any of the Data Mining Query Wizard dialog boxes. Figure F-1a shows a Select Model dialog box as an example. The Advanced Query Editor has two forms: a Query Builder (Figure F-1b) and a Query Editor within which you write DMX code. The Query Builder provides a structured user interface to more easily create and modify DMX queries than writing them from scratch in the Query Editor. In the figure the model initially displayed in the DMX Query panel is the Query Builder view for a prediction using the Classify - Decision Trees model selected the Figure F-1a.

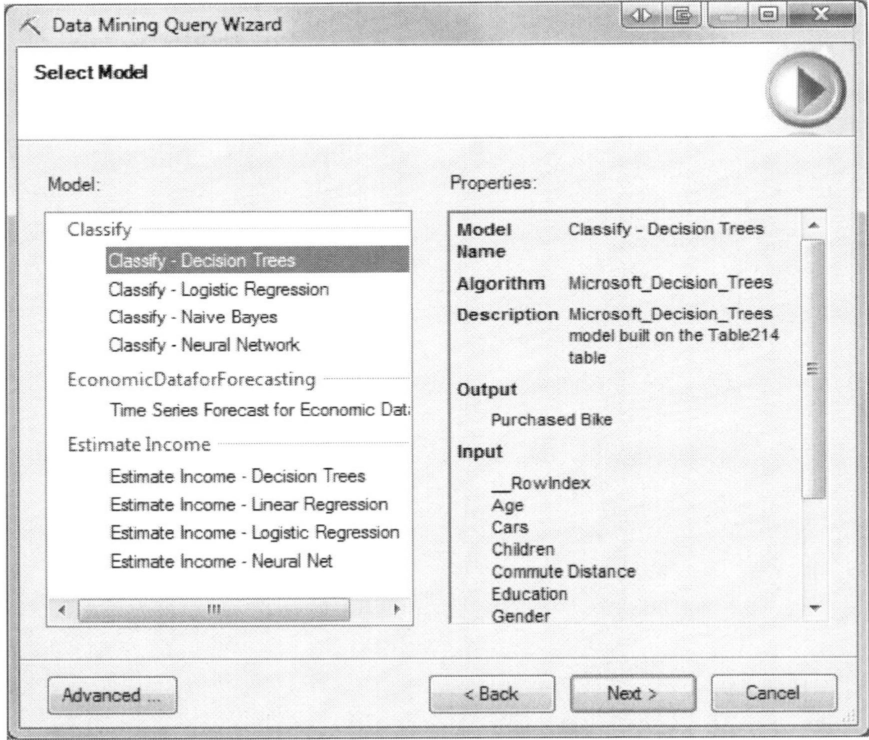

Figure F-1a Advanced Select Model Dialog Box with Advanced Button

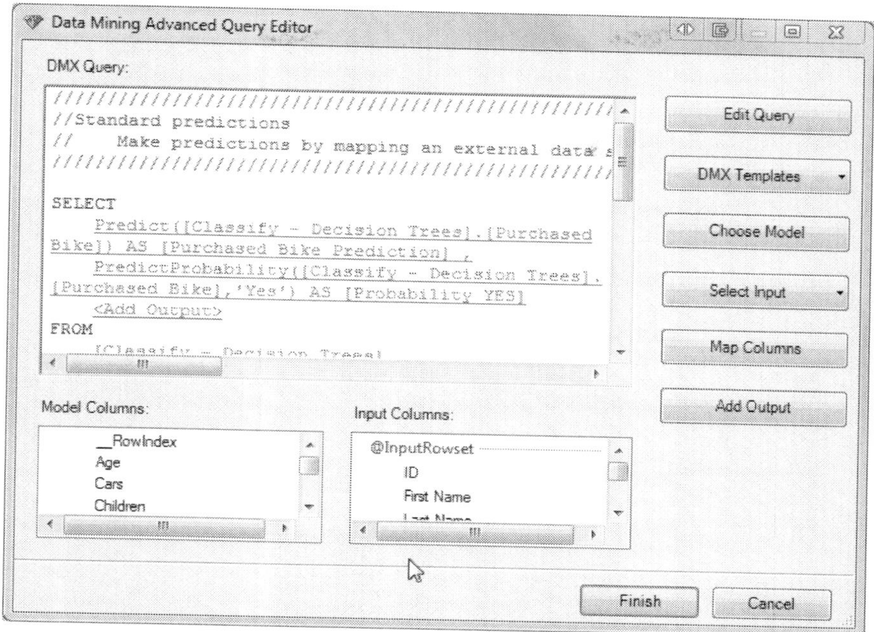

Figure F-1b Advanced Query Editor - Query Builder

The Query Builder has a number of buttons on the right side to assist in constructing a query. DMX Templates provides DMX templates that have areas to fill in to complete a query. There are four categories of templates as shown in Figure F-1c which also lists the templates for the Prediction category. Create, Model Properties, and Management template menus are shown in Figure F-1d.

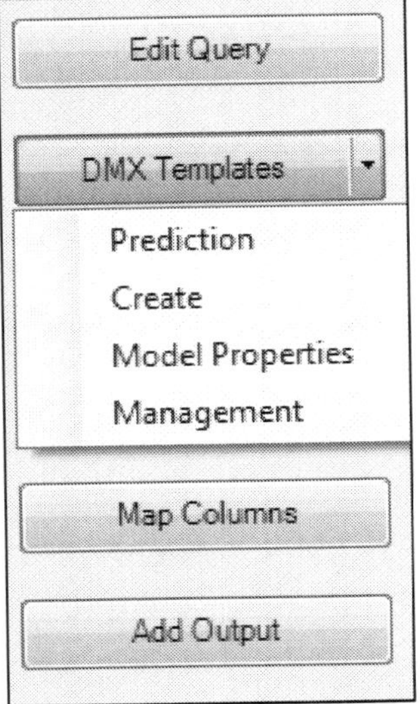

Filtered predictions
Filtered nested predictions
Nested predictions
Singleton prediction
Standard predictions
Time series predictions
TOP prediction query
TOP prediction query on nested table

Figure F-1c Prediction Templates

Mining model
Mining structure
Mining structure with holdout
Temporary model
Temporary structure

Create Templates

Mining model content
Minimum and maximum column values
Mining structure test/training cases
Discrete column values

Model Properties Templates

Clear mining model
Clear structure and models
Clear mining structure
Delete mining model
Delete mining structure
Rename mining model
Rename mining structure
Train mining model
Train nested mining structure
Train mining structure

Management Templates

Figure F-1d More Templates

The Choose Model button will display the Select Model dialog box as in Figure F-1a. You use the Select Input button to identify input columns for the model which are shown in the Input Columns listbox. The Map Columns button brings up the Map Input Columns to Model Columns dialog box (Figure F-1e) where Table Columns are matched to Mining [Model] Columns by using the drop down listboxes. In this case they are named the same so nothing needed to be changed. Finally, the Add Output button displays the Add Output dialog box as in Figure 10-31c and reproduced in Figure F-1f.

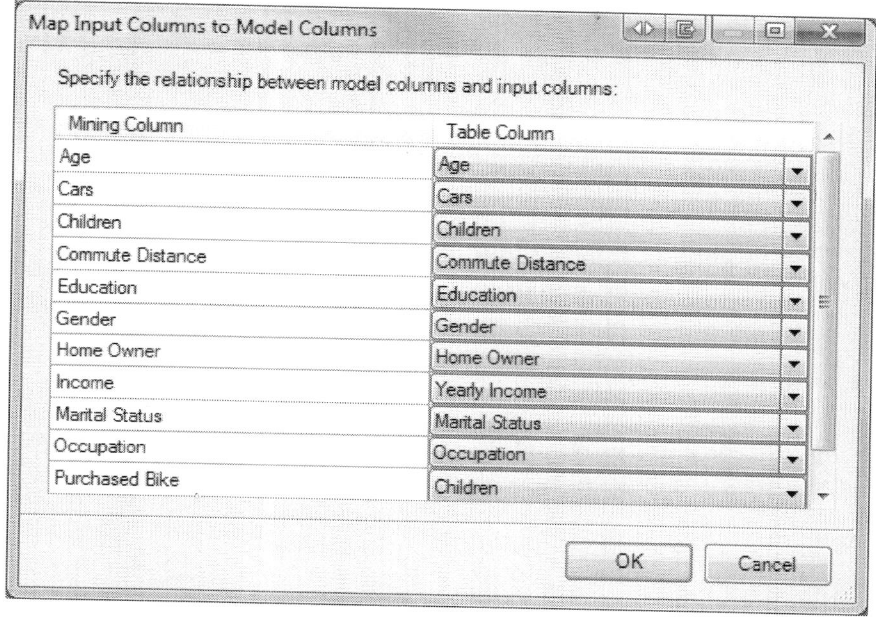

Figure F-1e Map Input Columns Dialog Box

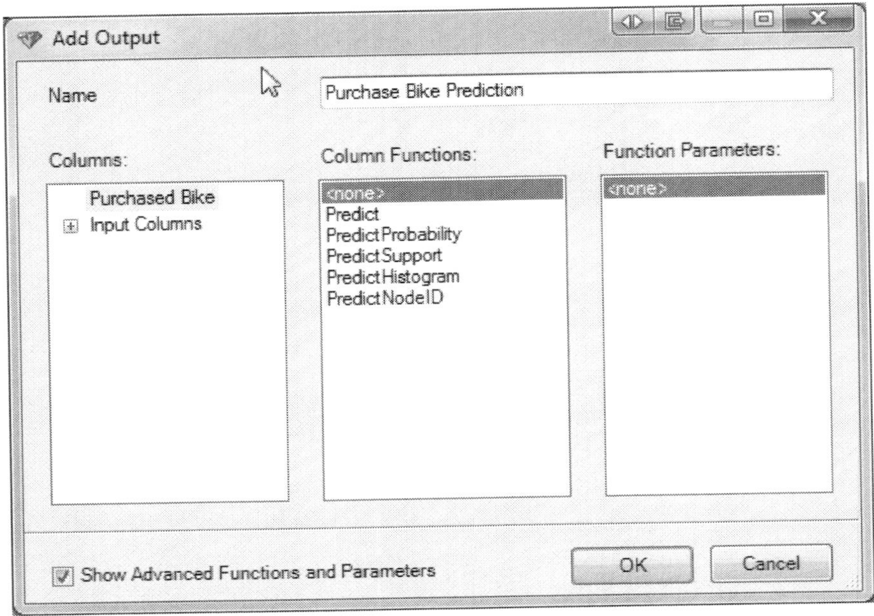

Figure F-1f Add Output Dialog Box

Filtering

Suppose AdventureWorks wants to explore bicycle buying behavior for its North American customers. With the data mining tools we've looked at so far the only way to do this is to create a table in Excel containing only North American customers or a similar query for use as the data source for a mining structure. While these approached are not difficult to use, the Advanced Query Editor allows us to limit the cases in a mining structure by adding a mining model filter. For an example we'll add a new mining model to one of the Table Analysis Tools Sample - Purchased Bike mining structures that we used in Chapter 10. In the Query Builder view I selected Mining Model from Create menu of the DMX Template button. Four lines in the DMX Query panel are shown in a red font—<Structure>, <Name>, Microsoft_Decision_Trees, and <No Drill-through>—indicating that these properties must be filled in or can be modified.

Clicking the <Structure> property in the DMX Query window displays the Select Mining Structure dialog box (Figure F-2b) that presents a list of the existing structures in the existing Analysis Services connection. I selected the Classify structure. Clicking the <Name> property brings up the Specify Name dialog box as in Figure F-2c where I entered a name for the new model.

Clicking the <Column> property will present the Model Columns, similar to the Select columns dialog box (Figure F-2d). (We saw this before in Figure 10-25c.) I changed the Purchase Bike column usage to Predict only. Clicking the Micorsoft_Decision_Trees property displays the Select Algorithm and Parameters dialog box (Figure F-2e) similar to what we have seen before. I kept the Decision Trees algorithm. And finally, clicking the <No Drill-through> property shows the Drill-through dialog box as in Figure F-2f where I left the property as is. Figure F-2g shows the DMX statement that automatically results from these entries. You may click on any of the entries for editing.

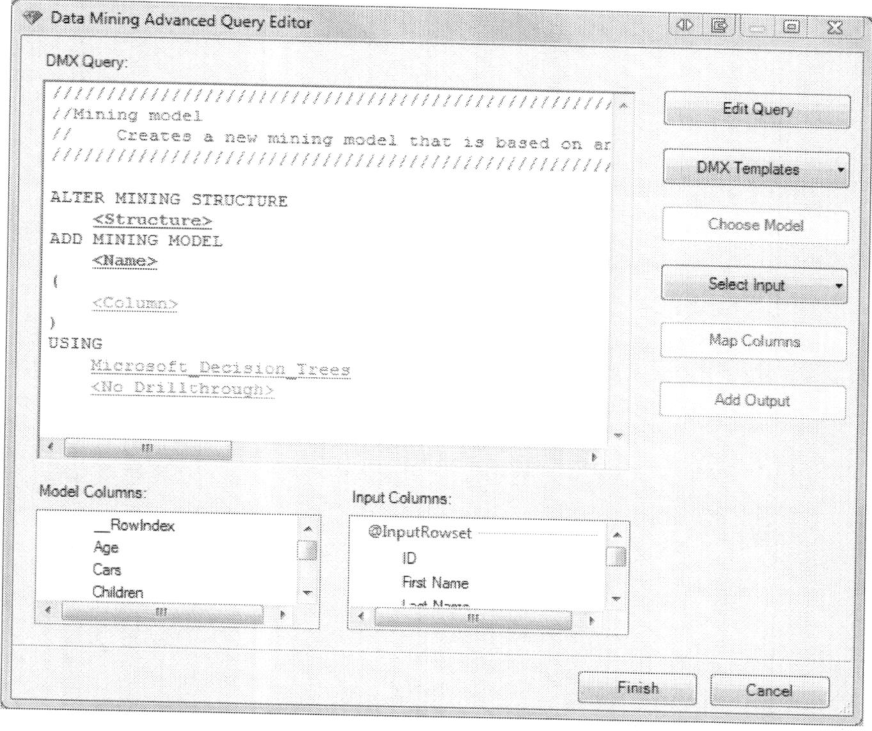

Figure F-2a New Mining Model

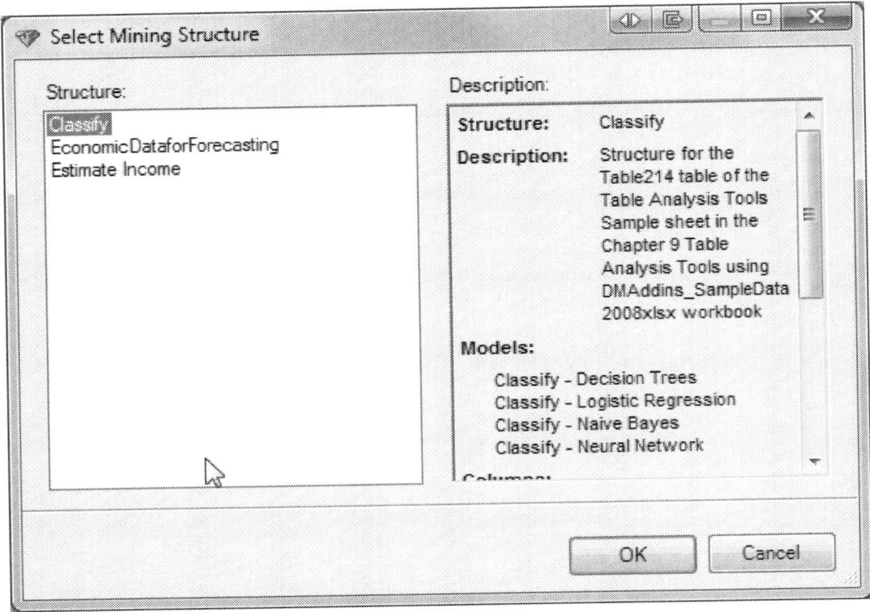

Figure F-2b Select Mining Structure Dialog Box

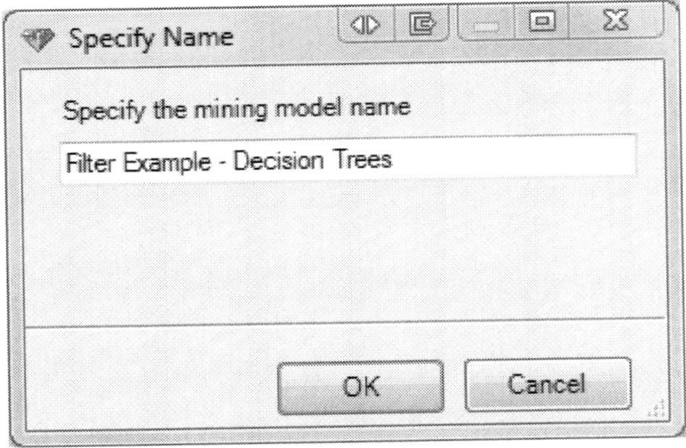

Figure F-2c Specify Name Dialog Box

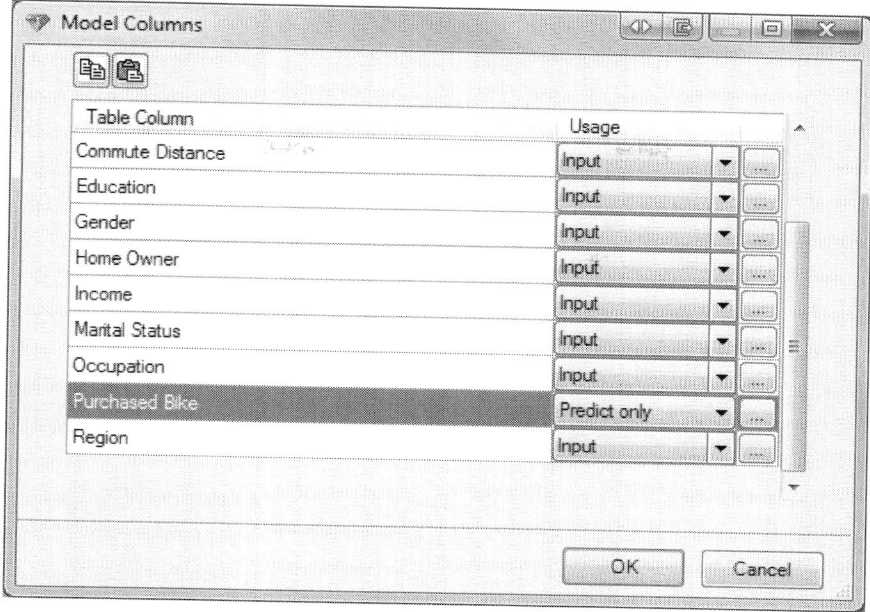

Figure F-2d Model Columns Dialog Box

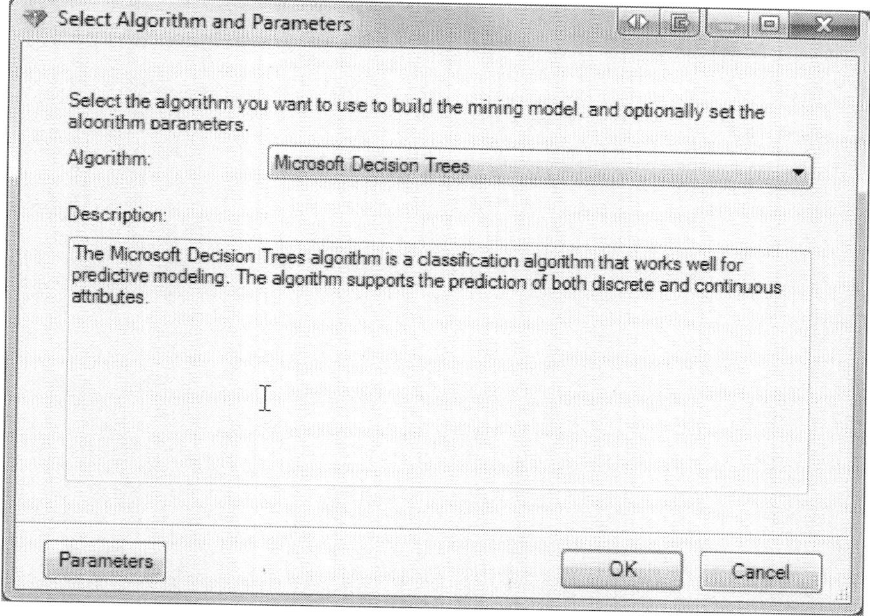

Figure F-2e Select Algorithm and Parameters Dialog Box

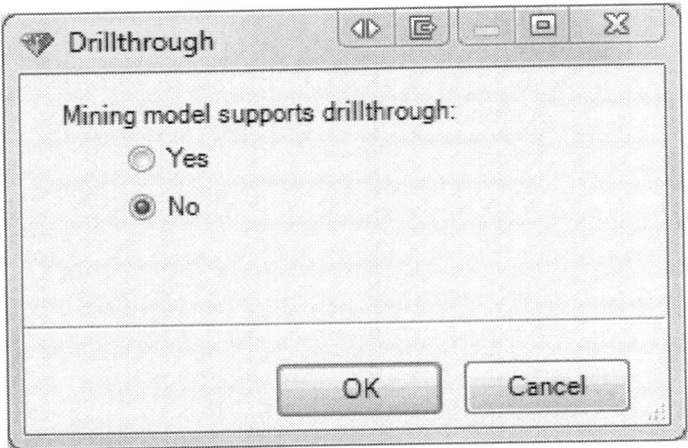

Figure F-2f Drill_through Dialog Box

```
//////////////////////////////////////////////////////////////
//Mining model
//     Creates a new mining model that is based on an
//////////////////////////////////////////////////////////////

ALTER MINING STRUCTURE
    [Classify]
ADD MINING MODEL
    [Filter Example - Decision Trees]
(
    [__RowIndex] ,
    [Age] ,
    [Cars] ,
    [Children] ,
    [Commute Distance] ,
    [Education] ,
    [Gender] ,
    [Home Owner] ,
    [Income] ,
    [Marital Status] ,
    [Occupation] ,
    [Purchased Bike] PREDICT_ONLY ,
    [Region]
)
USING
    Microsoft_Decision_Trees
    <No Drillthrough>
```

Figure F-2g Resulting DMX Statement

What we've done is to replicate the Classify - Decision Trees model that we created more easily in Chapter 10 using the Data Mining Wizard. The purpose of going to the additional effort here is to specify a model in the Query Builder that we can modify in the Query Editor. Unfortunately, there does not seem to be a way to access an existing model in the Editor.

We're finally ready to add the filter statement to the model by switching to the Query Editor by clicking the Edit Query button. Clicking Edit Query will display a dialog box warning saying that changes made will not be preserved. Click Yes to continue. In Figure F-2h I added the WITH FILTER expression and then clicked the Finish button. Note that if you return to the Query Builder by clicking that button you will lose the edit, i.e., the WITH FILTER expression will be missing. Continuing, if you try to Browse the new model (called Filter Example) you will get a message that the "Mining Model is not processed" so go to Manage Models, select model, click the "Process this mining model" task, and you're good to go.

You can create compound filters using logical operators. The one below filters on the Region, Commute Distance, and Age columns. Note that text values are delineated with apostrophes and column names containing blank spaces are enclosed in brackets. Also, columns in a Filter must be mining structure columns not mining model columns.

> WITH FILTER (Region = 'North America' and [Commute Distance] = '0-1 Miles' AND Age > 30)

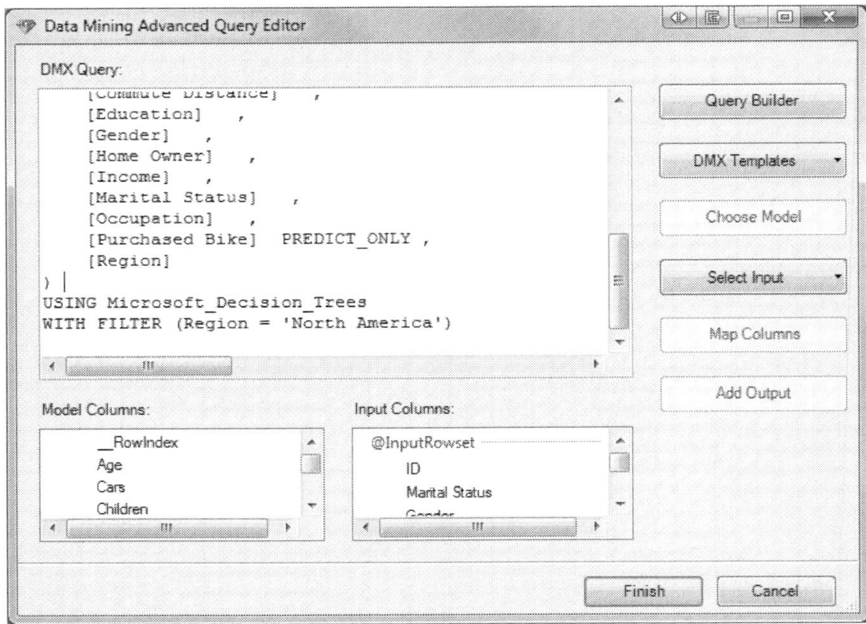

Figure F-2h DMX Statements In Query Editor

Nested Tables

Analysis Services uses case tables as a source for data where the cases are usually rows in a data table like the tables in the Sample Data Excel file from the Data Mining Add-Ins for Office 2007 used for examples in Chapters 9 and 10. However, at times the data cannot be contained in a single table such as when dealing with line items in orders. For example, in our example for Sequence Clustering in Chapter 10 the algorithm required order sequence data to be supplied in a nested table. A nested table (the child) provides details about rows in another table (the parent) very much like a many to one relationship in a relational database. The Sequence Clustering example uses two views from the AdventureWorks2008DW database: vAssocSeqOrders, the parent, on the left in Figure F-3a that contains the order data and vAssocSeqLineItems, the child, on the right that contains the items purchased in line number sequence. Figure F-3b represents a row in the mining structure case table for order number SO1178 with the nested table data shown in the Model column.

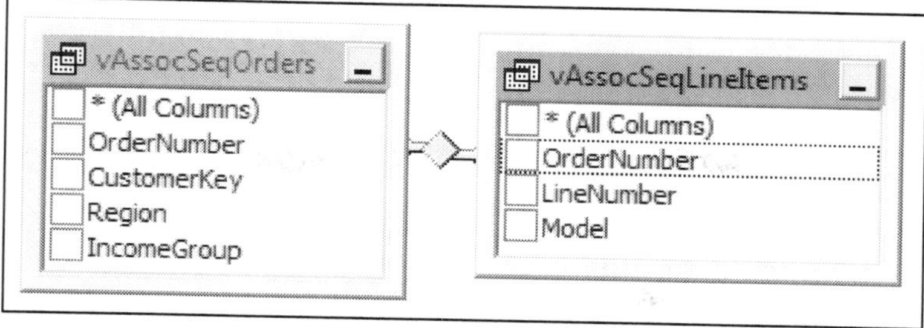

Figure F-3a SQL Views

OrderNumber	Region	IncomeGroup	Model
S051178	Europe	High	Mountain-200
			Mountain Bottle Cage
			Water Bottle

Figure F-3b Data Mining Table

Figure F-3 Sequence Cluster Case and Nested Tables Example

The example below uses the CREATE MINING MODEL statement to create a mining structure and model at the same time where the nested table (Products) is identified by the TABLE data type with its contents defined below it. This model recreates the Sequence Clustering mining model in Chapter 10 from scratch. The result of the DMX statement will be a mining structure called ProductSequence_Structure and a mining Model called ProductSequence.

You may be able to discern that the parent table contains the OrderNumber and IncomeGroup columns and the nested (child)table contains the Linenumber and Product columns. Sequence Clustering models require a column designated as a KEY SEQUENCE data type that indicates the sequence of events as in our product order sequence. Nested tables in other mining model types would not use the SEQUENCE part of the data type.

```
CREATE MINING MODEL ProductSequence
(
OrderNumber TEXT KEY,
IncomeGroup TEXT DISCRETE,
Products TABLE
(
   LineNumber LONG KEY SEQUENCE,
   Product TEXT DISCRETE PREDICT
)
)
USING Microsoft_Sequence_Clustering
```

To execute this DMX statement I ran it from the DMX Query Editor (not the Query Builder) as in Figure F-2f, i.e., I navigated to the Query Editor view, deleted the contents of the viewer, copied the above code into it, and clicked the Finish button.

At this stage a mining structure and model have been created but the structure is empty and the model is not trained. Binding the structure to data and training the model is done with the DMX code below.

```
INSERT INTO ProductSequence
(
OrderNumber,
IncomeGroup,
Products
(
SKIP,
Product,
LineNumber
)
)
SHAPE {OPENQUERY([Adventure Works DW], 'SELECT
OrderNumber,
IncomeGroup
FROM dbo.vAssocSeqOrders ORDER BY OrderNumber')
}
APPEND ({ OPENQUERY([Adventure Works DW], 'SELECT
OrderNumber,
Model,
LineNumber
```

```
FROM dbo.vAssocSeqLineItems ORDER BY OrderNumber,
LineNumber') }
RELATE OrderNumber TO OrderNumber) AS Products
```

In the code above the SHAPE command creates a table with nested tables by combining queries from multiple data sources. The SKIP command allows ignoring fields in the source queries that do not exist in the mining model. In our example we need to SKIP the Product and LineNumber columns in the case table because they only exist in the nested table. RELATE is a part of the SHAPE command with the form: RELATE <master column> TO <child column> AS <column table name>. The SHAPE command seems similar in function to the ADO command by the same name if you do any .Net programming.

We've only looked at two examples of the many possible uses for the Advanced Query Editor, and as you can see that writing DMX code is an advanced topic. Please refer to other sources for more information about DMX.

About the Author

Robert S. "Bob" Bussom retired early from academia where he served as a faculty member and administrator. He has other work experience in retail sales, heavy manufacturing, health insurance, and executive development. He earned a B.S., MBA, and Ph. D. from The Ohio State University and has additional graduate-level coursework in Information Systems.

Made in the USA
Lexington, KY
25 April 2015